# REPORTS OF THE UNITED STATES DELEGATION
## TO THE
## THIRD UNITED NATIONS CONFERENCE
## ON THE
## LAW OF THE SEA

# Reports of the United States Delegation to the Third United Nations Conference on the Law of the Sea

Editors:

*Myron H. Nordquist*

*Choon-ho Park*

Occasional Paper No. 33

Law of the Sea Institute
University of Hawaii • Honolulu

# ACKNOWLEDGMENTS

Publication of this paper is made possible in part through the support of


THE ANDREW W. MELLON FOUNDATION


DEPARTMENT OF PLANNING AND ECONOMIC DEVELOPMENT
STATE OF HAWAII

**Library of Congress Cataloging in Publication Data**

United States. Delegation to the United Nations
    Conference on the Law of the Sea, 3rd, 1973-1978,
    New York, N.Y., etc.
    Reports of the United States Delegation to the Third
United Nations Conference on the Law of the Sea.

    (Occasional paper / Law of the Sea Institute ; no. 33)
    1. Maritime law--Congresses. 2. Maritime law
--United States--Congresses. I. Nordquist, Myron H.
II. Park, Choon-ho. III. Title. IV. Series: Occasional
paper (Law of the Sea Institute) ; no. 33.
JX4408.U57 1983          341.4'5              83-875
ISBN 0-911189-07-6

This book may be ordered from:

The Law of the Sea Institute
University of Hawaii
Honolulu, HI 96822

# CONTENTS

# FOREWORD

The political and policy constraints of human societies make difficult the historian's task of accu-
rate assessment of the motivations which underlie national positions with respect to treaty negotiations.
All too often reliance is placed on anecdotal information and the human frailty of participant recollection.

Perhaps the most reliable record is to be found
in the official reports of the Delegations. These reports have undergone a careful policy screening before
publication and therefore represent a transform of the
fundamental considerations underlying the Government
decision. The perceptive and knowledgeable reader
will, however, be able to make an assessment of that
transform function and arrive at the fundamental policy consideration more closely than he or she would be
able to do by any other research technique.

Myron Nordquist and Choon-ho Park have thus rendered a most valuable service in the collecting and
editing of the Reports of the United States Delegation
to the Third United Nations Conference on the Law of
the Sea. These reports will complement the official
documents of the United Nations, the multi-volume report of the Australian Delegation, and Renate Platzoeder's ten-volume compilation of material of relevance (originally for the use of the West German Delegation). It is hoped that these publications will
inspire other similar compendia.

The editors of these reports are well know distinguished scholars of the law of the sea. Myron
Nordquist, Secretary of the United States Delegation
until 1978, is now with the law firm of Duncan, Allen
and Mitchell in Washington, D.C. Choon-ho Park is
Professor of International Law on the Faculty of Law,
Korea University, Seoul, and directs its East Asia
Law of the Sea Institute. Both editors have been in
attendance at all of the sessions of UNCLOS III and
have thereby acquired the intimate knowledge so essential to the editing of even the most formal documents.

The Institute is indebted to the State of Hawaii's
Department of Planning and Economic Development for
financial support in the preparation of the manuscript.

John P. Craven, Director
Law of the Sea Institute

BACKGROUND TO THE
THIRD UNITED NATIONS
LAW OF THE SEA CONFERENCE

# BACKGROUND TO THE THIRD UNITED NATIONS CONFERENCE ON THE LAW OF THE SEA

## Historical Background

The competition between shared and exclusive uses of the oceans has been the mainspring for the evolution of the law of the sea. For the last several hundred years, a dichotomy has been manifested between the freedom of the sea and the sovereignty of the coastal State. In 1625, a Dutch scholar, Hugo Grotius, published the treatise On the Law of War and Peace with a chapter of the book devoted to "mare liberum"-- the freedom of the seas. Grotius argued that the oceans were indivisible and so vast that States could not effectively occupy them. He stated that the resources of the high seas were inexhaustible and therefore open to utilization by all States.[1] The freedom of the seas concept espoused by Grotius well-suited the interests of the seafaring nations of the time. Ironically, however, the British, who were subsequently to become the staunchest defenders of the concept, were not a major maritime power in the early 17th century. In fact, they claimed exclusive fishing and trade rights over large expanses of ocean. The official rationale for the British coastal State position was developed by the scholar, John Seldon, who responded to Grotius' writings.

However, the dominant naval powers in Europe embraced the freedom of the seas doctrine, thereby bringing a stability to the law of the sea that was to last for nearly 300 years. During these three centuries, coastal State sovereignty was restricted to a narrow band of sea adjacent to the coast. Many maritime writers have suggested that the breadth of coastal State hegemony over this territorial belt was established by the range of a cannon shot--three nautical miles or one marine league.

The international law of the sea in the 18th and 19th centuries evolved mainly through State practice as interpreted and enforced by the then pre-eminent British Admiralty Courts. In 1930, the League of Nations convened the first major multi-nation international law codification conference at The Hague. The regime of the territorial sea was one of the three principal subjects selected for consideration by the

delegates from 47 nations. No one should have been
surprised that one month of deliberation at the Conference did not result in agreement on a uniform
breadth for the territorial sea. However, the Conference did agree on a future draft convention dealing with the character and extent of riparian State
rights over the territorial sea. In this connection,
the Committee of experts for the Progressive Codification of International Law that had prepared the
questions for the 1930 Codification Conference, referred to a number of earlier texts dealing with the
regime of the territorial sea.[2]

Between 1930 and the end of World War II, numerous States made unilateral extensions of their territorial sea beyond three miles to acquire greater control over foreign fishing.[3] But after the War, several
less directly related events of far-reaching significance started to converge. The founding of the United
Nations had provided a forum for newly emergent, mostly non-maritime power nations to assert their views.
Moreover, Article 13, paragraph 1, of the U.N. Charter
required the General Assembly to "initiate studies and
make recommendations" for the "progressive development
of international law and its codification". To discharge this mandate, the General Assembly established
the International Law Commission (I.L.C.) in 1947.
After adoption of the I.L.C.'s Statute and the election of members, the Commission met for the first
time in April 1949.[4] The I.L.C. determined forth-
rightly that the regime of the high seas and the regime of the territorial sea were ripe for codification.
However, it was not until its eighth session in 1956
that the Commission was able to present its final
draft afticles on the territorial sea.[5] At this same
session, all of the law of the sea provisions were re-
cast in a final report containing draft articles and
commentaries which was submitted to the General
Assembly.[6]

On February 21, 1957, the Assembly decided to
convene an international conference of plenipotentiaries "to examine the law of the sea, . . . and to embody the results of its work in one or more international conventions. . . ."[7]

First Conference

The First U.N. Conference on the Law of the Sea
met in Geneva from February 24 to April 27, 1958 with

3

86 States represented. The Conference decided to establish five main committees to deal with its agenda: First Committee (territorial sea and contiguous zone); Second Committee (high seas: general regime); Third Committee (high seas: fishing and conservation of living resources); Fourth Committee (continental shelf); and Fifth Committee (question of free access to the sea of landlocked countries). The General Assembly had referred the I.L.C.'s final report on the law of the sea to the First Conference containing 73 draft articles that had resulted from the Commission's seven years of preparatory work. The First Conference also had more than 30 preparatory documents, primarily consisting of specialized studies on particular issues.

At the conclusion of the deliberations, the five main committees each submitted a report to the plenary of the Conference that summarized the results of their work, including the draft articles that had been approved by majority vote. By a two-thirds vote, the plenary of the Conference then adopted draft articles, some in amended form, that resulted in four conventions: the Convention on the Territorial Sea and the Contiguous Zone;[8] the Convention on the High Seas;[9] the Convention on Fishing and Conservation of the Living Resources of the High Seas:[10] and the Convention on the Continental Shelf.[11] The landlocked States' issues in the Fifth Committee were not embodied in a separate convention but were incorporated in Article 14 of the Convention on the Territorial Sea and the Contiguous Zone and in Articles 2, 3, and 4 of the Convention on the High Seas.

In addition to the four Conventions, the Conference adopted an Optional Protocol of Signature concerning the Compulsory Settlement of Disputes and nine resolutions on various subjects, including the issue of convening a second U.N. Conference on the Law of the Sea.[12] The Final Act of the Conference was signed on April 29, 1958.

On September 30, 1962, the Convention on the High Seas and the Optional Protocol entered into force. The Convention on the Continental Shelf came into force on June 10, 1964; the Convention on the Territorial Sea and the Contiguous Zone, on September 10, 1965; and the Convention on Fishing and Conservation of the Living Resources of the High Seas, on March 20, 1966.

4

## Second Conference

On December 10, 1958, the General Assembly passed Resolution 1307 (XIII) requesting the Secretary General to convene a second U.N. Conference on the Law of the Sea. As in prior codification efforts, the First Conference had been unable to reach agreement on the breadth of the territorial sea and the extent of fisheries jurisdiction. Eighty-two States (four fewer than in 1958) attended the Second Conference that was convened expressly to settle these two outstanding issues. The Second Conference met in Geneva from March 16 to April 26, 1960 but again failed to reach any substantive agreement on either a uniform breadth for the territorial sea or on fisheries jurisdiction.

## Assessment of First and Second Conference

In spite of the failure of the Second Conference, the Geneva Conventions of 1958 were landmarks in the progressive codification of international law. Moreover, many of the provisions were expressions of existing customary international law, particularly those in the Convention on the High Seas. Important innovations were embodied in the Convention on the Continental Shelf, while the territorial sea articles were a mixture of well established and emerging rules. The fisheries articles were easily the least well received of the four Conventions, although the Optional Protocol on dispute settlement was nearly as weak on substance as it was on acceptamce by the international community.

As would be the case at the Third Conference, the outer limit of coastal State jurisdiction over the territorial sea, fisheries and continental shelf and the delimitation of boundaries between adjacent and opposite States were troublesome issues. These problems would increase in economic significance as advances in technology allowed offshore petroleum development in deeper waters and distant water fishing on a larger scale. Indeed, the gross underestimation of the rapid advances in marine technology by the First and Second Conferences coupled with the rising economic aspirations of numerous newly independent coastal States were two of the most instrumental factors in precipitating the convening of the Third U.N. Conference on the Law of the Sea.

5

## U.N. Activity, 1967-1969

In November 1967, Arvid Pardo of Malta spoke at
length in the General Assembly on the importance of
the oceans to the future of mankind and on the need
for the modernization of the legal regime for ocean
space. He also introduced a draft resolution to exclude the seabed beyond national jurisdiction from
national appropriation and to establish an international agency to control all seabed activities therein. The financial benefits derived from the exploitation of the deep seabed resources were to be used
primarily to aid the poorer countries of the world.

Pardo's ideas found immediate appeal with most
developing nations. Consequently, the General Assembly established an Ad Hoc Committee of 35 members to
study U.N. activities in the seabed area beyond national jurisdiction and to recommend means to promote
cooperation in the use of its resources.[13]

After three sessions of discussions ranging over
approximately two months, the controversial nature of
the subject matter was firmly established, and the Ad
Hoc Committee informed the General Assembly that further study was needed.[14] A harbinger of the future
was seen in that the Ad Hoc Committee conducted its
work on the basis of consensus among its members, although no formal decision was taken to that effect.

In December 1968, the General Assembly adopted a
resolution to create a standing 42-member Committee on
the Peaceful Uses of the Seabed and Ocean Floor beyond
the Limits of National Jurisdiction (Seabed Committee).[15] The Chairman of the Ad Hoc Committee was
Hamilton Shirley Amerasinghe, who later was elected
President of the Third Law of the Sea Conference. The
Seabed Committee was to study the deep seabed problem
and to submit a report to the General Assembly the
following year.[16] The Committee held three sessions
at U.N. Headquarters in 1969 for a total of eleven
meetings. Continuing the Ad Hoc Committee's organizational framework, the Legal Sub-Committee held 29
meetings and the Economic and Technical Sub-Committee,
25 meetings.[17] The Seabed Committee dealt primarily
with the legal principles governing the deep seabed
and the applicable international machinery. After
considering the Committee's Report, the General Assembly requested the Secretary General to ascertain the

views of member States on the desirability of convening, at an early date, a Conference on the Law of the
Sea.[18]

The "package deal" aspect of negotiations at a
comprehensive conference was seen early as illustrated
in the preamble of the 1969 Resolution which read,
inter alia:

> Having regard for the fact that the problems
> relating to the high seas, territorial waters,
> contiguous zones, the continental shelf, the
> superjacent waters, and the seabed and ocean
> floor beyond the limits of national jurisdic-
> tion are closely linked together . . . .[19]

Resolution 2564B asked the Committe to expedite
the preparation of draft principles governing the deep
seabed and to submit a draft declaration in 1970.
Resolution 2574C requested an international machinery
study and was non-controversial. In contrast, Resolution 2574D caused a furor by calling for a moratorium on deep seabed exploitation activities prior to
the establishment of an international regime. The
operative language of the Moratorium Resolution declared:

> (a) States and persons, physical or juridical,
>     are bound to refrain from all activities of
>     exploitation of the resources of the area
>     of the seabed and ocean floor, and the
>     subsoil thereof, beyond the limits of
>     national jurisdiction;
>
> (b) No claim to any part of that area or its
>     resources shall be recognized.

The Moratorium Resolution was adopted by 62 votes
to 28, with 28 abstentions. The voting pitted numer-
ically superior developing nations against economically advantaged developed States and identified one of
the most controversial issues for the upcoming negotiations at the Conference.

## Principles and Conference Resolutions

During 1970, the Committee worked intensively on
the elaboration of a draft declaration of principles
for the deep seabed. While the Committee was unable
to agree on a draft text in the time available, both

the formal and informal consultations contributed substantially to an emerging consensus on draft language. The Committee reported to the 25th session of the General Assembly that progress over the prior two years had been slower than it had hoped. Nonetheless, the progress was viewed as sufficient to maintain confidence in the emergence of a general agreement on an international regime in a future treaty. Such optimism was characteristic of the formal U.N. pronouncements about the Third Conference and its progress.

The twenty-fifth session of the General Assembly in 1970 set several landmarks for the Third U.N. Conference on the Law of the Sea. By Resolution 2749 the General Assembly adopted by 108 votes to none, with 14 abstentions, a Declaration of Principles Governing the Seabed and the Ocean Floor, and the Subsoil Thereof, beyond the Limits of National Jurisdiction.[20] In the Principles Resolution, the General Assembly declared the deep seabed area and its resources to be the common heritage of mankind. The area was not to be appropriated, and no rights were to be acquired with "respect to the area or its resources incompatible with the international regime to be established and the principles of this Declaration". The Declaration called for the establishment of an international regime and machinery through "an international treaty of a character, generally agreed upon".

Resolution 2750C noted that the responses from States indicated widespread support for holding a comprehensive conference on the law of the sea. The Assembly also observed that the problems of ocean space were closely inter-related and that technological advances had accentuated the need for early and progressive development of the law of the sea. Paragraph 2 of the Conference Resolution read:

> 2. *Decides* to convene in 1973, . . . a conference on the law of the sea which would deal with the establishment of an equitable international regime--including an international machinery--for the area and the resources of the seabed and the ocean floor, and the subsoil thereof, beyond the limits of national jurisdiction, a precise definition of the area, and a broad range of related issues including those concerning the regimes of the high seas, the continental shelf, the territorial sea (including the

question of its breadth and the question
of international straits) and contiguous
zone, fishing and conservation of the
living resources of the high seas (including the question of the preferential rights
of coastal States), the preservation of the
marine environment (including, inter alia,
the prevention of pollution) and scientific research;

The Resolution enlarged the Committee by 44 members, and instructed it to hold two preparatory sessions in 1971. The Committee was to prepare a comprehensive list of subjects and issues as well as
draft articles on such subjects and issues.[21] The
Committee was to report to the General Assembly on
the progress of its preparatory work to determine the
precise agenda for the conference, its definitive
date, location, and duration, and related arrangements.

Preparatory Sessions, 1971-1973

The first and second preparatory sessions of the
Committee were held in the spring and summer of 1971.
The Committee formed three Sub-Committees of the
whole, and allocated subjects and functions to them.
Sub-Committee I was to draft treaty articles on the
deep seabed regime. Sub-Committee II was to prepare a
comprehensive list of subjects and issues and draft
treaty articles on the traditional law of the sea, and
Sub-Committee III was to draft treaty articles on the
marine environment and scientific research. Twenty-
five Bureau members were elected to the Main Committee
and the three Sub-Committees after an allocation of
positions based on the "principles of equitable geographical distribution".[22]

The Committee held a general debate during 1971
and received a series of working papers, draft conventions, and draft treaty articles. The report of
the Committee for 1971 consisted of sections dealing
with the subjects and the issues allocated to each of
the three Sub-Committees. A considerable amount of
time was given to examining the relationship between
the 1958 Geneva Conventions and the anticipated results of the Third Conference. The general debates at
the first and second preparatory sessions demonstrated that the law of the sea was an extraordinarily complex subject upon which each State held different views.

On December 21, 1971 the General Assembly increased the Committee to 91 member countries, noted the "encouraging progress", and authorized the holding of the third and fourth preparatory meetings in New York and Geneva respectively, in 1972.[23] A pattern of work emerged: general debate followed by working group attempts to reconcile and consolidate the documents submitted by delegates into draft articles. The workload was overwhelming, and most delegates were confused by the subject's complexity. While the scope of common understanding was limited, it was not for want of trying; in fact, some 469 formal and countless informal preparatory meetings were held over 1971, 1972, and 1973.

The Committee continued to labor in 1972 pursuant to the agreed plan of work. Its most noteworthy achievement was the formal adoption of a comprehensive list of subjects and issues.[24] The list was to be the de facto agenda for the Third Conference, and the process of formulating it was highly controversial.

The General Assembly reaffirmed the mandate of the Seabed Committee at the end of 1972 despite noting only "further progress".[25] In reality, there were wide differences of opinion on virtually every substantive issue. Nevertheless, the Committee was requested to hold two further sessions in 1973, the fifth and sixth preparatory sessions, with a view to completing its work. A report and recommendations were to be submitted to the General Assembly at its 28th session. Resolution 3029-A also requested the Secretary General to convene the first session of the Third Law of the Sea Conference for a period of two weeks in November-December 1973, to deal with organizational matters. A second session of the Conference to deal with substantive work was to be held at Santiago, Chile for eight weeks in April-May 1974.[26] The General Assembly was to review the progress of the preparatory work at its 28th session in 1973 and, if necessary, take measures to facilitate the completion of the substantive work of the Conference.

The Committee did hold two sessions in 1973, the first in New York from March 5 to April 6, and the second in Geneva from July 2 to August 24. Early in its first session the Committee affirmed that the Sub-Committees should retain the same terms of reference. Indeed, most of the work accomplished in 1973 was done by the Sub-Committees.

## First Session, 1973

The first official act of the Third Conference was the election of H.S. Amerasinghe of Sri Lanka as its President.[27] Amerasinghe had served ably as the Chairman of the Seabed Committee and was widely respected by all regional groups. Thirty-one Vice Presidents were also elected as was a Conference Rapporteur General. Chairmen were also elected for Committees I, II, and III, the Drafting Committee, and the Credentials Committee. The President of the Conference would preside over the General Committee.

In addition to the election of officers and approval of organizational structure, the Conference considered the draft rules of procedure prepared by the Secretary General[28] together with amendments submitted by several delegations.[29] Unable to reach a consensus, the Conference decided to postpone adoption of the rules of procedure until the second session, thereby allowing time for informal, inter-sessional consultations.

## Second Session, 1974

The second session of the Conference opened with great fanfare on June 20, 1974 in Caracas with 138 States sending representatives. From June 21 to 27 the Conference considered its rules of procedure, adopting them on the exact deadline date set at the first session.[30] The Conference allocated subjects and issues to the Plenary and the three Main Committees largely along the lines of the work breakdown that had evolved in the Seabed Committee.

During the first six weeks of the Conference, 115 delegations and over a dozen representatives of intergovernmental organizations, specialized agencies, and non-governmental organizations spoke. Most delivered general statements in the Plenary providing the first overview of their positions on the law of the sea. It is worth recalling that the goal of the Conference was to adopt a comprehensive convention covering traditional law of the sea issues as well as a new regime for the international seabed area, marine pollution, scientific research, and dispute settlement. The Conference had been preceded by six preparatory sessions over three years, and hundreds of draft proposals were before it. Thus it should not have been surprising

11

that at the end of an exhaustive ten weeks of intensive negotiations in Caracas, the Conference found it
necessary to request the General Assembly to schedule
a third session at Geneva in 1975.

The President of the Conference was optimistic
about the results of the Caracas session.  He stated:

> There has so far been no agreement on any
> final text or on any single subject or
> issue, despite the lengthy deliberations
> in the Seabed Committee that formed the
> prelude to our discussions in the Conference
> itself.  We can, however, derive some
> legislative satisfaction from the thought
> that most of the issues or most of the key
> issues have been identified and exhaustively
> discussed, and the extent and depth of
> divergence and disagreement on them have
> become manifest.[31]

## Geneva Session, 1975

The third session of the Conference met in Geneva
from March 17 to May 9, 1975.  This session of the
Conference was the most historically important from an
interpretative point of view as well as the most productive in terms of concrete results.  As requested by
the Conference on April 18, 1975, each chairman of the
three Committees had drafted a single negotiating text
(SNT) on the subjects and issues within his mandate.[32]
In addition, the chairman of the dispute-settlement
group submitted a text to the President of the Conference.  The SNTs were portrayed as mere procedural devices to provide a basis for negotiation, and no nation's position was to be prejudiced by the document.
In fact, however, with respect to the articles examined in this dissertation, the SNT text as drafted in
1975 was decisive on every major issue.

For example, the Second Committee held two formal
meetings and 14 informal meetings during the third
session of the Conference.  The work of the Committee
began in 1975 with a second reading of the document
on main trends with a view toward reducing the excessive number of variants.[33]  The real negotiations, however, were taking place in a series of small consultative groups focused on particular issues.  The groups
dealt with the following subjects: baselines, historic
bays and historic waters, contiguous zone, innocent

passage, high seas, question of transit (landlocked
States), continental shelf, exclusive economic zone,
straits, enclosed and semi-enclosed seas, islands,
and delimitation.

The work of several informal consultative groups
in 1975 was described as follows:

> 10. The informal consultative group on baselines
> held three meetings, discussing provisions
> 4 to 20 of the document on main trends. On
> the basis of the discussion in the group and
> the work of a small working group, the Bureau
> prepared a consolidated text. Following
> further discussion, a revised text was issued
> and was studied by the group, provision by
> provision.

> 11. The informal consultative group on historic
> bays and historic waters held two meetings.
> A smaller working party was formed and held
> two meetings. The informal consultative
> group on the contiguous zone held one meeting.

> 12. The informal consultative group on innocent
> passage held six meetings. On the basis of
> the discussions in the group, the Bureau
> presented a consolidated text on provisions
> 24 to 46 of the document.[34]

Many other official and unofficial negotiations
were, of course, carried out.[35] Unfortunately, no official records exist of any of the informal consultations that played such a vital role in the formulation
of the precise terms of the SNT.

## Fourth Session, Spring 1976

The SNT was the subject of informal negotiations
both during the inter-sessional period and during the
entire fourth session that started on March 15, 1976.[36]
At the first meeting of the fourth session, the President of the Conference indicated that the next phase
should be the preparation by the chairmen of the three
Committees of a revised single negotiating text (RSNT).
In response, an RSNT was prepared which was the sole
responsibility of the chairmen and officers of the
Conference. Delegations were not precluded from moving for amendments or introducing new proposals. In
addition, following a general debate, the President

of the Conference took responsibility for the presentation of a Part IV dealing with the item "Settlement of Disputes".[37] By this procedure Part IV was
given the same status as other parts of the RSNT.

Since the mandate of this panel is to consider
jurisdictional aspects within 200-mile zones, the
remainder of this paper will focus on the activities
of the Second Committee which dealt with these issues
at the Conference.

In mid-March 1976 the Second Committee commenced
its article-by-article discussion of the SNT. It was
the input from this process that gave the Chairman
the necessary confidence to prepare a revised text.
The input from delegations was impressive, and during
53 informal meetings more than 3,700 interventions
were made.[38] Often over 120 of the 149 delegations at
the Conference were in attendance. The Chairman devised a pragmatic "rule of silence" for the informal
meetings. That is, silence on an SNT article meant
support for the article as drafted, while silence on
an amendment meant opposition to the amendment. In
effect, the Chairman created a presumption of acceptance for the SNT. As a result, few amendments commanded the necessary support.

## Fifth Session, Summer 1976

The fifth session of the Conference met in New
York from August 2 to September 17, 1976. The basis
of work was the RSNT issued after the spring session
in 1976. The conference as a whole chose to conduct
informal negotiations on the key outstanding issues
in each of the three main Committees.[39]

The key issues in the Second Committee identified
by Chairman Amerasinghe as suitable for small group
negotiations were:

(a) Definition and status of the exclusive
economic zone (Article 44 ff.);

(b) Delimitation of the exclusive economic zone
and the continental shelf between adjacent
or opposite States (articles 62 and 71);

(c) Definition of outer limit of continental
margin (a complex technical issue already

14

raised but not discussed in detail or
covered by article 64);

(d) Rights of landlocked and geographically
disadvantaged States to participate in
the exploitation of the living resources
of the exclusive economic zone (articles
50, 51, 58, and 59);

(e) Rights and duties of coastal States and
other States (articles 44, 46, 47, 75,
and 76);

(f) Revenue-sharing in respect of exploitation
of the continental shelf beyond 200 miles
(article 70);

(g) Straits used for international navigation
(articles 16, 33, 37, and 43);

(h) Right of access to and from the sea and
freedom of transit (article 110).[40]

All of the 58 Second Committee meetings held
during the fifth session were conducted informally.
Bear in mind that the process was intended to lead to
the formulation of successive versions of texts that
would command a consensus. The small negotiating
groups initially established were to deal with four
priority issues: the legal status of the economic
zone and the rights and duties of States in the zone;
the outer limit of continental margin and revenue-
sharing; and access to the sea by landlocked States.
Later, two additional open-ended negotiating groups
focused on straits and on the delimitation of the
territorial sea, exclusive economic zone, and continental shelf between opposite and adjacent States.
An informal group of coastal States and landlocked
and geographically disadvantaged States (LL/GDS)
formed outside the Conference structure to deal with
LL/GDS access to fishery resources in the 200-mile
zone. In addition, the Committee itself held a number of informal meetings allowing all delegations an
opportunity to comment on RSNT questions not described as "priority".[41]

Of the articles reviewed in this dissertation,
only incidental references were made in Negotiating
Group No. 5, at the fifth session, to the delimitation of the territorial sea provisions in article 14

of the RSNT. Otherwise, the territorial sea and contiguous zone text already commanded broad support at
the end of 1976.[42] At the same time, the Chairman of
the Second Committee observed that "(n)o concrete results were achieved at this session regarding any of
the questions considered by the various negotiating
groups".[43] He was, however, satisfied with the method
of work that had evolved, and he recommended that it
be continued at the sixth session.[44]

### Sixth Session, 1977

The sixth session of the Third U.N. Conference on
the Law of the Sea met in New York from May 23 to
July 15, 1977. Pursuant to a decision made at the end
of the fifth session, the Conference devoted the first
three weeks of the sixth session to the First Committee's deep seabed mining issues.[45] Thereafter, the
Second Committee concentrated on the already identified outstanding issues utilizing the small negotiating groups carried over from the fifth session. Unfortunately, delegations tended merely to restate
earlier positions in such groups, and additional efforts at reorganization were only moderately successful.[46] For example, an informal negotiating group convened under the Mexican Head of Delegation, Jorge
Castañeda, met during the last two and a half weeks of
the session. The "Castañeda Group" produced compromise formulations of the status of the economic zone.

A 21-State contact group having representatives
from both LL/GDS and coastal States dealt unsuccessfully with the issues of LL/GDS access to the living
resources of economic zones within their region. In
total, the Second Committee held over 30 informal
meetings in 1977.

The principal result of the sixth session was the
emergence of the informal composite negotiating text
(ICNT) after the session was over. Many of the compromise formulations that resulted from the small
group consultations were embodied in the ICNT. However, a general malaise had spread throughout the
Conference, and the prospects for a successful Convention were questionable at best as States contemplated
the opening of the seventh session in the spring of
1978.

## Seventh Session, Spring 1978

The first portion of the seventh session met in Geneva from March 28 to May 19, 1978. The seventh session was faced at the outset with the fact that a change in government in Sri Lanka had left President Amerasinghe unaccredited to any delegation. After two weeks of unsuccessful negotiation, he was reconfirmed as President of the Conference by a procedural vote of 75-18, with 13 abstentions and 21 States not participating. A third week of work was lost in debate about the organization of work, largely over procedural safeguards concerning settled articles in in the ICNT.

Seven negotiating groups (NGs) were established by the Plenary to deal with hard-core outstanding issues. Three of the NGs in the Second Committee considered problems regarding access to living resources by LL/GDS (NG-4, chaired by Nandan of Fiji); dispute settlement with respect to fisheries in the economic zone (NG-5, chaired by Stavropoulos of Greece); and the delimitation of maritime boundaries (NG-7, chaired by Manner of Finland). The Chairman of the Second Committee, Andrés Aguilar of Venezuela, chaired a fourth working group (NG-6) which dealt with the definition of the outer edge of the continental margin beyond 200 miles, and revenue sharing. To illustrate the pace of work in the NGs, the Aguilar Group held five informal meetings where 70 statements were delivered.[47]

The Second Committee convened informally on ten occasions at which delegations had the opportunity to explain difficulties with the ICNT outside the Negotiating Group's mandate. The first 40 articles were scrutinized, and comments were made on many of the 33 articles pertinent to this dissertation.[48] In spite of this, few changes to the ICNT were made, as the general rule was followed that textual changes would have to command overwhelming support before referral to Plenary.

One small change relevant to this dissertation did result from the Second Committee review process. At the suggestion of the Indonesian Delegation, the word "or" was inserted in Article 18, paragraph 1(b) between the words "roadstead" and "port facility".[49] Otherwise there was no directly relevant new language

to emerge from the NGs' deliberations during the first
part of the seventh session.

## Seventh Session, Summer 1978

The second part of the seventh session of the
Third Law of the Sea Conference resumed in New York
from August 21 to September 15, 1978.[50] Unlike the
Geneva phase of the seventh session, the New York
phase encountered no procedural or organizational
obstacles. Work began immediately in the Negotiating
Groups previously established.

It is noteworthy that the Second Committee met
five times to complete an article-by-article review
of the 115 articles within its mandate not assigned
to a Negotiating Group.[51]  NG-4 held two meetings on
the subject of access by LL/GDS to the living resources of the economic zones of their regions.  NG-6
met six times to discuss the definition of the outer
limit of the continental margin and revenue sharing.
NG-7 held seven meetings to consider maritime boundaries.

Overall, the results of the resumed seventh session were not significant from the point of view of
progress on Second Committee issues.  At the same
time, the article-by-article review was necessary, and
several compromise formulations in the NGs gained
stature by surviving the passage of another session
without being rejected outright.

## Eighth Session, Spring 1979

The first phase of the eighth session of the Conference convened in Geneva on March 19 and met until
April 27, 1979.  The session had been preceded by
three weeks of informal inter-sessional consultations
(not negotiations) held in Geneva from January 23 to
February 9, 1979.[52]  No substantive discussions on the
outer margin issues assigned to NG-6 took place, since
interested delegations preferred to confer directly
outside the Conference.  Five informal meetings were
devoted to the maritime delimitation issues falling
within the mandate of NG-7, with limited progress
being made.

One positive outcome of the inter-sessional consultations was that substantive work at the eighth
session began on the first day.  Negotiations

continued in the seven Negotiating Groups established
at the seventh session.  The hard-core Second Committee issues that remained were the definition of the
outer limits of the continental margin, delimitation
criteria for maritime boundaries, and the LL/GDS access to fishery resources in the economic zones in
their region.  The Nandan text produced in NG-4 during
the seventh session was finally acknowledged as enjoying widespread support, and it went forward into the
ICNT, Revision One (ICNT, Rev. 1).  Likewise, a text
on fisheries dispute settlement developed in NG-5 in
the prior session was incorporated into the revision.
Significantly, a compromise text on the outer limit
issue was produced by Chairman Aguilar at the last
minute, and this text was also included in the ICNT,
Rev. 1.  Throughout the first phase of the eighth session, intensive and fruitful private consultations
were underway on the hard-core issues.  However, no
new texts were produced by NG-7 on maritime boundaries.  As the first phase of the eighth session came
to a close, many delegations expressed doubt whether
any further progress was possible on this problem that
was essentially bilateral in nature.

The Conference had earlier determined that revisions of the ICNT found to have widespread and substantive support and to offer a substantially improved
prospect of consensus should be presented to Plenary.[53]
Hence, persuasive evidence of progress in the negotiations ensued from the agreement to issue a revision of
the ICNT.  New negotiating texts were incorporated on
various deep seabed issues, the definition of the continental shelf, protection and preservation of the
marine environment, access of landlocked and geographically disadvantaged States to surplus fisheries in
the economic zones of coastal States of the region,
conciliation with respect to certain disputes regarding conservation of living resources of the economic
zone, and management of anadromous species (salmon).
With these important steps toward a final agreement,
the Conference looked to a resumed eighth session in
1979.

Eighth Session, Summer 1979

The first three days of the second phase of the
eighth session held in New York from July 16 to August
24, 1979 were reserved for informal consultations.
The session was devoted to negotiations on the key
issues that remained unresolved after the issuance of

the ICNT, Rev. 1 the previous spring. The Chairmen of
Negotiating Groups 1, 2, and 3 conducted negotiations
under the Working Group of 21, chaired by the Chairman
of the First Committee. The Group of Legal Experts
on settlement of deep seabed disputes continued its
work. With respect to the Second Committee, the Conference concentrated on NG-6 (outer margin) and NG-7
(maritime boundary delimitation). NG-4 held no meetings.

Two informal meetings of the Second Committee
were devoted to matters other than those assigned in
A/CONF.62/62 to Negotiating Groups 4, 6, and 7.
Eleven specific suggestions to modify the text of
the ICNT, Rev. 1 were advanced by the Chairman of
the Second Committee.[54]

NG-6 held five meetings and then formed a smaller
open-ended Group of 38, which also had five meetings.
Despite extensive consultations, little headway was
made.[55] Intensive private and group efforts over ten
meetings were also undertaken in NG-7. But no new
text was allowed to emerge at this session, despite
the Chairman's conviction that compulsory conciliation
was the key to a compromise.[56] No other substantive
matters of particular relevance to this dissertation
resulted from the resumed eighth session.

On August 23, 1979, the Conference decided to
defer the issuance of a second revision of the ICNT
until the ninth session. The second revision would
still not be a "negotiated" text but rather a "negotiating" text.[57] The best that could be said is that
1979 ended with improved prospects that a Convention
could be achieved.

## Ninth Session, Spring 1980

The first portion of the ninth session of the
Third U.N. Conference on the Law of the Sea was held
in New York from February 27 to April 4, 1980. At
the conclusion of the eighth session, the Conference
had directed the chairmen of the Negotiating Groups
to seek compromise solutions on outstanding issues
during the first three weeks of the ninth session.[58]

The work of NG-6 was carried out primarily in
consultation with small groups of interested delegations. A compromise text on the outer limits of the
continental margin was formulated that excluded

submarine ridges and imposed a general outer limit of 350 miles.[59]   After discussion in NG-6, the new text was included in ICNT, Rev. 2

The Chairman of NG-7 was unable to find a consensus on the criteria to be applied in the delimitation of the boundaries of the exclusive economic zone or continental shelf between opposite or adjacent States.[60]   However, the Rev. 1 language of articles 74 and 83 was even less acceptable. Accordingly, Chairman Manner offered his own formulation, including a reference to international law. His proposal was included in ICNT, Rev. 2.

Other informal meetings of the Second Committee were convened to consider issues not assigned to NGs 6 or 7.  Sixteen proposals were considered at the spring ninth session, and three suggestions were determined to have widespread support and were incorporated into ICNT, Rev. 2.[61]

### Ninth Session, Summer 1980

The resumed ninth session of the Conference met in Geneva from July 28 to August 29, 1980.  The negotiations on outstanding issues were conducted in the three Main Committees and in an "Informal Plenary". The third revision of the ICNT was issued as the collective responsibility of the President of the Conference and the Chairmen of the Main Committees.[62] The revised text was given the title "Draft Convention (Informal Text)" since some issues needed further negotiations.  Affected delegations could thereby reserve their positions on the Convention package as a whole until satisfied on the particular issue considered vital.

The results of the resumed ninth session were sufficiently positive that the President of the Conference expressed the hope that "this revision will be regarded as bringing the Conference to the final stage of its deliberations and negotiations".[63]   Most of the new draft Convention text dealt with the major outstanding deep seabed issues such as decision-making procedures in the Council.  The Second Committee met only to consider drafting changes, none of which were incorporated.  However, intensive consultations took place on outstanding issues such as the delimitation of maritime boundaries between opposite and adjacent States.

21

The informal discussions in August 1980 confirmed the acceptability of Part II of the ICNT (Rev. 2).
Nevertheless, an effort was made to modify Article 21
to require prior authorization and notification for
warship transits through the territorial sea. While
the attempt to reopen the text was unsuccessful, the
issue remains a controversial one which could be
troublesome. Spanish amendments to Article 42 were
unopposed, but procedural reasons precluded their incorporation in the revisions. Argentina and Canada
pressed to strengthen Article 63 with respect to the
conservation of the same stock or stocks of fish
which occur both within and beyond the EEZ. The issue
involved protracted negotiations, including procedural linkages to the proposed Spanish amendments to
Article 43. The result was that no new textual language was advanced to the Informal Plenary.

A great deal of Second Committee time was spent
on negotiations between States favoring the equidistance line and those supporting equitable principles to determine the delimitation of maritime
boundaries. Representatives of Ireland and Spain
co-chaired meetings of nine advocates from each side,
and several draft compromise texts were eventually
produced that seemed headed toward a resolution in
1981.

## Tenth Session, Spring 1981

The first portion of the Tenth Session was held
at U.N. Headquarters from March 9 to April 24, 1981.
A new President had been elected in the United States,
and he had taken office in January of 1981. One of
the Reagan Administration's first law-of-the-sea decisions was to announce in late February that a review of U.S. policy at the Conference would be undertaken and that a new head of delegation would be appointed. Consequently, the U.S. was unable to negotiate on substance at the spring session, much to the
frustration of other delegations.

One procedural result was to elect Ambassador
Tommy Koh of Singapore as President of the Conference
to succeed the late Ambassador Amerasinghe. Most activities in the First Committee dealt with the formation of a preparatory commission. The Second Committee held four informal meetings which focused on warship passage in the territorial sea and maritime
boundary delimitation principles in the exclusive

economic zone. No changes were made in any of the committee texts. The most intensive work took place in the Drafting Committee which met frequently.

## Tenth Session, Summer 1981

The resumed tenth session was held in Geneva from August 3 to 28, 1981. The stated objective of the session was to finalize the Draft Convention on the Law of the Sea in 1981 with a signature ceremony in Caracas, Venezuela in 1982. Due to the review decision by the United States, the Conference was unable to meet the finalization schedule. Instead, a new schedule calls for finalization of the Draft Convention at the eleventh session in New York starting March 8, 1982.

The tenth session was preoccupied with negotiations on:

1. Delimitation of maritime boundaries;

2. Participation by liberation groups and other international organizations;

3. Protection of preparatory investment in deep seabed mining; and

4. The creation of a preparatory commission pending the entry into force for the treaty.

The Conference produced a new "neutral" provision on delimitation of the EEZ and continental shelf, thereby ending a long-standing controversy between proponents of the median/equidistance line on the one hand and of equitable principles on the other. A new text was also issued by the Conference President on participation by international organizations, including, in particular, the European Economic Community. Little substantive progress was made on deep seabed mining issues. However, the Drafting Committee, utilizing six open-ended language groups, significantly improved the text from a technical point of view.

## Eleventh Session, Spring 1982

The eleventh session of the Conference convened in New York on March 8 and met until April 30, 1982. On the last day of this session, the Convention and

four related resolutions were adopted by a vote of 130 in favor to 4 against, with 17 abstentions.

The United States was among the four countries voting against the Convention because it felt: (1) the seabed mining provisions of the Convention would deter the development of deep seabed mineral resources; (2) access to those resources was not assured; (3) the countries most affected did not have a proportionate voice in decision making on seabed policies; (4) the seabed amendment procedures allowing entry into force without a State's consent were incompatible with United States' treaty processes; and (5) mandatory transfer of seabed technology, potential benefits to national liberation movements, and seabed production limitations would face Congressional opposition.[64]

Venezuela also voted against the Convention because of unacceptable articles on maritime delimitation. Most of the abstentions were accounted for by the Soviet Union and its allies, but also abstaining were industrial States such as Belgium, the Federal Republic of Germany, Italy, the Netherlands, and the United Kingdom. The Convention was opened for signature by 168 States, 157 Members of the United Nations, and 11 other States which were members of one or more specialized agencies.

## Resumed Eleventh Session, Fall 1982

A resumed eleventh session was held at United Nations Headquarters in New York from September 22 to 24, 1982. The principal reason for the session was for the Conference to approve hundreds of textual changes recommended by the Drafting Committee after a grueling inter-sessional work period. These changes were intended to clarify and harmonize the text in its six official languages: Arabic, Chinese, English, French, Russian, and Spanish.

Venezuela withdrew its invitation to host the Conference-signing ceremony, since it did not plan to become a Party to the Convention. Jamaica, the site of the International Seabed Authority, was substituted by the Conference as host country for the signing session.

## Signing Session, December 10, 1982

On December 10, 1982, at Montego Bay, Jamaica, 119 delegations signed the United Nations Convention on the Law of the Sea. These signatories, plus 23 others and eight observers, signed the Final Act of the Conference which contained the text of the instruments and resolutions adopted by the Conference, and a formal account of its proceedings. Signatories to the Final Act did not commit themselves to the Convention but were thereby entitled to send an observer to the Preparatory Commission for the deep seabed regime. Four of the eight resolutions adopted complement the Convention: resolution I establishes the Preparatory Commission and defines its mandate; resolution II governs interim preparatory seabed investments; resolution III deals with dependent or non self-governing territories; and resolution IV allows national liberation movements to sign the Final Act.

The Convention will enter into force one year after 60 States have ratified or acceded to it. Among the signatories were five of the 11 States accorded a special status in the Conference as "pioneer" seabed investors: Canada, France, India, the Netherlands, and the Soviet Union. Six did not sign: United States, United Kingdom, Italy, Belgium, Federal Republic of Germany, and Japan. The Soviet Union and its Eastern European allies that had abstained on the adoption of the Convention, became signatories.[65]

## INTRODUCTION FOOTNOTES

1. See Dumbauld, E., *The Life and Legal Writings of Hugo Grotius* (University of Oklahoma Press, 1969).

2. League of Nations, *Committee of Experts for the Progressive Codification of International Law*, C.196.M.70.1927.V. pp. 31, 32.

3. 4 Whiteman *Digest of International Law*, 16 (1965).

4. *The Work of the International Law Commission*, U.N. Pub. 67.V.4, p. 5.

5. *Id*. at 32.

6. *Supra*, note 1.

7. G.A. Res. 1105(XI), 21 Feb. 1957.

8. Done at Geneva, April 29, 1958, 15 U.S.T. 1606, T.I.A.S. No. 5639, 516 U.N.T.S. 205. Text in Annex III.

9. Done at Geneva, April 29, 1958, 13 U.S.T. 2312, T.I.A.S. No. 5200, 450 U.N.T.S. 82.

10. Done at Geneva, April 29, 1958, 17 U.S.T. 138, T.I.A.S. No. 5969, 599 U.N.T.S. 285.

11. Done at Geneva, April 29, 1958, 15 U.S.T. 471, T.I.A.S. No. 5578, 499 U.N.T.S. 311.

12. 1 UNCLOS II 143-45.

13, G.A. Res. 2340 (XXII), Dec. 18, 1967.

14. See Report of the *Ad Hoc* Committee, 23 U.N. GAOR, A/7230 (1968).

15. G.S. Res. 2467A (XXIII), Dec. 21, 1968.

16. The groundswell building from Pardo's initiative was evident from related General Assembly activities in 1968. See G.A. Res. 2467B (XXIII), Dec. 21, 1968 on marine pollution study; G.A. Res. 2467C (XXIII), Dec. 21, 1968 on international machinery study; and G.A. Res. 2467D (XXIII), Dec. 21, 1968 in International Decade of Ocean Exploration.

17. See Report of the Committee, 24 U.N. GAOR Supp. 22 (A/7622) 1969. The Ad Hoc Working Groups were simply made Sub-Committees.

18. G.A. Res. 2574A (XXIV), Dec. 15, 1969.

19. Id.

20. G.A. Res. 2749 (XXV), Dec. 17, 1970

21. G.A. Res. 2750C (XXV), Dec. 17, 1950. G.A. Res. 2750A and 2750B dealt with UNCTAD studies concerning the economic implications of deep seabed mining and landlocked States access rights.

22. See Report of the Committee, 26 U.N. GAOR Supp. 21 (A/8421) 1971, pp. 6-7.

23. G.A. Res. 2881 (XXVI), Dec. 21, 1971

24. U.N. Doc. A/8721, Supp. 21, pp. 5-8.

25. G.A. Res. 2039A (XXVII), Dec. 18, 1972

26. The preamble expressed the optimistic expectation that the Conference might be concluded in 1974. G.A. Res. 3029B and C (XVII) asked for a study of the economic significance of the area based on various proposals. The Conference site was changed to Caracas, Venezuela after political upheavals in Chile occurred.

27. 3 UNCLOS I, 3.

28. U.N. Doc. A/CONF.62/2 and Add. 1-3, incorporated in U.N. Doc. A/CONF.62/1, 3 UNCLOS III 1.

29. U.N. Doc. A/CONF.62/4-14, incorporated in U.N. Doc. A/CONF.62/1, 3 UNCLOS III 1.

30. U.N. Doc. A/CONF.62/L.8/Rev. 1, para. 34, 3 UNCLOS III 97.

31. United Nations, Office of Public Information, Press Release SEA/150, Caracas, Aug. 30, 1974. On December 14, 1974 the General Assembly adopted Resolution 3334 (XXIX) that authorized the third session of the Conference in Geneva and designated Caracas as the site for the signing of the eventual Convention.

32. U.N. Doc. A/CONF.62/WP.8.

33. 3 UNCLOS IV 30, para. 4.

34. 3 UNCLOS IV 196, paras. 10, 11, and 12.

35. Id., para. 18.

36. G.A. Res. 3843 (XXX) authorized a fourth session of the Conference as well as a possible fifth session in 1976.

37. 3 UNCLOS V 125. The text of part IV is contained in U.N. Doc. A/CONF.62/WP.9/Rev. 1.

38. Id., at 153, para. 4.

39. U.N. Doc. A/CONF.62/L.12/Rev. 1, 3 UNCLOS VI 122.

40. Id., para. 11.

41. U.N. Doc. A/CONF.62/L.17, paras. 10-14, 3 UNCLOS VI 135.

42. Id., paras. 56, 57.

43. Id., para. 60.

44. Id., para. 62.

45. 3 UNCLOS VII 4, para. 18.

46. Status Report on Law of the Sea Conference: Hearings Before the Subcomm. on Public Lands and Resources of the Comm. on Energy and Natural Resources, United States Senate, 95th Cong., 1st Sess., 1973 (1977).

47. 3 UNCLOS IX 23, para. 15.

48. Id., para. 17.

49. 3 UNCLOS X, 86-87, para. 13.

50. 3 UNCLOS IX, 94, para. 154.

51. 3 UNCLOS X, 165, paras. 7, 8.

52. Letter from the Pres. of the 3rd U.N. Conference on the Law of the Sea dated 21 Feb. 1979 addressed to the Heads of Delegations of States Participating in the Conference. 1 Platzoeder, Dokumente der Dritten Seerechtskonferenz der Vereinten Nationen (Stiftung Wissenschaft und Politik, Forschungsinstitut für Internationale Politik und Sicherheit, June 1979) 254.

53. U.N. Doc. A/CONF.62/WP.10/Rev. 1, p. 17. The President of the Conference and the three main Committee Chairmen were given collective responsibility for the revision.

54. U.N. Doc. A/CONF.62/L.42, para. 10.

55. Id., para. 9.

56. U.N. Doc. A/CONF.62/91, p. 119 (NG7/45), 1 Platzoeder, supra, note 65, p. 99 (June 1979).

57. U.N. Doc. A/CONF.62/88, para. 3, id. at 89.

58. U.N. Doc. A/CONF.62/BUR./12, id. at 17.

59. U.N. Doc. A/CONF.62/L.5., para. 6, 3 UNCLOS III 88.

60. U.N. Doc. A/CONF.62/L.47, para. 7.

61. Supra, note 72, paras. 11-16.

62. U.N. Doc. A/CONF.62/WP.10/Rev.3/Add.1, 28 August 1980.

63. Id., para. 14.

64. U.N. Doc. SEA/498, Dec. 3, 1982, p. 6. (See Appendix I of this volume.)

65. U.N. Doc. SEA/MB/13, Dec. 10, 1982. (See Appendix IV of this volume.)

ANNEX

Chronology of Significant Law of the Sea Events

| Date/Place: | Event: | Significance: |
|---|---|---|
| 24 February - 27 April 1958; Geneva | First U.N. Conference on Law of the Sea | Produced four Conventions on Law of the Sea |
| 17 March - 26 April 1960; Geneva | Second U.N. Conference on Law of the Sea | Failed to reach agreement on breadth of territorial sea and extent of fisheries rights |
| 18 December 1967 | A/Res. 2340 (XXII) | Established Ad Hoc Committee to study peaceful uses of seabed |
| 18 - 27 March 1968; New York | 1st Ad Hoc Committee Session | Ad Hoc Committee met in Economic/ Technical and Legal Working Groups |
| 17 June - 9 July 1968; New York | 2nd Ad Hoc Committee Session | |
| 19 - 30 August 1968; Rio de Janeiro | 3rd Ad Hoc Committee Session | |
| 21 December 1968 | A/Res. 2467 (XXIII) | Established Committee on Peaceful Uses of Seabed and Ocean Floor Beyond Limits of National Jurisdiction |
| 15 December 1969 | A/Res. 2574 (XXIV) | Adopted Moratorium Resolution on deep seabed exploitation |

| Date/Place: | Event: | Significance: |
|---|---|---|
| 2 - 26 March 1970; New York | Spring Sea-Bed Committee Session | Solicited views toward convening a conference on law of the sea |
| 3 - 28 August 1970; Geneva | Summer Sea-Bed Committee Session | |
| 17 December 1970 | A/Res. 2749 (XXV) | Adopted Declaration of Principles governing sea-bed, ocean floor and sub-soil beyond national jurisdiction |
| 17 December 1970 | A/Res. 2750 (XXV) | Convened Comprehensive Third Conference on Law of the Sea for 1973; enlarged Sea-Bed Committee to 86 members and gave it Conference preparatory mandate. |
| 12 - 26 March 1971; Geneva | 1st Preparatory Session | Formed three Sub-Committees and allocated subjects and functions |
| 19 July - 27 August 1971; Geneva | 2nd Preparatory Session | |
| 21 December 1971 | A/Res. 2881 (XXVI) | Noted progress and authorized two more preparatory sessions |

ANNEX

| Date/Place: | Event: | Significance: |
|---|---|---|
| 28 February - 30 March 1972; New York | 3rd Preparatory Session ) | Agreed upon list of subjects and issues for Conference |
| 17 July - 18 August 1972; Geneva | 4th Preparatory Session ) | |
| 18 December 1972 | A/Res. 3029 (XXVII) | Authorized convening of Conference in 1973 |
| 5 March - 6 April 1973; New York | 5th Preparatory Session ) | Prepared comparative texts of proposals |
| 2 July - 24 August 1973; Geneva | 6th Preparatory Session ) | |
| 16 November 1973 | A/Res. 3067 (XXVIII) | Authorized 1st and 2nd Sessions, established Conference mandate, and dissolved Seabed Committee |
| 3 - 15 December 1973; New York | 1st Session of Third Conference | Organized work of Conference |
| 20 June - 29 August 1974; Caracas | 2nd Session of Third Conference | Produced Main Trends papers |
| 17 December 1974 | A/Res. 3334 (XXIX | Authorized 3rd Session |

| Date/Place: | Event: | Significance: |
| --- | --- | --- |
| 17 March – 9 May 1975; Geneva | 3rd Session of Third Conference | Produced informal Single Negotiating Text (SNT) |
| 12 December 1975 | A/Res. 3483 (XXX) | Authorized 4th Session and a possible 5th Session in 1976 |
| 15 March – 7 May 1976; New York | 4th Session of Third Conference | Produced Revised Single Negotiating Text (RSNT) |
| 2 August – 17 September 1976; New York | 5th Session of Third Conference | Identified principal unresolved issues in RSNT |
| 10 December 1976 | A/Res. 31/63 | Authorized 6th Session |
| 23 May – 15 July 1977; New York | 6th Session of Third Conference | Produced Informal Composite Negotiating Text (ICNT) |
| 20 December 1977 | A/Res. 32/194 | Authorized 7th Sessions |
| 28 March – 19 May 1978; Geneva | 7th Session of Third Conference | Formed Negotiating Groups (NGs) on outstanding issues |
| 1 August – 15 September 1978; New York | Resumed 7th Session of Third Conference | NGs met |
| 10 November 1978 | A/Res. 33/17 | Authorized 8th Sessions |

33

| Date/Place: | Event: | Significance: |
|---|---|---|
| 19 March - 27 April 1979; Geneva | 8th Session of Third Conference | Produced ICNT, Rev. 1 |
| 19 July - 24 August 1979; New York | Resumed 8th Session of Third Conference | Concentrated on deep seabed issues |
| 9 November 1979 | A/Res. 34/20 | Authorized 9th Sessions |
| 3 March - 4 April 1980; New York | 9th Session of Third Conference | Produced ICNT, Rev. 2 |
| 28 July - 29 August 1980; Geneva | Resumed 9th Session of Third Conference | Produced ICNT, Rev. 3 or Draft Convention on the Law of the Sea (Informal Text) |
| 10 December 1980 | A/Res. 35/116 | Authorized 10th Sessions |
| 9 March - 24 April 1981; New York | 10th Session of Third Conference | Intensive Drafting Committee work |
| 3 - 28 August 1981; Geneva | Resumed 10th Session of Third Conference | Focus on unresolved deep seabed issues; produced Draft Convention on the Law of the Sea |
| 9 December 1981 | A/Res. 36/79 | Authorized 11th Sessions |
| 8 March - 30 April 1982; New York | 11th Session of Third Conference | The Convention on the Law of the Sea adopted |

| Date/Place: | Event: | Significance: |
|---|---|---|
| 22 -24 September 1982; New York | Resumed 11th Session of Third Conference | Final Drafting Committee changes approved |
| 1 November 1982 | A/Res. 37/L.13/Rev./ | Authorized Signing Session in Jamaica |
| 6 - 10 December 1982; Montego Bay, Jamaica | Signing Session for the Convention on the Law of the Sea | 119 delegations signed the Convention on the Law of the Sea. |

35

SEABED COMMITTEE
GENEVA
July 2 - August 24, 1973

# I.   Summary and Organization

The United Nations Seabed  Committee which is
preparing for the Third U.N. Conference on the Law
of the Sea met in Geneva from July 2 until August 24.
The Committee completed its consideration of the articles dealing with the regime and the organization of
the new international authority for the deep seabeds.
These articles include both agreed texts and, where
agreement was not possible, agreed alternatives. Some
progress was made in drafting agreed articles on marine pollution.  Although work was begun on scientific
research articles, the Committee was unable to reach
agreement on any significant texts.  Because of the
complexity and sensitivity of the issues and because
of organizational problems, there was limited progress
in agreeing on treaty articles or an alternative text
on the territorial sea, straits, fisheries, coastal
State jurisdiction over offshore seabed resources and
related issues.  However, delegations did submit proposed texts on most of the important subjects and issues.  Despite the lack of progress in some areas, the
general view among delegations, with the possible
major exception of the Soviet Union and some others,
was that the Conference should proceed on schedule.

## SEABED COMMITTEE ORGANIZATION AND SCHEDULE

Sub-Committee I
>    Sub-Committee I Working Group (1): Mandate
>    includes regime and machinery for seabed
>    area beyond national jurisdiction.

Sub-Committee II
>    Sub-Committee II Working Group of the Whole:
>    Mandate includes territorial sea, straits,
>    archipelagoes, continental shelf resources,
>    fisheries, and related subjects.

>>        Informal Working Unit on Fisheries
>>            (met twice)
>>        Informal Consultations on Territorial Sea
>>            (met periodically toward end of session)

Sub-Committee III
>    Sub-Committee II Working Group (2):
>    Mandate includes protection of the environment.

>>        Informal Drafting Group on Marine
>>        Environment

Sub-Committee III Working Group (3):
Mandate includes marine scientific research
and transfer of technology.

Informal Drafting Group on Marine
Scientific Research

| Sixth Preparatory Meeting | 8 weeks | July 2-August 24, 1973 Geneva |
| Conference Organizational Session | 2 weeks | November/December 1973 New York |
| Conference | 8 weeks | April/May 1974 Santiago, Chile |

## II. Deep Seabed Regime

The Seabed Committee made discernible progress in
the preparation of draft treaty articles on the regime
for the deep seabed. A 33-member open-ended working
group (WG) was established at the end of the spring
1972 Seabed Committee session to prepare articles on
the seabed principles and machinery. Since then, it
has held 90 meetings and has produced over 50 draft
treaty articles. Sub-Committee I, which has responsibility for the seabed area beyond national jurisdiction, all but ceased to function during the latest
session. The WG, an informal drafting group, under
the excellent chairmanship of Christopher Pinto of
Sri Lanka, was able to develop alternative and bracketed texts reflecting the broad range of views within
the Seabed Committee.

Although there were no formal negotiations on
substantive issues, preparation of articles served to
highlight issues on which there are fundamental differences and those on which there appears to be common
ground. The Chairman of Sub-Committee I, Paul Engo of
Cameroon, attempted from time to time throughout the
session to encourage more basic negotiations and
greater compromise. However, most felt that the time
would be more usefully spent at the working group level in preparing clear draft articles.

There was solidarity among the developing countries on the issue of who may exploit the seabed and
who will control the Authority. The developed countries, i.e. US, UK, France, Japan, USSR, Canada, and

Australia, displayed great uniformity both in their opposition to a policy-making role for the Assembly of the Authority and in their support for inclusion in the treaty of rules and regulations governing resource exploitation.

In the closing weeks of the March session, the working group (WG) completed a second reading of the draft articles dealing with the international regime to govern deep seabed mineral exploitation and began the first reading of draft articles on the international machinery. During the first seven weeks of the July-August session, the WG continued consideration of these articles, which were contained in a working document prepared by its Chairman.

The machinery articles proved to be more complex than those on the regime, although there have generally been only two or three divergent views on each important item. Moreover, it was difficult to fit into the framework of the working paper some of the more lengthy and intricate concepts embodied in the US draft treaty, such as systems for adopting rules and regulations, for regulating resource exploitation and for settling disputes. The provisions on these questions are scattered throughout the US treaty, and it was necessary to redraft several important provisions in order to effectuate a coherent presentation in the format being used by the working group.

The major areas of disagreement arising during the recent session included:

A.  <u>Powers of the Assembly vs. Powers of the Council</u>

The preponderant developing-country view is that effective power in the new international organization should rest in the Assembly, in which all parties are represented with one vote; while the US and other developed countries maintain that the Council should exercise fundamental control over the operations of the Authority. The US explained its position on this issue in terms of the pragmatic necessity for having a smaller, permanent body deal with urgent operational matters arising from the Authority's role as resource manager. The US expressed its willingness to give the Assembly broad recommendatory powers as an alternative to other delegations' desire to give the Assembly policy-making functions.

### B. Rules and Regulations

In explaining the US position on the Council's role in the Authority, the US repeatedly emphasized the need for including in the treaty itself basic rules governing resource exploitation.

### C. System for Resource Exploitation

Early in the session the Latin American States introduced a detailed proposal on the Enterprise concept. In essence, their proposal would establish the Enterprise as the operating arm of the Authority exclusively empowered to exploit the deep seabed, either through service contracts or through joint ventures with companies or States. The developing countries reactivated the Group of 77 in order to garner unanimous support within the group for the Enterprise concept, but unanimity was not achieved. Throughout the discussions, the US representative pointed out the practical advantages of the licensing system versus an exploitation monopoly by the International Authority. As noted above, the US stressed that the basic conditions and terms of licensing should be established in the treaty itself and not left to an organ of the International Authority to determine, so as to avoid a subjective and possibly discriminatory and unpredictable licensing policy.

While the Latin American supporters of the Enterprise concept resisted efforts to acknowledge that there were any alternatives to the Enterprise, the US tried to highlight the practical differences and similarities between the Enterprise and licensing systems. It generally appeared that many of the Asian and African delegations were willing to engage in such a pragmatic comparison and found it helpful.

Several new proposals as to who might exploit the seabed were submitted. These include two proposals by Australia and Canada, both of which lean heavily toward the Enterprise but permit the Authority to issue licenses or enter into other contractual arrangements for exploitation. Japan, the UK, France, and the USSR maintained solidarity with the US in favoring a licensing system to the exclusion of other systems.

### D.  Production Controls

Virtually no substantive discussion took place
on the issue of production controls, although alternative texts now appear which grant various organs of
the Authority power over this question.  These proposals range from mere recommendatory power to power to
reduce production and fix price levels.  The US took
the position throughout that the International Authority should have no powers in the area of production
controls.

### E.  Composition of Council

One of the more difficult issues in the negotiation is the composition of the Council.  Many developing countries have made it clear that they will strongly support a Council consisting of countries selected
on an equitable geographical basis and in which decisions are made by a two-thirds majority.  The US and
several other developed countries, on the other hand,
have stressed the need for some formula by which those
countries which will have the greatest involvement in
deep seabed mining will be assured that their views
will be given proper weight.  Since at this stage in
the preparations there was no possibility of concession by either side on this issue, the WG passed over
the question without debate, simply including a set of
alternative treaty articles reflecting various approaches.

### F.  Tribunal

The WG thoroughly discussed the question of the
system for dispute settlement, although there was little substantive debate on the detailed US proposal for
a Tribunal.  General attitudes expressed in the discussion indicate that many delegations favor creation
of a Tribunal to settle seabed disputes, although the
scope of its powers and details of its organization
remain controversial.  The concept of compulsory settlement of disputes was presented by the US as one of
the cornerstones of the Sub-Committee I negotiations.

### G.  Provisional Regime

At the spring session of the Seabed Committee the
US proposed that the conference consider the possibility of having those portions of the LOS treaty affecting deep seabed mining go into effect on a provisional

basis immediately following signature, without waiting
for the treaty to enter into force, which might be a
matter of years. The purpose of the US proposal was
to assure that seabed mining, when it begins, will be
subject to an internationally agreed regime. The
Seabed Committee requested the Secretary General to
prepare a study on applicable precedents for the provisional application of treaties. This study was
prepared and circulated at the summer session. There
was very little discussion of the US proposal at this
session, although several delegations indicated serious interest in the suggestion.

In a statement on August 22, the US Representative stated that the US is prepared to support provisional application for both deep seabeds and fisheries aspects of the treaty and to consider provisional application in connection with other aspects of the
treaty as well.

III. Territorial Sea and Straits

There were three distinct approaches to the question of the breadth of the territorial sea which
emerged at this session. The first approach, which
was widely supported among all regional groups, was
for a 12-mile territorial sea. However, a number of
States conditioned their acceptance of the 12-mile
figure on satisfactory settlement on other issues in
an overall treaty. Backers of the OAU Declaration and
the Santo Domingo Declaration explicitly conditioned
acceptance of a 12-mile territorial sea on acceptance
of a 200-mile economic zone or patrimonial sea. The
US has repeatedly stated that our willingness to recognize a 12-mile territorial sea is contingent upon
satisfactory provisions ensuring free and unimpeded
transit through and over straits used for international navigation.

The second approach was advocated by Peru, Ecuador, and Uruguay. They envision a plurality of regimes under the term "territorial sea." In the first
zone out to 12 miles, the regime of innocent passage
would apply. In the second zone from 12 to 200 miles,
freedom of navigation, overflight, and the laying of
submarine cables and pipelines would apply.

The third approach was advocated by Brazil. It
supported a standard 200-mile territorial sea in which

the coastal State would exercise sovereignty subject to the regime of innocent passage.

The question of whether straits used for international navigation, which would be overlapped by a territorial sea of 12 miles, should be treated differently from other areas of the territorial sea remained a contentious issue. Major maritime States, such as the US, UK, France, and the Soviet Union, continued to stress the need for a guaranteed right of passage through and over international straits. Certain archipelago and "strait States," supported by others such as the People's Republic of China, Kenya, and Peru, continued to press for the application of the doctrine of innocent passage in the entire territorial sea. The vast majority of States, however, remained silent on this issue or at least did not take an active stance on either side. In general, at this session, there seemed to be a better comprehension of the rationale behind the US proposal and of the necessity for finding acceptable provisions on this issue in order to have a successful Conference.

There was considerable discussion on the archipelago concept. As in the past, Indonesia and the Philippines, supported particularly by Ecuador and Spain, were vigorous in their efforts to achieve acceptance of this concept. Fiji was an effective moderating influence on the question of notice for passage of military vessels and on defining the area within an archipelago as something other than internal waters. The UK introduced draft articles on the subject suggesting maximum baseline length (48 miles) and land-to-water ration (1:5) criteria for determining application of the archipelago concept. Australia endorsed the archipelagic concept in principle but stopped short of full acceptance on points such as prior notice for warships in sealanes. The Soviet Union laid down conditions which hinted that, if met, would enable it to recognize the archipelagic concept.

The status and maritime jurisdictional entitlement of islands clearly emerged at this session as one of the most troublesome and least understood issues in the negotiations. Turkey, which has Greek islands off its coast, made a number of long interventions arguing that ad hoc determinations based on equitable factors should be the basis for maritime jurisdictional entitlement for islands. Greece responded at length to the Turkish speeches, maintaining that islands should

have the same territorial sea and economic jurisdiction as coastal States. The strongly held positions of certain States on this issue materially affected the progress of the work in Sub-Committee III. The island issue illustrates--as well as any--that law-of-the-sea interests cut across regional group lines.

IV. Coastal State Resource Jurisdiction Beyond the Territorial Sea - Seabeds

On July 18, 1973, the US tabled draft articles which would give coastal States the exclusive right to explore and exploit seabed resources in a Coastal Seabed Economic Area. Coastal nations would have the exclusive right to authorize and regulate all drilling in the area as well as the construction, operation, and use of offshore installations such as offshore ports and airports affecting their economic interests in the area and the waters above. Coastal States would have to conform to internationally prescribed and agreed standards to prevent pollution and unjustifiable interference with other uses of the marine environment, although coastal nations could apply higher environmental standards to those activities under their jurisdiction. Investment agreements would have to be observed strictly and just and prompt compensation given in the event property were taken. Some revenue sharing from mineral exploitation of the area and compulsory dispute settlement were contemplated. The US proposed that the Coastal Seabed Economic Area extend beyond the 12-mile territorial sea, allowing for the fact that the Continental Shelf Convention already specified the 200-meter depth figure. The outer limit of the area was not specified, but the US noted that the preponderant view favored 200 miles. At the same time, the US observed that a sizable number of delegations preferred, in addition to this mileage limit, an alternative seaward limit which would embrace the full continental margin where it extended beyond 200 miles.

States generally reacted favorably to the US draft articles and introductory speech. In spite of this, we have experienced difficulty in getting other delegations to focus on the question of the international standards in the Coastal Seabed Economic Area. Some African States were critical of the provision for protection of investment and compulsory dispute settlement.

There were basically two controversial issues in connection with continental margin resources. The first concerned the so-called concept of "acquired rights." This concept referred to the fact that certain broad shelf countries such as Argentina, Australia, New Zealand, and Canada desired to retain exclusive rights to the resources of the continental margin where it extended beyond 200 miles. The African Group in particular resisted this approach as being inconsistent with the OAU Declaration. In addition, the acquisition of such rights was strongly opposed by landlocked and other geographically disadvantaged States who favored an intermediate zone with revenue sharing in any "acquired rights" areas. The second controversial issue related to the desire by landlocked and other disadvantaged States to share in the ocean resources of neighboring coastal States.

A 200-mile exclusive economic resource zone clearly had wide support. For example, such a zone was included, in the OAU Declaration, the Santo Domingo Declaration, and in a paper submitted by Norway and Canada. Certain archipelagic and strait States such as Indonesia and Spain also supported this concept. Other States, for example, India and Kenya, stated that the starting point of negotiations had to be an exclusive economic zone. Therefore, they were unwilling to discuss functional aspects of the zone, such as a fisheries regime, in great detail until there was acceptance of the exclusive economic zone principle. On the other hand, the USSR and its allies opposed not only the 200-mile exclusive economic zone but also the 200-mile boundary for the seabed.

V.   Coastal State Resource Jurisdiction Beyond the Territorial Sea - Fisheries

The United States continued to emphasize conservation, maximum utilization, and special treatment for anadromous and highly migratory stocks, (i.e., host State management and preferential rights to anadromous stocks and international management of highly migratory stocks) and compulsory dispute settlement. On August 22, the US Representative stated that we were prepared to support provisional application for both deep seabeds and fisheries aspects of the treaty and to consider provisional application in connection with other aspects of the treaty as well.

At this session, the most meaningful point-by-point exchanges on fisheries took place in two informal meetings chaired by Canada as spokesman for six co-sponsors (Canada, India, Kenya, Sri Lanka, Senegal, and Madagascar) of a draft fisheries proposal. There were detailed discussions on the issues of maximum utilization and conservation of fisheries resources. The US emphasized the equity of the maximum utilization concept, underscoring the world's need for high protein food from the sea. We pointed out that fisheries are a renewable resource, and that food is wasted when a fish stock is underutilized. Canada, Iceland, UK, Ireland, and the US strongly supported the need for host State control over anadromous fish stocks. Japan consistently resisted attempts to give coastal States control over anadromous stocks. The Soviet Union, Japan, and the UK were readily identifiable as the leading advocates for distant-water fishing rights in general.

Afghanistan, Austria, Belgium, Bolivia, Nepal, and Singapore urged acceptance of a right of neighboring States to participate in the exploration and exploitation of living resources of the zone on an equal and non-discriminatory basis. This effort was opposed by Kenya, Peru, and Cameroon. Ecuador, Panama, and Peru introduced draft articles on fisheries which would give the coastal State complete legal authority over living resources in national zones of ocean space. In what they termed the "international zone of ocean space" (presumably beyond 200 miles), the coastal State would enjoy preferential rights over living resources in a sector of the sea adjacent to the zone under its sovereignty and jurisdiction.

## VI.  Pollution

### A.  General

The US Delegation submitted a set of draft articles on the protection of the marine environment and the prevention of pollution. The articles were designed to demonstrate that satisfactory arrangements for environmental protection and an accommodation of coastal State concerns could be achieved without undue prejudice to navigational rights. The US pointed out in a statement of August 13, 1973, that the establishment of 200-mile zones of jurisdiction which included pollution-control competence would have the

unexpected and unintended consequence of cutting off
the majority of coastal States from direct access to
the high seas without going through another State's
zone of jurisdiction, thus making them "zone-locked."
Australia reacted sharply to the US statement, as did
several other supporters of broad marine pollution-
control jurisdiction such as Canada. However, a number of other States welcomed the initiative.

The Marine Pollution WG used the proposals of
the US, Canada, and others as a basis for its work.
In the March/April session, articles were drafted on
the general and particular obligations of States to
protect and preserve the marine environment.

At this session, alternative texts were prepared
on global and regional cooperation and on the source
of standards for controlling land-based, seabed-source
and vessel-source pollution. Agreed texts were provisionally adopted on monitoring and technical assistance, and there was consideration of articles on the
duty of States responsible to terminate activities
violating the Convention and the method of determining
whether a State had discharged its obligations under
the LOS Convention. Finally, there was considerable
discussion on enforcement issues but no agreement on a
narrowing of options or even on a method of presenting
alternative texts. There was no consideration of the
issues of State responsibility and liability, military
exemption, or compulsory dispute settlement, although
texts have been proposed by delegations on each of
these issues.

B. Economic Consequences of Pollution Control

A major development in the WG was the appearance
of a strong desire by developing countries to avoid
binding environmental standards which they feel could
restrict their economic development. This was characterized by a strong push to include language in many
articles indicating that economic development factors
must be taken into account when pollution-control
standards are established. While many developing
countries were willing to restrict their demands for
special treatment to standards for land-based marine
pollution (which could only be recommendatory in any
case), others wanted broader exceptions. Several
countries opposed the US proposal for minimum international standards for seabed resource activities, and
some, notably Brazil and Argentina, argued that

developing country flag vessels should not be subject
in any case to higher standards than those applied by
the flag State. (The US has proposed a floor of international standards with higher standards to be applied only by port or flag States.)

C.  Standards Discussion

A great deal of time was given to consideration
of pollution standards applicable to land-based,
seabed-source, and vessel-source pollution.  While the
US, in tabling the draft articles, did not include
articles concerning standards for control of land-
based sources of marine pollution, the informal drafting group, with US support, provisionally agreed on an
article obliging States to establish national standards and to endeavor to establish and adopt international standards.  On the question of standards with
respect to seabed sources of marine pollution, the US
draft articles called for the establishment of and
agreement to minimum international standards and the
right of coastal States to set higher standards.  Alternative texts reflect the view of some States (Tanzania, Kenya, and Brazil) that there need not necessarily be minimum international standards, and that
primary responsibility for establishing seabed standards should lie with the coastal States.  On the
questions of standards for vessel-source pollution,
the US--both in an earlier working paper and in draft
articles--favored exclusively international standards,
and proposed that IMCO should have the primary responsibility for establishing such standards.  In this regard, the US--supported by the UK, Denmark, Norway,
Sweden, Japan, and others--advocated that only port
States and flag States should be able to apply higher
standards.  Our proposals were attacked by Canada,
Australia, and the developing countries who opposed a
system of exclusively international standards.  Canada
and Australia favor primary reliance on international
standards but forcefully advocate a right for the
coastal State to establish supplemental standards for
special circumstances or for situations in which, in
their view, international standards are inadequate or
non-existent.  Some developing countries, notably
Kenya and Tanzania, and the People's Republic of China,
favored exclusive coastal State competence to set
standards both for seabeds and for vessels in their
economic zone.  The Soviet Union insisted that States
have the right to establish standards for their own
vessels, although they conceded that such standards

should not be lower than those agreed internationally. (The USSR, unwilling to consider an economic zone, is committed to coastal State standards only in the territorial sea and probably in the Arctic.)  The developing countries, in responding to US arguments, indicated they had no interest in interfering with navigation, but Tanzania, on at least one occasion, reserved the right to discriminate against certain unnamed States.  Several opposed IMCO as the primary source of international standards, and some felt that the Authority or UNEP should have a role.  Several alternative texts were laid out on these issues.

D.  Enforcement

The US proposed several general articles on enforcement based mainly on flag and port competence as well as bonding and other release measures.  In addition, the US draft articles contain extraordinary coastal State rights in three situations:

1.  A finding by the dispute settlement machinery of persistent flag State failure to enforce;

2.  Reasonable emergency enforcement measures to prevent, mitigate, or eliminate imminent danger to its coast from a violation of applicable standards;

3.  Intervention in circumstances spelled out in the 1969 Intervention Convention.

Canada, Australia, Kenya, and Peru, supported by certain developing countries, argued for a right of the coastal State to enforce standards within the limits of their national jurisdiction.  France and Japan proposed coastal State enforcement only against discharges or dumping in contravention of international rules in an unspecified zone.  The Soviet Union forcefully opposed any coastal State right of enforcement beyond the territorial sea and opposed forwarding any alternative texts on this subject to the Santiago Conference.

E.  IMCO

IMCO's role was a prominent topic in Sub-Committee III and its WG.  The US explained its proposal regarding a Marine Environmental Protection Committee (MEPC)

which could be empowered to adopt regulations on vessel-source pollution and send them directly to States. Ambassador Pardo of Malta responded to that proposal with a long speech attacking the proposition as being beyond the authority of the IMCO Charter. This attack was joined by Canada, Peru, Chile, Kenya, Tanzania, and others. Canada qualified its opposition to the MEPC by saying that its opposition was tied to exclusively international standards. In addition to the MEPC proposal, IMCO was attacked by some developing countries as not being representative of coastal States with an interest in marine pollution but rather only of flag States with a primary interest in shipping. These allegations were answered by various maritime States--including the US, UK, USSR, Greece, Norway, Sweden, and Denmark--who stated that IMCO had at least 50 developing countries as members; that almost all members were coastal States with coastal State interests; that IMCO had been effective in reduction of marine pollution from ships, and was the only international organization with the necessary expertise; that IMCO membership was open to all; that the 1973 Marine Pollution Conference was a plenipotentiary conference; and that the MEPC was open to all nations who were members of IMCO or who were signatories to a treaty administered by IMCO.

A letter was sent to the Secretary General of IMCO enclosing selected records and documents from the Seabed Committee and noting the relation to some areas being dealt with by Sub-Committee III and by the 1973 Marine Pollution Conference. Article 9 (2) of the IMCO draft on not prejudicing the LOS Conference was also noted.

This letter was not entirely satisfactory to the Group of 77 who are now sending a letter to their members encouraging attendance at the 1973 Conference to protect their LOS interests.


VII.  Scientific Research

The US delivered a statement in Sub-Committee III and introduced draft articles on marine scientific research on July 20. Other separate drafts were submitted by the Eastern Europeans (Soviet draft), Malta, Canada, China, and the Latin Americans, (Brazil, El Salvador, Ecuador, Peru, and Uruguay). A limited general debate occurred on the topic of technology

transfer with statements by Yugoslavia, USSR, France, US, Greece, Venezuela, and Malta. All of the draft articles were referred to a WG chaired by Andrzej Olszowka (Poland).

The US proposal calls for cooperation in facilitating research in the territorial sea and provides for a set of obligations for the conduct of research in areas beyond the territorial sea where the coastal State exercises jurisdiction over seabed resources and coastal fisheries. This obligation would be in lieu of consent and would include: advance notification; coastal State participation; flag State certification of the bona fides of the researcher; sharing of data and samples; assistance in interpreting the data; and compliance with international environmental standards.

The Chairman and the UN Secretariat produced an outline of a comparative table consisting of ten sub-sections with comparative texts for six of them. The organization of this table contributed significantly to the difficulties of the WG in subsequent efforts to achieve progress. The Latin American group attacked the titles of some sections, particularly one reading: "right to undertake marine scientific research." They considered this to be prejudicial to the question of whether such a right existed, especially within the limits of national jurisdiction.

The major dispute in the WG was created by an item which was subdivided into "consent," "participation," and "obligations." When the comparative table was distributed, the Chairman announced that these sub-items would be considered together; but when discussion commenced on this item, he stated the first concept to be considered would be "consent." When draft articles were being considered, the US insisted that its Article 7 (which does not mention consent but concentrates instead on detailed obligations of the researcher when conducting research in areas beyond the territorial sea) was, in fact, an alternative to the consent regime. Many delegations--particularly Brazil, Peru, Argentina, and Canada--actively opposed inclusion of the US article as an alternative to the consent regime. Others--including the Soviet Union and Tanzania--claimed further that by referring to jurisdiction in a zone between the territorial sea and the high seas, the US was prejudging the work of a different Sub-Committee. Some delegations indicated a willingness to accept the US proposal under the consent

heading but not the associated listing of obligations.
The WG could reach no agreement on this sub-section
but did produce texts on the definition and conduct
of scientific research.

During the discussions on the question of consent,
no delegation actively supported the US proposal, although France, Mexico, Australia, and Italy made suggestions which would qualify the right of the coastal
State to refuse consent. Kenya and Tanzania supported the consent regime, stating that such an adjunct of
sovereignty was necessary for consistency with the
concept of an exclusive economic zone.

## VIII. Dispute Settlement

Throughout the session in all Sub-Committees, the
US stressed that there was a need for an effective
dispute-settlement mechanism to ensure that conflict
could be avoided or resolved. All draft articles introduced by the US during this session contained a
cross-reference to a section of the overall LOS treaty
on dispute settlement. The US introduced general draft
articles on dispute settlement on August 22. In a
statement on the same day, the US emphasized that a
system of peaceful and compulsory dispute settlement
was an essential aspect of a comprehensive LOS settlement. We indicated that a system was needed that ensured, to the maximum extent possible, uniform interpretation and immediate access to dispute settlement
machinery in urgent situations while at the same time
preserving the flexibility of States to agree to resolve disputes by a variety of means. Thus, the US
articles reflected a system of settlement of disputes
by any manner agreed to by the parties with an LOS
Tribunal to settle disputes, if parties did not agree
to another method.

## IX. Procedural Aspects

The Seabed Committee has operated on a consensus
basis. In Sub-Committee I, the combination of a very
skillful Chairman of the WG (Christopher Pinto) and
the fact that more concrete draft articles were available at the outset resulted in largely satisfactory
completion of that Sub-Committee's preparation for the
Conference.

Procedural problems were also largely overcome in the Sub-Committee III WG on Marine Pollution, and approximately half of the draft articles were placed in an acceptable form for the Conference. This Group did, of course, have a relatively narrow mandate and far fewer drafts to work with than the Group in Sub-Committee II.

The Sub-Committee III WG on Scientific Research started late in the session, and little substantive progress was made. A great deal of time was spent sorting out procedural problems, as this WG had not established a work method before the start of this session.

Sub-Committee II and its WG continued to face a variety of time-consuming procedural obstacles at this session. Underlying the difficulties was the fact that unlike other Sub-Committees, Sub-Committee II has the broadest mandate for dealing with traditional law of the sea subjects upon which most States have strong, long-standing views. Moreover, the questions of off-shore fisheries and petroleum resources—as well as the questions of maritime commerce and navigation and straits passage—affect the hard economic and security interests of States.

The above factors, and others, combined to produce a bewildering number of draft alternatives under the various subjects and issues allocated to Sub-Committee II. The Procedure followed was to allow any State to introduce any draft article or articles that it desired under any list item. Unfortunately, draft alternative articles submitted at prior sessions, ones formally introduced at this session, as well as those informally or orally introduced at this session, were inserted in various places under comparative tables, in consolidated texts, and sometimes alone. The resulting documentation was voluminous and confusing.

SECOND SESSION
CARACAS
June 20 - August 29, 1974

# I. Summary and Overall Evaluation of Session

The object of the Law of the Sea Conference is a comprehensive Law of the Sea Treaty. This was not achieved at Caracas. It would be a mistake, however, to regard the Caracas session as a failure, as it accomplished a great deal: the foundations and building blocks of a settlement are now all present in usable form. A treaty can be achieved if detailed authentic negotiation takes place without delay.

Two underlying problems affect the evaluation of the session. First, events beyond the control of the Conference are tempting States to take matters into their own hands. Second, the Conference suffers from the carry-over of a negotiating style more suitable for General Assembly recommendations or negotiation of abstract issues than texts intended to become widely accepted as treaty obligations affecting immediate interests of States in a dynamic situation. Tactics, rather than negotiation, was the rule.

## A. Accomplishments

Accomplishments of the session are considerable. Among the most important are the following:

1. The vast array of law-of-the-sea issues and proposals within the mandate of Committee II was organized by the Committee into a comprehensive set of informal Working Papers reflecting main trends on each precise issue. The many formal proposals were introduced mainly as a basis for insertions in these Main Trends Papers. All States can now focus on each issue --and the alternative solutions--with relative ease. A similar development occurred with respect to marine scientific research in Committee III.

2. The transition from a Seabed Committee of about 90 to a Conference of almost 150 was achieved without major new stumbling blocks and with a minimum of delay.

3. The overwhelming majority clearly desires a treaty in the near future. Agreement on the Rules of Procedure is clear evidence of this desire to achieve a widely acceptable treaty. The tone of the

general debate and the informal meetings was moderate and serious. The Conference adopted a recommended 1975 work schedule deliberately devised to stimulate agreement.

4.  The inclusion in the treaty of a 12-mile territorial sea and a 200-mile economic zone was all but formally agreed, subject of course to acceptable resolution of other issues, including unimpeded transit of straits. Accordingly, expanded coastal States jurisdiction over living and non-living re-sources appears assured as part of the comprehensive treaty.

5.  With respect to the deep seabeds, the first steps have been taken toward real negotiation of the basic questions of the system of exploitation and the conditions of exploitation.

6.  Traditional regional and political align-ments of States are being replaced by informal groups whose membership is based on similarities of interest on a particular issue. This has greatly facilitated clarification of issues, and is necessary for finding effective accommodations.

7.  The number and tempo of private meetings has increased considerably and has moved beyond for-mal positions. This is essential to a successful ne-gotiation.

B.  Assessment

With few exceptions, the Conference papers now make it clear what the structure and general content of the treaty will be, the alternatives to choose from, the blanks to be filled in, and even the rela-tive importance attached to different issues. What was missing in Caracas was sufficient political will to make hard negotiating choices. The main reason was the conviction that this would not be the last session, which is the type of assessment that can easily be spread by treaty opponents. Nevertheless, the words "we are not far apart" were more and more frequently heard, at least in Committee II, insofar as the devel-oping country assessment of U.S. positions is concern-ed.

57

The Conference recommended to the UNGA that the next session be held "in Geneva from 17 March to 3 or 10 May, the latter date depending upon certain practical arrangements to be made with the World Health Organization, whose assembly was scheduled to open on 6 May in Geneva.

The Conference also agreed to recommend that the formal final session of the Conference should be held in Caracas for the purpose of signature of the final act and other instruments of the Conference. The successful conclusion of perhaps the most complex and divisive global negotiation ever held must be on the basis of States' real interests rather than abstract concepts. The momentum, albeit with fits and starts, tends to favor such negotiation. The United States can contribute to this by retaining its commitment to that end and sticking to a pragmatic approach to problems; but all must now make the ultimate choice between symbols and achievement.

## II. Committee I (Seabed Beyond the Limits of Jurisdiction)

### A. General

Unlike other Committees, the entire range of issues under Committee I's mandate, with only one exception, had been reflected in alternative treaty articles prepared by the Seabed Committee. The one exception was the preparation of treaty articles on
rules and regulations for deep seabed mining, a critical element of the US deep seabed position. In previous sessions of the Seabed Committee, which worked
on the basis of consensus, there had been considerable
opposition to even a discussion of rules and regulations, which were referred to in notes and footnotes.

The Committee held one week of general debate in
which the following trends emerged:

1. A number of African and Asian delegations
expressed their willingness to support an exploitation
system that permitted different types of contractual
arrangements in the early years of operation, coupled
with a gradual phasing out of these systems in favor
of direct exploitation. In this connection, the need
to provide security of tenure and conditions that
would attract entities with the necessary capital and
technology was a prevalent theme in their statements.

2. There was increased support among European
delegations for a parallel licensing/direct exploitation system. Australia and Canada maintained their
support for this approach.

3. A large number of developing country
delegations referred to the need to include dispute
settlement machinery in the Authority.

The general debate was followed by a rapid reading of the Regime Articles in an informal Committee of
the Whole, chaired by Christopher Pinto of Sri Lanka.
There were some reductions in alternatives and bracketed language on several articles. The majority received no alteration. The Informal Committee decided
to discuss in detail major issues of disagreement
rather than proceed to the texts on the machinery.
The three major issues selected were the exploitation
system (Article 9 of the Regime), conditions of

exploitation (Rules and Regulations), and economic implications.

B.  Exploitation System

The exploitation system (Article 9) was identified by many countries as the crux of the Committee I negotiations.  During the Caracas session, the Group of 77 agreed on a single text for Article 9 which would permit the Authority to enter into a variety of legal arrangements, provided it maintained "direct and effective control at all times."

A number of developing country delegations throughout the last weeks of the session began to call for serious negotiations on Article 9.  Three delegations threatened voting instead.

Several delegations indicated a willingness to discuss formulas which might include the concept that the Authority's control over resource exploitation would be exercised in accordance with certain broad general principles to be laid down in the Convention.

Jamaica introduced a proposal for Article 9 that includes such general principles, together with the requirement that the Authority promulgate rules and regulations within this framework.

In the closing days of the session, after earlier resistance to discussion of the context of general conditions of exploitation, Committee I established a Negotiating Group with the mandate to consider Articles 1-21, placing special emphasis on its work on both Article 9 and conditions of exploitation.  The Negotiating Group met several times and engaged in very constructive discussions on the Group of 77 text for Article 9.  There emerged in these exploratory talks a definite willingness on the part of a number of delegations supporting that text to explore changes in the text without commitment.

C.  Conditions of Exploitation (Rules and Regulations

After completing the debate on the exploitation system and three weeks before the end of the session, Committee I arrived at the agenda item of rules and regulations for deep seabed exploitation.

The US delegation made clear the importance which it attached to a full and comprehensive discussion of the issues involved in the conditions of exploitation. A lengthy, off-the-record statement was delivered that explained in detail the purpose of rules and regulations, why the US considered it important that they be included in the treaty, and our difficulties with moving further in the Committee I work without an agreed commitment that conditions of exploitation were to be included in the treaty.

The Group of 77 decided to prepare their own text of basic conditions of exploitation and indicated a willingness to create some formal mechanism for discussing and negotiationg this issue.

The draft text on basic conditions of exploitation that emerged from the Group of 77 was for the most part an elaboration of their proposal on Article 9, granting almost complete discretion to the Authority in very general terms to make decisions concerning exploitation, so as to protect land-based producers and give the Authority "direct and effective control" over all operators. In certain areas it described in greater detail how the Authority should maintain control, and sprinkled throughout were the seeds of ideas that might be converted into treaty articles to protect investment.

In addition to the Group of 77 proposal on basic conditions, draft rules and regulations were submitted to Committee I by the US, Japan, and eight members of the European Community.

D. Economic Implications

Committee I devoted several days of on-the-record debate to the issue of economic implications. Land-based producers of the metals contained in manganese nodules had in previous sessions of the Seabed Committee succeeded in winning widespread support for price and production controls, but the high profile given this issue during the Caracas session resulted in two new developments:

1. Detailed presentations and question-and-answer periods with representatives of UNCTAD and the Secretary General served to highlight the great uncertainty regarding any threat that the ocean mining

industry may pose for the economies of developing-
country producers of the metals contained in nodules.

2. Several developing country representatives made public statements on the need to protect
consumers from artificially high prices. This had
never occurred in the Seabed Committee.

The US delegation submitted a Working Paper and
made statements that pointed out the interests of all
consumers in encouraging seabed output, the unlikeli-
hood that the income of existing producers would de-
crease, even with seabed production, and the inherent
difficulties and adverse effects of schemes to protect
land-based producers. Several developing countries
expressed a willingness not to require protective
measures in the Convention itself, and an insistence
that a balance between consumer and producer interests
be structured into whatever machinery was created for
dealing with the potential problem.

E. Evaluation

The work of Committee I advanced during the Caracas session. The inclusion of conditions of exploitation in the Convention is widely accepted. However,
the proposals for such conditions are at considerable
variance with each other. Further, the Committee's
discussion of economic implications led to a greater
understanding of the complexity of the issue, coupled
with a growing awareness among developing country
delegations that the interests of their consumers
might be damaged in attempts to protect a small number
of developing country land-based producers who account
for a minority share of the world's output, although
the land-based producers continued to call for developing country solidarity. Most importantly, there was
a new, more serious mood in the Committee that indicated an understanding that genuine negotiation is
needed if an agreement is to be concluded. This mood,
although intangible, can be demonstrated in the following developments:

1. Most delegations opposed the Chairman's
initial plan for two weeks of general debate--they
wanted to get to work immediately.

2. During the third reading of the Regime
Articles, certain differences which were previously
insurmountable were easily removed, e.g.,

a. The key Article on the common heritage concept was reduced from four to two alternatives--it would have been unanimously agreed but for the refusal of only a handful of delegations to add language to the principle of the common heritage.

b. The differences over the Authority's power to regulate scientific research, which had been addressed in several different Articles, were restricted to only two Articles in the Regime.

3. The Group of 77 was able to agree among themselves on what they believe to be a more flexible approach to Article 9, and agreed to discuss Article 9 along with the conditions of exploitation.

4. An attempt by several land-based producers and a few others to prohibit reference to the conditions of exploitation in the debate on Article 9 was defeated.

5. The Jamaican proposal for Article 9, although significantly different from that of the Group of 77, was supported by several developing country representatives. This proposal was subsequently made a general footnote to the Articles.

6. Proposals for basic conditions of exploitation were presented, and a Working Group for negotiating this issue, together with Article 9, was established.

7. In various general statements and in all drafts of the basic conditions, the need to ensure an attractive and secure investment climate for deep seabed exploiters was acknowledged.

8. Efforts by a few delegations to rally support for a vote on Article 9 did not succeed.

9. Attempts by several land-based producers to prevent informal economic seminars on economic implications were unsuccessful.

10. Efforts by a few delegations to obstruct progress in the Negotiating Group did not succeed.

11. The principle of compulsory settlement of disputes and the establishment of a dispute settlement organ in the Seabed Authority was widely endorsed.

III.  Committee II

A.  General

The following are excerpts from the final summing up of the Chairman of Committee I on August 28
(DOC.A/Conf.62/C.2/L.86):

In 13 informal Working Papers the officers of
the Committee summarized the main trends with
respect to the various subjects and issues, as
they had been manifested in proposals submitted
to the United Nations Seabed Committee or at the
Conference itself....In view of the nature and
purpose of those papers, each of them had been
submitted to the Committee in formal working
meetings.  Thus all the members of the Committee
have had the opportunity to make observations on
these papers in their original versions and in
their first revised versions.  After considering
those observations in detail, the officers prepared a first and, in almost all cases, a second
revision of the papers which, by agreement of
the Committee, is the final version.

--Thus what we have is the collective work of the
Committee which, with the limitations and reservations to be indicated in the general introduction and, in some cases, in the explanatory
notes accompanying certain of the papers, is a
faithful reflection of the main positions on
questions of substance that have taken the
form of draft Articles of a convention.

--Assembling these papers in a single text, with
consecutive numbering makes it possible to present in an orderly fashion the variants which
at this state of the work of the Conference are
offered for consideration by States with respect to the subjects and issues falling within
the Committee's competence.

--This document, in my opinion, should serve not
only as a reference text relating to the most
important work done by the Committee at this
session but also as a basis and point of departure for the future work of this organ of
the Conference.  It would be senseless to begin
all over again the long and laborious process which
has led us to the point where we now stand.

64

--No decision on substantive issues has been taken
at this session, nor has a single Article of the
future Convention been adopted, but the States
present here know perfectly well which are at
this time the positions that enjoy support and
which are the ones that have not managed to make
any headway.

--The paper that sums up the main trends does not
pronounce on the degree of support which each
of them had enlisted at the preparatory meetings and the Conference itself, but it is now
easy for anyone who has followed our work
closely to discern the outline of the future
Convention.

--So far each State has put forward in general
terms the positions which would ideally satisfy
its own range of interests in the seas and
oceans. Once these positions are established,
we have before us the opportunity of negotiation based on an objective and realistic evaluation of the relative strength of the different opinions.

--It is not my intention in this statement to
present a complete picture of the situation
as I see it personally, but I can offer some
general evaluations and comments.

--The idea of a territorial sea of 12 miles and
an exclusive economic zone beyond the territorial sea up to a total maximum distance of
200 miles is, at least at this time, the key-
stone of the compromise solution favored by
the majority of the States participating in
the Conference, as is apparent from the general debate in the Plenary meetings, and the
discussion held in our Committee.

--Acceptance of this idea is of course dependent
on the satisfactory solution of other issues,
especially the issue of passage through straits
used for international navigation, the outermost limit of the continental shelf and the
actual retention of this concept and, last but
not least, the aspiration of the landlocked
countries and of other countries, which, for
one reason or another, consider themselves
geographically disadvantaged.

--There are, in addition, other problems to be
studied and solved in connection with this
idea, for example, those relating to archipelagos and the regime of islands in general.

--It is also necessary to go further into the
matter of the nature and characteristics of
the concept of the exclusive economic zone,
a subject on which important differences of
opinion still persist.

--On all these subjects substantial progress
has been made which lays the foundations for
negotiation during the intersessional period
and at the next session of the Conference.
(End of quotation)

B.  Territorial Sea

Agreement on a 12-mile territorial sea is so widespread that there were virtually no references to any
other limit in the public debate.  Major conditions
for acceptance of 12 miles as a miximum limit were
agreement on unimpeded transit of straits and acceptance of a 200-mile exclusive economic zone.  A variety
of articles have been introduced on the territorial
sea regime which, for the most part, parallel the provisions of the 1958 Territorial Sea Convention.

C.  Contiguous Zone

The contiguous zone is an area where the coastal
State may take measures to prevent and punish infringement of its customs and its fiscal, immigration, and
sanitary laws in its territory or territorial sea.  Its
maximum limit is 12 miles under the 1958 Territorial
Sea Convention.  Some States seem to feel that with
the establishment of a 12-mile territorial sea, the
contiguous zone has become superfluous.  Others would
like it extended to an area beyond 12 miles.

D.  Straits

The introduction of the UK Articles was the major
event of the session, as the UK--as both a maritime
power and a State bordering the most heavily used
strait in the world--necessarily sought an accommodation of the interests involved.  These articles were
well received.  The USSR and Oman also introduced
articles on straits.  In general, there was a trend in

the direction of unimpeded passage. While there was
little public movement toward conciliation on the part
of the straits States, debate was less heated. The US
made a statement reiterating the fundamental importance of unimpeded passage on, over, and under straits
used for international navigation, and addressed means
of accommodating the concerns of straits States with
respect to security, safety, and pollution. The US
also made it clear that distinctions regarding the
right of passage could not be made between commercial
vessels and warships.

E.  High Seas

Discussion centered on the issue of whether or
not the high seas regime, as modified with respect to
fishing, etc., would apply in 200-mile zones beyond
the 12-mile territorial sea. The US sponsored draft
articles on this issue, on fishing beyond the economic
zone, and also co-sponsored articles providing for hot
pursuit from the economic zone and continental shelf.

F.  Access to the Sea

There was little visible progress on the issue of
landlocked-State access to the sea, although there appears to be growing recognition among coastal States
that the question needs to be dealt with fairly. Negotiation of the issue is probably tied to some extent
to the question of access to and benefits from the resources of the economic zone.

G.  Archipelagos

The Bahamas, Fiji, Indonesia, Mauritius, and the
Philippines strongly advocated adoption of the archipelago concept. The issue has been complicated by the
addition of arguments for archipelagic treatment of
island groups belonging to continental States, with
substantial differences of view indicated in Conference statements on this issue. It is widely recognized that the key issues of definition and transit of
archipelagic waters must be resolved for a satisfactory accommodation on the issue.

H.  Economic Zone and Continental Shelf

1.  General

a. Over 100 countries spoke in support of an economic zone extending to a maximum limit of 200 nautical miles. With respect to the content of the zone, there is widespread support for the following:

(1) Coastal State sovereign or exclusive rights for the purpose of exploration and exploitation of living and non-living resources;

(2) Coastal State rights and duties with respect to pollution and scientific research to be specified, presumably in the Chapters of the Convention being prepared in Committee III;

(3) Exclusive coastal State rights over artificial islands and most installations;

(4) Exclusive coastal State rights over drilling for all purposes.

b. There is also general agreement that there would be freedom of navigation and overflight in the economic zone, as well as other third State rights such as laying and maintenance of submarine cables and pipelines. Provisions for the accommodation of uses in the zone would be included.

c. It is also widely recognized that a variety of detailed provisions regarding coastal State and third State rights in the economic zone will determine whether this overall framework can be translated into a generally acceptable treaty. Virtually all of these details, in alternative form, are now present in the informal Working Paper (No. 4 on the Economic Zone), thus laying a clear foundation for negotiation and decision of these issues. With a few exceptions, economic zone proposals have now been proffered from all conference groups, including the US. These proposals have been incorporated into the alternative texts on main trends.

d. The major problems encountered in the economic zone negotiation center on the following points:

(1) What are the rights of the coastal State with respect to scientific research and vessel-source pollution? The issues are being dealt with in Committee III and are discussed in Section IV of this Report.

(2) Do the rights of coastal States over the seabed and subsoil resources of the continental shelf extend beyond 200 miles where the continental margin extends beyond that limit? While a trend toward agreement on such jurisdiction is discernible, with some States declaring that such jurisdiction is a condition of agreement for them, there has been resistance from landlocked and geographically disadvantaged States, and from some African coastal States. The US proposal of an accommodation that includes coastal State jurisdiction over the margin coupled with revenue-sharing as a solution to the problem is picking up additional support, but is still strongly opposed by some coastal States with large margins. The idea proposed by some landlocked States that they have rights of access to mineral resources of adjacent coastal States has met strong and widespread opposition.

(3) What are the duties of the coastal States with respect to conservation and full utilization of fish stocks? What are the rights of access of landlocked States to fisheries? What is the role of regional and international organizations in fisheries management? What special provisions should be included for highly migratory species and for anadromous species? Section 2 below addresses the fisheries question.

(4) What principles apply to the delimitation of the economic zone or continental shelf between adjacent and opposite States? Any precise formula will tend to divide the Conference, since for each coastal State that supports a particular rule--e.g., equidistance--another naturally reacts in fear that it will lose some area. This problem has in turn given rise to arguments over the weight to be given to islands in such delimitation and, even further, to arguments that small or uninhabited islands are not entitled to an economic zone at all. The realization is growing that the Conference could become hopelessly bogged down if it tries to deal definitively with essentially bilateral delimitation problems.

(5) Collateral political and other issues. Numerous proposals have now been introduced regarding islands or areas under foreign domination or control. While most are now designed to ensure benefits

for the local inhabitants, some go farther and address
questions of administration or total denial of rights.
Similarly, other questions have been raised that are
more appropriately considered in other forums.

(6) The Legal Status of the Economic
Zone. It is clear to all that the economic zone is
not a territorial sea. It is equally clear that some
classic high seas freedoms will be eliminated (e.g.,
fishing) or modified, while others, subject to the
provisions of the Convention (for example provisions
on pollution), will be retained (e.g., navigation and
overflight). It appears that the provisions of the
Convention regarding coastal State rights will need
further elaboration before some States feel secure
enough to grapple with the issue in precise terms.

In an effort to allay such concerns, the US--
after consultation with a number of coastally-oriented
States--introduced the following text:

The regime of the high seas, as codified in
the 1958 United Nations Convention on the
High Seas, shall apply as modified by the
provisions of this Chapter and the other
provisions of this Convention, including,
inter alia, those with respect to the Economic Zone, the Continental Shelf, the
Protection of the Marine Environment,
Scientific Research and the International
Sea-Bed area.

(7) Dispute Settlement. Since the
heart of the economic zone negotiation turns on a
balance of rights and duties, the question of dispute
settlement becomes a critical element. On the one
hand, guarantees are sought against unreasonable interpretations, particularly as they affect navigation
and overflight. On the other hand, a measure of
coastal State resource management discretion is
clearly inherent in the exercise of resource jurisdiction. The dispute settlement question is also
examined in Section V of this Report.

There appears to be a genuine desire to negotiate
on these questions, and they are likely to dominate
regional and international consultations before the
next session.

## 2. Fisheries

The maritime nations, in particular the US, UK, and USSR, made significant moves toward increased coastal States rights. In early August the US tabled draft Articles setting forth in detail a 200-mile economic zone system, which implemented its earlier expression of a willingness to accept a 200-mile economic zone as part of satisfactory overall settlement of Conference issues including unimpeded transit of straits, and dependent on a concurrent negotiation and acceptance of correlative coastal State duties. These duties would include a duty to conserve fisheries and a duty to permit foreign fishing under coastal State regulation where a fishery resource is not fully utilized, and international and regional cooperation in establishing equitable conservation and allocation regulations for highly migratory species such as tuna, that includes fees and special allocations for the coastal State in the economic zone. Additionally, we reiterated our position on special treatment for anadromous species such as salmon. Three main approaches seem to have emerged with respect to fisheries in the economic zone. One is completely exclusive, with no coastal State duties. Another is the US-type approach, which couples exclusive coastal State regulation with conservation and full utilization duties. A third, exemplified by the Articles presented by eight EEC States, emphasizes the role of regional organizations.

While advocates of the first approach dwelt largely on conceptual arguments in the public meetings, private discussions tend to reveal more flexibility.

It is widely recognized that there should be special provisions regarding landlocked State access to fisheries. In the US Articles, this is presented in conjunction with the full utilization concept, but a coastal State is free to give special priority to neighboring landlocked and dependent coastal States.

The provisions on highly migratory species in the US Articles represent a large conceptual and substantive shift in the hope of finding reasonable accommodation. A large number of developing-country delegates have commented favorably on the US move.

In response to conceptual problems with jurisdiction following salmon beyond the economic zone, the

US has now proposed a ban on fishing for salmon beyond the territorial sea, except as authorized by the State of origin for purposes of ensuring full utilization.

Despite these positive signs, the failure to come to grips with the question of access and full utilization still plagues the negotiation, and is of central importance to the ultimate ability of the Conference to accommodate widely disparate interests on the subject.

### 3. Continental Shelf

Draft articles on the continental shelf were contained in L.4 (Canada, Chile, Iceland, India, Indonesia, Mauritius, Mexico, New Zealand, and Norway) and in L.47 (US). Coastal State jurisdiction beyond 200 miles, reflected in both submissions, was the major theme of debate. Other issues such as limits between States remain divisive.

Formal debate presented an opportunity for States favoring extension of coastal State jurisdiction beyond 200 miles and for those favoring a limit of 200 miles to present their positions. African States speaking, with the exception of Mauritius, generally advocated the position in the OAU Declaration against coastal State jurisdiction beyond 200 miles. Other opposition came principally from landlocked and other geographically disadvantaged States plus Japan. States in favor of coastal State jurisdiction over the continental margin beyond 200 miles included numerous Latin Americans and Asians, Western Europeans, Canada, Australia, New Zealand, and Mauritius. The Soviet Union supports jurisdiction beyond 200 miles to a depth of 500 meters. A number of States from different geographical groups made equivocal statements suggesting that they might be persuaded to accept coastal State jurisdiction beyond 200 miles.

The subject of revenue sharing from continental shelf resources was not extensively debated in formal Committee sessions. The US proposal for revenue sharing beyond 200 meters and the Netherlands proposal for a graduated revenue sharing dependent on a combination of distance and depth are the only two proposals under formal consideration by the Conference. Trinidad and Tobago, Ghana, and Jamaica referred to the concept as presenting a possible accommodation of interest, and Burma spoke in opposition.

The US proposal relating to integrity of investment is the only provision on the subject under consideration. It did not figure prominently in debate
but is contained in the alternative texts developed
by Committee II on the Economic Zone.

Numerous positions regarding delimitation of
continental shelf boundaries between adjacent and
opposite States were advanced. Treatment to be accorded islands greatly complicated this issue. Some
States are insisting that islands receive the same
treatment as continental areas. Others are seeking
to exclude or limit jurisdiction around islands.

## IV. Committee III

Committee III established two informal Working
Groups where most work was done. One, on pollution,
was chaired by José Vallarta of Mexico who chaired
the equivalent Working Group in the Seabed Committee.
The other, on scientific research and transfer of
technology, was chaired by Cornel Metternich of the
Federal Republic of Germany.

### A. Marine Pollution

Committee III met 22 times in informal session as
a small negotiating group to deal with marine pollution issues. Draft articles were completed on general
obligations to prevent pollution, particular obligations, global and regional cooperation, technical
assistance, rights of States to exploit their resources, and the relevance of economic factors to de-
veloping-countries' obligations. These texts were not
fully agreed, and the US, among others, opposed the
last two in their entirety. Work was begun on rights
to set standards and to enforce them, and on monitoring. The Committee did not begin consideration of
State responsibility and liability, sovereign immunity
or settlement of disputes.

The major item of contention in this discussion
was the double-standard issue raised by Brazil, India,
and several other developing countries. The focus of
discussion was on an Indian proposal to subject all
obligations of States to their national environmental
and national economic development policies. The US,
Japan, UK, and several other Europeans strongly opposed this approach. Some developing countries such

as Jamaica, supported a more restricted concept to give flexibility to developing countries only with regard to land-based pollution.

At the next session, the Committee will begin with the article on monitoring and then take up standard-setting and enforcement rights. The basic problem of vessel-source pollution remains to be addressed, although a trend against coastal State standard setting is already evident, particularly with respect to construction standards.

Negotiations have moved to the point of beginning on the major controversial issues of standards and enforcement, particularly regarding vessel-source pollution. Private negotiations and consultations indicated considerable detailed consideration of specific problems and a willingness to discuss realistic solutions.

B.  Scientific Research and Transfer of Technology

The Informal Working Group on Scientific Research and Transfer of Technology held 21 meetings during this session, either in informal session or as a negotiating group.

Initially there was an attempt to elaborate a definition of scientific research drawing from the definition elaborated by the Seabed Committee which excluded industrial exploration and specified that such research should be conducted for peaceful purposes. Several proposals were made by developing countries to delete these two qualifications. After inconclusive discussion, the informal committee decided to put the definitional question aside.

Agreement, however, was reached on general principles for the conduct of research as well as obligations for international and regional cooperation. The general principles include a requirement that scientific research be conducted exclusively for peaceful purposes; a clause dealing with non-interference with other uses; a requirement that research comply with applicable environmental regulations; and agreement that research activities shall not form the legal basis for any claim to any part of the marine environment or its resources.

The most important issues, and those on which
there was the greatest divergence of views, centered
on research in the economic zone and the international seabed area. As deliberations neared conclusion,
four major trends emerged. Those trends were set
forth in the Report of the Working Group which is expected to form the basis for negotiations at the next
session.

One of those trends was tabled by Colombia and
is stated to represent "the consensus of the Group of
77 of the Third Committee, without committing the
final position of the members of the Group." This
proposal provides that all research in the economic
zone--including that conducted by satellites and ODAS
--requires the explicit consent of the coastal State.
Research in the International Area would be conducted directly by the International Authority or under
its regulation or control.

The second trend, although not based on a formal
proposal, follows the language of the Continental
Shelf Convention and provides that while consent is
required to conduct research in the economic zone,
this consent shall not normally be withheld when certain conditions are met. It contains no reference to
research in the International Area.

The third trend provides for an agreed set of
international requirements for the conduct of research
in the economic zone in lieu of a requirement to obtain coastal State consent. Research in the International Area may be carried out by all States. Document A/Conf.62/C.3/L. 19, cosponsored by 17 countries,
reflects the substance of this third trend. The co-
sponsors include 11 developing countries.

The fourth and final trend provides for total
freedom to carry out research in the economic zone
"except that marine scientific research aimed directly
at the exploration or exploitation of the living and
non-living resources shall be subject to the consent
of the coastal State. In the International Area, all
States have the freedom to carry out marine scientific
research related to the seabed, subsoil, and super-
jacent waters."

In addition to the above, proposals were made
with respect to the legal status of marine research
installations and the responsibility and liability of

those conducting research. These proposals, however, were not formally discussed at this session.

With the identification of the four main trends of proposals for the conduct of scientific research in the ocean, it appears that the Conference at its next session will be in a position to concentrate on reducing these texts to a single set of articles on scientific research.

Nigeria and Sri Lanka introduced separate formal proposals on technology transfer. Sri Lanka formally withdrew its proposal and joined with Nigeria and about 20 others in cosponsoring a subsequent proposal on technology transfer (Document A/Conf.62/C.3/L.12). This proposal calls for transfer of technology, including the facilitation of transferring patented and non-patented technology, through agreements under equitable and reasonable conditions. It requires, inter alia, that the Authority ensure that legal arrangements with respect to seabed activities provide for the training of developing-State nationals, and that all patents on machinery and processes for exploiting the International Area be made available to developing States upon request.


V.   Dispute Settlement

   A.   General

     In the latter part of the session, about 30 States from all regions interested in dispute settlement met informally on a regular basis to discuss ideas and provisions for the dispute settlement chapter of the Convention. The group was chaired by Ambassadors Galindo-Pohl of El Salvador and Harry of Australia. The result is a Working Paper containing alternative texts on basic provisions introduced during the last week of the Conference by Australia, Belgium, Bolivia, Colombia, El Salvador, Luxembourg, Netherlands, Singapore, and the US (A/Conf.62/L.7), and supported by most members of the group.

     Aside from Committee I, there has not been much public debate in the Conference on dispute settlement, although there are many States that regard it as a critical aspect of the negotiations.

B.  Working Paper

The new paper (Doc. L.7) is likely to stimulate further study and discussion during the period before the next session of the Conference.

The paper resulted from some of the most serious and constructive meetings of the entire session.  It contains draft alternative texts and notes indicating relevant precedents on eleven points as follows:

1.  Obligation to settle disputes under the Convention by peaceful means

2.  Settlement of disputes by means chosen by the parties.  These texts deal with agreement by States to resolve a dispute by means of their own choice.

3.  Clause relating to other obligations. The issue dealt with is whether, in the absence of express agreement to the contrary, precedence is given to the procedures in the Convention or other procedures accepted by the parties entailing a binding decision.

4.  Clause relating to settlement procedures not entailing a binding decision.  In a situation in which a dispute is referred to non-binding procedures, these articles deal with the question of when a party is entitled to invoke applicable binding procedures under the Convention.

5.  Obligation to resort to a means of settlement resulting in a binding decision.  Three alternative forums are described in connection with the obligation: arbitration; a special Law of the Sea Tribunal; and the International Court of Justice.

6.  The relationship between general and functional approaches.  During the discussion, there was considerable support for special functional forums in connection with some issues.  The most widely discussed was a special Dispute Settlement Forum within the Seabed Authority.  The issue addressed here is whether, and to what extent, there is resource from a special functional forum to the general procedures established by the Convention.

7.  Parties to a dispute.  These texts establish that the dispute settlement machinery would be

open to States Parties to the Convention, and then addressed the issue of whether, and the extent to which, international organizations, and natural and juridical persons, could be involved.

8. Local remedies. The texts deal with the question of exhaustion of local remedies.

9. Advisory jurisdiction. The question addressed is whether a national court, duly authorized by domestic law, may request an advisory opinion from the Law of the Sea Tribunal on a question relating to the interpretation or application of the Convention.

10. Laws applicable. The question addressed is whether, and under what circumstances, rules in addition to the Law of the Sea Convention may apply-- including bilateral agreements, regulations of international organizations pursuant to the Convention, and the right of Parties to agree to seek a settlement ex aequo et bono.

11. Exceptions and reservations to the dispute settlement provisions. The issue addressed is whether, and with respect to what issues, there would be exceptions to the dispute settlement obligations of the Convention.

ANNEX I

OFFICERS OF THE CONFERENCE
and
MEMBERSHIP OF
THE GENERAL COMMITTEE
THE DRAFTING COMMITTEE
THE CREDENTIAL COMMITTEE


PRESIDENT:                 Mr. Hamilton Shirley Amerasinghe
                           (Sri Lanka)

VICE PRESIDENTS:           Algeria, Belgium, Bolivia, Chile,
                           China, Dominican Republic, Egypt,
                           France, Iceland, Indonesia, Iran,
                           Iraq, Kuwait, Liberia, Madagascar,
                           Nepal, Nigeria, Norway, Pakistan,
                           Peru, Poland, Singapore, Trinidad
                           and Tobago, Tunisia, Uganda, Union
                           of Soviet Socialist Republics,
                           United Kingdom, United States,
                           Yugoslavia, Zaire, Zambia

RAPPORTEUR GENERAL:        Mr. Kenneth O. Rattray (Jamaica)

## COMMITTEE I

CHAIRMAN:                  Mr. Paul Bamela Engo (Cameroon)

VICE CHAIRMAN:             Brazil, German Democratic
                           Republic, Japan

RAPPORTEUR:                Mr. H.C. Mott (Australia)

## COMMITTEE II

CHAIRMAN:                  Mr. Andrés Aguilar (Venezuela)

VICE CHAIRMAN:             Czechoslovakia, Kenya, Turkey

RAPPORTEUR:                Mr. Satya N. Nandan (Fiji)

## COMMITTEE III

CHAIRMAN:                  Mr. A. Yankov (Bulgaria)

VICE CHAIRMAN:             Colombia, Cyprus, Federal
                           Republic of Germany

RAPPORTEUR:                Mr. Abdel Magied Hassan (Sudan)

## GENERAL COMMITTEE

The General Committee consists of 48 Members:

The President
The 31 Vice Presidents
The Rapporteur General
The 15 Officers of the three Main Committees

## DRAFTING COMMITTEE

CHAIRMAN:   Mr. J. Alan Beesley (Canada)

MEMBERS:    Afghanistan, Argentina, Bangladesh,
Ecuador, El Salvador, Ghana, India,
Italy, Lesotho, Malaysia, Mauritania,
Mauritius, Mexico, Netherlands,
Philippines, Romania, Sierra Leone,
Spain, Syria, Union of Soviet Socialist
Republics, United Republic of Tanzania,
United States

## CREDENTIAL COMMITTEE

CHAIRMAN:   Mr. Heinrich Gleissner (Austria)

MEMBERS:    Chad, China, Costa Rica, Hungary,
Ireland, Ivory Coast, Japan, Uruguay

THIRD SESSION
GENEVA
March 17 - May 9, 1975

I.  Summary of Delegation Report

Following is a summary of the delegation report
on the Geneva Session of the Law of the Sea Conference
of March 17 - May 9, 1975.  The detailed delegation
report on the work of the main committees is included,
and the texts produced this season are appended.[1]

A.  Evaluation of Session

1.  The principal visible result of the
Geneva Session is the distribution of informal single
texts covering all subjects before the Conference.
The chairman of the dispute settlement group also submitted a text to the President of the Conference.  The
single texts were presented to the Conference President by the chairmen of the three main committees as a
basis for negotiation of a comprehensive treaty.
These texts do not represent agreed articles or consensus texts but represent the judgment of committee
chairmen based on their assessment of the negotiation
thus far as to the appropriate starting point for further negotiations during the intersessional period and
at the next session commencing March 29, 1976.  As
single texts were distributed on the last day, the
Delegation has not had an opportunity to review or
analyze them.  A detailed evaluation will be made in
Washington in the near future by the NSC Interagency
Task Force.  The test of the value of the single text
will be the extent to which it facilitates further
negotiations.

2.  The crucial question remains as to whether
there is a widespread genuine will to reach accommodation.  Without such will, the single text could provide nothing more than another vehicle to restate or
reintroduce fundamental differences.

3.  In the judgment of the Delegation, the
point has now been reached when a majority of States
must make an assessment in the interim period before
the next session as to whether a timely conclusion
of an overall treaty is in their interests.  There are
pressures in many countries, including the US, for
unilateral action to resolve immediate difficulties,
especially coastal fisheries, which may further com-
plicate negotiation of a comprehensive treaty.  There

appeared to be a general will to negotiate on major
economic-zone and pollution questions, with positions
drawing much closer.  On the other hand, with respect
to the deep seabeds, and to a lesser extent with respect to scientific research and the interests of
landlocked and geographically disadvantaged States,
positions are still far apart.  The remainder of
this report will review the course of negotiations
and the Delegation's assessment of current trends.

4.  Territorial Sea and Straits.  A substantial consensus continues on a territorial sea of
12 miles.  There appears to be a strong trend in favor
of unimpeded passage of straits used for international
navigation as part of a Committee II package.

5.  Economic Zone, Including Fisheries.
Negotiation of a balance of rights and duties in the
200-mile economic zone is one of the most important
elements of a satisfactory package.  The principal
efforts of this issue were made in the Evensen informal group, a group of some 40 nations from all regions,
chaired by Minister Jens Evensen of Norway.  The
Evensen group began work on the economic zone prior
to the Conference and completed work this session on
a chapter on the economic zone, including fisheries,
and the continental shelf.  With respect to fisheries
the Evensen group text includes articles on all fisheries issues including anadromous species (salmon) but
not highly migratory (tuna), and it reflects a general
consensus within the Conference on coastal State jurisdiction over coastal fisheries within a 200-mile economic zone.  Coastal States would have comprehensive
jurisdiction to manage coastal stocks in the economic
zone, coupled with a duty to insure their conservation
and to permit access by foreign States to fish stocks
in excess of the coastal State's capacity to harvest.
The text on salmon represents an accommodation that
contains new strong protections for the State of origin
while permitting some continuation of traditional
fishing.

6.  Deep Seabeds.  Efforts in the early weeks
which seemed likely to move toward accommodation with
developing countries on key questions of basic conditions of exploitation did not survive pressures within
the Group of 77 to return to original ideological positions.  Doctrinal differences have previously prevented progress on this subject, and the gap was not
bridged this session.  However, limited flexibility

was shown in efforts to reach an accommodation on basic questions involved in international machinery regarding powers and functions of the Assembly, Council, Tribunal, and Technical Commissions, as well as voting procedures and provisional application of the regime and machinery.

7. Dispute Settlement. The Text forwarded to the President by an informal group of about 60 states sets forth the dispute settlement procedures for inclusion in the Convention. While it proceeds on the principle that there will be some binding dispute settlement procedures, there is no agreement yet on what the scope of binding dispute settlement will be in the economic zone.

8. Detailed negotiations in the three main committees and in dispute settlement are summarized in paragraphs C, D, E, and F.

B. Future Work Program

The Plenary decided that the fourth session of the Conference should be held in New York for eight weeks commencing March 29, 1976. If the Law of the Sea Conference so determines, an additional session would be held in New York in 1976 with a final signing session in Caracas. The Evensen group decided to continue its informal negotiations, but it will now become an open-ended group for all interested participants. The group presently plans to meet during the last week of August and first week of September, with possible additional meetings during the General Assembly and in early 1976. Evensen announced that the subjects of marine pollution, scientific research, outer limit of the continental shelf, and revenue sharing would be discussed.

C. Committee I. Deep Seabeds

1. General

Serious negotiations occurred in Committee I (CI) during the Geneva Session, with a number of compromise proposals being explored, but the most striking feature of this session was the inability of the developing countries in the Group of 77 to make concessions on their more fundamental ideological positions.

Although the developing countries were somewhat receptive to our basic concerns in the area of
institutional structure and the need to limit the
Authority's powers over exploitation, we were not able
to bridge the ideological gap on the exploitation system. Despite a US effort to be forthcoming on some of
their demands for participation, the developing countries continue to support the view that only a system
in which the Authority directly exploits will protect
their interests.

2. Basic Conditions and the Exploitation
   System

The US entered the Committee I negotiations
at Geneva with a willingness to be more flexible on
issues of direct concern to the developing countries,
while at the same time preserving its most important
interest in access to deep seabed minerals. During
the first half of the session, we agreed to consider
including in the treaty basic conditions of exploitation as opposed to detailed regulatory provisions
(on the condition that detailed regulations for the
provisional period would be adopted by the Conference).
We also agreed to consider a system of joint ventures,
with the possibility of profit-sharing with the Authority, as the single method of exploitation, and proposed a reservation-of-areas system. Under this approach, an applicant for a joint venture would submit
two mine sites, one of which the Authority would designate as a reserved area. In the reserved areas, the
Authority could negotiate with applicants for the most
favorable financial terms and commitments to transfer
technology.

At mid-session, the Chairman of the Working
Group introduced a personal draft of basic conditions
that focused primarily on a contractual joint venture
system that included reservation of areas for States
and for direct exploitation by the Authority. This
elaboration of a parallel system (an approach in which
the Authority directly exploits at the same time that
States and their nationals exploit under a separate
system) was intensively considered by the Group of 77,
who eventually rejected the concept of designating
areas solely for State exploitation and also rejected
the parallel system as elaborated in the draft. The
reasons given by the Group of 77 for its rejection of
this concept related to their ideological difficulty in

establishing two separate regimes for the International Area.

## 3. Machinery

The Committee devoted only three formal sessions to consideration of machinery issues, although the Group of 77 developed a new, unified position on these questions. The most important aspect of this position was a willingness to include representation on the Council for developed and developing countries that have a special interest in the deep seabed and to submit the entire exploitation system to the control of the Council. The Group of 77 did not reach an agreed position on production controls, apparently as a result of the differing interests of producers and consumers within the group. The US delivered a statement in which we listed 12 critical elements of an acceptable international machinery.

## 4. Single Texts

The Committee concluded its activities this session with the introduction by its chairman of a draft of single texts on the regime and machinery, prepared as a personal effort. The Chairman of the Working Group also prepared a revised version of basic conditions which was not considered by the Working Group, although it was annexed to the Chairman's unified texts.

## 5. Conclusion

In marked contrast to previous sessions, Committee I engaged in intensive efforts to bring opposing views closer together. Little progress was made in bridging the ideological gap between nations on the basic aspects of the exploitation system, although greater understanding was developed on the relative needs and interests of States that must be accommodated in the structure and powers of the International Authority.

### D. Committee II. Territorial Sea, Straits, and the Economic Zone, including Living and Non-Living Resources

The basic structure of a 12-mile maximm territorial sea, unimpeded passage of straits, and a 200-mile economic zone with sovereign rights over living and

non-living resources and special treatment for anadromous species (salmon) has now been elaborated by specific texts. The Committee completed a review of the
paper, developed in Caracas to reflect the "main
trends" of the discussions, in informal meetings.
Working groups have dealt with virtually all of the
traditional details of the territorial sea question,
including baselines and innocent passage, and the high
seas regime, making some technical changes in the existing regime. The Evensen group text on the economic
zone reflects a broad trend of opinion; however, its
circulation was followed by efforts in the Group of 77
by extreme territorialists to make the economic zone
more coastally oriented and by efforts by landlocked
and geographically disadvantaged States to secure
greater rights of access to fisheries of neighboring
coastal States. On fisheries, the Evensen text includes conservation and full utilization articles and
an anadromous (salmon) article protecting the interests of the State of origin. While no agreement has
yet emerged on continental shelf jurisdiction beyond
200 miles, it is increasingly recognized by many mod-
erates that coastal State jurisdiction to a precisely
defined limit of the margin beyond 200 miles, coupled
with revenue sharing beyond 200 miles, is the only way
to achieve widespread agreement.

The main negotiating problems facing Committee II
in the future are likely to include the following:

1. Status of the economic zone. Assuming
all resource and economic activities (other than navigation, overflight, and submarine cables and pipelines)
are subject to coastal State jurisdiction, and that
pollution and scientific research questions are resolved, the question is whether the legal status of
the economic zone remains high seas.

2. Access of landlocked and geographically
disadvantaged States to fisheries in the economic
zones of their neighbors. The landlocked States are
numerous, and an increasing number of States, both
developed and developing, are regarding themselves as
geographically disadvantaged.

3. Right of access to the sea for landlocked
States. While in principle everyone agrees, the
strength and scope of the "right" is contentious
among concerned States.

4. Highly migratory species (tuna). No complete meeting of minds has yet been reached on this issue, although positions are closer. It seems that an organization which would establish mandatory conservation measures would be broadly acceptable, but there is still disagreement as to whether other measures adopted by an organization including allocation would be mandatory.

5. Continental shelf. What is still needed is an elaboration of a compromise on the continental shelf that includes coastal State resource jurisdiction over, and revenue sharing from, production on the continental shelf where it extends beyond 200 miles, although there are adamant positions by some delegations on both sides of the issue: those who oppose any jurisdiction beyond 200 miles; and some broad margin States who oppose the concept of revenue sharing.

6. Boundaries between adjacent and opposite coastal States and related islands problems. It is increasingly recognized that a precise resolution in a multilateral convention of these essentially bilateral issues will be very difficult. There is both strong support for, and strong opposition to, compulsory dispute settlement where the boundary location cannot be agreed.

7. Archipelagos. It is not yet clear whether agreement can be reached on an objective definition of archipelagos and on transit rights adequate to permit general acceptance of special provisions for archipelagos.

We believe the Conference must recognize that it will be impossible to go further to accommodate extreme territorialists and extreme straits States if the treaty is to be widely acceptable.

What most States want most out of the Committee II negotiation is reflected in texts that appear to have widespread support. What is now unresolved are special problems of considerable importance to some States on which a balance remains to be found. The cumulative total of States concerned with these special problems involves a substantial number; thus it will be necessary to resolve most of them, including the status of the economic zone, tuna, and the continental margin as well as landlocked and geographically disadvantaged concerns.

No State is likely to be fully satisfied by the single text prepared by the Bureau. If at the next session, States will accept the single text prepared by the Bureau as a basis for negotiation and press for changes of concern to them, there are reasonable prospects of success. If, on the other hand, a coalition forms of those dissatisfied that seeks to go back to the drawing boards and find a new basic text --the kind of maneuver that has already manifested itself in the Group of 77 economic zone recommended text submitted to the Chairman of Committee II for his consideration--then it is unlikely that a widely acceptable treaty can be produced.

    E.   Committee III. Marine Pollution, Scientific Research

        1. Marine Pollution

The pollution working group in the Third Committee completed texts on monitoring, environmental assessment, and land-based pollution, and moved close to completed texts on ocean dumping and continental shelf pollution. While these texts include meaningful obligations to protect the environment, there continues to be some opposition to accepting such obligations.

On vessel source pollution, negotiations continued in the Evensen group, but no final agreement was reached. There was a trend, however, against any coastal State standard-setting in the economic zone.

        2. Marine Scientific Research

During this session the four main trends developed in Caracas evolved into three approaches which the Chairman ultimately considered in producing the unified text. These three different approaches are:

        a. The proposal of some States within the Group of 77, which provides that all scientific research in areas under coastal State jurisdiction shall be conducted only with the explicit consent of the coastal State (L.13, Rev.2).

        b. A proposal by many Western European countries, with amendments by a group of landlocked and geographically disadvantaged States, that marine scientific research can be conducted if a list of

internationally agreed obligations are fulfilled,
subject to dispute settlement procedures (L.28, an
amendment to L.19).

        c. The Soviet proposal, later drawn upon
by Mexico and others, which distinguishes between research concerning resources and non-resource-related
research, requiring consent for resource-related
research and compliance with internationally agreed
obligations for research not concerned with resources
(L.26 and L.29).

        The informal sessions of Committee III
were devoted mostly to the question of the legal
status of scientific installations and State liability
for damage caused by scientific research. Meanwhile
an informal negotiating group, under the chairmanship
of Cornell Metternich of the Federal Republic of Germany, attempted to initiate negotiations on the major
issues of marine scientific research in the economic
zone and in the International Area. These efforts
focused mainly on research in the economic zone, and
were hampered by limited attendance. The private negotiations and new proposals formally introduced in
Committee III led to some narrowing of the negotiating
alternatives.

    F. <u>Settlement of Disputes</u>

    Although there were some members of the Working
Group on dispute settlement who opposed any binding
dispute-settlement procedures in areas of national
jurisdiction (e.g., economic zone), the concept was
supported by a majority of the more than 60 participating countries, at least for some important aspects
of the Convention such as navigation. The question of
the relationship between the exercise of coastal State
resource jurisdiction and the acceptance of dispute
settlement procedures is a particularly important and
delicate problem. It remains unclear whether there
will be a comprehensive dispute settlement mechanism
or whether, as some delegations prefer, each issue
will be dealt with separately. It also remains unclear
whether the mechanism for resolving disputes would be
the International Court of Justice, an arbitral body,
or a new Law of the Sea Tribunal. A proposal forwarded by the group sets forth a procedure which permits
States to elect to accept one or more of these alternatives. There is general support for special dispute
settlement machinery for the deep seabeds.

## II. Committee I, Deep Seabed

The Geneva Session commenced in a conciliatory mood. The Group of 77 began the Geneva Session with the view that it had made an important concession at Caracas in agreeing to include basic conditions of exploitation in the treaty. Moreover, its leadership indicated that they might have some new flexibility on machinery issues.

The US, also, came to Geneva prepared to be more flexible on issues of direct concern to the developing countries. We expressed our willingness to consider basic conditions in the treaty as opposed to detailed regulatory provisions (on the condition that detailed regulations for the provisional period would be adopted by the Conference) and to consider a system of joint ventures, with the possibility of profit-sharing as the single method of exploitation.

### A. Basic Conditions and the Exploitation System

The Committee devoted the first half of the session to consideration in its working group of basic conditions of exploitation. The group agreed to discuss basic conditions applicable to joint ventures, recognizing that the Group of 77 reserved its position on whether the Authority would directly exploit. A consensus emerged that the legal problems involved in establishing equity joint ventures might be very difficult. Accordingly, the working group chairman, Christopher Pinto (Sri Lanka) undertook to prepare a draft set of basic conditions that would be applicable to a contractual rather than an equity joint venture system.

In the working group, the US explored a system for the reservation of areas. Under this approach, an applicant for a joint venture would submit two mine sites, one of which the Authority would designate as a reserved area. In the reserved areas, the Authority could negotiate with applicants for the most favorable financial terms and commitments to transfer technology.

At the same time that the Group of 77 was considering the US banking system proposal and any implications it might have, the USSR formally introduced a draft of basic conditions that was applicable to a parallel system in which the Authority directly exploited a portion of the seabed--by itself or under contract with

private entities--while another portion of the area
was reserved exclusively for State access.

At mid-session the Chairman of the working group
introduced a personal draft of basic conditions that
focused primarily on a contractual joint venture system that included reservation of areas both for States
and for direct exploitation by the Authority. This
elaboration of a parallel system (an approach in which
the Authority directly exploits at the same time that
States and their nationals exploit under a separate
system) was intensively considered by the Group of 77,
who eventually rejected the concept of designating
areas solely for State exploitation and also rejected
the parallel system as elaborated in the draft.

B.   Machinery

The Committee devoted only three formal sessions
to consideration of machinery issues. The Group of 77
announced a new, unified position on these questions.
The most important aspect of this position was a willingness to include representation on the Council for
developed and developing countries that have a special
interest in the deep seabed and to submit the entire
exploitation system to the control of the Council. The
US delivered a statement in which we listed 12 critical
elements that would have to appear in an acceptable
version on the machinery articles:

1.  The Authority's control should cover only
activities directly related to exploitation and should
not extend to other activities, such as basic or fundamental research.

2.  The Authority's powers should be only
those specifically provided for.

3.  The Assembly's voting procedures should
protect minority interests, require efforts to reach
consensus, and provide for the suspension of Assembly
action if an advisory opinion on a legal matter were
requested of the Tribunal.

4.  The Assembly's powers should not overlap
those of the Council.

5.  Basic conditions that elaborated the
Authority's fundamental resource policies.

6. A rule-making procedure similar to ICAO's

7. The Council should have exclusive jurisdiction over the Authority's powers relating to exploitation.

8. A rules commission, supervisory commission, and a commission empowered to enter into contracts should have separate functions and report directly to the Council.

9. An effective dispute settlement system.

10. Stringent conflict-of-interests provisions and penalties for data disclosure to apply to the Secretariat.

11. A financially self-sufficient Authority with the power to borrow funds in the initial years.

12. Provisional application.

A key issue in the machinery discussion was the question of production controls. The Group of 77 did not arrive at a unified position on this issue, probably as a result of the differing interests of producers and consumer nations within the Group.

C. Single Texts

The Committee concluded its activities this session with the introduction by its chairman of a draft of single texts on the regime and machinery, prepared as a personal effort. In the time available, the delegation was unable to review this paper. The chairman of the working group also prepared a revised version of basic conditions which was not considered by the working group, although it was annexed to the chairman's unified texts on the regime and machinery.

D. Conclusion on Committee I

In marked contrast to previous sessions, Committee I engaged in intensive efforts to bring opposing views closer together. Little progress was made in bridging the gap between nations on the basic aspects of the exploitation system, although greater understanding was developed on the relative needs and interests of States that must be accommodated in the structure and powers of the International Authority.

III.  Committee II, Territorial Sea, Straits, Economic Zone, Including Living and Non-Living Resources

For easy reference this section of the report is organized in accordance with the "Main Trends" paper (A/Conf.62/C.2/WPI of 15 October 1974).

(a)  Territorial Sea

(1)  Nature and Characteristics

No formal discussion took place in Committee II on this topic. There was general acceptance of the Provisions of the 1958 Geneva Convention on the Territorial Sea and Contiguous Zone regarding this issue.

(2)  Historic Waters

Although a draft text, which attempted to define historic bays and other historic waters, was introduced by Colombia, the Consultative Group to which this was referred adjourned without taking any action on the text. There was strong opposition to a general doctrine of historic waters as proposed by the Philippines.

(3)  Limits

The Consultative Group considering baselines for delimiting the territorial sea agreed on the wording of Provisions 4 through 20 of the Committee II Main Trends paper; and although there was opposition by a few delegations to certain phrasing, these Provisions seemed to receive the approval of a majority of the members of the Consultative Group. The two principal changes between the revised text and the 1958 Geneva Convention articles are, first, the new provision that where, because of a delta or other natural conditions the coastline is highly unstable, appropriate points may be selected along the farthest extent of the low-water line and connected by straight baselines; and second, that straight baselines may be drawn to and from low-tide elevations with no lighthouses on them where the specific delimitation has received general international recognition. The Conference is proceeding on the assumption of a 12-mile territorial sea for which there is very broad support. The Ecuadorian proposal for a 200-mile territorial sea was supported by only a handful of countries most of

which have similar territorial claims of their own,
and even some of those supporting statements were
ambiguous.

(4) Innocent Passage on the Territorial Sea

The informal consultative group on Innocent
Passage completed its second reading of the Main
Trends Paper, A/Conf.62/C.2.WP.1. Straits are of
course dealt with in a different section of the paper.
There was broad support for retaining the relevant
provisions of the 1958 Convention on the Territorial
Sea and Contiguous Zone, Articles 14 through 23, in
all substantial respects except as follows:

(i) Rules Applicable to All Ships.

There was support for clarifying pas-
sage to mean navigation through the territorial sea
for the purpose of a. traversing that sea without
entering internal waters or calling at a roadstead or
port facility outside internal waters; or b. proceeding to or from internal waters or a call at such a
roadstead or port facility. The text of Article 16(2)
of the 1958 Territorial Sea Convention was changed so
as to provide a coastal State right to take necessary
steps to prevent any breach of the conditions to which
admission to roadsteads and facilities beyond internal
waters, as well as internal waters is subject.

With respect to the definition of innocent passage, there was support for an objective
list of activities by a passing ship prejudicial to
the peace, good order or security of the coastal State
and therefore non-innocent. Items receiving most support were the use or threat of force in contravention
of the UN Charter, and: (1) any exercise or practice
with weapons of any kind; (2) the launching or taking
on board of any aircraft; (3) the launching, landing
or taking on board of any military device; (4) the
taking on board or putting overboard of any commodity,
currency or person in contravention of the customs,
fiscal, immigration or sanitary regulations of the
coastal State; (5) any act aimed at collecting information to the prejudice of the defense or security of the
coastal State; (6) any act aimed at interfering with
any system of communication of the coastal State; and
(7) any act aimed at interfering with any other facilities or installations of the coastal State.

95

There was support for a list enumerating the competence of the coastal State to make laws and regulations, in conformity with the provisions of the Convention and other rules of international law, relating to innocent passage. Items receiving most support were: (1) the safety of navigation and the regulation of marine traffic, including the designation of sealanes and the establishment of traffic separation schemes; (2) the protection of navigational aids and facilities and other facilities and installations, including those for exploration and exploitation of the marine resources of the territorial sea and the seabed and subsoil thereof; (3) the protection of cables and pipelines; (4) the conservation of the living resources of the sea; (5) the preservation of the environment of the coastal State, including the territorial sea, and the prevention of pollution thereto; (6) research for the marine environment and hydrographic surveys; (7) the prevention of infringement of the customs, fiscal, immigration, quarantine or sanitary or cryptosanitary regulations of the coastal State; (8) the prevention of infringement of the fisheries regulations of the coastal State, including, inter alia, those relating to the stowage of gear.

Both of the lists are attempts to clarify possible ambiguities in 1958 Territorial Sea Convention which deals both with the issue of definition of innocence and coastal State regulatory power in general terms.

### (ii) Rules applicable to ships with special characteristics

Efforts to provide for advance notification for innocent passage of tankers and nuclear-powered ships or ships carrying nuclear weapons, and to provide for advance authorization in the latter case, received little support. Oil exporting and importing States stated strong opposition, noting that tankers are frequently rerouted.

### (iii) Rules applicable to merchant ships

There was no opposition to clarifying the text of Article 19 of the 1958 Territorial Sea Convention to add quote psychotropic drugs unquote to the provisions of Article 19-1(d) regarding suppression of traffic in narcotic drugs.

(iv) Rules applicable to government ships

There was support for State responsibility in the event of damage to the coastal State as a result of non-compliance with coastal State laws or regulations relating to passage through the territorial sea by a warship or other government ship on non-commercial service, in view of the sovereign immunity of such ships.

(5) Freedom of Navigation and Overflight Resulting from the Plurality of Regimes in the Territorial Sea

This subject received no discussion in the informal consultative group on innocent passage, other than an indication by Peru that the question should be kept alive pending resolution of economic zone issues.

(b) Contiguous Zone

There was one informal consultative session held on the subject of the contiguous zone. It was generally accepted that a contiguous zone of up to 12 miles from the coast could be declared for States not wishing to claim a 12-mile territorial sea. A few countries pressed for additional contiguous zone jurisdiction beyond a 12-mile territorial sea, primarily to combat smuggling, of limited distance, e.g., an additional 12 miles.

The confusion between the contiguous zone and the exercise of customs, fiscal, immigration, and sanitary jurisdiction over resource installations and artificial offshore ports has been eliminated by Article 1 of the Evensen economic zone text, which clarifies that such jurisdiction is part of coastal State jurisdiction over artificial islands and installations.

(c) Straits

Committee II held two informal consultations on straits. A clear majority of States participating in the debates favored a regime of unimpeded transit of straits, with a significant number of States endorsing the principle. The hard line straits States opposing unimpeded passage were more clearly isolated than in past sessions of the Conference. While there was little tendency to focus on specific treaty texts,

the dominant trend of the Conference now clearly favors an unimpeded transit regime.

In addition to the two public meetings, there were active negotiations on the straits issue this session in private, unofficial consultative groups and in bilateral discussions. The UK and Fiji jointly chaired an informal consultative group which met throughout the session, and included significant representation from developing countries in all regions. This group took as its basic negotiating texts the straits articles from the UK and Fiji proposals in Caracas (A/Conf./62/II/L.3 and L.18) and after numerous meetings, produced a draft straits chapter, adopted by consensus within the Group, which was forwarded to Ambassador Galindo Pohl, and circulated to Committee II.

The United States delegation has a number of problems with the UK-Fiji text primarily because the scope of permissible coastal State regulatory authority is too broad.

(d) Continental Shelf

It is generally agreed that coastal State exclusive sovereign rights over seabed resources would be co-terminous with the economic zone and extend at least to 200 nautical miles from the coast. The continental margin extends beyond 200 miles off the coasts of some States including the United States. With respect to areas of the continental margin beyond 200 miles, there are three positions:

1. The legal Continental Shelf ends at 200 nautical miles.

2. Where the continental margin extends beyond 200 miles, sovereign rights over seabed resources should extend to the outer limit of the margin.

3. Where the continental margin extends beyond 200 miles, sovereign rights over seabed resources should extend to the outer limit of the margin coupled with an obligation to share some revenues from mineral exploitation beyond 200 miles.

While some advocates of the first two positions remain adamant, there is growing support for the third solution as the only way to achieve widespread

agreement. The US, which has supported the idea of
jurisdiction coupled with revenue sharing beyond 12
miles or the 200-meter isobath, whichever is further
seaward, indicated that it could go along with applying revenue sharing only in the area of the margin beyond 200 miles, and suggested an illustrative schedule
as follows: after the first five years of production
at the site, the coastal State would contribute 1% of
the value of production of the site (well head value)
which would increase thereafter by 1% each year until
it reached 5% in the 10th year, where it would remain
thereafter. We indicated that if we assumed a given
field would produce 700 million barrels of oil through
a 20-year depletion period, and a value of $11 per
barrel, the total amount would be $140 million per
field. The oil and other minerals themselves, and
revenues collected by the coastal State would of
course remain with the coastal State.

The US explained that such a system would
permit some initial exploration and drilling costs to
be recovered before the commencement of the coastal
State obligation to make payments under the treaty.
During the more economically productive life of the
well, the rate of payments would increase, providing
the international community with certain and substantial revenues. A graduated approach is designed to
avoid onerous burdens on pioneering developments.

Other States favor a system of profit sharing,
which the US felt would produce uncertainty in view of
unpredictable costs in operating in great water depths
and great difficulty in reaching agreement among
States of differing economic systems on what costs can
be deducted from gross profits to compute net revenues.

Some landlocked and geographically disadvantaged States have presented a formula for distribut-
ing the revenues.

Another difficult issue is the precise definition of the continental margin where it extends beyond 200 miles. The US favors a formula which would
permit a coastal State to set the outer limit of the
margin within 60 nautical miles of the foot of the
slope. This is a relatively simple and inexpensive
determination. Other broad-margin States favor a direct geophysical definition which includes rocks derived from the land mass underlying the shelf, slope
and rise, but not the deep ocean floor. The problem

is that unless sediments overlying the deep ocean
floor are excluded from the definition of the margin,
its extent will be extremely and unnecessarily broad,
a result likely to meet with considerable opposition.
There is some lack of understanding that the object
of the negotiation is to fix a juridical boundary between the coastal and international resource regimes,
rather than to describe a scientific definition of the
margin; this is compounded by the link between land
and geology implied by the "natural prolongation" language used by the International Court of Justice.

Advocates of coastal State jurisdiction beyond 200 miles generally support independent and
binding international review of the coastal State's
delimitation of the outer edge of the margin in order
to ensure precision and avoid unreasonable claims.

Many delegations expressed environmental concerns over pipelines. It appears that the freedom to
lay and maintain pipelines will be qualified by coastal State rights with respect to routing and pollution
control, and that exclusive coastal State jurisdiction
over pipelines from its installations or entering its
territory will be expressly recognized.

In sum the textual material for a settlement
based on margin jurisdiction and revenue sharing beyond
200 miles is prepared. Precise formulas exist for defining the margin, with differences on texts being
narrowed, for a Continental Shelf Boundary Review Commission, and for revenue sharing contribution and distribution. Most broad margin advocates and many others
are prepared to negotiate on revenue sharing beyond 200
miles, and thus the negotiating prospects seem good
unless the numerous advocates of a straight 200-mile
limit feel that they cannot move until broad-margin
opponents of revenue sharing drop their opposition.

(e) Economic Zone

(1) General

After a long period of work, Chairman of
the Juridical Experts Group, Minister Jens Evenson of
Norway, submitted a text on the Economic Zone to the
Chairman of Committee II, and circulated copies to all
delegations. It is by far the major negotiating development on this issue. It deals with all the negotiating issues in the economic zone except for (1) a

blank article on highly migratory species that remains
to be negotiated, and (2) pollution and scientific research issues. The group is now working on pollution
and scientific research.

Article 1 summarizes the rights of the
coastal State in the economic zone, notably sovereign
rights over living and non-living resources, rights
over other economic activities such as production of
energy from winds, and rights to be specified with respect to pollution and scientific research. The pollution and research issues are to be considered without prejudice to the work of Committee III.

Article 2 establishes the maximum limit
of the economic zone at 200 nautical miles.

Article 3 deals with the rights of all
States in the economic zone. There was general agreement on freedom of navigation and overflight, and on
freedom to lay and maintain submarine cables and pipelines (which will probably be subject to subsequent
qualifications regarding pipeline routing and pollution). The highly contentious issue was whether "residual rights" would be accorded coastal States or to
all States or would be left open. The Evensen text
deals with the issue by according all States the right
to conduct internationally lawful uses of the sea related to navigation and communication, and by specifying that conflict over rights not given to the
coastal State or to all States should be resolved on
the basis of equity, taking into account the relative
importance to the States concerned and the international community. A footnote to Article 3 indicates
that scientific research remains to be dealt with.

Article 4 deals with artificial islands
and installations. This article, along with Article
3, was the major object of attack by the territorialists, who urged exclusive coastal State control over
all artificial islands and installations. The US and
others argued for jurisdiction over resource and other
economic installations only. The text deals with the
issue by giving the coastal State exclusive jurisdiction over (1) all artificial islands; (2) installations used for purposes subject to its jurisdiction
under Article 1 (e.g., deepwater parts); and (3) installations which may interfere with the exercise of
the rights of the coastal State in the economic zone.

The article specifies that safety zones, if any, must be reasonably related to the nature and function of the installation, thus introducing some flexibility, but includes a maximum breadth (to be specified) beyond which international action is needed, in order to protect navigation. It also introduces a new element of protection by requiring vessels to obey international standards in the vicinity of safety zones, thus permitting some measure of international protection without the need to establish unreasonably broad safety zones.

Although all regional and interest groups were represented in the Evensen group, the Group of 77 undertook to produce its own text. It appears that the dissatisfaction of extreme territorialists was a major factor in this, and they resorted to the usually effective tactic of appealing for Group of 77 unity. The irony is that certain territorialists were very active in the Evensen group but relied on the failure of some African members to attend consistently to argue that the Group was not fairly balanced. Another major factor was the dissatisfaction of the landlocked and geographically disadvantaged States with the Evensen text on access to fisheries. While both the territorialists and the landlocked and geographically disadvantaged seemed initially to favor the preparation of a Group of 77 text, the territorialists and those seeking to delay a treaty and stimulate unilateral action seem to have gotten the best of the tactic since the text forwarded by the Chairman of the Group of 77 is much more coastal in its orientation, contains new contentious substantive and political elements certain to arouse strong opposition, and was denounced by the group of landlocked and geographically disadvantaged States, most of whom are developing countries. Nevertheless, the structure of the paper is strikingly similar to the Evensen text, and it was forwarded to the Chairman of Committee II for his consideration in preparing the single negotiating text, presumably indicating an intent to work on the basis of the Chairman's text.

(2) Fisheries

As with other aspects of the Main Trends Paper (WP-1), public discussions of fisheries issues were conducted by Committee II in informal session. In general, this discussion was limited to restatements of national positions with no real negotiation

taking place. There were, however, significant developments as a result of private negotiations, and this session saw for the first time a willingness by many States to negotiate.

Although the Evensen text does not bind any delegation, it does represent a basis for ultimate compromise on the fisheries issues. The text contains provisions on all basic fisheries issues in the economic zone of importance, with the exception of highly migratory species, which proved to be too contentious an issue to resolve during the session.

The Evensen text has been attacked from several quarters. Members of the landlocked and geographically disadvantaged group, although represented in the Evensen negotiations, have formally stated to the Chairman of Committee II that the paper does not represent their views; their concern relates principally to access to fisheries. The Group of 77 formed its own negotiating group of the whole to produce another text on fisheries issues, although it is not clear to what extent there is agreement in the group.

On specific issues, the trend of the negotiation on fisheries is definitely in the direction of a more coastally oriented zone, although there is wide acceptance of a legal obligation to conserve the resources, and in principle to insure their full utilization.

The Evensen text includes both principles.

With respect to conservation (Evensen Article 5), the text expands upon the US view that environmental and other factors should be included in determining allowable catch, and in particular includes a clause on associated or dependent species.

Article 6 on full utilization in effect combines the principle of full utilization with the principle of coastal State regulation. The coastal State is required to permit access to that part of the allowable catch which exceeds it harvesting capacity, but its regulatory flexibility is expressed in great detail. There are no strict priorities of access for foreign States, but traditional fishing is one of the factors the coastal State must take into account.

The Evensen text on anadromous species (salmon) is the result of intensive negotiation among States most concerned; it represents a substantive accommodation of interests not only on the immediate issues but in response to general Conference pressure that the overall economic-zone framework be respected. The text establishes the special interest of the State of origin in anadromous species, gives the State of origin exclusive conservation authority in its own ecomonic zone and beyond the economic zone, and requires other States through whose waters anadromous species migrate to cooperate with the State of origin. At the same time, the State of origin must by agreement cooperate in minimizing economic dislocation in States that have fished these resources beyond the economic zone; this clause is intended to apply only to traditional fishing. The appearance of this text helped avoid a potentially bitter debate which could have been complicated by ideological and political factors not directly related to the specific problems of conservation and management of anadromous species.

Based on a US initiative, attempts were made in the Evensen group to negotiate an article on highly migratory species. One attempt centered on a compromise solution which would recognize the competence of an international or regional organization to set standards and make recommendations, but the organization itself would decide as to which were binding and which would only be recommendations. Special voting protections for coastal States were included in the proposal. This attempt proved unsuccessful, and the Evensen text remains silent on the issue.

There were discussions in the Evensen group as to how marine mammals should be handled in the treaty. Some States took a strong stand to preserve their whaling interests, and other nations have been active in attempts to ensure complete coastal State control over marine mammals within the zone. The US has taken a position which would allow both coastal States and international organizations as appropriate to exert strong regulatory measures over marine mammals, including a prohibition on harvesting.

(f) Preferential Rights

There was no discussion of this item as the economic zone in effect supersedes it.

(g) High Seas

Committee II held seven informal consultation meetings on the high seas and transmission (broadcasting) from the high seas, with a view toward developing agreed single texts on Provisions 136-177 of the Caracas Main Trends Paper. At its first meeting, the group decided to defer discussion of the definition of the high seas, the question of the freedoms of the high seas, and the regulation and the management and conservation of living resources, pending resolution of the issue of the economic zone. Single texts reflecting the existing law in other respects, as set forth in the High Seas Convention, were adopted, except as noted below.

An amended version of an EEC proposal setting specific flag state obligations and clarifying the requirement that there be a "genuine link" between the flag State and the ship was adopted.

A UK sponsored article dealing with suppression of unauthorized radio broadcasting from the high seas was provisionally accepted. After defining unauthorized broadcasting as "...transmission...intended for reception by the general public contrary to international regulations...," the article grants prosecution jurisdiction to "...any State where the transmissions can be received..."

The group also considered an article which would have permitted enforcement by all States against vessels under 500 tons engaged in trafficking in narcotics. However, a controversy developed over removal of the 500-ton limitation, and the Chairman announced that his private consultations convinced him the difficulty could not be resolved.

(h) Landlocked Countries and Geographically Disadvantaged States

This session of the Conference has seen a significant and coordinated effort by the Group of landlocked and geographically disadvantated (LL/GDS) States to establish themselves as a power to be reckoned with by the Conference. To a large extent this has been successful; and as the session closed, the issue of LL/GDS access rights to fisheries in Economic Zones of other states was recognized as a major issue in the Conference. This has been due to several factors.

First, the leadership of the group has been very effective in coordinating their efforts and presenting a position that is consistent in all fora. Additionally the group has been able to take advantage of fragmentation of views among regional groups, and the sheer number of States considering themselves members makes the group a potent force.

There were several informal meetings of the consultative group dealing with the question of the rights and interests of landlocked and geographically disadvantaged States. There are two principal issues which arise from consideration of this subject. The first concerns the strong efforts by landlocked and geographically disadvantaged States to have access to the living resources of the economic zones of neighboring States. In public debate, many coastal States took vigorous exception to this principle. The second issue relates to the subject of landlocked State free transit to the sea. While the informal meetings of Committee II dealt with both issues at length, small informal consultations were limited to this second issue. Landlocked States argued at length that "right" of transit was a logical consequence of landlocked State enjoyment of freedom of the seas and the common heritage. Certain transit States strongly resisted recognition of this idea as a "right."

Most of the controversy on the fisheries issue with regard to the LL/GDS problem centers on what legal obligation will be contained in the treaty to allow them to exploit the living resources of economic zones of their neighbors. The basic LL/GDS position is for the granting of such a right in the treaty, with the modalities of exercising it to be negotiated. Many coastal States, on the other hand, are opposing this basic position for political or resource reasons, and have instead proposed that the legal obligation should be to enter into good faith negotiations with a view to bilaterally granting exploitation rights. In addition, there are mutations of these positions, such as granting legal rights to landlocked but not to GDS.

In general, there is a trend to firmer fishing rights for LL States than for GDS. Nevertheless, the OAU position that LL States should have equal fishing rights in the economic zones of adjacent coastal States has been strongly opposed by some coastal States in other regions, particularly Peru.

The situation is made more complex by the differing political problems involved within regional groups, the difficulty of precisely defining "geographically disadvantaged," and the problems of making a developed/developing country distinction with regard to either the LL/GDS themselves, or to those in whose zones they would fish.

While the LL/GDS group has also raised the issue of a right of access to non-living resources of the economic zone and continental shelf in its draft articles, there is very broad opposition to this idea among coastal States.

(i) Archipelagos

Nothing new emerged during meetings of the working groups of the whole. Private discussions have taken place with a view to dealing with the critical issues of an objective definition of archipelagos and full transit rights adequate to permit general acceptance of the concept of the archipelagic States.

(j) Enclosed and Semi-Enclosed Areas

Consideration of this issue by the informal consultative Group was confined to definitions. There seemed to be a majority opinion to limit discussion to "semi-enclosed seas"; but the question of definition remained contentions, in part because it was unclear what purpose would be served by a chapter on the subject. The US and others noted that the item could require renegotiation of most general navigational and resource issues, which obviously should be avoided. There could be no question of affecting rights of all States as provided for in the general chapters of the Convention.

(k) Artificial Islands and Installations

(See discussion of economic zone.)

(l) Regime of Islands

Two aspects of islands were considered. The first was whether their entitlement to a territorial sea, economic zone, and continental shelf should be based on size, population, economic, or political status. No agreement was reached on this issue. The second problem was that of the weight to be assigned to

islands, islets, and rocks in the delimitation of boundaries between opposite and adjacent States. This question was referred to the consideration of delimitation issues.

Essentially, the basic problem is delimitation. However, States concerned with delimitation appear to be taking a double approach to the problem and are also questioning the entitlement of islands in principle to an economic zone. Many others argue that people on islands are even more dependent on marine resources than those on continents.

(m) Delimitation

There was considerable disagreement among delegations as to whether the articles on delimitation in the 1958 Geneva Convention remain adequate, or whether new provisions on delimitation are necessary. There are also some wide differences among those favoring new provisions.

IV. Committee III, Marine Environment and Scientific Research

A. Marine Environment

The Informal Working Group on marine pollution, chaired by José Vallarta (Mexico) devoted its efforts to non-vessel sources of marine pollution, on the understanding that contentious jurisdictional issues would be negotiated in the Evensen group. Taking up the plan of work where the group left off in Caracas, general agreement was reached on texts of articles on monitoring, environmental assessments, and land-based sources of pollution. The monitoring article, taken in conjunction with the US-proposed article on environmental assessments, should ensure that States assess in advance the environmental impacts of activities which may cause substantial marine pollution, and follow up with reasonable monitoring efforts. Both articles require appropriate communication of results to competent international organizations.

The article on land-based sources of pollution requires States to establish national regulations and includes special mention of toxic and persistent substances. The first of two alternate texts on the third paragraph would require States to endeavor to

establish global and regional rules to control land-
based pollution, but the second would modify such
efforts by requiring consideration of economic
factors.

The Working Group discussed but did not reach
complete agreement on pollution from the continental
shelf and from dumping.  On shelf pollution standards,
an impasse was reached on the jurisdictional issue
with a few coastal States (notably Brazil) taking the
position that the article should reflect their view
that all seabed activities within the economic zone
would be under the jurisdiction of the coastal State.
In spite of persistent corridor efforts by the Chairman to resolve this issue by a neutral reference to
the result of Committee II negotiations on the jurisdiction question, the article was deferred.  On dumping, agreement was close, but was prevented by India's
insistence on submitting an alternative to the Chairman's suggested text.  India opposed a binding obligation to accept international standards for dumping
in its economic zone, reserving in effect the right
to apply less stringent standards to such dumping.

B.  Marine Scientific Research

During this session the four main trends developed in Caracas evolved into three approaches which the
Chairman ultimately considered in producing the unified text.  These three different approaches are:

1.  The proposal of the Group of 77, which
provides that all scientific research in areas under
coastal State jurisdiction shall be conducted only
with the explicit consent of the coastal State
(L.13, Rev.2);

2.  A proposal by many Western European countries, with amendments by a group of landlocked and
geographically disadvantaged States, that marine scientific research can be conducted if a list of internationally agreed obligations are fulfilled, subject
to dispute settlement procedures (L.28, an amendment
to L.19);

3.  The Soviet proposal, later incorporated
in a formal proposal by Mexico and others, which distinguishes between research concerning resources and
non-resource-related research, requiring consent for
resource-related research and compliance with

internationally agreed obligations for research not
concerned with resources (L.26 and L.29).

The informal sessions of Committee III were devoted mostly to the question of the legal status of
scientific installations and State liability for damage caused by scientific research. Meanwhile an informal negotiating group, under the chairmanship of
Cornell Metternich of the Federal Republic of Germany,
attempted to initiate negotiations on the major issues
of marine scientific research in the economic zone and
in the International Area. These efforts focused
mainly on research in the economic zone, and were
hampered by limited attendance of States from the
Group of 77 in general, and Africa in particular. The
private negotiations and new proposals formally introduced in Committee III led to some narrowing of the
negotiating alternatives.

The Soviet Union, with cosponsorship by other
Socialist countries, introduced document L.26 early
in the session. The prior Soviet position, reflected
in L.31 (introduced in 1973 in the Seabeds Committee)
called for consent for shelf research, and freedom
for research in the water column and in the International Area. In L.26 the Soviet Union proposed that
in the economic zone, marine scientific research "related to the exploration and exploitation of living
and non-living resources" would be conducted only with
the consent of the coastal State, and research not so
related would be conducted subject to the fulfillment
of a series of obligations; a similar regime would
apply to research on the continental shelf beyond the
economic zone. Research in the International Area
could be conducted freely. As this approach focusing
on the purpose of the research had some appeal both
to those seeking a consent regime and those advocat-
ing marine scientific research under an obligation
regime, it was the center of discussion throughout the
session. The major criticism leveled at the Soviet approach by developing and some developed countries was
the practical difficulty of making such a distinction.
Some, led by Canada, concluded that all marine scientific research should be subject to a consent regime,
while others stated that they could accept a distinction if the coastal State had the exclusive right to
determine whether the research related to exploration
or to exploitation of resources.

The Netherlands served as chairman of the group
of landlocked and geographically disadvantaged States
in Committee III which group produced L.28 as an
amendment to L.19. This group consists of 48 countries, apparently not all of whom support L.28. L.19
provides that all research in the economic zone may
be conducted upon compliance with a series of internationally established obligations. L.28 provides
for notification of neighboring landlocked and geographically disadvantaged States and their participation, whenever feasible, in research projects conducted in the economic zone of neighboring coastal
States. A dispute-settlement procedure calls for a
panel of experts drawn from a list established by the
Director General of UNESCO to assist the researching
State and the coastal State in settling disputes concerning whether the obligations have been fulfilled
prior to the proposed project, or on prior projects
conducted in that State's economic zone. The decision of the experts is not binding, and if their
assistance does not result in agreement, either party
may resort to binding dispute-settlement procedures.

From a US perspective the most negative aspect
of the session was the reintroduction by the Group of
77 of their proposal, L.13/Rev.2. There was no change
of position from their earlier insistence on explicit
consent for research in the area under coastal State
jurisdiction and/or sovereignty and direct control by
the International Authority over all research in the
International Area. References to marine research
conducted by satellites was moved from the basic text
and placed in a bracketed note which stated that the
Group of 77 agreed to develop provisions on this issue in the future. The Group of 77 text also modified its wording from "marine scientific research" to
"scientific research in the marine environment," apparently to make the term more encompassing. The new
text also contains provisions with respect to rights
of landlocked States.

In the closing days of the session L.29 was introduced by Colombia, El Salvador, Mexico, and Nigeria. Elements of this proposal had been informally
circulated by Mexico for several weeks prior to its
formal introduction. Unlike the Soviet proposal which
distinguishes between research related to the exploration and exploitation of resources and research not
so related, L.29 distinguishes between fundamental
research and research related to the resources of the

continental shelf. If the research is fundamental, a
series of obligations must be fulfilled; while resource-related research may be conducted only with
the consent of the coastal State. Where disagreement
exists as to whether the research is fundamental, experts shall assist the parties to reach agreement.
If no agreement is reached, the coastal State shall
have the right to withhold its consent. In the International Area, information concerning the research
project shall be submitted to the International Authority or other appropriate international body prior
to the conduct of the research.

## V.   Settlement of Disputes

### A.   General

Effective provisions for the compulsory settlement of disputes arising from the interpretation or
application of the LOS Convention are an essential
part of a negotiated package. Without such provisions, the substantive provisions of the Convention
will be subject to unilateral interpretation, and the
delicate balance of rights and duties will be upset.

At Caracas, the recognition of the importance of
the issue led to the establishment of an open-ended
informal group on the settlement of disputes. A list
of eleven basic issues was prepared and, after considerable discussion, alternative texts were developed for each issue. The resulting document formed the
basis of the Geneva discussions under the cochairman-
ship of Ambassador Harry (Australia), Ambassador
Galindo Pohl (El Salvador), and Mr. Adede (Kenya), in
which more than 60 countries participated.

At Geneva an attempt was made to arrive at a
single negotiating text, selecting the more generally
accepted alternatives or combining them whenever possible, in an effort to develop an overall system for
the settlement of disputes arising out of the LOS
Convention. Difficulties, however, were encountered.
Various delegations argued for a single procedural
system--the International Court of Justice, arbitration, or a special Law of the Sea Tribunal; no group,
though, was able to rally strong enough support for
any particular solution. A compromise proposal, which
provided that a Contracting Party, when ratifying the
Convention, may choose one or more of these three

methods eventually proved acceptable to the vast majority of delegations. Under this proposal, a case
brought against a Contracting Party has to be brought
before the forum chosen by that party. It also allows special functional forums, such as a special
dispute-settlement procedure for the deep seabeds.

Objections were raised, however, by delegations
which thought that the method they preferred should
be imposed on everybody. Objections were also raised
by the "functionalists"--those delegations favoring
different machinery for different types of disputes,
e.g., deep seabed, fisheries, science, or pollution.
Objections were raised by a few delegations which,
while accepting binding decision-making in principle,
argued that there should be an exception for areas
under national jurisdiction (internal waters, territorial waters, economic zone, and continental shelf).
However, most of these apparently do not intend a
full exception (e.g., navigation rights and pollution
would not be excluded).

In addition, difficulties arose with respect to
the US proposal to establish a Law of the Sea Tribunal, since some delegations were completely opposed
to the idea of a permanent dispute-settlement machinery, as distinguished from the appointment of ad hoc
arbitration tribunals or special commissions, or the
use of the ICJ. Others opposed use of the ICJ.
There was also some confusion about the relationship
between this general tribunal and a specialized Seabed Tribunal to be established for the seabed beyond
the limits of national jurisdiction.

B. Annexes

The group forwarded to the President of the Conference four generally agreed introductory articles,
together with three annexes. Annex I presents Articles 5 to 17 for a comprehensive procedure, together
with three sub-annexes, dealing respectively with
conciliation, arbitration, and the special LOS Tribunal. Annex II illustrates the functional approach,
and Annex III sets forth a proposed preliminary chapter on information and consultation. The four generally agreed articles state that the Contracting Parties shall settle any Convention-related disputes by
the peaceful means provided in Article 33 of the UN
Charter; that they may choose the means to settle
their dispute; that they may resort to arbitration or

judicial settlement if they are party to another instrument which so provides; and that they shall expeditiously exchange views whenever a dispute arises or a procedure is terminated without a settlement of the dispute.

The principal merit of Annex I (Articles 5 to 17) is its flexibility. It does not try to confine all disputes into a single channel, but allows the parties to the dispute to make a variety of choices. Specifically, it contains the following provisions:

1. If the parties have agreed to settle a dispute by means of their own choice and a time limit has been set for the proceedings or if the Convention provides for special procedures (e.g., on deep seabeds), additional dispute-settlement procedures may be initiated only (a) upon the expiration of the time limit or completion of the special procedure; (b) if no settlement has been reached; and (c) further procedures are not precluded by the treaty (Articles 5 and 6).

2. There are flexible provisions for conciliation prior to judicial settlement in cases where the Convention does not provide for special procedures (Article 7).

3. A choice among three procedures entailing a binding decision--arbitration, a special Law of the Sea Tribunal, and the International Court of Justice--is permitted. Each State can, at the time of its ratification of the Convention, select one or more of these tribunals, depending upon its preference. If it does not care, it can agree to all of these procedures, leaving the choice in such a case to the plaintiff. Otherwise, the selection made by the defendant party is controlling (Articles 8 and 9).

4. The tribunal selected will exercise different kinds of jurisdiction: primary jurisdiction over disputes for which there is no special procedure; secondary jurisdiction in cases subject to preliminary procedures, after these procedures have proved unsuccessful; and appellate jurisdiction over disputes in which a binding decision has been rendered as a result of a special procedure and in which an appellate procedure is not excluded. Where a binding decision has been rendered in a special procedure, a party may appeal to the competent general tribunal

114

only in a few specified cases (lack of jurisdiction, infringement of basic procedural rules, abuse or misuse of powers, or gross violation of the Convention) (Article 10).

5. Scientific or technical matters arising out of certain chapters may be referred to a committee of experts or, alternatively, four technical assessors may be asked to assist the tribunal in its deliberations. If the dispute is not settled on the basis of the resulting opinion, either party may request that, on appeal, the findings be taken into account (Article 11).

NOTE

[1]Report and texts are not included in this paper.

FOURTH SESSION
NEW YORK
March 15 - May 7, 1976

## I.  Summary of Delegation Report

Following is a summary of the Delegation Report on the New York Session of the Law of the Sea Conference, March 15 to May 7, 1976.  The detailed Delegation Report of the work of the Main Committees is included.[1]

The fourth session of the Law of the Sea Conference met in New York from March 15 to May 7.  The basis of discussion and negotiation was the Single Negotiating Text prepared by the three Chairmen of the Main Committees, and by the President of the Conference with respect to dispute settlement.  After virtually complete discussion of these texts at the current session, revisions were released on the last day of the current session.  These revisions were prepared by the respective Chairmen, and with respect to dispute settlement, by the President of the Conference, taking into account discussions and negotiations at this session.

On April 8 Secretary Kissinger made a major statement on the LOS negotiations before an American audience which was circulated to all delegations.  He then met with the Conference officers and the heads of delegations, where he made additional remarks.  The Secretary's statement and appearance were widely welcomed as an indication of the high-level US interest in an early and successful conclusion to the negotiations, and his new proposals regarding the deep seabeds were welcomed as evidence of a real effort to accommodate the interests of developing countries.

The Conference has decided to convene another session in New York from August 2 to September 17.  Procedures are likely to emphasize negotiations on important outstanding issues leading to an overall package treaty.

Since the revised Single Negotiating Text was issued on the last day of the session, it is not possible to include an evaluation of it in this report.  An initial reading would indicate the following significant points.

COMMITTEE I

The new text contains refined ideas with respect to an accommodation of the interests of developing countries, industrialized countries, consumers, and producers. In particular it specifies conditions under which States and their nationals would have access to the exploration and exploitation of deep seabed minerals, the control of the Authority in this regard, and establishes a system under which prime mining sites would be reserved for exploitation by the Enterprise (the exploitation arm of the Authority) and developing countries. It also contains specific provisions, including an interim production limit, to protect developing country land-based producers of metals also produced on the seabed. New procedures for the Assembly designed to protect the interests of all concerned are included.

The text specifically notes that the important question of the composition and voting of the Council of the Seabed Authority "has not yet been fully dealt with by the Committee."

COMMITTEE II

No major changes were made in the Committee II text. As specifically noted in the introductory note of the Chairman to the revised text, certain important issues remain to be resolved. These include the question of the high-seas status of the economic zone and the question of the access of landlocked and other geographically disadvantaged States to living resources of the economic zone. The Chairman's basic approach to the revision of this text is indicated in paragraphs 7, 8, and 9 of his introductory note, which are as follows:

7. By far the largest category of articles consisted of those to which no amendments commanding other than minimal support were introduced. It was clear that these should be retained as they were in the single negotiating text.

8. A second group consisted of articles where there was a clear trend favoring the inclusion of a particular amendment or where I was given a mandate to make a change within agreed limits.

119

9. A third category consisted of articles dealing with issues which would be identified, on the basis of extensive discussion, as those on which negotiations were most needed.

My response to these issues varied according to my assessment of the state reached in the negotiations. In certain cases I felt I could suggest a compromise solution. In other cases I considered that negotiations would be advanced if I were to at least point the way to an eventual solution. In still other cases I felt that while there may be a need for a change in the Single Negotiating Text, any modifications to the test might prove counterproductive in the search for a solution.

## COMMITTEE III

1. Pollution: The major changes relate to vessel-source pollution. They include specific enforcement rights for port States for violations of international discharge regulation regardless of where they occur, and specified enforcement rights for coastal States with respect to discharges in the economic zone in violation of international standards.

2. Scientific research: With respect to marine scientific research, a major change has been made which would require the consent of the coastal State for marine scientific research for activities in the economic zone or on the continental shelf, provided that consent shall not be withheld unless the project bears substantially upon the exploration and exploitation of resources, involves drilling or the use of explosives, unduly interferes with coastal State economic activities in accordance with its jurisdiction, or involves the construction, operation, or use of artificial islands, and structures subject to coastal State jurisdiction. The procedures for settlement of disputes are elaborated further in this regard.

## SETTLEMENT OF DISPUTES

The new text contains new language on those cases in which the compulsory procedures would apply to disputes in the economic zone. It adopts a formula on procedures which permits a State to choose among the

following procedures in cases in which it would be
subject to suit:  (a) arbitration; (b) the International Court of Justice; (c) a new Law of the Sea
Tribunal; or (d) specialized procedures for particular kinds of disputes [although, if (d) is selected,
the State must also select (a), (b), or (c) for disputes not covered by the specialized procedures].

## II. Committee I, Deep Seabeds

Committee I completed a review of almost all articles of Part I of the Single Negotiating Text.

Toward the end of the session, the Chairman of
Committee I, Paul Engo of the Cameroon, issued as informal conference documents new texts which significantly modified the SNT he had issued in Geneva in
1975.  He characterized these texts as his personal
assessment of the emerging consensus in the Committee I
negotiations.  These texts were issued on the last day
of the Conference as the Revised Single Negotiating
Text, Part I.

### A. System of Exploitation and Access to Deep Seabed Resources

The Committee began the session by considering
Annex I (Basic Conditions of Prospecting, Exploration,
and Exploitation) to Part I of the LOS Treaty.  This
Annex elaborates the mechanism for obtaining contracts,
the qualifications and selection of applicants, the
rights and obligations under the contract, terms for
suspension and revision of contracts, and the scope
of the Seabed Authority's rules, regulations, and procedures.  It sets forth the objective criteria upon
which these rules and regulations must be based.

Annex I supplements the basic provision in the
body of the treaty on the system of access (Article 22).
This article lies at the heart of the deep seabed negotiations, as it determines the right of access of
States and their nationals to the mineral resources.

The system of exploitation included in the new
SNT consists of a system in which the Authority,
through its operating arm, the Enterprise, may exploit
the deep seabed directly; or exploitation may be carried out pursuant to contracts concluded with the

Authority in accordance with Annex I by member States or their nationals.

Annex I elaborates a new system of revenue sharing between the contractor and the Authority. The Committee did not complete its consideration of this issue. As a result, a formula including precise figures was not negotiated. The revised Annex provides two alternative formulas. One is based on a revenue sharing scheme widely used which includes a grace period for payments followed by a sliding scale based on profits or an alternative royalty system utilized at the discretion of the operator. A second alternative formula provides for revenue sharing or royalties at the discretion of the Authority.

B. Economic Implications

Committee I has for many years questioned the economic effect deep seabed mining may have on developing-country land-based producers of manganese, copper, nickel, and cobalt. A number of these land-based producers have attempted in the negotiations to provide protection for their countries by giving the Authority the power to control directly price and production of these metals mined from the seabed. The US and a number of other countries have strongly opposed giving the Authority the power to control prices or production. A failure to find a compromise on this issue has been one of the major obstacles to a successful conclusion of the negotiations on seabed issues. The new SNT issued by Engo includes an article (Article 9) which attempts to achieve a compromise on this point. It provides for a 20-year period during which time a production limitation would apply to ensure that ocean mining does not produce more than the projected cumulative growth segment of the nickel market.

C. Assembly and Council

Another difficult area in the negotiations has been the delineation of the relative powers and functions of the Assembly and Council of the Authority. The new SNT attempts a balance between these two organs of the Authority. The new Assembly is the supreme organ of the Authority with the power to prescribe general policies by adopting resolutions and making recommendations. The Council is the executive organ of the Authority with the power to prescribe specific policies to be pursued by the Authority.

D. Commissions

The new SNT establishes three commissions: the Economic Planning Commission, the Technical Commission, and the Rules and Regulations Commission. In addition, there are a number of general and housekeeping articles which were largely agreed upon.

E. Dispute Settlement System

Most delegations favor a system which includes a permanent organ of the Authority with the power and duty to take final, binding decisions regarding all disputes arising under Part I of the Convention, relating to the conduct of exploration and exploitation. The new SNT reflects this philosophy. However, a few delegations holding a different view--that all decisions should be made through a system of ad hoc arbitration--pressed their views strongly and will do so in the next session.

\* \* \* \* \*

A number of important issues were debated but only in a preliminary manner during this session and will have to be negotiated in more detail during the next session of the Conference.

F. Provisional Application

One such issue is whether the Law of the Sea Treaty, and particularly Part I, should be applied provisionally before the treaty as a whole enters permanently into force. Some delegations felt that this question can be more appropriately dealt with later or not at all. The majority view, however, supports provisional application of the treaty as a whole while recognizing that this concept may involve certain technical or juridical difficulties for some States.

G. The Enterprise

A major concern of developing countries is the establishment of a functioning Enterprise which would be the organ of the Authority which would exploit seabed resources directly. During the closing days of the Conference session, a draft Annex II (The Statute of the Enterprise) was circulated. While there was some discussion on this question, the debate was

inconclusive; and the details remain to be resolved
at the next session. The fundamental issue of concern to developed and non-developed countries is how
the Enterprise will be financed. The developed countries advocated a system in which the Enterprise could
borrow money in capital markets as well as receive a
portion of the Authority's revenue-sharing funds,
while some developing countries urged that there be a
mandatory fee levied on all States parties. The
Enterprise statute and the related articles in the
treaty on financing the Authority remain to be settled at a later date.

### H. Council Voting

The most important issue which was not resolved
concerns the composition and voting system in the
Council. The US and other developed countries clearly stated that they could not accept the system provided for in the SNT of March 1975. The US in December 1975 proposed amendments which would strengthen
this article from our point of view. However, our
representatives have made it clear that we are not
satisfied with our own amendments to the SNT, and have
said that we would propose a new article at the next
session. In light of this, Chairman Engo did not hold
consultations on this extremely important issue. The
SNT contains the text of the Geneva SNT, but there is
a clear understanding that this issue would be discussed and negotiated at the next session.

### I. Quota System or Anti-Monopoly Article

Several industrialized countries pressed vigorously for a limit on the number of minesites or contracts which any one State or its nationals could obtain from the Authority at any given time. This view
was resisted with equal vigor by the US, which explained that there are several hundred prime minesites
and thousands more of good quality for the future.
This issue remains as one of the most difficult in the
negotiations ahead. The developing countries side-
stepped this issue rather than take sides in a dispute
among and between developed countries.

### J. Secretary's Statement

During this session of the Conference, Secretary
Kissinger made a statement (April 8 before the Foreign
Policy Association) in which he outlined the major

remaining issues that had to be resolved in the LOS
negotiations, citing specifically the difficult problems in Committee I. Secretary Kissinger outlined
the compromise package proposal as an effort to bridge
differences in the negotiations. This speech was regarded as an important contribution to achieving an
atmosphere of accommodation.

III.  Committee II, Territorial Seas, Straits, the
      Economic Zone, the Continental Shelf, High Seas,
      Archipelagos, Landlocked States, Islands, and
      Enclosed and Semi-enclosed Seas

     The work of Committee II was organized to discuss
in informal working sessions of the full committee all
issues in the Informal Single Negotiating Text issued
at the end of the last session in Geneva. The discussion proceeded on an article-by-article basis. In an
attempt to expedite the work, a rule was adopted
whereby silence on the part of any delegation would be
interpreted as indicating support for the Geneva Single Negotiating Text and opposition to any amendments
proposed. While small group consultations were possible, and did in fact take place (tuna, landlocked and
geographically disadvantaged States), the committee
working sessions each day left little time for such
consultations. After six and one half weeks of intensive work, the consideration of all Committee II articles was completed, and the Chairman commenced the
preparation of a revised text. The clear overall impression of the debate was that Part II of the Geneva
Single Negotiating Text was broadly acceptable.

     The major contentious issues in Committee II
faced by the Fourth Session were:

     1.  The juridical status of the economic zone as
high seas; and

     2.  The access to the sea by landlocked States,
and the access to the resources in the economic zones
of States of a region by such States and geographically disadvantaged States of the Region.

     Other important issues on which there was signif-
icant division were:

1. Delimitation of economic zones and continental shelf boundaries between opposite and adjacent States including the question of islands;

2. The question of coastal State authority over construction, design, equipment, and manning standards for foreign vessels in the territorial seas, which is related to the Committee III pollution negotiations;

3. Highly migratory species;

4. Resource rights for territories under foreign occupation or colonial domination.

It will also be necessary to do further work with regard to the continental shelf beyond 200 miles, although the basic framework of a solution seems to be apparent at this point: a precise definition of the outer limit combined with revenue sharing beyond 200 miles.

It is clear that delegations now have a better grasp of the overall Committee II package, though a number of issues are still outstanding.

A. Territorial Seas

There was continued broad support within the committee for a 12-mile territorial sea as a part of an overall, widely accepted package. Some coastal States continued, however, to press for 200 miles, or reserved positions on breadth pending clarification of coastal States' rights in the exclusive economic zone. Neither proposals for 200-mile territorial seas, nor those for extensive historic waters received much support. Provisions on baselines received general approval with minor exceptions. In the discussion of delimitation between opposite or adjacent States the distinction surfaced, which appeared later as well, between the use of equity and equidistance as the proper criterion.

B. Innocent Passage in the Territorial Sea

There was general support in committee for retaining the regime for innocent passage as set forth in the Geneva Single Negotiating Text. There was some attempt to limit the right of innocent passage,

as a preliminary to the straits debate, but none of
the major amendments received significant support.
In addition, a group of States suggested amendments
making the list of non-innocent acts explicitly non-
exhaustive. Debate over whether the coastal State
could adopt laws and regulations concerning the design, construction, manning, and equipping of vessels
in innocent passage in the territorial sea was inconclusive, as was the debate over the retention of provisions concerning the documentation of nuclear-
powered ships. The former issue is a vessel-source
pollution issue being negotiated in Committee III.

C.  Straits Used for International Navigation

With the exception of vocal objections by a
small number of strait States, the discussion of
these articles reflected a general willingness to
accept the Single Negotiating Text. The majority of
States indicated this by remaining silent on the issue. An initial attempt to delete the entire part
and a suggestion that there be further consultations
among interested parties received little support.
As anticipated, a small number of States pressed
for amendments which would have the result of trans-
forming the transit passage regime to one of innocent
passage. Some States pressed for provisions for
State responsibility for loss or damage resulting
from passage of ships. Both efforts generated little
support.

D.  The Exclusive Economic Zone

Debate on the exclusive economic zone articles
of the Single Negotiating Text was extensive and
foreshadowed the general debate on the nature and
chafacter of the economic zone as high seas which
took place in connection with the high seas section.
Strong efforts by landlocked and geographically disadvantaged States to secure access to economic zones
on a regional basis also emerged in the debate.
Maritime States sought amendments that would limit
treatment of coastal State authority in the economic
zone regarding pollution and scientific research to
a cross reference to the work of Committee III.

While there was widespread support for sovereign
rights over resources, some coastal States sought to
achieve broader jurisdiction tantamout to a territorial sea. The group of landlocked and geographically

disadvantaged States strongly opposed the latter concept and proposed amendments that would ensure
strong language regarding their rights of access to
the living resources in the economic zones of States
on a regional basis. This evoked equally strong
coastal State reactions. Articles on fishing and
surplus of coastal State fish stocks received little
comment, while many States were still of differing
views on regional arrangements for the management and
conservation of highly migratory species. The article on anadromous species drew no substantial comment
and appears broadly acceptable. The question of delimitation again received committee attention with a
clear split between States favoring the median line
and those preferring to place emphasis on special
circumstances.

E. Continental Shelf

The primary issue in the Committee debate on the
continental shelf involved the extent of coastal
States jurisdiction. A number of States argued for
limiting such jurisdiction to 200 nautical miles,
while a number of States with broad margins pressed
for jurisdiction over the full continental margin
where it extends beyond 200 miles. Public debate and
private conversations indicated emergence of wide
support for a compromise including acceptance of
coastal State jurisdiction beyond 200 miles to a precisely defined limit combined with sharing according
to a treaty formula by the coastal State of revenues
generated from exploitation of the mineral resources
of the margin beyond 200 miles.

F. High Seas

The majority of the discussions on this topic
were devoted to a thorough airing of the question of
the juridical nature of the economic zone, with approximately three-quarters of the States present participating in the debate. States were evenly split
on whether the exclusion of the economic zone from
the high seas should be removed from Article 73, with
corresponding changes in other relevant articles.
The length and complexity of the debate showed a desire by many for some change in the article which
would preserve the high seas status of the economic
zone. Secretary Kissinger expressly stated that the
economic zone remains high seas. Attempts were made
by some delegations to find a compromise based upon

an exclusion from the regime of the high seas of those coastal States' rights expressly provided for in the Convention. Most other articles received little comment.

## G. Living Resources Beyond the Economic Zone

The provisions of this part were for the most part acceptable. Some support was generated for amendments calling for coordination of management and conservation of living resources beyond the economic zone through regional, sub-regional, or global organizations, and for minimizing conflicts between fishing within and outside the economic zone. In addition, some whaling States sought deletion of the reference in Article 53 to prohibitions or special limitations on exploitation of marine mammals.

## H. Landlocked-State Access to the Sea

The landlocked States opened debate on this subject calling for the right of transit through the territories of transit States for the purpose of access to the sea, subject to terms and conditions to be set by agreement. Such proposals were met by strong opposition from coastal transit States seeking a more limited version, suggesting that the principle of reciprocity should in all cases apply.

## I. Archipelagic States

There was little support for changes in the Geneva Single Negotiating Text. Attempts to alter the size of the envelope enclosing an archipelago, along with those designed to extend the concept by changing the land-water ratio, received little support. Debate centered upon the length of permissible archipelagic baselines with general support for limits set forth in the text with a small number of exceptions permitted. Several States pressed for extension of the archipelago concept to archipelagos of continental States, but attracted little support.

### J. Islands

This article was generally acceptable to the committee. The Geneva Single Negotiating Text provides that rocks which cannot sustain human habitation or economic life of their own shall not have an economic zone or continental shelf. A proposal to delete this reference drew strong, but not majority, support.

### K. Enclosed and Semi-Enclosed Seas

The text of these articles providing for States bordering on enclosed or semi-enclosed seas to co-operate in meeting common problems seemed generally acceptable to most States provided that the duty was not strengthened, and perhaps weakened a bit. Proposals in this area tended to be attempts to adjust the texts to deal with limited, special situations, and these suggestions received only limited regional support.

### L. Territories Under Foreign Occupation or Colonial Domination

Article 136 of the Geneva Single Negotiating Text would make special provisions for exercise of resource rights in certain categories of non self-governing territories. Discussion of this article tended to be highly politicized, and there was considerable support on the one hand for revising the text to make it less discriminatory (i.e. inclusion of reference to associated States), and for extending it to include liberation movements on the other. There was also some recognition that the issues involved cannot be resolved in the Law of the Sea forum. Several compromise proposals were suggested for the Chairman's consideration.

### M. Landlocked State Access to Marine Resources

Minister Jens Evensen of Norway convened a group of interested States during the session to attempt to find an acceptable formula for Articles 57, 58, and 59 dealing with access of landlocked and geographically disadvantaged States to the living resources of the economic zones of coastal States of their region. A text was produced for submission to the Chairman, but significant disagreement on the issues remains.

IV.  Committee III, Pollution and Scientific Research

A.  Protection of the Marine Environment

Objectives in this part of the LOS negotiations
have been to establish effective environmental protection obligations with regard to all sources of marine pollution.  In general, this would include standard-setting and enforcement rights for each source
and, with the exception of land-based pollution, to
require that domestic regulations be at least as effective as international regulations.  In addition,
much effort was devoted to finding a settlement on
vessel-source pollution which would ensure effective
enforcement of the regulations while not impinging on
navigation.  The negotiating process occurred mainly
within the informal working group of the whole and
through consultations conducted by Chairman José Louis
Vallarta (Mexico).

An important initial decision was not to reopen
the first 15 articles of the Geneva Single Negotiating
Text which were previously negotiated.  These cover
the general obligations to prevent pollution, global
and regional cooperation on pollution problems, technical assistance, monitoring, and environmental assessments.  A few changes were made to these texts based
on Evensen Group intersessional work.  Article-by-
article discussion then took place on Articles 16
through 19 and 21 through 25 with few changes being
made to the  Geneva Single Negotiating Text.  These
articles provide for the establishment and enforcement
of regulations on land-based pollution, continental
shelf pollution, and ocean dumping and indicate that
pollution from deep seabed exploration and exploitation of resources will be handled in Committee I.  On
the vessel-source pollution articles (20, 26-39), the
discussion took place on an issue-by-issue approach.
After general debate in the working group of the whole,
real negotiation took place in an informal consulting
group open to all countries.  There was movement toward
compromise on the part of both the coastal and maritime
States.  The tenor of the discussions permitted Ambassador Yankov to produce a new text which may be very
close to a final treaty on most issues.

In the area of vessel-source pollution, three
major aspects were addressed:  coastal State regulations
in the economic zone; enforcement generally against

131

vessel-source pollution; and coastal State rights in the territorial sea.

With respect to economic zone regulations, most countries agree that there should be only generally applicable international regulations in the economic zone, although there would be special areas, defined by criteria in the treaty, in which more strict international discharge regulations would apply. In general, the criteria and regulations in these special areas would be the same as those in the 1973 IMCO Convention. In addition, the text contains an article giving coastal States standard-setting and enforcement rights in ice-covered areas within the limits of the economic zone.

On enforcement of international discharge regulations, an accommodation has been generally supported along the following lines:

1. Strict flag State obligations to take effective enforcement action;

2. Port State enforcement rights to prosecute vessels in its ports for international discharge standard violations regardless of where they occur;

3. A coastal State right to take enforcement action in the economic zone against flagrant or gross violations of international discharge regulations causing major damage or threat of damage to coastal State interests;

4. A flag State right to pre-empt prosecutions for violations beyond the territorial sea by other States unless the flag State has disregarded its enforcement obligations or the violation has caused major damage; and

5. A series of safeguards including release on bond of vessels, liability for unreasonable enforcement, and sovereign immunity.

With regard to the territorial sea, a major split remains. The other major maritime powers (USSR, Japan, UK, and most Western Europeans) argue that the coastal State should not be authorized to establish construction, design, equipment, or manning regulations more strict than international regulations. Many coastal States and the US support complete coastal State

authority subject only to the right of innocent passage. The US view is already set out in domestic
legislation in the Ports and Waterways Safety Act.
The Third Committee text supports the US view while
the Second Committee text supports the maritime view-
point, thus requiring later resolution of the issue.

The major issue remaining to be resolved is coordination of the Committees II and III texts on territorial sea jurisdiction. The coastal State rights
to set manning, equipment, design, and construction
standards within the territorial sea will not see
final resolution until such coordination has taken
place.

## B. Marine Scientific Research

Committee III completed the first article-by-
article reading of the Geneva Single Negotiating Text
on marine scientific research (MSR) and on Technology
Transfer. The Chairman of the informal working group,
Cornell Metternich of the Federal Republic of Germany,
repeatedly stressed that the purpose of the sessions
was to obtain reactions to the SNT in order to aid
Chairman Yankov in redrafting the text.

With these ground rules, the main focus of the
marine scientific research discussions was Chapter III
of the Geneva text dealing with research in the economic zone and on the continental shelf. The US approach was that coastal State interests in the economic zone should be protected through a series of
agreed obligations upon the researcher. Many developed countries sought consent for all research in the
economic zone. The Geneva text set forth a mixed regime in the economic zone requiring consent for resource-oriented research and an obligations regime for
research not oriented toward resources. This distinction between categories of research came under question by 36 developing countries who claimed such a
distinction was impractical, and that consent should
apply to all research activities in the economic zone.
Most other countries defended the distinction concept
as the only practical basis for a compromise settlement on the question of MSR. In an attempt to find a
reasonable accommodation, Secretary Kissinger stated
a willingness to accept a reasonable distinction approach, subject to compulsory dispute settlement.

An important element of a regime for marine scientific research based on a distinction between resource and non-resource oriented research is the question of who decides the orientation of the research. Mexico continued to seek compulsory conciliation with the ultimate right in the coastal State to decide the issue. Many developing States who had attacked the proposal to distinguish between resource and non-resource oriented research indicated that the Mexican approach would make this distinction concept more acceptable. Many of the supporters of the distinction concept, on the other hand, said it was crucial to have disputed questions on the nature of the research subject to binding third-party settlement. There was no clear resolution of the issue in the informal meetings of the Committee.

Metternich, in his report to Chairman Yankov, referred to informal negotiations that had occurred during the session and offered the following personal conclusion:

1. A compromise will not be reached on a text which requires consent in all cases, nor on a text where consent is never required. A mixed regime subjecting some research activities to consent and some to an obligation regime appeared to be the only viable basis for compromise.

2. While there was no agreement as to the complete list, it appeared that at least the following should require consent: resource-oriented research, although there was no agreement as to the proper terminology to describe this form of research; drilling or the use of explosives; and utilization of structures referred to in Article 48 of Part II.

3. Central to the regime was the question of dispute settlement with no compromise on this issue readily apparent.

The revised Single Negotiating Text, however, reflects a different approach from those discussed in the negotiation. It requires consent for all scientific research in the economic zone but provides that consent shall not be withheld unless it is resource oriented, involves drilling and the use of explosives, or the utilization of artificial islands or installations subject to coastal State jurisdiction. The new text also provides that disputes regarding research will

first be referred to experts to aid the parties in
reaching agreement; but if those efforts are not successful, it will be referred to the binding dispute
settlement procedures set forth in Part IV.

C. Transfer of Technology

The discussion on transfer of technology was
lengthy but basically inconclusive. Several attempts
were made to ensure that the text reflected the view
that transfer of technology was an obligation of developed States not subject to normal economic principles. Contrasted to this view was the approach that
all transfer of technology involving technology in the
commercial sector must protect the interest of both
the recipient and the supplier of technology.

V. Settlement of Disputes

A. General Objectives

Effective provisions for the binding settlement
of disputes arising from the interpretation or application of the LOS Convention are an essential part of
a negotiated package. Without a provision for compulsory settlement of disputes, the substantive provisions of the Convention would be subject to unilateral
interpretation, and the delicate balance of rights and
duties achieved in a Convention would be quickly upset. Secretary Kissinger emphasized the importance
of this in his April 8 speech.

B. Background

An Informal Working Group on Settlement of Disputes was organized at Caracas, and at the end of the
1975 Geneva session this Group submitted a text to the
President of the Conference. Using that text and resolving some of the issues it left open, the President
prepared and circulated a Single Negotiating Text on
dispute settlement in July 1975.

In an effort to blend together the conflicting
approaches which were discussed at Caracas and Geneva
(one which would provide compulsory dispute settlement
only for certain disputes; the other which would apply
compulsory dispute settlement to all disputes), President Amerasinghe provided in his first text for a new
Law of the Sea Tribunal to resolve disputes involving

135

the interpretation or application of the Convention
(unless the parties to the dispute agreed to arbitration or the International Court of Justice); he also
provided for special procedures in the area of fisheries, pollution, and scientific research disputes
and for various exceptions to compulsory dispute settlement, including one which deals with the pivotal
question of dispute settlement in the economic zone.

### C. Plenary Debate

Dispute settlement was taken up in a Plenary
meeting of the Conference for the first time during
the fourth session. In six days of debate, 72 speakers expressed a wide range of views. Each speaker
acknowledged the need for a dispute-settlement system,
but discussion of the scope and competence of the system disclosed widely divergent viewpoints on basic details. Some States advocated a comprehensive system
that would apply to all disputes arising out of the
interpretation and application of the Convention.
Some States supported a comprehensive system with a
provision for limited and carefully defined exceptions
from the jurisdiction of the system. And some States
proposed that compulsory dispute settlement should be
totally excluded from the economic zone, although many
of those States also expressly acknowledged that navigation and overflight disputes in the zone should be
subject to compulsory dispute settlement.

Many delegations recognized that disputes arising
out of deep seabed mining activities, particularly
disputes over contract matters, would have unique features, and accordingly supported specialized procedures for such disputes. Some favored a completely
independent Seabed Tribunal which would be an organ of
the Seabed Authority with authority to make binding,
final decisions regarding all disputes arising out of
the activities in the area pursuant to Part I of the
Convention. Others suggested that an appellate relationship should be established between the Seabed Tribunal and the Law of the Sea Tribunal.

Speakers in the Plenary also discussed the structure of the dispute-settlement system. Some States
advocated arbitration as the sole mode of settling disputes; others advocated use of the International Court
of Justice; and others supported the creation of a new
Law of the Sea Tribunal (although some delegations opposed any new tribunal).

Some States advocated specialized procedures to handle disputes related to fishing, navigation, and research; other States advocated a system with general jurisdiction for handling all disputes. In the discussion of the type of forum or forums to be used, there was substantial support for a provision that would give a Contracting Party a choice among three tribunals (an arbitral tribunal, the Law of the Sea Tribunal, or the International Court of Justice). A Party's declaration at the time of ratification would determine the forum before which that Party could be brought by a claimant in a dispute.

At the close of the Plenary debate, President Amerasinghe obtained approval for his proposal to produce a revised text based on the remarks in Plenary and any suggestions subsequently submitted informally to him.

D. The Basic Issues

In the dispute settlement section of the Convention, the question of application of compulsory third-party dispute settlement in the economic zone is the most difficult and complex issue. States opposed to excluding compulsory dispute settlement from the zone contend that the Convention system must take account of both coastal and other States rights in the zone. The success of the Conference will depend on designing a provision that will accommodate both coastal State interest in resource management discretion and the major rights and interests of other States in the economic zone.

E. Group of 77

The Group of 77 undertook a serious and detailed study of dispute settlement for the first time during this session. A 12-member "contact group" conducted extensive discussion and debate over a period of several weeks. A position paper was produced by this contact group for the Group of 77.

F. Revised Single Negotiating Text

The fundamental question of protecting the rights of coastal States and the rights of other States in the economic zone is treated in Article 18. Subject to certain exceptions including interference with navigation and overflight, the new Article 18 excludes

from the Convention system disputes related to the exercise of sovereign rights, exclusive rights, or exclusive jurisdiction of a coastal State.

The new text must be carefully studied. If the economic zone is not to become the functional equivalent of a territorial sea, the dispute settlement system must provide adequate protection for the rights of both coastal and other States.

NOTE

[1] Reports are not included in this paper.

FIFTH SESSION
NEW YORK
August 2 - September 17, 1976

I. Summary of Delegation Report

The Fifth Session of the Third United Nations
Conference on the Law of the Sea met in New York from
August 2 to September 17, 1976.  The Conference decided to emphasize informal negotiations on outstanding
issues in the three main committees, with a more detailed review of the dispute settlement text in the
informal Plenary leading to the preparation of a revised dispute settlement text.  The bases of work
were the Revised Single Negotiating Tests issued at
the end of the spring session by the Chairmen of the
Main Committees, and a single negotiating text on dispute settlement issued by the President of the Conference.  It was decided that no further revisions of the
revised single negotiating texts would be proposed by
the Chairmen of the Committees.  However, the Chairmen
did issue reports the last day of the session.

The Third Committee has traditionally been able
to have smaller groups of effective size function on a
pragmatic basis.  For the first time, the Second Committee was able to establish similar limited groups of
interested delegations on selected issues.  However,
the First Committee, its workshop, even the workshop's
negotiating group, functioned in effect with very
large numbers of delegations present at all times.
While the difficulties faced in other Committees indicate that smaller groups are in and of themselves
no guarantee of quick results, the absence of a suitable negotiating vehicle in the First Committee clearly contributed to the problem.

The present Revised Single Negotiating Text (RSNT)
represents a consensus on a large number of issues before the Conference.  This text has been maintained in
this session as the basis for negotiations.  A broad
consensus already exists in certain key areas including a 12-mile territorial sea, unimpeded passage of
straits, establishing coastal State resource and other
rights in a 200-mile economic zone, protecting navigational rights, and marine pollution.  However, important issues are outstanding on which the Conference
concentrated.

The First Committee devoted most of its time to
the question of the system of exploitation for deep

seabed resources, evaluating the parallel-access system put forth in the RSNT. In an attempt to accommodate concerns regarding that system, Secretary Kissinger proposed a package approach which would include assured access in all its aspects to deep seabed mining sites by all nations and their citizens along with a financing arrangement to enable the proposed Enterprise (the independent operating arm of the International Seabed Authority) to get into business. As part of that package he further proposed that there could be a review, in perhaps 25 years, to determine if the provisions of the treaty regarding the system of seabed exploitation were working adequately. This was a significant move which generated considerable interest which we believe can be transformed at the next session into specific treaty language. A number of delegations, representing all concerned groups, have expressed to us their belief that our package proposal represented a constructive contribution in the negotiations. This reaction is encouraging, and we intend in the same spirit to follow up this initiative both during the period between sessions and at the next session. Some delegations chose tactics of confrontation. The Secretary noted that such tactics cannot work and will inevitably lead to deadlock and unilateral action.

The First Committee did not have time to discuss the questions of the decision-making process of the Authority, including the Assembly and the Council, or other matters in detail.

The Second Committee set up negotiating groups to deal with the following "priority questions":

1. The legal status of the exclusive economic zone. Rights and duties of the coastal State and of other States in the exclusive economic zone.

2. Rights of access of landlocked States to and from the sea and freedom of transit.

3. Payments and contributions in respect of the exploitation of the continental shelf beyond 200 miles.

4. Definition of the outer edge of the continental margin.

Later in the session, negotiating groups were set up on other matters.

Secretary Kissinger discussed the problem of the status of the economic zone with other delegations, emphasizing the importance of finding an accommodation that protects the rights of coastal States while preserving the high seas freedoms of all States.

In the Third Committee, most time was devoted to the problem of scientific research in the economic zone. We proposed a compromise which will give the coastal States the right to control marine scientific research directly related to resource exploitation but which will ensure the right to conduct other forms of marine scientific research. Secretary Kissinger reviewed the problem with a number of other delegations. While the RSNT on marine pollution commands general support, attention was devoted to certain particular problems such as standard-setting in the territorial sea.

The Plenary, in informal session, engaged in a detailed review of the articles on settlement of disputes. On this basis, the President of the Conference plans to issue a revised Single Negotiating Text on the matter. The debate indicates that the major issues revolve around the choice of procedures for dispute settlement and the extent of dispute settlement in the economic zone.

The Chairmen of Committees II and III have each commented on the inter-relationships between the work of their Committees and other Conference work which, of course, can be a complicating factor.

In his statement on the conclusion of the session, Secretary Kissinger commented on various issues, and then concluded:

We believe that equitable resolution of these and the other key issues in these negotiations can be found. Unless this is the case, various governments may conclude agreement is not possible, resulting in unilateral action which can lead to conflict over the uses of ocean space.

The United States has a major interest as a global power in preventing such conflict and thus will continue to seek overall solutions acceptable to all groups of countries. In so doing, however, we will continue vigorously to safeguard essential American interests.

142

We will work cooperatively with other nations, but we expect a reciprocal attitude of good will and reasonableness. There are limits beyond which the US will not go, and we are close to such limits now.

We must move toward businesslike negotiations and toward a recognition that the alternative to a treaty would serve no national or international community interest. I continue to believe that a Law of the Sea Convention can be achieved. The United States will seek to build on the progress made to date and will continue its intensive efforts to achieve a treaty. A successful outcome will bring major benefits to this nation and help shape a more peaceful and prosperous international community.

The General Committee decided on the following recommendations to the Plenary regarding future work and the next session to be held in New York:

1. The Conference should hold another session in 1977 for seven weeks, with the possibility of extending it to eight weeks.

2. The session should start on either May 16, 23, or 30.

3. The first two or three weeks of the session should be devoted to matters being dealt with by the First Committee to enable that Committee to reach the same stage as the other two Committees, but other meetings should not be precluded provided there was no interference with the First Committee and with the participation of Heads of Delegations in that Committee's work.

4. During the following two weeks of the session, the Second and Third Committees should meet along with the First.

5. Discussions should be held in Plenary meetings on the settlement of disputes as well as formal discussions on the preamble and final clauses of the Convention.

6. In the sixth week, the President and Chairmen of the Main Committees should prepare an informal

143

single composite text, on the basis of which the Conference should attempt to prepare a draft convention
on which it should act if possible by consensus and
without resort to voting.

As regards the intersessional consultations, the
Committee agreed to recommend that the Committee
Chairmen or individual delegations should organize
such consultations if they wish to do so. The Secretariat should inform all members and should transmit
the results of any such consultations to all members.

The Conference agreed.

II. COMMITTEE I

A. General

The US and a number of other countries expected
that the major issues to be discussed in Committee I
during this session would be those which had not been
the subject of previous negotiations in the Committee:
the composition and voting mechanism of the Council of
the Authority; the Statute of the Enterprise; and the
Statute of the Seabed Tribunal. The Group of 77, however, insisted upon reopening basic issues. The first
issue which was discussed was the system of exploitation of seabed minerals. As it turned out, this subject was the only item addressed during the session.

The formal position of the Group of 77 was that
the system of exploitation previously negotiated and
contained in the Revised Single Negotiating Text (RSNT)
was not acceptable. The RSNT provisions establish a
parallel system of exploitation with both the Enterprise of the Authority, and States and private entities having access on equal terms to the exploitation
of the seabed. The Group of 77 counter-proposed a system which would give the Authority broad discretionary
powers to refuse to conclude contracts with States and
their sponsored private entities and the power not to
open the Area at all. Under this proposal, the facade
of a parallel system was maintained; but the Enterprise
was given clear pre-eminence, and State and private
access was not guaranteed.

In response to this proposal, the US, supported
by a number of other industrialized countries, and
the Soviet Union, supported by other industrialized

States, submitted draft articles on a system of exploitation. The US in making its proposal emphasized that the parallel or dual access system was a method of accommodating the essential interests of all States and the international community in general.

Under the US system, the Authority is given supervision over all activities of resource exploration and exploitation in the Area. The Authority would enter into contracts with the Enterprise on the one hand, and States and private parties on the other, for the exploitation of seabed resources. The Authority would be required to enter into such contracts unless the applicant failed to meet a list of specific and exhaustive criteria contained in the treaty or its annex. The Soviet Union's proposal called for exploitation of the Area both by the Authority directly and by States and other entities under the effective fiscal and administrative supervision of the Authority.

The discussions in the Committee and its subsidiary bodies focused on these three proposals which essentially involved the system of exploitation applicable to States and private parties and did not touch upon aspects of Enterprise operations within the context of a parallel system. Since the question of the methods of operation for the Enterprise was not in the forefront of the Committee's work, its consideration of the parallel system of exploitation became somewhat unbalanced, with undue emphasis being placed in its deliberations on only the State and private party side of the access system established in the RSNT. Accordingly, many of the issues concerned with the system of exploitation which had formed an integral part of the compromise contained in the RSNT re-emerged as issues in dispute by the Group of 77.

Toward the end of the session, however, greater interest was expressed in the potential for strengthening the ability of the Enterprise to function within the context of a parallel system such as that established in the RSNT, a trend that was no doubt stimulated by the compromise proposals made in this area by Secretary Kissinger during his September 1-2 visit at the Conference. The Secretary noted that many countries had expressed doubts about the parallel system on the grounds that it did no good to set aside part of the minesites for the Authority if it did not possess the financial resources or the technology to exploit

these sites. In view of this concern, the Secretary said that the US Government would be prepared to agree to a means of financing the Enterprise so that it could begin mining operations in the same timeframe that State and private operators could begin exploitation of the seabed.

The Secretary also noted the concerns of some delegations that it was premature to establish a permanent regime for the deep seabeds in light of the many unknowns in this field, and he suggested periodic review conferences--perhaps at 25-year intervals--in which the system could be reexamined, although existing contracts would, of course, be respected. The Secretary emphasized that these new proposals were responsive to the legitimate concerns of the Group of 77, and that we now required similar responses to our concerns, particularly on the issues of guaranteed access, avoidance of production controls, and a suitable Assembly and Council.

These proposals of the Secretary were not discussed within Committee I because of the limited time remaining in the session, but a number of delegations expressed interest and a desire to pursue the subjects mentioned by the Secretary in greater detail at the next session. Following the Secretary's initiatives, a marked change occurred in the negotiating atmosphere of Committee I in that the tendency to consider State and private party access in isolation was reduced; and a more constructive willingness to address the entire complex of issues involved in the system of exploitation appeared.

B. Outlook

The outlook for the negotiations in Committee I is unclear. If one chooses to look only at the negative factors, the picture is glum indeed: this session produced no concrete results, and there is little hard evidence that the apparent gap in positions on the system of exploitation was narrowed; in addition to the system of exploitation discussed at this session, there are major issues yet to be negotiated, such as the composition and decision-making procedures of the Council. Further, members of the Group of 77 have identified other issues of concern, such as the powers and voting procedures in the Assembly, its relationship to the Council, production controls, and

146

the dispute settlement mechanism in Committee I.
These are complex issues which will take much time to
negotiate unless procedures can be developed which
permit negotiations among representative groups.
Moreover, a particularly disturbing development at
this session was the indication that a few developing
countries, for the first time in the negotiations, are
considering support of a State quota or anti-monopoly
provision, a trend that would seriously impede the
chances for reaching an acceptable deep seabed accommodation.

On the other hand, there are positive factors:
it is apparent that many of the problems this session
were caused by the insufficient time available between
the two New York meetings in which to digest the work
of the earlier conference and to formulate new positions. The result was a tendency to return to previous positions. In addition, at the end of this session there appeared to be widespread recognition that
the Committee could not afford another unproductive
meeting such as this one, and that at the next session
delegations and groups must come prepared to make the
hard political compromises necessary to reach agreement. Moreover, we believe that most delegations have
a better appreciation of the minimum requirements of
the various groups and recognize that the substance of
the RSNT on many of the issues involved in the system
of exploitation represents the probable outline of a
final compromise settlement which could meet the essential needs of all groups in the absence of ideology
and group politics.

As it turned out, this session gave an opportunity to those delegations in the Group of 77 holding more
extreme positions to dominate the 77 and attempt to obtain further concessions of substance from the industrialized countries. It became apparent that there is
no further give in these positions, however; and toward
the end, moderating influences in the 77 began to
emerge vocally and resume leadership. If this process
continues, we may find a somewhat better climate for
negotiation at the next session. Nevertheless, it
must be recognized that the issues which did not come
up at this session are at least as difficult and important as the system of exploitation; and that during
the session the Group of 77 adopted (though they did
not table) very tough, extremist positions on them.
These positions unless moderated before the next session
could cause the next session to end in stalemate, too.

147

It should be noted, as mentioned above, that there is some recognition that the negotiating difficulties in Committee I may be partially attributable to the procedures it has utilized, as well as timing factors. In this connection, the final report of the Chairman of Committee I, Paul Engo, emphasized that new procedural approaches, such as voting, may, in his view, be needed at the next session in order to encourage delegations to take the final decisions necessary to produce widespread agreement.

## III. COMMITTEE II

### A. Procedures

All negotiating at this session was conducted in open-ended negotiating groups established by the Chairman, and in small groups, when it appeared that the negotiating groups had carried issues as far as possible. The essential objective was to deal intensively with issues identified by the Committee as priority issues. Initially, the negotiating groups were set up to deal with four "priority" issues, i.e. the legal status of the economic zone and the rights and duties of States in the zone; the outer limit of continental margin, and revenue sharing; and access to the sea by landlocked States. Subsequently, two additional groups were established to deal with straits, and with delimitation of the territorial sea, exclusive economic zone, and continental shelf between opposite and adjacent States. Small groups of 30 States each further discussed the first three issues, and an informal group of coastal States and landlocked and geographically disadvantaged States (LL/GDS) was formed outside the Conference structure to deal with access to fishery resources in the zone by landlocked and geographically disadvantaged States.

### B. Status of the Economic Zone

Without a doubt, the most important outstanding issue for the United States in Committee II was, and remains, the juridical status of the economic zone. The US objective in this regard is to retain this traditional high-seas status of the zone, except for rights over resources and other limited rights (which had previously been high-seas freedoms) assigned to coastal States by the provision of the Treaty. This

objective has been made more difficult because:

    1. The present Revised Single Negotiating Text (RSNT) clearly states that the economic zone is <u>not</u> high seas.

    2. In his introductory note to the RSNT, the Chairman of the Second Committee wrote the following:

> Nor is there any doubt that the exclusive economic zone is neither the high seas nor the territorial sea. It is a zone <u>sui generis</u>.

He suggested that the solution was to be found in adjusting the articles dealing with the rights and duties of coastal States in the zone, and those of other States.

    The US made clear that the provisions of the RSNT on this subject are unacceptable as written, and that we cannot agree to any text which makes it clear that the zone is <u>not</u> high seas. On the contrary, the text must somehow explicitly accord high-seas status to the zone but with the recognition that the zone is not high seas with respect to the exercise of coastal State rights provided for in the Treaty. In addition, the summary of coastal State rights in the zone must be made consistent with the substantive articles.

    The negotiations have been made still more difficult by the extremists of the territorialist group who have insisted that the zone be characterized as one of national jurisdiction in which other States enjoy only subordinate rights of navigation, overflight, and communication.

    More moderate coastal States worked at this session of the Conference to seek an accommodation by experimenting with various formulations which might more satisfactorily specify the rights and duties of States in the zone.

    During two visits to the Conference, Secretary Kissinger met with various key delegations on this subject, stressing the importance of the issue to the United States, elaborating again the US position on the issue as set forth above, and encouraging moderate delegations toward an acceptable accommodation.

## C. The Continental Margin

Two questions were focused on during the negotiations: the first was the definition of the outer limits of the continental margin where it extends beyond 200 miles; the second involved revenue sharing from mineral exploitation on the margin beyond 200 nautical miles.

The resolution of these issues is important in clearing the way to a successful conclusion of a treaty. Although the US does not have an extensive margin beyond 200 miles, several other Conference participants, with very broad margins, consider this issue of great importance.

The two groups most seriously affected by these issues are the broad-margin States, who favor exclusive control over resources throughout the broadest reaches of the margin, and narrow-margin States (including landlocked and geographically disadvantaged States) who wish to ensure that significant resources be retained for the common heritage of mankind.

The US has supported a compromise which would define the legal limit of the continental margin where it extends beyond 200 miles, either at a fixed distance from the foot of the slope, or at a fixed thickness of sediment. As a necessary adjunct to this formula, the Treaty would provide for a sharing of revenues derived from mineral production from the margin beyond 200 nautical miles with the international community. The formula which was the primary focus of attention called for revenue sharing of one percent of the value of production at the site in the sixth year of production, increasing in annual increments of one percent to a maximum of five percent in the tenth year and thereafter.

The concepts of these formulas seem to be gaining substantial support. The organization(s) which would collect and distribute revenues has yet to be agreed. Discussion, however, did focus on both the regional and other development organizations and the International Seabed Resource Authority (ISRA) as mediums of distribution. It is an important element in the accommodation that all areas of the margin beyond 200 miles which would be recognized as under coastal State jurisdiction for resource purposes be subject to revenue sharing obligations. If certain larges areas of

the margin under coastal State resource jurisdiction
are excluded, the revenues for the international
community will be significantly reduced.

D.  Landlocked and Geographically Disadvantaged
States  (LL/GDS)

A significant number of LL/GDS at this Conference have pressed to have their interests accommodated.  A successful conclusion of the Treaty will have
to take these interests into account.  They have been
particularly active in seeking three objectives:

1.  Access to the sea and transit rights;

2.  Revenues from the continental margin
beyond 200 nautical miles; and

3.  Access and preferential rights to living
resources in the economic zones of neighboring States
or States in the region.

While some progress can be seen in the first two
categories, it is the third where there has been greater controversy.  At issue are such problems as whether
LL and GDS should have preference to fisheries over
third States in the region; whether that preference
should only be to the surplus; whether landlocked
should be treated differently from geographically disadvantaged; and whether a distinction should be made
between developing and developed States.

The US recognized this as an important issue,
and has encouraged attempts by the group of coastal
States and the LL and GDS group to find an appropriate
accommodation.  A small group of States representing
the respective interests has commenced negotiations
and has before it a text for consideration.  This is a
very encouraging development which will, we hope, come
to fruition.

In conjunction with the raising of fishery resource issues in the zone by LL and GDS countries, the
tuna article received some renewed attention, but
there was no widely displayed interest in amending the
article.  Principles were offered favoring a more
coastally oriented article, and were supported by a
limited number of States, several of whom may not have
had an interest in tuna, but did prefer the strengthening of the economic-zone concept.  The US maintains

that highly migratory species should be accorded special treatment in the economic zone within the framework of a regional regulating regime.

### E.  Straits Used for International Navigation

Late in this session, the Chairman opened the question of straits for discussion.  The straits articles provide for the regime of transit passage, which is an essential element in the adoption of a 12-mile maximum breadth of the territorial sea.

The discussions have clearly indicated that only a small number of States have difficulty with the articles.  A few, but not any substantial number, of strait States are seeking changes.  These changes vary according to each State's geographical location and configuration.

Because there is a long history of prior negotiation on the straits articles, substantive change in the text appears unlikely.

### F.  Delimitation Between Opposite and Adjacent States

This issue was also addressed late in the session. The major outstanding questions involve whether the primary method of delimitation should be according to equity, or by the application of the equidistance line; and as it is generally agreed that the solution is to be achieved by agreement between the parties, how the matter should be treated during the interval pending agreement.

The present text provides for agreement according to equitable principles taking into account, where appropriate, the median or equidistance line.  Since the underlying problems are essentially bilateral, the debates have been confused and involved.  No agreement was reached on whether or how the text might be amended.

### G.  Other Issues

The Chair provided limited time at the end of this session for countries to raise issues of importance to them other than those issues already discussed in specific informal negotiating groups.  The questions drawing the most comment were:

1. The right of the coastal State to establish design, construction, manning, and equipment standards for ships in the territorial seas;

2. Archipelagos;

3. The breadth of the territorial seas;

4. Enclosed and semi-enclosed seas;

5. Baselines; and

6. Mid-ocean archipelagos which are not States.

None of these discussions drew sufficient attention to warrant formal action by the Committee, although the Chairman encouraged further negotiations among interested States, and noted the need for appropriate coordination between the Second and Third Committees on the first issue. Questions concerning standards for management of living resources received scant attention; and marine mammals were not discussed. The transitional provision also was touched upon.


IV. COMMITTEE III

A. Marine Scientific Research

1. US Objectives:

The RSNT requires consent of the coastal State for all scientific research in the economic zone, but provides that the coastal State may withhold its consent only for certain specified scientific research activities. The US position is that there should not be an overall consent requirement, but that consent should be required only for specified marine scientific research activities--other scientific research activities should be conducted upon compliance with specified criteria designed to protect coastal State interests. These criteria include advance notification to the coastal State, their participation in the research project, and sharing of data and samples. In addition, the US has also sought to ensure that practical protections for researching and coastal States are improved. These protections include an effective tacit consent procedure and application of binding dispute-settlement procedures to all disputes concerning scientific research.

## 2. Negotiations at this Session

Most developing coastal countries supported a consent regime of some type for scientific research. Only one or two countries continued to argue for a total, unqualified discretionary consent regime. Most urged, as a compromise, an overall consent requirement with a specific list of criteria for denying consent. In particular, there was a general willingness to remove from the criteria research projects which interfere with economic activities, provided that a clear treaty obligation on researching States not to interfere was included.

On the question of tacit consent, there were only a few reservations, with most delegations indicating that this was not an issue of principle.

There was no detailed discussion of dispute settlement in the Third Committee, although the question of the application of dispute settlement to scientific research was discussed in the informal Plenary discussions on Part IV.

Secretary Kissinger met with a number of delegates to discuss scientific research in an effort to find an acceptable compromise. He underscored the importance of the issue to the United States and the strong opposition to ratification of the Treaty by the American scientific community which could result if the present text is not changed.

Throughout this session, the Chairman of Committee III (Yankov--Bulgaria) seemed intent on pushing the RSNT and an informal proposal he prepared as the basis for compromise. The report prepared by the Committee Chairman reflects only his own informal text, disregarding a variety of proposals that had been put forward. This is unfortunate, since informal negotiations had made it clear that his informal proposal could not serve as a basis for an acceptable compromise.

At the end of the session, Australia informally proposed a new compromise which required consent for all scientific research, but limited the criteria for denying consent. This proposal was circulated to all delegations, received some favorable comments, and the Chairman encouraged the Australians to continue their efforts.

In addition to substantive problems directly related to scientific research, the negotiations have been made more difficult by the perceived linkage of this issue with the question of the nature of the economic zone. The issues are linked in the Conference, and the negotiation of final solutions to both must be coordinated.

Overall, the Conference is not much closer to agreement on marine scientific research than we were at the beginning of the session. The US proposal of limiting consent to certain specified types of scientific research met with opposition. However, the position of a number of developing coastal countries to require discretionary consent in virtually all cases also met significant opposition.

B.  Marine Pollution

1.  US Objectives

The principal objective was to strike a balance between protection of the marine environment and facilitation of navigation and trade. In principle, Part III of the RSNT does so. The specific objectives of the US were:

a.  To ensure that the coastal State has authority to establish and enforce standards for all vessels navigating in innocent passage in its territorial sea;

b.  To strengthen the new port State enforcement regime;

c.  To preserve the careful balance between coastal State and navigational rights in the economic zone; and

d.  To extend the flag State obligation to include deepsea mining vessels. Additionally we had prepared a number of clarifying amendments to the vessel pollution and other articles.

2.  Negotiations at This Session

At the outset of the session, Chairman Yankov identified the issue of standard-setting in the territorial sea as the major outstanding issue. The US and several other States proposed deleting restrictions

not to hamper innocent passage. All of the maritime
States and a number of developing countries with maritime aspirations opposed this position. Chairman
Yankov indicated that the issue was not resolved and
that further discussions were needed.

Informal committee and small group negotiating sessions were held continuously during the session to discuss other aspects of vessel-source pollution. Large numbers of amendments were suggested,
most of which would upset the delicate balance between coastal and port State powers to protect the
environment and the rights of navigation. With few
exceptions, the amendments received little support,
and the existing text was confirmed.

A new paragraph relating to coastal State
rights to establish standards in special areas of the
economic zone was negotiated and generally agreed.
The text clarifies the procedure for establishing such
standards and assigns a major role to the competent
international organization (IMCO). Time and the
adopted procedure did not permit the discussion of
the other issues related to the US objectives. These
remain to be discussed at the next session.

C.  Transfer of Technology

The discussions on this issue were very brief,
and it is clear that the existing text does not provide an answer. A few developing countries continue
to seek to require the transfer of all deep seabed
mining technology, whether patented or not. Most
seem interested only in technology owned by the Seabed Authority and in gaining rights to that technology. However, the issue is clearly so intertwined
with Committee I negotiations that no progress was
made on this issue in Committee III.


IV.  DISPUTE SETTLEMENT

A.  General

The Plenary of the Conference met informally
throughout the fifth session under the chairmanship of
President Amerasinghe and, in his absence from August
5 to 23, Acting President Jens Evensen of Norway. The
informal Plenary completed an article-by-article review of the Single Negotiating Text, Part IV (A/CONF.

62/WP.9/Rev.1), with a view to the preparation by the
President of a Revised Single Negotiating Text concerning settlement of disputes. The President will
issue a Revised Single Negotiating Text on Part IV
shortly after the close of the session.

A broad cross-section of the membership of the
Conference participated actively in the debates. It
was generally accepted by those who spoke that a new
Law of the Sea Convention should include a comprehensive system for the obligatory settlement of disputes
relating to the interpretation or application of the
Convention, and that the procedures employed should
lead to final and binding decisions. The US strongly
supported this principle. For some delegations, however, acceptance of such a system was made contingent
on the satisfaction of their objectives with respect
to certain aspects of the system. Specifically, some
coastal States considered a satisfactory exclusion of
disputes relating to the exercise of certain coastal
States' rights in the economic zone (Article 18 of
the SNT) to be crucial to the acceptance of obligatory
dispute settlement. Other States considered the
availability of specific procedures favored by their
governments, particularly the Law of the Sea Tribunal
or the system of special procedures, to be similarly
essential.

B.   Choice of Procedures

Article 9 of the SNT set forth a procedure by
which each contracting party could choose to accept
the jurisdiction of one of four dispute-settlement
procedures: the International Court of Justice, arbitration, the Law of the Sea Tribunal, or the system
of special procedures contained in Annex II. The
principle of this article was widely accepted as the
essential core of a dispute-settlement chapter that
could be supported by a consensus of the Conference.
Many delegations did not favor one or another of the
four alternative procedures. Some delegations did
not wish to include as an alternative the system of
special procedures, and a few others did not wish to
include the Law of the Sea Tribunal as an alternative.
The US indicated that it had not decided which of the
procedures it would choose, and therefore would seek
to make each as effective as possible.

Article 9, paragraph 7 of the SNT deals with the
appropriate procedure in a case where the parties to

the dispute had chosen different procedures, in which case the plaintiff would be required to go to the procedure chosen by the defendant. A number of delegations, especially those that did not favor preconstituted tribunals, suggested that arbitration should be the proper procedure in such a case. A few favored the procedure chosen by the plaintiff. The US suggested giving the plaintiff a choice between the procedure chosen by the defendant and arbitration.

C. Exceptions

Article 18, paragraph 1 of the SNT excluded certain disputes relating to the exercise of sovereign rights, exclusive rights or exclusive jurisdiction by a coastal State from the obligation to settle disputes in accordance with the procedures in the Convention. A number of exceptions are then made to this exclusion for disputes relating to interferences with navigation, overflight, submarine cables and pipelines, substantive rights specifically established by the Convention and to certain environmental matters. The effect of this approach is that the exceptions to the exclusion describe the matters that would be subject to obligatory dispute settlement.

Generally speaking, the coastal States sought to restrict the exceptions to the exclusion, focusing in particular on a desire to delete the exceptions clause dealing with rights specifically established by the Convention. These States strongly opposed dispute settlement for fisheries. The US and several maritime and distant-water fishing States sought to broaden the exceptions, especially with respect to fisheries. There was insufficient discussion of a possible compromise whereby obligatory dispute settlement would apply to fisheries disputes with protection for the coastal State from harassing actions arising from the exercise of its discretion in accordance with the Convention.

A number of States insisted that disputes relating to maritime boundaries, dealt with in Article 18, paragraph 2(a) of the SNT, be excluded from the jurisdiction of any dispute-settlement procedure at the option of a contracting party. Several did not believe that an optional exclusion should be available for disputes concerning military activities, as provided by Article 18, paragraph 2(b) of the SNT.

## D. Access to Dispute Settlement Procedures

Most delegations generally accepted that the dispute settlement procedures should be available to all contracting parties and, with respect to disputes under contracts with the International Seabed Authority, to the Authority and its contractors. Many delegations opposed access for international, intergovernmental organizations, or private persons, natural or juridical. The US and several European States supported access for owners and masters of vessels to request release on bond of detained vessels as provided by Article 15, noting that this would not entail a decision on the merits of a detention, but only a procedure to facilitate prompt release of the vessel on bond. With respect to the Law of the Sea Tribunal, a few delegations suggested that entities that had been observers at the Third United Nations Conference on the Law of the Sea should have access to the procedures.

## E. The Law of the Sea Tribunal

Several delegations opposed the creation of a new Law of the Sea Tribunal, while many supported it. Those who did not like it insisted that the entire system be structured so that they could not be forced to go before it, in which case they would not object to its creation as an option for those who favored it. The US indicated that it could support the creation of a well-constituted tribunal.

With respect to the composition of a new tribunal, President Amerasinghe announced SNT amendments so that allocation of seats on the Tribunal by region would be deleted; and the selection would be made by a conference of contracting parties on the basis of assuring representation of the principal legal systems of the world and equitable geographical distribution, provided that each regional group would have at least two seats.

## F. The System of Special Procedures

Most delegations criticized, and several opposed, the system of special procedures contained in Annex II. Among the principal criticisms were the unworkability of the prohibition on interpretation (as distinguished from application of the Convention) by special committees, the limitation of membership on the committees

to scientific and technical experts, and the alleged developed-country bias of experts, and the delay and disputes that would be occasioned by the need for appeals and the reference of questions of interpretation to another procedure. Proponents of the special procedures agreed that the special committees could be authorized both to interpret and to apply the Convention, and may include juridical experts in their composition, thus eliminating the need for appeals or referrals.

G.  Relation to Part I Procedures

Several members of the Group of 77 took the view that the Seabeds Tribunal contained in Part I of the Revised Single Negotiating Text should be merged with the Law of the Sea Tribunal contained in Part IV of the Single Negotiating Test. Such a merger would result in a single Tribunal with a special chamber for disputes arising under Part I, and a general chamber for other disputes. For these delegations, large parts of the discussion on Part IV were undertaken subject to the subsequent resolution of this issue. It was not debated at this session of the conference and remains an important item for future consideration.

SIXTH SESSION
NEW YORK
May 23 - July 15, 1977

I. Summary

The Sixth Session of the Third United Nations
Conference on the Law of the Sea (LOS) met in New York
from May 23 to July 15, 1977.

Pursuant to a decision at the end of the Fifth
Session, the first three weeks were devoted to deep
seabed mining questions (Committee I). The work was
coordinated by Minister Jens Evensen of Norway, who
had led intersessional consultations on the subject,
and had successfully chaired informal work of the
Conference on other major issues at earlier sessions.
Evensen followed his normal procedure of producing
successive revised texts for consideration; his final
texts on such matters as the system of exploitation
and the system of governance of the International Seabed Authority were widely regarded among developing
and industrialized States as a sound basis for negotiation if not compromise.

After the first three weeks, the other Committees
and the Plenary resumed work on other matters. The
work of Committee II (which has considered the territorial sea and contiguous zone, straits used for international navigation, archipelagos, the economic
zone, the continental shelf, high seas, and rights of
landlocked States) was divided into groups concentrating on already identified outstanding issues--chiefly
the status of the economic zone and the rights and
duties of States in the zone; access of landlocked and
geographically disadvantaged States (LL/GDS) to fisheries in the zones of their neighbors; the precise
limit and revenue sharing with respect to the continental shelf beyond 200 miles; and delimitation of
economic zones and continental shelves between opposite and adjacent States. The tendency of delegations
to restate positions in such groups led to attempts to
organize more informal work, some of which was successful. The work of the Second Committee revealed
once again the broad measure of support enjoyed by the
texts generally. The number of States interested in
reopening the straits articles dwindled, and their
efforts did not succeed.

The Third Committee, which has dealt with the
marine environment and marine scientific research,

concentrated most of its efforts on vessel-source pollution. It became increasingly clear that the issue of scientific research in the economic zone could not be successfully resolved in isolation from related Committee II issues. The major items of controversy regarding settlement of disputes related to fisheries in the economic zone and the scope of review of actions of the Seabed Authority.

The Conference confirmed its decisions at the end of the Fifth Session that the President and the Committee Chairmen should prepare a new Informal Composite Negotiating Text (ICNT) of the Convention as a whole. Considerable debate was devoted to the question of the discretion of the President independent of the Committee Chairmen. Certain Latin American and East European countries successfully insisted in effect on a veto for the Committee Chairmen, at least for this round. Originally scheduled for release in the fifth or sixth week of the session, the ICNT was finally released on July 20, after the session ended.

In the last few weeks of the session, about 15 States representing the complete spectrum of positions met intensively to discuss ways to resolve the impasse on the status of the economic zone, scientific research, and fisheries dispute settlement. As a result of their discussions, new texts were presented in the last week; those relevant to the status of the zone were discussed in Committee II, and those relevant to science were discussed in Committee III. Initial reactions indicated a widespread view that they were a good basis for negotiation. Aside from a few extreme territorialist objections relating to maximizing coastal State offshore jurisdiction, most other reservations related to issues of LL/GDS access to fisheries which the texts did not purport to address. The texts discussed in the Second and Third Committees were generally incorporated into the ICNT (Articles 55, 56, 58, 86, 89, 247, 250, 254). The fisheries dispute settlement texts were not discussed and were more controversial, but some of the ideas discussed do seem to have been taken into account in preparation of the ICNT (Article 296). The Chairman of the Second Committee also presented anonymous new compromise ideas in the last week on LL/GDS issues. These proved controversial and were not included in the ICNT.

It is important to note that major changes were made in the Committee II texts only after substantial

discussion in the Committee. The result in Committee
I was precisely the opposite. The Evensen texts flow-
ed from discussions in which all delegations participated, and were available to all well in advance.
They were the subject of discussion in the Group of 77
and elsewhere. Nevertheless, substantially different
texts were placed into the ICNT on deep seabed mining.
These texts were not seen in advance and had not been
considered by a representative group or the Conference
as a whole.

Our initial assessment of the session is reflected in Ambassador Richardson's press statement
of July 20, 1977, which follows:

> The Informal Composite Negotiating Text re-
> sulting from this session of the UN Law of
> the Sea Conference evidences real progress
> on vital issues relating to international
> security and freedom of navigation. At the
> same time, it substantially sets back pros-
> pects for agreement on an international re-
> gime for the conduct of seabed mining. Both
> the substance of the text on this issue and
> the lack of fair and open processes in its
> final preparation require me to recommend
> that the United States undertake a most ser-
> ious and searching review of both the sub-
> stance and procedures of the Conference.
>
> It is with a sense of considerable frustra-
> tion that I make this accounting. For true
> progress was made during the past session:
>
> o  New provisions were negotiated to clar-
>    ify the legal status of the new 200-
>    mile economic zone. They seek to safe-
>    guard traditional high seas freedoms
>    within this zone except for specific
>    resource-related rights accorded coast-
>    al States by the Convention. These
>    provisions are a marked improvement
>    over previous texts and may help pre-
>    vent erosion of high seas freedoms by
>    coastal State attempts to extend their
>    sovereignty over ocean space.
>
> o  We successfully retained the generally
>    satisfactory previous texts on passage
>    of straits which a determined minority

sought to change. At the same time we
found a way to accommodate the real
need for environmental protection in
straits, particularly in areas such as
the Straits of Malacca.

o   The provisions of the text dealing with
    scientific research were improved. An
    effort by some delegations to increase
    the degree of coastal State control of
    scientific research in the economic zone
    was defeated. In the new text, the con-
    ditions for conducting scientific re-
    search are set out clearly, and are
    likely to be copied into national laws,
    thus regularizing what has until now
    been a capricious situation. Also, we
    successfully eliminated a clause that
    could have obliged the US to restrict
    publication of scientific data after
    the fact and without the consent of
    scientists, which was highly offensive
    to our concepts of free science and
    free speech. Now the coastal State,
    in granting consent, must indicate in
    advance if it wishes to impose such a
    restriction, and if so, the scientist
    can decide whether he wishes to proceed
    with the project under such circumstances.

o   We were successful in eliminating texts
    that could have prevented us from im-
    posing rules in our territorial sea to
    prevent pollution from foreign ships.
    At the same time, we retained our right
    to fix strict environmental conditions
    --including construction, manning,
    equipment and design regulations--for
    entry into US ports. These changes
    bring the text into full harmony with
    the Administration's anti-pollution
    program.

o   Continued progress was made in the
    design of a comprehensive system for
    peaceful settlement of disputes re-
    lating to ocean uses.

o   Under the fair and judicious leadership
    of Minister Jens Evensen of Norway, a

responsible and effective discussion of seabed issues took place.  This discussion and the texts formulated by Minister Evensen offered real prospect that the impasse on seabed mining issues could be resolved on terms acceptable to both the developed and developing nations.

Regrettably, however, the new "composite" text concerning the system of exploitation and governance of the deep seabed area (Part XI) is now fundamentally unacceptable. It deviates markedly from the proposed compromise text which had been prepared on the basis of full, fair, and open discussion under Minister Evensen's leadership.

The Evensen text, although not without problems, was generally viewed as a useful basis for further negotiation.  The newer text--produced in private, never discussed with a representative group of concerned nations, and released only after this session of the Conference terminated--cannot be viewed as a responsible substantive contribution to further negotiation.  Indeed, the manner of its production--treating weeks of serious debate and responsible negotiation as essentially irrelevant--raises an equally serious procedural problem: whether the Law of the Sea Conference can be organized to treat deep seabed issues with the seriousness they, and the Conference which depends upon their satisfactory resolution, demand.

Among the serious points of substantive difficulty in the latest deep seabeds text, and the system it would define, are the following:

It would not give the reasonable assurance of access that is necessary if we and others could be expected to help finance the Enterprise and to accept a "parallel system" as a basis of compromise.

It could be read to make technology transfer by contractors a condition of access to the deep seabed--subject,

at least in part, to negotiation
in the pursuit of a contract.

It could be read to give the Seabed
Authority the power effectively to
mandate joint ventures with the
Authority as a condition for access.

It fails to set clear and reasonable
limits on the financial burdens to
be borne by contractors; indeed, it
simply combines a wide range of alternative financial burdens, as if
such a combination could be a com-
promise--when, in fact, it is likely
to prove a compound burden sufficient
to stifle seabed development.

It would set an artificial limit on
seabed production of minerals from
nodules--which is not only objectionable in principle; it is also far
more stringent than would be necessary to protect specific developing
country producers from possible adverse effects, and is incompatible
with the basic economic interests of
a developing world generally.

It would give the Seabed Authority
extremely broad new, open-ended power
to regulate all other mineral production from the seabed "as appropriate."

It would appear, arguably, to give
the Authority unacceptable new power
to regulate scientific research in
the Area.

It would fail adequately to protect
minority interests in its system of
governance and would, accordingly,
threaten to allow the abuse of power
by an anomalous "majority."

It would allow the distribution of
benefits from seabed exploitation
to peoples and countries not party
to the Convention.

It would seriously prejudice the
likely long-term character of the
international regime, by requiring
that--if agreement to the contrary
is not reached within 25 years--the
regime shall automatically be converted into a "unitary" system,
ruling out direct access by contractors, except to the extent that the
Authority might seek their participation in joint ventures with it.

With this unfortunate, last-minute deviation
from what had seemed to be an emerging direction of promise in the deep seabed negotiations, I am led now to recommend to the President of the United States that our Government must review not only the balance among
our substantive interests, but also whether
an agreement acceptable to all governments
can best be achieved through the kind of
negotiations which have thus far taken place.

On the last day, the Conference decided to recommend that the UN General Assembly convene a further
session of seven or eight weeks commencing March 28,
1978. The Group of 77 (G-77) is planning to meet in
Dakar prior to the session. Jamaica offered to host
the next session, followed by an offer from Malta.
(Both governments have also offered to serve as sites
for the proposed Seabed Authority.) Both the G-77 and
its constituent regional groups were divided on the
matter. The Conference decided on Geneva by secret
ballot.

A significant number of members of both the
House and Senate attended the Conference, meeting
individually with the Conference leadership and
foreign delegates. The Congressional participants
conveyed the concern of the US Congress with respect
to the delay in reaching agreement on a Law of the
Sea treaty and expressed their views to foreign delegates on various aspects of the draft treaty of particular concern to them and to their constituents.

## II. COMMITTEE I

### A. Summary and Conclusions

Regrettably, the new "composite" text concerning the system of exploitation and governance of the deep seabed area (Part XI), as prepared by Chairman of the First Committee, Paul Engo of the Cameroon, is fundamentally unacceptable to the US. It deviates markedly from the proposed compromise text which had been prepared under Minister Evensen's leadership.

### B. Expectations

The impasse at the summer 1976 session convinced most participants that Committee I presented the most serious obstacle to achievement of a comprehensive LOS Convention. Despite disappointment that the Fifth Session had almost deteriorated into an exchange of polemics, the outlook for the Sixth Session seemed more hopeful for three reasons:

o The Kissinger package proposal on access to the seabed for States and their nationals, financing of the International Seabed Authority's operating arm (the Enterprise), and review of the deep seabed system after 25 years generated some positive response from developing countries at the end of the Fifth Session;

o The Geneva intersessional consultations in February-March 1977 produced a constructive atmosphere which, it was hoped, would carry over to the Sixth Session;

o Most delegations apparently recognized that a repeat of the Fifth Session impasse would doom the Conference.

Given the growing consensus that a parallel access system including a viable Enterprise represented the most promising approach to an acceptable accommodation, the US Delegation looked for substantial progress toward agreement on a concrete framework for the seabed regime. Through a restrained approach, emphasizing firmness on fundamental interests and flexibility on modalities, the US would seek to encourage a constructive negotiating process.

169

As agreed at the end of the Fifth Session, the first three weeks of the Sixth Session would focus almost exclusively on Committee I, with chiefs of delegations participating. It was thought that a breakthrough in Committee I at the outset would set the stage for reaching an overall agreement.

C.  The Evensen Phase (Weeks One to Three)

Chairman Engo installed Evensen as head of a "Working Group of the Whole" for the initial three weeks. Evensen continued the procedure that he had begun in the Geneva intersessional.

He introduced his personal compromise text dealing with key elements of the seabed regime--the basic system of exploitation, resource policy, financing of the Enterprise, and review. He then pushed the Committee through two- and three-day sessions, discussing each article line by line.

The US sought to deal concretely with developing country concerns about the viability of the Enterprise and the prospects for their sharing in the benefits from seabed exploitation. Elaborating on the US package proposal introduced at the Fifth Session, Ambassador Richardson outlined an Enterprise financing scheme which stressed loan guarantees by member States to fund the Enterprise's first operation. Richardson also tabled a proposal on financial arrangements, which would allow a mining operator to select either royalties or profit-sharing as a basis for payments to the Authority. For the first time, the US formally proposed specific methods and rates for determining those revenue-sharing payments. The loan guarantee proposal for the Enterprise received a generally positive reaction and was later incorporated into Evensen's text.

Another highlight of the early discussion was a Mexican proposal that would give the Authority discretion to condition access to non-reserved sites on the applicant's agreeing to exploit the corresponding reserved site in a joint arrangement with the Enterprise. With the notable exceptions of India and Singapore, the proposal failed to command much support.

Evensen's first revision to the compromise text evoked coordinated and sharply critical reactions from the industrial countries. In his sternest statement

170

of the Conference, Richardson asserted that the Evensen text was not pointing toward an acceptable compromise. He warned against the tendency to create
disincentives for investment in the seabed by imposing excessive front-end fees, restrictive production
controls, and mandatory technology transfer.
Richardson also faulted Evensen for ignoring US and
other industrial-country suggestions regarding financial arrangements between contractors and the Authority and financing the Enterprise. The UK, Federal
Republic of Germany, and Japan contributed strong remarks along lines similar to those of US.

Evensen's "final" revision, prepared on June 11,
was still unsatisfactory in a number of respects, and
substantially inferior to the Revised Single Negotiating Text (RSNT), produced in 1976, but could form
the basis for further negotiation. Evensen's revised
Article 22 of the RSNT retained the parallel system,
though not as clearly stated as in the RSNT; contracting procedures in a revised Annex I of the RSNT
tended to limit the Authority's discretion, though
banking of reserved sites could take place at the exploration rather than prospecting stage; the Enterprise would receive a large part of its startup financing from loan guarantees by Member States; States
would be obliged to "promote" technology transfer,
but it would not be an obligation of contractors;
and the 20-year review provisions would not necessarily lead to phase-out of the parallel system.
The revised Article 9 of the RSNT on resource policy
was the most troublesome aspect of Evensen's text,
allowing seabed mining to fill 100% of the projected
growth segment of the nickel market for the first
seven years but only two-thirds thereafter. Canada
had spearheaded the attack on the production limit in
Article 9, collaborating with developing copper and
nickel producers (Chile, Peru, Zaire, Indonesia, and
Cuba). The land-based producers insisted on limiting
seabed nickel output to half of the growth segment.

The three-week Evensen phase bustled with activity, and the evolution of his texts suggested that the
negotiating process was moving closer to a consensus.
The resulting Evensen text clearly commanded a wider
base of support that any previous text. As noted
above, however, the US and other industrial countries
found serious fault with the Evensen formulations.
The G-77 caucused to discuss the Evensen text but
could not reach a consensus.

D. <u>The Second Phase (Weeks Four to Seven)</u>

With Evensen's departure June 11 for a week's absence, the work in Committee I lost momentum. Meanwhile Engo withheld the Evensen text, threatening to revise it, before finally releasing it unchanged a week later as a set of "suggestions" not yet approved by the Chairman.

Evensen did resume leadership for part of the remaining weeks, and produced compromise texts on the institutional issues (Articles 24-32 of the RSNT), and Statute of the Enterprise (Annex II of the RSNT) and upon Dispute Settlement (Articles 33-39 of the RSNT).

Engo appointed Pinto (Sri Lanka) to head a technical group on Article 9 (2) of the RSNT on Production Controls. That group spent a week arguing over the best technique for computing projected growth rates, but never reached the core issue of whether and how to divide mineral production between sea and land.

Engo also appointed his rapporteur to head another ill-fated working group on financial arrangements. The text he produced revising Annex I, Paragraph 9, of the RSNT, represented a significant regression from the point that discussions on financial arrangements had reached last year.

Toward the end of the session, Engo came under considerable pressure from numerous delegations who made representations for specific provisions for inclusion in the Composite Text. Determined to make his mark on the text, Engo sought to respond to special pleas from the G-77 regarding mandatory technology transfer, dilution of the Evensen chambered Council proposal providing a degree of protection to the developed countries, resource policy, and the basic system of exploitation. He received important encouragement in these efforts from a core group of advisers, which did not include any representative of the developed countries.

E. <u>The Composite Text</u>

Chairman Engo and his advisers from the G-77 made their mark firmly on the Composite Text. Rather than submitting to the President of the Conference

the widely discussed and delicately balanced Evensen
compromise formula, Engo submitted his own formulations. While these consisted of changes or additions
to the Evensen Texts, rather than entirely new formulations, they fundamentally upset the balance achieved by Evensen. As such, they set back the prospects
for a negotiated resolution of the impasse on the design of a seabed mining regime.

F. Future of Seabed Negotiations

The last-minute alterations of the Evensen formulations by the Chairman of the Committee, and the
resulting text, raise the most serious questions
with regard to the future of the seabed negotiations.

These difficulties are compounded by the fact
that it is difficult to separate the seabeds negotiation into discrete elements which can be settled
individually. Virtually every important issue--pro-
duction controls, financial arrangements, nature of
the International Seabed Authority, contract procedures, review, quota/antimonopoly provisions--relate
to the core issue of access. In a sense, the negotiation is similar to playing a slot machine: all
the cherries must be lined up in order to win. All
of the issues noted above must be settled satisfactorily in order to achieve the objective of assuring
nondiscriminatory access for States and their nationals. Thus, the package deal approach has characterized the negotiations to date and will continue to
be necessary in future negotiating rounds.

In the Sixth Session, the US sought to state its
position clearly and unequivocally. There were no
new US substantive initiatives--though we did endeav-
or, with some success, to engage the G-77 in detailed
technical discussions on critical issues such as resource policy and financial arrangements. There is a
growing understanding about the nature of seabed mining and the basic requirements of industrialized and
developing countries.

The Evensen iterative process, beginning with
the Geneva intersessional, helped increase this common understanding by forcing delegations to reexamine
their positions at each successive stage. In addition to his capacity to "educate" through debate and
to cull from debate the elements of compromise, Evensen was able to persuade delegations that an essentially

173

open process was possible. Unfortunately, the process of open consensus-building that Evensen had started has now been fundamentally jeopardized by Engo's last-minute changes.

If the Third UN Conference on the Law of the Sea is to succeed in the design of a seabed mining regime acceptable to developed and developing nations, some new, more open, stable and effective process must be found for the conduct of negotiations. The prospects for the design of such a process are highly uncertain.

III.   COMMITTEE II

A.   Procedures

Committee II held no meetings during the first three weeks of this session while the Conference concentrated on work in Committee I. During this period, informal consultations were held. Beginning in the fourth week, the work was carried on in negotiating groups and small consulting groups which had been established by the Chairman during the last session. The small groups, each consisting of approximately 30 states, met throughout the next five weeks to deal with the legal status of the economic zone; the outer limit of the continental margin and revenue sharing; and delimitation of the territorial sea, the economic zone, and the continental shelf between opposite and adjacent states. In all the Committee held over 30 informal meetings to deal with these issues, as well as others deemed to be of importance to various delegations. The issue of landlocked and geographically disadvantaged State (LL/GDS) access to the living resources of economic zones within their region was dealt with by a 21-State contact group having representation from both LL/GDS and coastal States.

B.   Status of the Economic Zone

As in past sessions, the most important outstanding issue for the US was the status of the 200-mile offshore economic zone. The US objective in these negotiations is to retain the traditional high-seas status of the zone except for rights over resources and other specified rights assigned to coastal States by the provisions of the Convention. The negotiations were made difficult by the fact that the Revised

174

Single Negotiating Text (RSNT), which was the basis
for discussion, clearly stated that the economic
zone is not high seas. The Chairman's introductory
note to that text further stated that the zone is
neither high seas nor territorial sea but a zone <u>sui
generis</u>.

Attempts to change the texts in Committee were
met with strong opposition from the territorialists
who wished to strengthen the text in the direction
of making the zone a zone of national jurisdiction
with other States enjoying only limited rights of
navigation, overflight, and communication.

The debates made apparent the depth of the split
on this critical issue. In the seventh week it became apparent that no further progress could be made
in the small consulting group, and discussion of the
issue terminated.

However, a group of affected States was formed
to consider the status question informally outside
the Committee framework. The issue was discussed and
negotiated along with the questions of marine scientific research and dispute settlement for fisheries.
The result of these discussions was the production
of new texts which clarified the relative rights of
coastal and other States in the economic zone. These
texts were placed before the small consulting group
and then the negotiating group of the whole during
the final hours of the session. While the texts were
attacked by the territorialists and some others, the
bulk of the 37 States who spoke viewed them as a sufficient improvement over the RSNT that they should be
incorporated into the Consolidated Text for further
discussion at the next session of the Conference.

C. Highly Migratory Species

Two informal consultations were held which included States off whose coast highly migratory species
can be found, and States who fish those species, with
a view toward improvement of Article 53 of the RSNT.
While no agreement was reached, the discussions were
useful in clarifying the problem, and it was agreed
to continue the effort at the next session, as well
as to hold intersessional consultations as appropriate.

175

D.  Continental Shelf

The Committee discussed the question of the definition of the shelf where it extends beyond 200 miles and the related question of revenue sharing beyond 200 miles.  There was a broad perception that the accommodation would rest upon a precise definition coupled with revenue sharing based upon a royalty on the value of production at the site.  There was a broad base of support for the so-called Irish formula whereby the outer edge of the shelf would be determined at 200 miles or alternatively by a distance criterion from the base of the continental slope (a prominent feature) or by a depth-of-sediment test.  Other formulas were discussed but received less support.  No precise formula was, however, included in the ICNT.  The Secretariat has, in this regard, agreed to produce a preliminary study which, using both charts and figures, would give a general representation of the effect of the 200-mile limit, 500-meter isobath, Irish, and edge-of-the-margin formulas.

On the related question there is strong support for revenue sharing for the benefit of developing countries.  The formula which received broad support provides for the obligation to pay one percent of the value of production in the sixth year after commercial production begins beyond 200 miles.  This obligation is to increase in one percent increments annually up to a maximum rate.  Some States favored a maximum rate of five percent in the tenth year and thereafter, while others favored a maximum rate of seven percent in the twelfth year and thereafter.  The ICNT contains a five percent maximum rate in the tenth year.

Two main viewpoints were expressed on the question of which States should have the obligation to share revenues.  Some favor an exemption for developing countries with broad continental shelves which are net importers of the minerals exploited on the shelf.  Others favored no such exemption but believe that the position of these developing countries could be taken into account at the revenue sharing "distribution end."  Finally, there was much support for the proposition that the International Seabed Authority should be the distribution mechanism, although others felt that an appropriate entity of the UN should be used.  The ICNT provides for the Authority to be the distribution mechanism.  There was

complete agreement, however, that the revenues should be distributed to developing countries.

### E. Landlocked and Geographically Disadvantaged States (LL/GDS)

The 53 States which make up the Group of LL/GDS are seeking rights to participate in fishing activities in neighboring economic zones. A "Group of 21" (10 LL/GDS, 10 coastal States, and a Chairman) have met but have not been able to bridge the gap. The issues revolve about the "right" of participation, and whether the "right" applies to the surplus fish which the coastal State cannot itself harvest, or whether it should also apply to cases where there is no surplus. Further issues involve whether developed LL/GDS should be given different treatment than other LL/GDS and the definition of GDS.

### F. Delimitation of the Economic Zone/Continental Shelf Between Adjacent or Opposite States

The issue revolves around the question whether the equidistance/median line should be the primary method of delimitation or whether equitable principles/relevant circumstances (which include the equidistance line) should be emphasized. This issue related to bilateral situations and produced opinions on both sides of the question. It is clear, however, that an LOS treaty can only hope to provide a general framework within which agreement on such delimitation might be reached.

### G. Anadromous Species

A series of meetings were held among States interested in the question of anadromous species which spawn in the rivers of one State but migrate beyond the economic zone. While these meetings produced no agreed changes, they were productive in furthering an understanding of the problems involved.

### H. Other Issues

While there has been broad agreement on the straits articles, a very small number of States expressed a desire to modify the transit passage regime and to upset the delicate balance which is in the articles. There was virtually no support for such amendments. Proposed amendments to the coastal

fisheries articles received little support. In addition, there were proposed amendments to the articles on islands and on semi-enclosed seas, but no basis for any change to the RSNT emerged. The question of the competence of a coastal State to establish vessel pollution standards in the territorial sea is reported in the Section on Committee III.


IV.   COMMITTEE III

A.   Protection and Preservation of the Marine Environment

Discussion began in the fourth week of the session utilizing the same working procedure as previous sessions of the Conference. It was agreed that an informal working group of all interested Committee III delegations chaired by José Luis Vallarta (Mexico) would discuss outstanding issues with those not resolved being referred to a smaller private negotiating group under the same Chairman. It was agreed that discussion would first concentrate on key articles of the RSNT concerning vessel source pollution--Article 30 (coastal State enforcement), Article 28 (port State enforcement), Section VIII (enforcement safeguards), and territorial sea standard-setting. If time permitted, other articles of interest to specific delegations were also to be considered.

Discussion on Article 30 (coastal State enforcement rights in ports, the territorial sea, and the economic zone for vessel pollution violations) was directed to amendments proposed by several maritime States to limit all enforcement actions to violations of discharge regulations. These amendments and others attempting to limit coastal State enforcement rights in these areas were strongly opposed by a substantial majority of coastal States led by Canada. The US urged retention of the existing balance in the text. Similarly, amendments proposed to strengthen coastal State enforcement authority by increasing the number of cases in which vessel inspection could be undertaken received little support and substantial opposition.

A text for Article 30 (7) aimed at avoiding arrest of vessels for pollution violations in the economic zone if bonding or  other appropriate financial

security is provided was agreed by the private and
informal negotiating groups.

Discussion on Article 28 (port State enforcement)
centered on the issue of whether or not port State
jurisdiction should extend to discharge violations
occurring beyond 200 miles. Amendments to require
flag State consent for port State prosecutions of
such violations were supported by several maritime
States and opposed by the US, Canada, and many developing States. An amendment to increase port State
competence by allowing prosecution for discharge violations in other States' economic zones received some
support but substantial opposition from the maritime
States. No major change was made in the article.

Discussion on Article 21 (3) of Part III and
Article 20 (2) of Part II (Coastal State Standard-
Setting Competence in the Territorial Sea) became en-
tangled in an extensive procedural debate as to which
Committee was the appropriate forum for discussion of
the issue. General discussion elicited only limited
support for increased coastal State competence over
design, construction, manning and equipment of foreign vessels in the territorial sea and slightly more
support for competence over other matters regulated
by generally accepted rules and standards. The ICNT
text grants the coastal State competence in the latter
cases but not the former.

Discussion of coastal State standard-setting in
the economic zone (Article 21 (4)) was inconclusive
with most States supporting the present wording of
the RSNT which limits such competence to that necessary to carry out enforcement action.

A proposed compromise text to Article 21 (5)
(Special areas) makes clear that additional laws relating to discharges and navigational practice in a
special area could be approved by the Intergovernmental Maritime Consultative Organization (IMCO) at the
same time as the designation of the area. It was accepted by all but four delegations who objected to
submitting special areas to IMCO for approval.

The discussion of Article 38 (flag State pre-
emption) centered on two proposed amendments--increas-
ing the number of cases in which flag States could
pre-empt coastal State or port State prosecutions for
pollution violations. The amendments would allow

pre-emption even in cases of major damage to the
coastal State and even if the flag State had repeatedly disregarded its past enforcement obligations.
These amendments received little support and substantial opposition, with most States favoring the article as presently worded. No major changes were made
in the ICNT.

The US proposed an amendment to Article 19 requiring flag States to establish national laws no
less stringent than international rules to prevent
pollution from deep seabed mining activities including processing by vessels flying their flag. A major
purpose of the new ICNT language is to require national regulation of processing anywhere in the oceans,
supplementing International Seabed Authority regulations at the minesite. In this form, Article 19 received substantial support and little opposition and
is included in the ICNT.

A French proposal to specify in Articles 20 and
26 that incineration at sea be treated as ocean dumping received little support and substantial opposition
since most felt that was true in any case. The ICNT
is unchanged.

Another French amendment to Article 29 requiring
the port State to prevent an unseaworthy ship from
sailing but requiring immediate release of the vessel
upon rectification of the unseaworthy condition, received an equal amount of support and opposition and
was included in a compromise form.

A debate on several amendments to Articles 23
and 24, intended to make clear that States are not
bound to adopt and enforce national laws implementing
treaties to which they are not party, ended inconclu-
sively.

B.  Marine Scientific Research

The Chairman of Committee III, Yankov (Bulgaria),
chaired limited discussions on the regime for the conduct of marine scientific research (Article 60) and
other pertinent articles including researching State
obligations (Article 59), tacit consent (Article 64),
coastal State rights to stop ongoing projects (Article
65), and settlement of disputes (Article 76). Discussion on Article 60 elicited substantial support among
the G-77 for a Yankov test proposal revived from the

last session. The test proposal would markedly expand coastal State discretion to deny consent. Yankov
himself attempted to give his test proposal greater
status than proposals by individual countries. Under
pressure from the US and others he agreed that the
RSNT was still the basis of negotiation but stated
that he expected to use his test proposal in any
further negotiations.

The USSR again proposed that all marine scientific research be subject to coastal State consent
and suggested deletion of the second paragraph of
Article 60 (delimitation of cases in which the coastal State may withhold consent), and limitation of
Article 76 (settlement of disputes) to disputes regarding the conduct of research and not the issue of
whether consent should be granted or denied. Both
proposals received substantial support from the G-77.

The US reiterated its opposition to a general
consent regime and said that, in this regard, the
RSNT was unacceptable and the Yankov test proposal
even more so. The US stressed the importance of marine scientific research to the US and stated that it
was one of the most important issues remaining to be
resolved.

During the last Committee III session, a text
worked out by a cross-section of delegations was discussed. The major features of this text include the
following. It adopts the basic consent system but
states that "in normal circumstances," consent shall
be granted unless the research falls into one of four
specific categories. Those categories are equivalent
to those in the RSNT Articles 60 and 64 except that
paragraph (c) of Article 60 regarding interference
with coastal State activities is deleted and made an
obligation in a separate paragraph. The restriction
on publication (Article 61) is deleted, and tacit
consent (Article 64) is retained. Compulsory dispute
settlement applies to scientific-research disputes
except for disputes regarding the exercise of coastal
State rights and discretion in accordance with Articles 60 and 65.

The ICNT also contains a new paragraph requiring
only notification for projects sponsored by international or regional organizations if the coastal State
has agreed to the project within the organization.

181

A number of delegations said this text would be a good basis of negotiation and should be included in the Composite Text.


V.  COMPULSORY DISPUTE SETTLEMENT

The Conference President's informal note of 25 March 1977 to all delegations concerning dispute settlement procedures pinpointed the areas to be discussed during the meetings of the Informal Plenary on Part IV of the RSNT. The Part IV articles discussed in greater depth included Article 9 (choice of procedures); Article 12 (provisional measures); Article 18 (optional exceptions to jurisdiction); and Article 17 (limitations on jurisdiction). A concluding session of the Informal Plenary addressed other Articles in Part IV and its Annexes of particular concern to delegations, emphasizing certain articles in Annex II (Statute of the Law of the Sea Tribunal) and Annex III (Arbitration). The important issue of the relationship of dispute settlement procedures in Parts I and IV was discussed during three meetings of Committee I.

The single most fundamental decision reached was the acceptance by the G-77 and the overwhelming majority of other delegations of a single Law of the Sea Tribunal with a Seabed Disputes Chamber, the latter's members to be selected from the members of the full Tribunal. The Chamber would have exclusive and compulsory jurisdiction over all disputes arising under the articles of Part I of the RSNT. This would replace the Seabed Tribunal provisions under Part I and Annex III thereto.

Despite some opposition to Soviet-sponsored special functional tribunals (for fisheries, environment, and other questions), there was general agreement to allow States Parties to choose from among four dispute settlement procedures: International Court of Justice; Law of the Sea Tribunal; arbitration; and special arbitral procedure. When the parties to a dispute have chosen different procedures, arbitration may be resorted to as the residual forum, though some delegates expressed preference for the Law of the Sea Tribunal as the common forum. An amendment by the Chairman (President Amerasinghe) to Article 14 on release of vessels detained by the port State would provide that the question of release from detention could be brought before any Court or tribunal agreed upon

by the parties, and, failing such agreement, before a
forum accepted by the detaining State under Article 9
or before the Law of the Sea Tribunal.  Although the
owner, operator, or master would not specifically enjoy standing to bring such a suit, the revised articles would provide that such application could be
brought "by or on behalf of the flag State of the
vessel."

The optional exceptions to compulsory jurisdiction under Article 18 were retained, although modified
by proposals offered by the Chair.  The exception for
law enforcement activities will now be treated on an
equal footing with that for military activities, although the former will not apply to the exceptions
under Article 17.  Many States proposed the deletion
of the exception regarding disputes in respect of which
the Security Council is seized; they contended that it
was superfluous, given Article 103 of the Charter of
the United Nations.  Nevertheless, it was agreed to
retain it in a slightly revised form.  There was an even
division of views with respect to the provisions relating to maritime boundaries, the Soviet Union  and certain other States arguing for the right to completely
exclude such disputes from compulsory settlement.

The most difficult remaining issue was whether
fisheries disputes in the economic zone of a coastal
State should or should not be subject to compulsory
settlement.  This issue, as well as whether or not
scientific research issues arising in the zone should
be subject to compulsory dispute-settlement, directly
reflected the status of the economic zone negotiations
in Committee II.  Generally speaking, the coastal
States stood for the deletion of the provision submitting fisheries disputes to compulsory adjudication,
and some of them argued as well for the deletion of
the provision relating to scientific research in the
economic zone.  Various compromise proposals have
been suggested:  distinguishing between fishery conservation regulations and allocation provisions, submitting only the first to compulsory dispute settlement; adding a requirement that a prima facie case
must be established before resort to dispute settlement could be had (in order to avoid frivolous or
vexatious suits); the application of an abus de
pouvoir concept to the fisheries provision; or the
substitution of compulsory conciliation for adjudication.  There was little questioning of the applicability of dispute-settlement procedures to all coastal

State contraventions regarding freedom or rights of
navigation or overflight or of the laying or submarine cables and pipelines.

The relationship between the dispute settlement
provisions of Parts I and IV was discussed not only
in the Informal Plenary but also in the Chairman's
Working Group of Committee I.  It was decided to include all dispute settlement articles relating to the
structure and procedure of the dispute settlement
regime in Part IV, and to retain in Part I on Seabeds
only those articles referring to the jurisdiction of
the Seabeds Disputes Chamber to be provided for in
Part IV for all disputes relating to seabeds issues.
The principal debate revolved around the issue of
whether or not the discretionary acts of the Authority, including those of the Council, the Assembly,
and its organs, should or should not be subject to
compulsory adjudication.  The G-77 argued that the
Authority's discretionary acts should not be subject
to dispute settlement.  The articles prepared by the
Norwegian rapporteur (Vindenes) would not permit the
Seabed Disputes Chamber to adjudicate disputes as to
conformity with the provisions of the Convention of
any rules, regulations, or procedures adopted by the
Authority; nor would the Chamber have jurisdiction
with regard to the Authority's exercise of discretionary powers.  However, the Chamber would have jurisdiction over decisions or measures taken by the
Assembly, the Council, or any of its organs in cases
of lack of jurisdiction or misuse of power.

SEVENTH SESSION
GENEVA
March 28 - May 19, 1978

# I. Summary

The Seventh Session of the Third United Nations Conference on the Law of the Sea met in Geneva from March 28 to May 19, 1978.

Two events that occurred after the issuance of the Informal Composite Negotiating Text (ICNT) at the end of the sixth session dominated the Conference. One was the rejection by the United States and other industrialized countries of Part XI (Deep Seabed Mining) of that text, as well as the method by which it was produced.

The other was the change of government after elections in Sri Lanka, and the subsequent replacement of Hamilton Shirley Amerasinghe as Sri Lanka's Ambassador to the United Nations and head of delegation. (Amerasinghe was elected President of the Conference at its first session in 1973 and served in that capacity ever since.)

Intersessional consultation on the substance of the deep seabed problems commenced a pattern of negotiation that continued into the session. Consultations also produced a general understanding that any changes in the ICNT would in the future have to emerge from negotiations or be reviewed by the Conference in advance. However, during the intersessional period, the question of the presidency was not resolved, nor was the question of a veto for Committee Chairmen over changes in the text.

Thus, at its start, the Conference was forced to face the fact that President Amerasinghe had not been accredited as a member of the Sri Lanka delegation. Although the Sri Lanka delegation did not object to his continuation in office, many Latin American States opposed it as a matter of principle--that the president of a diplomatic conference must be a member of a delegation. The Asian and African groups strongly supported his continuation in office. After two weeks of unsuccessful negotiation, a resolution confirming Amerasinghe was adopted by a procedural vote of 75 in favor (including the US), 18 votes against, with 13 abstentions, and 21 delegations not participating.

The non-participants, mainly East and West Europeans, felt the matter should be decided only by consensus.

A further week was devoted to organization of work. With the Group of 77 (G-77) itself having re- jected attempts to secure a veto for Committee Chair- men over changes in the text, the main problem in organizing the work of the Conference lay in protect- ing the overwhelming number of articles in the ICNT that could command widespread support from splinter- group attempts to reopen them. This largely succeed- ed. Most of the additional time was consumed by pro- cedural difficulties attendant upon commencement of the final stages of negotiation on the access of land- locked and geographically disadvantaged States to fisheries.

A. Negotiating Groups

Seven negotiating groups (NGs) on outstanding hard-core issues were established as follows, the first three relating to Part XI of the ICNT on deep seabed mining.

1. NG-1. System of exploration and exploi- tation and resource policy, taking note of the work of the informal group of technical experts invited to consider the technical problems associated with any formula that might be used to limit production of minerals from the area. (Chairman, Frank Njenga, Kenya.)

2. NG-2. Financial arrangements. (Chair- man, Tommy Koh, Singapore.)

3. NG-3. Organs of Authority, their compo- sition, powers, and function. (Committee Chairman, Paul Engo, Cameroon.)

4. NG-4. *Right of access of landlocked States and certain developing coastal States in a sub-region or region to the living resources of the exclusive economic zone.

---

* The first part of the item is the formulation re- quired by the group of coastal States; the second part of the item is the formulation required by the group of landlocked and geographically disadvantaged States.

Rights of access of landlocked and geographically disadvantaged States to the living resources
of the economic zone. (Chairman, Satya Nandan, Fiji.)

5. NG-5. The question of settlement of disputes relating to the exercise of the sovereign rights
of coastal States in the exclusive economic zone.
(Chairman, Constantine Stavropoulos, Greece.)

6. NG-6. *Definition of the outer limits
of the Continental Shelf and the question of Payments
and Contributions with respect to the continental
shelf beyond 200 miles.

Definition of the outer limits of the continental shelf and the question of revenue sharing.
(Committee II Chairman, Andres Aguilar, Venezuela.)

7. NG-7. Delimitation of maritime boundaries between adjacent and opposite States and settlement of disputes thereon. (Chairman, E.J. Manner,
Finland.)

B. Other Groups

In addition, following upon the Amoco Cadiz
disaster off Brittany, and on the initiative of the
United States, France, and Canada, the Third Committee
revived its informal pollution working group under
José Vallarta of Mexico. The Third Committee also met
on scientific research.

The Second Committee devoted numerous meetings to an article-by-article review of the texts
within its mandate that were not assigned to negotiating groups.

The Plenary met to hear debate on the preamble and final clauses.

The basic procedural decision taken by the
Plenary regarding revision of the ICNT was as follows:

---

* The first part of the item is the formulation required by the group of coastal States; the second
part of the item is the formulation required by the
group of landlocked and geographically disadvantaged
States.

Any modifications or revisions to be made
in the Informal Composite Negotiating Text
should emerge from the negotiations themselves and should not be introduced on the
initiative of any single person, whether
it be the President or a Chairman of a Committee, unless presented to the Plenary and
found, from the widespread and substantial
support prevailing in Plenary, to offer a
substantially improved prospect of a consensus.

During the ensuing four weeks, the Conference
witnessed one of the most intensive periods of simultaneous negotiation in its history. With a few exceptions, Amerasinghe was accepted with good grace by
those who had opposed him on the issue of principle,
and bitterness over the presidential vote receded rapidly from view. Indeed, it is arguable that the reason why the Conference worked so intensively was in
part in an effort to make up for lost time. Whatever
the explanation, there was a genuine effort to find
compromises and accommodations that might prove acceptable to all.

C. When the results of the negotiations were
presented to Plenary in the last week of the Conference, it was clear that there had been considerable
success, but also that more work remained to be done.

1. NG-1. New texts were presented by the
Chairman of Negotiating Group 1 on the deep seabed
regime on Articles 150 (Policies Relating to Activities in the Area) and 151 (System of Exploration and
Exploitation), as well as on Article 140 (Benefit of
Mankind), 143 (Marine Scientific Research), 144
(Transfer of Technology), 150 bis (Production policies), 150 ter (non-discrimination), 153 (The Review
Conference), and Annex II, Paragraphs 4(c)(ii) and
5(j)(iv) concerning transfer of technology. These
texts do not represent a consensus, but are considered to offer a substantially improved prospect of
achieving consensus. The texts all represent improvement over the ICNT. In some cases, the improvement is significant, although in other important respects it can only be characterized as marginal. The
major features of the revised texts are as follows:

Transfer of technology is no longer a
condition of obtaining a contract, but
the contractor must undertake to transfer such technology to the Enterprise
(if the Enterprise so requests and after
he receives a contract) in good faith on
reasonable commercial terms and conditions, which are to be negotiated by the
parties. The fulfillment of this undertaking would be subject to conciliation
and arbitration. A clause has also been
added at the insistence of Brazil requiring transfer of technology in certain
quite limited cases to developing countries, but there is a possibility that
this provision can be eliminated at a
later stage.

On the Review Conference, Article 153,
considerable improvements were obtained
in Paragraphs 4 and 5. In Paragraph 6,
there is no longer automatic conversion
to a unitary system if the Review Conference fails to reach agreement after five
years, but the Assembly would then be
authorized to impose a moratorium on new
contracts and on new plans of work for
the Enterprise on sites not already reserved.

Although there was little discussion in
NG-1 on the production limitation, the
revised texts incorporate the provisional
US-Canadian agreement in a new Article
150 bis.

In Article 143 on marine scientific research, the revised text eliminates the
former mandate of the Authority to "harmonize" and "coordinate" such research.

Articles 150 and 151 contain both drafting and substantive improvements, including a provision in 150 bis under which
any production limitation on minerals
other than minerals from nodules could
be imposed only by Amendment of the Convention. The changes sought by the US
regarding commodity agreements were not
included.

2. NG-2. The Chairman of Negotiating Group 2 issued new texts that are significantly clearer on the complex questions of financial arrangements. In particular, these texts set forth a basis for calculating the financial obligations of miners, but omit specific percentages. Both the texts and, perhaps even more importantly, the improved common understanding of the complexities involved should clear the way for definitive negotiation of the financial obligations of miners.

3. NG-3. The issue of composition and voting of the Council of the Seabed Authority was seriously and intensively discussed within the context of Negotiating Group 3, but was not resolved at this session.

4. NG-4. The access of landlocked and geographically disadvantaged States to fisheries within the economic zones of other States in the same region or subregion has been one of the most divisive issues of the Conference. The Chairman of Negotiating Group 4 issued a new text which he characterized as offering a substantially improved prospect of consensus on the issue. However, the favorable reaction to that text was dampened by unanticipated difficulty in resolving the question of the precise outer limit of the continental shelf in Negotiating Group 6.

5. NG-5. One of the important contributions of a new Law of the Sea Treaty to international order would be the inclusion of a system for compulsory settlement of disputes under the Treaty. However, achievement of this goal has been complicated by widely divergent views over the degree and method of third-party settlement with respect to fishing in the economic zone. The Chairman of Negotiating Group 5 has issued a text providing for compulsory conciliation with respect to fisheries disputes of certain types. That text offers a substantially improved prospect of consensus on dispute settlement with respect to the economic zone as a whole, including binding settlement of disputes concerning violation of navigation and pollution provisions.

6. NG-6. While the principle of continental shelf jurisdiction over the continental margin beyond 200 miles remains in Article 76, a precise definition of the outer limit of the continental margin was not resolved by Negotiating Group 6. Moreover, believing

that the overall package between the coastal States
and the landlocked and geographically disadvantaged
States on living and non-living resources has been
upset by the Soviet attack on the so-called Irish Formula for defining the continental margin, the broad-
margin States have indicated an unwillingness to allow
the new NG-4 text on landlocked and geographically
disadvantaged State access to fisheries to go forward
into a revised ICNT until agreement has been reached
on the continental margin question.

7. <u>NG-7</u>. A large number of coastal States
have not delimited their fisheries zone and continental shelf boundaries with their neighbors. The Conference is thus more or less evenly divided on whether
any text on the subject of delimitation should emphasize equidistance methods or emphasize the equitable
principles elaborated by the International Court of
Justice. Given the nature of the issue, it was inevitable that the balance in Articles 74 and 83 would
be attacked from both sides. Negotiating Group 7 did,
however, make tentative progress on the unsettled
question of the extent, if any, of third party settlement procedures for delimitation disputes.

8. <u>Committee Three, Pollution</u>. Negotiations
on pollution produced significant improvements in the
text with respect to the prevention, reduction, and
control of pollution from ships. These resulted from
a concerted effort by the US, France, and Canada. The
new texts expand the duty to protect endangered species and fragile ecosystems from pollution, expand the
obligation to establish ship routing systems necessary
to protect the environment, clarify the right of the
coastal State to obtain prompt notice of events that
may result in pollution off its coast in adequate time
to act, and remove certain restraints on the power of
the coastal State to enforce anti-pollution measures
in the territorial sea and in the economic zone. The
new texts also clarify the right of the coastal State
to establish and enforce discharge standards stricter
than international standards for ships in innocent
passage in the territorial sea.

9. <u>Committee Three, Scientific Research</u>. The
US did not gain acceptance of the modest US amendments
derived exclusively from the text on scientific research which came out of package negotiations on the
economic zone at the last session. The Soviet Union
and a significant number of coastal States took the

position that the existing text on scientific research
represented a reasonable balance that ought not to be
disturbed. The US took issue with this position when
it was expressed by the Chairman of Committee Three
in Plenary, and indicated that it would review the
question of what elements should constitute a consensus on scientific research. (It should be noted that
the provisions in the deep seabed mining text with respect to scientific research were improved in NG-1.)

10. Preamble and Final Clauses. While the
Conference began discussion of the preamble and final
clauses, the US urged that further work on these formal provisions be deferred to a later stage. It is
customary for such provisions to be completed at or
near the end of a Conference.

11. Drafting Committee. For the first time,
the Drafting Committee of the Conference commenced
substantive work in informal session. It agreed on
the initial subjects of study and requested Secretariat assistance in preparing reports and materials on
these subjects.

D. The form to be given to the results of negotiations at the seventh session. The question of what
to do with the texts emerging from the various negotiations proved to be a delicate one. The number of
articles dealt with did not, in and or itself, seem
to necessitate the issuance of an entirely new informal text of the treaty as a whole. The Group of
77 and others concluded in effect that future negotiations on deep seabed mining would be based on the new
texts produced in NG-1. The same attitude existed in
the Conference with respect to most of the other new
texts. It would seem that the relevant provisions of
the ICNT are for practical purposes replaced by the
new texts emerging from the negotiations, but that the
implication of the new procedural requirements for revision of the ICNT have caused some delegations to refrain from taking formal steps in Plenary to confirm
this.

E. Conclusion of Session

The mood at the end of the session seemed to reveal a general view that the Conference was finally
coming to grips with the most intractable outstanding
issues and had commenced the inevitably painful process of attempting to resolve them in a generally

acceptable fashion. Delegates were sober but not dis-
couraged; optimistic that the job could be done, but
not heady about prospects; willing to find ways to
bridge the significant gaps between them,but unwilling
to sacrifice national interests. The Conference has
passed the nadir of the reaction to the deep seabeds
portion of ICNT and the Presidential problem at the
start of this session, and is now proceeding systemat-
ically to the completion of a treaty. However, since
the Conference is finally dealing in earnest with some
of the most controversial issues before it, criticism
of the accommodations that it reaches can be expected
to become ever more shrill. This may yet prove to be
its most severe test.

The basic procedural decision taken by the Plenary regarding revision of the ICNT is as follows:

> Any modifications or revisions to be
> made in the Informal Composite Nego-
> tiating Text should emerge from the
> negotiations themselves and should not
> be introduced on the initiative of any
> single person, whether it be the Pres-
> ident or a Chairman of a Committee, un-
> less presented to the Plenary and found,
> from the widespread and substantial sup-
> port prevailing in Plenary, to offer a
> substantially improved prospect of a con-
> sensus.

The actual route to ICNT revision involved several steps. The course proved to be so tortuous that
revisions were not produced at the session, even
though a number of new texts met the standard for inclusion in the ICNT. The negotiating groups on the
hard-core issues were organized at this session to be
of limited size, but open-ended, on the understanding
that these discussions of the issues did not prejudice
the position of any delegation. The Chairman of the
negotiating groups mandated by the Plenary reported
both to the competent Committee Chairman and to the
President of the Conference. The Committee Chairman
concerned, therefore, retained a considerable degree
of influence over the production of new texts.

It was noted that the negotiations on the settlement of disputes and on the preamble and final clauses
would pass through the Committee stage and Plenary, as
other issues allocated to the three main committees.

For this purpose in the first stage, the Plenary, in informal session, functioned as a main committee.

It was planned that the Plenary should aim at the completion of all substantive discussions for the production of a draft convention at the seventh session. The work program adopted by the Plenary tried to provide for the revision of the Informal Composite Negotiating Text and the discussion of the Revised Informal Composite Negotiating Text, but lack of working time following the Presidential fight prevented this.

The revision of the Informal Composite Negotiating Text was to be the collective responsibility of the President and the Chairmen of the Main Committees, acting together as a team headed by the President. This was the so-called "collegial" system. The Chairman of the Drafting Committee and the Rapporteur-General were to be associated with the team.

It was also agreed that in all negotiations held in Plenary, the President should have the Chairmen of the three Main Committees associated with him on the podium. In the event, however, this procedure was not followed.

## II. Negotiating Group 1 (NG-1). System of Exploration and Exploitation

### Summary and Conclusions

NG-1, under the chairmanship of Mr. Frank Njenga (Kenya), continued the work begun at the Intersessional in New York on Articles 150 (Policies Relating to Activities in the Area) and 151 (System of Exploration and Exploitation). Revised texts were issued by Mr. Njenga on these Articles, as well as on Article 140 (Benefit of Mankind), 143 (Marine Scientific Research), 144 (Transfer of Technology), 150 bis (Production Policies), 150 ter (non-discrimination), 153 (The Review Conference), and Annex II, Paragraph 4(c)(ii) and 5(j)(iv) concerning transfer of technology.

Although these texts do not represent a consensus, they offer a substantially improved prospect of achieving consensus. The texts all represent improvement over the ICNT. In some cases, the improvement is significant; in others, marginal. Negotiations both

195

in informal and formal negotiating groups and Committee I meetings underscored the deep suspicions and lack of trust of the Group of 77 with respect to the commitment of the developed countries to the workability of the Enterprise side of the system. These fears are reflected in the revised texts, particularly on transfer of technology and the review clause.

The revised texts are summarized briefly:

-- Transfer of technology is no longer a condition of obtaining a contract, but the contractor must thereafter undertake to transfer such technology to the Enterprise (if the Enterprise so requests) on reasonable commercial terms and conditions to be negotiated in good faith by the parties. The fulfillment of the undertaking would be subject to conciliation and arbitration. A new--and highly controversial--clause requires transfer of technology in certain quite limited areas to developing countries.

-- On the review Conference, (Article 153), considerable improvements were obtained in paragraphs 4 and 5. There is no longer automatic conversion to a unitary system if the Review Conference fails to reach agreement after five years, but the Assembly would be authorized to impose a moratorium on new contracts and on new plans of work for the Enterprise on sites not already reserved. The revised texts incorporate the provisional US-Canadian agreement on production controls in a new Article 150 bis.

-- The revised Article 143 (marine scientific research) eliminates the former mandate of the Authority to "harmonize and coordinate" such research.

-- Articles 150 and 151 contain both drafting and substantive improvements, including a provision in 150 bis under which any production limitation on non-nodule minerals could be imposed only by amendment of the Convention. Changes sought by the US regarding commodity agreements were not included.

There are two changes in the revised Article 140. The first is to insert the phrase, "and peoples who have not attained full independence or other self-governing status..." into the first sentence. The second adds a new paragraph 2, providing for equitable distribution by the Authority of the benefits derived from the Area.

The US Delegation sought to remove the Authority from responsibility for distribution of benefits by requiring the use of some already existing international mechanism rather than a new one created by the Authority. No objections were voiced to this proposal, but by the end of the session the desired changes had not appeared. The text is slightly improved by the change in wording from "shall establish a system for equitable sharing of benefits" to "shall provide for equitable sharing of benefits."

Marine Scientific Research. The major change in Article 143 is the insertion of a new paragraph 2 which helps consolidate the provisions on marine scientific research and eliminates the troublesome language directing the Authority to "harmonize and coordinate such research." This is replaced by language directing the Authority to "coordinate and disseminate the results of such research when available."

The only other change in revised Article 143 is the insertion in paragraph 3 of an explicit statement that "States Parties shall carry out marine scientific research." This addition balances the obligation of the Authority to carry out marine scientific research in the Area. The US Delegation made clear in the deliberations the right of States Parties to conduct marine scientific research in the Area irrespective of the Treaty.

Transfer of Technology. In the ICNT the obligations to assist developing countries through the transfer of deepsea mining technology are divided between the general obligations of States, and the more specific obligations of mining companies (in Articles 150, 151, and in Annex II). This general division remained intact throughout the seventh session.

No changes of substance were made in the general obligations of States and the Authority, although certain provisions found in Article 151 (8) were moved to a more appropriate place in Article 144. A number of changes, however, were made with respect to the specific obligations of private miners. In the ICNT, the private miner was required, apparently as a condition of being accorded the right to mine, to transfer (under fair and reasonable terms and conditions) to the Authority the technology he intended to use and to negotiate such terms and conditions as a part of the mining contract. If the terms and conditions

of transfer were a part of the contract, access to deepsea mining might become conditional upon arbitrary and excessive requirements. Further, the terms of the transfer might not be fair market value but some lower figure which seemed "fair" to the Authority. Finally, it was pointed out that at least a part of the technology involved would not be owned by the miner and thus could not be transferred to the Authority without the consent of the owner.

To meet these objections, changes were made in the text by Chairman Njenga which provided that the terms of technology transfer would be negotiated only after conclusion of the mining contract; that compensation would be based on "fair and reasonable commercial terms and conditions"; and that this obligation extended only to technology which the miner had the right to transfer.

While these are important improvements over the ICNT, some detrimental changes were also made. A miner would be required to give to the Authority, and to keep up-dated, a general description of his technology. Presumably this would allow the Authority to purchase the best technology. The miner would be allowed to use in the Area only that technology belonging to others which the owner had agreed could be purchased by the Authority. Finally, the miner would have the same transfer of technology obligations toward developing countries who start seabed mining in the corresponding reserved Area as he had assumed toward the Authority. This latter provision is particularly controversial in the Conference.

During the session, special efforts were made by the US Delegation to acquaint other delegates with the known facts about deepsea mining (including the diversity of concepts included in the word "technology" and the importance of trained personnel capable of dealing with new engineering and scientific problems). Despite these efforts, many developing countries continue to doubt that the Enterprise will be able to obtain the necessary technology unless it benefits from mandatory transfer.

Three fundamental concepts of the ICNT remained unchanged during the seventh session. First, the transfer of technology remained obligatory and not voluntary on the part of the miner. Second, any unresolved dispute on this subject would be resolved by

binding arbitration. Third, the obligations extend
only to technology used in mining (carrying out activities in the Area), and do not apply to subsequent
stages, such as processing.

General Policies Relating to Activities in the
Area. At the February intersessional meeting, the
policies in subparagraphs (a) - (g) of ICNT Article
150 paragraph 1 were put in a single article. Article
150 (a)-(b) was not discussed in NG-1 other than generally in comments on the package of revised articles
unchanged from the intersessional. The most important
change in this text is the substitution of the phrase
"with a view to ensuring" for the more absolute "in
order to ensure" in describing the purposes of the
policies in subparagraphs (a) - (g). This change reflects the reality that the policies in (a)-(g) are
objectives rather than mandates and helps avoid the
implication that the Article confers any power on the
Authority other than those contained in other treaty
articles. Other amendments in subparagraphs (a)-(g)
tightened the ICNT language slightly and can be viewed
as improvements, although the USDEL was not successful in securing all of the changes desired.

Production Policies. Paragraph 1 of Article 150
bis has been modified only slightly and does not contain changes sought by the US regarding commodity arrangements, in particular, the suggestion that it be
left for future decision whether the Authority could
represent all the production from the Area of only
that of the Enterprise.

The review paragraph 3 represents a significant
improvement over Article 150 paragraph C of the ICNT,
in providing that any production limitation on minerals from the deep seabed other than minerals from
nodules shall be subject to the procedures set forth
in the Convention for entry into force of amendments.

Paragraph 2 of Article 150 bis contains major
changes reflecting the results of US-Canadian negotiations on production controls.

These bilateral discussions were aimed at creating a "technical" framework for a production control
formulation that would be easier to interpret and
more workable than the ICNT's.

At the same time, the Archer Group of technical experts continued its work (begun at the Intersessional meetings). The Archer Group, now a sub-group of NG-1, was composed of a cross-section of States, with representation from industrialized States and land-based producers of nickel. The US and Canada worked together in the Archer Group to ensure that five of the basic points underlying the new text were incorporated in the Archer Group report. These are:

-- The production ceiling should be calculated by extension of a trend line.

-- Data should be updated annually.

-- The data base for each update should be the latest fifteen year period.

-- Growth should be calculated on an exponential rather than a linear function.

-- The calculations should be made on the basis of consumption data.

The US and Canada concluded that their interests would be served by early agreement on a complete production control formula. As a result, the pace of technical talks was accelerated, and a ten-point package was worked out. The ten points are the Archer Group five above, plus:

-- The interim period would begin five years prior to first planned commercial production, and would last 25 years;

-- The 100% build-up period would last five years;

-- The percentage split would apply to that portion of the growth segment accruing after the fifth year of the interim period;

-- The ceiling applicable to a plan of work would be that calculated for the year in which the project is projected to begin commercial exploitation, not the year in which the contract is approved;

-- Once a contract or plan of work is approved on the basis of a particular level of production, that level could not thereafter be cut back.

Agreement was reached between the delegations on a 60/40 percentage split, subject to reactions from capitals and from other friendly delegations.

Functions of the Authority. Article 151 contains a number of improvements over the ICNT such as deletion of the requirements of transfer of technology as a condition of obtaining a contract, and the sections on marine scientific research. In addition, transfer of technology and the system of compensation were deleted, leaving these subjects to be dealt with in Articles 143, 144, and 140 (along with 158) respectively. The troublesome phrases in paragraphs 1 and 2 (implying that all activities in the Area were to be carried out on behalf of the Authority) were replaced with more acceptable language. The delegation also succeeded in inserting a useful cross-reference to Article 139 in paragraph 4 regarding the obligation of States Parties to assure compliance with the Convention by entities under its sponsorship.

The Review Conference. Improvements in the revised text of Article 153 include the following:

-- In paragraph 1, the start of the Review Conference is advanced from 20 years after the entry into force of the Convention to 20 years after the approval of the first contract or plan of work.

-- In paragraph 4, the provision allowing the Conference to determine its own entry into force procedures is eliminated.

-- In paragraph 5, the provision permitting the contract period to be shortened in the years shortly before the Review Conference has been deleted.

However, paragraph 6, which provides for the contingency of the failure of the Review Conference to reach agreement, still presents serious difficulties for the US. While it eliminates automatic conversion to a unitary system, it gives the Assembly the power, if the Review Conference is deadlocked after five years, to impose a moratorium on new contracts and new plans of work for the Enterprise (except for areas already reserved). This text is designed to put pressure on both sides of the system to reach agreement in the Review Conference. The US voiced strong reservations on this provision and noted that US could not agree to the possible termination of its right of

access to seabed minerals just at the time the need
for them may become acute.

III.  Negotiating Group 2 (NG-2):
      Financial Arrangements

Summary and Conclusions

NG-2 made noticeable progress on the question of
financial arrangements, a subject which had not been
negotiated previously.  The articles regarding the
financing of the Authority and the Enterprise are much
improved over the ICNT (except for the transfer of
funds from the Enterprise to the Authority), and there
is now a solid framework for financial arrangements
between the contractor and the Authority.  The amount
of payments from the contractor to the Authority, however, is a hard issue still to be resolved.

The Negotiations.  NG-2 on financial arrangements
was established by Committee I and chaired by Ambassador Koh (Singapore).  His leadership of the working
group raised its status to an advanced political level
and therefore made the results of the group's work
more credible.    The active members of the group included representatives of both the industrialized
countries and the G-77.  From the latter came some
very constructive suggestions by delegates experienced
in the land-based production of minerals.

The work of the group was divided into three
parts:  financial arrangements of the Authority; financial arrangements of the Enterprise; and financial
arrangements between contractors and the Authority.
Articles on financial arrangements of the Authority
were redrafted by Ambassador Koh in a way which is far
clearer than the ICNT.  His changes provide that assessments of States for the administrative expenses of
the Authority will be based on the UN scale and that
these assessments will not be used to support the
Enterprise.

The Enterprise financial arrangements redraft is
also an improvement over the ICNT.  A vague reference
to "charges" in Annex II has been deleted, and States
Parties no longer are obliged to make appropriate
changes in the international financial organizations
(such as the International Monetary Fund) in order to
help the Enterprise.

Less desirable aspects of the redrafts appeared in the section which now gives the Assembly much more power to determine what income the Enterprise shall transfer to the Authority. The risk is that such power may result in the Enterprise retaining more money than a normal commercial operation and therefore having a competitive advantage over other miners.

Financial arrangements between the contractors and the Authority were by far the most difficult topic in NG-2, and the Chairman created a smaller group of technical experts to deal with them. The group recognized that there is a scarcity of reliable data on seabed mining but agreed that the Massachusetts Institute of Technology report (A Cost Model of Deep Ocean Mining and Associated Regulatory Issues) was the best report available, and it was used as a basis for discussion.

The ICNT provisions on financial arrangements between contractors and the Authority is less a framework than a recitation of all the possibilities. The first mode of payments considered by the expert group was the application fee. The EEC representatives favored a fee of $100,000; the developing countries and the US preferred $500,000. No dollar figure was inserted in the redrafts because no compromise could be reached. All delegations, however, agreed that the fee should be no higher than necessary to cover the expenses of processing an application, and that this should be reviewed every five years.

On the subject of an annual fixed fee to ensure miner diligence, the industrialized countries opposed it as superfluous given the large investment which seabed miners must make. The developing countries, on the other hand, argued that the main purpose of this charge was to provide a steady stream of income for the Authority, especially in the early years of the system. This charge was included (with the space for the specific number left blank) on the grounds that this would ensure the Authority some revenue before the commencement of commercial production.

The principal income question was focused on a plan for a royalty-only, and on a nominal royalty plus profit-sharing approach. The royalty-only system was favored by the USSR, Canada, Australia, and others; while the US, the EEC, and Japan favored the other system. The G-77 seemed to have no objection to

either approach provided it generated large amounts of income, much larger than first-generation mining sites could economically produce.

The US supported nominal royalty plus profit-sharing because it avoids heavy front-end payments to the Authority and because it provides a way to share risks. The Soviet Union preferred royalty-only system because this is more compatible with its economic ideology. Canada and Australia supported royalties because they are relatively easy to administer and are uniform in application.

Ambassador Koh incorporated both options (but without specific numbers) into the paper on financial arrangements. It was felt that this would better enable contractors to choose a system which is compatible with their social and economic system.

Within the issue of profit sharing another difficult issue was negotiated: the percentage of the miner's profits attributable to activities in the Area under the jurisdiction of the Authority. The developed countries stated that the percentage of total profits (from the sale of seabed minerals attributable to the mining activity) should be calculated as the ratio of capital investment in mining activities to total capital investments in mining, transportation, and processing activities (which according to the MIT study is approximately 20 percent). The developing countries felt that this percentage attributed an insufficient amount to the value of the nodules. Debate on this issue was intense, and no agreement was reached. Nonetheless, all the participating delegations (except India) acknowledged that this percentage should be less than 100 (G-77 delegates gave figures ranging from 38 percent to 80 percent).

One important issue not taken up--because it was felt to be beyond the group's mandate--was whether the same financial arrangements should apply both to the Enterprise and to other miners.

The explanatory memorandum accompanying the NG-2 redrafts did contain some numerical specifics which monetized some of the proposals. In this instance, they may have been somewhat misleading. For example, although the proposals made by Norway and India appear to produce more income than did the US proposal,

they would, in fact, produce no income because investors would be unlikely to risk capital on such terms.

Overall, although the redrafts on financial arrangements (between the contractors and the Authority) leave many important issues unresolved, they do at least provide a solid framework within which further negotiations can proceed. The jumble of the ICNT provisions has been clarified, and most technical matters (like the definition of such terms as development costs) have been agreed on. The way is now open for final compromises.

## IV. Negotiating Group 3 (NG-3), Organs of the Authority

Summary and Conclusions

NG-3, led by First Committee Chairman, Paul Engo, considered three subjects under its mandate: composition of the Council; the voting procedures of the Council (Article 159); and the relationship of the Council to the Assembly (Articles 158 and 162). The third subject was considered at only one meeting. On the other topics, discussions revealed that they were not ripe for settlement. A revised Article 159 was issued by the Chairman, but it contained only two minor changes.

Composition of the Council. Developing and developed country delegations hold divergent views on the purpose of the Council. The former regard the Council essentially as an executive committee for the Assembly in which the members drawn from special interest groups (seabed miners, major importers of minerals found in nodules, and major land-based producers of such minerals) serve merely in a representative capacity along with the members drawn from the regional groups. The latter consider it essential that the Council serve as a counterbalance to the Assembly and as the vehicle for the protection of the designated interests.

Discussion centered on variations of two proposals: the first, to raise the geographic representation in category 1(e) from one to at least two from each geographical region (in order to enhance the chances for Council membership for small WEO industrialized countries); and the second, to increase the number of representatives in category (a). In the end, however,

it did not prove possible to secure agreement on any of these proposals.

Voting Procedures. The US proposed that in addition to the three-fourths overall majority (now contained in Article 159), affirmative decisions of the Council must obtain concurrent simple majorities in three of the four special interest categories (a-d), or alternatively four of the five total categories. Developing countries, on the other hand, rejected the principle of a "veto" or "weighted voting" (which many regard as including concurrent majorities in any form), and sought instead to reduce the overall requirement to a two-thirds majority or to a simple majority.

For a time it appeared that broad support might be found for a compromise proposing a two-thirds overall majority with a two-thirds majority in categories (a-d) taken as one group and category (e) taken as a second group. Coupled with suggestions for a more favorable distribution of seats on the Council, this proposal or variants of it received expressions of interest from a number of industrialized countries. Others, however, sought to limit the concurrent majority requirement to a simple majority in each of the two above groups; and in the end, Chairman Engo concluded that no basis for settlement of this difficult political issue existed at this time.

## V.   Committee II

### A.   Summary and Conclusions

The work of Committee II was substantially advanced this session by the establishment of working procedures designed to accelerate the pace of real negotiations on key issues. Three special negotiating groups were established by the Plenary to deal with issues related to Committee II. The groups considered problems with regard to the access to living resources by the landlocked and geographically disadvantaged States--LL/GDS--(NG-4, chaired by Ambassador Nandan of Fiji); dispute settlement with respect to fisheries in the economic zone (NG-5, chaired by Ambassador Stavropoulos of Greece); and the delimination of maritime boundaries (NG-7, chaired by Judge Manner of Finland). In addition, a fourth working group (NG-6) was established by the Second Committee to deal with the definition of the outer edge of the continental

margin (beyond 200 miles) and revenue sharing. This group was led by Ambassador Andres Aguilar, Chairman of the Second Committee. In addition, the Second Committee spent considerable useful time in informal sessions reviewing issues not covered by the special groups whose work was given priority.

B. Informal Committee II Meetings

It was decided that there was a need for the discussion of other issues of importance to various countries. Thus the Chairman established a procedure whereby the Committee considered informal suggestions for changes to the ICNT in any articles not being considered by the negotiating groups. Ten meetings were used for this purpose, and over 40 articles were scrutinized. The general rule was established that changes would have to command overwhelming support before they could be considered for reference to the Plenary.

The topics commanding the greatest attention were those dealing with the legal status of the economic zone and straits used for international navigation. Others dealt with islands, enclosed or semi-enclosed seas, the territorial sea, and archipelagos. The tenor and content of the discussions made clear that on most of the articles there was no mandate for changes. One exception is the matter of anadromous species (primarily salmon). As a result of intensive negotiations among interested States, with the US acting as coordinator, a final version of Article 66 was agreed and submitted to Committee II and Plenary for approval.

Substantial progress was made in three of the four negotiating groups. Determination of maritime boundaries, involving so many bilateral difficulties, requires further efforts. In addition, the discussion on the Committee itself was valuable in making clear that it has reached a point where the successful conclusion of the Second Committee work is imminent. The remaining elements are interrelated, and the outlines of a broadly acceptable package are evident.

C. Negotiating Group 4 (NG-4), Right of access of landlocked States and geographically disadvantaged States to the living resources of the economic zone

This issue has long been identified as one involving the interests of a large number of States,

and so must be resolved before a treaty can successfully be concluded. On the one side, the LL/GDS (53
in number) are seeking access to the living resources
of the economic zones of their neighbors on favorable
terms. On the other side, the coastal States (numbering more than 80) have resisted.

NG-4 identified the questions to be resolved
as follows:

1. Whether the LL/GDS should be given
access as a matter of right rather than license;

2. How to deal with the question of
access above the surplus;

3. Whether the access of LL/GDS is on
a preferential basis with respect to third States;

4. Whether a distinction should be drawn
between developed and developing LL/GDS; and

5. The definition of geographically
disadvantaged State (GDS).

There were sharp clashes in NG-4 between the two
points of view, although the mood was positive, and both
sides worked diligently in seeking a successful conclusion.

As a result of extended negotiations, the Chairman was able to produce a document containing the
following elements:

1. A right for the LL/GDS to an appropriate
part of the surplus of the living resources of the
economic zone;

2. The criteria to be established by the
parties when entering into agreements with regard
to such participation;

3. A way of dealing with access of LL/GDS
when the coastal State has, through one means or another, utilized its surplus;

4. A definition of GDS, referred to as
"States with special geographic characteristics";

5. A distinction between developed and developing States, with preference for the latter.

At the concluding session, although many delegations offered comments, criticisms, and changes to the Chairman's document, he was able to conclude, without objections, that his text had substantial support and offered a substantially improved prospect of consensus, thus smoothing its path toward inclusion in a revised text.

Two final comments should be made. First, the resolution of this immensely complex and contentious issue has been significantly advanced through the skill and dedication of Chairman Nandan. Second, there has been a decided linkage, in the minds of many, between this issue and that of the continental margin, and the final resolution of both issues may have to be accomplished as a package.

D. Negotiating Group 6 (NG-6), The definition of the outer limit of the continental margin where it extends beyond 200 miles, and the question of revenue sharing.

A negotiating group (NG-6) under the Second Committee was set up to consider the question of the continental margin and the related question of revenue sharing. It was generally recognized by both States with broad continental margins and those with narrow or no margins that an accommodation would consist of three elements:

1. A precise definition of the continental margin beyond 200 miles;

2. Revenue sharing for the benefit of developing countries from exploitation of the margin beyond 200 miles; and

3. Agreement on the right of access of LL/GDS to the living resources of the economic zone (EEZ) of the same region or subregion.

The definition of the continental shelf contained in Article 76 of the ICNT is vague and was supported by few States. Several definitions of the margin are before the Conference, and to demonstrate their implications, the LOS Secretariat produced a map which showed:

1.  The location of the 200-mile line;

2.  The 500-meter isobath beyond 200 miles;

3.  The Irish Formula (base of the continental slope plus a maximum of 60 miles or, alternatively, the base of the continental slope and beyond to where the depth of sediments is at least one percent of the distance between that point and the foot of the slope);

4.  The outer edge of the margin, apparently (but not explicitly) defined on the basis of an unspecified gradient limitation.

Certain conclusions could be derived from the study. The 500-meter isobath beyond 200 miles and the 200-mile limit itself did not accommodate the interests of the many States with broad margins. The outer edge of the margin as defined by the unspecified gradient would give to certain coastal States jurisdiction very far out to sea (although Article 76 as drafted might extend even further seaward). Finally, the Irish Formula, using either alternative, was an accommodation between the 200-mile advocates and those who would seek jurisdiction to the edge of the margin undefined. Most States with broad margins supported the Irish Formula, and a very well defined trend exists among the LL/GDS toward that formula as a compromise.

The Soviet Union suggested a distance method formula which would permit coastal State jurisdiction over the margin where it extended beyond 200 miles, but only to a maximum of 100 miles beyond the 200-mile line. This formula was supported by the Eastern Europeans and Cuba. While it has a surface simplicity--a distance criterion--it suffered from the drawbacks that it did not accommodate certain key broad-margin States; it posed a very real possibility of evolving into a 300-mile economic zone; and it did not address the question of how to determine the outer edge of the margin between 200 and 300 miles. The Soviet suggestion did, however, make impossible a consensus on the definition at this session.

Moreover, Bulgaria and several other States proposed that the IOC prepare a new margin study with a larger scale chart which would include the Soviet suggestion. The Plenary agreed to indicate the Soviet suggestion on the Secretariat chart and to explore the implications (financial and otherwise) of a new study.

There was apparent recognition that sufficient information is, in fact, available to make the necessary
decision on the margin question.

The related question of revenue sharing based on
mineral production from the margin beyond the 200-mile
zone was barely discussed. It was, however, broadly
recognized that revenue sharing would be based on the
value of production at the site in respect of exploitation; that the revenue sharing obligation would
commence in the sixth year after exploitation began
at a site; and that it would increase annually in one
percent increments. Further discussion must be held
on the maximum rate to apply.

  E. Negotiating Group 7 (NG-7), The delimitation
   of the territorial sea, economic zone, and
   continental shelf between adjacent and
   opposite States.

A negotiating group (NG-7) was established by the
Plenary to consider the question of the delimitation
of the special maritime boundaries and was chaired by
Judge Manner of Finland. These issues are basically
bilateral, and therefore an LOS treaty can only establish a broad framework within which the parties can
reach agreement. The ICNT provisions concerning delimitation of the territorial sea follow the guidelines of the 1958 Geneva Convention on the Territorial
Sea and the Contiguous Zone, and are generally acceptable to the States concerned.

The heart of the controversy involved delimitation of the economic zone and continental shelf. On
the one hand, there are proponents of prime emphasis
on the application of equitable principles in delimitation. This view is reflected in the ICNT, and it
includes equidistance where applicable. On the other
hand, an opposing group advocates primary emphasis on
equidistance, but with provisions for taking special
circumstances into account. Clearly, some States are
concerned about protecting their position in existing
disputes. There is consensus, however, that the parties should settle their differences by agreement, and
that there should be an equitable result, regardless
of the principles of methods applied. It is also
clear that the predominant view favors application of
equitable principles. The existing text might be acceptable to more States if there were privision for
the compulsory settlement of disputes. In any event,

this issue will not likely be settled until the negotiations are in their final stages.

Dispute Settlement Aspects. The mandate of NG-7
included the dispute settlement aspects of marine
boundary delimitation as well as the substantive question. The ICNT (Article 297(1)(a)) contains an optional exception of delimitation disputes from settlement under the Convention, provided that a regional or
other binding procedure is accepted instead. While
this text was acceptable to the US, it became clear
early on in the negotiating group debate that a number of countries could not accept this text.

At the beginning of the seventh week of the session, there had still been no movement by either side
from their extreme positions: on the one hand, that
everything be subject to adjudication and, on the
other hand, that nothing be subject to it. At this
point the US suggested two possible compromises: the
first, that the court or tribunal should not finally
delimit the boundary but only issue guidelines to aid
the parties in negotiating a delimitation; the second,
that disputes arising before some particular date--
January 1, 1978, for instance--be excluded from compulsory settlement. The fact that although neither
side liked these compromises, they were willing to discuss them, indicated that they may be on the right
track.

Therefore, at the last minute an informal private
working group was set up to deal with the dispute settlement question. At the request of NG-7 Chairman
Manner, the US chaired this group of 14. In the two
meetings which were held, it was impossible to achieve
any consensus on a text. The foundations of a promising negotiation were laid, however, and a survey of
potential conciliatory formulas was prepared. Two of
these seem to show particular promise: one was a
staged or tiered process beginning with conciliatory
or advisory procedure and working up to more definitive solutions if these did not work; the second was
based on a suggestion that compulsory settlement would
be triggered by one party beginning exploitation beyond the median line or in the disputed area. It may
be hoped that the work of this informal group will
provide the basis for real progress at the next session, or possibly even earlier.

## F. Compulsory Settlement of Disputes

As anticipated, the living resources of the exclusive economic zone was the principal subject of
dispute settlement negotiations at the Seventh Session. The basic position of coastal States was that
no disputes related to their fisheries should be subject to any kind of compulsory procedure. On the
other side were the landlocked and geographically
disadvantaged States and the distant-water fishing
States (especially Japan and the Soviet Union). Their
position was that all disputes relating to living resources in the economic zone, and in particular those
concerning access of other States to those resources,
should be the subject of compulsory and binding settlement.

The ICNT provision which covered this matter (Article 296(4)) was so obscure as to defy interpretation, even by those familiar with its negotiating history. Its probable effect would have been to eliminate compulsory settlement for almost all disputes relating to coastal State rights or discretion with
respect to economic-zone fisheries

An alternative paragraph had been circulated at
the end of the Sixth Session in July 1977. That text
was clearer than the ICNT paragraph, but it was extremely limited in scope. It provided for no binding
settlement, offering compulsory conciliation* in only
a single situation where the coastal State was endan-
gering a species by over-exploitation. It was obvious
that at the Seventh Session this text could not, without change, be an acceptable replacement for the ICNT.
It failed to satisfy to a sufficient extent the legitimate demand of the LL/GDS and of Japan and USSR to

---

* A compulsory procedure is one to which either party
is obliged to go at the request of the other. Thus,
even negotiation can be compulsory. A binding procedure is one in which both parties are obliged to accept and to act upon the decision of a neutral third
party. Compulsory conciliation in the context of the
present negotiations is a procedure akin to arbitration except that the result would not bind the parties
absolutely. The report of the conciliation commission
would, however, contain findings of fact and, as appropriate, conclusions of law, which would become the
basis for further negotiations between the parties.

have a number of fisheries questions subject to compulsory procedure.

## G.  The Negotiating Group 5 Phase

The Conference referred the question of economic zone fisheries disputes to Negotiating Group 5 (NG-5), under the chairmanship of Ambassador Stavropoulos of Greece.  This group consisted of a core of 37 States plus about 20 other regular participants.

Work began with an attack by the coastal States, who proposed the deletion of paragraph 4.  This would have had the effect of complete elimination of all fisheries disputes from compulsory procedures.  The LL/GDS responded with proposals to strengthen the paragraph to bring more disputes within compulsory adjudication.  The US continued to support the principle of maximum compulsory and binding settlement.

After several days of debate, two potential bases of compromise began to emerge.  One was the notion of abuse of rights.  The idea behind this was that whenever a State abused rights conferred by the Convention, any other State affected by such abuse should have international legal recourse.

The second idea, and in the long run the more productive one, was that of compulsory conciliation. The suggestion was that, if one side wanted no compulsory procedure at all and the other wanted a compulsory and binding procedure, the best compromise might be a procedure which was compulsory but not binding.

## H.  The Group of 15 Phase

Chairman Stavropoulos adjourned the full NG-5 in favor of a small team of 15 (later expanded to 22). He indicated that this working group would attempt to draft a new text based on these compromise ideas, and it was successful in doing so.

The first few meetings of this smaller group were quite difficult, however.  The LL/GDS continued to insist on adjudication for all fisheries questions. The coastal States continued to insist that their sovereign rights were inviolate, and that no fisheries questions could be subject to settlement.  During this period it became clear that there could be no

general overriding provision for compulsory and binding settlement in all cases of abuse of rights, although certain States tried doggedly to push such a
provision through. The US then suggested a solution
based on the idea of compulsory enquiry or fact-find-
ing. Such a procedure would have provided a binding
but not necessarily conclusive result. Even this was
too much for the coastal States.

After several days and several near breakdowns,
it became apparent that only one middle position was
possible. The LL/GDS would have to give up all binding settlement, and the coastal States would have to
accept compulsory conciliation for an expanded range
of questions relating to fisheries in the economic
zone. As the inevitability of this course became
manifest, both sides seemed to resign themselves to
it, and a workmanlike atmosphere of honest bargaining
prevailed throughout the rest of the meetings. The
group proceeded in a ste-by-step fashion to see what
particular areas of dispute could be added to the list
of items submissible to compulsory conciliation. At
points in this process the groups had to consult with
Plenary meetings of their members to get authority to
budge on this or that position.

In the end, clauses were drafted making three
areas subject to compulsory conciliation. The first
is a substantially broadened and strengthened conservation clause based on the Article 61 concept of over-
exploitation. The coastal State will be obligated to
accept compulsory process whenever it has failed "to
ensure through proper conservation and management
measures that the maintenance of the living resources
. . . is not seriously endangered." The second clause
gives other States recourse when the coastal State has
arbitrarily refused to determine either the allowable
catch or its own harvesting capacity for a particular
species in which some fishing State is especially interested. The third provides for conciliation upon
arbitrary refusal to allocate surplus to any State in
accordance with Articles 62, 69, and 70 (which provide
for access by traditional fishing State and LL/GDS).

The clauses require that coastal State violations
be arbitrary or manufest before jurisdiction arises,
and they do not permit review of coastal State regulatory action within the proper limits of the regulatory power. By being so framed, the text ensures that

a coastal State which exercises its powers responsibly cannot be harassed by disgruntled fishing States.

### I.  The Final Negotiating Group Phase

Once the group of 15 agreed on these points and on the draft to replace present 296(4), the text sailed through the full negotiating group with relative ease, though some States continued to be dissatisfied with the compromise.

Despite one dissent, the text was accepted by the full negotiating group and passed along to Plenary where, after desultory discussion, it was approved for inclusion in any revised text.

It was noted in accepting the text that it was the subject only of "conditional" consensus.  This was intended primarily to signal the fact that final resolution of this question is related to and dependent upon achieving compromises in NG-4, concerning the rights of access of the LL/GDS and, to a lesser extent, in NG-6 delaying with the delimitation and regime of the continental shelf beyond 200 miles.

This new paragraph is one of the important successes of the Seventh Session.  It is an even-handed and balanced solution to a very difficult problem and both legally and politically superior to the ICNT. The ICNT masked fundamental disagreement with obfuscation.  It may have offered no compulsory settlement at all, or it may have offered too much.  The clarity and relative certainty of the new text signals real agreement on mutually acceptable limits of compulsory settlement in the economic zone.  It offers both sides procedural protection as part of the framework of a workable substantive regime.

### J.  Restructuring Article 296 Generally

After finishing with fisheries disputes, the mandate of NG-5 was extended to the general restructuring of the rest of Article 296.  A redraft was developed by the small group of 15 and passed directly to Plenary which agreed to its incorporation into any revised ICNT.  This was largely a non-political legal drafting exercise and was completed rapidly.

One important substantive problem did come up, and its solution resulted in an improvement over the

ICNT. The problem related to whether the complaining State would have to make a *prima* *facie* case before it could compel a coastal State to appear and defend a claim over an economic zone question. The new text properly balances the obligations of both parties with respect to preliminary determinations of submissibility.

Another problem in 296 concerned the ICNT limitation on compulsory settlement of scientific research disputes. Negotiating Group 5 decided that its action was dependent on action by Committee III, because the relevant paragraph in Article 296 corresponds to a similar provision in the scientific research portion of the ICNT (Article 265). In consultation with Committee III Chairman Yankov (Bulgaria) it was decided that Article 265 should be deleted and the issue referred to negotiations at the next session on dispute settlement.

### K. Abuse of Rights

The group also decided to recommend to Plenary that a general prohibition against abuse of rights be included at some appropriate place in the Convention. The specific language will be drafted at some later time. The Mexican proposal which has been the basis of discussion so far is unacceptable. It prohibits only "unnecessary" abuses.

### L. Seabeds Disputes

There are a number of very important seabeds disputes questions still outstanding. These include the power of the Seabed Chamber or an arbitral tribunal to review any abuse of regulatory and discretionary powers of the Authority, access to arbitration as an alternative to the Seabed Disputes Chamber, and the composition and method of election of that Chamber. Since this session had a full slate both of dispute settlement and Committee I matters, these issues were not put on the agenda. They should be included among the hard-core issues on the agenda of the next session.

## VI. Committee III

### A. Summary and Conclusions

The attempt to resolve the outstanding issues in pollution and marine scientific research was an up-hill struggle. Many delegations consider that the negotiations on these subjects have been closed; while others which may support modifications often seek an even more restrictive science regime or less helpful pollution changes. Despite these odds, advances were made in securing important pollution objectives, although efforts to improve the science text have not yet been successful.

### B. Protection of the Marine Environment

The prevailing view that negotiations on this subject had been concluded during the last session was exemplified by the fact that it was not listed as one of the outstanding issues identified during the intersessional meeting. Ultimately the Plenary, acting on a proposal by the US, called for meetings of the Third Committee to examine further the subjects under its jurisdiction. Initial meetings of the Committee showed a significant opposition to further negotiations which might upset the "delicate balance" embodied in the ICNT.

However, many delegations shared France's view that the recent Brittany coast incident necessitated close scrutiny of the ICNT, in particular the article dealing with intervention following a maritime casualty. This examination ultimately led to support for US proposals which called upon States (acting through the competent international organization) to promote the establishment of tanker routing systems and which would require compliance with the new international standards providing for notice to the coastal State of incidents causing or likely to cause pollution.

The US Delegation was concerned that the duty of States not to impair innocent passage, when read in conjunction with the articles specifying that passage remained innocent except in cases of wilful and serious pollution, could result in an unintended limitation on the coastal State's power to set discharge standards. This concern was alleviated by acceptance of an amendment in Part XII, which clarified the

applicability of coastal State discharge standards to
vessels engaged in innocent passage.

Similarly, a US proposal identifying particularly
the need to protect habitats and fragile ecosystems
was readily accepted. A US proposal to include in the
definition article a statement that marine environment
included marine life encountered procedural difficulties but no substantive disagreement. The Chairman of
the Third Committee made an interpretive statement on
the record that it was the understanding of the Committee that the term "marine environment" includes
marine life.

Another amendment to the definition section, advanced by other delegations, resulted in the deletion
of a provision stating that the Convention does not
deal with disposal of wastes from seabed activities
or offshore processing of seabed mineral resources.
In fact, the Convention does deal with these activities.

Other proposed amendments were more controversial. The US had sought several changes in the article dealing with arrest powers in the proposed economic zone. Many considered this to be a crucial article, and there was significant opposition to any
modification of it. Nonetheless, agreement was reached that certain ambiguities should be removed. The
amended article now provides that a coastal State may
arrest a vessel in its economic zone where there is
clear objective evidence that a violation (no longer
must it be a "gross and flagrant" one) has resulted
in a discharge which causes major damage or threat of
damage. An effort to eliminate or further confine the
qualified right of the flag State to preempt prosecutions by the coastal State for economic zone violations encountered significant opposition. No agreement could be reached on modifying this article.

The ICNT provides that only monetary penalties
may be imposed for pollution violations beyond internal waters. The US proposed allowing any type of penalties for pollution violations in the territorial sea.
The US garnered significant support--but also significant opposition. Deadlock would have resulted in retention of the existing text. A compromise based on
the definition of innocent passage (Article 19) was
generally accepted which would permit penalties other

than monetary ones for acts of wilful and serious pollution in the territorial sea.

Most controversial were a French and a related American proposal which would encourage States to enter into agreements harmonizing port entry requirements. If there were such an agreement, a State party to it could take the necessary measures for ensuring that a foreign vessel entering the port of another State party to the agreement complied with the port entry requirement of the latter State. Accepted in place of this proposal was a compromise which allowed a participating State to inquire of a foreign vessel in its territorial sea whether it was heading to the port of another participating State. If it were not, no further action could be taken. If it were heading to a participating State port, the inquiring State could then seek to determine whether the vessel carried documents indicating compliance with the port entry requirements of that State.

In the report to the Plenary, the proposals dealing with enforcement powers in the economic zone, pooling of port entry competence, increased penalties for acts of serious and wilful pollution in the territorial sea, and clarification of the right of intervention following a maritime casualty, were characterized as offering a substantially improved prospect of consensus. The other amendments referred to were characterized as having obtained a consensus. Following debate in Plenary, it was no longer clear that the pooling of port entry requirements provision could be described as one which had substantially improved prospect for consensus. The pooling text opposition was based to a significant extent on misunderstanding of its legal effects and background.

The US Delegation stated in a formal Committee Three meeting that if the amendments discussed above were accepted by the Conference, the US would not insist on further changes in the text dealing with marine pollution.

## C. Marine Scientific Research

Only one meeting on marine scientific research was held during the session under Chairman Yankov. The US, in a very strong statement supported by the Netherlands and the Federal Republic of Germany, proposed returning to the marine science language

negotiated in the Castañeda group during the last session. Denmark, speaking for the European Economic Community (EEC), supported this but only in regard to dispute settlement (Article 265). The US proposal met strong opposition from the USSR and Eastern Europeans and approximately 35 developing countries (led by Brazil, Tanzania, Pakistan, and Peru). Despite repeated requests by the US Delegation, Chairman Yankov did not include the US views in his Plenary report at the sixth week.

The US continued to press its proposal to revert to the Castañeda text on science during the Committee III meeting in the seventh week. This time there was support from the EEC, Australia, New Zealand, Israel, and Mexico. Strong opposition came from Brazil, Uruguay, Pakistan, and Argentina. The USSR and Eastern Europeans did not address this issue, and many developing States who had voiced prior objections were not present.

The Chairman's Plenary report did include a statement that some delegations preferred the language negotiated during the last session. However, the Chairman concluded that the ICNT still represented a "balanced" compromise and did not suggest any amendments to it.

VII.  The Preamble and Final Clauses

The ICNT includes a preamble and also final clauses on the less controversial legal points. These are, or were intended to be, mere place-holders inserted to give the text completeness. Prior to the Seventh Session there had been no negotiation on these topics. It had been agreed, however, that detailed and serious consideration of these questions would be preceded by a formal, on-the-record Plenary debate which occurred at this session.

The most widely held view was that the debate was still premature. Many delegations felt that no resolution or even sensible discussion of the more delicate legal problems--reservations, provisional application, signature or accession by entities other than States, and the relation of the Convention to other treaties--would be possible until the substantive text of the Convention was in nearly final form.

Nevertheless, there were indications of the important controversies to come.

Some States advocated an extended or "complete" preamble. By this was meant reference to and endorsement of the New International Economic Order, the Common Heritage concept, and related "guiding principles." Other States favored a more concise preamble along the lines of the ICNT draft.

There was scant support for a liberal reservations policy. Some delegations proposed that reservations be permitted only for a limited number of specific articles. The LL/GDS and scattered delegations from other groups came out in favor of prohibiting all reservations.

The most spirited discussion was addressed to the question of who should be permitted to sign and become party to the Convention. New Zealand introduced a proposal, on its behalf and that of four other Pacific entities, which would allow certain non-self-governing territories to become Contracting Parties. This set the stage for the Trust Territories of the Pacific Islands to suggest its inclusion as a Party. Eastern European, Arab, and certain other G-77 States advocated national liberation movements as Parties. The US opposed on legal grounds the inclusion of national liberation movements in the Convention. The EEC made an argument for having the EEC itself become a Party as to its areas of competence. Support for this last proposition was almost evenly balanced against opposition.

The Conference took no clear decision on the next step in the consideration of the preamble and final clauses. It is the US position that the matter should be handled in as expeditious and non-political a fashion as possible, preferably through the Drafting Committee. A decision on this point may be expected at the next session.

SEVENTH SESSION (Resumed)
NEW YORK
August 21 - September 15, 1978

I. Summary

The Seventh Session of the Law of the Sea Conference resumed in New York on August 21 and concluded on September 15, 1978. Work began immediately
where it had left off in Geneva, with no procedural
or organizational debate.

A. Negotiating Groups

Despite limited facilities, all seven Negotiating Groups (NGs) on outstanding hard-core issues
established in Geneva were able to meet.

1. NG-1. System of exploration and exploitation and resource policy, taking note of the work of
the informal group of technical experts invited to
consider the technical problems associated with any
formula that might be used to limit production of minerals from the area. (Chairman, Frank Njenga, Kenya.)

2. NG-2. Financial Arrangements. (Chairman, Tommy Koh, Singapore.)

3. NG-3. Organs of Authority, their composition, powers, and function. (Committee I Chairman, Paul Engo, Cameroon.)

4. NG-4. *Right of access of landlocked
States and certain developing coastal States in a subregion or region to the living resources of the EEZ.

Right of access of LL/GDS to the living resources of the economic zone. Chairman, S. Nandan, Fiji)

5. NG-5. The question of settlement of disputes relating to the exercise of the sovereign
rights of coastal States in the EEZ. (Chairman,
Constantine Stavropoulos, Greece.)

6. NG-6. *definition of the outer limit of
the continental shelf and the question of Payments

---

* The first part of the item is the formulation required by the group of coastal States. The second
part of the item is the formulation required by the
group of landlocked and geographically disadvantaged
States.

and Contributions with respect to the continental shelf beyond 200 miles.

Definition of the outer limits of the continental shelf and the question of revenue sharing. (Committee II Chairman, Andres Aguilar, Venezuela.)

7. NG-7. Delimitation of maritime boundaries between adjacent and opposite States and settlement of disputes thereon. (Chairman, E.J. Manner, Finland.)

The Second and Third Committees, and the Third Committee Marine Pollution group under José Luis Vallarta of Mexico, also continued their work. Negotiating Groups 1, 2, 3, 6, and 7 met most frequently.

C. The session was characterized by hard work, a sober atmosphere, and uneven progress. Its results could be divided into four categories.

1. First, with respect to matters other than the hard-core issues assigned to the seven negotiating groups, the Conference made steady progress toward completion of the Convention.

-- While negotiations on deep seabed issues were all conducted in Negotiating Groups assigned outstanding hard-core issues, most of the progress made in these groups at the resumed Seventh Session does not, in fact, deal with the fundamental hard-core issues. The amendments reported by the Chairman of NG-1 regarding Annex II, and by the Chairman of NG-3 on Articles 160 to 163, may, taken as a whole, be regarded in some respects as steps that might command broader support. Leaving aside the basic issue of adopting financial arrangements that are compatible with economic deep seabed mining, constructive work was done in NG-2 toward establishing common perceptions of the means and criteria for resolving the problem.

-- The Second Committee completed the article-by-article review begun in Geneva of some 115 articles of the ICNT within its mandate that do not deal with issues assigned to one of the seven negotiating groups.

-- Progress was made in informal discussions regarding increased protection for whales and other cetaceans and marine mammals. If the cooperation and

225

attitudes demonstrated in these discussions continue,
a new and improved article on the subject may emerge
at the next session.

-- The Third Committee has reported a group
of amendments that strengthen and clarify the rights
of countries to protect their coasts and the marine
environment from the danger of pollution from ships.
They substantially improve the prospects for consensus on the pollution texts as a whole.

-- With a few exceptions, the initial reaction to the new US amendments on marine scientific
research in the Third Committee was constructive.
These amendments are designed to improve and clarify
the text without altering the basic jurisdictional
framework, in particular in the exclusive economic
zone. Other countries indicated that they were prepared to consider improvements and clarifications on
this basis. Nevertheless, considerable negotiation
will probably be required to produce agreed changes.

-- The Drafting Committee commenced the task
of harmonizing references and terminology in a complex series of texts drafted and negotiated by different individuals at different times in different contexts. In forming various Language Groups, it has
found a practical way to harmonize views and engage
the energies of interested delegations that are not
members of the Committee.

2. Second, the proposals made in Geneva for
resolving some outstanding hard-core issues seem to
be taking hold.

-- This is particularly true of the texts
produced by the Chairman of NG-4, which deal with issues affecting the fishing interests of a large number
of countries. While the meetings of NG-4 revealed
reservations regarding the texts reported in May at
the end of the Geneva meeting, the general view seemed to be that these texts were a significant step toward achieving a consensus on the issue.

-- The reservations to the texts produced
last May in NG-5 seem to be related to the reluctance
of some delegations to discuss proposals on other
matters. Nevertheless, it must be noted that the
progress made in both of these groups is fragile; the

delicate fabric of the texts could unravel under conflicting pressures for changes in those texts.

3.  Third, there are outstanding hard-core
issues that have not been resolved, but which seem to
be amenable to some generally acceptable solution in
a reasonable time, although the nature of the solution
is not yet entirely clear.

-- On the question of defining the outer
limit of the continental shelf where it extends beyond
200 miles, NG-6 saw little more than a repetition of
positions, with broadening of support for the "Irish
Formula." While all delegations have recognized for
some years that agreement on the continental margin
beyond 200 miles and the Irish Formula is linked to
the sharing of revenues from that area, informal conversations in New York seem to reveal a set of additional considerations that might similarly facilitate
the resolution of the problem. While the potential
for consensus on any particular set of proposals is
not clear, all concerned delegations now seem better
able to understand how various different priorities
might be accommodated. The matter may soon be ripe
for further informal discussion.

-- The question of delimitation of the economic zone and continental shelf between States with
opposite or adjacent coasts is essentially bilateral
in character. With Newtonian certainty, every substantive proposal to amend the ICNT articles met with
a counter-proposal to amend the ICNT articles. Delegations are increasingly recognizing, as the ICNT itself indicates, that no automatic rules are possible:
delimitation can be effected only by bilateral agreement on the substance directly or by using an agreed
third party procedure. Some progress is being made on
the latter question, in particular in connection with
distinctions between disputes arising before and after
the Convention enters into force.

4.  Finally, there are the outstanding deep
seabed issues for which no solution emerged and for
which no generally acceptable solutions seem to be
emerging yet.

-- While NG-1 did not go back over the articles produced in Geneva, the European Community warned
against regarding those texts as a basis of agreement,
and the United States indicated that it had substantive

reservations that would eventually need to be considered. Moreover, the new texts on Annex II do not resolve critical outstanding problems, including those
related to the selection of applicants under paragraph
5. Discussion of the question of applying the Annex
to the Enterprise was deferred until the Eighth Session, despite persistent efforts by the US delegation.

-- The long hours and hard work put in by
delegations in NG-2 in an atmosphere of good will and
common purpose all served to emphasize the difficulty
of arriving at a common agreement on the limit of financial obligations compatible with economic deep seabed mining. However, Ambassador Koh's draft contains
some interesting ideas worthy of further study, along
with some amounts and percentages that are too
onerous.

-- NG-3, with US concurrence, felt it best to
defer consideration of certain basic questions regarding the system of governance of the Seabed Authority,
including composition and voting in the Council and the
capacity of the majorities in the Assembly to nullify
protections afforded States in the treaty and in the
Council. NG-3 discussed the subsidiary Commissions
to be established and, on the positive side, the
Chairman's text makes clearer the advisory character
of these bodies.

Since the major issues to be resolved by the
various Committees and Negotiating Groups are of differing importance to different States, the session
suffered to some degree from attempts to encourage
and attempts to forestall procedural and substantive
linkages among different issues. This has added to
the inherent difficulties of resolving the issues,
perhaps unnecessarily, as it is clear that all major
outstanding problems must sooner or later be addressed and resolved if there is to be a Convention.

At the first meeting of the General Committee, and in a longer statement on the final day in
Plenary, the Chairman of the Group of 77, stating that
he was speaking on behalf of 119 delegation members of
the Group, urged the industrialized States to refrain
from enacting unilateral legislation on deep seabed
mining. The statement argues that such legislation
and mining violate international law and would seriously prejudice the prospects for agreement on a Law
of the Sea Convention and adversely affect other North-

South negotiations. Similar statements were made by
the Soviet and Chinese delegations and some others,
mostly developing countries. Referring to legislation passed by the House of Representatives and currently before the Senate, the US delegation stressed
that all States have the right to explore and exploit
deep seabed resources as freedoms of the high seas,
reiterated its commitment to negotiation of a Law of
the Sea Convention, noted the interim character of the
legislation, and explained the need for enactment of
such legislation lest an infant mining industry feel
compelled to abandon plans and investments looking toward mining several years hence, hopefully under a
treaty. Other industrialized and potential mining
States made similar statements. Canada dissociated
itself from the US statements in the General Committee.

By the end of the session, a sentiment that
the Conference cannot continue indefinitely at the
same slow pace began to take hold. As might be expected, some--particularly those whose primary background is in the drafting of resolutions rather than
the negotiation of treaties--saw voting as the eventual solution. Others would at least keep alive the
threat of voting next year if consensus procedures
are "abused." Few seemed willing to accept the idea
of two full sessions in 1979 without some indication
that "the end is in sight." The US and others warned
against rigid deadlines, noted that much work remains
to be done on deep seabed issues, but expressed willingness to join others in a renewed and intensified
effort in 1979.

The Conference decided to meet again for six
weeks in Geneva beginning March 19, 1979. It would
decide then whether to hold further meetings that
year, but budgetary and space arrangements will be
made to permit a second six-week session in New York
in the summer. Its goal will be revision of the ICNT,
at which point the question of "formalization" of the
revised text would be considered. This decision was
taken in a sober mood, with increasing numbers of delegations becoming aware of the real potential for
failure unless, in 1979, obstacles to agreement are
removed and new attitudes and approaches are found to
resolve seemingly intractable problems.

## II. Negotiating Group 1

### Summary

NG-1, chaired by Frank Njenga of Kenya, discussed paragraphs 1-5 and 8-11(a) of Annex II. The product of these discussions was a revised text of paragraphs 1-5 and 8-10,* distributed at the final session of NG-1 as the Chairman's personal draft. The Chairman made clear that the draft was not intended to have any official status and that he recognized the need for further discussion. There was little opportunity for substantive discussion of this new text.

The revised text is an improvement over the ICNT in certain respects; however, there was insufficient time at this resumed session to study in depth the core issues of paragraph 5 relating to the selection of applicants. Accordingly, Njenga's proposals contain few revisions in paragraph 5. The texts also do not address paragraph 6, concerning the relationship of Annex II to the Enterprise, on which discussion was deferred because of insufficient time. The US made clear the need to consider this question and the need for further substantial work on paragraph 5 if an acceptable, workable system is to be achieved.

### The Negotiations

On the core issue of paragraph 5 and the selection of applicants, the US and other industrialized countries suggested a number of revisions designed to clarify the right of access on both sides of the parallel system and to address the difficult questions of how the banking system (and other aspects of the regime) can operate most efficiently for both sides of the system. The US stressed the importance of further study to devise a workable plan under which qualified applicants (who have invested large sums of

---

* It should be noted that while the Chairman's revised texts contain the relevant paragraphs from NG-1/10/ Rev.1. from the Geneva Session concerning transfer of technology, it was decided at the first meeting of NG-1 of the Resumed Session that further discussion of these texts would be deferred until a later time. This decision was taken after the EC-9, the US, and others stated their reservations to the Geneva texts.

money) can have the necessary confidence of being
awarded a contract. Furthermore, in the case of competing applications either for the same area or because of the operation of a production limitation, the
US said that the process of selection among qualified
applicants must be made on the basis of well-defined
and objective criteria.

A number of developing countries, on the other
hand, expressed the view that the Authority should
have broad discretion in the selection of applicants.
The qualifications for applicants and the criteria for
their selection, therefore, should be left deliberately vague and open-ended to give the Authority this
discretion. Frequent references were made to delicate
compromises and the general preference for leaving
controversial questions to be negotiated in the contract rather than in the proposed LOS treaty.

The difficult issues in paragraph 5 were further
complicated by the discussion of a quota/anti-monopoly
provision. The US made clear that it could not accept
any provision which would deny a contract to an American citizen on the basis of his nationality and
pointed out other difficulties with this kind of
approach.

In addition to the core issue of selection of
applicants, the discussion of Annex II covered a wide
range of subjects, including title of minerals; prospecting, exploration, and exploitation; transfer of
data; and training of personnel of the Authority.
The industrialized countries, and the US in particular, sought a number of clarifications and modifications in the ICNT on these subjects. These changes
were designed to achieve a higher degree of precision
and certainty of a workable system for both State and
private miners and the Enterprise. In particular,
the US wanted to establish clear rules that recovery
of minerals in accordance with the Convention confers
title to the minerals, that the rights of prospectors,
including their exclusive right to proprietary data
prior to the award of a contract for exploration and
exploitation, would receive adequate protection, and
that the text would provide for well defined and inclusive criteria for the qualification of applicants.
The US also sought to clarify the relationship of
paragraphs 8 and 9 on the transfer of data and the
training of personnel of the Authority to other provisions concerning the transfer of technology, and to

more coherently define and limit the obligations of miners under these supplemental paragraphs. The changes to paragraph 10 were sought to achieve greater precision regarding the exclusive right to explore and exploit the area specified in the approved plan of work, and to clarify the relationship of this and other provisions of Annex II to the Enterprise.

Many of the changes suggested by the US drew criticism from developing countries who stated a strong preference for leaving these matters to the Authority to be negotiated as part of the awarding of contracts. The Chairman's draft text reflects a number of suggestions made by the US but not others. As the Chairman stated in his report, the draft revised text will require careful scrutiny, and it will need to be further discussed and revised. For this purpose, the US considers it to be a very useful first effort.

## III. Negotiating Group 2

### Summary

The NG-2 meetings on financial arrangements exposed widely varying assumptions on the part of developed and developing countries. Much discussion during the latter part of the session centered on a Norwegian payments proposal (which was more realistic than its predecessor but still unacceptable to the developed countries). At the end, Chairman Koh issued a paper with figures even less acceptable than those in the Norwegian proposal. Nonetheless, this proposal, which was partly based on an MIT model of the seabed mining industry, was an improvement over earlier proposals by other delegations.

### The Negotiations

NG-2 on financial arrangements was led by Ambassador Koh of Singapore, who also chaired the group during the Geneva portion of the Session. He did an admirable job of trying to compromise the often sharply worded differences between developed and developing countries on financial arrangements issues.

The atmosphere in NG-2 was constructive, but vast differences in assumptions between the developed and the developing countries surfaced frequently.

The developing countries, for example, assume that seabed mining will be profitable, whereas the developed countries are hopeful but uncertain about the economic viability of this new endeavor. This difference results in the developed countries emphasizing profit-sharing in financial arrangements, while the developing countries emphasize front-end loading.

Another working assumption of the G-77 is that the Enterprise will get much of its financing from payments by contractors. The developed countries, on the other hand, feel that the Enterprise should be financed with borrowing and subscriptions by States of refundable paid-in capital. These different assumptions lead to financial arrangements of different orders of magnitude.

The position of the G-77 with regard to national taxation is that it should play a secondary role to the assessments of the Authority. The position of the US is that its taxation is purely a domestic matter not properly negotiated in an international forum. Again, these different approaches lead to widely varying financial arrangements.

The G-77 assumes that nodules have some intrinsic worth which must be paid for by those who mine them. The developed countries feel that the worth of the nodules must be arrived at through rational means and suggest that the best way to do this is for the miners to pay a moderate royalty and to take the capital costs devoted to mining and divide them by the capital costs of an integrated operation in order to get the percentage of value added by the mining sector. The Authority's profit share would be based on this percentage of value added, which is referred to in NG-2 as the "attributable net proceeds." Such a method, of course, would only be necessary until a market for nodules developed, at which time the market price could be used.

The G-77 also assumes that contractors will not report their income honestly to the Authority for purposes of profit sharing. Because of this assumption, the G-77 has been demanding onerous accounting procedures which are unprecedented in general commercial practice. The developed countries, on the other hand, feel that profit sharing, which is currently the trend in financial arrangements between developed and developing countries, can be properly and honestly managed

according to generally accepted accounting procedures. The developed countries feel that the onerous accounting procedures suggested by the G-77 not only would not be any more effective than generally accepted accounting principles, but also would take an unjustifiably long time to negotiate.

The first two weeks in NG-2 were taken up with the above subjects, and not much progress was made. In the third week, Minister Evensen of Norway made a proposal, and the rest of the time was taken up mainly with the discussion of that plan, which consisted of the following:

-- an application fee of $500,000 with monies not used refundable to the contractor;

-- an annual fee of $1 million creditable against production charges after production begins;

-- a production charge of 2 percent of the gross proceeds for the first 10 years of the contract and 4 percent for the remaining years;

-- an attributable net proceeds figure of 40 percent;

-- profit sharing of 40 percent of that 40 percent for the first 10 years and 75 percent of that 40 percent for the remaining years of the contract;

-- a depreciation period of 10 years;

-- a contract period of 5 years for preparatory work and 25 years for production.

Along with this proposal for a mixed system of royalty and profit sharing, Minister Evensen also proposed a royalty-only system. That system would require the contractor to pay to the Authority 7.5 percent of his gross proceeds for the first 10 years of the contract and 13 percent thereafter.

Although considering Minister Evensen's proposal as a step forward from the one he made in Geneva, the US made it clear that it was not acceptable for the following reasons:

-- the annual fee of $1 million is not eco-
nomically justifiable and would act as a deterrent to investment because it is a front-end
load unrelated to profit;

-- the royalty from the 11th year of the
contract forward is too high, especially in
view of the fact that it is unnecessary to
raise this charge at a time when substantial
profit-sharing payments will be coming onstream;

-- the attributable net proceeds figure is
too high, and it is not justified rationally.
Evensen himself stated that there was an element of "discretionary evaluation" in that
figure; and

-- the flat rates for profit sharing are
not sufficiently gradated to differentiate
between marginal and highly profitable operations.

In replying to US criticisms of his proposal,
Evensen stated that in a political context like that
at the Conference, one could not be too strictly logical. The US replied that financial arrangements
was an area not easily susceptible to political compromise because of the underlying economic realities
which must be recognized.

The Dutch delegation also put forward a proposal.
Only one aspect of this proposal received extended
comment: a so-called "safeguard" clause, which would
protect a contractor if his rate of return sank below
certain levels. The G-77 wanted this safeguard to be
applied to protect the Authority as well as the contractor. The US position was that a safeguard clause
was unnecessary if, as the US suggests, a system of
variable rates of profit-sharing is used. With such a
system, the Authority would receive high payments in
profitable times, and the contractor would not have to
pay much in times of low profit.

One other point which received attention was the
idea of reviewing various financial payments from time
to time. The G-77 favored review of every type of
payment made by the contractor. The US argued that
this would take away the stability which an investor
must be able to count upon before risking capital.

The US further argued that with a system based on variable rates of profit sharing, review was not necessary because the system was self-adjusting.

At the very end of the session, Ambassador Koh published a new paper on financial arrangements which somewhat revised his Geneva text and which contained the following figures:

-- a $500,000 application fee with portions not used by the Authority refundable to the applicant;

-- an annual fixed fee of $1 million which is creditable against royalty payments after production begins;

-- a royalty-only system with royalties of 7.5 percent for years 1-6; 10 percent for years 7-12; and 14 percent for years 13-20;

-- for those who choose a mixed system of royalty plus profit-sharing, a royalty of 2 percent for years 1-5; 4 percent for years 6-12; and 6 percent for years 13-20.

-- an attributable net proceeds figure of 40 percent;

-- profit-sharing percentages of 40 percent of that 40 percent for years 1-6; 70 percent of that 40 percent for years 7-12; and 80 percent of that 40 percent for years 13-20;

-- a so-called "safeguard" clause which would keep the contractor in the first stage of payments until he recoups his initial development costs and in the second stage of payments until he recoups double his original investment costs; and

-- a 15 percent rate of return if the baseline assumptions of the MIT model hold true.

The US believes that Ambassador Koh's report represents some progress because it leaves behind it some of the old financial-arrangements schemes which did not at all recognize the economic realities of seabed mining. Also, the report helps put the negotiation of financial arrangements on a rational basis

(with the help of such studies as that done by MIT), although the US believes that Ambassador Koh has leaned more heavily on the MIT figures than the authors of the MIT study say it is safe to do.

Although more logical than some previous financial-arrangements proposals, the US feels that some of the reasoning in the NG-2 report is questionable. For example, regarding the attributable net proceeds figure, the report states that it is logical to characterize transportation and processing (which make up 80% of the capital costs of an integrated seabed mining operation) as services for the mining sector, which make up only 20% of the capital costs. Truly, this is the tail wagging the dog.

By increasing profit-sharing and production charges based on the passage of time rather than on differences in rate of return, Ambassador Koh is assuming that a seabed-mining operation will get more profitable as time goes on. This may or may not be the case.

In moving away from variable rates of profit sharing based on rates of return, Ambassador Koh states that these raise accounting difficulties. It seems questionable, however, how much more severe they are than the accounting problems caused under his system.

The US does not believe that the annual fixed fee in the new text can be justified economically. Seabed miners, whose investment is hundreds of millions of dollars, do not need the incentive of an annual fee to make them diligent.

Finally, it is misleading to state, as Ambassador Koh does, that his proposal produces an internal rate of return of 15%. Fifteen percent is only the baseline case of the MIT study, and even the authors of that model have said that it is but one of many possibilities. The uncertainties are so great that there is no way to predict with confidence any rate of return. It is entirely possible that the charges suggested by Ambassador Koh would cause seabed miners to go bankrupt to the detriment of the common heritage of mankind.

The only way to avoid this undesirable situation is to lessen the front-end loading and the payments

required without regard to profitability and to put
emphasis on a self-adjusting system of profit sharing.
Such a system would be a safeguard clause in and of
itself, because the Authority would share heavily in
times of high profitability, while the contractor
would not be threatened with bankruptcy in bad
times.

## IV. Negotiating Group 3

### Summary

NG-3, led by First Committee Chairman Paul Engo, considered the subsidiary organs of the Council (Articles 161 to 164) and their relation to the Council (Article 160). Discussions in NG-3 and in a small informal group (which met on four occasions) centered on the number of Commissions which should be established, whether the Commissions should be advisory or executive bodies, and whether a Commission member should be a representative of a State or, insofar as possible, an independent expert. Revised Articles 160-163 were issued by the Chairman in the light of suggestions made in NG-3. Although the revisions of the ICNT are extensive and certain functions of the Commissions have been shifted, there is little substantial difference between the revised text and the ICNT. On the positive side, the new text more clearly establishes the Commissions as advisory bodies of experts. On the negative side, the important role of the Technical Commission in environmental matters has been de-emphasized.

### The Negotiations

The subject of the composition of the Commissions was the most contentious issue. Some contended that the Commissions were political bodies and that the text should clearly show and emphasize that members were representatives of States. Others, including the US, maintained that members should be experts in the relevant field of competence. Article 161 of the revised text provides for members elected by the Council having appropriate qualifications and experience. Articles 162 and 163 list illustrative qualifications. Article 161 provides that in electing members due regard shall be paid to the need for equitable geographic distribution and representation of special interests. No State may have more than one of its nationals as a member of a Commission.

It was determined that the Commissions should be advisory bodies. Accordingly, functions which were considered executive in nature were deleted from Articles 163 and added to powers and functions of the Council in Article 160(2), subparagraphs (xix) to (xxii) and (xxiv). These powers are: initiation of proceedings before the Seabed Disputes Chamber (xix);

initiation of proposals to implement decisions of the
Seabed Disputes Chamber (xx); issuance of emergency
orders to suspend mining operations for protection of
the marine environment (xxi); disapproval of areas
for exploitation to protect the marine environment
(xxii); and directing and supervising a staff of inspectors (xxiv).

The Chairman had suggested that in the interest
of economy, consideration be given to eliminating one
Commission and adding its functions to the remaining
two Commissions. Several delegations, including the
US, suggested elimination of the Rules and Regulations Commission and permitting each Commission to
draft rules and regulations within its jurisdictional
mandate. It was also suggested that responsibility
for financial matters be shifted from the Technical
Commission to the Economic Planning Commission to
balance the work of the Commissions, particularly in
view of the similarity in expertise needed for economic and financial matters. Several developing countries objected to any change in the function of the
Economic Planning Commission, as this Commission was
a specialized group whose attention should not be di-
verted from its principal duty. Some suggested that
a Finance Commission should be established. The revised text leaves the Economic Planning Commission
substantially the same as in the ICNT. The name of
the Technical Commission was changed to the Legal and
Technical Commission, and functions of the Rules and
Regulations Commission were added. Responsibility for
financial rules, regulations, and procedures was removed from the Technical Commission, and the Council
is charged in Article 160(2)(xxiii) to establish a
Commission responsible for financial functions.

Several developing countries attempted to open
debate on Article 160(2)(x), but the developed States
considered this inappropriate in a consideration of
the subsidiary organs and noted their opposition to
any change in the provision. The US indicated that
any change would be unacceptable. The Chairman's revised text made no change in this provision, and his
report noted that no negotiation of Article 160(2)(i)
- (xviii) had taken place.

The US repeatedly sought to focus attention on
environmental functions of the Technical Commission.
The US received little support for its proposals

which would have more clearly set forth environmental
responsibilities and emphasized the important and
continuing duty to monitor, assess, and recommend appropriate action to protect the marine environment.
These proposals are not reflected in the revised text.

## V.  Committee II

The work of Committee II during the New York
phase of the Seventh Session was organized along lines
established during the first phase in Geneva.   Three
Negotiating Groups, previously established, were continued.   NG-4, chaired by Ambassador Nandan of Fiji,
held two meetings on the subject of access by landlocked and geographically disadvantaged States to the
living resources of the economic zones of their regions.   NG-6, chaired by Ambassador Aguilar of Venezuela, met six times to discuss the definition of the
outer limit of the continental margin and revenue
sharing.   NG-7, chaired by Judge Manner of Finland,
held seven meetings on the subject of delimitation of
maritime boundaries between opposite and adjacent
States.   In addition, Committee II, in informal sessions, met five times to complete an article-by-article discussion of those items of interest to one or
more States not included in the scope of work of any
of the negotiating groups.

## VI.  Negotiating Group 4

The Chairman of NG-4, in consultation with the
coordinators of the Landlocked and Geographically Disadvantaged States Group (LL/GDS) and the Coastal
States Group, proposed at its first meeting that consideration of the Chairman's proposal from Geneva (NG-
4/9/Rev.2) with respect to suggested forms of Articles
62, 69, and 70, be postponed to permit other issues
before the Conference to reach the same level of progress.   Accordingly, substantive work was deferred.   At
the second meeting, the exchange of views made clear
that, while many delegations on both sides of the issue had reservations or even objections to parts of
the compromise formula, that text provided a sound
basis for future negotiations directed at further improvements.   NG-4/9/Rev.2 represents a substantial
step toward consensus, and it was recognized implicit-
ly that there is a possibility of unravelling the
progress made, leaving the pertinent articles of the

ICNT as drafted.  Some States urged that the work of
NG-4 should not be further delayed but begun as early
as possible in a future session, without regard to
progress in other forums.  Others saw a direct tie
between the NG-4 work and that on other issues.

## VII.  Negotiating Group 6

The Negotiating Group set up under the Second
Committee continued to deal with the problems of the
definition of the outer limits of the continental
margin and revenue-sharing beyond 200 nautical miles.
NG-6 continued to view the definition contained in
Article 76 of the ICNT as lacking in precision.  As
alternatives to this article, three formulas remain
on the table.

The Arab Group maintained the position that the
continental margin should be subsumed by the economic
zone, and thus the outer limit should be 200 nautical
miles.

The Soviet formula would permit coastal State
jurisdiction over the margin, where it extended beyond
200 miles, to a maximum additional distance of 100
miles if such extension is justified by sound geological or geomorphological evidence.

The Irish formula suggests that jurisdiction
might extend to 60 miles beyond the foot of the slope
or, alternatively, to a distance where the depth of
sediments is at least one percent of the distance between that point and the foot of the slope.

Discussions in the negotiating group elicited no
new ideas, nor were there many shifts in position.
The Soviet formula was supported by the Eastern Europeans countries and by Cuba and Haiti.  The already
widespread support for the Irish formula gained additional strength from States in all regions and could
form the basis for consensus after discussion of
revenue-sharing.

The question of revenue-sharing was touched upon
briefly in the closing hours.  The US reiterated its
views on this subject in support of the general principle as part of an overall package that should be
acceptable to broad-margin States, the LL/GDS, and
other States.  Several broad-margin States indicated

that they could consider modifications in the ICNT regarding revenue sharing as part of a package including
the Irish formula. This could form the basis for discussions at the Eighth Session.

The study proposed by the President in response
to a suggestion by Bulgaria, to examine and display
the implications of the Soviet proposal, was not completed during this session. Furthermore, the Intergovernmental Oceanographic Commission indicated that
it was having difficulty with the interpretation of
that formula and did not receive any adequate guidance.
Thus, it was not possible at this time to add a line
showing the formula on the existing Secretariat map.

## VIII. Negotiating Group 7

The consideration of the question of delimitation
between opposite and adjacent States was opened by the
chair posing three questions, to be examined in in-
verse order: (1) what criteria should be applied in
delimiting maritime boundaries; (2) what, if any,
interim measures should be effected pending final
resolution of such boundaries; (3) how should disputes
arising out of delimitation be dealt with?

The ICNT, Article 297(1)(a), contains an optional
exception of delimitation disputes from settlement
under the Convention, provided that regional or other
binding procedure is accepted instead. Since this
text was unacceptable to several delegations who wanted no compulsory settlement of such disputes, a small
informal private group was set up in Geneva under Professor L.B. Sohn (US) to consider various possible
models and variations in them. The group was able to
produce a survey consisting of seven compromise models
with some 15 variations.

At the beginning of the resumed session, Professor Sohn presented an annotated version of this sur-
vey--showing the use of the various models in existing international agreements--to the full negotiating
group. The three-day debate on this paper was encouraging. Twenty-eight delegations intervened and, without exception, did so in a positive way. Each found
at least one, and most found several of the models
worthy bases of further negotiation.

Those States who have, until now, been opposed to all compulsory settlement of maritime boundary questions tended to favor the models which exempted past disputes from compulsory process. Those who have wanted all boundary disputes subject to settlement tended to prefer models which inserted preliminary stages of non-binding decisions and further negotiations into the procedure.

On the basis of the debate Professor Sohn prepared two new models reflecting these trends and striking moderate positions on either side of the middle position. He reconvened the private expert group to work further on these, but some members of the group found the proposals unacceptable. Therefore, no new texts were circulated at this Session.

With respect to interim measures, NG-7 remained split between those who preferred such arrangements only by the voluntary agreement of the parties, and those who would apply the median or equidistant line for this purpose. No discernible movement was seen on either side. As a new element in the discussions, the question of a possible moratorium pending agreement, or for a specified time, received attention. The group was split on this question as well, but along different lines. It was clear, however, that the group could not agree on an imposed moratorium.

The core issue--the question of criteria to be applied in laying down boundaries, was addressed during one meeting. Again, the group was split between those preferring the application of equitable principles and those who would prefer the median line or equidistance approach. The debates confirmed once again that there is no consensus on the issue, although those favoring equitable principles continued to have broader support.


IX. Committee II Informal Meetings

Chairman Aguilar continued the exercise begun in Geneva to consider all those articles of the Committee II text of interest to one or more countries but not included within the scope of work of any negotiating group. Accordingly, informal suggestions were discussed, for Articles 73 bis, 73 ter, 86, 88, 90, 95, 98, 100, 109, 110, 111, 119, 120, 121, 122, and 124 to

132.  In addition, Peru suggested a reordering of
articles in the Committee II text.

Most of the proposed changes received little
support.  The most significant portions of the debates focused on the economic zone, islands, enclosed
and semi-enclosed seas, and marine mammals.

A Soviet proposal to delete Article 86, describing the scope of application of the high seas chapter
(a companion proposal to their previous suggestion regarding Article 55), received support only from the
Eastern European countries and was strongly opposed
by the Coastal States group.  Many countries were of
the view that there should be no further changes in
economic-zone-related articles.

A long debate over the status of islands focused
on two basic questions.  First, there was debate on a
proposal that there should be modification of the
status of zones surrounding islands where their geographical proximity to other land areas causes dis-
tortions.  The second focused on a suggestion to delete the paragraph to the effect that rocks which
cannot sustain human habitation or economic life of
their own shall have no economic zone or continental
shelf.  Neither of these suggestions received widespread support, and both received opposition.

The consideration of enclosed and semi-enclosed
seas was also lengthy and inconclusive.  Proposals
for change included a restriction of the article to
"small seas," and a modification of the regime in
such seas.  These were strongly opposed by many
States.

A US suggestion to clarify the conservation requirements under Article 65 for marine mammals received sympathetic attention.  In response to a request by one delegation, an informal consulting group
was established, and several suggestions were received for modification of the ICNT in this respect.  It
is expected that on the basis of these suggestions,
further meetings of this informal group will be held
next session with a view to modification of the
Article.

The conclusion of this article-by-article discussion lays to rest many issues.  Conclusion of this work
makes it possible to intensify work on the few remaining
hard-core issues.

## X.  Compulsory Settlement of Disputes

### Negotiating Group 5

NG-5 held one meeting during the resumed Seventh Session.  It was a procedural meeting, convened for the purpose of allowing delegations to "record" reservations to the compromise text negotiated at the Geneva part of the Session.  However, discussion expanded to the question of reopening the whole debate on settlement of economic zone fisheries disputes.  Chairman Stavropoulos (Greece) agreed to hold a meeting early in the Eighth Session to enable the group to deal with any matters before it.

## XI.  Committee III

### A.  Marine Pollution

The Chairman's report at the Geneva session divided proposals to modify the ICNT into three categories.  Category I dealt with articles on which consensus had been reached and included several clarifying amendments proposed by the US.  Category II, labeled compromise texts which offered an improved prospect for consensus, contained US amendments dealing with regional port entry requirements, enforcement in the economic zone and penalties in the territorial sea. Category III contained articles which, owing to lack of time or divided views, had not resulted in any compromise formulas.  The New York meeting reviewed Categories II and III.  Modifications of a non-substantive nature were made to proposals in Category II, and discussions of proposals in Category III produced compromise texts on some of these articles.

Following procedures used throughout the session, the individual proposals received a preliminary discussion at informal meetings of the Third Committee and then were referred to a small negotiating group. Following general agreement in the small group, the results were reported back to the Committee in informal sessions.  All proceedings were under the chairmanship of José Luis Vallarta of Mexico, whose serious and businesslike approach substantially contributed to the progress achieved.

The working paper containing the results of the negotiations was accepted by the Third Committee, and

246

the Chairman reported to the Plenary that compromise texts resulted from the negotiations in the Seventh Session which command a consensus or offer a substantially improved prospect of consensus.

A summary of the texts produced during the New York phase follows.

The US proposal relating to regional port-entry requirements was not altered from that set forth in the Geneva report. The enforcement rights of coastal States in the economic zone to cause proceedings, including the arrest of vessels where there is clear, objective evidence that a vessel has committed a violation in the economic zone resulting in discharge causing major damage or threat of major damage to the coastline and related interests of a coastal State or to any resources of its territorial sea or exclusive economic zone, was extensively discussed. It resulted in changing the word "arrest" to "detention." This revision followed discussions which reflected the understanding of the Committee that detention included delaying a vessel pending the issuance of an appropriate bond or other financial security. A conforming modification to Article 221(2) was also made. No substantive change was made to the proposal in the Geneva report that authorized other than monetary penalties for serious and willful acts of pollution in the territorial sea, but the proposal was redrafted.

In addition to the foregoing US proposals (which increase the effectiveness of the provisions dealing with the protection of the marine environment), coastal State inspection in the economic zone pursuant to Article 221(5) was clarified to permit inspection of vessels when there is a substantial discharge causing a threat of significant pollution, and the master has refused to supply information, or the information supplied is at variance with evident facts. The duty of a State in Article 211 to consult with States potentially affected by dumping activities under its control was modified by substituting "consideration of the matter with other States" for consultation with these States. The definition of dumping was amended by deleting the reference to incineration. In addition, Article 227 relating to release of foreign vessels was modified to strengthen the protection of flag States from unreasonable enforcement practices by ensuring prompt notification to flag States where release of a vessel has been refused or made conditional

247

along with a reference to the right to seek release in accordance with the dispute settlement articles.

In general, the American pollution initiative developed through the consultation between the US Congress and the Administration was favorably acted upon by the Conference, which responsibly considered these concerns.

At the conclusion of the session, Tanzania introduced additional amendments to the pollution part calling for: deletion of the article on flag-State preemption (Article 229); modification of the provision dealing with special areas; and a general amendment which would change the references in the ICNT from the competent "international organization" to competent "international organizations." Time did not permit extensive discussions, but several speakers found these proposals unacceptable. Tanzania and other delegations with proposals outstanding called for further discussions at future sessions of the Conference.

B. Marine Scientific Research

During the Geneva session, the US made clear its intent to submit amendments to the ICNT at the Resumed Session, and a set of proposed amendments was submitted on September 6, 1978. The amendments did not go to the fundamental juridical accommodation in the ICNT but rather were designed to clarify or improve the ICNT. Amendments were also included dealing with scientific research on the continental shelf beyond 200 miles--these amendments are designed to contribute not only to progress in Committee III but also in NG-6.

During this session only two informal meetings were devoted to marine scientific research. At the first meeting, the US amendments were introduced, and subsequent discussion focused upon reaction to them.

Virtually all delegations who spoke regarding these amendments did so in a preliminary manner and reserved detailed substantive comments for the Eighth Session of the Conference. The tone of the discussion was moderate with mostly constructive observations. The major researching States gave general support to the package, although all felt that the continental shelf amendments should not be dealt with outside the framework of NG-6, and that an article on dispute

settlement should be retained in the part dealing with
marine scientific research. Some delegations expressed general reservations about "reopening" in Committee
III fundamental issues such as coastal State rights
regarding scientific research in the economic zone and
dispute settlement.

Several delegations suggested that the US amendments fell into three categories: (1) stylistic and
drafting changes; (2) substantive amendments that do
not affect the fundamental character of the ICNT; and
(3) substantive amendments that alter the fundamental
character of the ICNT. Views differed widely on which
amendments fell into which category.

A few territorialists voiced extreme reservations
regarding any amendments to the ICNT and stated that
they would be prepared to submit amendments if the US
persisted in pursuing its proposals.

Discussion of the US amendments was incomplete.
The Chairman of Committee III in his final report
stated that there was a general view that marine
scientific research should be the subject of further
discussion at the next session.


XII.  Drafting Committee

The Drafting Committee met informally during the
resumed Seventh Session, with most of its efforts being devoted to consideration of a series of informal
papers prepared by the Secretariat. These papers attempted to highlight two problems of harmonization
common to the entire text:  internal references and
recurring expressions. No article-by-article review,
however, was attempted.

The preliminary work was handled by the formation
of informal groups in each of the six official languages. The groups were open-ended, and many States
not members of the Drafting Committee participated in
the deliberations. Generally, the individual Language
Group would study a paper, develop a general preference on each point raised, and report its results at a
Drafting Committee meeting. Each group selected a coordinator to chair the meeting and function as a liai-
son with the other teams. The Language Group Coordinators are Syria (Arabic), China (Chinese), USA (English), Italy (French), the USSR (Russian), and Spain

(Spanish). (France is not a member of the Drafting Committee.)

The Drafting Committee reached preliminary conclusions on Informal Paper 1, dealing with internal references. The Language Groups met through their coordinators in the final week, and exchanged reports detailing the progress achieved on Informal Paper 2, dealing with recurring phrases and clauses. The understanding was that Committee work will resume at this point in the next session on both Informal Paper 2 and its addendum.

The Drafting Committee has also solicited the assistance of the Secretariat to reproduce the text of the ICNT with articles in all six languages side-by-side. This would facilitate the comparison of parallel texts to evaluate proposed technical adjustments. It is hoped this document will be ready for distribution during the intersessional period.

Given the informal nature of Conference procedures and texts and the central role of consensus in the adoption of any text, it is considered useful for the Drafting Committee to do at least some of its work prior to the emergence of definitive substantive texts. At that point resistance to any change might be severe, and the possibilities for correction of substantive difficulties by the appropriate substantive Committee reduced. Moreover, since the Drafting Committee may be called upon to work very quickly at some future stage, the development of effective working tools, procedures, and relationships in advance is useful.

EIGHTH SESSION
GENEVA
March 19 - April 27, 1979

I. Summary and Overview

The Eighth Session of the Law of the Sea Conference met in Geneva from March 19 to April 27, 1979.
Substantive work began on the first day; as previously agreed, initial work was concentrated on Committee
I (deep seabed) issues. The Group of 77 (G-77) presented a statement on the first day challenging the
legality of any unilateral deep seabed mining, with
which the US Delegation naturally disagreed.

Consistent with the widely shared aim of completing substantive negotiations in 1979, the most active
developing and developed country representatives demonstrated a seriousness of purpose throughout the session. Nevertheless, some of the former were tempted
at times to reopen settled issues and indulge in ideological debate. While the leadership of the G-77 was
eventually successful in containing these problems,
more progress might have been made had they not arisen.

Negotiating Groups

Negotiations continued in the seven Negotiating
Groups (NGs) established at the Seventh Session, each
assigned one of the identified outstanding hard-core
issues (chairmen in parentheses):

1. NG-1. System of exploration and exploitation and resource policy. (Frank Njenga, Kenya)

2. NG-2. Financial arrangements. (Tommy
Koh, Singapore)

3. NG-3. Organs of the Authority, their
composition, powers, and function. (Committee I
Chairman, Paul Engo, Cameroon)

4. NG-4. *Right of access of landlocked
States and certain developing coastal States in a

_____

* The first part of the items is the formulation required by the group of coastal States; the second part
of the item is the formulation required by the group
of landlocked and geographically disadvantaged
States.

252

subregion or region to the living resources of the exclusive economic zone.

Rights of access of landlocked and geographically disadvantaged States to the living resources
of the economic zone. (Satya Nandan, Fiji)

5. NG-5. The question of settlement of disputes relating to the exercise of the sovereign rights
of coastal States in the exclusive economic zone.
(Constantine Stavropoulos, Greece)

6. NG-6. *Definition of the outer limit of
the continental shelf and the question of payments and
contributions with respect to the continental shelf
beyond 200 miles.

Definition of the outer limits of the continental shelf and the question of revenue sharing.
(Committee II Chairman, Andres Aguilar, Venezuela)

7. NG-7. Delimitation of maritime boundaries between adjacent and opposite states and settlement of disputes thereon. (E.J. Manner, Finland)

8. In addition, a Working Group of 21 was
charged with issues not yet resolved in NGs 1, 2, and
3; and other small groups were formed to consider certain discrete questions (see below).

It was decided on the final day to formally resume the Eighth Session in New York on July 19. The
G-77 and other groups will caucus July 16-18, and the
resumed session will end on August 24. On the basis
of debate in Plenary on new texts, agreement was
reached by the officers of the Conference to issue a
revision of the Informal Composite Negotiating Text
(ICNT/Rev.1) containing new negotiating texts on various deep seabed issues, the definition of the continental shelf, protection and preservation of the
marine environment, access of landlocked and geographically disadvantaged States to surplus fisheries in
the economic zones of coastal States of the region,

---

* The first part of the items is the formulation required by the group of coastal States; the second part
of the item is the formulation required by the group
of landlocked and geographically disadvantaged States.

conciliation with respect to certain disputes regarding conservation of living resources of the economic
zone, and management of anadromous species (salmon).

The new texts in effect represent completion of
the informal work of Committee III with respect to
protection and preservation of the marine environment
and related transfer of technology issues and of the
informal work of NG-4 and NG-5. The new texts also
represent substantial progress in the work of NG-1
and NG-2, although considerable work remains to be
done. While some progress was made in NG-3, the difficult and pivotal issue of composition of and voting
in the Council remains unsolved.

The new text issued for NG-6 has some serious de-
ficiencies, the most important of which is that it
does not deal with the problem of restrictions on marine scientific research on the continental shelf beyond 200 miles. Similarly, the work of Committee III
on marine scientific research remains to be completed.
In both cases that work relates to US proposed amendments regarding marine scientific research.

No agreement was reached in NG-7. A new text
strengthening protection for marine mammals is near-
ing completion. Little time was available for the
Informal Plenary on settlement of disputes, and none
on final articles. The Drafting Committee and its
Linguistic Groups accelerated their work.

In sum, the new text is a substantial further
step toward final agreement. Its major defects result from the fact that important outstanding issues
either were not addressed or were not completely resolved, rather than from any serious overall defects
in most of the new provisions. It remains uncertain
whether the resumed session can successfully complete
negotiation of these issues. Although NG-7 is still
deadlocked, the proposal on the limits of the continental shelf requires further work, and the critical
issue of final clauses has been addressed only super-
ficially, most of the remaining substantive negotiation in the Conference relates to deep seabed mining
and marine scientific research.

In the texts dealing with deep seabed mining,
more than 20 significant improvements have been made.
Perhaps five changes have been for the worse. For
the first time there is a satisfactory foundation on

which to build assurance of access to seabed minerals. Qualification standards for applicants are limited to financial and technical competence and performance under prior contracts. All plans of work proposed by all qualified applicants must be approved, except as limited by the production ceiling. There was some improvement in deep seabed dispute settlement provisions particularly as they relate to the question of fair and reasonable commercial terms and conditions for transfer of technology. Some of the proposed improvements in seabed mining environmental provisions were incorporated into the new text. There was some important tightening of the criteria for eligibility on the Council of seabed-mining States and of consumers and net importers of metals produced on the seabeds which should help ensure that the members of the Council in these categories will, in fact, represent those interests.

It was clear throughout the session that the overriding concern of the developing countries regarding the deep seabed mining text is that the Enterprise will not be a viable institution in reality. The question of how best to accommodate this concern affects many of the remaining issues. Among the more important outstanding problems are the following:

-- A politicized provision authorizing the proposed International Seabed Authority to share the financial benefits of mining with peoples who have not yet attained independence;

-- Remaining troublesome provisions on transfer of technology;

-- The question of contractor selection when production limitations force such selection, and the problems created by the efforts of some developing countries to accord absolute priority to the Enterprise over other applicants;

-- The unreasonably high financial burdens on contractors;

-- Unrealistic provisions regarding governmental contributions to the Enterprise;

-- Defects remaining in the production limitations provisions;

-- The problem of permitting a moratorium on private mining if the review conference (convened after 25 years) cannot agree on a new regime;

-- The pivotal issue of composition of and voting in the Council of the proposed Authority.

With respect to marine scientific research, the main substantive problem relates to the requirement of coastal State consent for the conduct of marine scientific research in the vast areas where the continental shelf extends beyond 200 nautical miles from the coast, particularly in light of the fact that resource development in most of those areas is unlikely for decades to come. In addition, despite several constructive meetings among concerned heads of delegations convened by the US, it was not possible to arrange serious negotiation on various clarifying and technical amendments to the text regarding scientific research in the exclusive economic zone and exceptions to dispute settlement, although the revised versions of the US amendments on many of these points seemed to be widely regarded by most coastal States as ultimately acceptable. There was no disagreement expressed in Plenary with the conclusion of the President and the Chairman of Committee III that further work is necessary on marine scientific research at the next session and that sufficient time should be allotted for such work.

Perhaps the principal benefit attaching to the issuance of the new text is the inclusion of the revised articles on protection and preservation of the marine environment. It was agreed in Plenary that informal negotiations of Committee III on this matter are concluded. While the 1958 Conventions on the Law of the Sea are virtually silent on environmental questions, the new text contains some 50 articles reflecting major developments in international environmental law. They are particularly important from the perspective of ensuring that global environmental problems are addressed by universal rules. They are equally important from the perspective of ensuring that navigation is not subject to a patch-quilt of inconsistent--and consequently costly--nationally imposed regimes. These texts give port and coastal States important new powers that put teeth into a system of international environmental standards, creating incentives for respecting them and disincentives for disobeying them.

Aside from deep seabed issues, the question of the definition of the outer limit of the continental shelf where it extends beyond 200 miles from the coast received the most attention. Three related matters were discussed: limits on the seaward extension of continental shelf jurisdiction of the coastal State under the "Irish Formula" presented at earlier sessions; marine scientific research on the continental shelf beyond 200 miles; and installations and high seas freedoms. The new text defines the continental shelf in terms of the "Irish Formula" but provides that it cannot extend beyond 350 nautical miles from the coast or 100 nautical miles from the 2,500-meter isobath, whichever is further seaward. It also provides that the exercise of coastal State rights over the continental shelf must not infringe upon or result in unjustifiable interference with navigation and other high seas freedoms. No change was made in the article dealing with artificial islands and installations. While no new text was presented on marine scientific research, the Chairman of Committee II said it was clear that final acceptability of the texts he presented would depend upon resolution of the scientific research question; and he stressed that it should be understood as part of his report that Committee III would resolve the question of marine scientific research on the continental shelf to the satisfaction of all concerned States at the earliest possible time.

One of the most promising, although ultimately somewhat disappointing, procedural developments at the Conference was the proposal of the G-77 to establish a Working Group on seabeds questions of 21 delegations (WG-21), consisting of ten developing countries, ten industrialized countries, and China. Alternates were added, and it became impossible to limit the number of persons present to a size conducive to negotiation. Moreover, the representatives of the G-77 found it impossible to avoid reopening matters that had already been tentatively resolved in the negotiating groups. Nevertheless, what eventually became an open-ended negotiating group did provide a useful procedural vehicle for the Chairmen of NGs 1, 2, and 3 to test ideas and propose texts. There is reason to hope that WG-21 will work better in the future if it can become less formal and meet without an audience of other delegates. NGs 1, 2, and 3 also continue in existence.

It should also be noted that the Chairman of Committee I established a group of legal experts to work on the important problem of settlement of disputes with respect to the deep seabed, including procedures for commercial arbitration. Similarly, a group of technical experts is working usefully but slowly on the question of production limitation. The emergence of smaller groups on matters requiring particular expertise is but one of the numerous signs of the seriousness with which participants approached this session.

## II. Committee I

### A. Overview

The first two weeks of the Eighth Session concentrated on matters relating to the system of exploration and exploitation of the minerals derived from the deep seabed (NG-1, Chairman Njenga of Kenya). Financial arrangements (NG-2, Chairman Koh of Singapore), and the organs of the Authority (NG-3, Chairman Engo of Cameroon) also were discussed during that period but more intensively during the third and part of the fourth week, when Njenga was absent in Kenya. A group of legal experts was also created to consider the issue of settlement of disputes relating to seabed matters, as was an expert group on the question of the production limitation.

The reports of the Chairmen of the three NGs and the two expert groups were considered in WG-21, representing ten States from developed countries, and ten from developing countries, and China. The group was created in response to the desire of a number of delegations to discuss pending issues in a smaller forum. The reports were then considered in Committee I and reported to the Plenary by the Chairman of Committee I in the form of document WG-21/1. After consideration of Engo's report and some discussion in Plenary, the texts in WG-21/1 were included in a revision of the ICNT, not as representing consensus but as offering an improved basis for further negotiation. The NGs of Committee I and WG-21 remain in being and will all continue to function at the resumed session in New York.

B.  NG-1 Matters -- System of Exploration and
Exploitation

Summary and Conclusions

NG-1 continued the work begun at the Seventh Session on the system of exploration and exploitation,
and new texts were presented on Article 140 (the sharing of the benefits of the resources of the Area); Article 143 (marine scientific research); Article 150
(policies relating to activities in the Area); Article 150 ter (non-discrimination); and Annex II provisions relating to the operation of the system of exploration and exploitation, including the most difficult issues of transfer of technology, the process of
selection from among applicants for a contract to exploit the resources of the Area, and the applicability of the provisions of the Annex to the Enterprise.

These texts were further discussed in WG-21 and
Committee I and were presented to the Plenary in WG-21
/1 as part of a revised Part XI of the ICNT. Under
the applicable Conference procedures, these texts were
not put forward as representing consensus but rather
are considered to offer a substantially improved prospect for achieving consensus. In fact, some of the
texts do bring the Conference significantly closer to
consensus while others do not advance the Conference
over the texts produced at the Seventh Session.

From the standpoint of US interests, almost all
of the texts are an improvement over the ICNT. Some
of the texts are significant improvements over those
produced at the Seventh Session. These include transfer of technology, in which the obligation on the contractor is now contingent upon the non-availability of
the technology on the open market, and revisions in
Annex II, clarifying and setting forth objective criteria for the qualification of and selection from
among applicants for a contract of exploration and exploitation of the resources of the Area. Satisfactory
results were also achieved in clarifying the applicability to the Enterprise of relevant provision of the
Convention, Annex II, and the rules, regulations, and
procedures of the Authority.

On the other hand, the difficult problem of the
clause was not advanced beyond its consideration by
the Seventh Session, and the present text thus permits
the imposition of a moratorium on mining if a Review

Conference convened 20 years after approval of the first contract or plan of work does not, within five years, produce agreement on continuation of the system in the Treaty. Also inserted was a provision giving preference to the Enterprise over private contractors in the event of conflict with other applicants under the production limitation. Moreover, further work is needed to resolve the issue of the Enterprise as a commercial competitor.

The US Delegation restated on a number of occasions its commitment to making the parallel system of access to seabed minerals viable both for States Parties and entities sponsored by them on the one hand, and for the Enterprise, as the operating arm of the International Seabed Authority, on the other. Positions taken by developing countries, however, continued to reflect their apprehensions concerning the parallel system and the successful operation under it of the Enterprise as a self-sustaining operator of integrated mining projects. The process of building understanding toward resolution of these difficult issues takes time, but the revised texts advance the Conference closer to the goal of a mutually acceptable seabed regime.

## The Revised Texts

A summary of the most significant provisions of WG-21/1 relating to NG-1 matters follows:

Sharing of Benefits from the Area. No significant changes were made in Article 140 during the Eighth Session, but the Seventh Session created an unresolved problem of possible distribution of benefits from the resources of the Area to other than States Parties, including peoples who have not yet gained independence, thus placing an unacceptably dangerous political burden on the Authority.

Marine Scientific Research. The revision of Article 143 contains major clarifications, making the role of the Authority one of coordinating dissemination of the available results of marine scientific research rather than one of coordinating the conduct of the research itself, and WG-21 further clarifies the right of States Parties to conduct such research in the Area. The article should now be non-controversial.

Policies Relating to Activities in the Area.  A
few drafting improvements have been made over the
Seventh Session texts in ICNT Articles 150 and 151
(revised Articles 150 and 153), although other drafting problems remain.

Production Policies.  The production control and
the related issue of Authority membership in International Commodity Agreements (Article 150 bis, revised Article 151) were considered by the "Nandan
Group" (chaired by Ambassador Satya Nandan of Fiji).
The group was formed by NG-1 Chairman Njenga and began
by meeting informally with over 25 delegations present.  It was then cut to a nucleus of 10 delegations
(Canada, Chile, Cuba, Indonesia, Australia, US, UK,
France, the Federal Republic of Germany, and Japan).
It was hoped that the smaller group could speak frank-
ly and expedite progress toward the "substantial improvements" the US Delegation and delegations of other
major consumers sought.

At the outset, consumer countries made available
a paper with a list of seven issues needing improvements and a redraft of Article 150 bis incorporating
the desired changes.  Several delegations were initially skeptical about the feasibility of progress.
Nevertheless, reasonably frank and useful discussions
proceeded to the point where the Chairman requested
that the delegations try to resolve some of the outstanding issues in private consultations outside the
Nandan Group meetings.

In these private consultations, several delegations discussed possible drafts.  The two issues considered first were "flexibility" and the "four metals
problem."  Briefly, "flexibility" refers to making explicit in the Treaty text the right of each minesite
operator in the Area to produce amounts approximating
his approved plan of work.  The "four metals" problem
(originally raised by Chile) results from the fear of
producers of metals other than nickel that seabed
miners could effectively exceed the intent of the production control by stockpiling or not recovering nickel and marketing other metals obtainable from manganese nodules.  This possibility is considered extremely remote by the US Delegation for economic reasons.
Nonetheless, to meet the concerns of several land-
based producers (chiefly copper and cobalt producers)
and to show good faith in the face of a forthcoming
land-based producer position on flexibility, the

consumers expressed readiness to consider drafts on
the four-metals problem.

At a deliberate pace, the Nandan Group went on to
consider other lesser issues before tackling three of
the most critical issues in Article 150 bis:  (1) the
land-based producers' desire to explicitly link the
Review Conference to the production control; (2) the
consumers' desire to improve the 60/40 split; and
(3) the consumers' attempt to have a "floor" or minimum growth rate under the ceiling.  No significant
progress was made on increasing the split or obtaining
downside protection (a "floor") although the concerns
of the consumers were clearly expressed.

Nandan's report is a conservative chairman's
summary of the little progress that was made and
presumably will form the basis for discussion of new
Article 151 at the Resumed Eighth Session.  It notes
that the group was able to reach agreement on a few
issues.  However, the two most critical issues remain.
These are improvement in the 60/40 split (to increase
benefits in periods of high growth rates) and downside protection against low growth rates (to avoid a
cut-off in access).  These issues proved difficult
even to approach.

The 60/40 split has almost become a political
slogan among land-based producers that will inevitably
be difficult to change.  We have pointed out that improvement would do little of a substantive nature to
hurt their position and would help consumers.  Downside protection, or protection of seabed miners' access to manganese nodules in extended periods of low
growth rates in the nickel market, will also prove
difficult to obtain.  We believe a method of protecting our access may be found that is more acceptable to
the land-based producers and also gives us sufficient
protection.  Discussion of other means is just beginning, and serious negotiations will have to continue
in the Resumed Eighth Session.

Attached to the end of the Nandan report is a
list of drafts which will serve as a basis for future
negotiation.  These concern the following issues:
flexibility, timing of Review Conference, four metals,
and using only ongoing production for the production
ceiling.

In addition to the foregoing, it should be noted that Article 151 in the revised text still does not contain changes sought by the US to make clear that the Authority's participation in commodity agreements will be limited to those in which all major producers and consumers participate. This issue will also have to be addressed at a later date.

The Review Conference. Article 153, paragraph 6 (new Article 155(6)) remains at an impasse in its perpetuation of the text as revised during the Seventh Session. The US Delegation made clear during the Eighth Session the unacceptability of a provision which could cut off access of countries needing the minerals to be derived from seabed resources at precisely the time in the future when these minerals are most likely to be needed. The G-77 continues to take the position that the parallel system must be a temporary one unless there is agreement at the Review Conference to continue it. We suggested a possible solution of a 25-year seabed regime, but this received no response from the members of the G-77.

Title to Minerals. The text of paragraph 1 of Annex II (revised Article 1) on title to minerals upon recovery was simplified and clarified during the Eighth Session. While the wording could still be improved, a number of ambiguities were removed.

Prospecting. Paragraph 2 (revised Article 2) of Annex II concerning prospecting was improved by clarifying the prospector's right to recover a reasonable amount of the resources of the Area as samples and by removing the requirement that the prospector transfer prospecting data to the Authority whether or not he applies for a contract of exploration and exploitation. A requirement for the prospector to train personnel of the Authority remains in the revised text despite strong US opposition to this provision. Another provision opposed by the US, permitting areas of the seabed to be closed to prospecting, also remains in the revised text.

Exploration and Exploitation. Paragraph 3 (revised Article 3) of Annex II concerning rights of exploration and exploitation still contains some drafting difficulties but generally improves and clarifies the previous texts particularly on the question of its applicability to the Enterprise.

Qualification of Applicants. Paragraph 4 (revised Article 4) of Annex II has been significantly improved to set forth objective criteria for qualifications of applicants for contracts. Qualification standards for applicants are limited to financial and technical competence and performance under prior contracts. These improvements, coupled with those requiring approval of all plans of work proposed by qualified applicants, except as limited by the production ceiling, provide for the first time a satisfactory foundation on which to build assurance of access to seabed minerals.

Transfer of Technology. Perhaps the most thorough discussion and most significant negotiation of NG-1 matters occurred on the provisions of Annex II dealing with the transfer of technology. During the Seventh Session we had succeeded in eliminating transfer of technology as a condition of obtaining a contract, but its sale on fair and reasonable commercial terms and conditions remained as an obligation which might be invoked after the award of a contract. The term "technology" was not defined, and the obligation could be invoked regardless of whether the technology was available to the Enterprise from other sources. Provisions concerning settlement of disputes relating to the transfer of technology were imprecise and badly in need of improvement.

The revised provisions of Annex II relating to transfer of technology (former paragraph 4 bis, revised Article 5) clarify a number of previous ambiguities and convert the obligation to transfer technology into an insurance clause to be invoked only if the Enterprise cannot obtain the needed technology on the open market. Disputes over whether the offers of the contractor to sell, and the Enterprise to buy, the technology fall within the range of fair and reasonable commercial terms and conditions would be settled by commercial arbitration under the UNCITRAL Rules or such other rules as may be prescribed in the rules and regulations of the Authority. Technology is defined, in essence, as the equipment, and the know-how necessary to use it, required to recover nodules from the seabed (which would not include the manufacture of such technology), and the license of the technology is expressly non-exclusive in nature. A US Delegation paper (see p. 293) was circulated without comment from other delegations making clear the US view of the meaning of "fair and reasonable commercial terms and

conditions." An additional provision sought by the
United States to impose a time limit on the obligation
to transfer technology was not included in the revised
text, but will be included at a later time, it is
hoped. In the case of joint ventures with the Enterprise, the transfer of technology shall be governed
not by these provisions but by the terms of the
joint venture agreement.

The very strong desire of developing countries to
assure that processing technology is available to the
Enterprise is met in the revised texts by an obligation on States having access to such technology to
consult and take steps to see that the Enterprise ob-
tains such technology if it cannot obtain it on the
open market. The US and other developed countries
refused to accept any obligations by a contractor
with respect to processing technology. It was generally accepted on the basis of a report of a Secretariat expert that this technology should be readily
available on the open market. Provisions were also
included to assure that technology used but not owned
by the contractor would be made available to the Enterprise by the owner by restricting his future rights as a
supplier if he fails to make the technology available
to the Enterprise on fair and reasonable commercial terms
and conditions. Efforts by contractors to frustrate
this transfer through devices such as vesting owner-
ship of the technology in subsidiaries would be taken
into account in a contractor's application for a second contract. The objectionable clause in the texts
of the Seventh Session requiring similar transfer of
technology to developing countries for exploitation
of areas reserved to the Enterprise remains in the
text, but a provision has been inserted precluding
the further transfer of such technology to a third
country or nationals of a third country. The US reiterated its opposition in principle to this provision.

Approval of Plans of Work and Selection of
Applicants. Annex II provisions concerning approval
of plans of work and selection of applicants (former
paragraph 5 and 5 bis, revised Articles 6 and 7) set
forth more clearly than before the procedures and
standards to be followed in approval of plans of work,
providing for consideration of such plans of work in
the order received and for their approval by the
Authority provided they have been found to conform to
the rules, regulations, and procedures of the Authority. Exceptions are set forth for cases in which

there may be more than one application for the same
site (in which case the "first come, first served"
rule applies) and for cases in which the same State
Party has already submitted or sponsored three plans
of work within a certain specified area of the seabed
not reserved to the Enterprise or has submitted or
sponsored plans of work covering more than three percent of the total seabed not reserved to the Enterprise.

Where there must be a selection from among applicants because of the applicability of the production
ceiling, criteria are specified which give priority to
applicants who give better promise of performance and
benefit to the Authority. A provision giving the
Enterprise an apparently absolute priority (to exploit
the reserved areas) over other applicants in the event
of a conflict under the production limitation was inserted in the text despite strong objections from the
US and other industrialized countries. The US Delegation supported a relative priority in this case (as
one among several factors).

Reservation of Sites. Annex II concerning reservation of sites (former paragraph 5 tertius, revised
Article 8) clarifies the procedure for reservation to
the Enterprise of one of the two sites covered by the
application for a contract. The revised text, however,
contains an undesirable provision permitting the Authority to require the prospector to do additional
prospecting before it chooses the reserved site. This
problem will have to be addressed in the future.

Joint Arrangements and Activities Conducted by
the Enterprise. The revised text retains provisions
from the Seventh Session and the ICNT regarding joint
arrangements with the Enterprise. The text adds a
provision that plans of work submitted by the Enterprise shall be accompanied by evidence supporting its
financial and technological capability. Additional
work needs to be done on this subject to achieve necessary clarity and precision, including provisions for
security of tenure of joint arrangements.

Rules, Regulations, and Procedures of the Authority. Article 16 of revised Annex II (former paragraph
11) contains several improvements over the text from
the Seventh Session and the ICNT, principally in its
delegation of rule-making power in areas already fully
covered by treaty provisions. These improvements do

not fully compensate for lack of a provision setting forth comprehensively in one place the exclusive functions of the Authority. Time and other factors, however, did not allow negotiation of such a provision. Article 16 also clarifies the application to the Enterprise of appropriate categories of rules, regulations, and procedures referred to therein.

Miscellaneous. Several clarifications and drafting improvements were negotiated in the paragraphs dealing with penalties, revision of contracts, applicable law and tort liability of contractors and the Authority.

C. NG-2 Matters -- Financial Arrangements

Summary and Conclusions

Financial arrangements were the subject of intensive and sustained negotiation throughout the session. NG-2 met eight times, and there were 12 meetings of related informal groups. Chairman Koh continued with his working method of questioning speakers, summing up arguments, and stimulating a constant flow of new ideas and background papers for delegates to consider. In addition, he tried a variety of devices to encourage negotiation and agreement, ranging from individual consultations to informal working groups. The system of financial arrangements was also the first topic addressed by the newly created WG-21 for Committee I matters.

At mid-point in the session, Koh issued a new draft text (NG2/12) which made certain modest improvements in the financial arrangements but which could not be accepted by the US.

Debate during the session moved through several distinct stages. The first centered on the level of financial contributions which contractors would be required to make. Discussion then moved to three alternate financing proposals which were of a more sophisticated nature than those contained in NG2/12 and which provided a needed element of flexibility. Finally, in response to proposals by the G-77, consideration was given to the capital structure of the Enterprise and the linkage between this structure and the scale of financial arrangements.

In the Chairman's final report, a new text was suggested which took into account most of the desires of the G-77 with respect to the capitalization of the Enterprise but which left the financial arrangements with only very minor improvements. The change with respect to the Enterprise was made over the objections of the US Delegation, which felt that the existing capital structure was quite adequate and that US could not consider changes in these financing provisions until the level of financial arrangements for contractors was reduced to a satisfactory point.

It is fair to say that the lack of substantial change in the financial arrangements does not fully reflect the activities of NG-2 and its ancillary groups. A much higher level of understanding of the probable financial structure of the deep seabed mining industry and of the various taxing structures which could be utilized by the Authority was achieved by developed and developing countries alike. It was the view of the US and other countries interested in seabed mining, however, that no changes should be made until a fully satisfactory text could be worked out. Efforts toward this goal will continue during the intersessional period and at the resumed session.

## The Revised Texts

Early discussions in NG-2 addressed the paper on financial arrangements produced by Koh at the end of the Seventh Session in New York (NG 2/10/Rev.1) suggesting a revision of Annex II, paragraph 7, of the ICNT. In order to accommodate the needs of different economic systems, this proposal allowed a contractor to make payments to the Authority either through a mixed system of royalty plus profit-sharing or a royalty-only system.

The mixed system (para.7 [sexies]), which is likely to be chosen by private contractors, proposed the following:

-- a $500,000 application fee, with portions not used by the Authority refundable to the applicant;

-- an annual fixed fee of $1 million to be creditable against royalty payments after production begins;

-- a production charge (royalty) on the gross
proceeds of the integrated project of two percent for
years 1-6; four percent for years 7-12; and six percent for years 13-20;

-- a share of the net proceeds attributable to
the mining sector of 40 percent for years 1-6; 70 percent for years 7-12; and 80 percent for years 13-20;

-- attributable net proceeds (ANP) at 40 percent
of the total net proceeds of the integrated project;

-- a so-called "safeguard" clause which would
hold the contractor at the first level of profit-
sharing until he recoups his initial development costs
and at the second level until he recoups double his
investment costs.

The royalty-only system (para.7 [quinquies]) also
called for a $500,000 application fee and an annual
fixed fee of $1 million. The royalty on the gross
proceeds amounted to 7.5 percent for years 1-6; 10
percent for years 7-12; and 14 percent for years
13-20. In his proposal, Chairman Koh attempted to
maintain rough equivalency between the royalty-only
system and the mixed system of financial arrangements
in terms of ultimate income of the Authority.

NG-2 first discussed the chapeau and then the
five objectives which will guide the Authority in the
preparation of regulations with respect to financial
arrangements and in the negotiation of contracts.
The US Delegation, supported by other industrialized
countries, criticized subparagraph (e), which stipu-
lated that the Enterprise should be able to engage in
seabed mining from the time the Convention entered
into force, as impossible of achievement. A Chilean
proposal for a new subparagraph (f) which would ensure equivalency of financial arrangements for sea-
based and land-based miners was not favored by the
industrialized countries and was criticized by some
developing countries, because of the lack of uniformity in land-based contracts and because such equivalency did not recognize the risks inherent in sea-
based mining.

In the course of discussions, the US stated that
the Koh text (NG-2/10/Rev.1) was unacceptable because:

-- the over-all effect of the system and rates was to allocate to the Authority more than the mining sector would actually earn;

-- the proposed scheme was inflexible because it was relatively unresponsive to both the overall profitability of the project and to the short-term fluctuations in profit;

-- the production charge rates place a heavy burden on seabed miners without regard to the profitability of the operation or the proceeds actually attributable to the mining sector;

-- the 40 percent ANP figure cannot be justified on any economic or accounting basis and would result in the Authority sharing in income generated in the non-mining stages of production that lie outside the Area;

-- the revenue-sharing rates of 40 percent, 70 percent, and 80 percent, especially the last two, are too high and would deter investment;

-- the so-called "safeguard" clause is an ineffective safeguard since the contractor pays a higher rate if he has recovered initial development costs but before he has earned any return on his investment.

The US, supported by Japan and some European Community (EC) countries, proposed the following financial arrangements:

-- a two-stage production charge system of one percent of gross proceeds in an early period and two percent in a later period (other EC countries proposed .75 percent and 1.5 percent);

-- an ANP figure of 20 percent, approximating the figure arrived at by dividing development costs in the mining sector by total development costs;

-- revenue-sharing rates on attributable net proceeds of 25 percent in the early period and 50 percent in the later period, the higher rate being triggered when the contractor recovered the present value of his investment computed at a 15 percent rate of return.

The G-77 stated that these rates were too low and did not provide adequate income for the Authority, and

that ANP should be more than 20 percent in order to take into account the value of the nodules in situ. Chairman Koh, who supported the G-77 position on ANP, released a paper which purported to justify an ANP rate of 40 percent. The industrialized countries attacked the methodology of the paper.

Koh did, however, recognize the inflexibility in his proposed financial arrangements, and he convened discussions to explore the possibility of introducing elements into the system which could deal with the problems of risk and low profits. Three alternatives were considered:

-- an incremental system in which the contractor's ANP would vary with his level of profitability, as measured by the ratio of his net proceeds to his gross proceeds;

-- an incremental system based on the contractor's profitability, measured by the ratio of his cash surplus to his development costs;

-- a flat rate system of two rate schedules in which the higher rates are triggered when the contractor recovers the actual value of his initial investment at an agreed rate of return.

Despite Koh's personal preference for a flexible system of financial arrangements, however, he was unable to achieve general acceptance in the G-77 for any of the three alternatives.

After NG-2 meetings concluded in the fourth week, Koh presented a new draft (NG-2/12) which contained the following revisions in the mixed system of payments:

-- a royalty on the gross proceeds of the integrated project of three percent in the first period (years 1-10) and five percent in the second period (years 11-20);

-- an ANP figure of 35 percent;

-- profit-sharing percentages on the ANP of 45 percent for the first period and 65 percent for the second period, with the higher rate being triggered when the contractor recovers double his investment costs.

271

In order to maintain the equivalency between the mixed system and the royalty-only system, the rates in the royalty-only system were adjusted to 8.5 percent in years 1-10 and 13.5 percent in years 11-20.

In addition, Koh made a number of other substantive changes in the text:

-- the five objectives outlined in paragraph 7 now enable the Authority to provide incentives for contractors "to train the personnel of the Authority and of developing countries";

-- the new text makes it clear that from the commencement of commercial production, the contractor shall pay either the production charge or the annual fixed fee, whichever is greater;

-- the contractor's choice between systems of financial arrangements may be revoked with the consent of the Authority;

-- the provisions on free market or arm's length transactions have been tightened to refer to the principles and interpretations of these transactions developed by tax experts in international forums;

-- the categories of monetary amounts to be calculated in constant dollars are now more clearly defined;

-- in cases of operations that are not fully integrated through the processing phase, the Authority has the discretion to establish the schedule of charges, bearing in mind equality of financial treatment and the schedules for fully integrated projects.

The texts which Koh finally issued, and which were incorporated in WG21/1, changed the NG2/5 provisions for financing the Enterprise (over the objection of the US) but, with the exception of one minor improvement, left the financial arrangement for contractors of NG2/12 substantially unchanged. The improvement was that the production charge in the first period was lowered from three percent to two percent.

In place of a requirement to pay "up to one third" of the Enterprise's financial needs as necessary to secure its borrowing, the new NG2/5 text

requires States to pay one half of the capital of the
Enterprise in refundable capital without regard to its
ability to borrow.  Thus, the character of the paid-in
refundable capital has been changed in principle;
while previously it provided additional collateral as
required for Enterprise borrowing, it now requires a
direct government contribution as "equity" (albeit
ultimately refundable) capital.  The financial obligation on States Parties has been increased substantially.

The US does not accept this new and unnecessary
provision for financing the Enterprise, and it seems
highly unlikely that many States will do so.

General Observations

The search for consensus on financial arrangements has been handicapped by the differing views of
the industrialized and developing countries on the
fundamental issues of the value of the nodules *in situ*
and the financing of the Enterprise.

As to the value of the nodules, which may also be
expressed as the value of the right to mine, the US
and other industrialized countries feel that the answer must await actual operations, since this value,
in any real economic sense, will depend entirely on
the profit which can be obtained from mining.  Since
the package of financial arrangements is commonly regarded as payment for the right to mine, and in view
of the risks, they insist that it be sufficiently flexible to relate the payment to the Authority to the
profitability of the mining operation.

While agreeing that financial arrangements are
payment for the right to mine, the developing countries desire to add the putative value of the minesite
to the capital structure of the mining operation and,
by so doing, increase the share of income of the integrated operation which is attributable to mining.  The
value of the minesite for this purpose is stated to be
in the range of 10 percent to 20 percent of the investment in the integrated operation.

The US believes that the financing of the Enterprise is adequately dealt with by the provisions of
Annex III, paragraph 10(bis), which call for a capital
structure of debt guaranteed by member States with the
possibility of up to one-third additional paid-in

refundable capital, to the extent needed for securing loans. Doubts about the sufficiency of this arrangement have now arisen among the G-77, which wants as much "equity" capital and as little debt as possible. They propose to link financing of the Enterprise to financial arrangements generally. This position led to demands for a higher liquid component of the capital structure and greater emphasis on front-end payments by contractors. It also led to a repetition of the $60 million bonus proposal, which soured the atmosphere in the early days of WG-21. As noted elsewhere, the demand for a larger liquid component was incorporated in NG21/1 over the objections of the United States.

The issue of national taxation also surfaces periodically in the discussion of financial arrangements. The G-77 believes that national taxation should be explicitly assigned a role which is secondary to the assessments of the Authority, while the US and other industrialized countries regard taxation as a purely domestic matter outside the scope and competence of an international forum. Despite repeated statements by the US that a tax credit for seabed mining is not part of existing US law nor something which can be predicted, and similar statements by other industrialized countries, the G-77 continues to predicate its approach to financial arrangements on the assumption of a tax credit.

### D.  NG-3 Matters -- Organs of the Authority

Summary and Conclusions

NG-3, led by Committee I Chairman Engo, met nine times to discuss Part XI, Section 5, of the ICNT (The Authority) and Annex III (Statute of the Enterprise). There was only limited debate on the controversial and most important subject, Article 159 (The Council). Seabed dispute-settlement provisions were referred to a group of legal experts under the Chairmanship of Professor Wuensche of the German Democratic Republic.

Composition of the Council and Voting Procedures

Only one negotiating session was devoted to this subject. It was immediately apparent that it would not be possible at this session to negotiate a reconciliation of the widely divergent views of

developed and developing countries on the key issues of numerical representation in the categories of special interests and of the voting mechanisms. Developing States remain unwilling to concede that States with special interests, particularly those with large investments in deep seabed mining and consumers of minerals, must be assured voting power in the Council sufficient to assure that the majority cannot take actions overriding the minority with special interests.

However, as a result of negotiations among developed States, significantly improved definitions specifying the criteria of eligibility in the categories of miners and consumers/importers were agreed and entered in the revised text. The new definitions set a limit on the number of States from which the representatives in each category will be selected and assure that those States which in fact have the most significant interests in the two categories will make up the group from which the representatives will be selected. Election to category (a), seabed miners, will be from among the eight States that have the largest investments in seabed mining. Election to category (b), consumers/importers, will be from among the ten or eleven States that are the largest consumers or net importers of the categories of minerals from the Area. At the resumed session, the US will pursue a proposal made informally at this session, which would require that the Council as a whole represent 50 percent of the value of production and 50 percent of the value of consumption of the minerals derived from the Area.

In the abbreviated discussions during the session on the question of voting procedures, the G-77 raised objections to Article 160 paragraph 2(x) regarding approval of plans of work reviewed by the Legal and Technical Commission unless specifically disapproved by the Council. Developed countries reiterated the necessity of this provision to assure approval of contracts of qualified applicants, and the provision remains unchanged in the revised text.

The Assembly

The ICNT Provisions on the powers and functions of the Assembly were left unchanged in the revised text. The US Delegation said that it could accept the characterization of the Assembly as the

275

"supreme organ" only on the understanding that no implications flow from that characterization. The exhaustive list of powers and functions of the Assembly remains in the revised text.

## The Enterprise

Article 169 (The Enterprise) was amended to include language clarifying the generally accepted view that the Enterprise should be authorized to engage in transportation, processing, and marketing, as well as the recovery of the nodules. Conforming changes were made in other articles in Annex III.

Other changes were also made in paragraph 1 of Annex III, clarifying that the Enterprise is subject to the entire Convention and all the rules, regulations, and procedures of the Authority. This alleviates previous US concern for clarification of the full applicability of environmental and other regulations to the Enterprise.

On the question of privileges and immunities for the Enterprise, the revised texts make clear that the Enterprise does not have the privileges and immunities accorded to the Authority, but only those specifically provided in Annex III. Paragraph 12(e) of Annex III grants the Enterprise immunity from taxation on its assets, property, and revenues. US efforts to delete this provision as improper for a commercial entity were strongly opposed by the G-77, and no change was made in this provision of the revised text.

## Environmental Provisions

The US introduced and succeeded in having included in the revised text two important amendments to Article 160 which would significantly strengthen environmental protection provisions. The first amendment is to Article 160(2)(xxi) and makes clear that the Council can require "adjustment" in deep seabed mining operations as well as suspend operations in order to prevent serious harm to the environment. The other amendment, which is to Article 160(2)(xxii), changes the standard for disapproval of areas for exploitation from the extraordinary standard "irreparable harm to a unique environment" to the more reasonable standard of "serious harm to the marine environment." Additional amendments sought by the US to

Article 163, concerning the "Legal and Technical Commission," would emphasize the environmental responsibilities of the Commission. Insufficient opportunity for discussion of these proposals resulted in objections by the USSR on procedural grounds to inclusion of the provision in a revised text. No opposition on the substance of the amendments was raised by any delegation, and they remain for further discussion at the resumed session.

### E. Group of Legal Experts on Seabeds Disputes

When the Conference created negotiating groups at the Seventh Session to deal with outstanding "hard-core" issues, no group was assigned to deal with the question of compulsory settlement of disputes concerning activities in the seabed area. It was generally understood, however, that the relevant texts, Section 6 of Part XI and related Annexes, were in need of revision. Accordingly, at the beginning of the Eighth Session a group of legal experts was formed within Committee I to consider the possibility of such revision. Dr. Wuenscho, a Vice Chairman of Committee I, was selected as Chairman.

The Group worked throughout the session and was able to produce a new text for Section 6 of Part XI. This text is incorporated in the revised text. It is understood, nevertheless, that the revised articles are only interim steps. Due to the limited time available for the Group's work, it was not able to give full consideration to all of the issues raised by revision. It is generally agreed, however, that they are a better basis for negotiation than the texts which appeared in the ICNT.

The US considers that the texts represent improvement over the ICNT in clarifying questions of access to and jurisdiction of the Seabeds Disputes Chamber and in clarifying the Chamber's jurisdiction to determine the non-applicability in a particular case of actions, rules, regulations, or procedures of the Authority which in that case would be inconsistent with the Convention or would involve an excess of the Authority's competence or a misuse of power. Improvements were also made in provisions relating to the availability of commercial arbitration as the appropriate dispute settlement mechanism for disputes concerning commercial questions, but further

clarification is needed in this regard. The US hopes these issues can be addressed in the Group at the resumed session.

## The Revised Texts

Notable features of the new text are as follows:

International Character of the Secretariat. This provision (Article 168, former Article 167) has been revised to make staff violations relating to wrongful financial interest in seabed activities or wrongful disclosure of proprietary information subject to redress through an appropriate national or international tribunal. The new provision obliges the Authority to take action against the staff member at the request of the State Party or a contractor. The affected party has the right to take part in the proceedings.

Jurisdiction of the Seabed Disputes Chamber. Article 187 is the basic jurisdictional provision for the Seabed Disputes Chamber. It reorganizes former Article 187 to focus on subject matter jurisdiction rather than parties. The Chamber's jurisdiction is limited in general to Part XI of the Convention and to matters relating to activities in the Area. It includes jurisdiction over disputes between States concerning interpretation and application of the Convention. It makes clear that violations of the Convention by the Authority or by a State Party can be questioned judicially by the other and specifies that compulsory settlement applies where a State Party alleges that the Authority has acted in excess of jurisdiction or has misused its power. Contractual disputes can be submitted to the Chamber by any party thereto, and prospective contractors who fulfill minimum conditions of application may take issue with the refusal of a contract and other issues arising in the negotiations for a contract.

Limitation on Jurisdiction with Regard to Decisions of the Authority. The limitations (Article 190, former Article 191) remain in the new version, namely those prohibiting the Chamber from substituting its discretion for the Authority's and preventing the the Chamber from invalidating Authority rules, regulations, and procedures. The revision makes clear, however, that the Chamber can decide that the application

of rules, regulations, or procedures in a particular
case would be in conflict with the Convention, and it
can determine whether decisions taken involved lack of
competence or misuse of power.

Submission of Disputes to Ad Hoc Chambers of
the SBDC and to Binding Arbitration. Paragraph 1 of
Article 188 represents a change from the ICNT and includes a provision for submission of disputes between
States Parties concerning the interpretation or application of Part XI to an ad hoc Chamber of the Seabed
Disputes Chamber. The provision was changed in the
report of the Chairman of Committee I to the Plenary
to provide for such submission at the request of "the
parties" to the dispute instead of at the request of
"any party" to the dispute. This paragraph will require further discussion at the resumed session.

Paragraph 2 of Article 188 specifies that
commercial arbitration of contract disputes shall be
available to the extent provided in the contract at
the request of either party. There is provision for
the use of an as yet unspecified set of commercial
arbitration rules if the parties cannot agree on a
procedure. Although the work done on this article
has resulted in an improvement over the ICNT, the
precise legal effect of the new text is not yet certain. Further work needs to be done to clarify the
circumstances in which commercial arbitration will be
available and the nature of such arbitration.

III.  Committee II

A.  Overview

Committee II continued work on those issues previously identified by the Conference as hard-core issues in the Negotiating Groups specially established
for the purpose. Primarily, attention was focused on
the question of the definition of the outer limits of
the continental shelf, delimitation of maritime boundaries between opposite and adjacent States, and the
access of landlocked and geographically disadvantaged
States (LL/GDS) to the living resources of the economic zones of the region or subregion.

The text of NG-4 relating to LL/GDS, produced at
the Seventh Session, received broad support and went
forward into the revision. Similarly, the text on

fisheries dispute settlement developed in NG-5 last session was incorporated into the revision. Most significantly, Ambassador Aguilar during the final hours produced a compromise text on the shelf issues that is included in the revised text. In comprises the Irish formula with maximum limits, a new article to protect other uses, and new figures on revenue sharing. The text was widely discussed in the Plenary and, although generally opposed by the Arab States, appeared to offer an improved prospect of consensus. There will be further negotiations on this subject. The text regrettably did not include any provision on scientific research, but the Chairman made clear that an accommodation on science was essential to resolution of this issue.

   B.   NG-4 Matters.  Landlocked and Geographically
        Disadvantaged States (LL/GDS) Access to
        Fisheries

   NG-4 held only one substantive meeting during this session of the Conference, because there was a widespread feeling that the texts developed earlier by the group under the leadership of Ambassador Satya Nandan (Fiji) were as close as possible to an eventual compromise. These texts are reflected in NG-4/9/Rev.2 produced during the Seventh Session. During the single meeting held, it was clear that a number of States would still prefer improvements from their perspective. Some concentrated their comments on the fact that qualifying LL/GDS were entitled to rights only with regard to the surplus of fish above the catch capacity of a coastal State in its economic zone. On the other hand, certain coastal States were of the view that the word "right" should not be used at all when speaking of access to living resources for the LL/GDS. Comments were also made with regard to any distinction to be drawn between developed and developing countries. By and large, however, the closely balanced nature of the discussion, coupled with an absence of total rejection of the texts, led Chairman Nandan to conclude that the articles contained in NG-4/9/Rev.2, possibly with some minor non-substantive drafting changes, should be included in any revision of the ICNT or its equivalent, and he so recommended to Chairman Aguilar of Committee II in that Committee's final meeting. On that occasion, there was widespread support for going forward with the text as recommended by Nandan provided that there could be an opportunity for further discussion of

improvements. Since only a small handful of States felt that further work needed to be done before taking that step, Aguilar felt able to suggest the inclusion of the text in the revision. It is clear that the Nandan proposals embody the essence of the final compromise on the issue.

C. NG-5 Matters -- Settlement of Disputes in the Economic Zone

NG-5 had completed substantially all of its work at the end of the Geneva part of the Seventh Session. Some question was raised, however, at the resumed session as to whether the issues which it had considered should be reopened for discussion. At the Eighth Session the Group held one meeting at which it appeared that it was in fact unnecessary to reopen negotiations. Accordingly, the main products of the Group's work--revised Articles 296 and 296 bis--were submitted and approved for inclusion in the revised ICNT.

The Group had also considered in 1978 a general substantive provision on abuse of rights for insertion somewhere in the Convention. It decided upon reflection, however, that a recommendation regarding such a provision was beyond its specific mandate. Therefore, no such provision was incorporated in the revised text but was reserved instead for consideration at some future time.

D. NG-6 Matters -- Definition of the Outer Limits of the Continental Shelf and Revenue Sharing Beyond 200 Nautical Miles

Discussions in NG-6, under the guidance of Ambassador Aguilar, took place in the latter part of the session, although intensive private consultations were held throughout. At issue in these discussions were three basic questions:

-- the outer limits of the continental shelf beyond 200 miles;

-- revenue sharing beyond 200 miles; and

-- the regime of the shelf beyond 200 miles.

The basic proposals before the group with respect to limits were the following:

281

-- the so-called Irish formula, which would provide a limit on Article 76 of the ICNT by the use of
either a thickness-of-sediment test or one utilizing
a fixed distance from the foot of the slope;

-- a Soviet suggestion of further limitation to
the Irish formula of a fixed distance (e.g., 300 or
350 miles) from the baselines from which the breadth
of the territorial sea is measured, or a maximum of
60 or 100 miles seaward of the 2500-meter isobath,
whichever is further seaward but not extending beyond
the Irish formula;

-- the proposal of the Arab Group that the continental margin be cut off at 200 nautical miles, the
outer limit of the economic zone.

Of course, a fourth alternative would be Article
76 as it appears in the ICNT. Discussions demonstrated strong support for the Irish formula, although the
Arab Group formally held to their 200-mile position.
At the same time there was widespread and substantial
recognition of the need to provide for margin jurisdiction to extend beyond 200 miles where the margin
so extends. Of particular significance is the fact
that the USSR has publicly endorsed the Irish formula
albeit with a maximum limit.

Because some delegations were of the view that
the Irish formula could be improved, they were willing to consider a way to impose a further limitation
on the continental margin as defined by that formula.
At the end of the session, the Chairman of NG-6 introduced a compromise text which incorporated the Soviet
amendment. This text found substantial support in the
Plenary and was incorporated into the revision of the
ICNT.

The revenue-sharing question remained an integral
part of continental shelf discussions. According to
the ICNT, coastal States, after a five-year period of
grace, would share revenues from shelf production beyond 200 miles with developing countries at a rate beginning at one percent in the sixth year of production
and increasing at one percent annual increments to
five percent in the tenth year, there to remain. The
Chairman's compromise text retained this approach but
increased the final percentage to seven percent.
Broad support was given to this proposal.

The question of the regime for the continental shelf beyond 200 nautical miles received much attention. On the one hand, broad-margin States were unwilling to agree to any new provisions which might allow construction by others of artificial islands on the continental shelf beyond 200 miles. They were, however, willing to consider amendments that insured protection for other uses. The Chairman's compromise text contains language drawn from the 1958 Shelf Convention which protects other uses. No alteration was proposed in the ICNT article on installations and structures.

E. NG-7 Matters -- Delimitation of Maritime Boundaries

NG-7 continued its work at the Eighth Session under the chairmanship of Judge E.J. Manner (Finland). As at previous sessions, the Group was unable to produce any new texts which represented sufficiently better bases for compromise or justified changing the relevant portions of the ICNT.

As a result of the continued inability of the Group to make substantial progress, there was at the end of the session considerable doubt expressed, both within and outside the Group, about the appropriateness of continuing discussion in this forum in the future.

Nevertheless, there were some developments during the session which may offer promise for the future. One was the emergence of groups of so-called "neutral" States who actively sought ways of bringing the opposing sides closer together on the questions of substantive criteria and the interim regime. The US Delegation continued to play such a role with regard to dispute-settlement aspects of the Group's work.

The Group took up its subject in three categories:

-- the question of the proper rules or criteria for delimitation, on which the States divided between those favoring equitable principles as a rule and those that would give preference to the median line as modified by special circumstances;

-- the question of the provisional regime to apply in the period before a final delimitation is achieved, on which the States divide between those

favoring a provisional regime determined by agreement (generally the equitable principles States) and those who would use the median line;

-- the question of the submission of delimitation disputes to compulsory and binding settlement. On this issue the equitable-principles States tend to oppose compulsory settlement, and the equidistance States tend to favor it, although there is by no means a one-to-one correlation.

## The Substantive Rules of Delimitation

As usual this, the principal concern of NG-7, occupied most of its meeting time. Although at the outset it appeared that the opposing sides might continue to hold adamantly to their extreme positions, the debate soon showed some willingness in both groups to move to positions somewhat closer to a genuine middle ground. It was at this point that first Mexico and then Peru (States which are "neutral" on this question) and later Ivory Coast and Brazil began offering compromise formulas. The approach which nearly all of these took was to combine references to equitable principles, equidistance, and special circumstances in such a way as to try to avoid giving any clear preference to any of thm.

Toward the end of the session, a joint Mexican/Peruvian proposal seemed to elicit interest from both sides. The equidistance advocates saw in it a new basis of negotiations which could create a parity between equitable principles and equidistance. The equitable principles advocates, in part fearful of being accused of complete intransigence, made a nod to this proposal if amended in certain key respects. At this point in the proceedings, it was suggested by the Chairman that a contact group be formed. NG-7, however, declined to give its approval to the organization (even informally) of any sort of sub-group.

Following the failure to establish this contact group, the Mexican and Peruvian delegations offered revisions to their proposed compromise which were not received favorably by the full Group. Mexico and Peru eventually withdrew these amendments, and the unfavorable debate put the entire future of the original Mexican/Peruvian proposal in doubt. Paragraphs 1 of Articles 74 and 83 remain unchanged, and there was no basis for revising the ICNT provisions. There is

broad recognition that this issue can be solved, if at all, only when it is clear that a treaty will be concluded.

## Provisional Measures

At the resumed Seventh Session there had been considerable discussion about the possibility of an exploitation moratorium as part of the interim regime. At the Eighth Session it became clear that a moratorium could not form an acceptable part of a provisional regime.

With respect to provisional measures, India, Iraq, and Morocco came forward to offer "neutral" assistance in finding an acceptable middle ground. They offered an article which would have provided for provisional arrangements by agreement and would have enjoined any State from taking measures which might aggravate the situation or jeopardize the interests of another. The article would have ensured that the interim regime would be without prejudice to the final delimitation. Again, the debate showed a willingness on the part of both sides to consider compromise positions, and several delegations offered suggestions and amendments with a view to finding a truly acceptable compromise. On the basis of this debate, Chairman Manner met with the proposal's sponsors and produced a reformulation. The reformulation was not well received as a potential basis for a compromise. Moreover, it was offered and considered too late in the session for further work to be done along these lines. Thus, no progress could be reported in this area either.

## Settlement of Disputes

As at previous sessions, Professor Sohn (US), joined now to some extent by Ambassador Rosenne (Israel), took the lead in trying to suggest ways in which the two sides might approach compromise on this issue. At this session, work focused on three possibilities which it was thought might be useful elements in a compromise. The first was the idea of using a preliminary settlement procedure to identify the circumstances, methods, and principles to be considered in the context of a particular delimitation. On the basis of this preliminary determination, parties might then make a second attempt at a negotiated settlement before proceeding if necessary to a final

285

third-party settlement. The second element was the possible use of conciliation rather than a binding procedure as the compulsory method of settlement either in the preliminary stage, in the final stage, or in both. The third element was the distinction between past and future disputes.

At the beginning of the session, Professor Sohn offered a compendium of 45 possible provisions incorporating almost every conceivable permutation and combination of these three elements, from the extreme of no settlement to compulsory and binding settlement on everything. This approach proved to be a bit too complex for a Plenary negotiating group. As a result, Professor Sohn submitted a further paper selecting four of the 45 possibilities, representing a range of choice from one side of the question to the other. Again, due to a lack of time, these proposals were not taken up in full debate. Nevertheless, consultations suggest that some combination of these three elements may eventually produce a compromise on this point. In the end, Chairman Manner concluded that there was no basis for revising the relevant provisions of the ICNT.

## Marine Mammals

This subject, not being one of the "hard-core" issues designated as such by the Conference, was nonetheless the focus of two unofficial meetings (approximately 20 States) convened by the US. The objective of these meetings, attended by all affected interests, was to seek improvement in the language of Article 65 of the ICNT to make clear that there is a minimum conservation standard for marine mammals both within and without the economic zone. The meetings showed that there was substantial unanimity for proposed changes reflecting such a conservation objective. Also discussed was the need for textual improvements with respect to cooperation in an appropriate international organization for the conservation of cetaceans. Discussions in this area focused on the need to accommodate appropriate regional organizations for the conservation of stocks where those stocks need not be addressed on a global scale. A great deal of progress was made in the direction of a final accommodation, and it is anticipated that a final solution will be reached at the resumed session.

IV. Committee III

A. Overview

Of the three issues within the mandate of Committee III, two are now considered closed: protection of the marine environment, and transfer of technology. On the question of marine scientific research, the US actively pursued the matter at senior level. Although no changes were made in Conference texts, it is clearly understood by all that further negotiations are required, and this was made explicit by President Amerasinghe, Committee III Chairman Yankov, and the US Delegation at the final Plenary.

B. Protection of the Marine Environment

The negotiations on this subject are closed. The revisions of the negotiating text incorporate the US amendments introduced during the Seventh Session. These are the proposals referred to in the Report of the Seventh Session as having achieved consensus or an increased prospect of consensus (Categories 1 and 2).

During this session, negotiations on pollution focused on those remaining proposals introduced during the Seventh Session "on which, owing to lack of time or divided views, no compromise formulae emerged." These were the so-called Category 3 proposals. (See Chairman's Report C.3/1 Rev.1 of 13 Sept 1978.) Past discussions of these proposals indicated that, with one or two exceptions they were probably too controversial to command the necessary support to be incorporated in any revision of the ICNT. The two exceptions were a proposal relating to Article 236 (Responsibility and Liability) submitted by 18 Arab States and Portugal, and a Soviet proposal to create a new Part in the Convention establishing General Safeguards. The Soviet proposal would broaden the application of certain safeguards articles presently contained in Part XII to the entire Convention.

Active negotiations took place on Article 236 and resulted in a compromise text. Revised Article 236 accommodates the desires of its proponents for a greater emphasis on the elaboration of international law relating to the compensation of victims for damage caused by pollution of the marine environment. The change, however, does not inject the Law of the Sea Conference into the process of creating substantive

law relating to liability and compensation. Many
States believe further elaboration should properly be
left to other competent technical organizations. The
compromise text was incorporated in the revision of
the ICNT.

The Chairman of Committee III in his final report
stated: "In view of the progress of the negotiations
made during this session, and the very important positive results that were achieved, I would venture to
state that the substantive negotiations on Part XII--
protection and preservation of the marine environment
--could be considered completed." This conclusion
was not challenged by any delegation.

C.  Marine Scientific Research

In contrast to marine pollution, results on marine scientific research were disappointing. Even
though the US Delegation revised its amendments on
scientific research to meet concerns expressed by
other delegations, substantive negotiations in the
Committee did not prove possible. Unwillingness on
the part of several delegations to conduct real negotiations on scientific research stemmed less from
opposition to our amendments than from the situation
in the rest of the Conference. Many see the science
amendments linked to other issues either substantive-
ly or tactically. Despite the negative outcome of
this session, there is now a clear understanding in
the Conference of the need for further negotiations
on marine scientific research at the resumed session.
President Amerasinghe and Chairman Yankov left no
doubt about this in statements in General Committee
and Plenary, emphasizing that consensus on research
had not yet been achieved.

Initial efforts to obtain support for US science
amendments took place at a series of unofficial meetings with a representative group of States. These
meetings, convened by the US at the head-of-delega-
tion level, were chaired by Ambassador Richardson.
Discussions in this group resulted in a revised set
of amendments attached to this report. The revised
amendments were introduced into Committee III and
discussed thereafter in several informal Committee
meetings chaired by Chairman Yankov. Comments on the
revised amendments were made by some 50 countries.
Honduras, speaking on behalf of the G-77, stated that
further negotiations on the issue of scientific

research did not appear warranted at this stage. Developing country representatives thereafter expressed agreement with the statement of the G-77 Chairman and then proceeded to make substantive comments. There was strong opposition to modifying Article 247(1), which speaks of the right of coastal States to authorize and regulate science in the exclusive economic zone. Most developed countries spoke in favor of those of our proposals relating to the economic zone.

Broad-margin States, whether developed or developing, either opposed our proposals for the shelf beyond the economic zone, or stated they were an inherent part of discussion on outer limits of the shelf. The USSR submitted an informal proposal in NG-6 which dealt with several continental shelf issues including Article 258(bis) on research. Their proposal required consent for research of direct significance to exploration and exploitation, and notice plus obligations for all other research, a result which was unacceptable to the US. This proposal was also opposed by some broad-margin States in NG-6, because it did not contain adequate protection for coastal State interests.

The final report of Chairman Yankov stated that "some of the US proposals, especially those referring to the conduct of marine scientific research on the continental shelf, were of a substantive nature, while others entailed drafting modifications, further clarification of existing provisions, or their interpretation." He stated his personal view that although this session of the Conference had not attained sufficient consensus to revise the ICNT, further negotiations could broaden the basis for agreement. He concluded by saying that it was very important not to preclude the option for further attempts to improve the prospect for consensus. The US stressed that further amendments to the marine scientific research text are necessary and that we will pursue negotiations toward this end at the resumed session.

D. Transfer of Technology

The Committee accepted the following amended version of Article 275(bis) designed to promote the establishment of national marine scientific and technological research centers:

## Article 275 bis

New Section 3:   Establishment of national centres

1.  States, through competent international
organizations, and the Authority shall, individually or jointly, promote the establishment specially (sic) in developing coastal
states, of national marine scientific and
technological research centres and strengthening of the existing national centres, in
order to stimulate and advance the conduct
of marine scientific research by developing
coastal states and for strengthening their
national capabilities to utilize and preserve their marine resources for their economic benefit.

2.  States, through competent international
organizations and the Authority shall give
adequate support to facilitate the establishment and strengthening of such national
centres:   for the provision of advance training facilities and necessary equipment, skills
and know-how as well as to provide technical
experts to such states which may need and request such assistance.


## V.  Drafting Committee

The Drafting Committee met informally during the
Eighth Session.  Efforts were devoted primarily to
consideration of harmonization problems in the present
text that were identified in several papers prepared
by the Secretariat.  Efforts in this direction culminated in at least an initial reading by all six
Language Groups of each of the Secretariat papers.
Preliminary preferences were developed by the Groups
which if implemented would resolve some of the difficulties brought into focus by the informal papers.

The Language Groups themselves were formed at the
resumed Seventh Session, and represent each of the six
official languages (English, French, Spanish, Arabic,
Chinese, and Russian).  Widespread participation is
encouraged by both the open-ended composition of the
Groups and the informal character of their deliberations.  The modest volume of work completed during
the session was due to scheduling conflicts and

personnel shortages in many of the smaller delegations.
Each language group met in informal session to consider the Secretariat papers. The conclusions, if any,
of the group were noted by the Coordinator in a report
circulated to all other groups and the Drafting Committee itself.

At this session, the Committee, meeting informally, reached certain conclusions regarding the structure of the Convention and seems to agree on certain
internal cross-references. The Secretariat also distributed a document comprising an ICNT text in the
English language which had been marked up to reflect
these conclusions. Unfortunately, the time available
to the Language Groups and the Drafting Committee did
not allow consideration of this document, as priority
was given to completion of a first reading of all the
informal papers dealing with harmonization problems.

At the conclusion of the resumed Seventh Session,
the Language Groups circulated reports of their preliminary conclusions on the 33 categories of harmonization problems identified in Informal Paper 2. At
this session, the Coordinators met several times to
review the preliminary positions of the Groups, in an
attempt to resolve differences, referring certain
problems back to the Groups. While this process was
under way, the Groups themselves were working on Informal Paper 2/Add.1, which catalogued 15 more harmonization problems. To maximize the progress of the
Drafting Committee, problems raised by the Coordinators' meetings were reserved for consideration until
the Language Groups completed their study of Informal
Paper 2/Add.1. Some Groups were unable to complete
both tasks in the time available but promised to
raise and resolve these problems either at intersessional meetings (Arabic Group) or after further study
(Chinese). Although deferring some items, the English Language Group was able to complete both tasks,
and final reports were prepared to reflect the preliminary decisions taken. The latter Group also established a small group of volunteers to study the
problem of references to "generally accepted" international standards and "applicable" international
standards in item 20, Informal Paper 2.

The Secretariat at this session distributed a
concordance text (A/CONF.62/DC/WP.1) which contains
the text of the ICNT with each article in all six
languages side-by-side. This document, while costly

and available only in limited copies, was helpful in both Drafting Committee work and substantive negotiations, as it allows rapid comparison of parallel texts to evaluate proposed technical adjustments or substantive revisions. In view of the utility of the concordance text, the Committee has investigated the possibility of keeping it up-dated through some inexpensive means to reflect future revisions to negotiating texts.

The discussion of future scheduling of work at the final meeting revealed some desire for an acceleration of Drafting Committee and Language Group activity at the resumed session. The Committee also seemed willing to see work start early.

Because of the technical nature of the reports of the Drafting Committee, a series of documents is available in a Drafting Committee Supplement to enable interested readers to consider more closely the work of this group.

March 26, 1979
INFORMAL WORKING PAPER

FAIR AND REASONABLE COMMERCIAL TERMS AND CONDITIONS

During the Intersessional period the United States Delegation undertook to ascertain with a greater degree of clarity what was meant by the phrase "fair and reasonable commercial terms and conditions". Although it was not possible to come up with a precise definition of this terminology, the United States Delegation was able to compile a number of examples of terms which would in general be regarded in commercial terms as fair and reasonable. These examples have been drawn from practices firmly established in commercial licensing agreements and transactions involving technology transfers.

It is not possible or appropriate to set out in advance what would be fair and reasonable commercial terms and conditions in all circumstances, or for all such transactions. Rather the list compiled here represents examples which, in light of commercial practices in relevant trades, are generally considered fair and reasonable measures to protect the technology being transferred, to ensure fair compensation to its owner and to protect the recipient of the technology. These provisions include terms that:

(1) establish a price - in specie, in kind or in other appropriate form - which provides a fair return to the owner for the transfer of the technology and any related services provided and which may be based on factors such as the cost of developing the technology (including direct research and development costs, overhead and other indirect costs, and taking into account the cost of the total development effort including unsuccessful projects), the risk to which the owner was exposed in developing the technology, the uniqueness of the technology, the profit or benefits to be derived or passed on by the Enterprise, and a reasonable profit to the owner;

(2) provide security for payments by means of letters of credit or other devices;

(3) limit the use of the technology by the Enterprise to exploration and exploitation of the deep seabed;

(4) provide for termination of the agreement in the event of substantial breach of the agreement;

(5) require that the Enterprise provide to the owner, on an exclusive or non-exclusive basis and without royalties, any improvements which it makes in the technology transferred to it (known as "grant-backs");

(6) ensure appropriate protection and proper handling of leased equipment;

(7) protect the secrecy of the technology, including restrictions on sub-licensing or assigning the technology to third parties;

(8) require indemnification by the Enterprise to the owner in the event the Enterprise causes damage to others by misuse of the technology and the owner is held liable;

(9) make appropriate provisions for the protection of the Enterprise in its use of the technology, such as warranties as to the validity of any patent;

(10) ensure that if there are any warranties of new technology, they take into account the untested nature of the technology;

(11) provide for a commercial arbitration mechanism to adjudicate any disputes arising within the scope of the contract for the transfer of technology including question of financial or other damages to be awarded.

COMMITTEE III SUPPLEMENT

MSR/2/Rev.1
2 April 1979
Original: ENGLISH

THIRD COMMITTEE (Informal Meeting)
(SCIENTIFIC RESEARCH)

INFORMAL SUGGESTION BY THE UNITED STATES

Amendments to the texts on marine scientific research

## Article 1(6)

Original U.S. Proposal

Restore the following definition from the RSNT:
"Marine scientific research" means any study or related experimental work designed to increase mankind's
knowledge of the marine environment.

Revised U.S. Proposal

"Marine scientific research" means any study or
related experimental work in the marine environment
designed to benefit all mankind by increasing mankind's knowledge thereof.

## Article 242 bis

Original U.S. Proposal

The coastal State in the application of this Part
shall provide other States with a reasonable opportunity to obtain from it, or with its co-operation, information necessary to prevent and control damage to
the health, safety and environment of persons not subject to the jurisdiction of the coastal State, such as
research and monitoring data regarding weather, current, pollution and other general processes and their
causes and effects.

Revised U.S. Proposal

[Without prejudice to its rights and duties under
this Convention,] a [coastal] State in the application
of this Part shall provide other States with a

reasonable opportunity to obtain from it, or with its co-operation, information necessary to prevent and control damage to the health, safety and environment of persons not subject to its jurisdiction, [such as research and monitoring data regarding weather, currents, pollution and other general processes and their causes and effects].

## Article 244 bis

Original U.S. Proposal

States shall establish, through competent international organizations, international rules and standards to facilitate consent for and the conduct of marine scientific research projects of importance to the international community that require the consent of several coastal States.

Revised U.S. Proposal

States shall cooperate through competent international organizations in the establishment of international procedures to facilitate consent for and the conduct of marine scientific research projects of importance to the international community that require the consent of several coastal states.

## Article 247(1)

Original U.S. Proposal

Coastal States have jurisdiction to regulate, authorize and conduct marine scientific research in their exclusive economic zone in accordance with the relevant provisions of this article.

No Changes:

Note: This amendment may be unnecessary if appropriate changes are made in article 296.

## Article 247(6)

Original U.S. Proposal

"The absence of diplomatic relations does not,

in and of itself, justify the conclusion that normal circumstances do not exist between the researching State and the coastal State for purposes of applying paragraph 3 of this article."

No Changes

## Article 250(1)(d)

Original U.S. Proposal

"if requested, provide the coastal State, as soon as practicable, with an assessment of such data, samples and research results...".

Revised U.S. Proposal

"if requested, provide the coastal State with an assessment of such data, samples, and research results or assist in their interpretation."

Note: The record should expressly confirm that in cases where time is necessary to complete an obligation, the term "outstanding obligations" in article 247, paragraph 4(d) and 253(d) refers to the absence of timely efforts to commence and complete performance of the obligation in good faith.

## Article 250

Original U.S. Proposal

Delete from paragraph 1(e) "subject to paragraph 2 of this article," and redraft paragraph 2 as follows:

"The coastal State, if it decides to grant consent under Article 247 for a project of direct significance for the exploration and exploitation of natural resources, may require prior agreement on reasonable conditions for making the research results internationally available."

Revised U.S. Proposal

Delete from paragraph 1(e) "subject to paragraph 2 of this article" and redraft paragraph 2 of the ICNT

as follows:

"This article is without prejudice to the conditions established by the [laws and regulations of the] coastal State for the exercise of its discretion to grant or withhold consent pursuant to article 247, paragraph 4."

## Article 254

Original U.S. Proposal

1. Delete "and compliance is not secured within a reasonable period of time" in subparagraph (b), and redraft the chapeau of Article 254 to include the underlined words as follows:

The coastal State shall have the right, where it has been unable to secure compliance by any other means within a reasonable period of time, to require the suspension of any research activities in progress within its exclusive economic zone, if:

2. In subparagraph (a) delete "initially."

Revised U.S. Proposal

1. In the chapeau, substitute "suspension" for the word "cessation."

2. Revised paragraph (a) as follows:

"the research activities are not being conducted in accordance with the information communicated as provided under article 249 [regarding the nature, objectives, method, means or geographical areas of the project] upon which the consent of the coastal State was based and compliance is not secured within a reasonable period of time;"

3. Add a paragraph 2 as follows:

The coastal State may require cessation of research activities if the conditions provided for in paragraph 1 are not complied with within a reasonable period of time after suspension has been invoked, subject

to any proceedings which may have been instituted pursuant to section 2 of Part XV.

## Article 256

Original U.S. Proposal

Redraft the article as follows:

States shall adopt appropriate measures to facilitate access to their harbours and to promote assistance for vessels engaged in marine scientific research
in accordance with the present Convention.

Revised U.S. Proposal

For purposes of giving effect to bilateral or re-
tional and other multilateral agreements and in a
spirit of international cooperation, coastal States
shall endeavour to adopt reasonable rules, regulations,
and procedures to promote and facilitate marine scientific research activities conducted in accordance
with the present Convention, and to facilitate access
to their harbours and promote assistance for marine
scientific research vessels.

## Articles 257 and 258

Original U.S. Proposal

Combine these two articles as follows:

States, irrespective of their geographical location, as well as competent international organizations, shall have the right, subject to and in conformity with the relevant provisions of the present
Convention, to conduct marine scientific research beyond the limits of the exclusive economic zone.

No Changes

Note: The question of terminology and drafting
could be dealt with in the Third Committee or in the
Drafting Committee.

## Article 258 bis

Original U.S. Proposal

1. Insert the following new article:

Articles 249 and 250 shall apply <u>mutatis</u> <u>mutandis</u> to marine scientific research that is of direct sig-nificance for the exploration and exploitation of the natural resources of the continental shelf beyond 200 nautical miles from the baselines from which the breadth of the territorial sea is measured.

2. Delete the references to the continental shelf in articles 247 to 250 and articles 254 to 256. (N.B. There would be no change in article 81, which applies to drilling "for all purposes.")

No Changes

## Article 265

Original U.S. Proposal

(see art. 296(3) (a))

No Changes

## Article 296, paragraph 3(a)

Original U.S. Proposal

1. Delete the words "a right or" and add the phrase "to withhold consent" after the word "discretion."

2. Delete the words "and 254" and the clause "or a decision taken in accordance with Article 254."

Revised U.S. Proposal

1. Delete the words "a right of" and add the phrase "to withhold consent" after the word "discretion."

2. After "or a decision taken in accordance with Article 254", add "paragraph 2 to require cessa-tion of research activities".

EIGHTH SESSION (Resumed)
NEW YORK
July 19 - August 24, 1979

I.  Summary

    A.  Overview

        The Resumed Eighth Session of the Third United
Nations Conference on the Law of the Sea was held in
New York from July 16 to August 24, 1979, with the
first three days devoted to informal consultations.
The session ended with the issuance of reports by
the Committee Chairmen that reflect substantial progress toward agreement on most outstanding issues.
The Conference decided to hold its final substantive
session in two five-week stages next year, the first
in New York beginning February 27, and the second in
Geneva beginning July 28.  Intersessional consultations are also contemplated.

        The work of the Conference was devoted to the
major outstanding issues not resolved by the Informal
Composite Negotiating Text/Rev. 1 issued at the end
of the spring meeting in Geneva.  The organization of
the work of the Conference was much the same as in
Geneva, except that certain outstanding issues had
been largely resolved by the ICNT/Rev. 1.  The Chairmen of Negotiating Groups 1, 2, and 3 conducted negotiations within the framework of the Working Group
of 21 on deep seabed issues established under the
Chairman of the First Committee, with the Group of
Legal Experts on settlement of deep seabed disputes
also continuing its work.  The rest of the work of
the Conference was concentrated largely in Negotiating
Groups 6 (continental shelf) and 7 (delimitation of
maritime boundaries between States with opposite or
adjacent coasts), the Informal Third Committee (marine
scientific research), the Informal Plenary on Final
Clauses, and the Drafting Committee and its Language
Groups.

        The major achievements of the Resumed Session
are reflected in the Chairmen's reports issued at
the end of that session.

        The new texts on deep seabed mining move signif-
icantly toward a consensus that can accommodate the
objective of establishing a viable international seabed mining Enterprise with that of assured access for
States and their nationals under reasonable terms and

conditions; this is particularly the case with respect to financial arrangements, the system for obtaining contracts, and the powers of the Seabed Authority and its principal organs. The Chairman of the First Committee also expects that there will be general agreement on a new text of Article 165 strengthening the environmental provisions regarding deep seabed mining which emerged at the end of the session. There are also new texts on marine scientific research that remove or reduce unnecessary and objectionable restrictions on scientific inquiry and communication. There is a new text strengthening the protection of whales and other marine mammals that essentially resulted from consultations among interested States, although some further discussions will take place.

While a second revision of the ICNT incorporating these new texts was not issued, they were the result of intensive negotiation and were presented to the respective committees. One should expect that their substance and delicate balance would be preserved at a ninth session determined to achieve final agreement.

Significant progress was also made with respect to the narrowing of differences on an interim ceiling on seabed mining production that adequately accommodates the interests of consumers and potential seabed producers with those of land-based producers. Similarly, the Chairman of Negotiating Group 7 has issued a text on conciliation of delimitation disputes that could help resolve the disagreements between those favoring and those opposing compulsory third-party settlement of delimitation disputes.

The debates in the Second and Third Committees revealed a widespread desire to avoid tampering with the texts. Indeed, the Second Committee significantly narrowed the scope of an amendment introduced into the ICNT/Rev. 1 in Geneva regarding suspension of innocent passage. Nevertheless, the Second Committee debates were an uneasy reminder of the willingness of some delegations to risk unravelling the overall package. Considerable restraint and discipline will be required to deal with this problem as the Conference approaches its formal stages.

The Drafting Committee approved the first set of recommendations prepared by the Language Groups for revising the text. While modest, these recommendations harmonizing terminology reflect the general

opinion that the time has come for careful review of the drafting of texts prepared at different times by different people.  A second set of harmonization recommendations is in preparation.

For the first time, this session saw extensive debate on the question of final clauses in the Informal Plenary on Final Clauses and in the Group of Experts set up under Minister Jens Evensen of Norway. Debates on complex problems such as entry into force, preparatory arrangements, reservations, amendments, relationship to other agreements, denunciation, and participation are now the subject of articulate summaries prepared by the President.  Most reflect a common desire to protect the integrity and balance of the overall accommodation reflected in the treaty (the so-called "package deal") while promoting the broadest possible ratification at the earliest possible time. Considerable intersessional efforts are comtemplated. While the problems are serious, they can be overcome if political issues that transcend the law of the sea are not pressed.

News reports regarding exercise of freedom of navigation and overflight by US forces beyond the three-mile territorial sea currently recognized by the US caused something of a stir at the Conference. The Group of Coastal States made a statement during the last week in which it referred to the position that the high seas commence beyond three miles as an "anachronism" and noted that a majority of States claim 12-mile territorial seas.  The US statement reaffirmed our legal position as well as our willingness, within the context of an overall acceptable Law of the Sea treaty, to accept a 12-mile territorial sea coupled with transit passage of straits.  At a conference which has not dealt with these basic issues of the traditional law of the sea for some years, and which regarded them as resolved while it devoted its attention to other questions such as deep seabed mining, this exchange seemed to be a sober reminder to all concerned of the persistence of the underlying problems that originally gave rise to the need for a widely ratified Law of the Sea Convention.

On the last day of the session, the Chairman of the Group of 77 made a statement reiterating the Group's opposition to unilateral deep seabed mining legislation, challenging its legality and arguing that it would violate the rule of good faith in the

negotiations and have wider impact on economic cooperation between developing and developed States.  The US delegation reiterated our view that the contemplated legislation is consistent with existing  international law and compatible with our commitment to the conclusion at the earliest possible time of a generally acceptable Law of the Sea Convention.

B.  Deep Seabed Mining

Since most of the serious outstanding issues of the Conference relate to deep seabed mining, it is significant that this is the area where most progress was achieved, and where the most serious problems remain.

The improvements regarding the Seabed Authority include:  the limitation of its powers and functions to those "expressly conferred upon it" by the Convention and those "implicit in and necessary for" their performance; the added requirement that one organ may not derogate from or impede the exercise of specific powers and functions conferred upon another organ; and the explanation of the phrase "supreme organ," including the limitation of the accountability of other organs to the Assembly by the phrase "as specifically provided in this Part."  The Seabed Disputes Chamber would be elected by the full Tribunal rather than the Assembly of the Seabed Authority, and there is a provision for ad hoc chambers  to be formed to hear disputes between States Parties.

With respect to the system of exploitation, the text clarifies the nature of the inquiry to be made by the Authority into proposed plans of work, which is limited to their compliance with the terms of the Convention and the rules, regulations, and procedures. Such a limitation is fundamental to the concept of assured access.  There are substantial improvements in the financial terms of contracts, including the production charges and their terms of application, and the profit-sharing rates and their calculation. The voluntary character of joint ventures is made clear.  Unnecessary burdens on prospecting are removed.

The most difficult remaining issue is the question of decision-making by the Seabed Authority.  At this session, discussions centered on a three-tiered system of voting in the proposed 36-member Council of

the Seabed Authority. The text issued by the Chairman would require a majority of those present and voting for procedural decisions; require a two-thirds majority of those present and voting (including a majority of the members of the Council) for certain substantive decisions and also require for other substantive decisions that a specified number of members have not cast negative votes. In this connection, Article 162, paragraph 2(j) would be changed so that a plan of work would be deemed to have been approved by the COuncil unless a proposal for its approval or disapproval has been voted upon within 60 days.

The key question regarding this proposal is the number of negative votes necessary to prevent a decision. The US indicated that it could support the number 5. Various developing countries supported figures in the range of 7 to 9. The Soviet delegation continued to support the existing ICNT, whose voting provisions have been completely rejected by the Western delegations. The Western delegations objected to the new text so long as it did not contain a specific and satisfactory blocking number. It seems clear that the issue of voting in the Council will remain unresolved until the next session of the Conference.

While there was little discussion of the composition of the Council, the US delegation reiterated its proposal that members of the Council include countries representing 50 percent of world production and 50 percent of world consumption of the categories of minerals that will be produced from deep seabed mining.

Assuming that the changes contained in the report of the Chairman of the First Committee, other than those relating to the Council, would be included in the ultimate revision of the ICNT, the Delegation has identified the following as the most important problems remaining in the deep seabed mining provisions:

     1. Article 140 -- Sharing of benefits with "peoples who have not attained full independence or other self-governing status."

     2. Article 150 -- Making clear that provisions regarding policies relating to activities in

the Area shall be implemented as specifically provided in this Part.

3. Article 151 -- Agreement on the numbers in the production ceiling.

4. Article 155, paragraph 6 -- the moratorium.

5. Article 161 -- Voting in the Council (including Article 162, paragraph 2(j)).

6. Article 188 -- Providing access to commercial arbitration for contractual disputes.

7. Annex II, Article 4 -- Sponsorship where nationality and control are separated.

8. Annex II, Article 5 -- Technology transfer: the Brazil Clause, time limits, dispute settlement recourse for third party owners, and avoidance of warranty implications.

9. Annex II, Article 7 Selection of applicants: the priority accorded the Enterprise by paragraph 4.

10. Annex II, Article 10 -- Joint arrangements: the failure to make clear that they have the same security of tenure as other contracts.

11. Annex II, Article 10 or 11 -- Payments by the Enterprise: the failure to state that the Enterprise is liable for the same payments as the contractors, at least with respect to activities in non-reserved sites.

12. Annex III, Article 10 -- Financing the Enterprise: the failure to require that payments and guaranties be in convertible currencies.

13. Annex III, Article 12 -- Tax immunity for the Enterprise.

C. Marine Scientific Research

With respect to marine scientific research, the Chairman's amendments (1) confine discretion to withhold consent on resource grounds for scientific research on the continental shelf beyond 200 miles to specific areas where exploitation, or exploratory

activities such as drilling, are occurring or are
about to occur; (2) require conciliation for scientific research disputes that are not subject to adjudication or arbitration; and (3) remove unnecessary
encouragement to restrict publication of scientific
information while preserving the right of the coastal
State to control dissemination of information of direct significance for resource exploration and exploitation. The amendments also require appropriate cooperation in supplying or allowing access to information necessary to prevent harm to persons or the environment, and allow a reasonable time for projects
already under way to be brought into compliance with
relevant requirements before they can be ordered to
stop.

### D. Continental Shelf

The new definition of the continental shelf in
Article 76 of the ICNT/Rev. 1 was generally accepted.
Work centered on the problems identified in the footnotes to that article, namely the question of under-
water oceanic ridges and the special question raised
by Sri Lanka regarding the geological and geomorphological conditions off its coast.

There was general agreement that the continental
margin does not include ridges composed of oceanic
crust (such as the mid-Atlantic ridge), where coastal
State resource jurisdiction is limited to 200 miles.
The Soviet delegation also urged limitations for other
ridges as well; these other ridges are, however, in
fact features of the continental shelf. As for the
Sri Lanka proposal, it appears that delegations may be
prepared to deal with the unique problem posed if this
does not lead to extensions of the limits of the continental shelf elsewhere. Discussion of revenue sharing revealed widespread support for the existing text;
the US delegation proposed what we believe is a more
equitable substitute for the existing exemption for
developing country importers.

While not resolved at this session, these remaining continental shelf problems seem amenable to fairly
rapid solution.

### E. Delimitation

Next to deep seabed mining, the problem of delimitation of the economic zone and continental shelf

between States with opposite or adjacent coasts seems to be the most intractable. By the very nature of the issue, coastal States are paired against their neighbors with nothing more uniting each side than a perceived interest in emphasizing "equitable principles" or in emphasizing "equidistance." The political problems of delegations that must avoid the perception that they have yielded on the issue have long since overtaken the underlying issues of substance. All realize that the underlying delimitation issues between neighbors cannot in any event be resolved by any general provision in the LOS COnvention.

This situation was complicated by the fact that some coastal States favor compulsory adjudication, while others insist that they will not accept a treaty that requires adjudication of delimitation disputes. While seeking a solution to the dispute settlement problem in some conciliation mechanism, the Chairman of NG-7 has until now, perhaps understandably, also sought some means of revising the statement of substantive principles governing delimitation in such a way that could prove generally acceptable. It is now clear that any such text would be meaningless.

In this situation, the US delegation decided to concentrate its efforts on promoting recognition of the fact that few coastal States are prepared to yield their positions on unresolved bilateral delimitation questions in this treaty, nor is there any particular need to compel them to do so in this context. Moreover, any perception of a coastal State that the "balance" has been "tilted" against it in a redrafted text will simply have the effect of discouraging its ratification of the treaty. Therefore, a redrafted text cannot contribute to the resolution of any particular dispute, and can only deter ratification of the Convention. A generally acceptable resolution of the problem would seem possible only if each State is allowed to preserve its position on the interpretation and application of the relevant rules.

F. Conclusion

In brief, completion of the treaty now awaits only the following:

1. Resolution of the remaining problems regarding deep seabed mining;

2. Realization that political objectives such as those regarding liberation movements cannot be significantly furthered by a Law of the Sea Convention and that the attempt can only harm the prospects for its acceptance;

3. Recognition that bilateral delimitation disputes cannot be solved or prejudiced by texts in a Law of the Sea Convention that is to be widely ratified;

4. Finalization of the amendments on marine scientific research and marine mammals;

5. Technical clarification of the continental shelf provisions;

6. Preparation of final clauses that protect the substantive balance of the treaty and promote its earliest and most widespread acceptance;

7. Intensive drafting review;

8. Recognition that actual voting on amendments or articles during a "formal" state is likely to be unmanageable and might well destroy the substantive balance of the treaty and the prospects for its acceptance.

The forward momentum generated now seems sufficient to enable the Conference to resolve the difficult remaining issues next year in a generally satisfactory manner. At this point, the major potential obstances to achievement of a generally acceptable treaty are the danger of reopening compromises already reached, the loss of sufficient will to resolve the remaining issues, or the unraveling of the intricate and delicate package during formal proceedings on a final text. There is a substantial risk that one of these obstacles will emerge. But if a "critical mass" of leaders determined to achieve and protect a consensus can be maintained, there is no longer any reason to believe the obstacles will prove to be insuperable.

## II.  Committee I

### A.  Overview

The Working Group of 21 (WG-21) continued its work on Committee I matters under the chairmanship of the Chairman of the First Committee, Paul Engo (Cameroon), who also coordinated negotiations within the Group on the Council and Assembly.  Although no meetings were held of NG-1, NG-2, or NG-3 as such, Ambassador Tommy Koh of Singapore coordinated the negotiations on financial arrangements, and Ambassador Frank Njenga of Kenya coordinated the negotiations on the system of exploration and exploitation.  The WG-21 conducted its work both through formal meetings (during about half of the resumed session), informal meetings, and consultations.  The Group of Legal Experts on Seabeds Disputes Settlement also continued its work under the chairmanship of Harry Wuensche of the German Democratic Republic, as did the negotiating group on production limitation under the chairmanship of Ambassador Satya Nandan of Fiji.

The Report of the Chairman of the First Committee incorporated the suggestions resulting from his consultations and the suggestions resulting from the consultations of the other Coordinators of the work of the WG-21, except for the report on the production limitation, which is a separate document.  The reports were considered in the WG-21 and the First Committee.  No new revision of the ICNT was produced at the session, although the texts contained in the suggestions of the Chairman and Coordinators are considered as offering an improved basis for further negotiations.

### B.  System of Exploration and Exploitation

Useful WG-21 discussions were held on a wide range of issues, and revised texts were issued (WG-21/2) which improved and clarified a number of points in the ICNT/Rev.1.  These include passing of title to minerals upon recovery (Annex II, Article 1); training obligation of prospectors and closure of areas to prospecting (Annex II, Article 2); applicability of the system of exploration and exploitation to the Enterprise (Annex II, Articles 3 and 8); approval of plans of work (Annex II, Article 6); data required to be submitted by an applicant (Annex II, Article 13); joint arrangements (Annex II, Article 10); and protections for proprietary data transferred

311

to the Authority and/or the Enterprise (Annex II, Article 13).

No new texts were issued on transfer of technology (Annex II, Article 5), or selection of applicants (Annex II, Article 7), and further work needs to be done on these articles. The questions of sharing of financial benefits from the minerals derived from the Area (Article 140) and the review conference (Article 155) also remain outstanding. Clarification that commodity arrangements referred to in Article 151, to which the Authority may become a party, are limited to those in which all major producers and consumers participate has been included in the report of the small group chaired by Ambassador Nandan of Fiji on production limitation (dealt with separately below). A new quota/antimonopoly provision introduced by the French delegation, which would make more restrictive the provisions now contained in Annex II, Articles 6 and 7 (and which would be unacceptable to the US), was left for future discussion.

Revised Texts -- A summary of the most significant provisions of the new Njenga texts follows:

## Article 140 - Benefit of Mankind

New language sought by the Arab States has been included limiting "peoples who have not yet attained full independence or other self-governing status" to those so recognized by the United Nations. This does not affect the fundamental US difficulty with the text, i.e. that it does not limit the sharing of financial benefits of the resources derived from the Area to States Parties to the Convention.

## Revised Annex II

### Article 1 -- Title to Minerals

The revised article provides that title to minerals shall pass upon recovery in accordance with the Convention. This clarifies that no special action is needed for title to pass and that the same rule applies for contractors, the Enterprise, joint venturers, and prospectors (with respect to samples).

### Article 2 -- Prospecting

The undesirable provision in the ICNT/Rev. 1

permitting the Authority to close areas of the seabed for prospecting has been eliminated in the new text. In addition, the requirement in the ICNT/Rev. 1 that prospectors undertake to train personnel nominated by the Authority has been changed to a requirement of "cooperation in training programs according to Articles 143 and 144." The US has consistently opposed training obligations for prospectors, and the new text is a significant improvement over the ICNT/Rev. 1 in this regard.

### Article 3 -- Exploration and Exploitation

The revised Article 3 clarifies the applicability of the Annex to the Enterprise in applying for plans of work.

### Article 4 -- Qualifications of Applicants

Paragraph 3 clarifies that the responsibility of States Parties under Article 139 to ensure compliance with the Convention is to be carried out "within their legal system" and is met by the enactment of appropriate implementing legislation and administrative procedures. Paragraph 6(c) clarifies that "a written assurance" by the contractor is sufficient evidence of his good faith intention to fulfill his contract obligations. Article 4 also contains a new provision requiring sponsorship of multi-national applicants by all States involved. An additional new provision requiring a State Party that "effectively controls" the applicant to join in sponsoring the application, however, raises new problems and requires further consideration in the Conference.

### Article 6 -- Approval of Plans of Work

Paragraph 3 of Article 6 represents an important improvement over the ICNT/Rev. 1 in clarifying the obligation of the Authority to approve plans of work when the necessary conditions have been met. It limits the inquiry of the Authority to the question of compliance of the proposed plan of work with the Convention and the rules, regulations, and procedures of the Authority and eliminates the imprecision and confusion in the prior text.

### Article 8 -- Reservation of Sites

The revised text makes clear that the

obligation of the applicant to submit data to the
Authority concerning the area covered by his application is limited to that data which already has been
obtained by him.  This clarification is accompanied
by a new provision which permits the Authority to defer action on the application for an additional 45-
day period if the Authority requests an independent
expert to assess whether all data required has been
submitted to the Authority.  This provision would presumably permit the Authority to verify that the applicant has not withheld data already obtained by him
but, unlike the earlier text, does not authorize the
Authority to require the applicant to obtain additional data for submission to the Authority.

### Article 8 (bis) -- Activities in Reserved Sites

Article 8 (bis) is a new article concerning
activities in reserved sites.  It clarifies that the
Enterprise may decide to exploit areas reserved to it
at any time, except that a developing country applicant may notify the Enterprise that it wishes to exploit a reserved site, and its application shall be
considered if the Enterprise does not decide within a
reasonable time to exploit the site.  The new article
also clarifies the ability of the Enterprise to carry
out its activities through contracts or joint ventures
in accordance with rules and regulations to be prescribed by the Authority.

### Article 10 -- Joint Arrangements

Article 10 clarifies that joint arrangements
may be provided for in a contract only when the parties to the contract so agree.  A new subparagraph 3
makes clear that joint venture partners of the Enterprise in the reserved sites shall be liable for the
payments required by Article 12.  Unfortunately,
neither an additional provision that the Enterprise
is liable for such payments, nor a compromise that it
is liable when exploiting sites on the non-reserved
side, was included in the revised text despite warn-
ings that the absence of such provisions could have
the effect of converting the parallel system into a
unitary system of joint arrangements with the Enterprise by forcing private contractors into joint arrangements of some sort other than joint ventures to
obtain the benefit of the Enterprise exemption from
payments to the Authority.

## Article 13 -- Transfer of Data

Article 13 on transfer of data has been
amended to make clear that proprietary data shall not
be disclosed by the Authority to the Enterprise, or
vice-versa, or outside the Authority. These provisions are important to the protection of proprietary
data acquired at considerable cost, the value of which
would be lost or greatly diminished by unauthorized or
unnecessary disclosure.

An additional clarification sought by the US
delegation specifying that proprietary data is that
data which is deemed to be proprietary by the trans-
ferrer was not included on the ground that this goes
without saying.

### French Anti-Monopoly Proposal

The new anti-monopoly proposal introduced by the
French delegation at the Resumed Session is far more
restrictive than the provision contained in the ICNT/
Rev. 1 Annex II, Articles 6 and 7. First, the proposal changes the density control area from a circle
of approximately 400,000 km$^2$ to a rectangle of approximately 435,000 km$^2$ when near the equator. Second,
the number of work plans which the applicant may have
awarded to him in the controlled area is decreased
from three to two. Third, work plans on reserved
sites are included for the first time. Fourth, the
three percent area limit of Article 6, paragraph 3(d)
has been abandoned in favor of a limitation to 20 percent of the total area within the rectangle defined
above. The earlier text had reserved to the applicant
the right to define the location of the controlled
area, a right that has been eliminated. Finally, the
proposal would modify Article 7 providing for selection of competing applicants when the production control limits the number of sites so as to give an absolute preference to an applicant with no existing
sites over an applicant which already has two or more
approved plans of work.

These additional restrictions, which were not debated at any length during the Eighth Session, are unacceptable to the US since they go far beyond the requirements of a reasonable anti-monopoly provision and
would discriminate unfairly against American companies
on the basis of their nationality and US sponsorship.

## Production Limitation

The work of the production limitation group, chaired by Satya Nandan (Fiji), may conveniently be divided into three periods: (1) early period of position-taking by all participants; (2) period of Nandan's absence when William Okoth (Kenya) chaired; and (3) final period of intense negotiations. From the beginning of the session the group appeared to be building toward resolution of the outstanding issues of production limitation (Article 151 of the ICNT/Rev. 1.) In the last moments of the session, however, the Canadian delegation raised objections to any report that would have been agreeable to the US delegation. The group ended its work on the last day of the session without a final compromise.

The first period of the Nandan group was used to review the status of the report resulting from the Geneva session. Delegations then moved to discuss the issues Nandan had identified as the highest priority: the floor (a minimum for the production control), and the level of the ceiling. Before leaving for a two-week absence, Nandan attempted to produce a Chairman's proposal but was apparently blocked by some members of the land-based producer group. Okoth was chosen to be Chairman in Nandan's absence by NG-1 Chairman Frank Njenga (also of Kenya).

It was clear after a few sessions that Okoth would make an attempt to produce a Chairman's proposal. Okoth produced two drafts: the first was stillborn due to land-based producer objections; the second was read orally in English to the group and then presented in writing after having become part of the Okoth report to the Chairman of NG-1. The Okoth proposal had two alternative floors: a percentage minimum growth rate for an unspecified period less than the interim period, or a minimum tonnage for the first few years.

Due to structural problems, the Okoth proposals were useful only as a means to begin serious discussions on the issues which both Nandan and Okoth had identified as key.

Nandan's return began the final period. The Canadian delegation stated in the WG-21 that the Chairman should not produce a draft on the production limitation. However, Nandan made it clear that he

considered a Chairman's draft a useful device. He immediately began working toward a compromise text with an intensive series of meetings and frequent private consultations with the various parties on both sides of the issues.

Chairman Nandan produced a draft Chairman's proposal which he presented to the group on August 20. His proposal makes three important changes in Article 151. First, it provides for a maximum period of five years between allocation of the production ceiling and commercial production. Second, it provides for minimum tonnages regardless of ceiling restrictions on the following schedule:

| Year of commercial production | Tonnages of nickel |
|---|---|
| 1 | 185,000 |
| 2 | 202,500 |
| 3 | 220,000 |
| 4 | 255,000 |
| 5 | 290,000 |
| 6 | 325,000 |
| 7 | 360,000 |

Third, it provides for increasing the segment of the market for which seabeds can compete from 60% to 65% over the last ten years of the interim period. Other lesser technical changes were made to make the draft acceptable to both sides.

At about the same time, Okoth organized an informal land-based producer/US meeting in which, after an intense series of meetings among themselves, the land-based producers offered a 100,000-ton initial floor. The offer was rejected by the US when made but was quickly overtaken by successive land-based producer offers of 136,000 and 250,000 tons for the first few years (exactly how many years was in doubt, but 5-10 years were figures bandied about).

In the last three days of the session, Ambassador Brennan of Australia, supported by other moderate land-based producers, made an extraordinary effort to reach agreement on at least one fundamental issue -- an initial tonnage minimum floor. Chairman Nandan worked closely with land-based producers such as Brennan and also with many consumer delegations, especially the US and the UK, in an unsuccessful, last-minute effort to produce a positive result. Despite this

effort, the group was unable even to agree on a report of the meeting. Suggestions for compromise on wording of a report were put forward unofficially by Chile, the USSR supported by Cuba, Australia, and the US. However, none of the above were acceptable to the Canadian delegation.

For the first time in the negotiation of the production limitation, the USSR delegation became active. The USSR expressed concern that the production control may be so restrictive in the latter part of the interim period as to eliminate access except through joint ventures with

[sic]

A new idea discussed during the final days of the session was that of a split that changes over time. The US delegation welcomed Chairman Nandan's proposal that the split increase from 60 percent beginning in the tenth year of commercial production to 65 percent in the twentieth year in annual increments. This idea in principle holds some promise for alleviating fears concerning access to the deep seabed in the later stages of the interim period. The discussions revealed, however, that negotiation of the growing split will be difficult.

C. Financial Arrangements

Attention was focused on the financial terms of mining contracts and the financial structure of the Enterprise. The developing countries had emphasized the linkage between these two issues at Geneva. After extended discussion in the WG-21, which produced no result, intense consultations took place under the leadership of Ambassador Tommy Koh. These consultations led to a new proposal by Koh which makes substantial improvements in the arrangements for payments by contractors and for financing the Enterprise.

This new proposal on financial arrangements is a major effort to reconcile the need of the Authority for adequate and reliable revenues, and the need of the contractor for flexibility. It must be recognized that the level of payments to the Authority still represents a heavy burden on deep seabed miners and is considerably higher than those under any proposal which the U.S. previously had tabled, but it also represents a substantial reduction from payments

contemplated in earlier texts. During the intersessional period the U.S. and other industrial countries must consider whether this level of payments
would deter investment in deep seabed mining.

By contrast, there were few changes made in the
provisions for financing the Enterprise. States
Parties are to provide one-half of the Enterprise's
first-site financial requirements in interest-free
loans and one-half in loan guarantees. Repayment of
interest-free loans is subordinated to repayment of
the guaranteed loans, and it is to take place in accordance with a schedule to be adopted by the Assembly upon recommendation of the Governing Board of
the Enterprise.

## Financial Terms of the Contracts

WG-21 opened its consideration of financial issues by debating the text which Koh had prepared on
financial terms of contracts in Geneva. The major
components of the financial package were:

-- Production charges of 2% in the earlier period and 5% in the later period on the gross value of
the metals processed from the seabed nodules.

-- The portion of net proceeds of a fully integrated project attributed to the mining sector (ANP)
set at a flat rate of 35%.

-- Revenue-sharing rates on the ANP of 45% in
the early period and 65% in the later period.

-- An automatic mechanism triggering the higher
rates of the second period when the cumulative cash
flow was equal to twice the amount of development
costs.

The U.S. criticized the Koh text, arguing that
the revenue-sharing regime was confiscatory as well
as excessively burdensome. To underscore this argument, the United States distributed a paper which
analyzed the effects of the financial arrangements
on seabed mining projects under a variety of assumptions as to profitability. The analysis showed a
larger drop in the internal rate of return in marginal cases than it did for highly profitable cases.

The U.S., along with the EC countries and Japan, further stressed the importance of having a correct determination of the net proceeds attributable to mining (ANP), since this would represent the revenue-sharing base for the Authority. The flat rate of 35% was well above the 20% - 25% figure which was supported by the financial projections. Since a flat rate could not account for projects organized on any basis other than three-metal integrated production, the U.S. Delegation recommended a formula based on the allocation of proceeds among stages of production in proportion to the investment in each stage (cost-ratio method). Thus, a formula for ANP for mining would be the ratio of the contractor's mining development costs to total development costs.

Finally, the U.S. pointed out that the financial terms that mining operations would likely be

[sic]

Comments of other western industrialized countries mirrored those of the United States. They reminded Koh that the production charge rates of 2% and 5% on the gross proceeds of an integrated project amounted to charges of 10% and 25% on the proceeds from mining. Since the proceeds were levied without regard to profitability, these rates represented a significant deterrent to investment. Industrialized countries also requested improvements in the mechanism which triggered the higher rates of the second period.

In rebuttal, developing countries (G-77) outlined the changes which they in turn required in the text:

-- a surcharge on excess profits;

-- a requirement that only fully integrated operators could be granted contracts;

-- revision of the mechanism for triggering the higher rates of the second period;

-- acceptance of the principle of equivalency between the financial terms faced by land-based producers and seabed miners.

-- periodic review and revision of the financial terms of contracts.

Near the end of WG-21 discussions, Evensen (Norway) made a new proposal on financial arrangements. It included a trigger clause similar to that in the existing text. Royalty rates would be 2% in the early period and 4% in the later period. The ANP percentage would rise from 20% in the early period to 40% in the later period. Finally, the Authority's share of ANP would be 40% in each period, but during the second period an additional profits tax of 35% would be charged on the whole of the mining sector income if the annual return on investment exceeded 10%. Although the proposal contained major defects, it nonetheless represented some improvement over the ICNT/Rev. 1 in view of its partial cognizance of annual return on investment, lower production charges, and a lower ANP for part of the contract period.

After the full WG-21 completed discussions on the financial terms of contracts, Koh convened a group of financial experts from the WG-21 countries to explore further various approaches to solving the ANP problem and to study ways of increasing the flexibility of the revenue-sharing system. To facilitate the discussions, Koh produced two papers which proposed alternative means for calculating ANP, and one paper which proposed a more flexible system.

The papers on ANP outlined four basic approaches to determine the ANP of the mining sector:

-- A flat ANP rate;

-- The cost-ratio formula;

-- The net-back formula;

-- The cost-plus formula.

Extended discussion of each of the formulas took place, a signal that the participants recognized the inadequacies of a flat rate. The net-back formula, which had some appeal among the G-77 and to Koh, subtracts both the costs of downstream activities and a predetermined return on downstream investment from the gross proceeds of the integrated project. The residual amount is assigned as the gross proceeds of mining. The cost-plus approach starts with the costs

of mining and adds a predetermined return on mining
investment in order to calculate the gross proceeds
of mining. The industrialized countries argued that
both of these approaches could lead to arbitrary and
unpredictable results, depending on the chosen return
on investment. For instance, the net-back procedure
could result in a negative ANP in bad years, and, in
good years, the formula could attribute all additional profits to the mining sector. The cost-plus approach creates similar problems in reverse. While
industrialized countries insisted that the cost-ratio
method was therefore the only workable formula, the
G-77 could not accept it because they believed that
the approach did not recognize the "value of the nodules in situ." Koh's initial attempts to break this
logjam by proposing that various methods and formulas
be combined to determine ANP were unsuccessful.

Koh's last paper on flexibility in the revenue-
sharing system represented a major step forward. It
recognized that payments to the Authority should be
structured so that when the contractor's overall
profitability is low, the level of these payments results in only a small reduction in the profitability
of the project; when the profitability of the project
is high, the level of payments rises to a point at
which the Authority gets a substantial share of the
profits. Another encouraging aspect of the paper was
a new mechanism to trigger the second period, and a
revenue-sharing schedule loosely based on the annual
return on investment.

After these deliberations, Koh engaged in exhaustive consultations. The text which Koh developed
from these consultations contains the following major
elements:

-- There is a production charge of 2% in the
first period of commercial production and 4% in the
second period. If the annual return on investment in
the second period falls below 15%, the production
charge drops back to 2%.

-- ANP is based on the ratio of development
costs of mining to the contractor's total development
costs. The product of this ratio and the total net
proceeds determines the attributable net proceeds of
mining. ANP, however, may not fall below 25% of the
total net proceeds in a three-metal integrated project. In other cases, the Authority may adjust the

floor so that it bears the same relationship to those cases as the 25% floor does to the three-metal case.

-- The Authority's share of net proceeds is based on the following incremental schedule applicable to that part of the ANP falling within each increment:

| Return on Investment | First Period of Commercial Production | Second Period of Commercial Production |
|---|---|---|
| Greater than 0% Less than 10% | 35% | 40% |
| Greater than 10% Less than 20% | 42.5% | 50% |
| Greater than 20% | 50% | 70% |

-- The higher rates of the second period are triggered only when the contractor has recovered his development costs with interest of 10%.

In addition, Koh's text adds a new objective to the effect that the financial incentives provided to contractors by Part XI could not place seabed miners at an artificial competitive advantage over land-based miners.

The structure of the new article represents a carefully balanced package which attempts to meet the concerns of the potential seabed-mining countries and the developing countries. The incremental rates based on annual returns on investment, the mechanism for triggering the second period, and the production charge trigger in the second period give the system the crucial element of flexibility which all previous texts had lacked. When the contractor's profitability is low, payments to the Authority will result in a smaller reduction in profitability. When the contractor's profits are high, the Authority will share in a proportionately higher part of those profits.

Many of the problems associated with a flat ANP rate, such as the determination of ANP for a partially integrated project or a four-metal project, have been reduced by the introduction of the cost-ratio method. A floor of 25% for a three-metal project is provided to meet the concerns of the G-77 that unusual

or continued circumstances might drastically reduce
the income of the Authority. Since the U.S. and
other industrialized countries believe that the cost-
ratio for a three-metal project would be in the area
of 20%, the floor provision has in effect guaranteed
the Authority a substantial revenue-sharing base.

An incremental schedule of rates introduces a
needed element of flexibility. Lower rates apply
when the annual return on investment is low, which
will help miners in bad years. Higher rates apply
when the annual return is high, meeting the G-77 demand for a form of excess profits surcharge. Finally,
the fears of the G-77 land-based producers that incentive clauses in the text would result in subsidization of seabed miners by means of financial arrangements have been allayed by the new subparagraph (f)
in paragraph 1.

### Financing the Enterprise

The WG-21 debate on financing the Enterprise
centered on three issues:

-- The portion of Enterprise first-site financing which would be composed of direct interest-free
loans from States Parties and what the terms of those
loans would be;

-- The scale of assessments for guarantees and
loans;

-- The value of government guarantees.

Under the ICNT/Rev. 1, States Parties would provide one-half of the Enterprise's first-site financing needs in long-term interest-free refundable loans,
and the other half in loan guarantees. The U.S. and
other industrialized countries objected to this formula, and argued that the financing program provided
in an earlier document (NG-2/5) was entirely adequate
to meet the financial needs of the Enterprise for one
mine site. In NG-2/5, States Parties would guarantee
Enterprise borrowing for its first mine site and provide, as necessary, "up to one third" of its needs in
paid-in capital "to secure the borrowing of the Enterprise." The U.S. reminded the Conference that it
would not subsidize its own miners, and thus would
have difficulty obtaining funds from Congress which
had the appearance of a grant or subsidy for the

324

Enterprise. In addition, the U.S. pointed out that
government guarantees would enable the Enterprise to
command better terms and conditions than mining companies receive in project financing. State Party
loans and guarantees must, of course, be in freely
convertible currency.

Concern was expressed by the G-77 over the financial viability of the Enterprise under the NG-2/5
formula, particularly with respect to its ability to
service its debt under a 2:1 "debt-equity" ratio.
Supported by China and the Eastern European countries,
the G-77 also argued that seabed-mining countries
should bear the entire burden of financing the Enterprise, rather than basing assessments on the U.N.
scale, since the seabed mining countries would, in
their view, receive the bulk of the benefits from
mining.

Koh made several changes with respect to financing the Enterprise. The funds will be available for
funding Enterprise participation in several projects,
rather than limited to a single fully integrated
project. The measure of funding, however, remains
the cost of one fully integrated four-metal project.
Determination of the cost of such a project would be
made by the Assembly on recommendation of the Council.
A repayment schedule for the interest-free loans
would be adopted by the Assembly. Finally, the proposal adopted the U.N. scale of assessment for all
State Party financial obligations.

If this proposal were adopted, it would require
the United States, in accordance with the U.N. scale,
to bear 25% of the cost of a single four-metal project, one-half in interest-free loans, and one-half in
debt guarantees. Total costs of a fully integrated
project are estimated to be close to $1 billion.

Certain technical changes and modest changes of
substance would improve the financing proposal. Among
these would be a specification of the total financial
obligation, an explicit requirement that State Party
loans and debt guarantees be in freely convertible
currency, the provision of interest in at least a nominal amount on the proposed interest-free loans, and
the establishment with the participation of the Council of a repayment schedule for these loans. One or
more of these issues may, if circumstances are appropriate, be brought forward in the next session.

D. Organs of the Authority

The first item of business in the WG-21 was the question of decision-making in the Authority. This included three elements: the relationship of the Council and the Assembly, the composition of the Council, and voting procedures in the Council. Negotiations were held in both formal and informal meetings of WG-21 and in consultations among members of the Group and with the Chairman.

Revised texts were issued in WG-21/2 (as "Suggestions Resulting from Consultations Held by the Chairman") on certain provisions of Article 157 (Powers and functions of the Authority), Article 158 (Organs of the Authority), Article 160 (Powers and functions of the Assembly), Article 161 (Composition, procedure and voting in the Council), and Article 162 (Powers and functions of the Council).

These texts represent considerable improvement in the definition of the relationship of the Council and the Assembly and the functions of the Authority. The texts of the voting procedures for the Council represent one approach to the problem of protection of the interests of the special interest categories of seabed miners, major consumers and land-based producers, whereby a minimum number of members in the Council (a blank in the text) could block decisions adverse to their interests. Certain specified issues would be excluded from this special procedure. Article 162 (2)(j) would be revised to provide for automatic approval of a plan of work only if the Council had not acted on the plan of work within 60 days. Earlier texts specified automatic approval of all plans of work unless explicitly disapproved by a three-quarters majority of the Council.

The U.S. made it clear that there could be no agreement on the texts or the approach to voting taken in them unless and until they included a satisfactory blocking number. We also reiterated our proposal that the Council represent overall 50% of consumption and 50% of production of the categories of minerals derived from the seabeds as well as a proposal that all the rules and regulations of the Authority be established according to the procedures specified in Article 162(2)(p). These items remain for further discussion at the next session.

The Revised Texts

Article 157(1)(bis) - Article 157(1)(bis) is a
new provision clarifying that the powers and functions of the Authority are those expressly conferred
upon it by the Convention.  Further, the Authority
shall have only those implied powers which are necessary for the performance of these express powers.
These provisions usefully limit the scope of permissible activity of the Authority and will serve to
prevent the Authority from lawfully claiming powers
and functions not either expressly granted in the
Convention or necessary for their performance.
(These provisions should be read in conjunction with
Articles 187 and 190 concerning dispute settlement
for ultra vires acts of the Authority).

Article 158 - The second sentence of paragraph 4
of Article 158 has been revised to provide that the
Assembly and Council shall avoid actions "which may
derogate from or impede the exercise of specific powers and functions conferred upon (each other)."  This
is a significant improvement over the previous text
which provided for actions "compatible with the distribution of powers and functions" and makes clear
that the Assembly cannot, e.g., by the exercise of
general or implied powers, interfere with the Council's exercise of the important powers and functions
conferred upon it by Article 162.

Article 160 - The first sentence of paragraph 1
of Article 160 has been revised substantially to provide that "[t]he Assembly, as the sole organ consisting of all members, shall be considered the supreme
organ of the Authority to which the other principal
organs shall be accountable as specifically provided
in this Part."  While the text still contains the
"supreme organ" characterization which the U.S. and
other industrialized countries had sought to eliminate, the phrase has been helpfully elaborated and
placed in a context which clarifies its intended purpose.  In addition, the final sentence of the first
paragraph in the ICNT/Rev. 1 text, relating to questions not specifically entrusted to a particular organ, was moved to a more appropriate place as paragraph (2)(o) in the listing of powers and functions.

Article 161 - Although the revised texts of
"suggestions" of the Chairman appear to place paragraph 7(c) of Article 161 in a more tentative position

327

than paragraph 7(b) of Article 161 (voting in the
Council) and Article 162 paragraph 2(j) (approval of
contracts), the U.S. Delegation, as stated above,
made clear that these provisions can be considered
only as a package in which a satisfactory number is
put in Article 161 paragraph (7)(c) which would permit blocking of Council decisions adverse to the major interest categories by an acceptable number of
Council members.  In this context, paragraph 7(b)
represents an attempt to define those issues on which
the interests of industrialized countries require
special protection and to meet G-77 concerns that
special voting procedures not be given across the
board and on matters in which all members will have
an equal interest.

The developing countries made clear that special
voting protections for industrialized countries could
be considered only in conjunction with some modification of paragraph 2(j) of Article 162 of the ICNT/
Rev. 1, which they had long considered unsupportable
in that it provided for automatic Council approval
after 60 days of plans of work reviewed by the Technical Commission even if the Commission recommended
against approval and a majority of the Council (up to
one member fewer than a three-fourths majority) voted
against approval.  Moreover, as drafted, it could
have been read as applicable to plans of work where
selection must be made among applicants because of
the production limitation, which would be unworkable.
The revised text removes this ambiguity and provides
that the Council must act on a plan of work within 60
days of its submission by the Commission.  In the
event it is not brought to a vote within the 60-day
period, it shall be deemed approved except where selection is required.  If, however, it is brought to a
vote and that vote is not decisive on approval or disapproval, it will not be deemed approved.  This provision must be read in conjunction with Articles 4
and 6 of Annex II which provide for approval of all
qualified plans of work when selection among applicants is not made necessary by the application of the
production limitation.

## Composition of the Council

Relatively little discussion was held during
this session on the question of Council composition,
although there were repetitions of previously stated
desires by developing countries, by the mining and

consuming countries, by the potential land-based producers, and by the small industrialized countries for
increases in the allocations made to them by the text
in the ICNT/Rev. 1. The U.S. Delegation also reiterated its proposal to revise paragraph 2 of Article
161 to require that members of the Council represent
at least 50% of world production and 50% of world
consumption of the categories of minerals that will
be produced from the Area. There was little discussion of this proposal during this session and it, as
well as the other composition questions, will remain
for resolution, along with the issue of voting, at
the next session of the Conference.

### E.  Seabed Disputes Settlement

The Wuensche Group of Legal Experts met regularly throughout the session and issued revised texts
concerning the manner of selection of the members of
the Seabed Disputes Chamber (SBDC) of the Law of the
Sea Tribunal) Annex V, Article 36, paragraphs 1 and
2); the use of an ad hoc chamber as an alternative to
the SBDC for disputes between States Parties (Article
188, paragraph 1, and Annex V, Article 36 (bis)); the
problem of jurisdiction of dispute settlement mechanisms over questions of the liability of the Authority for its wrongful acts (Article 187, paragraph 4,
and Annex II, Article 21); and the participation and
appearance of a State Party in a dispute brought by a
person or entity sponsored by it against another
State Party (Article 191, paragraph 2). The revised
texts represent improvements over the ICNT. Unfortunately, time did not permit the issuance of a revised text on the important matter of commercial arbitration of contractual disputes as an alternative
to the SBEC (Article 188, paragraph 2).

### The Revised Texts

A summary of the revised texts follows:

Annex B, Article 36 -- Selection of the SBDC:
The revised text provides for selection of the SBDC
from among the members of the LOS Tribunal by the
Tribunal itself. This text represents a compromise
between the preference of developing countries for
selection by the Assembly as provided in the ICNT/Rev.
1, and the preference of the developed countries for
selection by the Council.

329

The developing countries nevertheless considered it appropriate for the Assembly to have a role in the process to reflect the generally shared perception that the SBDC should have among its members representatives of all the world's principal legal systems and that seats should be equitably distributed among the world's geographic regions. A proposal of the G-77 that the Assembly be empowered to assure that these criteria were met raised concern among developed countries that such power would restrict the judicial independence of the Chamber. The compromise text empowers the Assembly to make recommendations of a general character with regard to the criteria for selection, it being understood that these would be guidelines only and would not relate to specific membership. Thus, the sole discretion of the Tribunal in selecting the SBDC is preserved.

The developed countries, particularly the United Kingdom and France, have considered that disputes relating to seabed questions arising between States Parties are legally indistinguishable from disputes arising under the rest of the Convention and therefore should be referred to the procedures in Part XV rather than to the SBDC. It had been clear from the beginning, however, that such a result would not be acceptable to the G-77, who have consistently advocated broad and fundamentally exclusive jurisdiction for the SBDC over all seabeds matters. As a consequence a proposal was introduced that seabeds disputes between States Parties be referred at the request of either of them to an ad hoc chamber to be composed of three or five members selected from the whole LOS Tribunal. This proposal was supported by the Western European States.

At the final meeting of the Group, the G-77 stated that they could accept the use of ad hoc chambers at the request of either party, if no national from either disputing party were allowed on the Chamber and if the membership were limited to a selection from among members of the SBDC. Alternatively, they said they could accept selection form the full LOS Tribunal and the inclusion of nationals if agreement of both disputing parties were secured. The compromise text incorporates both of these ideas, but it was not clear at the end of the session whether all of the concerned States could accept this result.

330

Article 188, paragraph 1 and Annex V, Article 36 (bis) -- <u>Ad Hoc Chambers</u>: The revised text contains two alternatives. Perhaps the more useful of the two provides that in the case of disputes between States Parties, at the request of either party the SBDC shall form an <u>ad</u> <u>hoc</u> chamber. The composition shall be determined by the SBDC with the approval of the parties. Failing agreement of the parties on the composition, each party shall appoint one member, and they shall agree on the remaining member. Nationals of the parties to the dispute (or persons in their service) cannot be members of the <u>ad</u> <u>hoc</u> chamber.

Article 187 and Annex II, Article 21 -- <u>Liability of the Authority</u>: The question of liability of the Authority gave rise to complex legal discussions about the drafting of various technical provisions of the Convention and the Annexes. The principal result of these discussions was an agreement that the basic jurisdictional article (187) should make reference to disputes concerning liability of the Authority for its wrongful acts. An additional paragraph was inserted into the text to cover this point.

Article 191 -- <u>Disputes Between States Parties and Natural or Juridical Persons</u>: The revised text eliminates the requirement in the ICNT/Rev. 1 that a State Party intervene in a dispute brought by its national against another State Party at the request of the respondent State Party. Instead, such intervention is discretionary, and if the intervention request is declined, the respondent State Party may arrange for the appearance on its behalf of a juridical person of its nationality. This text represents a compromise between the USSR and others who were concerned that the Convention not create a precedent for actions by a natural or juridical person against a sovereign power in an international tribunal, and the opposition, as a matter of principle, of Western States to any obligation for intervention.

Article 188, paragraph 2 -- <u>Commercial Arbitration</u>: The United States and some Western European States argued strongly that commercial arbitration should be available for contract disputes at the request of either party, whether or not the contract contains an arbitration provision. They pointed out that this remedy is essential if contractors are to have the necessary confidence in the system and its

equitable implementation. Contract disputes are essentially commercial matters which should be settled
in an expeditious fashion with the necessary expert
technical analysis of issues of vital economic importance to their substantial investments.

Initially, the G-77 opposed making commercial
arbitration available at the request of either party,
primarily because of their concern that questions relating to the Convention itself might go to commercial arbitration along with contract questions. Toward the end of the session, support developed for a
compromise approach in which commercial arbitration
would be available at the request of either party
for disputes relating to the interpretation and application of the contract, with the explicit proviso
that related questions concerning the interpretation
and application of the Convention could only be decided by the SBDC. However, due to insufficient time
and lack of full understanding and agreement in the
Group concerning the proposal, it was not possible
for the Chairman to introduce a new text. In his report to the First Committee, Chairman Wuensche noted
that this would be the first priority of the Group at
the next session.

## Other Outstanding Issues

In addition to the above issues, the Wuensche
Group undertook an article-by-article review of the
entire section on seabeds dispute settlement (Section
6 of Part XI). After a number of proposals for radi-
cal amendments to the basic jurisdictional articles
(187 and 190) it was agreed that, at least for this
session, those provisions would remain essentially as
they are in the ICNT/Rev. 1. It was noted, however,
that basic questions remained about jurisdiction over
disputes involving non-States Parties relating to activities in the Area. It was agreed that these matters would, if possible, be reviewed at the next session. This review would include consideration of (1)
the implications of the possibility of disputes between the Enterprise and the Authority; (2) jurisdiction over disputes arising from or relating to any
plan of work between the Enterprise and the Authority
(including the possibility of a third party challenging the validity of such plans of work); and (3) the
coverage of disputes between two separate contractors.

## F. Environmental Issues

During the first part of the Eighth Session in Geneva, the United States introduced a number of proposed amendments to Article 165 to clarify and reinforce the environmental functions of the Legal and Technical Commission. These proposed amendments were revised during the Resumed Session in New York to take account of the views of one delegation. They were reintroduced by the U.S. at the Resumed Session, and the Chairman of the First Committee noted that they had engendered no opposition.

The U.S.-proposed amendments would give recognition to the important work to be done by the Commission in the environmental field by renaming it the Legal, Technical, and Environmental Commission. In addition, they would restore to the Commission the function of making recommendations to the Council regarding the initiation of proceedings before the Seabed Disputes Chamber, the measures to be taken following a finding by the Dispute Chamber, the issuance of emergency orders to prevent serious harm to the marine environment, and the disapproval of areas for exploitation where substantial evidence indicates the risk of serious harm to the marine environment.

The Commission would also have the duty to make recommendations to the Council regarding the establishment of a monitoring program designed to measure the risks of activities in the Area to the environment and regarding the direction and supervision of a staff of inspectors to determine compliance with contracts and rules and regulations of the Authority. Finally, the Commission would be responsible for coordinating the implementation of the monitoring program approved by the Council. (The earlier U.S. proposal would have given the Commission itself the responsibility for establishing and implementing the monitoring program and directing and supervising the staff of inspectors.)

## III. Committee II

### A. Overview

Second Committee work focused on a limited number of issues, although these issues were of importance to a large number of States and to the success of the Conference. Most of these issues were dealt with in the context of Negotiating Group 6 (NG-6) (The Outer Limits of the Continental Margin and related subjects) and Negotiating Group 7 (NG-7) (Delimitation of Maritime Boundaries between opposite and adjacent States), although some issues were handled through private consultations or in informal Committee II itself.

### B. Definition of the Continental Shelf and Revenue Sharing Beyond 200 Miles

Debates in the negotiating group centered on the text of Article 76, ICNT/Rev. 1, which had been produced at the close of the Geneva portion of the Eighth Session. The debates reflected general support for the new text regarding the limits of the continental margin, although some States continued to prefer a flat 200-mile cutoff of all continental margins. However, collateral questions were raised with respect to the questions of mid-ocean ridges, revenue sharing, a Boundary Review Commission, and the Sri Lanka exception.

The problem of oceanic ridges was generated by a misunderstanding of the 2,500-meter plus 100-mile cutoff in Article 76, paragraph 5. It became clear that a misapplication of the formula, as elaborated in the new text, might be used by some States to claim extension of continental shelf jurisdiction over large areas of oceanic ridges formed of oceanic crust, particularly mid-ocean ridges, even though these ridges are, in fact, part of the deep seabed.

To offset this possible result, several proposals were placed before the group. The first, a proposal by the Soviet Union, would limit the shelf in areas of oceanic ridges (of both continental origin and oceanic origin) to a maximum of 350 miles. The second proposal, by the ten "margineer" States, called for a similar maximum limit, but narrowed the definition of the area of applicability to ridges formed of oceanic crust (basically mid-ocean ridges).

Both proposals came under heavy fire from members of
the landlocked and geographically disadvantaged
States (LL/GDS) since, they claimed, both would extend coastal State jurisdiction over ridges from 200
to 350 miles. It was not fully appreciated that
ridges of continental origin were included within
coastal State resource jurisdiction in the Secretariat study produced last year, while ridges formed of
oceanic crust were not so included. A Bulgarian
variant of the USSR proposal did not meet the mar-
gineers' point that ridges of continental origin
should be permitted to be extended to the full scope
permitted by the ICNT/Rev. 1, Article 76.

At the close of the session, consultations were
being undertaken designed to reach an accommodation
to the problem. Time did not permit a final solution,
but a proposal by Japan that would cut off mid-ocean-
ic ridges at 200 miles received broad support within
the negotiating group, as at least a partial solution.

A proposal by Sri Lanka designed to permit an
exception in its case, and its case only, from the
application of Article 76 as drafted received considerable attention and much sympathy. Sri Lanka
believes that Article 76 unduly restricts its continental margin to approximately 300 miles, while it
maintains that because of geological/geomorphological
factors it should extend approximately 600 miles from
shore. Its proposal was not warmly received, however, by States that felt that the text should not be
cluttered with single State exceptions. The suggestion was made that the problem be dealt with outside
the text in some appropriate manner at a later stage
in the Conference.

A related problem was the question of the Boundary Review Commission referred to in Article 76, paragraph 7. That provision was criticized as putting
into the hands of the coastal State unlimited discretionary power to place its outer shelf boundary
where it pleased. As a result, private consultations
took place among a number of delegations with a view
to working out the details of how the body would be
constituted and what its mandate would be. As a result of those consultations, a text was drafted which
will be considered at the next session of the Conference.

The question of revenue sharing had two facets:
the first reflected the system and rate of revenue-
sharing beyond 200 nautical miles; the second, the
identification of States that should make contributions based upon that system. Most States were of
the view that the system of revenue-sharing contained in ICNT/Rev. 1, Article 82 was the appropriate
system, although some States suggested that the Committee should consider a system of revenue-sharing
similar to that being negotiated in Committee I or,
alternatively, a Netherlands' proposal contained in
NG-6/7, which is of like effect.

While there was broad support for the system
contained in Article 82, paragraphs 1 and 2, some
differences were noted on both the grace period and
the rate. The margineer group held fast on the five-
year grace period, but some of them felt that the
rate of 7% was too high. On the other hand, some
LL/GDS felt the rate was too low. All agreed, however, that the rate should not be so high as to in-
hibit exploitation. One small group of States proposed that coastal States should make contributions
to a Common Heritage Fund from the proceeds accruing
from the exploitation of non-living resources of the
economic zone, as well as of the shelf beyond. This
proposal, however, was strongly opposed by many coastal
States and cannot form the basis for agreement.

The United States submitted a proposal designed
to deal with the problem raised by the provision in
Article 82, paragraph 3 that exempts developing countries which are net importers of hydrocarbon resources from making contributions. The suggestion
would give the developing coastal State the option
of staying in the revenue-sharing system, in which
case it would make regular payments with any necessary adjustments made in the distribution of funds
to it in order to achieve an equitable result. Alternatively it could opt out of the system for a
fixed number of years, in which case it would neither
make payments nor receive contributions. Foremost
among the problems with the existing text are the
following: (1) it exempts certain States from a
treaty obligation (the only such provision in the
text); and (2) the more advanced developing countries benefit while the less developed countries
do not.

## C. Delimitation of Maritime Boundaries

Delimitation of maritime boundaries between opposite and adjacent States continued to be a contentious item in the committee's work. Because the Chairman of NG-7, Judge Manner (Finland), did not arrive in New York until three weeks into the session, no meetings of the group took place before that time. Instead, this period was occupied with informal consultations directed to the question of how future negotiations should proceed. When convened, NG-7 continued dealing with the problem in three related segments: (1) criteria to be applied in delimiting boundaries; (2) interim measures to be applied pending agreement; (3) dispute settlement in the event of disagreement.

The discussions on criteria, supplemented by private consultations between the Chairman and selected States, once again failed to produce an agreement. Deep differences remained between States favoring the equidistance or median line approach and those preferring a solution based on equitable principles. Although the Chairman tried various formulations in his attempt to find a "neutral" solution, it was quite clear that no such formulation would be acceptable. Clearly there is no incentive for States to agree to a modification of the criteria if other States might reserve to the article in any event.

With regard to interim measures to be applied pending final agreement, several meetings were held utilizing Judge Manner's formulation in his last report, NG-7/39, as a basis for negotiation. The second sentence rapidly became the focus of attention, with several States seeking its deletion, and others preferring to keep it with some modification. The final suggestion by the chair, as reflected in NG-7/45, was to attach this sentence as a final phrase in the first sentence so that States would "during this transitional period not [act in a manner] to jeopardize or hamper the reaching of final agreement." This seemed to command a good deal of support.

At the end of the Geneva part of the session, Judge Manner introduced a suggestion for a compromise text on dispute settlement. It would have provided that delimitation disputes arising after the entry into force of the Convention for that State be submitted to compulsory conciliation. All other

delimitation disputes could be excepted from any form of compulsory settlement. The U.S. and several other States had opposed the inclusion of Judge Manner's text in the ICNT/Rev. 1 and, therefore, the ICNT text was left unchanged. (The ICNT ensures that there will be some form of compulsory and binding settlement for delimitation disputes.)

The informal consultations at the beginning of this session suggested that the Soviet Union and equitable principle advocates were strongly in favor of using the Manner text on dispute settlements as a new basis of negotiation. The U.S. and others realized, however, that this text was too close to the position of the dispute settlement opponents to be a finally acceptable compromise. Therefore, when the formal NG-7 meetings began, the U.S. proposed several changes in the Manner text designed to bring it closer to a reasonable compromise position. These changes would have clarified the exception of mixed marine and land territory disputes, reserved the controlling effect of other dispute settlement agreements on the subject of maritime boundary delimitation, and, most importantly, changed the critical date for the division between the past and future disputes from the date of entry into force of the Convention between the disputing parties to the date of entry into force of the Convention as a whole.

When formal meetings of the negotiating group began, discussion centered around Manner's text. Predictably, the advocates of dispute settlement (primarily the equidistance States) were strongly critical of this text and were generally of the opinion that the U.S. amendments did not bring the text close enough to a true middle position.

After a week and a half of full group discussion in which little progress was made, Judge Manner announced his intention to set up, under his chairmanship, a small consultative group of interested States to work on the dispute-settlement aspects of this problem alone. The group worked for several days on the basis of the Manner text and produced a revision incorporating the substance of two of the three U.S. amendments and parts of the third (relating to mixed land and sea disputes). However, the advocates of dispute settlement did not participate actively in this small group, primarily because of Judge Manner's stated intention to work on the basis of his text.

Therefore, when the results of that small group's work were presented to the full group, the dispute settlement advocates did not accept the text. Despite last minute efforts by Manner to develop a compromise provision in further small group negotiations, no new text emerged from this session. A suggestion was made to add a paragraph to the substantive Articles 74 and 83, which would permit a State to declare at the time of ratification or accession that it interprets the Article in a certain way. In that event no other interpretation could be applied against that State without its consent.

D. Marine Mammals

The U.S. continued efforts to negotiate improvements in Article 65 regarding the conservation of marine mammals. After intensive consultation, a meeting of approximately 25 interested States was held, as a result of which the U.S. redrafted its suggested amendment. The text reads as follows:

> Nothing in this part restricts the right of a coastal State or the competence of an international organization, as appropriate, to prohibit, limit, or regulate the exploitation of marine mammals more strictly than provided for in this part. In this connection, States shall cooperate with a view to the conservation of marine mammals and in the case of cetaceans shall in particular work through the appropriate international organizations for their conservation, management, and study.

Time did not permit a final negotiation, but the U.S. tabled the text as a working document in Committee II and it is reflected in the Chairman's final report as the basis for further discussion in the next session. It was clear that the proposed draft commanded the support of a large majority of those States which participated in the consultations and formed a good basis for a final outcome.

E. Miscellaneous

During the informal meetings of Committee II, the Chair permitted wide-ranging discussion of various proposals put forward by States. Amendments were suggested for Articles 25, paragraph 3, 36, 56,

62, 63, paragraph 2, 65, 77, 98, paragraph 3 and 121.
A new Article 121 (bis) was proposed by Ecuador regarding archipelagos that are part of a State. An
amendment to Article 25, paragraph 3 was proposed to
clarify the intent of the amendment introduced into
the ICNT/Rev. 1 that added the element of the "safety of ships" as a reason for suspending innocent passage in the territorial sea. The present proposal
was to delete the words "or for the safety of ships"
and to substitute therefor "including weapons exercises." This proposal was further amended by adding
"by such State," and, in that form, was accepted by
the committee. All other proposals, except for Article 65 (marine mammals), drew sufficient opposition to reflect a lack of ability to achieve a consensus. Article 121 (bis) was not discussed but had
in prior sessions been opposed.


IV.  Committee III

Marine Scientific Research

Negotiations on marine scientific research moved
forward at this session. This area of negotiations
in the Conference has always been disappointing because of the concerns and suspicions of developing
countries in particular. The ICNT, however, went too
far in the direction of coastal States and provided
inadequate protection for research interests. This
necessitated our introducing proposed amendments to
the ICNT. To prevent unbalancing the text, the
amendments proposed were of necessity modest, but
they would accomplish essential improvements. At
this session, these amendments were given serious
consideration. While the results of the negotiating
process were somewhat less than we had hoped, the
package of amendments represents, on balance, a distinct improvement over the ICNT.

The Chairman of Committee III (Yankov of Bulgaria), in his report to the Plenary, included the
texts which emerged from the negotiations. In his
report, he stated his view that they improved the
prospect of achieving consensus and that several
amendments could be considered generally accepted.
He also stated that most delegations could accept the
other amendments in substance, but some drafting
changes were required.

The first amendment contained in the Chairman's
Report adds a sentence to Article 242 and obligates
States to provide other States "when appropriate"
with information necessary to prevent damage to the
health and safety of persons or the environment. It
serves, therefore, as a useful adjunct to the more
generalized obligation upon parties to promote and
facilitate marine scientific research.

Under the Chairman's Report, a new article would
be added dealing with two aspects of the basic regime:
the "in normal circumstances" exception and the regime
for research on the shelf beyond 200 miles.

Under the basic regime article, a coastal State
must give its consent "in normal circumstances" subject to four specific exceptions. The purpose of the
normal circumstances language is to allow a coastal
State to refuse consent when the overall relations
between the researching State and the coastal State
are strained. The proposed amendment makes clear
that the absence of diplomatic relations does not
necessarily mean that normal circumstances do not
exist. If there are no diplomatic relations because
the overall relationship is strained, circumstances
clearly are not normal. On the other hand, circumstances could be normal where the absence of a diplomatic relationship is due to some reasons other than
strained relations between the researching State and
the coastal State.

The regime for research on the continental shelf
was one of the most intractable issues this session.
The broad margin states were reluctant to consider
any regime which implied that the shelf beyond 200
miles was different from the shelf within. The compromise text, while accomplishing considerably less
than we had originally proposed, is clearly better
than the ICNT/Rev. l. All marine scientific research
projects on the continental shelf must comply with the
duty to provide notice and undertake the normal research State obligations, e.g., participation by the
coastal State, data sharing, etc. Consent also must
be obtained, but the largest category of research activities over which the coastal State has discretion
to withhold consent has been substantially narrowed.
A research project of direct significance for exploration and exploitation of resources is subject to discretionary consent of the coastal State only when undertaken "in specific areas of the continental shelf

beyond 200 miles which the coastal State has publicly designated as areas in which exploitation or exploratory operations, such as exploratory drilling, are occurring or are about to occur."

One minor amendment would insure that special procedures for obtaining coastal State consent for research projects conducted by global and regional organizations only apply if such organizations are "intergovernmental." Another would seek to make more specific the obligation of researchers by substituting "providing an assessment and assisting in their interpretation" as opposed to "assisting in assessing" research data and results.

The restriction on publication contemplated by the ICNT has been considerably relaxed. Under the ICNT, the coastal State could restrict publication of all research findings, and indeed the text virtually invited the coastal State to do so. The amendment, while making clear that the coastal State can impose different conditions for research projects subject to its discretionary consent, limits the coastal State's ability to restrict the international availability of research results to projects of direct significance for the exploration and exploitation of natural resources.

Under the ICNT, a marine scientific research project could be stopped while in progress under certain specified conditions. The amendment introduces additional flexibility by allowing for either suspension, or cessation, but provides that cessation may be instituted only after the expiration of a reasonable period of time. "Reasonable time" when there has been a gross violation of the Convention would presumably be far different than when a minor infraction had occurred. Another amendment which would improve the ICNT insures that suspension and cessation can be invoked only if a project varies materially from all information available to the coastal State at the time it granted its consent, not just that initially communicated to it.

The article dealing with facilitating access to harbors has been substantially modified. While all agreed on the desirability of facilitating such access, many delegations displayed great sensitivity on this point. The compromise text sets forth the principle of facilitating access to harbors for marine

342

scientific research vessels but substantially dilutes any obligation to do so.

Negotiations regarding dispute settlement on scientific research in the economic zone and on the continental shelf were difficult. The compromise amendment subjects those disputes which are excepted from binding settlement to compulsory conciliation, with the exception of exercise of discretion to with-hold consent for specified projects, e.g., resource-oriented research. Our ability to accept this com-promise would be possible only if a decision by the coastal State to terminate a project were subject to compulsory conciliation.

At the next session, successful conclusion of the negotiation on marine scientific research will be conditioned upon maintaining the substantive balance reflected in the compromise proposals. As the Chair-man indicated in his report, drafting changes may be required; but substantive changes will destroy the fragile compromises now reflected in these amendments

V. Dispute Settlement

One informal plenary meeting during the session was devoted to consideration of several proposed changes to Part XV of the ICNT/Rev. 1 and associated annexes which had been presented in 1978 by Switzer-land and the Netherlands. Most of these related to the conciliation procedure set out in Annex IV and were of a technical nature, designed to conform that procedure to its use as a principal dispute settle-ment mechanism in several parts of the text. One substantive change in the procedure--the reduction of national members of the five-person conciliation com-mission from two per party to one per party--met with some opposition and requires further consultations. The remainder were approved. The Netherlands and Switzerland also supported changing the order in which alternative procedures for dispute settlement are listed in Article 287 so that the International Court of Justice (ICJ) would appear before the LOS Tribunal. This was not approved. It was argued that that LOS Tribunal has a special role in the field covered by the Convention and that one cannot con-clude from its being listed first that there is an intention to detract from the role played by the ICJ as the principal judicial organ of the United Nations.

## VI.  Drafting Committee

The Drafting Committee's work was primarily devoted to the production of a set of provisional recommendations regarding harmonization problems in the
ICNT/Rev. 1.  Efforts in this direction culminated
in an informal paper containing general preferences
on 26 of the 33 problem areas identified in the Secretariat's Informal Paper 2.

Initially, the coordinators of the six language
groups labored to piece the various group recommendations into a preliminary document.  They were guided
in this effort by the reports on Informal Paper 2
previously submitted by each of the language groups.
The coordinators then took the result of their efforts back to the language groups and incorporated
the few suggestions raised during that exercise into
Informal Paper 8.  The sole meeting of the Drafting
Committee itself during the Resumed Eighth Session
adopted the paper without substantive alteration.
The Committee also authorized Chairman Beesley of
Canada to present the paper to the Plenary of the
Conference as suggestions of the Committee to improve
the quality of the text.

A substantial amount of work was also done by
the English Language Group on some of the more difficult harmonization problems posed by Secretariat
Informal Papers 2 and 2/Add.1.  Although provisional
recommendations were not reached on all of these
points, the discussions served to increase the understanding of all the participants of the nature of the
problems and bodes well for their eventual resolution.
These efforts were assisted a great deal by a series
of non-papers on specific points, prepared by the
secretariat in response to the Group's requests.
Further work in both the Language Groups and the Coordinators Group will be required to allow the preparation of a document similar to Informal Paper 8 to
proffer solutions to the harmonization problems identified in Informal Paper 2/Add.1.

At the Eighth Session in Geneva, a volunteer
study group was proposed to consider the problems of
reference to "generally accepted" international standards and "applicable" international standards in
item 20, Informal Paper 2.  At the New York Session
the group was expanded to include participants from
all language groups, as some of the other groups also

experienced difficulties in dealing with the subject.
Unfortunately, scheduling difficulties plagued the
volunteers throughout this session to such effect
that only one working meeting was held. All the
participants noted their intention to continue to
study this matter in hopes of developing a satisfactory recommendation.

The concordance text issued by the Secretariat
at the Geneva Session, A/CONF.62./DC/WP.1, was out-
dated by revision of the ICNT. In view of the utility of the concordance text as a working tool of the
Drafting Committee, the Secretariat is preparing a
series of loose-leaf revisions which will reflect the
present status of the negotiating texts. Competing
demands on the translation and printing facilities
prevented the supplements from being available at the
present session.

The discussion of future scheduling at the final
meeting revealed some support for intersessional work
by the Drafting Committee and its adjuncts. Although
everyone recognized the potential problems with any
intersessional meetings by an organ of the Conference,
the conviction that the Committee's work required additional time and effort was apparent.

An intersessional meeting would probably be devoted to completing work on the second set of harmonization problems (Informal Paper 2/Add.1). The
Committee would then be free to commence an article-
by-article review at the next session in each language and to compare all six languages. Weeks of
intensive work will be required, given the sheer
volume of the Convention and the diversity of sources
for its provisions.


VII. Final Clauses

The Conference began extensive work on the Final
Clauses at the resumed Eighth Session. The negotiations were organized into two forums--the Informal
Plenary on Final Clauses and a Group of Legal Ex-
perts--for which some 55 delegates volunteered. The
Informal Plenary took up each issue for consideration before it was turned over to the Legal Experts
for further discussion. The mandate of the Group of
Legal Experts is to develop draft texts after due
consideration of the technical, non-political aspects

of the issues presented.  The Informal Plenary reserved to itself the resolution of all political
questions.

At the suggestion of the Conference President,
two categories of issues were established:  controversial and non-controversial.  The respective lists
appeared as follows:

Category (a) [Controversial]:

    (i) Amendment or Revision
   (ii) Reservations
  (iii) Relation to other Conventions
   (iv) Entry into Force (including Preparatory
                 Commission)
    (v) Transitional Provision
   (vi) Denunciation
  (vii) Participation in the Convention

Category (b) [Non-controversial]:

    (i) Signature
   (ii) Ratification
  (iii) Status of Annexes
   (iv) Authentic Texts
    (v) Depository
   (vi) Testimonium Clause

The Informal Plenary took up consideration of
Category (b) first and then proceeded to the more
controversial items in Category (a).  The Group of
Legal Experts followed the same route, but reached
only item (i), Amendment or Revision, in Category
(a).  The President of the Conference issued summaries of the substance after debate in the Informal
Plenary on each point.

Since the subject of amendment/revision was considered in both forums, it was the most thoroughly
considered.  Much time was lost trying to distinguish
between revision and amendment.  Central to the entire
discussion was the argument that the elements constituting the "package deal" should not be susceptible
to disruption.  It was further recognized that the
key issues are the entry into force of amendments and
the problem of objecting States.  Generally States
favored some amendment mechanism to provide needed
flexibility, circumscribed by substantial entry into
force requirements designed to protect the overall

balance of the treaty. The subject of reservations
was closely linked to the amendment issue. Although
some delegations still support the concept of no
reservations, as a political reality it is clear that
at least some reservations will have to be allowed
unless Negotiating Group 7 adopts an approach permitting States to make declarations of interpretation
that are effective for them. Many of the delegations
noted that liberal reservation provisions would destroy the consensus procedure of the Conference. One
solution proffered would categorize the provisions of
the treaty according to their status vis-a-vis reservations. Those provisions embodying "jus cogens," or
reflecting customary international law, or fundamental to the package deal would not be subject to reservations. No effort was made to identify all the
articles which would compromise such categories. By
way of example, however, some States cited the seabed
regime, exclusive economic zone provisions, and the
marine scientific research articles. Immediate response was heard from others, suggesting that many
provisions concerning rights of navigation and overflight and protection of the marine environment
should also receive this treatment.

"Relation to Other Conventions" was raised with
respect to three issues:

(i) The extent to which the 1958 Law of the
Sea Conventions will be superseded by the new treaty;

(ii) The effect of the new treaty on other UN
sponsored treaties dealing with related subjects;

(iii) The effect of the treaty upon bilateral
agreements on related subjects.

Although no firm decision was taken, the trend
emerged against abrogation of agreements which do not
impair the rights and duties of third parties under
the new treaty. For example, it was assumed that
Article 2 of the Convention on Civil Aviation would
be applied to the territorial sea under the LOS Convention, and Article 12 would continue to apply beyond the territorial sea.

"Entry into Force" raised three issues:

(i) Entry into force of the Convention;
(ii) Provisional application of the treaty;

(iii) The formation of a Preparatory Commission.

Universal participation in the Convention coupled with early entry into force was the admitted
aim of the majority of the speakers. The proposals
on specific numbers of States required for entry into
force ranged from a low of those 36 which would qual-
itatively allow for the functioning of the Council of
the Seabed Authority, to a high of 70. No firm view
emerged on this point. There was agreement, however,
that entry into force--provisional or otherwise--
should be of the Convention as a whole and not of
selected portions. A proposal was made which would
allow a State to accept the treaty provisionally with
a later right either to accept it permanently or to
cease to be bound. Although discussed at some length,
the initial reaction was cool to such a mechanism.

The subject of the Preparatory Commission was
not discussed in detail, due to lack of time in the
later sessions of the Informal Plenary. However, it
was an accepted fact that a Commission would be established and would have drafting functions; it would
not have regulatory powers and would not be a provisional Authority. It would draft proposed rules and
regulations for the future Authority, but not authorize or regulate exploration or exploitation of seabed
resources.

The subject of a "transitional provision" for
areas under foreign occupation or colonial domination
evoked widespread comment. While for political reasons many favored such a provision in the text of the
Convention with status equivalent to other articles
in the text, strong opposition also emerged with some
States warning that it would preclude ratification.

With respect to "denunciation," general agreement on certain preliminary points emerged quickly.
It was generally agreed that such a right is fundamental to the concept of the sovereignty of a State
in international law. Many felt that an express provision should accordingly be inserted in the text,
perhaps with time periods and procedural mechanisms,
to regulate the use of the right.

The final point discussed by the Informal Plenary was related to "Participation in the Convention."
Six major categories emerged: (1) States; (2) regional economic communities like the EEC;

(3) associated States that have the relevant international and domestic legal capacity to become parties and whose participation is supported by the
State with which they are associated; (4) Trust Territories; (5) non-self-governing territories generally; (6) liberation movements. As might be expected,
the debate on this point in the Informal Plenary was
the most politicized. It was characterized by little
if any attention to the legal consequences of permitting entities other than States to become party to a
global convention of this sort.

The U.S. supported an "all States" clause, accompanied by a resolution interpreting the clause to
cover entities such as the EEC and associated States
enjoying the international and domestic legal capacity of States with respect to matters covered by the
Convention. We noted, however, that among the problems to be dealt with was the question of full reciprocity of obligations if a regional organization
were permitted to be a party only with respect to
matters within its competence.

The UK and France distinguished between the EEC
and other entities, opposing the inclusion of non-
self-governing territories and liberation movements
as parties. It would seem that the debate at this
stage on the question of participation amounted to
little more than an opportunity for delegations to
state their preferences. It is widely understood at
the Conference that allowing entities other than
States to become parties is a complex problem, and
that inclusion of dependencies and liberation movements would probably preclude ratification essential
to the viability of the Convention. In this connection, some delegations taking strong public positions
in favor of inclusion of such entities were indicating privately that it might be sufficient that those
permitted to attend the Law of the Sea Conference as
observers have the same status at the Seabed Authority, assuming they had not achieved statehood by
that time.

Other issues, such as a general abuse of rights
clause, a non-disclosure of information clause (derived from the Treaty of Rome and related to dispute
settlement), and a provision on <u>jus cogens</u> were raised by the informal submissions of several States.
These items will be considered at some future working
session.

Interim intersessional work on a draft text by the Group of Legal Experts is contemplated.

NINTH SESSION
NEW YORK
March 3 - April 4, 1980

SUMMARY


The first half of the Ninth Session of the Third
United Nations Conference on the Law of the Sea met
in New York from February 27 to April 4, 1980.

A second revision of the Informal Composite Negotiating Text has been issued by the officers of the
Conference that includes amendments proposed by the
various chairmen. The amendments emerged from intensive negotiations at this meeting and during the Resumed Eighth Session. They were found, in light of
debate in plenary, to afford a substantially improved
prospect of consensus. The result is a very substantial reduction in the number of issues that remain to
be resolved at the Resumed Ninth Session to be held
in Geneva from July 28 to August 29.

While these negotiations necessitated a decision
to relax somewhat the optimistic timetable set in advance for the meeting, the substantive results justify that decision. The deadlines were a useful device
for stimulating intensive work, but in the end the
need for negotiated solutions prevailed.

Committee I

The most extensive changes were made with respect to deep seabed mining (Part XI and related annexes). In addition to those included in the reports
at the end of the Eighth Session, and those dealing
with a host of important technical problems, these
new changes include the following:

-- The provision in Article 155, paragraph 6 enabling the Assembly to impose a moratorium on seabed
mining after 25 years, if the Review Conference fails
to reach agreement on the system of exploration and
exploitation, has been deleted in favor of a provision
enabling the Review Conference, by a vote of two-
thirds of the States Parties, to propose and submit
to the States Parties for ratification amendments to
the system of exploration and exploitation. Such
amendments would enter into force upon their ratification, accession, or acceptance by two-thirds of the
States Parties. The new provision ensures the possibility of meaningful review of and, if necessary,
changes in the system of exploration and exploitation

and eliminates the need some delegations saw for a moratorium provision in the Treaty.

-- Extensive revisions were made on the question of technology transfer to accommodate the desires of both developing and industrialized countries for increased certainty regarding their respective concerns consistent with the purpose of these provisions, namely to make the parallel system work and, to that end, to help the Enterprise get into business. Thus, the technology transfer obligations will be included in all mining contracts issued before, but not after, the Enterprise begins commercial production, and those obligations can then be invoked only for a further period of ten years. The controversial "Brazil clause" imposing the same technology transfer obligations with respect to a developing country planning to exploit the reserved site banked by the contractor has been narrowed so that it does not apply where the Enterprise has already asked to buy the technology from that contractor. Detailed provisions have been added to deal with the situation where a contractor does not own the technology he plans to use, and the blacklisting system of the earlier text has been discarded. There is increased protection for proprietary data. The obligations of States now include mining technology but are collective and relate only to taking such measures as are feasible within their respective legal systems; only the obligations of States, not those of contractors, include processing technology.

-- The anti-monopoly provisions have been clarified so that they exclude sites no longer under contract to a State or its nationals and relate only to recovery of manganese nodules from non-reserved sites; the area of the total seabed now available to any State at one time is 2% instead of 3%.

-- Joint ventures with the Enterprise enjoy the same security of tenure as other contracts.

-- Monetary penalties have been added as an alternative to suspension or termination of a contract, even in the most serious cases.

-- Technical accounting problems regarding financial obligations of contractors have been eased.

-- Financing of the Enterprise must be in convertible currencies. The Preparatory Commission would recommend the overall amount necessary to finance one fully integrated project, which would therefore be known before a State is bound by the Convention. There is provision for supplemental assessments if there is a shortfall in Enterprise financing resulting from less than universal accession to the treaty.

-- The revised Statute of the Enterprise emphasizes its autonomy and commercial character, and deals sensibly with the difficult problems of taxation and payments to the Authority.

-- The interim production limitation would not restrict production below a minimum "floor," thus affording miners protection against rigid application of the production ceiling formula in the event of depressed markets. The new text also allows contractors some flexibility in production levels to take account of inevitable year-to-year variations.

-- The new Legal and Technical Commission will provide a focus for environmental concerns.

-- Commercial arbitration of all contractual disputes at the request of a contractor has been provided.

While some controversy continues regarding these new texts, in general they seem to command widespread acceptance. From our perspective, the remaining problems include:

-- Sharing of benefits with "peoples who have not attained full independence or other self-governing status."

-- Representation of production from the Area in commodity agreements; lack of clarification that the Authority may become a party to commodity agreements only when all major producers and consumers have become parties; and absence of a pro-production policy statement.

-- A scattered system for adoption of all rules, regulations, and procedures of the Authority.

-- The "Brazil Clause" and an excessive time
period for technology transfer obligations after the
beginning of commercial production by the Enterprise.

-- The potentially substantial increase in
United States contributions to the Enterprise, which
poses obstacles to early ratification, and failure to
stipulate that the repayment schedules for the interest-free loans shall be set forth in the rules and
regulations.

The main outstanding deep seabed problem concerns the decision-making procedures of the Authority,
in particular the Council. It was widely recognized
that while this question is crucial and exceedingly
difficult, completion of the work on the vast number
of other deep seabed problems could help focus the
necessary time and attention on this matter at a
later stage. The few meetings that did occur on
this issue afforded the United States and other Western industrial countries the opportunity to make clear
their determination to ensure that they can prevent
decisions adverse to their major economic interests
at stake. Along with the related problem of ensuring
that contracts that satisfy the treaty requirements
cannot be blocked by political or interest-group action in the Council, this is the major substantive
issue facing the Conference when it resumes its work.


Committee II

The new Second Committee texts largely resolve
outstanding issues facing that Committee. The articles
on the precise outer limit of the continental shelf
have been completed by the addition of texts dealing
with the question of ridges and by the inclusion of
an annex on the Commission on the Limits of the Continental Shelf. The Second Committee report indicates
that the text of a statement to be included in the
Final Act on the continental shelf of Sri Lanka remains to be completed.

The Second Committee itself considered a wide
range of amendments. It agreed, most notably, to an
amendment strengthening the protection for marine mammals, including whales, that had long been sought by
the United States and environmentalists.

355

Unfortunately, the Second Committee debate also revealed a considerable tendency on the part of delegations to press amendments that would alter the basic jurisdictional balance in the text and an apparent willingness on the part of a large number of delegations to see such changes made without negotiation. While this did not occur, this attitude will represent a very serious problem if it persists once formal proceedings of the Conference begin.

A proposal by several countries on archeological and historical objects, while laudable in its purpose, would have altered the very delicately constructed and carefully negotiated list of coastal State powers in the economic zone and the continental shelf with a new, and open-ended, category of sovereign rights or jurisdiction. Proposals are being made to incorporate texts drawn in whole or in part from the United Nations Charter in isolation from other relevant provisions of the Charter and with the evident intent of alterning the rights enjoyed by all States in the exclusive economic zone. Apparently unconcerned that the issue itself nearly destroyed the 1958 Conference on the Law of the Sea, some delegations have launched an effort in effect to eliminate the right of innocent passage for warships by making that right subject to prior notification to and authorization by the coastal State.

For the moment, the fact that these efforts did not succeed indicates that the spirit of consensus continues. But if it becomes apparent that numerical majorities are going to use the threat of voting to obtain alterations in carefully negotiated texts that have remained unchanged for a long time, the implications for entry into force of a treaty would be grim.

Efforts to resolve the question of the substantive principles applicable to delimitation of the exclusive economic zone and the continental shelf between states with opposite or adjacent coasts have finally borne fruit, with the inclusion in the ICNT, Rev. 2 of a new text that may well offer better prospects of consensus. Moreover, it is widely accepted that the new texts on conciliation with respect to delimitation disputes and on interim measures pending resolution of those disputes will be part of a final settlement.

Committee III

The long and occasionally difficult negotiations in the Third Committee on marine scientific research came as a surprise to many delegations that had believed that the texts contained in the Chairman's report at the end of the Eighth Session basically resolved the matter. The most serious potential retrogression came from the effort by some States with broad continental shelves beyond 200 miles to reverse the protections for scientific research in that area contained in the Chairman's report at the Eighth Session. Fortunately, the resulting text, while accommodating the concerns of these States, does not seriously erode these protections.

With respect to other provisions, on the positive side there were several drafting clarifications which both enhanced the acceptability of the text to others and, to the extent they affect the overall balance at all, provided more clarity from the perspective of marine scientific research. This is particularly true of the new text on suspension and occasation of marine scientific research which, while expanding on the nature of the rights of the coastal State, does so in the context of a rational procedure for enforcement of those rights.

Unhappily, the amendments also contain setbacks for marine scientific research. The most distressing of these was the addition of a further limitation on the settlement of disputes. Also troubling was the addition of a potential roadblock to the conduct of marine scientific research by regional organizations in which the coastal State concerned participates. This well may remove a major incentive for countries with advanced marine scientific research capability to cooperate in regional scientific research projects organized by developing coastal States.

The United States was able to acquiesce reluctantly in the report of the Chairman of the Third Committee, because he proposed that all the revised articles contained in the annex to his report be incorporated in the second revision of the ICNT, and because of his conclusion that, with these changes, the Third Committee has successfully completed the consideration of the question of marine scientific research and has--in light of the earlier completion of its work on other issues--accomplished its tasks at

this stage of the Conference. The revised articles appear in the ICNT, Rev. 2.

## Settlement of Disputes

The major outstanding issues facing the informal plenary on settlement of disputes have been resolved.

## Final Clauses

This session witnessed a very considerable expansion of the work of the Informal Plenary on Final Clauses with respect to matters normally dealt with toward the end of a negotiation on a convention of this sort. The Informal Plenary essentially completed work on a non-controversial Preamble in an extraordinary display of cooperation and restraint among all delegations in a context where the debate could easily have deteriorated into ideological confrontation.

The Group of Legal Experts on Final Clauses continued intensive work on drafting articles on the matters delegated to it by the Informal Plenary. Although the texts produced by the Chairman of the Group have not yet reached the stage where they could be incorporated into the ICNT, they represent a considerable advance on issues which had not previously been the subject of precise textual negotiation. Nevertheless, next to the Council of the Seabed Authority, both the substantive and the political aspects of the Final Clauses probably constitute the most important hurdle that must be overcome before the text is completed.

The Informal Plenary also conducted substantial work on a resolution to establish a Preparatory Commission whose major functions would relate to preparations necessary for the establishment of the Seabed Authority when the Convention enters into force. This would include the drafting of provisional rules, regulations, and procedures, without which the Seabed Authority could not perform its functions under the treaty. In this connection, at the end of the session the United States circulated an informal working paper dealing with the protection, under the Convention, of investments made in deep seabed mining in contemplation of its entry into force. Inclusion of provisions on this matter is essential if there is to be continuing development of technology during the

period prior to entry into force enabling both private miners and the Enterprise to be assured of the
capacity to go forward as soon as the treaty enters
into force

## Drafting Committee

The Drafting Committee of the Conference continued its work on harmonization of texts at this
session. There was a growing appreciation of the
importance of that work, and of the need to accord
sufficient time to the Committee and its language
groups for completion.

## Outlook for Geneva

While the major substantive problems that remain for the Geneva meeting are critical, they are
few in number and generally well understood. A
larger number of technical and drafting problems remain, but these could be resolved in a reasonable
period of time, perhaps with special procedural arrangements.

Thus, there is no reason why a final informal
draft, in effect the Draft Convention, could not be
completed after a few weeks of work in Geneva. If
this is done, however, the resultant euphoria could
itself amplify the danger that the Conference faces
as it enters a stage of formal debate and formal
proceedings.

There appear to be some delegations that believe
that the text will in fact be subject to voting on
amendments or to article-by-article voting. If they
are correct, it is unlikely that there will be a Convention. This seems to be understood by many, but
not all, of those who have worked the hardest over
the years for a treaty that can be adopted by consensus and can be widely ratified.

## COMMITTEE I

### Overview

The Working Group of 21 (WG-21) continued its work on Committee I matters, commencing where it left off at the end of the Resumed Eighth Session. It proceeded under the overall chairmanship of the Chairman of the First Committee, Paul Engo (Cameroon), who also coordinated the negotiations on issues involving the Assembly and Council. Negotiating Group 1 (NG-1) Chairman Frank Njenga (Kenya) coordinated the negotiations on matters relating to the system of exploration and exploitation through both formal meetings and informal consultations, and NG-2 Chairman Tommy Koh (Singapore) coordinated discussions concerning financial arrangements and the Statute of the Enterprise. The Chairman of the Group of Legal Experts on Seabeds Disputes Settlement, Harry Wuensche (German Democratic Republic) held discussions on remaining outstanding seabeds disputes settlement issues in intensive informal consultations as well as in meetings of the full group at the end of the session, and Satya Nandan (Fiji) continued negotiations in his group on the production limitation.

The Chairman of the First Committee, as Principal Coordinator, received reports from all of the coordinators on the above-mentioned negotiations and consultations conducted by them, and these reports were considered in two meetings of the First Committee. The texts contained in the Report of the Coordinators were incorporated into the ICNT, Rev. 2 and are considered as offering an improved basis for further negotiations and the achievement of consensus of the Conference. Unfortunately, a text developed informally at the Eighth Session on Article 162, paragraph 2(j) (award of contracts) was included in the ICNT, Rev. 2 despite the clear statement of the Committee I Chairman that it had insufficient support (A/CONF.62/C.I/L. 27 (Part IV)) and in contradiction of the criteria for inclusion of new texts laid down in A/CONF. 62/62.

### System of Exploration and Exploitation

Useful WG-21 discussions were held on outstanding issues in Part XI and Annex II on the system of exploration and exploitation and a number of revised

texts were issued. Of particular note were A/CONF.
62/C.1/L.27 (Part II), which clarified and improved
various provisions in the ICNT, Rev. 1 and texts contained in A/CONF. 62/91. These included the definition of terms (Article 133); the Review Conference
(Article 155, paragraphs 1 and 6); transfer of technology (Annex II, Article 5); anti-monopoly (Annex
II, Article 6, paragraph 3 (d); selection among applicants (Annex II, Article 7); reservation of sites
(Annex II, Article 8); joint arrangements (Annex II,
Article 10); transfer of data to the Authority (Annex II, Article 13); and imposition of penalties (Annex II, Article 17).

These revisions dealt with most of the major
outstanding issues on the system of exploration and
exploitation. While there are still problems remaining on some of these subjects, most notably the
provision requiring transfer of technology to developing countries (Annex II, Article 5 (e)), in general
the revisions can be considered as significantly ad-
vancing our efforts to create a viable parallel
system.

Regarding other matters of concern to the United
States,no new texts were issued on sharing of financial benefits from the minerals derived from the area
(Article 140) or the policies relating to activities
in the area (Article 150), except for the introductory clause. In addition, the question of the ra-
tionalization of procedures for the promulgation of
the rules, regulations, and procedures of the Authority (Articles 160, 162, and 167, and Annex II, Article 16) remains for further discussion.

Revised Texts

A summary of the most significant provisions of
the new Njenga texts follows:

Article 133 - Definition of Terms

Article 133 was redrafted to eliminate a dupli-
cative reference to "activities in the Area" and to
better define the term "resources," including making
specific reference to "polymetallic nodules."

## Article 150 - Policies Relating to Activities in the Area

Article 150 was usefully revised to clarify that the policies relating to activities in the Area as listed in Article 150 are to be carried out "as specifically provided" in the Convention and, thus, to imply that the policies are not intended to be the source of additional functions of the Authority.

## Article 155 - The Review Conference

Article 155 was revised in two respects. First, the particularization in paragraph 1 of the aims of the system of exploration and exploitation was redrafted to reflect a more balanced view of the system, and it now contains a reference to the development and use of the Area and its resources. Second, the provision in paragraph 6 enabling the Assembly to impose a moratorium on seabed mining after 25 years if the Review Conference fails to reach agreement on the system of exploration and exploitation has been deleted in favor of a provision enabling the Review Conference, by a vote of two-thirds of the States Parties, to propose and submit to the States Parties for ratification amendments to the system of exploration and exploitation. Such amendments would enter into force upon their ratification, accession or acceptance by two-thirds of the States Parties. The new provision ensures the possibility of meaningful review of and, if necessary, changes in the system of exploration and exploitation, and eliminates the perceived need for a moratorium provision in the Treaty.

## Annex II, Article 5 - Transfer of Technology

Following introduction of a new G-77 proposal and detailed discussion of the problems associated with transfer of technology, Article 5 was extensively revised. Major concerns of the G-77 related to making the obligation to transfer technology binding both on the contractor and on his supplier of technology so that the Enterprise would be assured of obtaining the technology needed by it to become a viable seabed miner. The United States and other industrialized countries, on the other hand, viewed the obligations to sell technology to the Enterprise as extraordinary obligations to which they had agreed because of the developing countries' concern that the few companies and States which possessed seabed mining technology at

the outset would conspire to keep the technology from the Enterprise. However, there were limits on the extent to which they could bind themselves and their nationals within their own legal systems to assure the availability of the technology. The revised text represents a new approach to these important issues and makes more precise from the standpoint of both the Authority and the applicant/contractor, the timing, nature, and limits of the obligation.

First, the applicant is to provide the Authority with a general description of the equipment and methods to be used by him in his plan of work if it is approved. The revised Article makes clear that this requirement relates only to non-proprietary information, and not to the technology which the operator would later make available to the Enterprise on fair and reasonable commercial terms and conditions. If the applicant's plan of work is approved, this general description would be kept up to date if there is a substantial technological innovation. The revised text has been further clarified so that these obligations apply to the Enterprise as well as to the contractors.

Second, the revised article provides that the undertakings required to be made by the operator are to be contained in his contract. The basic obligation to make available to the Enterprise on fair and reasonable commercial terms and conditions, if requested by the Authority, that technology which the contractor is legally entitled to transfer remains the same as in the ICNT. Despite the initial view of some developing countries that this obligation should apply whether or not the technology is available on the open market, the explanation of industrialized countries was persuasive, i.e. that there is no need to obligate the contractor if the Enterprise finds that technology is available on the open market.

Concerning the technology which the contractor intends to use but does not himself have the legal right to transfer, several obligations pertain which have now been made a part of the contract. Following the approach of the ICNT, Rev. 1, the contractor must obtain a written assurance from the owner of such technology, if it is not generally available on the open market, that the owner will, if requested by the Authority, make the technology available to the

Enterprise on fair and reasonable commercial terms
and conditions. No technology for which such a
written assurance is not obtained may be used by the
contractor. In addition, if the contractor is able,
without any additional cost to him, to secure a legally binding and enforceable assurance by the third
party supplier, he must do so.

If a contractor is not able to secure such a legally binding assurance at no additional cost to him,
the Enterprise itself may seek to pay the additional
cost required to secure such a legally binding assurance. If, however, it chooses not to do so, or if
the owner of the technology remains unwilling to provide a legally binding assurance to the contractor,
two alternative procedures are provided. First, if
the Enterprise so requests, the contractor is required to take all feasible measures to acquire the
legal right to transfer the technology to the Enterprise. If the corporate relationship between the contractor and his supplier is such that the contractor
exercises effective control over the owner of the
technology and the contractor does not acquire the
right to transfer the technology to the Enterprise,
failure to do so shall be considered relevant to the
contractor's qualifications for any subsequent contract. Alternatively, should the Enterprise prefer
to negotiate directly with the owner of the technology
rather than obtain the technology through the contractor at a possibly higher cost, the contractor is
obliged simply to facilitate the acquisition of the
technology by the Enterprise if the Enterprise requests such facilitation.

It was generally considered by both developed
and developing countries that in most cases these
procedures should be sufficient to assure transfer of
technology to the Enterprise but that there should be
an additional provision against the unlikely contingency that a contractor might still be unable or unwilling to transfer technology to the Enterprise.
The ICNT, Rev. 1 sought to ensure against this contingency by providing that a third party owner of
technology who refused to make his technology available to the Enterprise would be "blacklisted" and
could not have his technology used in the future in
seabed mining. Because this provision still might
not assure the transfer of technology for the Enterprise, and because it presented particular difficulty
for the developed countries, the blacklisting

provision was dropped. Notwithstanding the contrary
reference in the WG-21 Report, it is the firm view of
the United States Delegation that failure of the
third-party owner of the technology to make the technology available to the Enterprise could not legally
result under Article 5 in a blacklisting of either
the third party or of the contractor (providing, of
course, that the contractor had lived up to his obligations to obtain a written assurance and other obligations specified in Article 5).

Instead of blacklisting, therefore, a different
approach was followed that would create an obligation on States Parties having access to such technology, as a group, to take effective measures to
ensure that the technology is made available to the
Enterprise on fair and reasonable commercial terms
and conditions. This is the same obligation which
was contained in the ICNT, Rev. 1 with respect to
processing technology; however, it has been restated
to make clear that it involves a collective obligation on all States Parties having access to the technology. Any individual State is required to take
only those measures which are feasible under its own
legal system. It was understood that feasible measures might differ substantially according to what
was practically possible within the legal system of
the particular State, e.g., that while a State that
itself owned the technology could presumably sell it
to the Enterprise, a State such as the United States,
which did not itself own seabed mining technology,
might only be able to take such enforcement measures
as might be possible under its antitrust and other
relevant laws, should its nationals fail to make
technology available to the Enterprise.

Two other important changes were also made in
the revised text. First, paragraph 7 imposes a time
limit on the obligation to transfer technology, so
that the obligation applies only to contracts concluded before the Enterprise begins commercial production and ceases ten years after the Enterprise has
begun such commercial production. While we consider
that five years would be a sufficient and more appropriate period, the addition of the time limit on the
duration of the obligation is a major improvement in
the text. Second, the dispute settlement procedure
specified in paragraph 4 of the revised text has been
greatly simplified and now provides that disputes
concerning the undertakings to be included in the

contract specified in paragraph 3, like other provisions of contracts, shall be subject to compulsory dispute settlement in accordance with Part XI. While inclusion of the technology obligations in the contract has the advantage of making all disputes concerning them subject to commercial arbitration as contractual disputes--not just questions of the range of fair and reasonable commercial terms and conditions--it has the disadvantage of permitting contract suspension or termination in the event of "serious, persistent and willful violations of the fundamental terms of the contract" (Annex II, Article 17).

Several developing countries had pointed out the unnecessary complexities of the dispute settlement provisions in the ICNT, Rev. 1, and the new text is a clear improvement. It should also be noted in this connection that these dispute settlement procedures apply to disputes which may arise concerning whether technology requested by the Enterprise is otherwise available on the open market in all cases where this is a condition of the transfer obligation, with the exception of paragraph 3(a) where the finding concerning availability is to be made by the Enterprise.

Although both developed and developing countries continue to have some difficulties with the revised text, it appeared to be generally accepted that the revised text offers an improved basis for consensus on this difficult issue, and better assurance that needed technology will in fact be transferred to the Enterprise under workable procedures. A major problem remains for the U.S. and other developed countries in paragraph 3(e), which, as in the ICNT, Rev. 1, requires the contractor to take the same measures as prescribed for transfer of technology to the Enterprise to transfer technology to developing countries operating in the reserved site, providing such transfer would not involve transfer of the technology to a third country or nationals of a third country. A further limitation on this obligation was added, however, stipulating that the obligation shall apply to any given contractor only where technology has not been requested by or transferred by him to the Enterprise.

Finally, it is noted that the definition of technology in paragraph 8 of Article 5 was revised to make clear that it is intended to refer to specialized equipment and know-how necessary to operate a "viable"

seabed mining system. The addition of the adjective
"specialized" should help reduce the problems concerning technology owned by third parties. The WG-21
Coordinators' Report states that the term "viable,"
which did not appear in the ICNT, Rev. 1, was inserted to make clear that the definition was intended to cover all paragraphs of Article 5, including
in particular paragraph 5, which contains the collective obligation of States Parties with respect to
mining and processing technology. It is clear from
the text of Article 5 that this collective obligation is the only obligation regarding processing
technology, despite the continued desire of developing countries to impose obligations on contractors
with respect to processing technology.

### Annex II, Article 6, paragraph 3(d) and Article 7 - Anti-Monopoly

Frank Njenga, Chairman of NG-1, convened a small
but open-ended group to consider proposed French
amendments to the quota/anti-monopoly provisions contained in Article 6 and 7 of Annex II of the ICNT,
Rev. 1 that had been introduced but not discussed in
the WG-21 during the Resumed Eighth Session at New
York. Far more restrictive than the ICNT, Rev. 1,
the French proposal in Article 6, paragraph 3(d)
would have prohibited the granting of a contract to
a country that already had been awarded contracts
that, together with the new contract, would either
(1) cover more than 20% of a movable 400,000 km
square, or (2) give that country "more than two"
plans of work within such an area. The French proposal in Article 7 would also have given an absolute
priority to a State applying for the first time over
a State that already had two sites, wherever situated.

Both the Soviet Union and the United States suggested that clarifying changes might be made to the
formula contained in Article 5, paragraph 3(d) of
Annex II of the ICNT, Rev. 1 text to meet some of the
French concerns. To this end, the Chairman requested
that the United States, the Soviet Union, France, the
Federal Republic of Germany, Japan, and India confer
to consider possible revision of that paragraph.

As a result of these consultations, which were
coordinated by the United States, a proposed new text
was submitted to Mr. Njenga. The new text represented

both a clarification of the ICNT, Rev. 1 and, from
the point of view of the United States, an improvement on that text in at least one important respect:
it makes clear that sites to be counted for anti-
monopoly purposes are limited to those which a State
seeking a further contract "already holds." Ambiguities in the earlier text could have made it possible that all sites ever held by a State Party over
time could be included in the calculation, including
even those which had been exhausted and abandoned.
The new text also made clear that it applied only to
the mining of manganese nodules.

In place of the ICNT, Rev. 1 and the French
text, which had called for both a numerical and a
percentage limitation, the revised formula provides
that the limitation would apply only to a State which
"already holds" plans of work that "together with
either part of the proposed site, would exceed in
size 30% of a circular area of 400,000 km surrounding
the center of either part of the area covered by the
proposed plan of work."

Japan, the Federal Republic of Germany, and the
Soviet Union agreed with the new formula as drafted.
France could agree only if it were understood that
activities undertaken in conjunction with the Enterprise in reserved sites within the 400,000-km area
were to be included in the 30% calculation. India
could agree to the formula so long as it did not include reserved sites as proposed by France. India
also objected strongly to the second subparagraph of
paragraph 3(2) of the ICNT, Rev. 1, which limited the
total area of mine sites held by any one State Party
or its nationals to 3% of the total seabed area,
India asserted that this was an inadequate limitation.

The text that the Chairman put forward retained
the 30% size limitation as proposed in the new formula, but did not include reserved sites as proposed by
France. To meet the objection of India and other developing countries, the Chairman reduced the total
seabed area beyond which any single country could
hold concurrent sites from 3% to 2%. The Chairman
rejected the proposed French amendments to Article 7
that would have rendered the entire text unacceptable
to the United States.

## Annex II, Article 7 - Selection of Applicants

The priorities to be accorded by the Authority, when selection among applications is required because of the production ceiling or because of the obligations of the Authority under a commodity agreement or arrangement to which it has become a party, have been revised to include a priority for applicants who have already invested most resources and effort in prospecting and exploration (paragraph 2(c)). In addition, applicants who have made a pre-application but have not yet received approval are given priority until they receive a contract (paragraph 3). Finally, the preference for the Authority to exploit the reserved areas either solely or through joint ventures has been limited to situations in which fewer reserved sites than non-reserved sites are under exploration. These changes represent significant improvement in rationalizing the procedure for selection among applicants where such selection is necessary for the above reasons. It is noted that the text of this Article will have to be adjusted in order to implement the split contracting system contained in the report of Ambassador Nandan on the production limitation.

## Annex II, Article 8 - Reservation of Sites

The revised Article 8 contains a new provision describing the kinds of data concerning the proposed site to be transferred to the Authority by an applicant and refers to mapping, sampling, and density and metallic content of nodules. This reflects the desire of developing countries to assure that sufficient data is transferred to the Authority to enable it to decide which part of the proposed area to reserve for the Enterprise, while at the same time preserving for the applicant the necessary decision as to when he has sufficient data to submit his application and obtain assurance of receiving his site.

## Annex II, Article 10 - Joint Arrangements

The revised Article 10 contains the same security of tenure for joint arrangements with the Enterprise as is provided for contracts with the Authority. The article has also been revised to make clear that joint arrangements may cover all stages of operations (e.g., including processing and refining as well as exploration and exploitation).

369

## Annex II, Article 13 - Transfer of Data

Paragraph 3 of Article 13 has been usefully re-vised to clarify the provisions on transfer of data to the Authority and protection of proprietary data. All data on the reserved site may be transferred by the Authority to the Enterprise, but other proprietary data may not be transferred by the Authority to the Enterprise or outside the Authority. "Equipment design data" may now be accorded the protection of proprietary data, even when it is necessary for promulgation of safety of environmental regulations.

## Annex II, Article 17 - Penalties

Article 17 has been clarified to provide expressly that monetary penalties may be awarded by the Authority as an alternative to termination or suspension of contract in the case of serious, persistent, and willful violations of the contract or the rules and regulations of the Authority.

## Article 151 - Production Policies

The Production Control Group continued to meet under the Chairmanship of Ambassador Satya Nandan (Fiji) as it had in the Eighth Session. At this session, however, the Chairman was able to include in his report (after protracted discussions) a proposal which, in the view of most delegations, increased the prospects for consensus. This proposal includes a floor (protection for consuming countries against the vagaries of a production control under certain low growth rate projections) and, as a balancing element, a growth segment "cap" (protection for land-based producers).

At the outset of the Ninth Session, the group met fairly regularly while Nandan conducted bilateral consultations in an attempt to expedite progress. Early on it became clear that the fixed tonnage type floor proposed by some delegations (and by Nandan himself at the Eighth Session) held little prospect as a basis for compromise. Nandan thus sought other means of meeting the concerns of the participating consumer delegations, including that of the United States. He concentrated on ensuring adequate access under the production control during the early years of seabed mining and toward the end of the interim period (20 years after first commercial production),

and protection for land-based producers during possible periods of extremely low growth in nickel consumption. Land-based producers also sought to pro-
scribe subsidization of seabed mining by governments
and to assure non-discriminatory access for themselves to markets in seabed-mining countries.

The United States sought to improve substantially the production control formula contained in the
ICNT, Rev. 1 by making its own position known and by
seeking to meet the problems of other delegations.
The United Kingdom presented a thoughtful and novel
approach to Article 151, paragraph 2, that was acceptable in principle to the other consumers but did
not command enough support in the group to supplant
the ICNT, Rev. 1 text as the basis for discussion.
The Australian Delegation put forth a proposal to
eliminate all production limits in favor of provisions to prevent subsidization of seabed mining.
Finally, Cuba and Zambia jointly formulated an informal proposal that, although not accepted in principle by all land-based producers, helped focus the
group's efforts on resolving the problems faced by
both sides.

With this background, the Chairman presented his
own suggestion to a small group of delegations he had
assembled in the fourth week to assist him in defining areas of potential compromise. This group met
with the Chairman several times. Although inconclusive, these discussions were useful and increased
Nandan's confidence that his proposal would further
prospects for eventual consensus. The proposal is
based on the ICNT, Rev. 1, but it provides that the
production ceiling as calculated by the Authority
shall not be less than it would be if the rate of
growth of nickel consumption were 3% per year beginning with the trend line value for the first year of
the 15-year data set used to calculate the trend line
(as specified in Article 151, paragraph 2, of the
ICNT, Rev. 1).

Nandan felt it necessary to balance the text for
the benefit of land-based producers with a "cap." The
cap specifies that the floor can in no case exceed
the total growth segment no matter how small. The
cap will thus lessen the protection of the 3% floor
in periods of long-term low growth rates of nickel
demand, and it is therefore undesirable to potential
seabed mining countries.

371

The Nandan text changes the contracting system set out in the ICNT, Rev. 1. Land-based producers and most major consuming nations agree that the new system is a significant refinement, although several, headed by Canada, urged that the figures should be replaced by lower numbers. In brief, the new text separates the approval of a plan of work from a subsequent granting of a permit to produce. The permit to produce (actually, an allocation of the production control for the relevant period) will be issued only when a contractor is within five years of beginning production rather than ten or more years before commercial production as in the old text. The effect of the change is to make the production control system more efficient from the point of view of both major land-based producers and consumers.

As mentioned above, the Australian Delegation suggested early in the session that the production limitation be replaced by anti-subsidy and anti-discrimination provisions. When this approach did not bear fruit, they modified it by calling for anti-subsidy and anti-discrimination provisions in addition to a production limit. To this end, texts were drafted which the participants have agreed to take back to governments for consideration prior to resumption of the Ninth Session in Geneva.

Several clarifications were made in the text of Article 151, paragraphs 1, 2, and 3. Although the changes were not very substantive, they improve the overall acceptability of the text.

## Financial Arrangements

### Financial Terms of Contracts

The financial terms of contracts (Annex II, Article 12), which were negotiated during the Resumed Eighth Session, emerged substantially unchanged from discussions in the group of financial experts convened by Chairman Tommy Koh within the framework of WG-21. The proposed text withstood criticism by France and Belgium, which supported substantially decreased rates, and by India, which argued for substantially increased rates.

It appeared that the system of financial payments was acceptable to all delegations, while the rates of financial payments were acceptable (though

not always welcome) to the majority of industrial
market-economy countries, to all the industrial
Socialist countries, and to the majority of the
members of the G-77.

The United States proposed a number of modest
changes to the text of Article 12. The most important of these, together with the action taken on
them, were as follows:

> The annual fixed fee which the Contractor
> must pay after receiving a contract and prior
> to commercial production should be adjusted
> to conform to the split-contract system de-
> veloped in the negotiations on production
> limitation, so that payment is not required
> during periods prior to the actual alloca-
> tion. Action taken: If the commencement of
> commercial production is postponed because
> of a delay in the allocation of a production
> quota, the fixed fee shall be waived for the
> period of postponement.

> The production charge should be levied
> as a percentage of gross nodule value rather
> than as a percentage of gross value of metals.
> (This proposal did not affect the amount to
> be paid by the contractor.) Action taken: None.

> The use of the 25% floor on attributable
> net proceeds, while acceptable in the calcu-
> lation of the Authority's share of net pro-
> ceeds, creates a serious distortion in the
> calculation of return on investment. Action
> taken: None.

> The Contractor should be permitted to
> carry losses backward as well as forward.
> Action taken: Net operating losses can
> now be carried backward as well as forward.

> Financial terms for the exploitation of
> seabed minerals other than nodules should be
> spelled out in rules and regulations. Action
> taken: None.

Another effort will be made at the summer
session to obtain the changes on which no action
was taken at this session.

In addition to these items, Chairman Koh made a number of drafting and minor technical amendments which have improved the text on financial arrangements, including specific new provisions dealing with contractors engaged only in mining.

## Financing the Enterprise

As in the case of the financial terms of contracts, the essential elements of the text on financing the Enterprise negotiated last summer remained intact. Despite an attempt by some industrialized countries to reopen the discussion of the ratio between interest-free government loans and government guarantees of commercial loans, Chairman Koh continued to maintain that the 1:1 ratio was required to put an infant Enterprise on a sound footing and, in any case, was an integral part of a delicately balanced financial package.

Prior to discussions in the WG-21, Chairman Koh circulated an informal paper which focused on four issues: determination of the amount of capital to be contributed to the Enterprise by States Parties; determination of the repayment schedule applicable to interest-free loans; the convertible currency clause; and use of Enterprise capital in joint ventures.

Of these issues, the last two proved to be the least difficult. Agreement was easily reached that States Parties should meet their obligations to the Enterprise in freely usable currencies or currencies convertible into freely usable currencies on major foreign exchange markets. It was also agreed, despite limited objections from the Soviet Union and France, that the Enterprise would be permitted to use its funds for one or more joint ventures in addition to or in place of exploitation of a site itself.

Major discussions centered on the total amount of Enterprise financing and on the repayment schedule for the interest-free loans. All representatives from industrialized countries emphasized the need to know the extent of their obligations with respect to financing the Enterprise prior to ratification. Both the EEC countries and Japan urged that the amount and the repayment schedule be specified in the treaty text. Members of the G-77, on the other hand, insisted that if an amount were specified, it must be indexed to avoid the effect of inflation. Indexation,

however, has always been unacceptable to the United
States in international agreements, and proved equally so to other industrial countries. Instead, the
United States proposed that the amount be specified
in the rules and regulations of the Authority to be
prepared by the Preparatory Commission prior to the
ratification process. This suggestion eventually
proved to be acceptable.

A schedule for the repayment of the interest-
free loans proved to be a much more difficult problem. Many of the G-77 view the prospects of the
Enterprise as marginal at best, and they are reluctant to load it with debt service which they fear it
will not be able to meet. They regard the interest-
free loans as a form of equity financing which bears
another name only to avoid the connotation of the
control inherent in common stock. A fixed repayment
schedule is, of course inconsistent with this view.

On the other hand, the developed countries in
the position of contributing most of the interest-
free loans and guaranteeing most of the interest-
bearing loans, see a repayment schedule as an integral
and necessary part of this or any loan, and one which
bears in an important way on its value. They wish
therefore to take this schedule into account when
deciding whether to ratify the treaty.

Debate on this issue led to a change in the
text, which now provides that the repayment schedule
will be determined by the Assembly on the recommendation of the Council and with the advice of the Governing Board of the Enterprise. While this solution
does give roles to the major bodies concerned, it
does not meet the problem of setting the repayment
schedule in advance so that States can examine it
before ratification.

Another serious problem related to the financing of the Enterprise arises from the possibility, indeed the probability, that some States will not become parties to the Convention. In that event, the
States that do adhere to the Convention will find
that their share of the capital of the Enterprise has
increased proportionately, and unpredictably. Any
effort to provide States in advance with exact information as to their obligations could thus be
defeated.

To deal with this eventuality, the United States and the Soviet Union suggested that each State's share under the United Nations scale would represent a cap on its assessments; thus, if a State would owe 10% if all the States of the United Nations adhered to the Law of the Sea Convention, it would owe no more that this sum if a smaller number became parties. This formula produced an effective cap but would almost certainly leave the Enterprise short of funds. France suggested that a special conference of States should be called if Enterprise funds actually proved to be inadequate. G-77 countries, on the other hand, felt that each State should be assessed proportionately to make up the short-fall.

Chairman Koh dealt with these conflicting views by a compromise that did in fact provide for additional assessments in the event of insufficient funds but limited the additional obligation to a total of 25% of the cost of one fully integrated project, to be apportioned on the UN scale of assessments. States acceding to the Convention at a later date would reimburse the early comers. In any event, the compromise text needs redrafting as it is incompatible with the scale of assessments set forth in Article 160, paragraph 2(3).

Thus, while the new text on financing the Enterprise resolves many of the outstanding issues, it does leave States with the possibility of being required to pay substantially more than their United Nations contributions, which is 25% in the case of the United States. It also requires States to make a decision on accession without knowing what the repayment schedule of the interest-free loans will be. Both of these points must be regarded as serious defects in the text; the repayment schedule could be dealt with by the Preparatory Commission in rules and regulations.

One notable omission with respect to the Enterprise is any provision for the conduct of affairs in the event of a default. The problems involved in consideration of this possibility are so complex that it has seemed wise not to attempt to deal with them in the Convention text.

## Statute of the Enterprise (Annex III)

For the first time there was extensive debate on Annex III, which contains the constitutional provisions for the Enterprise analogous to the charter and by-laws of a private corporation. In the course of the debate there were numerous statements reflecting the views of the delegates concerning the goals which the Enterprise was to pursue and the independence which it might enjoy in doing so. While opinions differed in detail, with the Soviet Delegation in particular insisting that the Enterprise must be given policy guidance by the Council and the Assembly, there emerged a consensus that the Enterprise should have operational autonomy and that in developing the resources of the seabed it should function on commercial principles. One corollary of this was that the members of the Governing Board should be elected and act in their individual capacities and not as representatives of governments.

Prior to the debate Chairman Koh had circulated an Informal Paper which, in addition to incorporating provisions establishing the Enterprise and its Governing Board on an autonomous operating basis, listed the specific powers and functions of the Board (previously scattered in the text), required the Enterprise to make the same financial payments to the Authority as do private miners after an initial period required for it to become "self-supporting," and made a number of other drafting and technical changes which tightened and improved the existing provisions.

Despite the general agreement that the Enterprise should be an autonomous commercial entity, some difficulties could be expected in converting these generalities into actual language that measured the extent of autonomy and accountability. The Soviet Union, France, and Belgium emphasized the need for a Council role in the policy decisions of the Enterprise, whereas some members of the African group demanded elimination of any Council role and the need for detailed guidance by the Assembly. The United States and a large majority of delegations continued to support the concept of the Enterprise as responsible for the conduct of its affairs within the provisions of the Convention and subject to only general policy guidance. To reflect the existence of some differences on this point, references to policy making

functions in the article dealing with powers of the Board were deleted.

Extended debate also took place on the related questions of the selection of the members of the Board and of the Director-General. A French proposal that the Board be selected for a limited time by those States which account for 70% of Enterprise financing met severe opposition from the G-77. Some of the G-77, notably Sierre Leone and Madagascar, insisted that there be no Council role in selecting the Governing Board.

The final topic discussed by the group concerned the liability of the Enterprise for financial payments to the Authority and national taxation. Koh's paper subjected the Enterprise to financial payments (after an initial period required for the Enterprise to become self-supporting) but retained Enterprise immunity from taxation. The United States made strong interventions favoring Enterprise liability for both financial payments and national taxation in order to ensure a competitive balance between the Enterprise and private seabed miners, pointing out that tax immunity for the Enterprise might present a major obstacle to ratification by the United States. Representatives from the G-77 (India, Madagascar, and Sierre Leone) opposed liability for payments to the Authority or to States, arguing that the Enterprise was in fact an arm of the Authority with a "social/ political function." and thus should not be liable for financial payments to the Authority or for national taxes.

In his report, Koh retained the substance of the changes he had suggested in his preliminary report. He did, however, add two major amendments: the Enterprise exemption from the payment of financial terms of contracts until it becomes "self-supporting" shall not exceed 10 years from the commencement of commercial production; and the provision which granted the Enterprise immunity from taxation was deleted. Instead, the Enterprise "shall negotiate with the host countries in which its offices and facilities are located for immunity from direct and indirect taxation."

## Organs of the Authority

Negotiations on decision making in the Authority were deferred in the WG-21 until after discussion of NG-1 and NG-2 matters, and only two WG-21 meetings were held on the issues of composition and voting in the Council (Article 161, paragraphs 1 and 7), the procedure for the award of contracts (Article 162, paragraph 2(j)), and the relationship between the Assembly and the Council (Articles 157, 158, and 160). Although useful discussions were held on the critical question of voting in the Council, no resolution of this difficult issue could be found at this session, and the ICNT, Rev. 1 text of Article 161 was retained in the ICNT, Rev. 2 with a footnote that these issues remain under negotiation. The ICNT, Rev. 1 text of Article 162, paragraph 2(j) on the award of contracts was also to have been retained in Rev. 2 with a similar footnote. Nevertheless, the Collegium substituted a text of no standing that had been developed informally at the previous session although the Chairman of Committee I had been advised explicitly that the substitute text was unacceptable to the United States and other industrial countries. This action was taken in direct violation of A/CONF. 62/62, the document produced precisely to preclude the disregard of due process and to ensure that only those texts would be included in revisions of the ICNT that (a) had been put before Plenary and (b) had received support sufficient to indicate an enhanced prospect for achieving consensus. Neither condition was satisfied with respect to the text of Article 162, paragraph 2(j) that was included in the ICNT, Rev. 2. The revised texts in the Chairman's Report of the Resumed Eighth Session (A/Conf. 62/91) on Articles 157, 158, and 160 concerning the relationship of the Council and Assembly, which contain a number of improvements over the ICNT, Rev. 1, were included in the ICNT, Rev. 2 with only minor modifications. Finally, amendments introduced by the United States at the Eighth Session to strengthen the environmental functions of the Legal and Technical Commission were included in the ICNT, Rev. 2.

### Council Voting

In addition to discussions in the WG-21 under Chairman Paul Engo, informal consultations were held in an effort to resolve the question of the voting system in the Council (Article 161, paragraph 7). In

the first instance, delegates addressed their comments to the proposal on page 57 of the Chairman's
Report from the Resumed Eighth Session (A. Conf. 62/
91), which was considered at that Session to represent a trend for revising paragraph 7 of the ICNT,
Rev. 1. That proposal, which would have divided issues on matters of substance into two categories, i.e.
substantive and particularly sensitive issues, and
would have provided for a blocking vote by a still to
be negotiated number of States, posed serious difficulties for a number of delegations, and it was concluded that this approach did not offer a likely basis for achieving consensus.

Several new proposals were also advanced which,
it was felt, might point to possible avenues for
fruitful negotiations; however, no resolution emerged.
The United States and other Western industrialized
countries made clear their requirement to be able to
prevent decisions in the Council adverse to their major economic interests at stake in the seabed mining
regime under negotiation. The Soviet Union and Eastern European Socialist States also emphasized their
need for adequate protection for the political and
economic interests of their group. Developing countries, on the other hand, while recognizing the need
for some protection for the special interest categories of seabed miners, consumers, and land-based
producers, remained opposed to any system which would
have the effect of giving a veto to any one group or
category of special interests. Several approaches
considered at past sessions as well as new approaches
and variants on these approaches were discussed, but,
in the end, questions of principle and numbers prevented agreement among the various concerned interests at this session.

## Council Composition

Relatively little discussion was held during
this session on the question of Council composition,
although there was repetition of previously stated
desires by certain smaller industrialized countries
to increase their representation on the Council in
category (e) of paragraph 1, Article 161. The sponsors of this proposal considered that discussion
should be deferred until after a resolution could be
found for the voting mechanism in the Council.

The United States proposed, in connection with
composition of the Council, that the special interest
groups in the Council be composed of States nominated
by those eligible for membership in each category.
Although this proposal did not meet with serious objection, there was little discussion of it and it was
not included in the ICNT, Rev. 2. It will be considered further at the Resumed Ninth Session.

Award of Contracts

Considerable discussion was held in the WG-21
concerning Article 162, paragraph 2(j), which deals
with the award of contracts. Industrialized countries stated the need to retain the ICNT, Rev. 1 text
under which plans of work reviewed by the Legal and
Technical Commission would be deemed to be approved
unless the Council voted to disapprove within 60
days of receiving the plan from the Commission.
(The Chairman's Report from the Resumed Eighth Session (A/CONF. 62/91) would change this provision to
eliminate the assumption of approval in the absence
of disapproval.) Developing countries, on the other
hand, opposed the ICNT, Rev. 1 formulation on the
argument that decisions whether or not to approve
plans of work should be made by the Council. As
noted above, the A/CONF. 62/91 text was inserted at
the last minute in the ICNT, Rev. 2 instead of the
ICNT, Rev. 1 formulation, coupled with a footnote
that this issue remains under negotiation.

Relationship between the Council and Assembly

The ICNT, Rev. 2 contains revised texts on Articles 157 (Powers and Functions of the Authority), 158
(Organs of the Authority), and 160 (Powers and Functions of the Assembly). These revised texts are the
same as those contained in A/CONF. 62/91 with only
minor drafting changes. The revised texts represent
considerable improvement in clarifying the relationship of the Council and Assembly and the functions of
the Authority. (See U.S. Delegation Report, Resumed
Eighth Session, July 16-August 24, 1979, p. 24 and
following.)

Environmental Provisions

At the Eighth Session, the United States introduced certain amendments to Article 165 (Legal and
Technical Commission) to clarify and reinforce the

381

environmental functions of the Legal and Technical
Commission. (See U.S. Delegation Report, Resumed
Eighth Session, p. 31 and following.) These amendments were reintroduced by the United States in the
WG-21 at this session, encountered no opposition, and
were included in the ICNT, Rev. 2 with the exception
of the proposal to change the title of the Commission
to "Legal, Environmental and Technical Commission."

## Seabeds Dispute Settlement

The only text emerging from the group was the
text on commercial arbitration, which was the most
important issue from the standpoint of the United
States. However, other issues were also raised.

### Commercial Arbitration

The Group of Legal Experts on Seabed Dispute
Settlement, headed by Harry Wuensche (German Democratic Republic), completed its work at this session
with a successful resolution of the commercial arbitration issue. A new text emerged from the Group's
discussions, and received sufficient support in Plenary to be included as Article 188, paragraph 2 in
the ICNT, Rev. 2.

The article states the fundamental rule that
contract disputes will go to commercial arbitration
at the request of either party to the dispute. Thus,
this procedure is made compulsory and mandatory by
the Convention itself, and requires neither negotiation at the time of the award of the contract nor
special contractual provision. The arbitration will
be conducted under the UNCITRAL rules unless the parties agree on some other rules or the Authority pre-
scribes otherwise in the rules and regulations of the
Authority.

The provision preserves the jurisdiction of the
Seabed Disputes Chamber (SBDC) with respect to interpretation of the Convention itself and its associated
Annexes. When such a question is involved in a commercial dispute and its resolution is necessary to
the tribunal's award, the arbitral tribunal is obliged to refer this interpretative question to the SBDC
for a binding ruling. It is, however, for the arbitral tribunal to determine whether a question of
treaty interpretation is involved in the dispute and
whether a ruling is necessary for the tribunal's

award. It should also be noted that questions arising under the rules and regulations of the Authority
are not reserved to the SBDC.

The structure of the provision proceeds from
the general statement of principles to particulars
of implementation. Article 188, subparagraph 2(a)
states the general principle of compulsory commercial
arbitration of contractual questions, and the parallel principle of compulsory referrals of conventional questions to the SBDC. Subparagraph 2(b) covers
the terms and procedure for the separation of the
two types of questions. Subparagraph 2(c) specifies
the particulars of the arbitral procedure itself.

The negotiations on the commercial arbitration
issue involved essentially three interests. The
United States and several Western European States
considered it important to provide for commercial
arbitration for contractual disputes. The G-77 was
concerned with maintaining the integrity and unity
of the jurisdiction of the SBDC over the interpretation of the Convention. The Soviet Union was concerned that, in preserving this integrity, the text
should not inadvertently permit entities other than
States to use the arbitral tribunal to raise issues
of the interpretation of the Convention (which such
entities could not do under Article 187). The text
is carefully drawn to take account of the concerns
of the the Soviet Union and the G-77, while satisfying the United States and other Western European
States on the establishment of commercial arbitration as the mechanism for the settlement of contractual disputes at the request of any party to the
dispute.

Other Issues

Several delegations wished to see the potential
membership of ad hoc chambers (Article 188, paragraph
1) broadened to include any member of the LOS Tribunal, rather than being limited, as it now is, to the
SBDC members only; and they wanted also to broaden
the jurisdiction of ad hoc chambers to include disputes between States and the Authority. The United
States supported, and the G-77 opposed, these efforts,
and there was little time for discussion of the proposal. The Report of the Chairman retains the provision as reported at the end of the Resumed Eighth
Session (A/CONF.62/91). Another issue raised was the

standing of joint ventures. An examination of the text of Article 187, paragraph 3 yielded the conclusion that they are covered by the term "juridical persons" and are thus already protected. A third question concerned possible provision for settlement of labor disputes. It was agreed that, insofar as necessary, provision for such disputes could be made through the regulatory processes of the Authority.

Finally, the United States pointed out that certain drafting changes to Article 190 would be desirable to make its meaning clearer. It is generally agreed that the third sentence thereof means that the SBDC should not apply rules, regulations, or procedures where doing so would violate the Convention, and that it should not enforce allegedly discretionary acts of the Authority which constitute abuses or misuses of power. However, the text could be improved by minor drafting changes. It was nevertheless difficult at this time to reopen this text, and it remains as in the Chairman's Report of the Resumed Eighth Session (A/CONF. 62/91).

COMMITTEE II

Overview

Committee II, under the chairmanship of Ambassador Andres Aguilar (Venezuela), virtually completed its work at this session, and a number of changes in the texts with regard to marine mammals, submarine ridges, the Commission on the Limits of the Continental Shelf, maritime boundary delimitation criteria, and others were inserted into the ICNT, Rev. 2. These changes, as described below, constituted final recommendations on most of the outstanding problems before the committee. A number of other problems were raised by delegations but did not achieve the support necessary to justify their inclusion in the ICNT, Rev. 2. The Committee II package has thus emerged in near final form.

Definition of the Continental Shelf and Revenue-Sharing Beyond 200 Miles

The question of the outer limits of the continental margin was resolved through the medium of a compromise text on submarine ridges prepared by Chairman Aguilar:

384

Amend the last sentence of Article 76, paragraph 3, to read as follows: "It does not
include the deep ocean floor with its oceanic
ridges or the subsoil thereof."

Add a new paragraph 5 bis to read as follows:

"Notwithstanding the provisions of paragraph
5, on submarine ridges the outer limit of
the continental shelf shall not exceed 350
miles from the baselines from which the
breadth of the territorial sea is measured.
This paragraph does not apply to submarine
elevations that are natural components of
the continental margin, such as its pla-
teaux, rises, caps, banks and spurs."

This text was discussed in NG-6 and included in
the ICNT, Rev. 2.

The Representative of the United States, Ambassador Richardson, put the following statement on the
record in Plenary session on April 3:

Our support for the proposal regarding the
continental shelf contained in Ambassador
Aguilar's report rests on the understanding
that it is recognized--and to the best of
our knowledge there is no contrary inter-
pretation--that features such as the Chukchi
plateau situated to the north of Alaska and
its component elevations cannot be considered a ridge and are covered by the last
sentence of the proposed paragraph 5 bis.

Also included as a part of the package was an
amendment to Article 76, paragraph 7 of the ICNT,
Rev. 1 (paragraph 8 in Rev. 2) to change "taking
into account" to read "on the basis of," thus
strengthening the recommendatory powers of the Commission on the Limits of the Continental Shelf, and
a new annex spelling out the structure and functions
of the Commission.

Sri Lanka's suggestion for an exceptional method
of definition of the outer edge of its shelf applicable to the unique conditions off its coasts was discussed, and there was a widespread understanding that
such an exception would be accommodated by means of a
"Statement of Understanding" of the President of the

Conference to be incorporated in an annex to the
Final Act of the Conference. Consultations are continuing with regard to the precise content of the
statement.

Some discussions took place with regard to
revenue-sharing, but no change to the present text
emerged. The United States sought to change paragraph 3 of Article 82, which exempts developing
countries from the revenue-sharing obligation if
they are net importers of the minerals exploited.
The United States proposal would permit developing
countries to opt out of the revenue-sharing system
(in which case they would make no contributions and
receive no benefits) for a fixed period of years.
Continued opposition on the part of some broad margin States prevented inclusion of the proposed
change in the final package.

This package received broad support as part of
an overall final accommodation, although some reservations were expressed by the Arab group and the
Landlocked and Geographically Disadvantaged States
group.

Delimitation of Maritime Boundaries

NG-7 finished its work close to agreement on a
text concerning the criteria to be applied in the delimitation of maritime boundaries of the exclusive
economic zone or continental shelf between opposite
or adjacent States. On the basis of his conclusion
that the language contained in paragraph 1 of Articles 74 and 83 of the ICNT, Rev. 1 could not form
the basis of a consensus on the issue, Chairman
Manner (Finland) offered his own suggestion in an
attempt to advance work toward a consensus, as
follows:

> The delimitation of the exclusive economic
> zone/continental shelf between States with
> opposite or adjacent coasts shall be effect-
> ed by agreement in conformity with interna-
> tional law. Such an agreement shall be in
> accordance with equitable principles, employ-
> ing the median or equidistance line, where
> appropriate, and taking account of all cir-
> cumstances prevailing in the area concerned.

The inclusion of a reference to international law and other changes in the text increase the prospects for consensus and represent a positive step toward a successful accommodation on the issue. The proposal was included in the ICNT, Rev. 2.

Since the entire time available for NG-7 was devoted to the issue of criteria, there were no negotiations with regard to interim measures or settlement of delimitation disputes, and the texts previously prepared by Judge Manner on these subjects were carried forward in his report. There was, however, widespread support for the Manner text on interim measures during the Eighth Session of the Conference.

It was generally assumed that, if the text on delimitation criteria could be agreed, all sides would accept the dispute settlement text set out in Judge Manner's report from the Resumed Eighth Session.

Marine Mammals

The United States reintroduced its revised Article 65 on marine mammals, which was the product of negotiations with approximately 25 States of all persuasions and geographic regions. It was supported (or not objected to) in informal Committee II and Plenary and was included in the ICNT, Rev. 2. There were no objections voiced to the text, which reads as follows:

> Nothing in this Part restricts the right of a coastal State or the competence of an international organization, as appropriate, to prohibit, limit or regulate the exploitation of marine mammals more strictly than provided for in this Part. States shall cooperate with a view to the conservation of marine mammals and in the case of cetaceans shall in particular work through the appropriate international organizations for their conservation, management and study.

The text provides a sound framework for the protection of whales and other marine mammals, with needed emphasis on international cooperation. It preserves and enhances the role of the International Whaling Commission (or a successor organization) especially, but not exclusively, with regard to whales. It recognizes the role of regional organizations in the

protection of marine mammals, which are often taken
incidental to fishing operations.

## Archeological and Historical Objects

While all nations recognize the importance of
the need to protect objects of an archeological and
historical nature, a seven-nation proposal to this
effect was not included in the ICNT, Rev. 2 because
it was perceived as having the potential for upset-
ting the delicate balance between coastal State
rights and obligations and the rights and obligations of other States. The text was also vague and,
if adopted, could have led to disputes between States
with no guidelines as to how they might be resolved.
The United States submitted a proposal which avoided
these pitfalls, but it was not debated at this session. This proposal read as follows:

> All States have the duty to protect objects of
> an archeological and historical nature found
> in the marine environment. Particular regard
> shall be given to the State of origin, or the
> State of cultural origin, or the State of his-
> torical and archeological origin of any ob-
> jects of an archeological and historical nature
> found in the marine environment in the case of
> sale or any other disposal, resulting in the
> removal of such objects from a State which has
> possession of such objects.

## Other Issues

Included in the ICNT, Rev. 2 was an amendment to
Article 25, paragraph 3 (rights of protection of the
coastal State) regarding temporary suspension of innocent passage. The clarifying amendment which was
negotiated at the Eighth Session would delete "or for
the safety of ships" and substitute "including weapons exercises," thus adding precision to the condition justifying suspension.

An Indonesian amendment to Article 111 (the
right of hot pursuit) to add a reference to archipelagic waters was accepted by the Conference. The
amendment was of a technical nature reflecting the
fact that Article 111 was negotiated prior to the
completion of discussions on archipelagoes. Other
amendments of this sort may be handled by the Drafting Committee.

All other proposals in Committee II outside the mandates of NG-6 and NG-7 were opposed by a number of States sufficient to preclude their incorporation in the ICNT, Rev. 2.

## COMMITTEE III

Marine Scientific Research

The Resumed Eighth Session of the Conference in Geneva ended with the Chairman of Committee III, Alexander Yankov (Bulgaria), setting forth in his report compromise formulas on several articles. These formulas emerged from intensive negotiations and had acquired a considerable degree of support as a basis for a subsequent agreement. While some reservations were expressed, the overall debate appeared to sustain the Chairman's conclusion. Thus, the United States Delegation, which considered these amendments minimally acceptable, did not expect further debate on these texts with the possible exception of Article 253 (cessation of research activities). The Ninth Session, however, began with several delegations criticizing even the most non-substantive amendments.

It took Chairman Yankov much of the first week of debate to get agreement on slightly weakened texts for Article 242 (cooperation in obtaining marine scientific research information necessary to prevent damage to the health and safety of persons and the environment), Article 247 (promotion of research projects under the auspices of regional or global organizations off the coasts of member States), and Article 255 (facilitation of access to harbors for research vessels). The length and nature of this debate did not augur well for the more substantive articles.

Discussion on Article 246 bis (a), dealing with the interpretation of the term "normal circumstances" in Article 246, paragraph 3, was lengthy. Many developing countries argued that the Chairman's text was redundant and unnecessary. They argued that if relations between the two countries concerned were good, research would not be precluded in any event. At Chairman Yankov's urging, the United States Delegation held private negotiations with several of the objecting delegations, and agreement was finally reached on reformulated language. This language does

not alter the basic thrust of the Chairman's original text.

Marine scientific research on the continental shelf beyond 200 miles (Article 246 bis (b)) was the most contentious issue of the session. During the committee debate several countries joined broad margin States in opposing the Chairman's text. Surprisingly, some of the opposition was voiced by States that had participated in last year's session in the drafting of the changes which were included in the Chairman's report. Opposition focused primarily on three areas. Several broad margin States feared that the test for designation of areas was too stringent, arguing that the term, "such as exploratory drilling," although only illustrative, suggested a stage of development too close to exploitation. They argued that the test for designation should be more general. Several Latin American countries also expressed concern that the Chairman's text would not permit the coastal State to deny consent for marine scientific research projects even if political relations between them and the researching State were not normal. Finally, several delegations expressed opposition to the words "or are about to occur" because exploitation or exploratory operations might not immediately follow the designation of an area.

As negotiations moved from the full Committee to a smaller negotiating group of 40 States and then to an even smaller group of approximately 10 States (chaired by Ambassador Andres Rozental of Mexico), the United States indicated it might be able to be flexible on these points if it were possible to reach a satisfactory agreement on the definition of the term "normal circumstances" (in 246 bis (a)), the dispute settlement article (264) and the article dealing with the suspension and cessation of research results (253). As a result, Ambassador Rozental agreed to produce a text on each of these articles.

On the shelf, the text from the prior session had said that the "discretion shall be deferred and consent shall be implied" with respect to certain research activities undertaken outside specific areas designated by the coastal State. The compromise formulation now states that coastal States "may not exercise their discretion to withhold consent" for such research. With respect to when a coastal State may designate specific areas, the test in the prior text

390

had been when "exploitation or exploratory operations such as exploratory drilling, are occurring or are about to occur." The compromise text states that such designation may take place when "exploitation or detailed exploratory operations focused on those areas is occurring or will occur within a reasonable period of time." Canada and Norway remained troubled by the word "detailed."

The principal objection to the Chairman's text of Article 253 was that it left the implication that coastal States must invoke suspension in some cases before they could order cessation of the project. Developing coastal States wanted to be able to invoke either remedy at any time. Some of these States also wanted to prevent the dispute settlement procedures in Article 264 from applying to a decision to suspend a research project. The coastal State may now invoke cessation only if the change in activities from that which the coastal State had approved was a major change or if the researching State did not bring itself back into compliance within a reasonable period of time. A duty is imposed to lift suspension if the researching State does bring itself back into compliance. Any dispute relating to either suspension or cessation is subject to the dispute settlement procedures outlined in Article 264.

The question arose as to whether the designation of specific areas under Article 246 would be subject to compulsory dispute settlement. There seemed to be general agreement in the Committee that the power to designate areas should not be subject to dispute settlement procedures under Article 264, paragraph 1; but the question of whether such designation was made in accordance with the criteria set forth in Article 246 bis (b) would be subject to compulsory conciliation under 264, paragraph 2. The text finally submitted by Ambassador Rozental attempted to take these points into account. Although this text narrowed the gap, small group negotiations continued and produced a somewhat more ambiguous final text.

While the small group negotiations were continuing, the full Committee continued its discussion of Article 249, paragraphs 1 (e) and 2 (publication of research results). The Committee accepted the Chairman's text on paragraph 2, but several developing countries insisted on retaining the cross reference to it in paragraph 1(e). The Committee also agreed

to the Chairman's text in regard to assisting the coastal State in assessing research results (Article 249, paragraph 1(d)) with the addition of the words "assessment and" before "interpretation." Thus, the researching State must provide assistance in the assessment or interpretation of such results.

Chairman Yankov in his report to the informal meeting of Committee III characterized the texts of Article 242, 247, 249, and 255 as achieving consensus. Moreover, he characterized the texts on Articles 246, paragraph 4 (formerly 246 bis (a)), 246, paragraph 6 (formerly 246 bis (b)), 247, paragraph 7, 253, and 264 as compromise formulas providing a better prospect for agreement than his compromise text from the Eighth Session. He noted some reservations and objections to these articles but stated that in his opinion they met the test for inclusion in a revision of the ICNT. He also stated that a last-minute compromise formula on the rights of landlocked and geographically disadvantaged States (Article 254) fell into this category. All appear in the ICNT, Rev. 2.

In his summation, Chairman Yankov stated that in his opinion Committee III had completed its work at this stage of the Conference.

INFORMAL PLENARY

Preparatory Commission

The Informal Plenary held two meetings during the first week of the session and three meetings during the third week to consider an informal proposal and a draft resolution by the President of the Conference, H.S. Amerasinghe, concerning a Preparatory Commission to function between the time of the conclusion of negotiation of the Convention and its entry into force. The specific task of the Preparatory Commission would be to prepare for the establishment of the International Seabed Authority and its various organs.

General agreement was expressed on the desirability and need for such a Commission to be established by resolution of the Conference. In addition, a considerable degree of agreement was expressed concerning the content of the resolution. A number of

specific issues, however, arose concerning the membership, structure, and functions of the Commission.

The United States and a number of other delegations (both developed and developing) urged that the Commission be composed of one representative from each State signatory to the Convention, arguing that this degree of seriousness of identification with the Convention should be a requirement for membership. Other delegations asserted that such a provision was too restrictive because their domestic political systems envisioned ratification closely following signature, and they preferred membership on the Commission to be based on signature of the Final Act of the Conference. These delegations and others further argued for signature of the Final Act as the criterion for membership in order to give the Commission the broadest possible composition from the beginning. The draft resolution distributed by Amerasinghe called for membership in the Commission on the basis of signature of the Convention.

A number of States, both developed and developing, also urged that the Resolution on the Preparatory Commission provide for an executive body, possibly paralleling the Council of the Authority, to facilitate decision making; the United States considered that flexibility concerning its structure could be given to the Commission and that it would be likely in practice to function with several expert groups which might most efficiently report to the full Commission. In any event, this decision could be left to the Commission. This approach prevailed in the draft resolution.

The major sources of controversy regarding the Preparatory Commission involved the questions of functions and the status of the rules, regulations, and procedures to be drafted by the Commission. Concerning functions, a number of delegations pointed out the impossibility of drawing up a definitive list of functions until the conclusion of substantive negotiations on the Convention; and one delegation, supported by the United States, alluded to the possibility that these negotiations might result in the Treaty assigning functions to the Commission other than those contained in the draft resolution. Need for a catch-all provision was also expressed.

Concerning the status of the rules and regulations drafted by the Commission, the United States
and a number of other industrialized countries expressed the strong view that these rules and regulations should serve provisionally as the initial set
of rules and regulations of the Authority, unless and
until the Council might act to change them. This
position is based upon both the need to avoid delay
in the functioning of the Authority when the Treaty
enters into force and the necessity of predictability
in the initial functioning of the Authority as related to the decision of States whether or not to ratify
the Treaty. A number of developing States expressed
the contrary view that the integrity of the organs of
the Authority should not be compromised by giving
legal effect to rules and regulations adopted by the
Commission before the Authority has had an opportunity
to consider them. These delegations argued that the
rules and regulations drafted by the Preparatory Commission should be merely recommendatory for the consideration of the organs of the Authority. The draft
resolution of the President leaves the issue open by
providing that the rules and regulations prepared by
the Commission shall be adopted by it and transmitted
to the Authority along with the final report of the
Commission.

The issue of the status of these rules and regulations was concurrently considered in the Group of
Legal Experts on Final Clauses and is commented on
further in that section of this report.

Preamble

During the second week of the Ninth Session, the
Informal Plenary met to consider the ICNT, Rev. 1
Preamble and the Group of 77 text of October 1978 on
the Preamble (A.CONF/62/L.33). From the ensuing discussions it was agreed that the President would draft
a revised text, which he presented on March 19 as
Preamble 1.

The President, while rejecting the preference of
the United States for a very brief Preamble, produced
a non-controversial text based on the Group of 77
proposal that was widely praised on all sides and
that was not substantially changed during successive
meetings. As an example, the text described one purpose of the Convention as promoting the equitable and
efficient utilization of marine resources, thereby

394

harmonizing and synthesizing different values in what could otherwise have been a highly controversial passage. There was general agreement that the text represented a judicious and balanced response to the conflicting desires of some countries for a substantive, even "political," text and the wishes of other countries (including the United States) for a brief, non-substantive statement in order to avoid controversy.

The United States supported additional clauses to the text emphasizing that among the objectives of the Convention was the realization of a just and equitable international economic order which would take into account "the needs and interests of mankind as a whole," not only the "special interests and needs of developing countries." In addition, express references to promoting study, protection, and preservation of the marine environment and conservation of its living resources were adopted. A great deal of time was devoted to consideration of whether reference to the Declaration of Principles in the text should be to "develop" the principles contained therein or to "give effect" to them, with the former solution emerging in the end accompanied by an explanatory statement that the reference did not affect the status of the Declaration.

In his introductory remarks, President Amerasinghe made three important points which were not questioned by delegations and therefore served to defuse whatever controversy might have remained in the preambular text. The points were: (a) the clause on promotion of the peaceful uses of the seas and oceans represents an objective and should not be construed to preclude traditional high-seas rights and usage by vessels of all kinds; (b) the clause, "contribute to the realization of a just and equitable international economic order," in paragraph 5 should not be interpreted to mean insurance of such an order; and (c) the term "take into account" as related to the needs and interests of all mankind as well as the developing countries should not be construed as an obligation.

The resultant Preamble received very widespread support.

## Final Clauses

The subject of Final Clauses of the draft LOS Convention was extensively reviewed. Ambassador Jens

Evensen (Norway), Chairman of the Group of Legal Experts on Final Clauses, submitted three successive sets of draft texts, the last in FC/20 of March 29, 1980. Despite intensive discussions and progress on some issues, some of the texts clearly need considerably more work.

The texts do contain a number of provisions that should facilitate ratification of the Convention while protecting its substantive integrity and balance. Article 302 (Entry into Force of the Convention) stipulates that the Assembly will be convened on the day the Convention enters into force and that rules, regulations, and procedures drafted by the Preparatory Commission will then apply provisionally, pending formal adoption or amendment by the Authority. Article 303 prohibits reservations, while permitting States to make other types of declarations. Article 306 provides for a simplified procedure that would permit rapid and universally acceptable amendments to the Convention.

Article 308 confirms the right of denunciation although it may unnecessarily discourage or delay ratification by purporting to restrict the right of denunciation during the first five years that the treaty is in force.

The text includes a variety of other troublesome provisions. Article 302 provides an unusually high threshold for entry into force of the Convention (70 States). The provision that "The first Council shall be constituted in a manner consistent with the purpose of Article 161 if the provisions of that Article cannot be strictly applied" is vague and offers no protection for the very interests that the Council is designed to protect. Moreover, pending completion of the Council negotiations, a final negotiation on this matter is premature. Article 304 provides that "This Convention shall prevail, as between States Parties, over the Geneva Conventions on the Law of the Sea of 1958" when in fact the new Convention replaces the 1958 provisions in every instance where it does not specifically repeat them.

The complex amendment provisions (Articles 305 to 307) present a special problem. They include an unnecessary ten-year moratorium on amendments and a low percentage (50 percent) of States Parties required to convene a Conference of plenipotentiaries. There is

also no need to restrict the right of the Authority to propose amendments directly to States Parties.

Aside from the Review Conference, where the substantive consensus expressly includes the possibility of change after 25 years, the percentage of States required to bring an amendment into force ( 66-2/3%) is too low, and there is no specific protection of different interests that is necessary to ensure a balanced process that would preserve the consensual, package-deal character of the Convention.

The United States has sought to reshape Article 307 in such a way as to reemphasize and strengthen the integrity of the Convention. The United States has also sought a higher entry into force percentage ( 75 percent ) for all amendments while elaborating a system that also identifies broad interest groups within the law of the sea community (coastal, maritime and landlocked and geographically disadvantaged States) and stipulates their concurrence in amendments at the same percentage threshold. If anything, the three-group approach is not specific enough to protect minorities of States with substantial common interests.

At the close of discussion, there was general awareness that the Final Clauses issues needed further work. The issue of participation in the Convention has yet to be tackled in a detailed manner. President Amerasinghe noted that new Final Clause articles would not be included in the ICNT, Rev. 2 at this time.

General Provisions

During the final week of negotiations the Informal Plenary began initial consideration of several general provisions. The idea of a section containing general or miscellaneous provisions, as in the United Nations Charter, is gradually gaining support as a useful tool for resolving technical problems, provided it does not become a vehicle for reopening substantive issues. Several clauses were extensively discussed.

A text on good faith and abuse of rights put forward by Mexico and the United States received considerable attention. Toward the close of discussion

Mexico circulated a revised text that removed the more controversial phraseology, but agreement was blocked by the Peruvian Delegation after the United States proposed to defer consideration of a Peruvian proposal on the use or threat of force that in fact was designed to offset the balance of the economic zone texts.

A Chilean proposal to declare the concept of "the common heritage of mankind" a peremptory norm of international law (Jus Cogens) was deferred after a brief debate. A Turkish proposal entitled "General Principles" contained language regarding the special application of general principles to specific geographic areas that other delegations deemed too controversial. The United States proposal that nothing in the Convention should be deemed to compel a State to divulge information contrary to its essential national security interests was endorsed by a wide range of developed and developing countries in principle; however, there was concern about abuse of the right if the United States texts were added as drafted to the Convention. Because of probably objections at this time, the United States decided to withhold a revised text that had been discussed with developing country leaders.

Further work can be expected on general provisions which may include some new, and hopefully noncontroversial proposals that could promote consensus.

## PREPARATORY INVESTMENT PROTECTION

For some time it has been recognized that the United States must seek a mechanism within the LOS Treaty structure that will accommodate continuing seabed mining development and investment in the interim between signature and entry into force of a treaty, probably a period of several years. Such a mechanism would have to provide a significant measure of certainly to seabed mining investors that, when the treaty comes into force, they would be granted a contract on the specific site they had developed during the interim. Site overlap questions would have to be resolved in the interim period, and a compatible site would have to be set aside for subsequent development by the Enterprise or developing countries after the treaty had entered into force.

Discussions with representatives of both the seabed mining industry and the Group of 77 on the need for such a mechanism started in November 1979 and were accelerated during this session. These informal consultations culminated in meetings with representatives of industry on March 3, 1980 and with a group of G-77 delegation members on April 1, 1980. Two meetings were also held with delegations from potential seabed-mining nations to discuss the informal United States proposal for Preparatory Investment Protection as well as related domestic seabed-mining legislation amendments. During the last week of the session, the United States submitted to the Conference an informal working paper including a suggested treaty provision and language to be inserted into the Conference resolution establishing the Preparatory Commission. (A copy is attached.) The approach suggested by the United States would charge the Preparatory Commission with the task of receiving State-sponsored applications from potential seabed miners and granting such miners a priority to the site requested. The Preparatory Commission would also oc lect the site to be reserved (or banked) for the Enterprise or developing countries. The priority accorded by the Preparatory Commission to an applicant with regard to a specific site could, however, be invoked only during an initial period after entry into force of the treaty.

Although most of the delegations approached on the preparatory investment protection issue reserved their positions on the specific features of the United States proposal, there was a general recognition that the problem outlined by the United States must be satisfactorily resolved. These initial consultations have laid a basis for further negotiation of the proposal at the Geneva session.

## DRAFTING COMMITTEE

The coordinators of the six Language Groups of the Drafting Committee met on several occasions with the Chairman in efforts to resolve the different positions taken by the Language Groups with respect to certain problems of harmonization. The issues that they addressed are more difficult than those dealt with in the earlier report of the Drafting Committee, and thus progress was somewhat slower. It is expected that the Coordinators and the Chairman will attempt

to complete this part of their work before the meeting in Geneva. Meanwhile the Language Groups of the Drafting Committee continued their work on the texts. Some, like the English Language Group, have essentially completed their work on the existing harmonization problems and are ready to proceed with a review of the text, generally in the order in which the articles appear. Some, like the Arabic and Spanish Language Groups, are still dealing with difficult and extensive problems of translation, but that work should doubtlessly facilitate the subsequent scrutiny of the texts by those groups.

Attachment

IA/1
2 April 1980

ORIGINAL: ENGLISH

Informal working paper by the United States

An approach to interim protection
of investment

The Problem

Although investment by potential seabed miners
in prospecting and in research and development is not
related insignificantly to any one or more potential
mining sites, the major investment that must precede
the beginning of commercial production becomes site
specific at a relatively early stage.  This is obviously true of detailed site exploration, but it is
also true of the final design and acquisition of
dredge heads, refining plants, and, to some extent,
ships and lift systems.  To a significant degree the
key components of a seabed mining and refining system
must be tailored to the topography and location of a
specific site, and to concentration and composition
of nodules on that site.

Most of the companies that have been investing
in the development of seabed mining systems during
the past decade have reached or are reaching the
point where further investments will have to be very
large in dollar terms and will have to be related to
certain specific potential sites.  Prudent financial
management will preclude such investments unless the
companies can be assured that the sites to which they
relate will be available to them once the Convention
has entered into force.  Even to the extent that investments are not site specific in a technical sense,
none of the really major pre-production investments,
such as the construction or acquisition of mining
vessels, the construction and operation of pilot
processing plants and the construction of full-scale
processing plants, will be undertaken until the company concerned has a legally secure exclusive right
to a mine site.  This is, of course, the traditional

practice of the mining industry, and it is a rule of
financial prudence that would be followed strictly by
any commercial lending institution.  This means that,
absent agreement to provide such assurance, these
companies will be forced to choose either to disband
their technical staff and abandon seabed activities
indefinitely, or to opposed the Law of the Sea Convention with a view to engaging in seabed mining outside of the Convention.

A system that would allow these site-specific
investments to go forward prior to entry into force
of the Convention must accomplish three tasks:

(a) Create a priority for the pre-Convention investor in the event that a subsequent applicant requests part or all of the same site;

(b) Create a similar priority for the Enterprise
on a prospected area of equivalent potential economic
value to that identified for the pre-Convention investor;

(c) Transmute the priorities created in tasks
(a) and (b) into legal rights secured by the Convention when it enters into force.  That is, ensure that
priority in the event of conflicting claims is, in
fact, given to an otherwise qualified applicant on
the non-reserved side of the parallel system who has
received a priority in the pre-Convention period and
has made certain specified minimum investments in
anticipation of receiving a contract on that site, and
that the area selected to be reserved is in fact reserved when the plan of work is approved and the contract signed.

It should be noted that such a priority would extend only to potential conflicting applications covering the same areas, not to other questions such as the
qualifications of applicants, the requirements applicable to all proposed plans of work, the production
limitation or the anti-monopoly provisions:  all of
these requirements would still have to be satisfied
and the priority would in no way affect them.

A Possible System

One way of creating such a system would be by
entrusting tasks (a) and (b) to the Preparatory

Commission by means of a resolution of the Conference, while taking care of task (c) in the Convention
text itself.

The Preparatory Commission or its Executive Secretary, who presumably would be appointed by the Secretary-General of the United Nations, would receive
from any person or State desiring to establish priority an application covering two seabed areas which
the applicant believes to be equivalent in potential
economic value. A panel of technical experts, retained by the Preparatory Commission or by the Executive Secretary, would review the prospecting data
which the applicant would have to submit and would
choose one of the areas to receive an Enterprise priority, and the other to receive a priority for the
applicant. In the event two applications were received for overlapping areas, the application accompanied by the most complete data would be acted on,
while the other would be returned for modification
to eliminate the overlap. Prospecting data would be
available only to the panel. Once the choice had
been made, the data on both areas, other than their
coordinates, would be sealed until the miner applied
for a contract under the Convention, when they would
be given to the Authority.

Once the Convention enters into force, applicants for contracts who had earlier received priorities and whose State sponsor had become a Party to
the Convention, would be entitled to submit applications covering the same areas covered by those priorities. In order to maintain the priority, they
would have to act within six months after entry into
force of the Convention and demonstrate that they
complied with the minimum investment requirements set
out in the Convention. Assuming they had complied
with these requirements and were otherwise qualified,
their applications would be deemed to be first in
time as against any other application covering part
or all of the same area. Under Article 6 of Annex II,
overlapping applications are resolved by accepting
the earlier application. Since the applicant with
the priority would be deemed to be first in line, the
priority would guarantee that any overlaps would be
resolved in his favour. As noted above, the applicant and his proposed plan of work would still have
to meet all the other requirements, including those
relating to anti-monopoly and the production limitation. The Convention would also require that the

site selected by the panel of experts for future use
by the Enterprise would be reserved when the plan of
work is approved and the contract is signed.

## The Enterprise

A corresponding but somewhat different problem
exists for the Enterprise. Considerable work will
have to be done prior to entry into force of the Law
of the Sea Convention if the Enterprise is to assume
its role early within the treaty period. The Preparatory Commission will have to develop detailed
plans for the establishment of the Enterprise including questions of staffing and management, financial
matters, training, sources of technical data and
technology, sources for the procurement of equipment
and services, selection of mine sites, possible
processing locations and joint venture arrangements.
The Enterprise will benefit, as well as the private
side, from the continued orderly development of the
seabed mining industry in anticipation of a treaty
in force. The United States believes that this
problem, as well as preparatory investment protection, will have to yet be addressed by the Conference.

## Conclusion

If a system along these lines were implemented,
it would allow those who wish to begin preparations
in the near future for seabed mining to do so even
while the Convention was moving through the ratification process in the signatory States. It would
thus advance significantly the date when commercial
production can begin and financial and technological
benefits flow to the world community from both sides
of the parallel system. It would ensure that the
Enterprise would have available at the outset half
of the earliest discovered prime mining sites. Without such protection for interim investment, site-
specific investment--and indeed any really major pre-
production investment--would be so risky as, in effect,
to be precluded prior to entry into force of the Convention for any company whose country intended to
become a Party to the Convention. Thus, the provision, or not, of this interim investment protection
is likely to have a significant impact on the views
of potential investors concerning the desirability
of the Convention.

## Informal suggestions by the United States for a Treaty provision regarding preparatory investment protection

1. In order to promote a continuing development of seabed mining technology, equipment, and expertise so as to ensure that common benefits can be derived from activities in the Area as early as possible after entry into force of this Convention, and as an interim measure to accommodate such investment as has been made prior to the entry into force of this Convention, the Third United Nations Conference on the Law of the Sea established an advance site designation system by resolution dated _____.

2. Notwithstanding the provisions of paragraph 3, Article 6, Annex II of a proposed plan of work submitted by a qualified applicant during the six months following entry into force of this Convention for an area which has been given advance designation as a non-reserved area pursuant to the advance site desig nation system established by such resolution shall be deemed to have been submitted prior to all proposed plans of work which have not been accorded such an advanced designation.

3. Notwithstanding the provisions of Article 8 of Annex II, the area submitted by such applicant which has been given advance designation as a reserved area pursuant to such system shall be designated by the Authority as the area to be reserved solely for the conduct of activities by the Authority through the Enterprise or in association with developing countries.

## Informal suggestions by the United States for language to be included in the resolution of the Conference establishing the Preparatory Commission

1. The Preparatory Commission shall, as soon as proposed rules and regulations pertaining to the size of areas to be subject of plans of work have been agreed to, receive applications from signatory States, on their own behalf or on behalf of their nationals, seeking advance designation of areas for conduct of

activities under the Convention pursuant to Articles
153 (2)(a) and 153 (2)(b) respectively.

2.  Each application shall cover a total area which
need not be a single continuous area, sufficiently
large and of sufficient estimated commercial value
to allow two mining operations.  The application
shall indicate the coordinates dividing the area into
two parts of equal estimated commercial value and
include all the data obtained by the signatory State
or its national with respect to both parts of the
area.  Within 45 days of receiving such data, the
Preparatory Commission shall designate one part to
be reserved pursuant to the Convention after it
enters into force when a contract for the non-reserved part is signed.  The other part shall be designated for the conduct of activities by the applicant
pursuant to the Convention.

3.  The Preparatory Commission shall inform the prospective miner in writing of his determination which
shall also be forwarded to the International Seabed
Authority upon the entry into force of the Law of
the Sea Convention.

4.  In the event two or more applications are submitted covering part or all of the same area before
the designations described in paragraph 2 have been
made, the application containing the most detailed
data with respect to the area of conflict shall be
chosen.

5.  All proprietary data received by the Preparatory
Commission pursuant to this resolution shall be safe-
guarded.  They shall be made available only to persons responsible for making the designation called
for under this resolution.  After such designations
are made, the data shall be sealed.  They shall be
turned over to the Authority upon entry into force
of the Convention.

6.  The Preparatory Commission shall prepare a detailed plan concerning the establishment of the
Enterprise.  The plan shall contain a recommendation
for the operations of the Enterprise which will permit it to engage in activities in the Area as soon as
possible after the Law of the Sea Convention has entered into force.  This plan shall include detailed
proposals regarding the staffing and management of
the Enterprise, financial matters related to the

Enterprise, training, sources of required technical data and technology, source for the procurement of equipment and services, selection of mine sites, possible processing locations, and joint venture arrangements. In addition, the Preparatory Commission shall, at the earliest practical time, promote arrangements for training of United Nations and developing-country personnel and the planning and development of programmes which will promote cooperation between States Parties and will facilitate the establishment of the Enterprise at the earliest possible time.

---

NINTH SESSION (Resumed)
GENEVA
July 28 - August 29, 1980

SUMMARY


The Resumed Ninth Session of the Third United
Nations Conference on the Law of the Sea has completed substantive negotiation of texts on virtually
all major outstanding issues.  These texts have been
incorporated into a new informal Draft Convention
that seems likely to command general acceptance in
principle.  It is likely that the Convention on the
Law of the Sea will be completed and opened for signature in 1981.

The Conference has proposed a schedule for 1981
that provides for the Drafting Committee to meet
intersessionally for seven weeks, commencing January
12 in New York, in order to complete its review of
all articles in all languages before the start of the
Tenth Session.  After a one-week interval, the Tenth
Session would then meet in New York, if facilities
are available, commencing March 9, for six weeks, with
a possible one week extension, to complete the final
text of the Convention.  A final session would then
be held in Caracas, presumably later in the year, for
formal statements and the opening of the Convention
for signature.

As a result of the work of the Ninth Session,
the major questions outstanding are the three deferred at this session of the Conference:

1.  Preparatory Commission:  The Conference
needs to complete the resolution establishing a Preparatory Commission for the establishment of the International Seabed Authority and the drafting of
rules, regulations, and procedures.

2.  Preparatory Investment Protection:  Prospects
for support of the Convention could be significantly
improved if means were found to ensure that those who
make investments in seabed mining prior to the entry
into force of the Convention will, if qualified, be
accorded priority in seeking a contract from the
Authority.

3.  Participation:  Various proposals have been
made to allow entities other than States to become
parties to the Convention.  The questions involved
range from the justifiable juridical requests of the
European Community, the associated States that are

emerging in the Trust Territories of the Pacific Islands and a small number of other associated States, to the explosive and potentially destructive issue of liberation organizations.

In addition, the question of the precise wording of the articles regarding delimitation of economic zones and continental shelves between neighboring States has yet to be settled, although it seems clear now that any settlement will not entail drastic substantive modifications to the current text.

There are a number of problems in all Committees at the margins of the basic settlement where some modifications that could command a consensus would significantly help one or a few countries to become party to the Convention. The next session of the Conference will have to find a means of making such modifications without running the risks of disturbing the balance of the Convention by reopening matters that are settled.

It is also possible that on the basis of closer examination of some of the present accommodations on such issues as voting in the Council and financing the Enterprise, governments may want to seek improvements in certain respects.

Finally, the Drafting Committee of the Conference must complete its work before the next session if the Conference is to be in a position to debate and adopt a Convention.

It is not unrealistic to expect that all of this can be achieved by the end of the Tenth Session. There is, however, a significant danger as the Conference approaches it final stages, i.e. the misguided belief that substantive changes affecting the balance of the Convention can be effected through voting or the threat of voting. The United States and other delegations have made it clear that this would destroy the Convention.

## Seabeds

The negotiation of new texts dealing with the major outstanding deep seabeds issues constitutes the decisive breakthrough of this session of the Conference. These new texts provide for the decision

making procedures of the Council of the Seabed Authority and related matters, and also contain improvements and clarifications of other texts dealing with the system of exploration and exploitation as well as with financial matters.

The single most significant obstacle facing this session of the Conference was the impasse over voting in the 36-member Council of the Seabed Authority. The fundamental question in our view was how to ensure that important decisions could not be taken contrary to the interests of States most affected, particularly the western seabed-mining and consumer nations. The developing countries were strongly insistent upon equal weight being given to each member's vote, and the negotiations were further complicated by the refusal of the Soviet Union to accept any result which it considered discriminatory.

The deadlock was broken by a proposal to make decisions on the most sensitive issues subject to consensus. Given the risks of paralysis in a system under which each Council member would have an equal, potentially blocking vote, it was essential that the number of issues requiring a consensus be limited. Other important issues could then be made subject to a three-fourths vote; the remainder, a lower majority.

Under the final compromise, substantive issues requiring decision by the Council are divided into three categories. Depending on their sensitivity, decisions require either a two-thirds or three-fourths vote, that includes a majority of the total membership of the Council, or consensus (defined to mean the absence of any formal objection).

The decisions subject to the consensus procedure are those concerning production policies and limitations, the adoption of rules, regulations, and procedures of the Authority, and the adoption of amendments to Part XI of the Convention, including Annexes III and IV. This result is combined with a technical streamlining of the provisions of the Convention dealing with rules, regulations, and procedures which makes clear that the procedure requiring consensus in the Council applies to the three decisions noted above. The emergence of this compromise in turn made it possible to resolve certain other substantive issures by providing that their solution would be set

forth in the rules, regulations, and procedures of the Authority.

A critical element in this overall First Committee settlement is found in the paragraph of the final clauses which states that the draft rules, regulations, and procedures adopted by the Preparatory Commission shall apply provisionally from the date of entry into force of the Convention pending adoption by the Authority of rules, regulations, and procedures. Many governments may not, therefore, deposit instruments of ratification or accession to the Convention until the draft rules, regulations, and procedures are completed by the Preparatory Commission.

The question of Council voting posed a different type of problem with respect to approval of mining contracts. It is basic to the system set up in the treaty that a qualified applicant who satisfies the requirements of the Convention, and whose project would not exceed the specified production limitations or anti-monopoly requirements, should receive a contract. Accordingly, approval of plans of work should not be politicized in the Council. The text specifies that the Legal and Technical Commission must evaluate plans of work strictly on the basis of the criteria set forth in the treaty. If the Commission recommends approval, the proposed plan of work will be deemed approved unless the Council disapproves it by consensus (excluding the State or States making the application or sponsoring the applicant). On the other hand, disapproval of the proposed plan of work by the Commission could be reversed by a three-fourths vote of the Council. The rules, regulations, and procedures of the Authority will establish the decision-making procedures of the Commission.

There were a significant number of other changes in the seabeds text. The distribution of benefits from the seabeds, while effected by the Assembly, is subject to rules, regulations, and procedures which must be adopted by both the Council and the Assembly. The so-called split contracting system has been fully implemented throughout the text, thus ensuring that early investors will not be frustrated by the production limitation or face premature procedures for selection among competing applicants. There is no longer automatic liability for any shortfall in financing the Enterprise resulting from the delay or failure of some States to ratify the Convention.

There have also been some improvements in other provisions regarding the financing of the Enterprise, including the call-up of funds as needed, default procedures and improved repayment procedures. The power of commodity conferences to decide the question of what production from the Area the Authority will represent has been protected. The tax immunity provisions have been replaced by much better ones virtually identical to those included in the recent Common Fund Agreement. Seabed amendments do not enter into force until one year following the deposit of the necessary instruments of ratification, the same one-year period required for notice of denunciation.

## Second and Third Committees

The Second and Third Committees, the texts of which deal with the substance of the Law of the Sea Convention aside from deep seabed matters, met only to consider drafting questions. There were no significant attempts to alter the substance. Nevertheless, some delegations are continuing to threaten votes on such matters as authorization for innocent passage of warships in the territorial sea or changes in the economic zone regime. The United States and other delegations have made it clear that there is no possibility of a Convention on the Law of the Sea with such provisions added, and that pressing these points will result either in the destruction of the Convention or in a "negative record" that makes it obvious that the proper interpretation of the Convention is the opposite of what the proponents seek.

The atmosphere created by these extreme proposals made it difficult to consider largely technical questions that do not alter the balance of the text and that could command a consensus. This can probably be done at the next session.

## Dispute Settlement

With a final reorganization of some of the provisions, the negotiations on settlement of disputes are completed. It is possible that minor changes may emerge as a result of the completion of negotiation on delimitation of the economic zone and the continental shelf between opposite and adjacent States, and

with respect to certain technicalities regarding the seabed dispute settlement system.

## Final Clauses and General Provisions

The Informal Plenary has essentially completed the task of arriving at a set of final clauses that can command general agreement. The texts that emerged provide for entry into force of the Convention after the deposit of 60 instruments of ratification or accession. They protect the integrity of the overall "package deal," involving different priorities of different States, by making clear that reservations and exceptions are only permitted when expressly provided in a particular article of the Convention. At the same time, the new texts facilitate ratification by giving broad latitude to States to make declarations that do not purport to modify the Convention, and by removing restrictions on the right to denounce the Convention.

An element of flexibility is introduced by allowing amendments. The procedures both for adoption and for entry into force of amendments are quite stringent, and are designed to protect the underlying premise that all relevant interests must be balanced and accommodated. Given the complexity of the Convention, a helpful provision has been inserted allowing rapid adoption of amendments if no party to the Convention objects within 12 months, after which they would be circulated for ratification or accession. The stability of the seabed system has in particular been preserved by making clear that amendments pending the Review Conference can only be adopted if approved in identical form by the Council and the Assembly of the Authority. Under the new First Committee text, a consensus would be required in the Council for approval.

There are several new general provisions. They prohibit abuse of rights or the use or threat of force in violation of the United Nations Charter, protect classified information, and provide for the protection of archeological objects and objects of historical origin.

## Drafting Committee

This session demonstrated once again that it is difficult for delegations to give undivided attention to Drafting Committee matters during a regular session of the Conference. The Drafting Committee, having completed much of its initial harmonization efforts at its intersessional meeting in June, will proceed during the next intersessional period to the completion of the formidable task of textual review and concordance of the six language versions of some 400 articles.

COMMITTEE I

Overview

The Working Group of 21 (WG-21) began its work
with a broad review of the status of the hardcore
issues still unresolved at the end of the first part
of the Ninth Session. It then proceeded to intensive
consultations in smaller groups. The WG-21 was
chaired by First Committee Chairman Paul Engo (Cameroon). In the absence of Frank Njenga (Kenya),
Professor Harry Wuensche (German Democratic Republic),
First Committee Vice-Chairman and Chairman of the
Group of Legal Experts on Dispute Settlement, coordinated the consultations on matters relating to
the system of exploration and exploitation. Ambassador Tommy Koh (Singapore) coordinated consultations
on financial arrangements and the Statute of the
Enterprise. Chairman Engo, with the assistance of
Ambassador Koh, coordinated consultations on decision
making in the International Seabed Authority, including procedures for the approval of plans of work.
Ambassador Satya Nandan (Fiji) coordinated consultations relating to the production policies and quota
anti-monopoly provisions. Due to Professor Wuensche's
responsibilities for other matters referred to above,
there was no time for any meeting of the Group of
Legal Experts on Dispute Settlement.

The Chairman of the First Committee, as principal coordinator, received reports from the other coordinators including revisions in the text of the
ICNT Rev. 2 (A/CONF.62/C.1/L.28 and A/CONF.62C.1/L.28
/Add.1). These reports and texts were considered in
a meeting of the First Committee and have been included in the Draft Convention (Informal Text). Although some delegations expressed difficulties and
reservations regarding certain provisions, no delegation objected to the inclusion in the Draft Convention of the new texts as a package satisfying the
criteria of A/CONF.62/62 and bringing the Conference
close to the achievement of consensus and a final
text on First Committee Matters.

## System of Exploration and Exploitation

WG-21 discussions were held on a number of outstanding issues in Part XI and Annex III on the system of exploration and exploitation. Consultations
followed in a smaller group coordinated by Professor
Wuensche. These consultations had wide participation
from among both developed and developing countries
and the Eastern European Socialist countries, including the United States, the United Kingdom, the Federal Republic of Germany, France, Japan, Peru, Brazil,
Trinidad and Tobago, Jamaica, India, Sri Lanka, Egypt,
Tunisia, Tanzania, Madagascar, Sierra Leone, Senegal,
the Soviet Union, and the German Democratic Republic.
Due to the extensive consultations being conducted by
Chairman Engo and Ambassador Koh on Council decision
making, it was impossible to schedule enough meetings
of the Wuensche group to complete work on the system
of exploration and exploitation in that forum. Consequently, some of these matters were taken up in the
consultations conducted by Ambassador Koh with the
participation of Professor Wuensche after the discussions on decision making had been completed. The two
groups had similar membership.

Revised texts were issued on most of the major
outstanding issues (A/CONF.62/C.1/L.28/Add.1). Some
of the texts offer solutions to problems that have
long plagued the Conference, such as Article 140 on
the sharing of financial and other economic benefits
and a uniform system for adoption of the rules, regulations, and procedures of the Authority (Article
160(2)(f), 162(2)(n), 167, 168, and Annex III, Article 17).

A number of other improvements and clarifications of both a substantive and purely drafting nature, were made. These include: conforming the period for entry into force of all Review Conference
amendments to the one-year period specified in the
final clauses for entry into force of other amendments
and for notice of denunciation (Article 155); making
clear that the requirements for sponsorship of applicants
is to be further defined in the rules, regulations, and

procedures of the Authority (Annex III, Article 4);
and a number of wording improvements concerning the
transfer of technology (Annex III, Article 5). Some
improvements were also made in the small group coordinated by Ambassador Nandan concerning production
policies (Articles 150, 151), and drafting changes
were made in Part XI and Annex III (Articles 6 & 7)
to implement the split contracting system proposed
in Ambassador Nandan's report from the first part of
the Ninth Session (A/Conf.62/C.1/L.27 (Part II)). In
addition, a revised text was issued on quota/anti-
monopoly (Annex III, Articles 6 & 7), a subject which
the United States Delegation now regards as closed.

## Revised Texts

A summary of the most significant provisions of
the new texts relating to the system of exploration
and exploitation follows:

### Article 140 - Sharing of Benefits

The revised text of Article 140, combined with
the revised texts of Articles 160(2)(f), 160(2)(j),
162(2)(n), and 161(7)(d), reflects a resolution of
the thorny political problem of the sharing of financial and other economic benefits derived from activities in the Area. This resolution involves three
elements.

First, the general principle contained in Article 140, that peoples who have not attained full independence or other self-governing status are eligible for financial and other economic benefits derived
from activities in the Area, was retained.

Second, a new procedure was adopted for the establishment of the rules, regulations and procedures
of the Authority concerning distribution of such benefits which involves Council formulation, Assembly
consideration and approval, and Council reconsideration if the Assembly decides not to approve. Unlike
the other rules, regulations, and procedures of the
Authority (the new Articles 160(2)(f) and 162(2)(n)),
these rules and regulations would not be effective
until approved by the Assembly; however, like the
other rules, regulations, and procedures of the Authority, the Council's original formulation could not

be changed by the Assembly itself, but could only be returned to the Council for reconsideration. Under the new Article 161(7)(d), decisions of the Council on all rules, regulations, and procedures of the Authority would be taken by consensus. A new paragraph, 160(2)(j), was also added giving the Assembly the function of deciding upon the equitable sharing of financial and other economic benefits derived from activities in the Area, consistent with the Convention and the rules, regulations, and procedures of the Authority.

Third, a reference to payments and contributions made pursuant to Article 82 on revenue sharing from the continental shelf beyond 200 miles was included in the provisions establishing the new procedure for adoption of rules, regulations, and procedures for the sharing of financial and other economic benefits (Articles 160(2)(f) and 162(2)(n)). Although the Report of the Chairman (A/Conf.62/C.1/L.28 p. 28) may be read as implying a different result, this reference does not change the text of Article 82, which provides that payments shall be made "through the Authority" but limits the eligible recipients to States Parties.

The above solution represents a compromise between the developed countries, which wished to limit to States Parties the distribution of financial and other economic benefits derived from the seabed under Article 140, and the developing countries which opposed any change in the ICNT Rev.2 on this matter.

It should also be noted that helpful drafting changes were made in Article 140 to make clear that the principle is implemented only as specifically provided and that the benefits referred to in the Article include both financial and other economic benefits derived from activities in the Area.

## Article 147 - Accommodation of Activities in the Area and in the Marine Environment

The words "in the Area" were deleted from subparagraph (b) concerning stationary and mobile installations used for the conduct of activities in the Area in order to make clear that the Article applies to all such installations, whether or not located in the Area as defined in Article 1, i.e., the seabed or

ocean floor and subsoil thereof beyond the limits of national jurisdiction.

### Articles 150 and 151 - Policies Relating to Activities in the Area and Production Policies

Discussions on Article 150 and Article 151 were held in the Production Limitation Group, again chaired by Satya Nandan of Fiji. There was relatively little debate on the production limitation formula itself. Most attention was instead focused on the chapeau, subparagraphs (d) and (e) of Article 150 and new subparagraphs of that article dealing with market access and development policy.

In negotiations on Article 150, the United States emphasized that one stated goal of the Seabed Authority should be to develop the resources of the Area. The EC insisted on clarifications in Article 150, sub-paragraphs (d) and (e), and was supported by the United States. They contended that some might mistakenly read subparagraph (d) to mean that seabed mining was meant to be a residual supplier. Land-based producers sought a clause requiring States to keep mineral and metals markets in consumer countries open to land-based suppliers on a non-discriminatory basis vis-a-vis suppliers from the seabed. Land-based producers also asked for a clause which would have prevented subsidization of seabed mining.

The outcome was an addition of two subparagraphs to Article 150. The first, (h), makes explicit the developmental aspect of the Authority's role. The second, (i), restrains States from establishing conditions of market access for seabed production better than the best available to land-based sources.

Efforts by Canada and several African countries to lower the floor percentage (the minimum growth rate for the production control trend line) or to change the safeguard (protection for land-based producers against a possible loss of their preexisting market) did not succeed. Many delegations, including several important land-based producers, were quite ready to accept the production control formula as it appeared in Article 151 of the ICNT Rev.2. The United States Delegation made clear that any change in the formula would put the entire text of Article 151 in jeopardy. The new text of Article 151 includes some drafting

changes useful to a clearer reading, but changes nothing of substance.

At the request of the USSR, changes were made in the text of Annex III, Articles 6 & 7 to allow quota/ anti-monopoly provisions to extend past the end of the interim period by means of rules and regulations of the Authority adopted at that time. Other changes were made in Annex III to ensure that the entire text would be consistent with the split contracting system embodied in Article 151, paragraph 2 of the ICNT Rev.2.

At the very end of the session several African land-based producers sought changes in the text of Article 151, paragraph 4, and the new market access clauses of Article 150. The changes would require among other things creation of a compensation scheme for certain land-based producers to be funded by the developed countries. These proposed changes differ from the present text which envisages a compensation system funded from revenues of the Authority. We are opposed to this change, and we do not believe that these proposals enjoy widespread support in the Conference. Drafting changes in Article 151, however, may be needed to remove ambiguities that the African land-based producers have identified.

## Article 155 - The Review Conference

Article 155, paragraph 4 (formerly paragraph 5) was revised to change the period for entry into force of amendments adopted in the sixth year of the Review Conference after ratification by two-thirds of the States Parties from 30 days to 12 months. This change conforms this time period to the time period specified in the final clauses for entry into force of seabeds amendments and for notification of denunciation.

Two other changes were made in this Article. In the first sentence of paragraph 4, the words "changing or modifying" were included to make clear that the Review Conference might decide either to change the system of exploration and exploitation or to modify it. Additionally, the word "decisions" in paragraph 5 (formerly paragraph 4) was changed to "amendments" to avoid any implication that the Conference could take any decisions affecting the system other than by proposing amendments or treaty revisions. It was understood that the Conference might decide either to

propose no changes, to amend the system in the Convention, or to adopt a new Convention on the matter.

## Articles 160(2)(f), 162(2)(n), 167, 168, and Annex III Article 17 - Rules, Regulations, and Procedures of the Authority

An important improvement in the revised text is provision for a single system for the adoption of rules, regulations, and procedures of the Authority governing financial rules, including the rules on borrowing, the transfer of funds from the Authority to the Enterprise, and the transfer of funds from the Enterprise to the Authority, and administrative rules as well as those governing the system of exploration and exploitation. This uniform procedure is now contained in Articles 160(2)(f) and 162(2)(n) which provide that all rules, regulations, and procedures will be adopted and provisionally applied by the Council pending consideration and approval by the Assembly. Article 160(2)(n) and Article 162(2)(p) were deleted as no longer necessary, and drafting changes were made in Article 160(2)(x), Article 167, and Article 168 to implement the new uniform procedure.

As an element of this package, Article 17 of Annex III was amended to make open-ended the formerly exhaustive list of aspects of the system of exploration and exploitation subject to rules, regulations, and procedures of the Authority. This change had long been sought by the Group of 77, which argued persuasively that all matters on which rules, regulations, and procedures might be needed could not reasonably be foreseen. In order to make possible this flexibility, limitations stated in general terms were incorporated in Articles 160 and 162.

## Article 162(2)(a) and (k)

Changes in these subparagraphs ensure that the Council's supervision and control is limited to matters within the competence of the Authority and is exercised in accordance with the rules, regulations, and procedures of the Authority.

Annex III

## Article 4 - Qualifications of Applicants

Although we were unsuccessful in our efforts to delete the sentence in paragraph 2 requiring sponsorship by more than one State in cases where a corporation's nationality and effective control are different, the provision was improved by the addition of a sentence providing that "the criteria and procedures for implementation of the sponsorship requirements shall be set forth in the rules, regulations, and procedures of the Authority."

## Article 5 - Transfer of Technology

A number of useful improvements were made in this Article.

First, in paragraph 3(a), the phrase "which is used by him" was changed to "which he uses" to make clear that the obligation to transfer technology pertains only to that technology which the contractor actually uses and to avoid any implication that he might be required to transfer technology before he has used it himself.

Second, the last sentence in paragraph 3(b) was deleted in order to avoid the implication that the general assurance covered by that paragraph could ever be made legally binding.

Third, the first sentence of paragraph 3(c) was redrafted to alter the possible ambiguous obligation to take "all feasible measures" to acquire a legal right to transfer technology requested by the Enterprise into an obligation to acquire a binding legal right to transfer the requested technology "whenever it is possible to do so without substantial cost to the contractor." It was understood that the Enterprise would bear any substantial cost resulting from carrying out these obligations if the Enterprise requested the contractor to acquire such a legal right.

Fourth, although the United States and other developed countries continued to oppose the provision in paragraph 3(e) for transfer of technology under certain circumstances to developing countries, developing country insistence on its retention remained

unshakable. Nevertheless, it was possible to revise the text to state more clearly that this obligation extends only to the site banked by the contractor.

Fifth, paragraph 4 was revised to make clear that only the offers made by the contractor (and not those by the Enterprise) are subject to arbitration on the question of whether they are within the range of fair and reasonable commercial terms and conditions. In addition, the text clarifies that an adverse decision of the Arbitral Tribunal will not of itself result in the initiation of proceedings against the contractor. Such proceedings can be invoked only if the contractor refuses to revise his offer and thus violates his contract by being unwilling to sell on fair and reasonable commercial terms and conditions.

One change extends the contractor's obligation to transfer technology. The revised paragraph 7 provides that the undertakings required by paragraph 3 shall be included in each contract for the conduct of activities in the Area until 10 years after the Enterprise has begun commercial production. The text formerly provided that such undertakings would be included in contracts only until the Enterprise had begun commercial production. The limit on the enforceability of such undertakings remains the same, i.e., until 10 years after the Enterprise has begun commercial production. The United States and other industrialized countries attempted to reduce this period to five years; the developing countries wished to eliminate the time limit entirely. The resulting compromise was accepted in the light of developing country assurances that they would not press for other changes they had sought in Article 5, such as inclusion of processing technology in the transfer obligation. It was understood that the United States and other industrialized countries would continue to oppose paragraph 3(e).

### Articles 6 and 7 - Quota/Anti-Monopoly

Early in the resumed Ninth Session, the French delegation reintroduced three changes in the anti-monopoly texts which they had pursued without success in the New York session of the Conference last spring.

The first of these involved the computation of the maximum density permitted to any one State Party within the basic control area of 400,000 square kilometers by including in the count plans of work undertaken in conjunction with the Enterprise in reserved sites within the Area (Annex II, Article 6, paragraph 3(d)).

The second would have inserted the concept of "effective control" in the method of computing prorata shares where a plan of work is undertaken by a consortium sponsored by more than one State Party (Article 6, paragraph 4).

The third, and most significant, proposed a fixed numerical quota where selection is required among competing applications because of the production limitation in Article 151. The French proposal would have provided that an application sponsored by a State that has not yet received a production allocation "shall have priority" over an application sponsored by a State already in possession of two or more such allocations (Article 7, paragraph 4).

During the discussions in WG-21, these proposals were supported by the Soviet Union and opposed by the United Kingdom, the Federal Republic of Germany, and the United States, which took the position that the texts to which they had agreed in New York already represented a negotiated solution to the problem and did not merit any further change. Consultations coordinated by Dr. Wuensche failed to bring any of the interested parties closer to agreement.

The Soviet Union took the position that the introduction of the split contracting system in Article 151 provided sufficient reason for re-examination of the anti-monopoly texts. Subsequent discussions between the United States and Soviet delegations coordinated by Ambassador Nandan led to compromises on two new provisions for insertion in Articles 6 and 7 of Annex III.

The new paragraph 5 of Article 6 provides that following expiration of the interim period covered by the production limitation, the Authority may adopt through rules, regulations, and procedures "other procedures and criteria" in addition to the maximum density provisions.

Paragraph 5 of Article 7 (formerly paragraph 4) has been re-worded to make clear that, where selection among applications is made necessary by the production limitation, it shall "avoid discrimination against any State or System" as well as prevent monopolization of such activities, as already provided in the text.

Both of these provisions were included in the report of the Coordinators of WG-21 to the First Committee (A/Conf.62/C.1/L.28/Add.1) and were included in the Draft Convention. Although a new effort may be made to reopen the quota/anti-monopoly issue at the next session, the United States regards the present text as final.

## Article 18 - Penalties

In paragraph 2, the word "or" was deleted to make clear that monetary penalties are an alternative to suspension or termination of contract in cases of serious persistent and willful violations of the fundamental terms of the contract.

## Other Issues Deferred

A few other changes that were proposed to make drafting or modest substantive changes in the text were deferred for further consideration at the next session. These included revision of the title of Section 3 of Part XI to read "Conduct of Marine Scientific Research and Activities on the Area"; revision of Article 168 to authorize the imposition of monetary penalties on staff members who violate their obligations; and some drafting amendments in Articles 4 and 9 of Annex III.

## Financial Arrangements

### Overview

Ambassador Tommy Koh of Singapore, acting on behalf of Paul Engo, Chairman of the Working Group of 21, presided over negotiating sessions on financial issues related to the seabed mining regime. After consultations with individual countries and intensive negotiations both in WG-21 and in a small group where

the interests of industrial countries were represented by the United States and the Soviet Union, Koh produced a new text on financing the Enterprise (Annex IV, Article 11) which extensively revised the provisions on (1) the determination of the <u>amount</u> of the total capital of the Enterprise, (2) the measures to be taken in case there is a <u>shortfall</u> in Enterprise financing because of insufficient adherence to the Convention, (3) the procedures for <u>call-up</u> of State Party financial obligations, and (4) the <u>repayment</u> of the interest-free loans. In addition, Article 183 on the tax immunities of the Authority was replaced in its entirety with a new provision based on a similar provision in the Common Fund arrangement. The substance of the financial terms of contracts (Annex IV, Article 13) was not discussed, and the previous text remained largely intact.

## Amount of Total Capital of the Enterprise

There was no change in the general understanding that the capital should be equal to the cost of a four-metal project. At issue, however, was the desire of the industrialized countries for a definite figure at the time of ratification, and the desire of the G-77 to make sure that the initial figure would not be eroded by changes in costs to an extent that would cripple the Enterprise.

In order to make the figure available at the time of ratification, it was agreed that the Preparatory Commission would include the amount in the draft rules, regulations, and procedures of the Authority. (Under Article 304 of the Draft Convention, the draft rules, regulations, and procedures prepared in the Preparatory Commission will be the provisional rules, regulations, and procedures of the Authority when the treaty enters into force.) To partially meet G-77 concerns, it was agreed that the Preparatory Commission would also set forth in the rules, regulations, and procedures the "criteria and factors" to be considered in adjusting the figure. It was also understood, however, not to address in the treaty the means (either institutional or otherwise) by which the amount may be adjusted.

## Supplementary Financing

Near the end of the last session, Koh added a new provision which would obligate States to make supplementary financing available to the Enterprise in case it faces a shortfall because not all States have adhered to the Convention. The total supplementary financing was limited to no more than 25% of the total financing of the Enterprise.

The industrialized countries, including the Soviet Union, objected strenuously to any text which mandated additional contributions. They argued that such a provision severely strained budgetary processes, since it amounted to an additional financial obligation of uncertain amount. In addition, application of the provision would run directly contrary to the long-standing reluctance of the United States Congress to authorize appropriations for more than 25% of the cost of any international organization.

There was extensive debate on the original United States proposal, supported by the western and eastern industrialized nations, that the request for any supplementary funds should be the subject of a non-binding Council recommendation. The G-77 rejected this proposal. After further debate, however, the G-77 stated that it could accept a provision requiring the Assembly to adopt by consensus measures for dealing with the shortfall. The United States Delegation, although preferring a Council role, was able to support this proposal. It protects the financial interests of all States Parties, since measures adopted by the Assembly require consensus. Further, since the Convention establishes no obligations to contribute to the Enterprise beyond the initial contribution, any supplementary fund established by the Assembly would have to be voluntary.

## Call-Up Procedures

Previous texts contained no specific provisions for calling up the funds which States Parties had agreed to provide for the financing of the Enterprise. In order to relate the call-up procedures to the Enterprise budget and make more certain that the Enterprise would call up funds only as needed for its operations, the United States proposed that such procedures be specified in the draft rules, regulations,

and procedures prepared by the Preparatory Commission.
The G-77 rejected this approach as offering the possibility of a veto over Enterprise operations by industrial countries, and insisted that the States Parties make the entire amount of interest-free loans
and debt guarantees available upon entry into force
of the Convention.

Koh thereupon produced a new text which drew
upon a proposal by the Netherlands delegation in ob-
ligating States Parties to deposit promissory notes
with the Enterprise at the time of ratification in
the amount of their total share of interest-free
loans. The Governing Board of the Enterprise is required to prepare a schedule of its financial needs,
on an annual or appropriate basis, and to draw against
the notes on the basis of this schedule. States would
be notified of their obligation under the schedule
"through the Authority." Although the new provision
does not explicitly state the ratio of interest-free
loans and debt guarantees in the call-up, the requirement that the call-up be in accordance with subparagraph 3(b) permits the view that one-half of the
Enterprise annual financial requirements will be met
by interest-free loans and one-half by borrowings
guaranteed by States Parties.

### Repayment Procedures

The ICNT Rev.2 provided that the repayment
schedule of interest-free loans which States Parties
make available to the Enterprise be based on a schedule adopted by the Assembly upon the recommendation
of the Council. This would of course take place
after the treaty came into effect. The United States
argued that the terms and conditions for financing
the Enterprise, in particular the repayment schedule
for interest-free loans, had to be known in advance,
so that States could evaluate their financial obligations when considering ratification. The United
States Delegation therefore proposed that the repayment schedule be specified in the rules, regulations,
and procedures of the Authority to be drafted by the
Preparatory Commission. The G-77 felt, to the contrary, that the terms of repayment could not be determined by the Governing Board until a later date,
when the financial situation of the Enterprise was
clearer.

The new text retains the old formula that the repayment schedule be adopted by the Assembly on the recommendation of the Council, but <u>adds</u> the requirement that the Assembly and Council <u>also</u> act on the advice of the Governing Board. Under the decision-making procedures which also emerged at this session, recommendations as to the repayment schedule would be adopted by a three-quarters majority of the Council. The Governing Board must be guided by the relevant rules, regulations, and procedures of the Authority, which in turn must take into account the importance of ensuring the financial independence and success of the Enterprise. It was understood that these rules, regulations, and procedures will address such matters as the priority, maturity, and rate of repayment.

A number of other issues related to financing the Enterprise were dealt with during the session:

-- The formulation of the basic scale of assessments was amended (and thus clarified) to state explicitly in Article 11 of Annex III that assessments would be based on the UN scale adjusted for States not members of the United Nations.

-- The provision requiring that funds made available to the Enterprise be in convertible currency was amended to conform with similar language in the Common Fund.

-- The text now requires that the procedures for calling up funds in case of an Enterprise default on the repayment of debts guaranteed by States Parties be specified in the rules, regulations, and procedures of the Authority.

-- The United States Delegation proposed that the provision by which States Parties "make every reasonable effort to support application by the Enterprise for loans in capital markets and from international financial institutions" should be amended by adding the words "where appropriate." The G-77, and ultimately Koh, rejected this proposal, but it was clearly understood that no State would feel constrained by this provision to support loans in cases that were inappropriate, for example, because of the nature of the international financial institution in question.

## Tax Immunities of the Authority (Article 183)

The industrialized countries found Article 183 concerning the immunity from taxation of the International Seabed Authority to be wholly unacceptable. To correct the situation, the Netherlands delegation suggested that all articles on the privileges and immunities of the Authority be deleted, and that a separate protocol be negotiated. Alternatively, the Netherlands proposed a complete revision of Article 183.

The United States Delegation and other western delegations agreed that the text would have to be revised to ensure that (1) the Authority should only be exempt from direct taxation within the scope of its official activities; (2) the Authority should not be exempt from taxes which are no more than charges for services rendered; and (3) States should only be obligated to the extent practicable to reimburse the Authority for indirect taxes. Regarding the treatment of employees of the Authority, however, the United States and EC countries differed. The United States insisted that States Parties reserve the right to tax their own nationals and permanent residents. The EC wanted the staff of the Authority to be subject to a tax proposed by the Authority for its own benefit on salaries and emoluments paid by the Authority.

The United States and EC resolved their differences by agreeing to propose the language on tax immunities contained in the Common Fund Agreement, since all Conference participants had already agreed to such language. After minor modifications, the G-77 agreed to allow the Common Fund language to be included in the text. Essentially, this text incorporates the suggestions of the western industrialized States and resolves the United States/EC differences along the lines of the United States proposal.

## Decision-Making in the Council

Decision-making in the Council, the most difficult of all the seabeds issues, was given the highest priority during this session. In view of the total lack of progress on the issue at the first part of the Ninth Session, the WG-21 reviewed all the suggested alternatives. After discussions in the WG-21

intensive consultations were undertaken with the various interest groups by Chairman Engo, and, under his
direction, by Ambassador Koh. These consultations
began with the Chairman consulting separately with
different interest groups, followed by formation of a
small group which was later joined by others. The
United States participated actively throughout these
consultations, which continued through the fourth
week of the session, with an unparalleled concentration of effort by all who participated.

Discussion in the WG-21 quickly resulted in
further deadlock. The Group of 77 remained adamantly
opposed to any voting mechanism based on weighted
voting or a veto for any interest or geographical
group; the western industrialized countries remained
firmly committed to the need for a mechanism which
offered protection for potential seabed miners and
consumers of the types of minerals derived from the
seabed against decisions adverse to their major economic interests; and the Soviet Union emphasized that
any formulation which accorded the desired protection
for the western industrialized countries would have
to also accord similar protection to the Eastern
European Socialist countries. Previous proposals for
chambered voting, possibly in combination with a
blocking vote for regional groups, or for a three-
fourths majority vote to include 50% of production
and 50% of consumption of the types of minerals derived from the seabed accounted for by members of the
Authority, were shown to be unacceptable to the G-77.
Similarly, it did not appear possible to agree on a
formula by which a specific number of States (proposals ranged from four to nine) could block decisions
adverse to their interests, or on any formulation
based on according such a blocking vote to a combination of interest groups.

Two themes, however, emerged from the WG-21 discussions which offered some direction to the consultations that followed. One was a revival of a reference to the principle of consensus and the desirability of a voting mechanism which would encourage decisions to be taken on that basis. Sentiment was also
strong in the G-77 for a voting mechanism keyed to
the importance of specific issues to be decided by
the Council and for limiting to only the most sensitive category the number of issues which would be
decided by a majority higher than a two-thirds majority.

Revised texts were issued on the voting mechanism in the Council (Article 161, paragraph 7); the procedure for approval of plans of work (Articles 162(2)(j), 163(10), and 165(2)(b)) and creation of a uniform system for adoption of rules, regulations, and procedures, discussed above; a new procedure for nomination of members of the Council (Article 161(2) (c)); and other provisions concerning functions of the Assembly and Council (Articles 160 and 162), the Commissions of The Council (Articles 163 and 165), and the provisions concerning the Secretary General of the Authority (Article 166).

The revised texts on decision-making provide for a three-tiered categorization of issues of substance to be decided respectively by a two-thirds majority of Council members present and voting, a three-fourths majority of Council members present and voting, and consensus, which is defined as the absence of any formal objection. Decisions not listed for which no voting majority has been specified in the rules, regulations, and procedures of the Authority would be decided by consensus. Plans of work recommended for approval by the Legal and Technical Commission (by a decision-making process to be specified in the rules, regulations, and procedures of the Authority), would be deemed approved by the Council unless disapproved by consensus provided that the sponsoring State of the contractor may not be the barrier to consensus. Plans of work not recommended for approval by the Commission would require a three-fourths majority of Council members present and voting for approval. Decisions of the Commission and objections to approval in the Council would be based solely on the requirements for approval of plans of work specified in Annex III. Other helpful revisions were also made in the text concerning the Commissions of the Council (Articles 163 and 165), although time did not permit thorough discussion of this matter.

While many delegations, including the United States, expressed reservations to the new texts on decision-making, it was generally recognized that no other approach seemed likely to command general support.

The Revised Texts

A summary of the most important revised texts follows:

## Article 161(2)(c) - Caucus Nomination

The revised text contains a new Article 161(2)(c), which provides that each group of States Parties to be represented on the Council shall be represented by those members, if any, which are nominated by the group. This provision applies to both the special interest groups in categories (a) through (d) and to the regional groups in category (e) to be represented on the Council pursuant to Article 161(1). The addition of this provision assures that the members of the various interest groups can, in fact, assume that the group interests will be represented adequately by those it selects to represent them.

## Article 161(7) - Voting in the Council

The revised text on the voting mechanism in the Council is based on a division of the issues to be decided by the Council into categories, with different majorities specified for each category. Procedural issues, as in the ICNT Rev.2, would be decided by a simple majority of members present and voting. Substantive issues would be divided into three categories according to their sensitivity: the least sensitive substantive issues would be decided by a two-thirds majority of members present and voting; more sensitive substantive issues, by a three-fourths majority of members present and voting; and the most sensitive substantive issues by consensus. Consensus is defined as the absence of any formal objection, and conciliation procedures are specified in order to try to achieve consensus in the event of such an objection.

The United States, of course, had previously put forward and would have preferred other solutions to the problem of protection in the Council of our major economic interests. The device of decision by consensus on most sensitive issues poses greater danger for paralysis of the Council than previous proposals for chambered voting or, as advanced by the United States, a vote based on shares of production and

consumption of the types of minerals derived from the seabed accounted for by members of the Authority. Nevertheless, it became apparent that no other approach, as previously noted, seemed likely to command general support.

Considerable controversy arose in deciding which matters would be placed in the various categories, with the developing countries pressing for most matters to be in the two-thirds category and the United States and other western industrialized countries seeking to have a large number of issues in either the consensus category or the three-fourths category. The texts place in the consensus category three items --the adoption of necessary and appropriate measures in accordance with Article 150(g) to protect against adverse economic benefits apecified therein (Article 162(2)(l)); the adoption of the rules, regulations, and procedures of the Authority (Article 162(2)(n)); and adoption of amendments to Part XI. Most of the remaining issues were placed into the three-fourths category. While the list is the product of a major effort to accommodate and balance the views of all concerned groups, it was, of course, impossible to satisfy all delegations, and some further shifts of issues among categories may occur at the next session.

It should also be noted in this connection that in the process of drawing up the list, changes were made in the statement of several functions of the Council and Assembly, including Article 162(2)(a) and (k), as noted above, and Article 160(2)(n) (formerly (2)(o)). The latter change was intended to clarify that any decision by the Assembly to assign to an organ of the Authority any question or matter falling within the competence of the Authority which has not previously been assigned, must be in accordance with the rules, regulations, and procedures of the Authority.

Two other important and difficult elements of the package were the question of the majority required for residual issues not listed in any of the three categories of substantive issues and the questions of resolving disputes as to the category into which an issue falls. The revised text provides that decisions on residual issues shall be taken in accordance with the rules, regulations, and procedures of the Authority if specified therein, and if not specified therein, then under whichever voting rule is decided

by consensus. When a question arises as to whether an issue falls within the simple majority, two-thirds majority, three-fourths majority, or consensus category, the question shall be treated as falling within the category requiring the higher or highest majority as the case may be, unless otherwise decided by the Council by the said majority.

Finally, it should be noted that in paragraph 7(c), the reference to the time period for which emergency orders may be issued under Article 162(2) (v) to prevent serious harm to the marine environment arising out of activities in the Area has been changed from 10 (as specified in the so-called "Brennan Text" of August 1979) to 30 days. In addition, the United States Delegation is considering whether a distinction should be made between emergency orders for suspension of operations and emergency orders for adjustment of operations, and, in particular, whether the 30-day period should apply in the case of an emergency order for the adjustment of operations.

Article 162(2)(j) - Approval of Plans of Work

Despite the incorporation into the text of the split contracting system, under which approval of plans of work no longer includes allocation of a production authorization, negotiation of the procedure for approval of plans of work proved extremely difficult. Controversy arose over the procedure to be followed in both the Legal and Technical Commission and the Council.

The revised text has two elements. First, if the Commission recommends the approval of a plan of work, it shall be deemed to have been approved by the Council unless a Council member objects in writing within 14 days alleging non-compliance with the requirements of Annex III, Article 6. In the event of such an objection, recourse is provided to the conciliation procedure specified in Article 161(7), which calls for a report within 14 days by the Conciliation Committee. If the objection is still maintained, the plan of work shall be deemed to have been approved by the Council unless the Council disapproves it by consensus among its members, excluding the State or States, if any, making the application or sponsoring the applicant.

If, on the other hand, the Commission recommends disapproval of a plan of work or does not make a recommendation, the Council may decide to approve the plan of work by a three-fourths majority of members present and voting provided that such majority includes a majority of members participating in the session.

The revised text represents a compromise between the developing countries, which considered that a plan of work should have to be approved by a high majority in the Council after being recommended for approval by the Commission, and the United States and other western industrialized countries which considered that it should be made difficult for the Council to disapprove a plan of work. The preference of the United States Delegation was a system under which the Commission would review a plan of work without making a recommendation, and the plan of work would be deemed approved by the Council unless disapproved. The Group of 77, however, argued persuasively that if it is made difficult for the Council to disapprove a plan of work by specifying a high majority for Council disapproval and a presumption in favor of approval, there should at least be a requirement for recommendation of approval by the Commission. The resulting text seeks to accommodate the concerns of both groups as well as the concerns of the Eastern Socialist countries. The question of the decision-making procedures in the Commission pursuant to Article 163(11) is to be decided by the rules, regulations, and procedures of the Authority.

It should be noted in this connection, that several improvements were made in the texts of Articles 163 and 165 concerning the Commissions, and, in particular, the Legal and Technical Commission, as discussed below. These improvements afford additional protections in the process of approval of plans of work. The United States Delegation will be giving further consideration prior to the Tenth Session of additional ways to better safeguard the legitimate rights of duly sponsored applicants during the approval process.

Article 163 - Organs of the Council

The revised text adds to paragraph 3 on the qualifications of members of the Commissions, a

requirement that in submitting nominations for the
Commissions, States Parties shall bear in mind the
need to submit candidates of the highest standard of
competence and integrity with qualifications in relevant fields. The terms of members of the Commissions
specified in paragraph 7 were also increased from
three to five years to enhance their independence.
In addition, paragraph 8 now contains a provision
prohibiting conflicts of interest by members of the
Commissions and requiring the protection by members
of the Commissions of proprietary data or other con-
fidential information.

## Article 165 - The Legal and Technical Commission

A provision has been added to paragraph 2(b) to
require that in reviewing plans of work, the Commission shall base its recommendations to the Council
solely on the grounds stated in Annex III and shall
report fully thereon to the Council. This provision
helps assure that the Commission will indeed make its
decisions on technical rather than political grounds
and that adverse decisions can be appealed under the
dispute settlement procedures of the Convention.

## Article 166 - The Secretary General

The revised text makes clear that the residual
functions of the Secretary General referred to therein are administrative functions entrusted to him by
the organs of the Authority and that the Enterprise
cannot use him and his staff to supplement its own
staff.

## COMMITTEE II

### Overview

Committee II, under the Chairmanship of Ambassador Andres Aguilar of Venezuela, held only one meeting during the second half of the Ninth Session and
that to review certain Drafting Committee recommendations. Nevertheless, intensive consultations took
place among interested States in an effort to deal
with issues of particular concern to one or more
States in the Conference. Notable among these

outstanding issues, as discussed more fully below, was the question of the delimitation of maritime boundaries between opposite and adjacent States. Despite an earnest effort on the part of the interested States, they did not succeed in reaching a final solution at this Session, although the outlook for resolution of the problem was enhanced. Other issues included small changes to Article 42, desired by Spain and supported by the major maritime countries, a proposal made by Canada and Argentina with respect to stocks of fish that are to be found both within and beyond the limits of the exclusive economic zone, and a declaration regarding the continental zone, and a declaration regarding the continental shelf off Sri Lanka setting forth an exception from the limits in Article 76 in part of the Bengal Bay area, because of its peculiar shelf characteristics. With respect to this latter issue, it is anticipated that this declaration will be appended to the Final Act of the Conference.

The informal activity related to Committee II was successful in consolidating previous gains and compromises with respect to the texts under its jurisdiction, providing time for negotiating the final few issues, and in keeping some delegations from reopening sensitive issues which could result in making the entire package unacceptable to many States in the Conference. Exemplary of the latter category was the attempt by a number of States to generate support for an amendment to Article 21 to require prior authorization and notification for warship transits through the territorial sea. This proposal was completely rejected by the major maritime powers and others as a Conference breaker, which cannot be permitted. Some of the sponsors of the proposal recognize that they cannot succeed and realize the burden that they would bear for destroying the entire treaty if they press the amendment.

The Spanish amendments to Article 42 and the Argentine and Canadian concerns regarding fish were not included in the Draft Convention although no objections were stated to the substance of the Spanish changes. Procedural problems stymied the adoption of the Article 42 amendments at this time.

## Stocks of Fish Occurring Both Within and Beyond the Exclusive Economic Zone

Argentina and Canada continued to press their position in favor of strengthening Article 63 with respect to the conservation of the same stock or stocks of fish which occur both within and beyond the economic zone. Their position which favored the coastal State in the area beyond 200 miles caused difficulties for many delegations concerned about expanding coastal State jurisdiction. In addition, both countries wanted to clarify the applicability of the dispute-settlement procedures, including provisional measures.

While it was clear that any approach which included the expansion of coastal State jurisdiction would not be acceptable to the Conference as a whole, it appeared initially that an approach which focused on dispute settlement would have some reasonable chance of success. The negotiations on this issue were somewhat protracted, and the initial acquiescence of certain States in a much scaled-down proposal turned into opposition at the end of the Session. Thus, no new text was included in the Draft Convention. It seems clear, in any case, that the provisions for the compulsory and peaceful settlement of disputes are applicable to situations where actions are taken beyond 200 miles that are in violation of the applicable international standards regarding conservation; and this includes the power to prescribe provisional measures under Article 290 where necessary to insure conservation.

It should be noted that because resolution of this issue was in part tied by its sponsors to other issues in Committee II, including the suggested non-controversial drafting changes to Article 42, a complex procedural tangle resulted. Moreover, certain States believe that Committee II, except for the principles regarding delimitation of offshore boundaries, should be closed as soon as possible and that no substantive issues should be injected at this late date. Nevertheless, the question of conforming the text of Article 63(2) with that of Article 117 merits further study, since both provisions may apply to the same fishing activities.

## Delimitation of Maritime Boundaries

During the Geneva session, negotiations were carried on between the group of States favoring the equidistance line (supporters of NG 7/2) and the group favoring equitable principles (supporters of NG 7/10). These negotiations were publicly conducted by nine representative States from each side, with meetings co-chaired by Ireland and Spain. The procedural problem of identifying the precise text which would be accepted as a basis for negotiations was avoided by focusing the debate rather upon the elements of the problem. Hence, it was possible to have a full discussion of the meaning of international law and its relevance to the problem, such as the kinds of circumstances which might be taken into account when delimiting boundaries. While these debates produced no concrete formula, they served to clarify misunderstandings which delegations on each side of the debate may have had concerning the positions of those on the other.

Following the general discussions, more intensive negotiations were carried out in private consultations, resulting in various draft texts. While none of these proved entirely acceptable, it was encouraging that negotiations were carried out with such intensity. It appeared by the end of the Session that a good start had been made toward a final solution that might make the eventual treaty more acceptable to a substantial number of delegations which might otherwise feel compelled to seek a reservation on the issue. In this regard, the provision on reservations in the final clauses contains a footnote specifically noting that the final outcome of delimitation negotiations might include the possibility of reservations on that issue. On the other hand, it was somewhat disappointing that so much time was spent discussing the procedures to be followed that true negotiations did not begin until so late in the Session that tangible results were difficult to obtain.

COMMITTEE III

The conclusion reached this spring in New York
that Committee III had completed substantive negotiations on the issues under its jurisdiction--marine
pollution, marine scientific research, and transfer
of technology--was confirmed during this resumed
Ninth Session of the Conference. No substantive negotiations were undertaken, and, with few exceptions,
no delegation seriously proposed that substantive negotiations be resumed.

The major activity of the session was a series
of meetings to examine drafting changes prepared by
Chairman Yankov and the Secretariat. The changes by
and large were of a drafting nature, although a limited number had substantive effects. Of the 169
changes proposed, 135 were accepted by the Committee.
About five amendments were proposed from the floor,
but only two were accepted. The Chairman prevented
reopening substantive negotiations by applying the
rule that no change would be adopted over the objec
tions of any single delegation. Although he held
open the possibility that the Committee might examine
other drafting suggestions at a future date, he left
no room for doubt that the present texts of Parts
XII-XIV will become the texts of the Convention.

The major problem that arose was related to the
selective incorporation of Drafting Committee harmonization proposals, which defeats the purpose of
such proposals, and can result in abuse of the process for substantive ends. These new problems will
have to be resolved by the Drafting Committee, which
in the future may have to present harmonization suggestions on each point as a package.

INFORMAL PLENARY

General Provisions

The Informal Plenary, chaired by President
Amerasinghe, met eight times to consider General
Provisions. Five articles gained widespread support
and were incorporated in the Draft Convention.

The following articles dealing with good faith
and abuse of rights, peaceful uses of the seas, and

disclosure of information, were considered as a package and accepted by the Informal Plenary:

## Article 300

### Good Faith and Abuse of Rights

The States Parties to this Convention undertake to discharge in good faith the obligations entered into in conformity with this Convention, and to exercise the rights, jurisdictions and freedoms recognized in this Convention in a manner which would not constitute an abuse of rights.

## Article 301

### Peaceful Uses of the Seas

In exercising their rights and performing their duties in accordance with the provisions of this Convention, all States Parties shall refrain from any threat or use of force against the territorial integrity or political independence of any State, or in any other manner inconsistent with the principles of international law embodied in the Charter of the United Nations.

## Article 302

### Disclosure of Information

Without prejudice to the right of any State Party to resort to the procedures for the settlement of disputes provided in this Convention, nothing in this Convention shall be deemed to require a State Party, in the fulfillment of its obligations under the relevant provisions of this Convention, to supply information the disclosure of which is contrary to the essential interests of its security.

By presenting these articles as a package, it was made clear by the first article that the third article may not be abused. This is the point made in the report of the President where he emphasizes

that it was understood that the third article does not detract from obligations under the Convention.

Chile pressed a proposal to the effect that the principle of the common heritage of mankind was a rule of jus cogens, i.e. a peremptory norm of international law. While many less developed States favored the proposal, several States observed that it raised serious legal questions, including the impossibility of creating a rule of jus cogens in the manner suggested, as well as the need to consider other principles, including freedom of navigation and overflight, transit passage through straits, and the duty to protect the marine environment as equally entitled to such status. At the same time, no one maintained that the parties to the Convention could enter into agreements in derogation of the principle set forth in Article 136. This is reflected by a new paragraph 6 in Article 305 of the final clauses which provides:

> The States Parties to this Convention agree that there can be no amendments to the basic principle relating to the common heritage of mankind set forth in Article 136 and that they shall not be party to any agreement in derogation thereof.

The Informal Plenary considered the question of archeological objects. Initially a proposal that would establish coastal State sovereign rights, or alternatively jurisdiction, over such objects on the continental shelf was considered, but it was rejected because it upset the balance between the rights and obligations of coastal States and other States in the economic zone and the continental shelf. A compromise was struck and accepted by consensus as follows:

## Article 303

1. States have the duty to protect archeological objects and objects of historical origin found at sea, and shall cooperate for this purpose.

2. In order to control traffic in such objects, the coastal State may, in applying Article 33, presume that their removal from the seabed in the area referred to in that

article without the approval of the coastal
State would result in an infringement within its territory or territorial sea of the
regulations of the coastal State referred
to in that article.

   3. Nothing in this article affects
the rights of identifiable owners, the
law of salvage or other rules of admiralty, or laws and practices with respect
to cultural exchanges.

   4. This article is without prejudice
to other international agreements and rules
of international law regarding the protection of archeological objects and objects
of historical origin.


Paragraph 2 refers to the power of the coastal
State, in a contiguous zone extending up to 24 miles
from its coast, to take measures to prevent and punish infringement of its customs, fiscal, immigration,
or sanitary regulations in its territory or territorial sea.

Questions relating to salvage, title, and other
private law matters are not affected by this article.
The coastal State power granted by this article is,
moreover, both meaningful and circumscribed in a manner that addresses the real problem faced, particularly in the area of the Mediterranean Sea.

The Informal Plenary accepted the following text
to emphasize that the Law of the Sea text does not
address all of the questions related to responsibility and liability under international law.


## Article 304

   The provisions of this Convention
regarding responsibility and liability for
damage are without prejudice to the application of existing rules and the development of further rules regarding responsibility and liability under international
law.

This text was accepted on the tacit understanding that it facilitated acceptance of the Convention, including the straits provisions, by the Spanish and Moroccan delegations and might be removed if this proved not to be the case.

A proposal by Ecuador on use of terms and a proposal by Turkey on the application and interpretation of the Convention were not accepted.

Dispute Settlement

The Conference completed substantive negotiations on the dispute-settlement portions of the text. No substantive changes were made in these provisions. The Informal Plenary did consider and adopt a proposal by the President to restructure Part XV.

The restructured text emphasizes that while in some disputes parties will be obliged to submit to arbitral or judicial procedures entailing a binding decision, in others the parties will be obliged to submit to a procedure leading to a non-binding report, i.e. compulsory conciliation. The latter category embraces disputes relating to certain economic zone fishery issues, certain marine scientific research matters, and maritime boundary delimitation. The revised text divides Part XV into three sections-- one covering the procedures to which all disputes are subject as a preliminary step, one prescribing procedures for binding decisions and one for conciliation.

The revision also includes a new Section 2 to be added to Annex V (conciliation). This section incorporates the procedural machinery appropriate to the special use of conciliation under the Convention. Notable in this section are provisions which allow the conciliation to proceed regardless of the cooperation of the "defendant" party. Another provision makes clear the conciliation commission's jurisdiction to decide questions of its own competence.

Most of the dispute-settlement portion of the text may now be regarded as closed. The Informal Plenary recognized, however, that some desirable changes in Article 298 may become possible after the conclusion of the delimitation negotiations. Professor Wuensche announced his intention to consider a

few small issues in Section 6 of Part XI at the Tenth
Session, and, of course, further small drafting
changes may be required in Part XV, or associated
Annexes.

## FINAL CLAUSES

As a result of intensive work in the Informal
Plenary, the substantive texts of the final clauses
are in essence complete. This is a substantial
achievement by the President of the Conference in
light of the controversial nature of some of the
provisions that emerged at the end of the New York
session from the Group of Legal Experts in document
FC/20, which formed the initial basis of negotiation
at the Geneva session.

At the start of the session, the President of
the Conference announced that the question of participation in the Convention was best deferred. Accordingly, there was no debate or drafting by the Conference on various proposals to allow entities other
than fully independent States to become party. Thus
the Conference will have to deal at the next session
with the legal issues necessary to accommodate participation by the European Community and associated
States such as those that emerge from the Trust Territories of the Pacific Islands as well as the Cook
Islands and Niue, while fending off efforts to exploit
the Convention for the purely political issues of dependencies and liberation movements.

The President also postponed further consideration of the resolution on the Preparatory Commission
and, with it, the question of preparatory investment
protection. These will be the major issues facing
the next session.

## Entry into Force of the Convention

Two problems were posed with respect to entry
into force of the Convention:

(1) The number of ratifications needed; and

(2) The question of composing the first Council
of the Seabed Authority if the initial States Parties
were insufficient to fulfill the requirements of

Article 161 regarding different categories of States.

With positions on the first issue generally divided between 50 and 70, a compromise on 60 ratifications for entry into force emerged naturally.

It was recognized that the second issue was closely connected to the negotiations on the Council. Accordingly, the President sent a letter to the Chairman of the First Committee requesting that Committee's advice. Deeply engaged in substantive negotiations, the First Committee recommended no change in the text pending further negotiations on the matter. Thus the existing text retains the proposal of the Chairman of the Group of Legal Experts that the first Council shall be constituted in a manner consistent with the purpose of the article on composition of the Council, if its provisions cannot be strictly applied. In this regard, the new text extends from six to twelve months the delay in entry into force after the necessary number of ratifications have been deposited, thus giving additional States time to ratify and perhaps thereby avoiding or reducing the problem.

The text provides that the rules, regulations, and procedures drafted by the Preparatory Commission will apply provisionally from the date of entry into force of the Convention until the Authority itself adopts rules, regulations, and procedures. This provision is integral to the package settlement that emerged in the First Committee; it is essential if States are to understand what it is they are ratifying and if the Authority is to function when the Convention enters into force.

## Reservations

Since the Convention is an overall "package deal" reflecting different priorities of different States, to permit reservations would inevitably permit one State to eliminate the "quid" of another State's "quo." Thus there was general agreement in the Conference that in principle reservations could not be permitted.

There was also agreement on a provision allowing declarations or statements that do not purport to exclude or to modify the legal effect of the provisions

of the Convention. At the same time, it was recognized that in certain very limited and specific instances, a substantive article might itself permit reservations. Thus, although not strictly a question of reservations, Article 298 on optional exceptions to dispute settlement itself authorizes certain defined exceptions to the general requirements regarding dispute settlement. As the footnote in the text indicates, the most frequently mentioned possibility of a specific provision allowing reservations concerns the provision regarding delimitation of the economic zone and continental shelf between States with opposite or adjacent coasts. Whether or not this comes to pass will presumably be known at the conclusion of negotiations on delimitation.

There was some scattered dissent to the general view that reservations should be prohibited in principle. In most cases, this dissent seemed to be merely for the record or in order to bring pressure to bear on other substantive negotiations, particularly those on delimitation.

Relation to Other Conventions

Article 311 deals with the relation between the Law of the Sea Convention and other treaties, and draws heavily on the rules on this subject set forth in the Vienna Convention on the Law of Treaties. This article contains the new clause mentioned above which specifies that there can be no amendments to the basic principle of the common heritage of mankind. This is in essence a particular application of the general rule set forth in this Article. It emerged after it had become clear that there could be no agreement on any provision, such as that proposed by Chile, dealing with peremptory norms of international law.

Amendments

After very extensive work, the new text rationalizes the amendment system. It makes clear that all amendments to the Convention are subject to ratification or accession after their adoption. It also distinguishes between amendments relating to First Committee matters (amendments relating to "activities in the Area") and other amendments.

Amendments that do not relate to "activities in the Area" can be adopted at a conference of the parties, which could be called by a majority of the parties no sooner than ten years after entry into force of the Convention. Alternatively, they can be adopted at any time by a simplified procedure in which the amendment is circulated to all States Parties, and is considered adopted if there are no objections within 12 months. In either case, such an amendment would enter into force for States ratifying or acceding to it once instruments of ratification or accession are deposited by two-thirds of the States Parties.

Amendments relating to deep seabed matters are treated differently. Aside from the review conference convened under Article 155, they can be adopted in identical form by both the Council and the Assembly of the Authority at any time. Since it is generally not possible to have two different sets of legal provisions governing deep seabed mining, deep seabed mining amendments would enter into force for all States Parties one year after they have been ratified by three fourths of States Parties. The one-year time period was included to permit States that did not favor the amendment to take action once it was clear the amendment was entering into force. It was recognized that under the constitutional systems of some States the choice would then be between ratifying the amendment and denouncing the Convention.

Amendments regarding the Law of the Sea Tribunal (Annex VI) also enter into force for all parties once ratified by three-fourths. Such amendments can only be adopted, pursuant to the new text of Article 42 of Annex VI, in the Council and Assembly of the Seabed Authority for seabed matters, or by consensus of all the parties for other matters.

## Denunciation

The text now provides that a State may denounce the Convention at any time by giving one year's notice. A five-year freeze on denunciation contained in earlier texts was eliminated, it being recognized that it was unlikely in practice that States would ratify a Convention of this sort with the intention of denouncing it shortly thereafter. The technical provisions dealing with the effects of denunciation

were drawn largely from the Vienna Convention on the
Law of Treaties.

## Authentic Texts

The final clauses contain a standard provision
specifying that the texts of the Convention in all
official languages are equally authentic. In this
connection, the United States statement in Plenary
on August 26, 1980, contained the following sentence:
"Since virtually all of the original texts of the
ICNT and its predecessors were drafted in English,
the Conference will wish to review the proposed Article 313 of Document FC/21/Rev.1 in light of the
further work of the Drafting Committee." The intersessional meeting of the Drafting Committee early
next winter is expected to devote the major portion
of its time to article-by-article textual review and
concordance in preparation for completion of the
Convention.

### DRAFTING COMMITTEE

The coordinators of the six language groups of
the Drafting Committee, meeting informally with the
Chairman, devoted most of their time to harmonization
problems. Relatively few new recommendations emerged
from the process. At the end of the session it seemed generally understood that the work of the coordinators and the Committee as a whole would be most
productive if they now proceeded directly to an
article-by-article review of the text.

Most of the language groups, meanwhile, devoted
themselves to textual review and are now well along
in the process. Each group has proceeded independently on the basis of its own language version of the
text. These texts already differ among themselves to
some extent. This procedure has thus begun to suggest the probable difficulty of conforming the six
different language versions with the original English
which will ultimately be necessary.

### PREPARATORY INVESTMENT PROTECTION ("PIP")

Not unexpectedly, early in the session it became
clear that the passage of national seabed mining

legislation by the United States and the FRG had complicated the negotiation of the protection of interim
investments. Indeed, the G-77 reiterated its position
in opposition to deep seabed mining in the absence of
a Law of the Sea treaty, while the United States and
several developed States reiterated their previously
stated views. A United States-sponsored meeting on
the subject failed to attract a significant number of
G-77 participants. However, a number of useful small
group discussions did take place during the session.
While representatives of the seabed mining industry
continued to emphasize the inadequacies of the original "PIP" concept, attention was also drawn to the
reserved side of the system. The G-77 are plainly
concerned that treaty provisions aimed at protecting
the continuity of operations of existing private ventures would serve to move these activities even farther out in front of the Enterprise than they are already. The USSR also indicated a fear that under a
"PIP" arrangement, early applicants could corner the
prime sites to the disadvantage of later entrants,
although their concern presumably has been reduced by
the addition of new anti-monopoly language to Article
6 of Annex III.

Under the circumstances, the Conference leadership decided that the "PIP" issue, together with the
Preparatory Commission itself, should be carried over
to the next negotiating session. An active program
of consultations is slated for the intersessional
period.

TENTH SESSION
NEW YORK
March 9 - April 24, 1981

SUMMARY

The tenth session of the Third United Nations
Conference on the Law of the Sea was dominated by reactions to the United States announcement on March 2
that it was undertaking a policy review with respect
to the Convention and that the United States delegation would be instructed to seek to ensure that the
negotiations would not be completed at this session.
As a result, while there was some intensive discussion of a few issues, no new texts or agreements
emerged.

As its start, the Conference elected Tommy T.B.
Koh of Singapore as its President to succeed the late
Hamilton Shirley Amerasinghe of Sri Lanka, who died
in December.

At the ninth session, the Conference had identified three major outstanding issues:  preparatory investment protection, the resolution on the preparatory commission, and participation in the Convention.
With respect to preparatory investment protection,
the immediate reaction of the Group of 77 to the
United States policy review was to refuse to discuss
this issue so long as the United States was unable to
make commitments.  With respect to the preparatory
commission, there was considerable discussion in the
First Committee and in its Working Group of 21, but
no new drafts were proposed.  With respect to participation, there was a further debate in the informal
plenary, followed by intensive consultations held by
the President, which served to clarify the legal issues involved in participation by entities other than
States.  Again, no new texts were proposed.

While work continued between the two interest
groups concerned with respect to delimitation of offshore zones between States with opposite and adjacent
coasts, no agreement was reached.

The informal plenary met and approved almost all
of the proposals of the Drafting Committee regarding
Second and Third Committee texts.

The tenth session of the Conference will resume
in Geneva on August 3 for four weeks.  The Conference
may decide to extend that session for a fifth week.
The Drafting Committee will hold an intersessional

meeting in Geneva from June 29 to July 31; it will
direct its attention to Parts XV, XVI and XVII of the
text, turning back to Part XI and Annexes III and IV
in the last two weeks.

## REACTION TO U.S. POLICY REVIEW

The reaction to the U.S. policy review was characterized by bewilderment and frustration. Many Conference participants had believed that this would be
the last negotiating session of the Conference; those
who were skeptical thought remaining matters could be
cleared up this summer in time for signature in
Caracas soon thereafter.

The announcement of the U.S. review was followed
by widespread endorsement of the basic package embodied in the Draft Convention as it stands by developing countries, the Soviet bloc, and some Western
countries.

Three motivations appear to be prevalent in this
reaction among foreign delegates:

1. A desire to conclude the treaty quickly.
The reasons for this range from fatigue and frustration with the length of these negotiations and the
need to show a tangible end product to a concern that
existing trends in the law of the sea toward expansion of coastal State controls of navigation are prejudicial to their national interests and may soon
render the existing provisions on navigational freedoms unratifiable by coastal States.

2. A desire to avoid making further concessions
to the United States with respect to deep seabed mining.

3. A desire to avoid encouraging their own governments, or third States, to reopen other matters in
the Convention in response to U.S. proposals for
changes.

No delegation seriously questioned the right of
the U.S. Government to carry out such a review.
While some were annoyed at its timing and our inability to give more notice, most were much more concerned about the outcome. Thus, statements of foreign
delegations were characterized by efforts to affirm

the basic "package deal" as it stands and stress the difficulty of considering any fundamental changes in that deal. Nevertheless, they stopped short of presenting the draft as it stands on a "take it or leave it" basis, and were keenly aware of the need to avoid provoking a sharp negative reaction to the Convention. This led to numerous statements toward the end of the session that the reservoir of good will for the United States was not inexhaustible and that the United States should not misinterpret moderation at this session as a sign of weakness.

The arguments stressed two basic themes. The first was the issue of the credibility of U.S. participation in long-term negotiations, in this case, negotiations that were begun in 1967 and carried on under presidents of both parties. The second theme was that "a single State" could not be permitted to stop the entire world from concluding such a long-range effort. While recognizing the classic problem of reconciling inequalities of wealth and power with the sense of national dignity inherent in the legal equality of States, some of the delegates seem to be warning that public embarrassment would not be tolerable to them or their governments whatever the consequences of defiance.

There is widespread recognition of the need to deal with the United States if at all possible. Thus, for example, it is now generally recognized—as the United States stated—that the resumed tenth session in Geneva will be for the purpose of considering the problems identified in the U.S. review, but that the review may well not be finally completed until after the session. President Koh speaks of "benign pressure" on the U.S. to complete its review before August.

## ELECTION OF THE PRESIDENT

The death of the long-time President of the Conference, Hamilton Shirley Amerasinghe of Sri Lanka, necessitated the election of a new President. Since the previous President was Asian, and since the various chairmanships were distributed among the regions, it was generally expected that the primary responsibility would fall on the Asian Group to select a candidate generally acceptable to the Conference.

The principal candidates were Satya Nandan of
Fiji and Christopher Pinto of Sri Lanka. Repeated
polling in the Asian Group revealed a split between
the candidates, with a significant number of delegations casting votes for neither candidate. There
were persistent rumors that the Soviet Union was attempting to maneuver a "compromise" on Dr. Jagota of
India, but this did not materialize.

As expected from the outset, in the end Ambassador Tommy T.B. Koh of Singapore emerged as the consensus candidate of the Asian Group and was elected
by the Conference by consensus. Laos, Mongolia, and
Vietnam reserved their positions within the Asian
Group, but did not block a consensus.


NEXT SESSION

Considerable time was devoted to the question of
the next session of the Conference. The issue was of
interest because of its effect on the expectations of
States regarding the outcome.

There was a general desire among developing
countries to schedule a long resumed session of six
weeks this summer to complete the negotiations. This
reflected in part a genuine frustration by developing
countries with the length of time that these negotiations have taken, and in part tactical considerations
related to the United States review.

The United States indicated that since it was
doubtful that final decisions could be taken in the
review before August, it would be preferable to hold
a session next year. In acceding to the general desire to hold a session in August, the United States
made clear that it viewed such a session as an opportunity for informal consultations rather than definitive negotiation on texts, and that it did not expect
to complete its review until after the August session.

The resultant compromises on the timing of the
next session reflect a general, but not explicit,
acceptance of the desirability of avoiding confrontation on the issues at this point. Thus, while the
four-week session can be extended to five weeks, the
decision on whether to extend it will be taken by consensus if at all possible. While the Drafting Committee will work for five weeks prior to the session,

it will not turn to deep seabed mining texts until
the last two weeks.


## COMMITTEE ONE

The First Committee held two formal meetings and
four informal meetings before shifting to an informal
WG-21 format. Events in the First Committee at this
session were significantly affected by U.S. positions
announced before the Conference. While discussion of
the Preparatory Commission resolution continued, no
serious negotiations were conducted. The Group of 77
itself precluded any work on preparatory investment
protection so long as the United States was unable to
commit itself to the package.

First Committee Chairman Paul Engo held private
consultations with the EEC countries, Zambia, Zaire,
Zimbabwe, and Canada, on the production limitation.
The consultations were based on papers prepared by
Zaire, Zimbabwe, and Zambia attaching the Secretariat's report (see below). No changes occurred in the
text as a result. U.S. participation in all work was
minimal and was expressly qualified by our position
regarding review of the Convention.


### Secretariat Reports

The Secretary-General's representative for Law
of the Sea presented two reports to the conference in
the First Committee. One, which had been requested
at the last session of the conference by certain
land-based producers of seabed metals, was a definitive study of the operation of Article 151, paragraph
2--the Production Limitation (A/Conf.62/L.66). It
was accompanied by voluminous tables showing how much
production would be allowed under certain assumptions.

A second report on financial implications of a
Preparatory Commission and start-up of the International Seabed Authority (A/Conf.62/L.65) was also
presented in the First Committee. This report gave
costs for the operation, administrative support and
housing of the PrepCom given assumptions made by the
Secretariat about its size and duration. It also
costed out start-up of the Enterprise under certain
assumptions.

During discussion on the Production Limitation paper, Zaire, Zambia, and Zimbabwe, with Canadian support, urged that the report be supplemented with work on the implications of Article 151 for metal markets and the economies of relevant countries. There was no broad support for this request.

The Canadian Delegation followed this up with a proposal that a technical group be formed to continue work on Article 151, paragraph 2, without specification of the Technical Group's term of reference. This proposal was rejected by all speakers except Zimbabwe, Zaire, and Zambia.

## Working Group of 21

The Working Group of 21 (WG-21), of which the United States is a member, met in sessions open to all delegations to discuss the draft resolution to create the Preparatory Commission contained in A/Conf. 62/L.55. This group was co-chaired by Paul Engo of Cameroon in his capacity as Chairman of the First Committee and T.T.B. (Tommy) Koh of Singapore as President of the Conference. The WG-21 then moved through the Preparatory Commission resolution in a general fashion.

The WG-21 began with a substantive debate on the status of Preparatory Commission drafts of rules, regulations, and procedures. G-77 delegates in general attacked Article 308, paragraph 4, of the ICNT, Rev. 3, which specifies that the PrepCom drafts of rules, regulations, and procedures will be the provisional rules, regulations, and procedures of the Seabed Authority until others are adopted by the Authority. Generally, developed countries defended this approach as the only way to assure those ratifying the treaty that the Seabed Authority would operate in the manner foreseen by them.

The decision-making procedures of the PrepCom were also vigorously debated.

Participation in the PrepCom (the so-called Ticket of Admission problem) was thoroughly debated. Industrialized countries expressing a view preferred that signatories of the Final Act be full participants in the work of the PrepCom and its decision-making procedures, since that would provide the

461

broadest possible participation in the PrepCom. Developing countries demanded that full participation
be reserved for signatories of the Convention so that
only those who had already indicated their intent to
become parties to the Convention could become full
members of the PrepCom.

The WG-21, after reviewing the broad issues involved in the PrepCom, shifted to a more private atmosphere in which only members of the WG-21 and the
co-chairmen were present. Chairman Engo then led the
group through a paragraph-by-paragraph review of the
resolution text with a view toward producing another
iteration.

The process proved to be slow and contentious.
Nevertheless, the WG-21 came close to completing a
sentence-by-sentence review of the text.

Chairman Engo's report on the session contained
no new drafts or suggestions for the text. The report described in a general manner the activities of
the session and noted efforts made to develop consensus.

The U.S. Delegation confined its participation
in the debate to noting our need to review Law of the
Sea issues. In the case of PrepCom issues, the U.S.
Delegation noted that the PrepCom could not be discussed in isolation from other issues which would be
under review in the U.S. in coming months.

### Other Issues

Other Committee I issues were referred to in
passing only, and the texts of Part XI and Annexes III
and IV were given no substantive discussion. Private
conversation indicated that most delegates were
awaiting the outcome of the U.S. review before making
any further moves.

The site of the Seabed Authority was discussed
and support was registered for Jamaica. The African
Group and the Latin American Group stated that it was
the consensus of their groups that Jamaica should
eventually be chosen. Fiji and Malta (the other
countries which have offered to host the Seabed Authority) found discussion of the issue at that time
inappropriate.

COMMITTEE TWO

The Second Committee held four informal meetings
without agenda to permit delegations to raise any
questions deemed important to them. The articles receiving primary attention were 21 (warship passage in
the territorial sea), 58 (warship activities in the
200-mile economic zone), 60(1) (military installations and structures), 60(3) (duty to remove installations), and 63 (straddling fish stocks). Private
consultations were also held among delegations on the
subject of delimitation of maritime boundaries between opposite and adjacent States. No changes in
text emerged as a result of work related to Committee
Two subjects.

At the conclusion of the meetings, Chairman
Aguilar (Venezuela), drew three conclusions: (1)
while there were widely divergent views expressed,
a practical consensus exists along the basic lines
of the Committee Two package; (2) there remain only
a very few questions of interest to a substantial
number of delegations; (3) it was not the time, under
the circumstances, to establish any working groups.

The committee was held together, once again, by
the strong and able leadership of Ambassador Aguilar.
Interventions in plenary on the record following his
report were lengthy, followed by the same lines as in
committee debates, and constituted a clear indication
that many coastal States delegations were ready and
willing to do battle on a number of military-related
issues should the text be reopened. Peru stated that
there was no consensus on certain contentious provisions such as Article 21. The U.S. stated that our
views regarding navigation rights, including those of
warships, and other uses of the sea related to international peace and security were well known, and that
we reserved our position regarding any efforts to
alter these rights under customary or conventional
law.

Warship Passage in Territorial Sea - Article 21

Discussion on this article centered on a proposal by the Philippines and others (C.2/Inf.Mtg./58)
which had the effect of permitting coastal States to
require prior authorization or notification before

warships may enter the territorial sea. This article
absorbed the attention of the committee for most of
the four meetings. Of the approximately 70 speakers
on the subject, roughly one-half favored the amendment and one-half opposed. Among those favoring the
amendment, a small number thought that notification
only might be acceptable. Those opposed were split
between those who spoke to the substance of the article (it upset the balance of the text) and those
who thought that the Committee Two text had, as a
package, been highly negotiated and should not be
reopened. Western States were joined by the Eastern
bloc in opposition to the change. Several delegations pressed for the formation of a small consultation group on this subject.

## Warship Activities in 200-mile Economic Zone - Article 58

Brazil argued that Article 58 should be revised
to make clear that it does not authorize military exercises in the exclusive economic zone without the
authorization of the coastal State. This proposal
received support and opposition along the same lines
as the proposed change to Article 21, but it received
less attention.

## Military Installations and Structures - Article 60(1)

Brazil and Uruguay suggested that, in accordance
with their amendment contained in C.2/Inf.Mtg/11, the
limitations on coastal State jurisdiction over artificial islands, installations, and structures contained in subparagraphs (a), (b), and (c) should be
deleted.

## Duty to Remove Installations - Article 60(3)

The U.K. raised the problem created by the requirement in the present text that all installations
in the EEZ (and on the shelf) be "entirely" removed.
It was suggested that a new form of words be used to
allow partial removal, based on international standards and provided that navigation and fishing interests are adequately protected. In principle, this
proposal received widespread support, particularly

among broad-margin States, and no opposition. Wording remains a problem.


### Straddling Fish Stocks - Article 63

Argentina pressed its suggestions for a change
in the text to provide for cooperation among affected
States for the conservation of so-called "straddling
stocks," that is, stocks found both within and beyond
the exclusive economic zone. This change would incorporate the thrust of the language in Article 117
dealing with the same subject on the high seas. The
suggestion was supported by others, including Canada,
who pointed out that consultations were under way on
the subject but was opposed by a number of distant-
water fishing States.


### Common Heritage Fund

Nepal drew the committee's attention to its suggestion contained in C.2/Inf.Mtg/45, Rev.1, for the
establishment of a "common heritage fund," contributions to which would be made by payments occurring
from the exploitation of the non-living resources of
the exclusive economic zone. Payments would be made
from the fund to developing countries and would be
used for other beneficial purposes. The proposal was
supported by ten other countries, most of which were
co-sponsors. There is broad opposition among coastal
States.


### Delimitation of Maritime Boundaries Between Opposite or Adjacent States

The two delimitation groups, those favoring a
solution based on equitable principles (Group of 29)
and those preferring emphasis on the median or equidistance line (Group of 22), met separately and
jointly on several occasions. The focus of the joint
discussions was a lack of agreement on a text as a
basis for negotiation. The G-22 wished to utilize
the text contained in the Draft Convention, while the
G-29 rejected that approach. Accordingly, the discussions proceeded along the lines of previous discussions with both sides concentrating on the various
elements contained in any possible solution. When
the G-22 insisted on inclusion of a general reference

to principles of international law, the other side agreed on condition that the term be accorded suf- ficient clarity. Subsequent discussions indicated that the two sides were in fact little closer to a final solution than before. The basic disagreement as to the relative weight to be placed upon "equita- ble principles" and the "median or equidistance line" remains. The group concluded its work, deferring future negotiations to the summer session.

### COMMITTEE THREE

Committee Three met only once during the session. Chairman Yankov convened a brief informal meeting to elicit the views of the committee on whether any is- sues within the mandate of the committee remained to be discussed or negotiated. He stressed that, in his view, negotiations had been completed at the Ninth Session and that any attempt to reopen substantive negotiations would seriously endanger the delicate compromises already achieved. He stated that the only reason that he could see for further meetings of the Committee would be in the event that additional mat- ters were referred to it by the plenary. There was general agreement expressed by several delegations with the views of the Chairman.

The United States representative intervened to state that the United States reserved its position on the status of the work of the committee pending the outcome of our review of the draft convention. Fur- ther, he made clear that there remained several tech- nical changes that needed to be discussed at some point. (This was in reference to the technical straits amendments to Articles 221 and 233, and to adding "generally accepted" in Article 208(3).)

### INFORMAL PLENARY

#### Participation

The question of participation in the Convention by various entities was a substantive issue on which President Koh tried to make some progress toward resolution during this session.

It is generally agreed that all States may become party to the Convention. The "all States"
clause will presumably be applied by the UN in traditional fashion. The question discussed was what
entities other than States may become party to the
Convention.

The legal aspect of this problem involves two
situations. The first concerns regional economic integration organizations such as the European Economic
Community to which members have transferred the internal and treaty-making competences of States with
respect to some matters regulated by the Convention.
The second concerns associated States, such as the
Cook Islands, Niue, and those that may emerge in the
Trust Territory of the Pacific Islands, that have the
independent internal and treaty-making competences of
States with respect to matters regulated by the Convention in accordance with the relevant instruments
of association.

The political aspects of the question relate to
proposals to permit areas that have not yet attained
full independence generally, and so-called national
liberation movements, to become party to the Convention.

At the first of two informal plenary meetings,
President Koh reviewed the history of this item and
presented his summary of the issues as participation
by five entities:

1. All States, which he called non-controversial;

2. Fully self-governing associated States which
have chosen that status in an act of self-determination supervised and approved by the United Nations,
and which have full competence in matters falling
within the sphere of the Convention;

3. Territories which have not yet attained full
independence, a more heterogeneous category of entities, which comprise:

    a. Trust territories;
    b. Territories over which there are disputes;
    c. Non-trust territories.

4. Intergovernmental organizations and economic
integration groups; and

5. National liberation movements recognized by the United Nations and by regional intergovernmental organizations concerned. (Note by the President: informal document FC/23)

During the informal plenary meetings, many delegations urged that the questions of participation should be examined from legal and juridical rather than from political perspectives. Some delegations viewed the five entities as part of a package which would require a comprehensive solution. There was no opposition to participation by all States.

In dealing with entities other than States, several delegations felt that objective criteria should be applied, in a uniform way, to determine whether those entities had the legal capacity to become a party to the Convention.

As to the category of "fully self-governing associated States," two important criteria emerged in the discussion: (1) whether the entities contemplated in this category have competence over the matters falling within the scope of the Convention; and (2) whether they possess the legal personality to enter into treaties in respect of those matters.

In the case of the Cook Islands and Niue, as well as the associated States that may emerge in the Trust Territory of the Pacific Islands, it was argued that both criteria were satisfied.

As to the category of "territories which have not yet attained full independence," the discussion again focused on legal and administrative competence over subject matters of the Convention and sufficient legal personality to make treaties on their own with respect to such matters. With respect to disputed territories, some delegations believed such territories could not enjoy the benefits of the Convention while other delegations saw no reason why peoples of such territories should not enjoy those benefits. Finally with respect to other territories that are not independent, there was again no general consensus because some territories may not have competence and may lack capacity to enter into treaties on matters within the scope of the Convention.

A representative of the Trust Territory of the Pacific gave a full account of the status of the three States--the Federated States of Micronesia, Palau, and the Marshall Islands--so far as participation in and signature of the Convention were concerned (Statement to the Conference: informal document FC/24). He stressed their competence and capacity, citing their 200-mile fishery zones and fisheries agreements with other States and describing their Compacts of Free Association with the United States.

As to the category "international organizations and economic integration groups," the European Economic Community (EEC) submitted a proposal (informal document FC/22) which was explained at some length. Several questions were raised regarding: whether all the member States of the organization should become parties to the Convention; the areas of competence transferred by members to the organization with respect to matters falling within the sphere of the Convention; the information to be obtained or notification to be made to third States with regard to competence of the organization; rights and benefits that a member of the organization may or may not obtain when not itself a party to the Convention; dual representation; who would be responsible for infringement of the rights of third States or for failure to comply with obligations; and the application of dispute settlement provisions to the organization.

As to the category "national liberation movements recognized by the United Nations and by the regional intergovernmental organizations concerned," opinion was strongly divided. Arguments made in favor of participation included the fact that they have been granted full membership by the Non-Aligned Conference, the Islamic Conference and the League of Arab States, and observer status by the UN General Assembly and UNCLOS III. Arguments against participation were the facts that they lack legal and administrative competence in the subject matter of the Convention and lack sufficient legal personality to enter into treaties in respect of such matters.

President Koh convened a small group of about 20 countries (including the United States) for informal consultations to examine further the participation issues from a legal, not political perspective. The basic documents examined were the EEC proposal (FC/22)

and another put forward by the Group of 77 (unnumbered, dated 25 March 1981) which incorporated prior proposals dealing with the Cook and Niue Islands, TTPI entities, modifications of the EEC proposal and its own proposals on other territories not yet independent and on national liberation movements.

During seven informal consultation meetings, each of the various entities was discussed in detail. There emerged from these consultations two criteria (same as those in the informal plenaries--legal competence in LOS subject matters and treaty-making capacity with regard to such matters) which should be applied as a test to determine whether a non-State entity could participate in the Convention. Some expressed the view that these criteria should not be strictly applied and that other factors should be taken into account.

In applying these criteria to self-governing associated States (as described in the Philippines/Solomon Islands proposal: informal document FC/19), it was found that they would satisfy the two criteria. In this regard, a strong case was made that the Cook Islands, Niue, and the associated States that may emerge in the TTPI would satisfy both criteria.

Because of variations with respect to territories which have not attained full independence in accordance with UNGA resolution 1514 (XV), discussions revealed that:

1. Participation cannot be allowed to all dependent territories as a class;

2. Disputed territories and those to which the transitional provision applies should be deferred for the moment; and

3. Some territories, which have achieved significant autonomy, can satisfay both criteria.

With respect to national liberation movements, some delegations suggested that these groups had the potential to fulfill the criteria even though they could not presently do so, arguing that other criteria should be applied to them. Other delegations questioned the application of these criteria to these groups. The Arab Group States and others tried to ascribe legal competence and legal personality to the

PLO by describing a growing jurisprudence with regard
to them (i.e. a certain degree of recognition by States,
the United Nations, and regional organizations; establishment of diplomatic missions in several States
in accordance with the Vienna Convention on Diplomatic Relations; and signature, though on a separate
page, of the Final Act of the Diplomatic Conference
on the Reaffirmation and Development of International
Humanitarian Law Applicable in Armed Conflict). However, there was no consensus that the two criteria
applied to the PLO or other national liberation movements.

Because of the many questions regarding participation by organizations (outlined above at the informal plenary), the EEC proposal and that part of the
G-77 proposal pertaining to international organizations were debated most thoroughly but without reaching consensus. To make participation by such organizations more restrictive, the USSR offered three
proposals: making participation by all members of the
organization a mandatory prerequisite for participation by the organization; requiring accession by an
international organization only through an instrument
filed with the depositary listing all powers delegated
to it by member States in areas regulated by the Convention and immediate notice of subsequent changes
thereto; and making the organization and its member
States jointly and severally responsible with respect
to obligations arising under the Convention. The
Soviets apparently did not realize that their proposal might give each member of an organization the power to prevent ratification by all members. Although
there was no consensus on most of the questions,
there was agreement that there must be evidence of a
transfer of competence to the organization, the fundamental criterion qualifying the organization to
participate at all. The other criterion of treaty-
making capacity would depend on the nature and extent
of the powers transferred to the organization by member States with respect to third States.

The G-77 spokesman reiterated that all elements
of the question of participation form a package requiring comprehensive solution.

Finally, it was agreed to defer consideration of
the question of the so-called transitional provision
that appears after the text of the Convention pending

further consultations with the most interested delegations.

After some informal consultations, it quickly
became obvious that no negotiations could be conducted at this session on the first two topics.
There was some interest in starting the formidable
task of coordinating the texts in Part XV, first
through the language groups and then through the
Drafting Committee.  It did not prove possible, however, to allocate the necessary time for that purpose
at this session.  In consequence, priority will be
given to the subject at the presessional meeting of
the Drafting Committee.  Some meetings of the informal plenary on this subject will also be required.

## Drafting Committee

At its seven-week intersessional meeting prior
to the commencement of the tenth session, the Drafting Committee recommended over 1,000 changes to the
Second and Third Committee Texts.  A report on that
intersessional meeting is attached.  During the session, these recommendations were considered in informal plenary.  The meetings were informal so as to
avoid the problem of creating interpretive records
during consideration of Drafting Committee recommendations.  Virtually all of the Drafting Committee
recommendations were approved.  A few were referred
back to the Drafting Committee, some of which have
been reconsidered and submitted to plenary and approved.

During the session, the Drafting Committee continued its work on Part XI texts.  It submitted a few
recommendations on the initial articles to informal
plenary, which were approved.  That work continued in
more intense fashion during the last week of the session, which was devoted exclusively to the Drafting
Committee and its organs.

As in the past, proposals were presented initially in one of the six language groups to all Conference participants.  If recommended by that language
group, the proposal was reviewed by the others.  The
six coordinators of the language group would then
meet to harmonize the positions of the language
groups and make recommendations to the Committee.

The Committee then considered texts recommended by the coordinators.

As of the end of the session, remaining Drafting Committee work includes:

1. A number of items still pending in the Committee and in the language groups with respect to the Second and Third Committee texts;

2. The significant portions of Part XI and Annexes III and IV which have yet to be addressed, including a number of the more difficult drafting problems that remain to be resolved regarding texts already reviewed;

3. The preamble, Article 1, and Parts XV, XVI, and XVII, which have yet to be considered.

## DISPUTE SETTLEMENT

Three issues were discussed among delegates during the tenth session: some changes in seabed mining provisions concerning dispute settlement sought by some Western European countries; two technical changes in Part XV (relating to the exhaustion of local remedies in case of a seizure of a vessel and the clarification of provisions relating to disputes concerning maritime boundaries); and drafting changes in the more than 100 articles in Part XI, Section 6, Part XV, and related annexes.

## SITES OF THE AUTHORITY AND OF THE TRIBUNAL

The candidates for the site of the proposed International Seabed Authority are Fiji, Jamaica, and Malta.

The candidates for the site of the proposed Tribunal on the Law of the Sea are the Federal Republic of Germany, Portugal, and Yugoslavia.

The question of the site of the Seabed Authority was raised during one of the First Committee meetings. Questions were raised as to whether that matter would be resolved by the First Committee or by Plenary.

473

The President informed the Conference that the candidates have agreed that the matter would be taken up during the third week of the resumed tenth session in Geneva. The options facing the Conference at that time will be to select one of the sites for each of the two institutions, defer the matter for future consideration by the Conference or refer the matter to the proposed Preparatory Commission.

ATTACHMENTS:

1.  Report of the Chairman of the First Committee dated April 16, 1981

2.  Report of the Chairman of the Second Committee dated April 15, 1981

3.  Report of the Chairman of the Third Committee dated April 17, 1981

4.  Drafting Committee Report: January 12 - March 2, 1981

ATTACHMENT 1
(A/CONF.62/L.70, 16 April 1981)


REPORT TO THE PLENARY ON THE NEGOTIATIONS IN THE FIRST
COMMITTEE BY PAUL BAMELA ENGO (UNITED REPUBLIC OF
CAMEROON), CHAIRMAN OF THE FIRST COMMITTEE


1.  At the end of the resumed ninth session I reported that there had been what I consider to be a
breakthrough in our negotiations on the outstanding
hard-core issues before the First Committee. It was
clear from the reactions of all delegations, in the
First Committee and in the Plenary, that the proposals which were later incorporated in the Draft Convention enjoyed a consensus. The report I submitted
therefore outlined only a few issues which required
attention before the First Committee could terminate
its mandate.

2.  It is common knowledge that the United States
delegation announced at the commencement of this session their decision to review the Draft Convention
and insisted that the Conference must await the end
of such a review before any fruitful negotiations
could take place with a view to formalizing the Draft.
The Group of 77 expressed the opinion that no useful
negotiations therefore could be undertaken to resolve
the issue of preliminary investment protection. Consequently, the work of the First Committee at this
session proceeded with an unhappy cloud hovering over.
My consultations left me in no doubt, however, that
it was the will of the delegates to proceed with the
negotiating effort on all outstanding issues, bearing
in mind the effect of the reservations expressed.

3.  During this session the First Committee held
four meetings, all formal. The first two were devoted to general debates on the Preparatory Commission.
The other two meetings provided opportunity for general comments on two reports of the Secretary-General
of the United Nations:  one on potential financial
implications for States Parties to the future Convention on the Law of the Sea (document A/CONF.62/L.65),
and the other on the effect of the production limitation formula under certain specified assumptions
(document A/CONF.62/L.66 and Corr.1).

4.   In addition, the issue of the Seat of the Authority (Art. 156(3)) was taken up for the first time.
The opportunity was also given for the examination of
all or any matter that delegations felt had not been
or had never been dealt with formally in the First
Committee.

5.   As may be recalled, the question of the Preparatory Commission had been considered by the Plenary of
the Conference at its informal meetings, as part of
the late President Shirley Amerasinghe's consultations on the final clauses.  It became clear that the
issues involved were so closely related to the issues
negotiated on Part XI that the forum of the First
Committee was the more appropriate for the negotiating process.

6.   Consequently, following consultations with the
President at this session, the matter was taken up
formally for the first time.  In order not to lose
the valuable contents of the late President's report
on the subject, and also to facilitate our examination, it was decided that those contents be made the
basis for discourse.  Furthermore, it was agreed that
in order to avoid duplication, the negotiating effort
should be co-chaired by the President and the Chairman of the First Committee, using the established
system of a Working Group of 21.

7.   The Working Group of 21 held four meetings and
discussed, inter alia, critical issues relating to
the composition, mandate, decision-making system, and
the financing of the Preparatory Commission.  Consistent with the understanding, it took as a basis
for negotiation, the report of the President on the
work of the Informal Plenary of the Conference on the
question of the Preparatory Commission (document
A/CONF.62/L.55 and Corr.1) in particular the annexed
draft resolution proposed for adoption by the Conference providing interim arrangements for the International Seabed Authority and the Law of the Sea Tribunal (see Annex II of the same document).

8.   Following an extensive and, I must add, illumi-
nating discussion on the issues in the Working Group
of 21, the President of the Conference and I commenced preliminary consultations with the members of the
Working Group of 21 with a view to updating the ideas
contained in the said draft resolution.  I am of the
opinion that the efforts made by the First Committee

at its various negotiating forums on the Preparatory
Commission, though preliminary, have achieved some
constructive results in identifying major issues and
the interrelationships among them. I am encouraged
consequently to make the following observations:

9.  First, there appeared to be general agreement
that the Preparatory Commission should be established
by a resolution of the Conference included in the
Final Act.

10. Secondly, the objective in establishing the
Preparatory Commission was broadly recognized, that
is to say the purpose of making provisional arrangements for the first session of the Assembly of the
International Seabed Authority, and of its Council.
The objective included such arrangements regarding
the establishment of its other organs, namely the
Secretariat and the Enterprise, as well as the convening of the International Law of the Sea Tribunal.

11. The title of "Preparatory Commission for the
International Seabed Authority and the International
Law of the Sea Tribunal" may prove to be the most ap-
propriate.

12. On the issue of the membership of the Commission,
the text of the President's draft appeared to present
difficulties for some of the industrialized countries.
They would prefer that it be opened to all signatories
to the Final Act. The other participants insisted
that only States which demonstrate an intention to be
bound by the Convention should be members. They submitted consequently that signature to the Convention
would be a minimum criterion, as this would also induce early commitment to the treaty and consequently
prevent participation by those States who may have
reached the decision not to be party to it anyway.

13. The Group of 77 appears to be ready to accept a
compromise granting observer status to States which
sign only the Final Act, granting them power to participate fully in the deliberations of the Commission
but denying them a right to participate in the decision-making procedures.

14. This first reading also focused on the broad
question of the decision-making process and the adoption of the Commission's rules of procedure. Three
relevant areas were:

    (i)    the rules of procedure to be applied in the Preparatory Commission pending the adoption of its own rules of procedure;

    (ii)    the majority required for the adoption of its rules of procedure; and

    (iii)    provisions for voting on substantive issues.

15. The exchange of views, especially on the latter two, was somehow inconclusive. It would appear that the Western industrialized countries and the Eastern (socialist) countries would insist on the consensus rule. The Group of 77 would favour a two-stage approach by which the failure of a quest for consensus would be followed by a voting procedure. It is clear that more consultations in the negotiating process will be inevitable.

16. The function, or the mandate, of the Commission was examined. While it appeared that general agreement existed for the proposition that the Preparatory Commission would have the broad mandate of preparing for the establishment of the International Seabed Authority and the International Law of the Sea Tribunal, the industrialized countries considered that the discussion of the issue of the establishment of the Enterprise was premature, as it had to be taken up in discussion on the preliminary investment protection proposals. The Group of 77 and other members of the Working Group of 21 consider this to be an imperative item, as the Enterprise would be a main organ to effect the agreed working of the parallel system.

17. The exchange of views appeared to have been more productive on the substantive question of the function of the Commission, especially as it related to its role in the preparation of rules, regulations, and procedures. It is my impression that further reflection will be desirable to determine the scope of this function.

18. There appears to be general agreement for the proposition that the Secretary-General of the United Nations should be empowered to convene the Commission, certain criteria being satisfied with regard to the timing. That which was recommended in document A/CONF.62/L.55, requiring 50 signatures to the

Convention or the same number of States depositing
instruments of accession, received widespread support.
It was suggested, however, that the wording proposed
in paragraph 10 should be harmonized with what is specified in Article 307.

19. There is general agreement that the life of the
Preparatory Commission should not be unduly long,
having regard to the nature of its mandate and also
of the need for the Authority to be established expeditiously to perform functions assigned by the
Convention. The view was expressed by some, however,
that if that life must be extended beyond the convening of the Assembly, the latter, that is the Assembly,
alone must decide to grant it.

20. The issue of the financing of the Preparatory
Commission presented some difficulties. It was clear
that all sides would support that the United Nations
should provide the funds for the initial costs. Yet
the terms found a divergency of views. The concept
of loan proposed by the late President's text was ro-
jected by those who saw fundamental legal as well as
practical difficulties involved. The Group of 77 and
the Eastern (Socialist) countries argued further that
until the Authority was established the United Nations
regular budget should finance the Commission in the
same way as with the present Conference. Others
pointed to the fact that observers or Member States
of the United Nations who are not signatories of the
Convention would be compelled to contribute to the
financing. It is my feeling that the second reading
on this issue might, hopefully, be more fruitful.

21. The Special Representative of the United Nations
Secretary-General introduced two reports that were
relevant to the mandate of the First Committee. They
are contained in documents A/CONF.62/L.65 and A/CONF.
62/L.66 and deal respectively with "potential financial implications for States Parties to the future
Convention on the Law of the Sea" and "the effects of
the production limitation formula under certain specified assumptions."

22. With regard to document A/CONF.62/L.66, the Committee decided to postpone detailed discussion until
the resumed session. During the discussion of this
report, some delegations proposed that a group of experts be established, which could utilize the report
of the Secretary-General as the basis for an evaluation

of the production limitation formula. Since there was no consensus with respect to establishment of such a group, I suggested that I be authorized to hold informal consultations with a view to reaching consensus on how to proceed.

23. The report on the financial implication of the future Convention contained in document A/CONF.62/ L.65 offered a preliminary estimate of the cost involved in the functioning of the following organs of the Authority:

(a) The Authority - including the Assembly, Council, its Economic Planning Commission, and Legal and Technical Commission and the Secretariat.

(b) The Enterprise - including Governing Board and the Secretariat.

(c) The International Tribunal for the Law of the Sea - including the Seabed Disputes Chamber, Special Chambers, the Ad Hoc Chamber and the Office of the Registrar.

(d) The Commission on the Limits of the Continental Shelf.

(e) The Preparatory Commission, and any subsidiary bodies it may establish.

24. In introducing the report the Special Representative made the following observations:

1. Costs of the Authority and the Enterprise could be reduced considerably if both organizations are located at the same site and share the staff and institutional facilities on the reimbursement basis;

2. With regard to the Preparatory Commission: Cost estimate was based upon the assumption that the Preparatory Commission would be located at a site of United Nations Headquarters. If the Commission is located at a site other than the United Nations Headquarters, extra cost must be taken into account, depending upon the extent of offers made by the host country;

480

3. The manning table of the Secretariat of the Authority is lower than such specialized agencies as the World Intellectual Property Organization and the United Nations Environment Programme.

25. The majority of States, in commenting on the report, stressed the necessity for cost-efficiency of the new organization, and expressed the view that the report is a sound basis for a careful study by the Conference.

Other Matters

26. The First Committee provided opportunity for the discussion of all outstanding matters, including those never before dealt with under its mandate.

(i) The Site of the Authority

As I indicated above, this matter was dealt with for the first time since the announcement at the Caracas Session of the candidacy of Jamaica, its formal endorsement by the Group of 77, and subsequent introduction of the subject in the Informal Single Negotiating Text. Article 156(3) in the present Draft Convention shows that in addition to Jamaica, there are two other candidacies: in order of presentation, Malta and Fiji.

During the discussion the Jamaican delegation presented their case, concluding that construction work for receiving even the Preparatory Commission is well under way. The summary records of that meeting reflect the arguments and information presented by that delegation.

The delegation of Malta stated that they could not participate in the debate on the grounds that the First Committee was not the proper forum. There had been an agreement with the President and other candidates that a decision on the issue would be taken in Plenary at the tenth session. This view was broadly speaking supported by the Fiji delegation.

During the discussion, the Chairman of the Latin-American Group, as well as other delegations

from Latin America who spoke on this issue, many African countries and Yugoslavia spoke out in favour of Jamaica. A number of speakers did not find it expedient to declare a choice at this stage.

It is important to note from the debate that all three candidates declared that preparations were afoot to receive the Authority, although only Jamaica undertook to state details of such preparations.

## (ii) Production policies

Although our main business at this session was to deal with the issue of the Preparatory Commission, I felt that delegations should be given an opportunity to raise any other issues which are of concern to them.

At the 50th meeting of the First Committee held on 19 March 1981, the delegation of Zambia, supported by the delegations of Zimbabwe and Zaire, made an appeal that the issue of production policies be examined. Intensive consultations at various levels, within and across interest groups, have since been launched and may be expected to continue at the resumed session.

The specific issues in question were the impact of the production limitation formula set out in Article 151 of the Draft Convention on the existing and future land-based nickel, copper, cobalt, and manganese industries and the measures for the protection of developing countries from adverse effects on their economies or on their export earnings likely to result from seabed mining.

## (iii) Unfair Economic Practices

Among other matters, the delegation of Australia made a suggestion about provisions dealing with unfair economic practices which may cause injury to the trading interests of the economy of another State Party. An exchange of views took place during an informal meeting of the interested delegations, and consultations on this issue are continuing.

(iv) Composition of the Council

During the session, I encouraged continuing informal contacts between interested parties concerning the problem raised by some less developed western States concerning an increase in minimum representation for geographical groups in the Council. While these continue, I have nothing to report at this stage.

27. Finally I should like to conclude with the same concern I expressed at the commencement of this session. The First Committee has, for nearly a decade, grappled with perhaps the most complex problems that ever faced any Conference sponsored by the United Nations. It has had to achieve accommodation of global conflicts of interests, inspired by an incredible sense of dedication to the loftiest ideals of a generation desperate for international peace and security.

28. So far not a single nation, large or small, definitely not the rich, has been left out of the negotiating effort. The negotiating texts produced through the years have shown a clear attempt to meet the needs and interests of all States, and more realistically those of the industrialized States.

29. This Conference cannot at this late stage, when at least we have provoked passions of hope in the international community, afford to indulge in any exercise in futility or any backward or destructive step. We must at all cost preserve that which we have succeeded in accepting by consensus. The packages worked out may have been delicately put together, but it is clear that they are made strong by the consensus they enjoyed.

30. At the resumed session we must all bear this in mind. We must maintain our spirit of accommodation on outstanding issues and any pleas that may be made of additions. But what we must not do is to destroy directly or indirectly the results of our fruitful labours so far. It is in the fact of universal accommodation and compromise that our nations can hope to draw strength for individual survival.

ATTACHMENT 2
(A/CONF.62/L.69, 15 April 1981)

REPORT TO THE PLENARY BY AMBASSADOR ANDRES AGUILAR
(VENEZUELA), CHAIRMAN OF THE SECOND COMMITTEE

1. During the first part of the tenth session, the
Second Committee held four informal meetings. This
served to meet the desire expressed by a number of
delegations for an opportunity to refer to certain
questions within the mandate of the Second Committee,
that is to say, relating to parts II to X inclusive
of the Draft Convention on the Law of the Sea (informal text) (A/CONF.62/WP.10/Rev.3).

2. These meetings were held without any pre-estab-
lished agenda, so that the delegations participating
in them could express their views and present or reiterate informal suggestions for amendments with complete freedom on all issues and questions within the
competence of the Committee, the sole exception being
the problem of the delimitation of maritime space between States with opposite or adjacent coasts, because at this stage of the work of the Conference,
that matter is being dealt with by the two groups of
countries directly concerned, which have established
a procedure for consultations on the subject. I
deemed it necessary, however, to point out at the
first informal meeting that the Committee's work in
this final phase of the Conference should be directed
toward supplementing or improving the Draft Convention
(informal text), and not toward reopening discussion
on the basic elements of the agreements reached after
many years of effort.

3. Nearly all the informal suggestions considered at
these meetings had already been submitted to the Committee at previous sessions. It should be noted,
however, that on this occasion a revised version of
one such suggestion was presented.

4. The number of statements made at these meetings
totalled 119, and many of the articles in parts II to
X of the Draft Convention (informal text) were referred to or touched on. It may be said, however, that
most of those statements focused on very few questions.

5. One of these questions, a very controversial one,
was the subject of lengthy debate, during which

detailed explanations of the various positions were given, and alternative means of achieving reconciliation were suggested. In connexion with this question, a number of delegations requested the establishment of a working group or the holding of consultations among the most interested delegations with a view to harmonizing the different positions. In response to that request, I carried out consultations on the subject and found that there was, at least for the present, no agreement on the establishment of a working, negotiating or consulting group for that purpose.

6. The informal suggestion presented in the Committee for the first time by one delegation was also given special attention in these discussions. The delegation making the suggestion announced at the end of the meetings that it would hold consultations with the other delegations which had shown an interest in it with a view to submitting to the Committee in due course, for its consideration, a precise formulation taking into account the comments that had been made on the subject.

7. During these meetings, the delegations interested in some of the informal suggestions made at previous sessions stated that they were continuing the consultations aimed at finding generally acceptable formulae.

8. As I said by way of summing up at the end of the last of these meetings, the following conclusions may be drawn from these discussions:

(a) There is a virtual consensus on the fact that it is not desirable or practical to reopen discussion on the basic Second Committee issues, which, while they do not in all cases represent a consensus, are the formulae that come closest to commanding general agreement and that have been arrived at through long and arduous negotiations.

(b) It is possible to introduce, at such time as the Conference may decide, minor changes designed to supplement, clarify, or improve the Draft Convention, always provided, of course, that they command the necessary support and will help to facilitate acceptance of the text by the largest possible number of delegations.

485

(c) Although some of the draft articles, as now worded, present difficulties of various kinds for some delegations, the draft as a whole is acceptable to the great majority of delegations. There are actually, in the view of a significant number of delegations, very few questions that require further discussion and negotiation.

9. Lastly, it seems to me appropriate to note in this report that as Chairman of the Second Committee I participated, along with the President of the Conference and the Chairman of the Drafting Committee, in three of the informal meetings of the Plenary to consider and adopt the recommendations of the Drafting Committee concerning parts II to X of the Draft Convention on the Law of the Sea (informal text) (A/CONF.62/WP.10/Rev.3).

ATTACHMENT 3
(A/CONF.62/L.71, 17 April 1981)

REPORT OF THE CHAIRMAN OF THE THIRD COMMITTEE
A. Yankov (Bulgaria)

1. I have the honour to report briefly to the Conference on the work of the Third Committee at the current session. It may be recalled at the outset that in my last report to the plenary (A/CONF.62/L.61 of 25 August 1980), the substantive negotiations on part XII (Protection and preservation of the marine environment), part XIII (Marine scientific research), and part XIV (Development and transfer of marine technology) were completed. The results of these negotiations are reflected in the Informal Text of the Draft Convention on the Law of the Sea (A/CONF.62/WP. 10/Rev.3). It was also stated that the Third Committee had attained a level of agreement which could offer a substantially improved prospect for consensus. This assessment, which has emerged from the Third Committee's deliberations, was subsequently confirmed by the Conference itself at the end of the resumed ninth session.

2. At this session, an informal meeting of the Third Committee was held on 25 March 1981 in order to ascertain whether there were still any issues which could be discussed by the Committee.

3. I am now pleased to inform the Conference that the Third Committee reiterated its previous conclusion, namely that the substantive negotiations had been completed. It was agreed that the Draft Convention on the Law of the Sea with respect to parts XII, XIII, and XIV constitutes a compromise based on a sound balance which should not be upset by reopening issues which had already been extensively negotiated.

4. It was also agreed that if and when called upon by the Conference the Third Committee should be available to consider any issue within its terms of reference.

5. I wish to take this opportunity and place on record my appreciation of the excellent work done by the Drafting Committee, its language groups and the coordinators. On this occasion, I wish to extend my congratulations to the Chairman of the Drafting

Committee, Mr. Beesley.  The recommendations advanced by the Drafting Committee did not affect the substance of the text, and altogether they constitute a distinct improvement from a drafting point of view.

6.  Since the recommendations of the Drafting Committee have been considered in informal meetings of the plenary, the adopted suggestions should be issued in a document in order to keep a clear record.

7.  I would like to express my sincere gratitude to all the members of the Third Committee for their understanding and cooperation which has been the main feature of the atmosphere in the Committee throughout the long years of arduous negotiations.

8.  Finally, I wish to pay special tribute to the Secretariat for their exemplary diligence, dedication, and most valuable service rendered to the Committee and to its Chairman.

ATTACHMENT 4

REPORT OF THE U.S. DELEGATION ON THE MEETING OF THE
DRAFTING COMMITTEE OF THE THIRD UN CONFERENCE ON
THE LAW OF THE SEA, JANUARY 12 - MARCH 2, 1981

## Summary

The Drafting Committee approved over a thousand
amendments to the text of the Draft Convention on the
Law of the Sea (Informal Text) (UN Doc. A/CONF.62/WP.
10/Rev.3). These resulted from an article-by-article
review of Second Committee texts (Parts II-X and Annexes I and II) and Third Committee texts (Parts XII
to XIV). The amendments are technical and stylistic.
They are designed to improve the style and clarity of
the texts in each language and to enhance the concordance of texts in the six official languages.

Because of time pressures, the Committee was able
only to begin the process of an article-by-article
review of First Committee texts (Parts XI and related
annexes), and could not deal with the preamble, Part I
(definitions) and the Informal Plenary texts (Parts XV
to XVII). Attempts to prepare, and forward to the
competent organ of the Conference, a list of technical
questions that might have substantive inplications did
not succeed.

Despite a very intensive schedule frequently running from 9:00 a.m. to 10:00 p.m., the Drafting Committee still faces a large amount of work on deferred
items with respect to texts on which recommendations
have been made, and with respect to an initial review
of texts on which no recommendations have been made.

## Procedure

The Drafting Committee and all its organs functioned by consensus. The Committee, chaired by Ambassador Beesley of Canada, has limited membership that
does not include delegations that wish to, and might
be expected to, participate in its work (e.g. China,
France, and the U.K.). Moreover, it was recognized
at an early stage that any attempt to do initial
drafting work in several languages at once would lead
to confusion. Accordingly, the Drafting Committee

489

established six language groups, one for each of the
official languages, all of which are open to all conference participants. The chairmen or coordinators
of the language groups are as follows:

| | | |
|---|---|---|
| Arabic | - Professor Yasseen | (UAE) |
| Chinese | - Dr. Ni | (China) |
| English | - Professor Oxman | (USA) |
| French | - Professor Treves | (Italy) |
| Russian | - Dr. Yevseev | (USSR) |
| Spanish | - Dr. Lacleta | (Spain |
| | Alternate: | |
| | Dr. Yturriaga | (Spain) |
| | Ambassador Valencia | (Ecuador) |

Drafting proposals were first discussed in a
language group. After discussion, each language
group submitted its recommendations on the articles
in question. These were then collated on an article-
by-article basis in all six languages. Each language
group then discussed the recommendations of the other
language groups. All of this was accomplished without the need for interpretation.

The coordinators of the language groups then met
together under the Chairman of the Drafting Committee
to discuss all of the changes, with interpretation.
These meetings were open to all participants, although
discussion was usually carried on only by the coordinators. Once the coordinators approved recommendations in the six languages, they were forwarded to
the Drafting Committee for action. At that point,
most were approved without discussion.

The effect of this procedure is that every proposed drafting change in at least English, French,
and Spanish is scrutinized many times before it is
finally recommended. A single objection or hesita-
tion at any stage is sufficient to stop the proposal,
despite the fact that the precise text in the language in question was never in fact negotiated closely, if at all. In part because it is the largest and
most diverse of the groups, the English Language
Group proved to be a substantial hurdle, particularly
with respect to any change that would affect the
English Text.

## Concordance

Efforts to improve concordance among the six languages were initiated almost exclusively by the Arabic, Chinese, French, Russian, and Spanish language groups with respect to their own language texts. While each worked largely from the English text, as the original text of negotiation, for political reasons this was not made explicit.

Each language group showed considerable deference to the stylistic preferences of the others, even where this resulted in an absence of strict linguistic concordance. To cite one example, most of the references to coastal States in the Spanish text are in the plural; in the French text, many are in the singular. Any effort to achieve stylistic consistency in the English text on this kind of question was doomed to failure.

A very large percentage of the changes recommended by the Committee affect the Arabic, French, and Spanish texts only. In essence, the respective language groups have been redoing what Secretariat personnel had been compelled to do on short notice when texts were originally issued. The Arabic Language Group faces the additional problem that earlier instruments on the Law of the Sea did not have official Arabic version.

In order to ensure that the consideration of drafting changes not give rise to substantive implications or interpretive records, the Committee and its organs have followed the practice of avoiding records of discussion of drafting changes and the reasons therefor.

## Working Atmosphere

The atmosphere was highly professional and workmanlike throughout the seven weeks. There were few occasions on which the political or substantive differences between participating States or groups of States affected the work. The intense schedule created fatigue and strain but surprisingly little friction. While problems arose from time to time regarding the potentially substantive implications of a particular change, and while certain changes were rejected because one or more participants felt they

might alter the substance, it appears that most, if
not all, of the participants limited their proposals
to drafting suggestions very narrowly defined.

## Mixed Questions of Drafting and Substance

The Drafting Committee has yet to find a technique for dealing with, or even indicating that it
has identified, a technical problem in the text whose
resolution may have substantive, albeit non-controversial, implications. Its efforts on harmonization
of terminology have already been hampered by this difficulty. At this meeting, the Committee was again
unable to make recommendations on, or even refer to
the continuing problems associated with the use of
different words or phrases to deal with the same
question in different parts of the Convention (e.g.
the description of ships entitled to sovereign immunity in Articles 31, 32, 96, and 236) or technical
problems arising from texts incorporated without negotiation from earlier treaties (e.g. the removal requirement in Article 60(3)).

Throughout most of the session there was a great
deal of talk about referring at least some of these
questions to the competent Conference organ in a so-
called "third basket." The coordinator of the English Language Group circulated a possible list of
items (attached to this report). However, agreement
could not be reached on doing this, nor could agreement be reached on a different kind of list simply
enumerating items still pending.

Should this situation continue, the Conference
may have to develop an alternate way of identifying
and disposing of questions that are technical, non-
political, and non-controversial. The problem is
that if doing so requires an essentially open-ended
meeting of a substantive committee, some delegations
may prefer to avoid the risk that such a meeting
would reopen substantive matters more broadly. Specific referrals from the Drafting Committee could
have helped avoid open-ended agendas of the substantive committees.

## Notes on Some Recommendations or Lack Thereof

By their nature, drafting amendments on hundreds
of articles cannot be summarized. The appended Drafting Committee Report is by its nature the essence of
this report. Several points are however of some note.

The drafting recommendations for the English
text emphasize the use of the present tense rather
than the imperative "shall" except where the latter
is essential to convey the meaning. Thus, for example, the standard terminology is "nothing in this
article affects. . ." rather than "nothing in this
article shall affect. . ."

Except where qualified by an adjective, the
term "the provisions of" is generally removed. It
has been retained in some places for reasons of style
or simply because of oversight.

For the first time extensive work has been done
on the more formidable of the long and repetitive
texts on pollution (Part XII). This has resulted in
some simplification and lightening of the texts, particularly in Articles 211(6), 220(3)(5) and (6), and
226.

Some of the recommended changes affect terminology in texts prepared by more than one main Committee. Should the Drafting Committee recommendations
be reviewed in committee, and should some of these be
rejected by one Main Committee but not another, there
will be problems.

The Drafting Committee report contains an important disclaimer to the effect that no substantive
implications should be drawn from the fact that the
Committee made or failed to make a recommendation.
In the limited time available, the Committee did what
could be done most easily. In many situations, lack
of harmonization in a single language or lack of concordance among languages has been allowed to remain
because it was not felt that the point was important
enough to warrant the time it would take to deal with
it, either because of the inherent complexity of the
matter or because of the concerns of one or more
participants.

Mutually cancelling objections were the most
common problem. An example can be found in a

comparison of Article 7, paragraph 6 with Article 47, paragraph 5. While both provisions set forth prohibitions that are in substance identical, the former uses the term "may not" while the latter uses the term "shall not." Supporters of the former generally oppose changes in terminology in texts drawn from the 1958 Geneva Conventions unless they are essential. Supporters of the latter generally oppose changes in the closely negotiated texts on archipelagic States unless they are essential. Functioning by consensus, the English Language Group was unable to recommend a change in either provision, although no participant suggested that there was any difference in meaning between the texts. The same kind of problem arose regarding the choice between deleting the words "which are" in Article 37 or inserting them in other articles on straits.

There were serious problems in dealing with the English term "as appropriate" in other languages; in French, in particular, it was exceedingly difficult to achieve concordance. The words "facilities" and "maintenance" have also given rise to questionable translations.

## Outstanding Problems

As already noted, no means have been found for dealing with, or even referring to the Conference, the problems identified in the attached "third basket" list. Work has just begun in the Language Groups on First Committee texts. Informal Plenary texts remain to be addressed.

In addition, a significant number of questions remain unresolved that relate to Second and Third Committee texts. Among them are the following:

1. <u>Flag and Registry</u>. The Second Committee texts, particularly Part VII on the High Seas, consistently refer to flag when referring to ships having the nationality of a State. This is Geneva Convention terminology. The Third Committee texts on pollution refer to both flag and registry with respect to both ships and aircraft. This is at best cumbersome and at worst a harbinger of legal confusion. The English Language Group has proposed that the texts be revised so as to use "flag" alone in connection with vessels and "registry" alone with aircraft. The Spanish

Language Group has made a counter-proposal that the term "nationality" be used in connection with both. Either faces the prospect of Third Committee resistance on what is in fact a Second Committee issue.

2. <u>Definition of the Area</u>. The definition of the Area in Article 1, paragraph 1 bears no textual relationship to the Second Committee articles. It refers to the ocean floor, whereas Articles 56 and 76, which also cover parts of the ocean floor, refer only to the seabed and subsoil. Moreover, the Convention does not indicate what is meant by the limits of national jurisdiction, since the term "national jurisdiction" is not used in any of the articles on the territorial sea, exclusive economic zone, or continental shelf. In this connection it should be noted that the Convention therefore prohibits national claims beyond limits that are nowhere defined <u>expressio</u> verbis.

3. <u>Government Non-Commercial Ships</u>. Three different terms are used in four articles (31, 32, 96, and 236) to refer to ships entitled to sovereign immunity: one inherited from the 1958 Territorial Sea Convention, one from the 1958 High Seas Convention, and one from the 1973 Marine Pollution Convention.

4. <u>Sealanes</u>. The term "sealanes" is used in at least three substantially different contexts. Moreover, the term "sealanes and traffic separation schemes" is not the preferred technical terminology--IMCO recommends "routing systems."

5. <u>Coastal State Obligations</u>. The premise of the High Seas Convention (Article 10) and the carefully drafted articles drawn from it (Articles 94(5), 211(2) etc.) is that a party to the Law of the Sea Convention may automatically be bound by an international safety or pollution standard arising from another instrument if that standard is "generally accepted." The words "generally accepted" are however omitted in connection with pollution from continental shelf and other coastal State seabed activities (Article 208(3)) as well as dumping (Article 210(6)). The result is a legal anomaly that could hurt the Convention and restrain efforts to promote the gradual elaboration of environmental recommendations and measures in UNEP and elsewhere.

6. <u>Installations</u>. A comparison of Articles 60, 147, and Part XIII, Sec. 4 leaves one in doubt as to the significance of their divergent texts on the same subject. Moreover, the text of the removal requirement in Article 60(3) was copied without negotiation from the 1958 Convention, and reflects neither state practice, nor modern technological and environmental considerations, nor the definition of "dumping" in Article 1. The notion that a "recommendation" of an international organization is sufficient to expand a safety zone (Article 60(5)) and impede navigation is inconsistent with the rest of the Convention.

7. <u>Function-less Articles</u>. Possible candidates for this category include Article 85 (tunneling) (copied from Geneva) and 264 (a remnant that is the only general dispute settlement cross-reference of its kind in a substantive text).

8. <u>Relationship between Third Committee Texts and those of the other Committees</u>. Since the Third Committee was the first to complete work, some problems of integrating its texts with the rest of the Convention inevitably arise. Third Committee texts ignore the existence of archipelagic waters; do not match First Committee terminology on rules, regulations, and procedures of the Authority or Second Committee terminology on nationality of ships; fail to cross-reference expressly the detailed provisions of Part XI and related annexes on transfer of technology; and incorrectly imply that only Part XI, and not even Parts XII and XIII apply to marine scientific research in the Area.

9. <u>Verbosity</u>. The Convention texts will be reproduced thousands of times in international and national instruments, books, and articles. Stripping the texts of repetitive litanies would help to prevent, reduce, and control pollution.

<u>Part XI</u>

The language groups have generally completed initial recommendations through Article 149. The English Language Group has continued through Article 151. However, the groups have not yet reviewed each other's proposals. Moreover, at least in the English Language Group, it was clear that the presence of technocal personnel on delegations during the tenth

session could facilitate work on certain articles
either in a Drafting Committee or First Committee
context.


/s/ Bernard H. Oxman
U.S. Representative


Attachments:

1. "Third Basket" list prepared by ELG
   Coordinator

2. ELGDC/13

3. Report of the Chairman of the
   Drafting Committee

## Attachment 1   ("Third Basket" list prepared by ELG Coordinator)

### Articles 16(2), 47(6), 75(2), 76(9), and 84(2)

Whether the word "deposit" in these articles should be replaced by a word such as "transmit" in light of the use of "deposit" and "depositary" in Articles 306, 307, 308, and 319.

### Articles 22, 41, and 53 (paragraphs 6-11)

Whether a reference to "routing systems" should, where appropriate, replace references to sealanes and traffic-separation schemes in these provisions (while retaining the term "sealanes" where it is used in other contexts, such as the designation of sealanes and air routes for the exercise of the right of archipelagic sealanes passage under Article 53, paragraphs 2-5 and 12, or in Article 60, paragraph 7). (See letter of 23 May 1980 from the Secretary-General of the Intergovernmental Maritime Consultative Organization, Appendix III, paragraph 3(a).)

### Articles 31, 32, 96, and 236

Whether the references in these articles to ships other than warships should be harmonized, for example, by referring to ships owned or operated by a State and used for exclusively non-commercial purposes.

### Article 36

Whether the text should be elaborated by adding a clause such as "; in such routes, the other relevant Parts of this Convention, including the provisions regarding the freedoms of navigation and overflight, apply."

### Article 42(1)(b)

Whether the word "applicable" should be changed to "generally accepted" in this sub-paragraph to conform to related texts (see Articles 39(2), 41(3), and 211(2)). Whether the adjective "oily" should be deleted in the clause "oil, oily wastes and other noxious substances."

## Article 60(3)

Whether a reference to artificial islands should be added to the second sentence.

## Article 60 (3)

Whether the exception to removal when navigation is not infringed should be expressly referred to in the second sentence, for example as authorized by generally accepted international standards or the competent international organization (see paragraph 5).

## Article 60(5)

Whether the words "as recommended by" should be deleted in order to conform the text to other similar provisions affecting freedom of navigation in the Draft Convention.

## Article 63(2)

Whether this paragraph should be harmonized with Article 117 with respect to the duty to cooperate in taking measures to conserve living resources beyond and adjacent to the exclusive economic zone.

## Article 73(1)

Whether this paragraph should refer to natural resources, whether living or non-living.

## Article 85

Whether this article (copied from the 1958 Convention, which contained the exploitability criterion) should be omitted from the new Convention in light of the provisions regarding the exclusive economic zone, the continental shelf, and the Area.

## Article 208(3)

Whether the specific environmental obligations of the coastal State (in respect of its territorial sea, exclusive economic zone, and continental shelf) under this paragraph should be expressly stated to arise only from international rules and standards that are generally accepted (see Articles 94(5), 211(2), etc.).

## Article 210(6)

(Same general point as with respect to Article 208(3).)

## Article 221

Whether this article should be amended to make the point that the words "beyond the territorial sea" do not affect the right of a State to take measures in its territorial sea.

## Article 233

Whether this article should state that it is without prejudice to Article 38(3).

## Part XII

Whether a provision should be added applying Sections 5, 6, and 7 to archipelagic waters.

Attachment 2    (ELGDC/13 of 25 February 1981)


DRAFTING COMMITTEE

Recommendations of the English Language
Group to the Drafting Committee


A.    GENERAL RECOMMENDATIONS


The English Language Group makes the following
recommendations with respect to some of the General
Comments contained in Informal Paper 19, to be implemented in the course of article-by-article review:

1.  Throughout Part XI, where there is a reference to
"this Part," this should include a reference to the
annexes relating thereto.  Since this matter pertains
to several Parts of the Convention, the Group pro-
poses the amendment to Article 318 contained in Sec
tion B of this report.

2.  The Group recommends that wherever "General"
stands alone as a section or subsection heading, the
word "Provisions" should be added to conform to the
style of other Parts.

3.  The Group recommends that everywhere there is a
reference to "nodules," the reference should be to
"polymetallic nodules."

4.  The Group recommends that everywhere there is
reference to "regulations" or "rules and regulations"
of the Authority, the reference should be to "procedures" as well.  Such reference should read, in all
cases, as "rules, regulations, and procedures of the
Authority" or "its rules, regulations, and procedures."

5.  As to General Comment No. 5, the English Language
Group has deferred other aspects of this matter, but
its General Recommendation 1 on page 1 of ELGDC/12 of
19 February, which reads as follows:

"1.  The first letter of subparagraphs should not
be capitalized (unless word is ordinarily capitalized or is the first word of a sentence)."

501

6. The Group recommends that where there is a reference to "protection of the marine environment," the
reference should in principle be to "protection and
preservation of the marine environment." However,
the Group has not recommended this change in the
chapeau of Article 145 because of the way in which
that clause in drafted.

7. The Group recommends that all titles of annexes
should be in block capitals.

8. The Group recommends that where "immunities and
privileges" appears, it should read "privileges and
immunities."

9. The Group recommends that throughout Annex IV,
where there is a reference to "Governing Board of
the Enterprise," it should appear as "Governing
Board."

### B. SPECIFIC RECOMMENDATIONS

| | |
|---|---|
| Article 318, line 3 | Delete the full stop after annexes. After annexes add and a reference to a Part of this Convention includes a reference to the annexes relating to that Part |
| Article 133 (b), line 1 | Replace Resources shall include by "Resources" includes |
| Article 133 (b), lines 3, 5, 6, 9, and 10 | Replace surface by seabed |
| Article 134, para. 1 | Replace shall apply by applies |
| Article 134, paragraphs 2, 3, and 4 | Delete paragraphs 2, 3, & 4 |
| and | |
| Article 84, paragraph 2, line 4 | After United Nations add and the Secretary-General of the Authority |

| | |
|---|---|
| Article 137, paragraph 2, line 4 | Replace minerals derived from the Area by minerals recovered from the Area |
| Article 137, paragraph 3, line 3 | Replace minerals of the Area by minerals recovered from the Area. |
| Article 139, title | Replace by Responsibility and Liability |
| Article 139, paragraph 1, lines 5 and 6 | Replace shall be carried out by are carried out |
| Article 139, paragraph 1, line 11 | After failure to comply add with this Part |
| Article 139, paragraph 2 | Revise to read Two or more States Parties or international organizations acting together shall be jointly and severally responsible in accordance with paragraph 1 |
| Article 140, title | Replace Mankind by mankind |
| Article 140, paragraph 1, line 6 | Delete the before developing. Add of before peoples |
| Article 142, paragraph 1, line 5 | Replace resources by deposits |
| Article 142, paragraph 3, lines 7 and 8 line 8 | Replace hazardous occurrences by hazards Delete any |
| | Authority and Zone should be capitalized in the French text when referring to the International Seabed Authority or to the International Seabed Area |
| Section 3, title | Revise to read MARINE SCIENTIFIC RESEARCH IN THE AREA |
| Article 143, paragraph (b) 3(iii), line 2 | Delete activities of |

| | |
|---|---|
| Before Article 144 | <u>Insert new heading</u> Section 3 bis* CONDUCT OF ACTIVITIES IN THE AREA |
| Article 144, paragraph 2, line 1 | <u>Delete</u> the <u>before</u> States Parties |
| Article 144, paragraph 2(b), line 3 | <u>After</u> particularly <u>add</u> by providing |
| line 6 | <u>Add</u> for <u>before</u> their full participation |
| Article 145, chapeau, first sentence, lines 1-5 | <u>Revise to read</u> Necessary measures shall be taken in accordance with this Convention to ensure effective protection for the marine environment from harmful effects which may arise from activities in the Area |
| line 5 | <u>Replace</u> that <u>by</u> this |
| line 6 | <u>Delete</u> appropriate |
| lines 6 and 7 | <u>Replace</u> for inter alia; <u>by</u> ,inter alia, for: |
| Article 146, line 2 | <u>Delete</u> in order |
| line 3 | <u>Replace</u> that <u>by</u> this |
| line 4 | <u>Delete</u> appropriate |
| line 5 | <u>Replace</u> reflected <u>by</u> embodied |
| line 6 | <u>Replace</u> specific treaties <u>by</u> relevant treaties |
| | <u>After</u> treaties <u>delete</u> which may be applicable |
| Article 148, line 4 | <u>After</u> in particular <u>add</u> to |

---

\* Renumbering of sections would be done when full text is issued.

| | |
|---|---|
| Article 148, line 6 | <u>Replace</u> them, in overcoming <u>by</u> them with a view to overcoming |
| Before Article 149 | Insert new heading Section 3ter*, ARCHAEOLOGICAL OBJECTS AND OBJECTS OF HISTORICAL ORIGIN FOUND IN THE AREA |
| Article 149, title | <u>Revise to read</u> Archaeological objects and objects of historical origin |
| Article 149, line 1 | <u>Replace</u> All objects of an archaeological and historical nature <u>by</u> Archaeological objects and objects of historical origin |

---

\* Renumbering of sections would be done when full text is issued.

Attachment 3   (A/CONF.62/L.67 of 26 February 1981)

REPORT OF THE CHAIRMAN OF THE DRAFTING COMMITTEE
J. Alan Beesley

## Meetings

1.   An informal intersessional meeting of the Drafting Committee was held in New York from 12 January to 27 February 1981 in accordance with the decision taken by the Conference at its 141st meeting on 29 August 1980[1] and on the basis of the timetable proposed by the Conference.   The meeting was extended to 2 March 1981.   The Drafting Committee conducted an article-by-article textual review of the Draft Convention on the Law of the Sea (Informal Text)[2] and directed its attention in particular to:

>   (1)   continuing the process of harmonization of words, expressions, and terminology recurring in the Draft Convention;
>
>   (2)   considering drafting and editorial points relating to the Draft Convention; and
>
>   (3)   improving concordance of the Arabic, Chinese, English, French, Russian, and Spanish texts of the Draft Convention.

2.   There were 240 meetings of the language groups open to all delegations, 33 meetings of the coordinators of the language groups under the direction of the Chairman of the Drafting Committee and 14 meetings of the Drafting Committee as a whole.   Representatives of 50 delegations participated in the meetings, and the Drafting Committee maintained its previously established informal working methods, but altered the procedures for the meeting of the coordinators of the language groups under the direction of the Chairman of the Drafting Committee by opening such meetings to all members of the Drafting Committee and all members of the language groups.

---

1.   A/CONF.62/SR.141, p. 15.

2.   A/CONF.62/WP.10/Rev.3.

Documentation

3. The Drafting Committee had before it the Draft
Convention on the Law of the Sea (Informal Text);
it also had before it a concordance text of the Draft
Convention in the six official languages of the Conference: Arabic, Chinese, English, French, Russian,
and Spanish;[3] a series of informal papers prepared by
the Secretariat; a series of papers embodying proposals of a drafting nature arising out of the consideration by the respective language groups of the Draft
Convention; and a series of documents outlining the
recommendations of the coordinators of the language
groups under the direction of the Chairman of the
Drafting Committee. The documentation prepared during the intersessional meeting was extensive, and the
pace of work and volume of documentation were without
precedent in the history of the Conference. The
Drafting Committee expresses its appreciation to the
Special Representative of the Secretary-General, the
Secretary of the Committee, and the other members of
the Secretariat for their truly remarkable and tire-
less efforts throughout the intersessional meeting.
The availability of a computerized text greatly
facilitated the task of identifying and dealing with
recurring words and phrases.


Textual review progress

4. The complexity and importance of the task of the
Drafting Committee, coupled with the extraordinary
volume of documentation, made it necessary from the
opening days of the meeting for the language groups,
the coordinators, and the Drafting Committee to maintain an intensive schedule of meetings in the early
morning hours, evenings, weekends, holidays, and
luncheon periods in addition to the regular meetings
during United Nations working hours. As a consequence,the Drafting Committee was able to carry out
an article-by-article textual review of Parts II to
X and Annexes 1 and 2, and Parts XII to XIV. The
recommendations on these Parts which the Drafting
Committee has adopted in the course of this meeting
are set out in Addendum 1 to this report. Other matters regarding these Parts are still under review.

---

3. A/CONF.62/DC/WP.2

During the final two weeks of the session, the Drafting Committee began its article-by-article textual review of Part XI, in accordance with the timetable proposed by the Conference. Progress has been made by the language groups in the preparation of the article-by-article textual review of Part XI by the Drafting Committee. For lack of time it did not prove possible to commence an article-by-article textual review of the Preamble, Part I (Use of Terms), Part XV (Settlement of Disputes), Part XVI (General Provisions), and Part XVII (Final Clauses) and the related annexes. A list of the Informal Papers and Language Group Recommendations is set out in Addendum 2 to this report.

5. Because of the large volume of work, the Drafting Committee concentrated on those drafting suggestions that could be prepared and considered most expeditiously. The fact that the Committee decided to propose or not to propose a drafting change does not imply either agreement or disagreement with reasons proferred therefor orally or in writing, nor does it imply any conclusion regarding the meaning of any existing text. Moreover, the decision to propose, or not to propose, harmonization of or a distinction between terms used in different provisions implies no conclusion as to whether the terms have the same or a different meaning.

6. In order to ensure that the consideration of drafting changes not give rise to substantive implications or interpretive records, the Committee and its organs have followed the practice of avoiding records of discussion of drafting changes and the reasons therefor.

7. It should be noted that a number of recommendations made in this report are applicable to the texts prepared in more than one main committee of the Conference. Agreement to such recommendations was premised on their application to all relevant parts of the Draft Convention and not on a partial or selective basis.

8. It should also be noted that, with respect to the requirement for concordance of the six official language texts of the Draft Convention, the Drafting Committee sought to improve linguistic concordance, to the extent possible, and juridical concordance in all cases.

## Future work

9.  It is recommended that the Drafting Committee meet during the tenth session of the Conference with a view to early completion of its work.

TENTH SESSION (Resumed)
GENEVA
August 3 - 28, 1981

REPORT OF THE UNITED STATES DELEGATION TO THE
RESUMED TENTH SESSION OF THE
UNITED NATIONS CONFERENCE ON THE LAW OF THE SEA
Geneva, August 3 - 28, 1981

## Summary

This delegation report describes the principal
activities of the US delegation to the Third United
Nations Conference on the Law of the Sea during its
tenth session held in New York from March 9 to April
24 and in Geneva from August 3 to 28, 1981. The membership on the US delegation to the conference is
attached at Appendix A (not included here).

It was the stated intention of the Conference to
finalize the Draft Convention on the Law of the Sea
in 1981 with a view toward opening it for signature
in Caracas, Venezuela in 1982. The Conference was not
able to meet this schedule and has prepared a new
schedule which calls for finalization of the Draft
Convention in an 11th session to be held in New York
March 8 to April 30, 1982. The Conference has further
requested the Secretary General of the United Nations
to arrange with the Government of Venezuela for the
Convention to be opened for signature in Caracas in
the fall of 1982.

## Deep Seabed Mining Issues

In 1980, at the ninth session of the UNCLOS, the
Conference determined that, but for the continuing
negotiation on four outstanding issues, negotiations
could be concluded at the tenth session in 1981.

The four outstanding issues identified by UNCLOS
as requiring further negotiation were:

1. Delimitation of maritime boundaries;

2. Participation by liberation groups and other
   international organizations;

3. Protection of preparatory investment in
   deepsea mining; and

4. The creation of a preparatory commission
   pending the entry into force of the treaty.

512

At the New York session in early 1981, the US delegation announced that the Draft Convention was under review by the Reagan Administration and that under these circumstances, it was not possible for the US delegation to engage in active negotiations. It was announced that the US policy review extended to all issues in the Draft Convention and not only to those related to deepsea mining. Reactions to the US decision were in the main less than favorable, and virtually all countries expressed the hope that the US would conclude its policy review as quickly as possible and avoid reopening any fundamental questions which had previously been agreed to and supported by the US delegation.

Conference participants generally agreed that the new US Administration should have a limited opportunity to review its position on these difficult and complex issues. Nevertheless, the United States was urged to return to the negotiating table at the resumed Geneva session in August. The US delegation indicated that the policy review would not be completed in time for the August resumed Geneva session and that it would prefer the UNCLOS to schedule its next session in 1982 when the policy review would be completed. In the hope that the United States would conclude its review and the Conference would be able to complete its work, a four-week session was scheduled from August 3 to 28. The US policy review process was, in fact, accelerated between the two sessions so that the principal missing ingredient was an assessment of the negotiability of the areas of concern with the Draft Convention that the Administration had identified in its review process. Accordingly, at the Geneva session, the US delegation came prepared to explain those concerns to Conference participants. The delegation also sought to determine from other delegations the extent to which it might be possible at a further session of the Conference to improve the Draft Convention in those areas of concern.

The principal objectives of the US delegation to the Geneva session, therefore, were first, to make the negotiability assessment described above, and second, to participate in the Conference in a manner that preserved all options available to the US with respect to law of the sea. The US considered it important to take no action inconsistent with a possible decision to return as a full-fledged partner to the UNCLOS deliberations or to undertake other options and

was instructed to seek to avoid any final decisions which might otherwise have been taken.

The US delegation placed primary emphasis on finding opportunities in which reasoned debate and discussion could occur so as to assist in assessment of the negotiability which it was instructed to make. At the end of the first week of the session, it was clear that delegations to UNCLOS would not agree to insert into the formal structure of the Conference an opportunity for the US to reopen issues which all countries felt had been settled previously. Instead, the President of the UNCLOS and Chairman of the First Committee arranged for an informal dialogue outside the normal working hours of the Conference in which the US could present its concerns and hear the responses of other countries.

Before this dialogue could take place, however, the US was asked to deliver a statement to the informal plenary of the UNCLOS on August 5 giving a <u>tour d'horizon</u> of its concerns. That statement is attached at Appendix B. The reaction to the statement was generally sympathetic, and the Group of 77 requested more detail about the US position. The Group of 77 indicated that it would not be able to address the US areas of concern until they had been fully disclosed in ample detail so that the Group of 77 could make an assessment of the negotiability of US concerns.

The US delegation on the other hand took the position that if it were to lay out detailed areas of concern as requested, it might appear to be entering into negotiations which it did not have authority to conduct. In addition, the delegation believed it would not be likely to engender a constructive dialogue. The delegation also sought to avoid a situation in which there would be a general debate between the Group of 77 and the US. Such a debate might have led to an unfavorable climate at the Conference. The US delegation, therefore, indicated that it might engage in a detailed discussion on a point-by-point basis, encouraging dialogue with the Group of 77 on each of the points.

When the informal consultations were convened by the President of the UNCLOS and Chairman of the First Committee, however, the Group of 77 continued to insist on a comprehensive and detailed statement. This insistence apparently was a condition of the dialogue

once the consultative mode had been established. For the reasons already stated, the US refused to engage in such a sweeping detailed review and, instead, chose to make a general statement containing more specifics than had been set out on August 5. An eight-point statement was delivered on August 13 by Ambassador Malone and is attached at Appendix C (not included here, its summary following below). The statement indicated the following serious problem areas in the Draft Convention:

1. The delegation said that the US view that its role in the decision-making organs of the Seabed Authority should approximate the economic stake which it would have as a major consumer and producer of resources and as a major contributor to the Authority and the Enterprise. In this connection, it was noted that as the Draft Convention is presently written, the main powers of the Seabed Authority are vested in the Assembly and that the Assembly is in turn controlled by the developing countries without any special provisions to protect the interests of the United States and other industrialized countries. The US delegation considered this to be inconsistent with its national interests.

2. The US delegation also said that the executive Council of the Seabed Authority also poses serious problems. The delegation indicated that industrialized countries should have a stronger voice in the Council's decisions. It also noted that the Assembly had overriding policy powers which could undercut the effectiveness of the executive Council. The delegation also pointed out that the method of decision making could lead to a paralysis of the Council and become disadvantageous to those countries with deepsea mining technology who wished to have affirmative decisions made by the Council. The delegation stated that the US should have a stronger role in the Council's decisions. The US would also seek an arrangement for permanent representation by the US on the Council, as is the case under the present draft convention for the socialist group of Eastern European countries.

4. The US delegation questioned the adequacy of the technical procedures for the approval of applications. This particular aspect of the Draft Convention had been highlighted in the policy review, although it was noted that this problem must be considered in

connection with the Authority's discretionary powers, the production limitation provisions and the discrimination built into the system. Taken together, these elements contribute to the belief that access of US nationals could not be assured under the Draft Convention. The issues of discretion and discrimination were raised as separate points and are mentioned below.

5. The US delegation explained its concern that a number of major provisions of the Draft Convention established discrimination in favor of the Enterprise and, accordingly, were contrary to the interests of US nationals. This discrimination, seen as a package, gave rise to an assessment that the Enterprise would have significantly lower operating costs than other operators in the absence of government subsidies. In this situation, the assessment could be made that the parallel system would not function as a truly parallel system but over time could put private or State-owned companies at a competitive disadvantage. Moreover, it was also pointed out that a substantial share of the discriminatory subsidies which the Draft Convention gave to the Enterprise would be coming from the highly industrialized countries. It was noted that this aspect of the Draft Convention created significant political difficulties in our Congress since it would appear that the US was subsidizing the Enterprise, and in doing so the prospects for American companies to have profitable access to the resources would be diminished.

6. The US delegation raised problems with Article 155 which deals with the review conference. This article provides that 15 years after commencement of commercial production under the Treaty, a conference to review the provisions of Part XI will be convened by the Seabed Authority. If agreement had not been reached after five years of negotiations, the review conference could adopt proposed amendments to the treaty. These amendments could then enter into force for all States parties to the treaty if two-thirds of them ratified the amendments. The delegation pointed out that this procedure raises significant constitutional issues for the US. More importantly, it also creates a situation in which the US would have joined a treaty regime established through 15 years of negotiations under the rule of consensus. Fifteen years after commencement of commercial production under the Treaty, however, ratification by two-thirds of States

parties could alter fundamental aspects of the treaty. Under this system, the US would be bound to these changes regardless of whether it ratified the amendments and regardless of the effects such a change would have on US interests.

7.  The US delegation pointed out that there were many discriminatory provisions in the Draft Convention which, when taken together with the powers and functions of the Assembly and the Council, could give rise to opportunities for interference with the conduct of mining operations.  Thus, even if access were guaranteed, an investor, once having obtained access, could not be assured that he would be able to develop a mine site without additional economic burdens.  The US delegation indicated that this was an area in which the treaty should state clearly that one of its policy objectives is to avoid unreasonable interference with mining operations once a contract has been awarded so that operators can expect to see the fruits of their investments.

8.  The US delegation also raised questions concerning the financial obligations imposed by the Draft Convention, both on governments and private parties. The delegation indicated that the US was troubled by uncertainties with respect to the total cost of the treaty to the US Treasury and by the effect of financial obligations on the profitability of mining operations.

The Group of 77 responded to Ambassador Malone's statement on August 17.  On the surface, the statement delivered by Ambassador Inam-Ul-Haque of Pakistan, speaking as Chairman of the Group of 77, would appear to foreclose the types of changes to the Draft Convention that the US would presumably seek if it were to pursue further negotiations.  Nevertheless, careful reading of the statement coupled with an impression created by many public and private discussions would indicate that some flexibility does exist and that it would be possible to re-examine some of the provisions of the treaty.  A number of proposals were made privately for intersessional work on the possibilities for repairing Part XI, and these proposals are under consideration.

The important highlights at the Resumed 10th session were these:

- The UNCLOS was prepared to delay its work in order to make a good-faith effort at either accommodating US concerns or at least give the US an opportunity to study carefully both the draft Convention and its national interests in a Law of the Sea Treaty.

- Many delegations indicated a willingness to work with the US to improve the draft Convention.

- The Western industrialized countries publicly stated the importance to them of US participation in the treaty.

- The Group of 77, while understandably resentful of the US review, was willing to expend some effort to listen to our concerns.

- The Draft Convention was not finalized at the Geneva session despite strong feelings that it should be. Indeed, Soviet efforts to finalize the text were decisively defeated.

- Three weeks of additional negotiating time has been specifically set aside in 1982.

The US is now evaluating these considerations and many others with a view toward making final decisions in the next few months.

## Other Work of the Tenth Session

Work on outstanding issues continued in the WG 21, which is a working group of limited membership co-chaired by the President of the UNCLOS and the Chairman of Committee One. Primary emphasis at the Geneva session was devoted to the question of creating a Preparatory Commission pending the entry into force of the treaty. A new draft conference resolution was prepared on this subject, but most of the important issues under debate were not resolved. The most difficult issue which arises out of those negotiations involves membership and decision-making in the Preparatory Commission. If the Preparatory Commission is given important functions, such as the preparation of the first draft of rules and regulations for deep seabed mining, then it becomes vital to know which countries will be members of the Preparatory

Commission and how influential each of them will be in those decisions.

If, on the other hand, the Preparatory Commission is vested with ministerial functions, this issue becomes less important. The Conference will need to devote further attention to this subject. The WG 21 did not deal with the question of protection of preparatory investments. This issue will require considerably more consultation among industrialized countries whose nationals are presently involved in the exploration of deep seabed resources so as to enable a coordinated position to be put forward at the negotiations. Further, the Group of 77 is not anxious to negotiate on this subject until it becomes clear whether the US is committed to the treaty process. Under these circumstances, it was not judged a good subject for discussion in Geneva.

Other Issues Raised at the Geneva Session

1. Delimitation of the Economic Zone and the Continental Shelf Between States with Opposite or Adjacent Coasts

The Conference produced a new provision on delimitation of the Economic Zone and Continental Shelf:

The delimitation of the exclusive economic zone between States with opposite or adjacent coasts shall be effected by agreement on the basis of international law, as referred to in article 38 of the Statute of the International Court of Justice, in order to achieve an equitable solution.

The Conference achieved agreement on the elimination of any express reference to median or equidistance line, and limited the entire provision to a rule of delimitation by agreement that does not, as such, purport to lay down a normative rule to be applied in the absence of agreement. The reference to "equitable principles" was changed to a vaguer formulation providing that agreements should achieve an equitable solution.

Additionally, the Conference included an express cross-reference to article 38 of the Statute of the International Court of Justice. That article contains the 60-year-old reference to "civilized" nations that

is regarded by some developing-country lawyers as a
product of colonialist attitudes.

## Participation of International Organizations

As a result of several meetings held on the subject, the Conference President issued a new text on
participation of international organizations. His
report makes clear that this excludes "agencies of
the United Nations System", and that the European
Economic Community was the principal organization in
mind.

Procedurally, for an organization to become a
party to the Convention, a majority of States members
must be parties. In its instrument of acceptance, the
organization must file a declaration "specifying the
matters governed by this Convention in respect of
which competence has been transferred to the organization by its members which are States Parties."
States Parties that are members of the organization
must do the same. The declarations must be kept up
to date.

An organization is a party "to the extent that it
has competence in accordance with the declarations".
Therefore States members may not exercise that competence. The organization takes the place of States
Parties with respect to matters on which they have
transferred competence to it.

Responsibility for failure to comply with obligations under the Convention is divided between the
organization and its members. However, joint and several responsibility is imposed for failure to provide
information on request as to who has responsibility
in respect of any specific matter or if contradictory
information is given. The obligations of the organization under the Convention to "third States" (non-
members) prevail over its obligations under the agreement establishing the organization.

Provision is made for situations where the organization and a member State "are joint parties to a
dispute, or [presumably separate] parties in the same
interest." Were they allowed to be separate parties
not in the same interest, the odd arithmetic of Annex
VII, article 3(g) would come into play, giving the organization and its members more arbitrators than a
single adversary.

This is one example of the overall difficulty with that article, which can accidentally produce arbitration panels tilted against one of the parties in disputes involving more than two parties asserting they are not in the same interest. In this treaty, arbitration would be the residual compulsory dispute settlement mechanism. The English Language Group of the Drafting Committee recommended a technical solution. The Drafting Committee was able to deal in part with a similar problem in Annex V, article 3(g) on the compulsory conciliation by eliminating the reference to the possibility of expanding the conciliation panel to accommodate parties not in the same interest. This is significant because of the provision for compulsory conciliation of certain delimitation, fisheries, and marine scientific research disputes which might involve more than two States.

## Drafting Committee

The work of the Drafting Committee has resulted in a text that is significantly better drafted and more internally consistent within each language and among the six language versions. The Drafting Committee uses six open-ended language groups that meet separately, but simultaneously, on the same articles to make proposals in their respective languages and to consider the proposals of other language groups. This reduces the need for simultaneous interpretation, allows non-members and Secretariat experts to participate actively, and expedites consideration of proposals in a given language. Moreover, it channels most joint discussion with interpretation to open meetings of the coordinators where virtually all debate is limited in fact to the six coordinators and the Chairman, arguably to advantage.

Most proposals of most language groups affect only the text in their language, although this is least true of the English Language Group. In effect, when that Group is ahead of the others, the system approximates the more traditional approach in which the first text--usually the English text these days--is drafted for meaning, and the remaining texts are then brought into conformity with it.

The Drafting Committee has experienced problems arising from its limited mandate and time constraints. Proposals to correct serious defects in the text are met with objections that they affect substance or will

take too long to consider. When this is coupled with
a strict and very rapid "no objection" procedure for
dealing with proposals, the chances of making an important correction are seriously reduced.

At the conclusion of the tenth session, the Conference issued a revised text incorporating over 1500
Drafting Committee changes covering all Second and
Third Committee texts and some First Committee and
dispute-settlement texts. Without making it a formal
text closed to negotiation and open to formal amendment, it gave the text a "higher status" by deleting
the words "informal text" in its title and giving it
an official limited document number. The existing
procedure for changing the text is retained, namely a
finding of a substantially improved prospect of consensus.

President Koh gave the following statement in
connection with the status of the new text:

It will be the official Draft Convention of
the Law of the Sea of the Conference subject,
however, to the following three conditions:

First, the door would be kept open for the
continuation of consultations and negotiations
on certain outstanding issues. The results
of these consultations and negotiations, if
they satisfy the criterion in A/CONF.62/62,
will be incorporated in the Draft Convention
by the collegium without the need for formal
amendments.

Second, the Drafting Committee will complete
its work, and its further recommendations,
approved by the Informal Plenary, will be
incorporated in the text.

Third, in view of the fact that the process of
consultations and negotiations on certain outstanding issues will continue, the time has,
therefore, not arrived for the application of
rule 33 of the Rules of Procedure of the Conference.

At this stage, delegations will not be permitted
to submit amendments. Formal amendments may only be
submitted after the termination of all negotiations.

## Summary

The tenth session of the UNCLOS was a difficult one for all States. Discussions were awkward and relations strained. Nevertheless, in a spirit of realism, it was possible for the US to hold many fruitful and informative discussions and communicate more directly its concerns with the draft Convention. The US delegation sought to avoid antagonizing other delegations with its policy review and to preserve the opportunity for negotiations in the future. Nevertheless, there was a clear mood at the Conference concerning the future course of the Conference work.

First, virtually the whole of the UNCLOS is impatient with the protracted nature of the negotiations and the current US position. The mood of the Conference clearly favors finalization of the draft Convention so that it can be opened for signature in 1982, although the Conference could delay that schedule under certain circumstances.

Second, virtually no delegation appeared publicly willing to support changes of a fundamental character in the Draft Convention. Many delegations--including representatives of other industrialized countries-- exhorted the US to avoid reopening fundamental questions because, in their judgment, this would make agreement with the US impossible.

It is possible to interpret these two factors in a variety of ways. Sometimes, public statements are intended, in part, as negotiating tactics. We must always be alert to the need to distinguish between tactical statements and those that genuinely reflect Conference sentiment. Thus, in evaluating the results of the tenth session and forecasting the events of the eleventh, these two factors need to be carefully understood.

APPENDIX B


STATEMENT BY AMBASSADOR JAMES L. MALONE
Special Representative of the
President of the United States for the
Third United Nations Conference on the Law of the Sea
Plenary, August 5, 1981


Mr. President,

   As you and other Conference leaders are aware, I
had been reluctant to make a broad statement reporting
on the progress we have made in our review because of
my conviction that this Conference can benefit most
from structured and sober discussion of these matters
in a series of informal meetings. However, many delegations, including the Chairman of the Group of 77,
told us that such a dialogue could best follow a general statement by my delegation. It is in this spirit that I present these remarks today.

   Mr. President, the United States is keenly aware
of the importance which all nations attach to the work
of this Conference. We have no wish to retard the
progress of the Conference, nor do we wish to delay
the successful conclusion of its work. We, like all
of our colleagues, have come here to ascertain what
can be done to achieve this end, including satisfactory resolution of the issues first raised in the
Declaration of Principles in 1970.

   Mr. President, I want to emphasize that the
United States has not yet taken any decision with
respect to its policy, strategy, or tactics. We are
here in Geneva to learn from others whether it is
possible to find accommodations and explanations which
may meet some of the concerns I will identify today
and those which I will discuss in more detail during
the next several weeks.

   As most of you know, my government undertook its
review of the Draft Convention because the people of
the United States, through their electoral process,
have expressed their preference for a variety of policies that affect the work of this Conference. Mr.
President, my country's political leaders cannot and
should not ignore that mandate. We have nevertheless
tried to be mindful of the fact that a great deal of

work has been done by this Conference over the last decade. As we conduct the review, we are therefore making every effort to avoid burdening the Conference with issues that are not vitally important to the acceptability of a treaty to the United States Administration or the United States Senate.

The review of the Draft Convention has not been completed. Indeed, it is now entering its most crucial stage.

Substantial time has been devoted to identifying those areas which give us concern. Most of that work has been completed. We do not believe, however, that it would be prudent for us to recommend that the President make decisions about our final position without fully understanding how other nations feel about the issues raised by these areas of concern.

It may well be that after we have engaged in a dialogue here in Geneva we will discover that a number of issues which gave rise to concern in Washington have been misunderstood or can be resolved. If this is the case, we would be able to avoid problems which could delay the work of the Conference.

In this regard, we find ourselves in some sympathy with the views expressed at the Plenary on Monday by the distinguished representative of Sierra Leone. He stated more eloquently than I can his view that it would be undesirable to force the United States to raise issues which could be avoided. That is why we believe that if we can talk through our concerns in depth in a workmanlike atmosphere, we may help rather than hinder the Conference. We regret that our intentions were deliberately misinterpreted in a few polemical statements.

Mr. President, we are especially cognizant of the desire of all countries for a cooperative and harmonious approach to North-South issues. We are hopeful that during the August session, working together with the Group of 77, it will be possible to create an atmosphere conducive to achieving our mutual objectives not only here in Geneva, but in other forums as well.

Our review of the Draft Convention has revealed that Part XI of the text would, in its present form, be a stumbling block to treaty ratification. I know

this comes as unwelcome news to most of you. But, in the spirit of goodwill and cooperation, I know that you would not wish me to conceal the political facts of life which we confront.

I am aware that many have assumed that our difficulties with Part XI are stimulated by private companies. They believe that, were it not for the views of a few companies, the United States might be able to agree to the present text. Mr. President, that assumption is without foundation. The questions and doubts that have emerged during this review relate to issues of principle. These principles follow from widely shared American attitudes toward the creation of global regulatory institutions, the availability of resources for an industrial economy, the financial and economic burdens of an unbalanced budget, and the role which the United States should play in decisions affecting its vital interests.

We have been asked to be as specific as possible in our comments on the Draft Convention so that at the outset all delegations may assess the scope of the issues we would like to discuss. We intend at this session, if we are given the opportunity to do so, to engage in intensive discussions to elaborate with precision and detail the points which have been raised in our review. We cannot easily do that in a single opening statement to the Plenary. We are anxious to discuss these points and to hear other views on the merits of our concerns and on possible ways to alleviate them.

Allow me, then, to describe in a general way the kinds of questions that have occurred to us in our review in the hope that by sharing these questions with our colleagues at the Conference some answers may also begin to emerge.

One of our concerns relates to the complex of issues related to decision making in the International Seabed Authority.

It is widely recognized that all countries should feel that the principles governing the machinery do not create the apprehension that one country or group of countries could dominate others in a decision-making process where vital interests are at stake.

During our review, the question has been raised
whether the balance of decision making in the Draft
Convention may be somewhat askew. In particular,
concern has been expressed about the scope of the
Assembly's powers and its relationship to the Council.

Is it possible, for example, that the Assembly,
in pursuit of its general policy-making function and
acting as a "supreme organ," might seek to use ambiguous treaty provisions providing wide discretion and
permitting discrimination in such a way as to have a
substantial impact on the Council's executive function or even the rights of States under the Treaty?
We think that risk exists. It is an area we would
like to discuss further with our colleagues.

We are aware that there have been intense and
difficult negotiations leading up to the preparation
of Article 161 on composition, procedure, and voting
in the Council. A number of doubts exist in my government, however, regarding the extent to which the
interests of a country like the United States, which
is one of the world's major consumers of raw materials
and which has played perhaps the largest role in the
development of deep seabed mining technology, is fully
protected.

I am sure many delegations have the impression
that Article 161 ensures that the United States and
other technologically advanced Western countries will
be appropriately represented on the Council at all
times. Mr. President, a fair reading of the text
leaves that result uncertain. Our government, in
reviewing this particular text, has discovered a
certain lack of equilibrium in the Council which we
believe could benefit from more intense discussion.

Questions have also been raised about the Council's voting system. It may surprise many of our colleagues to know that one of those questions concerns
the ease with which the voting system could be used to
paralyze the Council. As a country with an active interest in carrying out seabed mining, we have examined
whether it would not be possible to create a more balanced voting system--one in which decisions on some
subjects could be taken more easily while ensuring
that countries in a minority position will have an effective voice on issues of vital interest to them. If
there is a will to correct this possible imbalance, we

the lingering impression that, in sum, the overall objective of the Draft Convention is contrary to such a
policy. Perhaps this is not a fair reading of these
two articles. In fact, it may be that most delegations intend that the Seabed Authority would create a
favorable and fertile climate in which resource development would flourish--indeed that resource development would be the Authority's overriding policy objective. One of our problems is that we have difficulty
in finding that objective clearly stated in the Draft
Convention. We would also be prepared to go into
great detail on the other problems we find with these
two articles.

Mr. President, there has been much thought given
to the provision which relates to the Review Conference. Questions have been raised whether this Conference intends that, after 10 years of difficult negotiation to reach a consensus text, Part XI of the
Treaty may be altered by amendments ratified by two-
thirds of the States parties.

This system would in effect allow an amendment to
come into force for the United States over our objection. This raises a constitutional question and we
believe it is something our Senate could well refuse
to do in this circumstance.

Some delegations have said to us that one of the
principal values of the Law of the Sea Conference is
that it has established the rule of consensus as a
precedent for global conferences. We share that view,
to the extent it has been possible to make great progress in these negotiations and in other forums where
the rule of consensus was used, it is because States
with vital interests knew that their views would not
be overridden by a large majority of States seeking to
protect contrary interests. This precedent has served
us well, and we are concerned that it would be abandoned for the entry into force of amendments to Part
XI of this Treaty.

Mr. President, the Treaty contains a number of
financial and budgetary implications which have drawn
significant attention not only in the United States
but in other Western countries. Our government is em-
barked on a course of action designed to reduce inflation and stimulate productivity. It is also attempting to reduce burdensome regulations that impede industrial activity. Many have viewed the Draft

Convention as being inconsistent with these basic goals.

The Draft Convention appears to impose significant regulatory burdens on productivity and requires budget outlays not only to assist in the creation of the Authority but to assist in the creation of the Enterprise. At the same time, the financial and regulatory burdens imposed on mining companies by the Convention would increase the pressures for direct or indirect subsidies.

Thus, the Draft Convention may create a situation in which the Enterprise, using funds provided in part by the United States Government, eventually would eclipse mining activity by private companies. This possibility makes it all the more difficult to generate the political will to provide funds for the Enterprise when their ultimate use may be contrary to the United States' desire to increase domestic productivity. Perhaps there are other ways of synchronizing these potentially contradictory objectives. This too could prove to be a useful subject of discussion during the coming weeks.

Mr. President, I cannot in one statement reasonably develop all of the questions raised about Part XI. There are, for example, the question of the mandatory transfer of technology, the question of the moratorium on development of mineral resources other than manganese nodules, the criteria for distribution of revenues, and the imposition of penalties. These and other specific questions can be more usefully addressed at another time--perhaps in meetings of the WG-21 during the coming weeks.

What I have tried to do is simply to indicate general categories in which we have identified concerns and to provide a few concrete examples of the problems which give rise to our doubts that our government could react favorably to this Treaty in its present form. We have come to Geneva knowing that the Conference will not greet with enthusiasm the reopening of important issues. But we also know--because so many of you have told us--that if it is possible to accommodate our concerns, you would want to try to do so.

We do not want to conclude our review without gaining concrete information on the possibilities

for our concerns to be accommodated. We want to be able to base our judgment on reasoned discussions, not on general debate or rhetoric. This Conference has labored with extraordinary diligence for many years. In our judgment, with some additional work at this session, exploring these areas of concern which we believe may be shared by other delegations, the prospects for a successful outcome--satisfactory to all nations--could be greatly enhanced.

We hope that the Conference will continue to demonstrate patience with these new developments. More importantly, we hope that the Conference will consider these concerns and offer candid and creative reactions to them. For our part, I can assure that before any final decisions are made by the United States, we will weigh heavily and take most seriously the views other delegations express during the coming weeks.

Thank you, Mr. President.

ELEVENTH SESSION
NEW YORK
March 8 - April 30, 1982

## I.  INTRODUCTION

This report describes the principal developments at the Eleventh session of the Third United Nations Conference on the Law of the Sea, held from March 8 to April 30, 1982, at the United Nations in New York.

After a detailed review of the Draft Convention on the Law of the Sea, the United States (US) returned to the Eleventh and final negotiating session of the law of the sea negotiations.  In a statement made on January 29, 1982 (Appendix B), President Reagan emphasized that the US was committed to the multilateral treaty process for reaching agreement on the law of the sea and that the non-seabed mining sections of the Draft Convention were acceptable. The President stated that major elements of the deep seabed mining portion of the Convention were unacceptable and that the US would return to the Conference to seek changes necessary to satisfy six objectives important to the US.

The final treaty text that was adopted at the Conference failed to meet any of the US objectives in regard to seabed mining.  Consequently, the US called for a vote on the adoption of the text.  On April 30, 1982, the Conference adopted the Law of the Sea Convention by a vote of 130 in favor, 4 against (US, Israel, Turkey, and Venezuela), with 17 abstentions (FRG, UK, Belgium, Luxembourg, Netherlands, Italy, Spain, Thailand, Mongolia, and the Eastern European Bloc, except Romania).

## II.  DEEP SEABED MINING:  PART XI AND RELEVANT ANNEXES

The principal aim of the US at the Conference was to obtain improvement in the seabed mining provisions of the treaty (Part XI and Annexes).

### A.  Intersessional Meeting: February 24 – March 2

The first phase of the US delegation's efforts coincided with the intersessional meeting, February 24 – March 2, called by Tommy Koh, Permanent Representative of Singapore to the United Nations and President of the Law of the Sea Conference, to deal with the three issues not resolved in prior sessions of the Conference: Preparatory Investment Protection, the Preparatory Commision, and participation in the

Convention. Negotiations of these issues are discussed more fully as separate topics under Parts III,
IV, and V of this report.

During the intersessional meeting, the US circulated a comprehensive paper outlining its major
concerns and suggesting alternative solutions. The
paper marked the culmination of a process intended
to inform industrialized countries and allies, the
Soviet Union, and the developing countries about the
specific concerns raised in President Reagan's
January 29 statement.

The paper elicited strong reactions from most
interest groups at the Conference. In particular,
the breadth and scope of the US paper created a
widespread impression that the US was not serious in
its claim to have returned to the Conference to negotiate in good faith, even though the core issues
presented in the paper were few in number and ones
with which all delegations were by then familiar.
The G-77 leadership, in both public and private, expressed concern that the US proposals were not in
the form of specific textual language. The G-77 insisted that no considered response could be expected
from them unless specific language was forthcoming.
Although the US would have preferred to leave its
proposals in their existing, more flexible format,
the US delegation complied with the G-77 request and
the additional suggestion that the package be completed around March 8, the opening day of the Conference.

B. The "Green Book"

The second phase of the Conference began around
March 5. Following an intensive drafting effort, the
US presented a set of amendments, referred to as the
"Green Book" due to the color of its cover, to the
Conference on March 11. In presenting the "Green
Book," the US made clear that since the proposed
amendments were only one of a number of possible
solutions, no ultimatum was intended that the specific changes proposed were insisted upon by the US.
Rather, the US emphasized that the sole purpose of
the "Green Book" was to be responsive to the request
from the G-77 for specific textual language. Drawn
from the US alternative approaches paper circulated
during the intersessional meeting and proposing
treaty language, the book made clear to other

delegations that the six US objectives could not be satisfied without substantive changes being made to the Draft Convention, thus producing a significant adverse reaction at the Conference. Some delegations were of the view that the US had made a frontal assault on the foundations of the parallel system.

## C. The Group of Eleven Proposals

The "Green Book" was strongly resisted by the G-77, which rejected it as a basis for negotiation. Their recalcitrance galvanized a group of eleven States (Australia, Austria, Canada, Denmark, Finland, Iceland, Ireland, New Zealand, Norway, Sweden, and Switzerland). After a week of consultations and drafting, this group of eleven nations (G-11) produced a package of amendments (Appendix C) (initially made a part of the Conference record on March 25) which, they believed, could serve as a basis for negotiations between the US and the G-77.

After careful analysis, the US delegation concluded that certain elements of the G-11 proposals provided adequate bases for addressing US concerns (e.g., contract approval, technology transfer, and separation of powers) but that other elements fell short of US objectives (e.g., review conference). More importantly, several of the US concerns were not addressed at all by the G-11 paper (e.g., production limitation, decision-making, and theoretical eligibility for sharing in benefits by national liberation groups).

Further complicating the negotiating environment was the insistence of the G-77 that the US and its allies accept the G-11 proposals as an exhaustive negotiating agenda. Since the US could not negotiate on the basis of an agenda which did not cover all of the US objectives, the G-77 demand introduced a further element of rigidity into the Conference. Consequently, the only meetings scheduled toward the end of March and first part of April were pro forma in nature; the US and its close allies set forth their concerns, and the G-77 leadership did little more than listen.

While informal discussions were taking place outside regular Conference sessions, delegations made official presentations in the Plenary sessions, held from March 29 through April 1, concerning their

position on those changes to the text suggested during the informal consultation period. On April 1, the Chairman of the US delegation set forth the US position in a statement made before the Plenary (Appendix D), emphasizing the US desire for substantive negotiations.

### D. Modified US Amendments

For the US delegation, the third stage of the Conference began with the recognition that tangible evidence of US good faith was necessary if the negotiating impasse were to be broken. The US delegation's instructions were modified to reflect additional flexibility in two areas: the US would not insist on complete elimination of the production limitation nor on affirmative voting power for the US and a few of its closest allies regarding the adoption of rules, regulations, and procedures by the Council of the International Seabed Authority (ISA).

The US delegation proceeded to engage in a series of meetings with Conference leaders and interest groups, including US allies, the G-77, the European Community, the G-11, and the USSR. At these sessions, the US described the minimum contents of a seabed mining package that could serve as a negotiating agenda for the short time remaining before April 13, the last day on which formal amendments to the text could be tabled.

In a further attempt to improve the atmosphere, the US agreed to the inclusion in the treaty text of a proposal submitted by a group of African nations concerning Article 171 (Funds of the Authority). This group, interested in securing compensation for land-based producers of seabed minerals, wanted to include a reference to a compensation fund whose sources would be recommended by the Economic Planning Commission of the ISA.

Unfortunately, no substantive negotiations took place on the US seabed regime proposals during the April 5-13 period. The only substantive negotiations that did occur during this time concerned the Resolution on Preparatory Investment Protection, discussed in Part III of this report.

### E. Formal Amendments

The fourth stage of the Conference began on April 31 with the tabling of formal amendments. Plenary meetings were scheduled from April 15 to 17 for delegations to introduce their formal amendments.

Thirty-one sets of amendments were submitted. The most significant amendments were those sponsored by the US and six of its closest supporters (Belgium, France, FRG, Italy, Japan, and the UK) (Appendix E) and those put forward by the G-11 (Appendix F). The US amendments, covering Part XI, the Annexes, Preparatory Investment Protection, and the Preparatory Commission, represented modification of the "Green Book." To foster co-sponsorship by the allies, these amendments drew upon the G-11 proposals, while tailoring them in such a way as to make them consistent with the President's objectives.

The number and breadth of the amendments which various delegations submitted caused concern that voting could lead to far-reaching changes in the Draft Convention, sufficient to unravel what were perceived by the Conference leadership as the delicate compromises embodied in the text. Consequently, the Conference leadership attempted in the days that followed the introduction of the amendments to induce sponsors to withdraw their amendments or to agree not to press them to a vote. The leadership succeeded in avoiding votes on all but three amendments. These three amendments, described in more detail in Part VI of this report, concerned non-seabed mining provisions and were defeated. The US and its co-sponsors decided not to press for a vote on their amendments, in the interest of promoting the possibility of substantive negotiations on US concerns with Part XI of the treaty text.

### F. Final Stages

The fifth and final stage of the Conference began on April 23. Since the Preparatory Investment Protection negotiations were the principal focus of the final weeks of the session and the G-77, particularly the African group, continued to resist negotiating on Part XI, little time was available for achieving improvement in the seabed provisions of the text. Recognizing this, Conference President Koh

established himself as an arbiter between the US and the G-77. During a day and a half of intensive discussions, negotiators representing the US, the G-77, and the Soviet Union put their cases to each other and to President Koh. These discussions constituted the sole instances of substantive negotiations on the seabed mining provisions during the entire Conference session.

Working with the Collegium of the Conference, President Koh subsequently issued two reports (Appendix G) which incorporated those changes that he believed would offer a better prospect than the existing text for adoption of the treaty by consensus. President Koh's final reports contained changes that (a) modified the composition of the Council of the ISA by guaranteeing a seat to the largest consumer of seabed minerals (intended to meet the US concern for a guaranteed seat), (b) made the objectives of the ISA more production-oriented, and (c) raised from two-thirds to three-fourths the votes needed for treaty amendments to enter into force at the review conference. Additional minor changes were made dealing with other minerals and the award of contracts. Conference President Koh's proposal on the transfer of technology was more troublesome to the US than the existing text. Upon being made aware of this, President Koh withdrew the proposal before the final vote, leaving unchanged the existing provisions of Annex III, Article 5 (Transfer of Technology).

G. Adoption of Treaty Text

When Conference President Koh's last report appeared on April 29, it became clear that the changes to the seabed mining provisions of the text failed to meet any of the US objectives. Consequently, the US demanded that a recorded vote be taken on the adoption of the Convention.

On April 30, the Convention was adopted by a vote of 130 in favor, 4 against, with 17 abstentions (see Appendix H for a chart showing the vote cast by each delegation). The US statement explaining the US vote against adoption of the text, given in the Plenary, is contained at Appendix I.

## III.  PREPARATORY INVESTMENT PROTECTION

### A.  Negotiations

A major focus of activity during the intersessional period was the formulation of a resolution on preparatory investment in pioneer activities relating to polymetallic nodules (referred to as Preparatory Investment Protection or PIP), intended to offer protection for investments made in deep seabed mining prior to entry into force of the LOS Treaty.  As a major element of unfinished Conference business, the Conference leadership was impatient to receive a specific proposal dealing with the protection of pioneer investors.  Consequently, during the intersessional meeting and into the Conference session itself, the US and four other key industrialized countries engaged in intense negotiations to develop a PIP proposal.  The major issues in these negotiations included Japan's concerns over mine-site size and its "second tier" status in the process of mine-site conflict resolution, France's concern that PIP be limited to a specified group of entities, the size and number of pioneer mine-sites, and a requirement that a prospected site equal in value to the applicant's mine-site be made available to the Preparatory Commission by such applicant for future use by the Enterprise (the operating arm of the ISA).

On March 16, 1983, the US, UK, FRG, and Japan put forward a PIP proposal.  Because the proposal used objective criteria rather than a list for identifying pioneer investors, it did not attract French co-sponsorship.  The proposal would have established a two-tier system of conflict resolution, giving priority to those consortia with site specific claims and obliging those without specific claims to recognize that priority.  States with prospective miners would ensure that conflicts were resolved prior to registration for PIP status.  The PIP proposal contained a reference to areas of equal value being provided by an applicant upon registration.

The PIP proposal submitted by the US and other industrialized nations provoked a counterproposal from the G-77.  The G-77 draft proposal was significant for its recognition that pioneer miners warranted special treatment and that conflict resolution was a responsibility of prospective certifying States.  However, in other respects, the G-77 proposal imposed

onerous burdens on prospective investors. The G-11. as they had in the case of the "Green Book," attempted to narrow the gap between the industrialized countries and the G-77 by producing a compromise draft proposal on PIP. All three PIP proposals were used by Conference President Koh to form the basis of his own proposal.

During the April 5-13 period, the only substantive negotiations that took place at the Conference concerned the PIP Resolution. Conference President Koh held a series of meetings at which he tried to resolve the principal issues: the size of an exploration area, the definition of a pioneer investor, and the relationship of pioneer investors to the seabed mining regime embodied in the Draft Convention.

The G-77 presented the principal opposition in these negotiations, insisting that pioneer investors not be allowed to exploit the seabed minerals until after entry into force of the Convention, that pioneer investors be subject to the treaty's production limitation found in Article 151 (Production Policies), and that pioneer investors be required to submit a plan of work for exploration and exploitation to the ISA for approval. The G-77 also demanded that the provisions of the text relating to the reserved area apply to pioneer investors, that each pioneer investor be obligated to respond to Preparatory Commission requests to explore the reserved area it had proposed, and that pioneer miners pay a total of $500,000 in application fees and a fixed annual fee of $1 million. The US and its allies resisted these demands, arguing that pioneer investors should receive production authorizations prior to any new entrant, plans of work should be automatically approved upon certification of the applicants' qualifications by the sponsoring State, and only one reserved area need be fully explored.

During the negotiations on PIP, Japan's demands for a smaller exploration area of 60,000 square kilometers were resisted in favor of an initial exploration area of 150,000 square kilometers.

A provision allowing a multinational mining consortium to be certified by a single country, as long as that State had signed the Convention, proved to be a highly contentious issue. This provision would allow an entity participating in a consortium to obtain

pioneer investor status without requiring the country, of which it is a national, to be a signatory to the Convention. The Soviet Union, which had earlier announced by letter to Conference President Koh that it would qualify as a pioneer investor, was particularly troubled by this provision. The Soviet Union argued that the provision unfairly prejudiced its interests since it required it to sign the Convention in order to obtain pioneer status, while US pioneers could qualify without US signature of the Convention. The Soviet contention was put to the Legal Counsel of the United Nations who concluded that indeed only one country need sign the Convention for a multinational consortium to receive PIP treatment, but that this was a political judgment the Conference was empowered to make. President Koh did not include language to change that provision. The specific PIP categories are explained more fully below.

B.   Final PIP Resolution

The final PIP Resolution adopted on April 30 creates three categories of pioneer investors:   (1) four countries (France, Japan, India, and USSR); (2) four consortia (nationals of Belgium, Canada, FRG, Italy, Japan, Netherlands, UK, and US); and (3) developing countries.

The PIP Resolution requires that pioneer investors must have spent $30 million in pioneer activities prior to January 1, 1983, with not less than 10% of that figure spent on survey and evaluation of the pioneer area. Developing countries have until December 1, 1985 to meet the same financial qualification.

Under the PIP Resolution, pioneer investors have the following obligations:

1.   Pioneer investors must obtain certification by a State signatory to the Convention before applying for registration with the Preparatory Commission.

2.   Certifying States must ensure that overlapping claims are resolved prior to registration with the Preparatory Commission. Conflict resolution, if not accomplished by negotiations between the certifying States, is to be performed through binding arbitration using principles of equity, set out in the Resolution, with final awards to be made by December 1, 1984.

3. Each application must cover an area sufficient for two mining operations. The Preparatory
Commission is to allocate an exploration area to the
pioneer investor which cannot exceed 150,000 square
kilometers.

4. The pioneer investor must relinquish at
least 50% of his exploration area within eight years
after allocation for reallocation to the international area reserved for the Enterprise.

5. Financial obligations include:

    a. $250,000 on registration by the
       Preparatory Commission.

    b. The accrual of a one million dollar
       annual fee payable upon approval of
       a plan of work when the Convention
       enters into force.

    c. $250,000 for processing a plan of work.

    d. Diligence requirements to be established
       by the Preparatory Commission.

6. Other obligations for pioneer investors
include:

    a. Exploration of the reserved area at the
       request of the Preparatory Commission.
       Costs incurred to be reimbursed plus
       10% annual rate of interest.

    b. Training for personnel designated by
       the Preparatory Commission.

    c. Transfer of technology prior to enter-
       ing into force of the treaty.

The PIP Resolution also sets forth certain rights
of pioneer investors:

1. Registration as pioneer investor, if certified by a signatory to the Convention.

2. One pioneer area of 150,000 square kilometers.

541

3. Production authorization after entry into force with priority over all other applicants except the Enterprise. If production limitation ceilings (Article 151: Production Limitation) are in force, pioneer investors may apportion the available authorization among themselves.

The Enterprise is entitled to two guaranteed production authorizations in the first round of allocation for pioneer investors.

While not every State with a national participating in a consortium must sign the Convention for the consortium to be registered as a pioneer investor, every State must ratify the Convention in order for that consortium to obtain an approved plan of work including production authorization when the treaty enters into force. Without such ratification, a pioneer investor must alter its nationality within a specified period to that of any State party to the Convention which has effective control over the pioneer investor and which has proper PIP status.

For the US, the PIP Resolution might have been acceptable had the negotiations on the seabeds provisions of the treaty text led to significant improvement. However, those provisions were so little changed that the PIP Resolution, because of all of its linkages to Part XI and the relevant Annexes, does not alter our difficulty with the Convention.

## IV. PREPARATORY COMMISSION

The specific tasks of the Preparatory Commission are (a) to administer PIP; (b) to prepare for the establishment of the ISA and its various organs; and (c) to develop rules and regulations for deep seabed mining to permit the ISA and the Enterprise to commence their functions upon entry into force of the Convention. These rules and regulations may be changed when the Convention enters into force only by consensus in the Council of the ISA.

### A. Negotiations

The Preparatory Commission was one of the three unresolved issues left to be negotiated after the August 1981 Conference session. At that session, a text was submitted to the Conference by President Koh

and First Committee Chairman Engo. A revised version of the Koh-Engo text was presented to the Eleventh session of the Conference on April 2 after a series of discussions in the Working Group of 21. Later in the New York session, the Collegium introduced additional provisions as a result of formal amendments submitted by delegations on April 13. Two major additions were the establishment of a special commission to study the problems of the land-based mineral producers likely to be most seriously affected by the production from the Area and the provision for participation by certain "national liberation movements" in the Preparatory Commission as observers.

Membership in the Preparatory Commission is limited to those States which sign the Convention. States which sign only the Final Act may participate as observers but may not participate in the taking of decisions. The Collegium took this position on Preparatory Commission membership over the objections of the US and other industrialized States who had pressed for signature of the Final Act as the qualification for voting membership. Additionally, entities which were observers at the Conference (e.g., the International Maritime Consultative Organization and certain "national liberation movements") are allowed to participate as observers, consistent with UN practice in other organizations.

Various views were expressed on the issue of decision-making in the Preparatory Commission, ranging from requiring a simple majority to consensus voting. The US proposed that decisions on matters of substance be taken by a two-thirds majority of 36 States, to be elected by the Conference according to the system used for the composition of the ISA Council.

B.  Final Resolution

The negotiated solution, adopted by the Conference on April 30, provides that the Preparatory Commission will:

- Exercise the powers and functions assigned to it in Resolution II on Preparatory Investment in Pioneer Activities.

- Undertake studies on the problems encountered by developing land-based producers likely to be most seriously affected by the production of the Area.

- Establish a special commission for the Enterprise, which will "take all necessary measures for
early entry into effective operation" of that organ.

- Begin meeting between 60 and 90 days after 50
States sign or accede to the Convention.

- Apply the Law of the Sea Conference Rules of
Procedure with respect to the adoption of the Preparatory Commission's rules; thereafter, the Commission determines its own rules for decision-making.
(The Conference's rules provide for the taking of
substantive decisions by a two-thirds majority--
including a simple majority of all participants--but
with no voting to take place unless the Conference
decides, also by a two-thirds majority, that all efforts to achieve consensus have been exhausted.)

The Preparatory Commission is to be financed
from the United Nations' regular budget and serviced
by the United Nations Secretariat. It will remain in
existence until the end of the first session of the
Assembly of the ISA.

Only States and other entities such as associated States (e.g., the European Economic Community),
which sign the Convention can be members of the Preparatory Commission and participate in its decisions.
States which have signed the Final Act of the Convention and other entities, which were observers at
the Conference and which have signed the Final Act,
may participate in the Preparatory Commission as
observers.

V.   PARTICIPATION IN THE CONVENTION

A. Negotiations

Conference President Koh conducted a number of
informal Plenary sessions to complete work on the
question of what entities can participate in the Convention, one of the issues formally designated as remaining to be negotiated. The basis for negotiation
was contained in reports of the Conference President
on Article 305 (Signature), Article 306 (Ratification
and Formal Confirmation), Article 307 (Accession) and
Annex IX (Participation by International Organizations). Debate focused on three separate categories
of potential participants: intergovernmental

organizations (primarily integrated economic organizations); associated States and territories which enjoy full internal self-government; and "national liberation movements" which are recognized by the Organization of African Unity or League of Arab States and which were observers at the Conference.

Negotiations at previous sessions of the Conference had actually brought the questions of intergovernmental organizations and associated States and territories to near-completion, with few issues regarding them left to be resolved at this final negotiating session. Thus, the delicate question of participation by "liberation movements" was a major focus of the final consultations. Following the Plenary sessions on March 29 to April 1, a number of small group consultations, chaired by Conference President Koh, were held to consider these issues.

B.  Final Resolution

The negotiated solution, adopted by the Conference on April 30, includes the following elements.

International intergovernmental organizations, such as the European Economic Community, and associated States and territories that "enjoy full internal self-government recognized by the United Nations" can be signatories to the Convention. In addition, the Convention is subject to formal "confirmation" by the international organizations or "ratification" by the associated States and territories, and shall be open for accession by each of these entities.

"National liberation movements" which have participated in the Law of the Sea Conference will be entitled to sign the Final Act in their capacity as observers; they may not sign, ratify, or accede to the LOS Convention. Observers who have signed the Final Act, but who are not referred to in Article 305 (b), (c), (d), or (e) (Signature), have the right to participate in the ISA as observers.

Finally, all signatories of the Final Act may participate in the deliberations of the Preparatory Commission as observers.

At a late stage in the proceedings, the United Nations Council for Namibia proposed that the treaty be amended to include Namibia in the category of

States in Article 305 (Signature). After consultations, it was agreed that Namibia, represented by the Council, would be eligible for participation in the Convention (Article 305, as amended) and for membership in the Preparatory Commission.

## VI. COMMITTEE II

Committee II, which was responsible for traditional non-seabed mining issues, held three informal sessions and one formal meeting during this final negotiating session of the Conference. At those meetings, further debate took place on issues that various delegations viewed as not yet commanding a consensus in the Conference. Many old issues were revived, but most of the debate centered on only a few articles.

### A. Navigation Through Territorial Seas

The most significant of the informal debates was on the proposal to amend Article 21 (Laws and Regulations of the Coastal State Relating to Innocent Passage) to require prior authorization or notification for warships entering the territorial sea. This proposal was pressed by a number of delegations, including Romania, Morocco, the Philippines, and Panama, all of whom perceived prior notice or authorization as necessary for the protection of coastal State security interests. The proposal was strongly opposed by a number of delegations, including the US and other major maritime States. The Soviet Union and the Eastern European States (excluding Romania) opposed the proposal on the merits and on the additional ground that there should be no changes whatsoever to any of the texts. Many States, in fact, took the position that the delicately negotiated balance reflected in the Draft Convention should not be disturbed.

In response to appeals by the proponents of the amendment, the Chairman of Committee II held a series of informal consultative meetings with interested delegations in order to explore the possibilities of a compromise. During these meetings, the proponents of the amendment alluded to a number of possible compromise solutions, including a requirement for prior notification only, a requirement for prior notification outside of generally recognized sealanes, or the

addition of a reference to "security" in Article 21
(1)(h). None of these suggestions drew widespread
support. Thus the Committee Chairman was forced to
conclude that there was no possibility of a consensus
change to the text concerning the Article 21 issue.

During the fourth stage of the Conference's work
program (April 13 to 22), two formal amendments were
submitted relating to this subject. The first proposal, sponsored by Gabon, would have changed Article
21 to permit coastal States to require prior authorization or notification for warships entering the territorial sea. The second amendment, co-sponsored by
approximately 30 States, sought the inclusion of a
reference to "security" in Article 21 (1)(h), so as
to permit the coastal State to promulgate "security"
regulations that would cover warships (or even commercial vessels) entering the territorial sea.

As part of his overall efforts to minimize the
number of votes on substantive issues, Conference
President Koh conducted intensive consultations concerning withdrawal of the proposed changes to Article
21. As a result, the sponsors of the amendments
agreed not to press the amendments to a vote on the
understanding that President Koh would make a statement in the Plenary to the effect that the sponsors
were of the view that the existing text of Article 21
was without prejudice to the right of coastal States
to safeguard their security interests in accordance
with the provisions of Article 19 (Meaning of Innocent Passage) and Article 25 (Rights of Protection
of the Coastal State). The statement was compatible
with the provisions of the draft text, which were
carefully negotiated to preserve pre-existing law,
precluding coastal State discrimination against warships in their exercise of the general right of innocent passage.

B.  Straits Provisions

Although there was no direct reference to the
straits articles in the Committee II debates, Spain
submitted four formal amendments concerning straits
and pressed two of them to a vote. The first of
these two amendments attempted to delete the word
"normally" from Article 39(3) (Duties of Ships and
Aircraft During Transit Passage) which would have had
the effect of making absolute the requirement that
State aircraft comply with International Civil

Aviation Organization rules of the air regarding safety measures. The second amendment, more technical in nature, would have replaced the word "applicable" by the words "generally accepted" in Article 42(1)(b) (Laws and Regulations of States Bordering Straits Relating to Transit Passage). The first amendment, which the US strongly opposed, was soundly defeated by a vote of 21 in favor, 55 against, with 60 abstentions. The second amendment failed to receive a simple majority of States registered at the session and thus, under the Conference Rules of Procedure, was not adopted.

Negotiations concerning the correct interpretation of the straits provisions with respect to the Malacca and Singapore straits continued between the maritime user States and the littoral States and were concluded at this session of the Conference. Malaysia, on behalf of the littoral States, submitted a letter to the Conference President containing a statement relating to Article 233 (Safeguards with Respect to Straits Used for International Navigation). The statement incorporates an understanding which takes cognizance of the peculiar geographic and traffic conditions in these straits, and which recognizes the need to promote safety of navigation and to protect and preserve the marine environment in the straits. This understanding was subsequently confirmed by letters from major user States. These letters constitute a part of the permanent records of the Conference.

C.  Abandoned Installations, Structures

The Chairman of Committee II reported out only one informal amendment as being conducive toward enhancing the possibility of consensus. This was the UK proposal concerning Article 60(3) (Artificial Islands, Installations and Structures in the Exclusive Economic Zone). The amendment modified the requirement that abandoned installations in the exclusive economic zone and on the continental shelf be entirely removed. Debate in the Committee and in the Plenary demonstrated that the proposal had widespread support once the UK delegation made clear that the amendment contemplated the expeditious adoption of binding international standards, and that the UK intended to cooperate immediately in the development of such standards. Accordingly, the Conference President and the Collegium were able to recommend that the

proposed amendment be incorporated into the treaty
without a vote as follows:

> Any installations or structures which are
> abandoned or disused shall be removed to
> ensure safety of navigation, taking account
> of any generally accepted international
> standards established in this regard by the
> competent international organization. Such
> removal shall also have due regard to fish-
> ing, the protection of the marine environ-
> ment and the rights and duties of other
> States. Appropriate publicity shall be given
> to the depth, position, and dimensions of any
> installations or structures not entirely re-
> moved.

### D. Fisheries

An effort also was made at the final negotiating
session of the Conference to encourage increased cooperation for the conservation of "straddling stocks"
by incorporating a change in Article 63 (Stocks Occurring Within the Exclusive Economic Zones of Two or
More Coastal States or Both Within the Exclusive Economic Zone and in an Area Beyond and Adjacent to It).
While this suggestion promoted by Canada and Argentina, among others, received widespread support in
the Committee, the possibility of consensus approval
was blocked by Soviet Union objections on both procedural and substantive grounds. A formal amendment
on this issue was proposed by eight States, but not
pressed to a vote as a result of Conference President
Koh's efforts to avoid as many votes as possible on
substantive issues.

### E. Delimitation of Maritime Boundaries

Venezuela put forward a proposal that would permit reservations to three articles regarding the delimitation of maritime boundaries: Article 15 (Delimitation of the Territorial Sea Between States with
Opposite or Adjacent Coasts), and Article 83 (Delimitation of the Continental Shelf Between States with
Opposite or Adjacent Coasts). Venezuela, however,
decided not to press for a vote on its proposal,
throwing its support instead to a Turkish proposal to
delete Article 309 (Reservations and Exceptions).
This article prohibits all reservations unless expressly permitted elsewhere in the Convention. Opposition to the Turkish proposal was widespread, since

an open door on reservations would have frustrated the "package deal" underpinnings of the entire Committee II text. The proposal was overwhelmingly defeated by a vote of 19 in favor, 100 against, with 26 abstentions.

### F. Conclusion

All other amendments affecting Committee II issues were not pressed to a vote at the final stage of the Conference. In sum, the carefully negotiated balance reflected in the Committee II texts, particularly those dealing with navigation and overflight issues, was preserved at the Eleventh and final negotiating session of the Conference.

## VII. Transitional Provision

### A. Negotiations

The Transitional Provision in the Draft Convention had provided that rights established or recognized by the Convention to the resources of a territory would vest in the inhabitants thereof, even though the people had not attained either full independence or some other self-governing status recognized by the United Nations or were inhabitants of another, specified type of territory. The second paragraph of that provision in the Draft Convention stated that parties involved in a dispute over the sovereignty of a territory should refrain from exercising the rights vested in them by the provision until settlement of the dispute is achieved under the auspices of the UN Charter.

Throughout the work of the Conference, the US and others voiced strong objection to the inclusion of this Transitional Provision regarding the resource rights of dependent territories, in that it raised questions of a political nature that transcended the law of the sea negotiations. Because of this opposition, the subject was injected into the consultations conducted by Conference President Koh. As a result, the Transitional Provision was substantially modified in form and substance.

## B. Final Resolution

The Transitional Provision adopted at the Conference was incorporated into a separate Conference Resolution. The revised provision eliminates the reference to vesting of rights in the inhabitants of territories and, instead, states that the rights and interests under the Convention shall be implemented for their benefit, with a view to promoting their well-being and development. The second paragraph of the provision was modified as follows:

> Where a dispute exists between States over the sovereignty of a territory to which this resolution applies, in respect of which the United Nations has recommended specific means of settlement, there shall be consultations between the parties to that dispute regarding the exercise of the rights referred to in sub-paragraph (a). In such consultations the interests of the people of the territory concerned shall be a fundamental consideration. Any exercise of those rights shall take into account the relevant resolutions of the United Nations and shall be without prejudice to the position of any party to the dispute. The States concerned shall make every effort to enter into provisional arrangements of a practical nature and shall not jeopardize or hamper the reaching of a final settlement of the dispute.

## VII. DRAFTING COMMITTEE

Meetings of the Drafting Committee's six language groups and coordinators continued throughout the session, although a severe shortage of facilities hampered the work of the coordinators in the last three weeks of the Conference. The US continued to serve as English language coordinator.

Having completed Part XI during the intersessional meeting, the Drafting Committee worked on Annexes III and IV. In addition, it was directed by the Collegium to take up, as a priority matter, the PIP, Preparatory Commission, and Transitional Resolutions, as well as the new Annex IX. Although these texts prevented the Drafting Committee from making very much progress in its other work, the Collegium

insisted that the Committee continue to concentrate on them. This was the case even after it became clear that the PIP Resolution was being fundamentally renegotiated.

The English Language Group completed its analysis of the English version of the text, with the exception of Article 1 and the Preamble. In addition, the Group completed work on all proposals from other language groups through Article 7 of Annex III. The Coordinators were significantly further behind and, in fact, did not complete work on Annex VI, which the language groups finished during the Tenth Session.

The US delegation, supported by other members of the English Language Group, insisted on receiving translations of changes proposed by other language groups even if such changes were intended to apply to that language only. The US delegation believed that, if drafting a treaty in six equally authentic languages were to succeed, it was vital that the US be in a position to examine the texts in all languages for substantive harmonization and concordance.

The Drafting Committee will meet for five to six weeks in July-August 1982 in Geneva to complete all outstanding issues. An informal Plenary will meet in New York from September 22 to 24, 1982 to review and adopt Drafting Committee recommendations.

## APPENDICES

* Not included; easily available from other sources.

*Editor*

## APPENDIX B

*Following are statements by President Reagan on January 29, 1982, and by Ambassador James L. Malone, Special Representative of the President for the Third United Nations Conference on Law of the Sea, before the House Merchant Marine and Fisheries Committee on February 23, 1982.*

Statement by President Reagan:  January 29, 1982

The world's oceans are vital to the United States and other nations in diverse ways.  They represent waterways and airways essential to preserving the peace and to trade and commerce; are major sources for meeting increasing world food and energy demands and promise further resource potential.  They are a frontier for expanding scientific research and knowledge, a fundamental part of the global environment balance, and a great source of beauty, awe, and pleasure for mankind.

Developing international agreement for this vast ocean space, covering over half of the Earth's surface, has been a major challenge confronting the international community.  Since 1973 scores of nations have been actively engaged in the arduous task of developing a comprehensive treaty for the world's oceans at the Third UN Conference on Law of the Sea. The United States has been a major participant in this process.

Serious questions had been raised in the United States about parts of the Draft Convention, and last March I announced that my Administration would undertake a thorough review of the current draft and the degree to which it met US interests in the navigation, overflight, fisheries, environmental, deep seabed mining, and other areas covered by that Convention. We recognize that the last two sessions of the conference have been difficult, pending the completion of our review.  At the same time, we consider it important that a Law of the Sea treaty be such that the United States can join in and support it.  Our review has concluded that while most provisions of the Draft Convention are acceptable and consistent with US

interests, some major elements of the deep seabed mining regime are not acceptable.

I am announcing today that the United States will return to those negotiations and work with other countries to achieve an acceptable treaty. In the deep seabed mining area, we will seek changes necessary to correct those unacceptable elements and to achieve the goal of a treaty that:

- Will not deter development of any deep seabed mineral resources to meet national and world demand;

- Will assure national access to these resources by current and future qualified entities to enhance US security of supply, to avoid monopolization of the resources by the operating arm of the international Authority, and to promote the economic development of the resources;

- Will provide a decision-making role in the deep seabed regime that fairly reflects and effectively protects the political and economic interests and financial contributions of participating States;

- Will not allow for amendments to come into force without approval of the participating States, including in our case the advice and consent of the Senate;

- Will not set other undesirable precedents for international organizations; and

- Will be likely to receive the advice and consent of the Senate. In this regard, the Convention should not contain provisions for the mandatory transfer of private technology and participation by and funding for national liberation movements.

The United States remains committed to the multilateral treaty process for reaching agreement on law of the sea. If working together at the conference we can find ways to fulfill these key objectives, my Administration will support ratification.

I have instructed the Secretary of State and my Special Representative for the Law of the Sea Conference, in coordination with other responsible agencies, to embark immediately on the necessary consultations with other countries and to undertake further preparations for our participation in the conference.

Ambassador Malone's Statement:   February 23, 1982

I am pleased to appear before this committee today to brief you on the President's recent decision to resume US participation in the Law of the Sea Conference. With your permission, I will introduce the full text of the President's statement for the record.

In his public statement, the President made clear several points, which I would like to reiterate.

- It is important that a Law of the Sea treaty be fashioned so that the United States can join in and support it.

- Major elements of the deep seabed mining regime are not acceptable to the United States.

- We have six broad objectives with regard to the deep seabed mining regime, and we will be seeking changes in the draft treaty in order to achieve them.

- The United States remains committed to the multilateral treaty process and will support ratification if our six objectives are fulfilled.

We are now consulting with our principal allies, the Soviet Union, the leadership of the conference, and influential delegates from the conference, including the leadership of the Group of 77.

Beginning tomorrow, we will participate in a formal intersessional meeting of the conference. That will be an important opportunity to explore potential solutions to the problems we have raised with Part XI of the Draft Convention. During the first week of March, we will assess the results of our consultations and the intersessional meeting, determining whether we believe it is possible to negotiate satisfactory changes to the Draft Convention which meet the President's objectives. The assessment will describe what the US delegation believes to be an achievable package of improvements in Part XI. This assessment will be reviewed carefully before we proceed further.

During the February informal consultations, we have explained our problems with the Draft Convention in a clear and precise way. We have discussed those potential solutions which we believe would meet our

national interests and make the treaty acceptable to
the US.  I will make available a compendium of the
approaches to problems in Part XI which we are placing before the conference leaders in order to evaluate the prospects for successfully negotiating
changes that satisfy the President's objectives.
Let me turn now to those objectives.

The President stated that we will seek changes
necessary to correct unacceptable elements of the
draft treaty and to achieve our six objectives.

First, the treaty must not deter development of
any deep seabed mineral resources to meet national
and world demand.

The United States believes that its interests,
those of its allies, and, indeed, the interests of
the vast majority of nations will best be served by
developing the resources of the deep seabed as market
conditions warrant.  We have a consumer-oriented
philosophy.  The draft treaty, in our judgment, reflects a protectionist bias which would deter the
development of deep seabed mineral resources, including manganese nodules and any other deep seabed minerals such as the polymetallic sulfide deposits which
have received considerable publicity recently.

Many different provisions of the draft treaty
discourage development of seabed resources.  Chief
among them are:

- The production policies of the Authority which
place other priorities ahead of economically efficient
resource development;

- The production ceiling which limits the availability of minerals for global consumption;

- The limit on the number of mining operations
which could be conducted by any one country, thus potentially limiting our ability to supply US consumption needs from the seabed; and

- Broad areas of administrative and regulatory
discretion which, if implemented in accordance with
the Authority's production policies, would deter
seabed mineral development.

To meet the President's first objective, these and other related areas of Part XI would require change and improvement.

Second, the treaty must assure national access to those resources by current and future qualified entities to enhance US security of supply, avoid monopolization of the resources by the operating arm of the international Authority, and promote the economic development of the resources.

The draft treaty provides no assurance that qualified private applicants sponsored by the US Government will be awarded contracts. It is our strong view that all qualified applicants should be granted contracts and that the decision whether to grant a contract should be tied exclusively to the question of whether an applicant has satisfied objective qualification standards. We believe that when a sovereign State sponsors an applicant and certifies that the applicant meets the treaty's qualification standards, the Authority should accept such a certification unless a consensus of objective technical experts votes that the applicant's qualifications were falsely or improperly certified.

The Draft Convention also should make specific provision for the rights of private companies that have made pioneer investments in deep seabed mining. We are all aware that a few companies have devoted substantial resources to prospecting for deep seabed minerals and developing new technologies for their extraction. We recognize that there are different views as to the rights which pioneer investors have acquired, but practicality should guide us in this matter. Deep seabed mineral resources will not be made available for the benefit of mankind without the continuing efforts of pioneer miners. I am confident, therefore, that the conference can find ways and means to accommodate their special circumstances.

In addition, the draft treaty creates a system of privileges which discriminates against the private side of the parallel system. Rational private companies would, therefore, have little option but to enter joint ventures or other similar ventures either with the operating arm of the Authority, the Enterprise, or with developing countries. Not only would this deny the United States access to deep seabed minerals through its private companies because the private

access system would be uncompetitive but, under some scenarios, the Enterprise could establish a monopoly over deep seabed mineral resources.

To meet the President's second objective, therefore, qualified applicants should be granted contracts, the legal and commercial position of pioneer operators should be accommodated, and the parallel system should be designed to permit private miners to operate independently.

Third, the treaty must provide a decision-making role in the deep seabed regime that fairly reflects and effectively protects the political and economic ineterests and financial contributions of participating States.

The United States has a strong interest in an effective and fair Law of the Sea treaty which includes a viable seabed mining regime. As the largest potential consumer of seabed minerals, as a country whose private firms could invest substantial amounts in seabed mining, and as potentially the largest contributor to the Seabed Authority and to the financing of the Enterprise, our political and economic interests in any new international organization are far-reaching. The decision-making system in the Seabed Authority must reflect these realities. For example, a treaty which makes American access to natural resources of the seabed dependent on the voting power either of its competition or of those countries which do not wish to see these resources produced would not meet the President's objectives.

Similarly, the President's objectives would not be satisfied if minerals other than manganese nodules could be developed only after a decision was taken to promulgate rules and regulations to allow the exploitation of such minerals. In our judgment, the development of other seabed resources should proceed without restraint pending the development of rules and regulations.

We must be candid--many countries do not wish to see new sources of minerals produced from the seabed, because they believe that such production will jeopardize their own competitive position in the world markets. We do not criticize them for holding this view but do expect them to understand that the US national interest is not consistent with impediments to the

production of seabed minerals. A seabed mining regime which deters production is antithetical to the
interests of all nations in the economically efficient development of resources.

A way must be found to assure that any nation
like the United States, having a vital stake in the
Authority's decisions, has influence sufficient to
protect its interests. The decision-making system
should provide that, on issues of highest importance
to a nation, that nation will have affirmative influence on the outcome. Conversely, nations with
major economic interests should be secure in the
knowledge that they can prevent decisions adverse to
their interests. We will make detailed proposals to
the conference on ways to achieve these objectives.

Fourth, the treaty must not allow for amendments
to come into force without approval of the participating States, including in our case the advice and
consent of the Senate.

The draft treaty now permits two-thirds of the
States parties acting at the review conference to
adopt amendments to Part XI of the treaty which would
be binding on all States parties without regard to
their concurrence. It has been argued that a State
which objects to an amendment has the option to withdraw from the treaty if the amendment is imposed
without his consent. This proposal is obviously not
acceptable when dealing with major economic interests
of countries which have invested significant capital
in the development of deep seabed mining in an international treaty regime. We believe there are ways to
solve this problem, and we will be exploring them during the negotiations.

Fifth, the treaty must not set other undesirable
precedents for international organizations.

Most, if not all, of the adverse precedents
which would be established by the draft treaty could
be avoided by achieving the six objectives set out by
the President. Our negotiating efforts, however,
should not result in offsetting or replacing one undesirable precedent with another. Our task in returning to the negotiating table is to satisfy all of the
President's objectives. The job would not be complete if, for example, adverse precedents related to
artificial production limits and protection of land-

based minerals are avoided at the price of acquiescence on other issues of principle such as the mandatory transfer of technology.  In solving problems in
the draft treaty, we will be alert to the possibility that a particular solution may be viable in the
context of the Law of the Sea treaty but inappropriate as a precedent for some future negotiation.
As we proceed to seek solutions to problems in the
Law of the Sea negotiations, we will be mindful of
the broadest national interests and the relationship
of these negotiations to US participation in other
global institutions.

Sixth, the treaty must be likely to receive the
advice and consent of the Senate.  In this regard,
the Convention should not contain provisions for the
mandatory transfer of private technology and participation by and funding for national liberation movements.

The comprehensive policy review process was initiated because this Administration recognized that
the Senate could not and would not give its consent
to the emerging draft treaty on the Law of the Sea.
It is, however, our judgment that, if the President's
objectives as outlined are satisfied, the Senate
would approve the Law of the Sea treaty.  It would be
necessary, of course, to demonstrate concretely how
any renegotiated treaty texts have solved the problems raised by Members of the Congress and the public
which led to the review and how they have met the
President's objectives.

In this regard, there are certain issues to
which special attention must be called.  The President highlighted these in his sixth objective.  The
mandatory transfer of private technology and participation by and funding for national liberation movements create commercial and political difficulty of
such consequence that they must be singled out as issues requiring effective solutions.  These solutions
will have to be clearly defensible as total solutions
to the problem.

There is a deeply held view in our Congress that
one of America's greatest assets is its capacity for
innovation and invention and its ability to produce
advanced technology.  It is understandable, therefore,
that a treaty would be unacceptable to many Americans
if it required the United States or, more particularly

private companies to transfer that asset in a forced sale. That is why the problem must be solved.

I would like to emphasize the President's statement that, if his objectives are successfully met, he will support the ratification of this treaty. We will work with all Members of Congress, particularly those who have shown a special interest in this subject, in order to insure that they will be given an opportunity to give us their advice in advance of any commitments we make. We will encourage Members of Congress to participate actively in the work of our delegation and to keep abreast of developments at the conference. We will continue to work with members of the advisory committee and other interested Americans. We will do everything possible to avoid a situation in which we agree to draft treaty provisions which will later face political opposition.

What we want to do now is return to the bargaining table with a clear and firm position that meets our national interests. We believe there is a reservoir of good will at the conference, and we will work cooperatively and diligently at the conference to seek a result acceptable to all.

---

Published by the United States Department of State, Bureau of Public Affairs, Office of Public Communication, Editorial Division, Washington, D.C., February 1982. Editor: Phyllis Young.

A/CONF.62/L.132
22 April 1982
ORIGINAL: ENGLISH

REPORT OF THE PRESIDENT TO THE CONFERENCE
IN ACCORDANCE WITH RULE 37 OF THE RULES OF PROCEDURE

## Introduction

1. In accordance with the programme of work contained in document A.CONF. 62/116, the door was closed to the submission of amendments on Tuesday, 13 April at 6:00 p.m. By the deadline 30 amendments, viz. A/CONF. 62/L.96 to A/CONF.62/L.126 were duly received.

## Period of deferment

2. In accordance with rule 37, paragraph 2(a) of the rules of procedure, the President informed the Conference of his decision to defer the taking of a vote on the amendments for a period of eight calendar days, commencing 14 April and terminating on 21 April 1982.

## Debate on the amendments

3. In accordance with the programme of work, the Plenary met from 15 to 17 April 1982 in order to enable delegations to make statements on the amendments. Altogether 87 delegations took part in the debate. In addition, a number of delegations submitted written statements.

## The President's efforts to achieve general agreement

4. Both the programme of work and rule 37, paragraph 2(c) require the President, during the period of deferment, to make every effort with the assistance, as appropriate, of the General Committee to facilitate the achievement of general agreement.

5. In view of the large number of amendments submitted and the limited time available, the President addressed a letter to the sponsors of the amendments.

*[Items 6 through 15 are omitted, since they are irrelevant to this section.]*

## Treatment of preparatory investments

16. A number of delegations submitted amendments to Draft Resolution II of A/CONF.62/L.94.

17. The sponsors of these amendments collectively requested the President and the Chairman of the First Committee to undertake consultations on the amendments with a view to enhancing the prospects of achieving general agreement on the Draft Resolution.

18. The President, with the able assistance of his fraternal colleague, Chairman Engo, held a series of intensive consultations involving representatives of all the sponsors of the amendments and representatives of the different regional and interest groups.

19. As a result of these intensive consultations an ad referendum agreement was reached on the text of the Draft Resolution which would replace Draft Resolution II in A/CONF.62/L.94.

20. In the view of the President and of Chairman Engo, the new text of the Draft Resolution enjoys widespread and substantial support and offers a substantially improved prospect of achieving general agreement. The text of the draft resolution is contained in annex IV to this report.

## Modifications to Part XI of the Draft Convention

21. A number of amendments were submitted to the provision of Part XI of the Draft Convention and to Draft Resolution I in A/CONF.62/L.94.

22. At the request of the sponsors of these amendments and with the concurrence of other delegations, the President and Chairman Engo conducted intensive consultations on these amendments.

23. In assessing the results of these consultations, the President has borne in mind that the basic texts of the Conference are contained in A/CONF.62/L.78, A/CONF.62/L.93 and A/CONF.62/L.94, and any modifications thereon must offer a substantially improved prospect of achieving general agreement.

24. Guided by this criterion, the President felt able to recommend only three modifications to the provisions of Part XI in A/CONF.62/L.78.

25. The modifications to Articles 150, 155, and 161 are contained in annex V to this report.

Amendments to other parts of the Draft Convention

26. The President requested the Chairman of the Second Committee, H.E. Mr. Andres Aguilar, to assess the extent of support for the amendments submitted to Parts I to X of the Draft Convention.

-----

A/CONF.62/L.132/Corr.1
23 April 1982

REPORT OF THE PRESIDENT TO THE CONFERENCE
IN ACCORDANCE WITH RULE 37 OF THE RULES OF PROCEDURE

Corrigendum

Page 3, paragraph 19 should read

19. As a result of these intensive consultations, the President and Chairman Engo have proposed a new text.

-----

A/CONF.62/L.132/Add.1
22 April 1982

REPORT OF THE PRESIDENT TO THE CONFERENCE
IN ACCORDANCE WITH RULE 37 OF THE RULES OF PROCEDURE

Addendum

ANNEXES

ANNEX I

Proposed modifications to document A/CONF.62/L.93/ Corr.1

Article 156 as changed in document A/CONF.62/L.93/
Corr.1

Paragraph 3, lines 2 and 3

delete entitled to become Parties to the Convention
and substitute referred to in Article 305(b),
(c), (d), or (e),

Paragraph 3 will read:

3. Observers at the Third United Nations Conference
on the Law of the Sea who have signed the Final Act
and who are not referred to in Article 305(b), (c),
(d), or (e), shall have the right to participate in
the Authority as observers, in accordance with its
rules, regulations and procedures.

Draft Decision of the Conference in document
A/CONF.62/L.94

1. Delete the titles

   DRAFT DECISION OF THE CONFERENCE

   NATIONAL LIBERATION MOVEMENTS

   and substitute

   DRAFT RESOLUTION IV

   THE THIRD UNITED NATIONS CONFERENCE ON THE
   LAW OF THE SEA,

2. Add a preambular paragraph to read

   Bearing in mind that national liberation movements
   have been invited to participate in the Conference
   as observers in accordance with rule 62 of its
   rules of procedure,

3. The text of the Draft Decision becomes the operative paragraph of the Draft Resolution

4. In the paragraph of the text of the Draft Decision, line 1

   delete The Conference decides
   and substitute Decides

The Draft Resolution will read:

## DRAFT RESOLUTION IV

The Third United Natins Conference on the Law
of the Sea,

**Bearing in mind** that national liberation movements have been invited to participate in the
Conference as observers in accordance with rule
62 of its rules of procedure,

**Decides** that the national liberation movements,
which have been participating in the Third United
Nations Conference on the Law of the Sea, shall
be entitled to sign the Final Act of the Conference, in their capacity as observers.

-----

## ANNEX II

Proposed modifications to document A/CONF.62/L.93

Annex IX, article 4, paragraph 6

    1.  Delete paragraph 6.

    2.  Renumber paragraph 7 accordingly.

-----

## ANNEX III

Proposed modifications

    1.  Article 171 of A/CONF.62/L.78 add a new
        subparagraph (f)

        *(f) payments to a compensation fund, in
            accordance with article 151.4, whose
            sources are to be recommended by the
            Economic Planning Commission."

    2.  Draft resolution I (document A/CONF.62/
        L.94)

## Add a new paragraph 8 bis

8 <u>bis</u>  "The Commission shall establish a special commission on the problems which would be encountered by developing land-based producers likely to be most seriously affected by the production of the Area and entrust to it the functions referred to in paragraph 5(i)."

———

ANNEX IV    A/CONF.62/L.132/
            Add.1    English

DRAFT RESOLUTION II GOVERNING PREPARATORY INVESTMENT
IN
PIONEER ACTIVITIES RELATING TO POLYMETALLIC NODULES

The Third United Nations Conference on the Law
of the Sea,

Having this day adopted the Convention on the
Law of the Sea (the "Convention"),

Having this day also established by resolution
the Preparatory Commission for the International Seabed Authority and the International Tribunal for the
Law of the Sea (the "Commission") and directed it to
prepare such draft rules, regulations and procedures
as it deems necessary to enable the Authority to commence its functions, as well as to make recommendations for the early entry into effective operation
of the Enterprise,

Desirous of making provision for investments by
States and other entities made in a manner compatible
with the international regime set forth in Part XI of
the Convention and the annexes relating thereto,
prior to the entry into force of the Convention,

Recognizing the need to ensure that the Enterprise will be provided with the funds, technology
and expertise necessary to enable it to keep pace
with the States and other entities referred to in
the preceding paragraph, with respect to activities
in the Area,

Decides as follows:

1.  For the purposes of this resolution:

(a)  "pioneer investor" refers to:

(i)  France, Japan, India and the Union of
    Soviet Socialist Republics, or a State
    enterprise of each of those States or
    one natural or juridical person which
    possesses the nationality of or is ef-
    fectively controlled by each of those
    States, or their nationals, provided

that the States concerned sign the Convention and the States or State enter-
prises or natural or juridical persons
have expended, prior to 1 January 1983,
an amount equivalent to at least $US
30 million (United States dollars calculated in constant dollars relative to
1982) in pioneer activities and have expended no less than 10 per cent of that
amount in the location, survey, and
evaluation of the area referred to in
paragraph 3(a);

(ii) four entities, whose components being
natural or juridical persons possess the
nationality of, or are effectively controlled by, one or more of the following
States: Belgium, Canada, the Federal Republic of Germany, Italy, Japan, Netherlands, the United Kingdom of Great Britain and Northern Ireland and the United
States of America or their nationals,
provided that the certifying State or
States sign the Convention and the entity concerned has expended, prior to
1 January 1983, the levels of expenditure and for the purpose stated in subparagraph (i);

(iii) any developing State signatory of the
Convention or any State entity or natural or juridical person which possesses
the nationality of such State or is effectively controlled by it or its nationals, or any group of the foregoing
which, prior to 1 January 1985, has expended the levels of expenditure and for
the purpose stated in subparagraph (i);

The rights of the pioneer investor may devolve upon its successor in interest.

(b) "pioneer activities" means undertakings, commitments of resources, investigations, findings, research, engineering development, and
other activities relevant to the identification, discovery, and systematic analysis and
evaluation of polymetallic nodules and to the
determination of the technical and economic

feasibility of exploitation. Pioneer activities include:

(i) any at-sea observation and evaluation activity which has as its objective the establishment and documentation of:

a the nature, shape, concentration, location and grade of polymetallic nodules;

b the environmental, technical, and other appropriate factors which must be taken into account prior to exploitation;

(ii) the taking from the deep seabed of polymetallic nodules with a view to the designing, fabricating, and testing of equipment which is intended to be used in the exploitation of polymetallic nodules;

(c) "certifying State" means a signatory of the Convention standing in the same relation to a pioneer investor as would a sponsoring State pursuant to Annex III, article 4 of the Convention and which certifies the level of investment specified in subparagraph (a);

(d) "polymetallic nodules" means one of the resources of the Area, consisting of any deposit or accretion on or just below the surface of the deep seabed consisting of nodules which contain manganese, nickel, cobalt, and copper;

(e) "pioneer area" means an area allocated by the Commission to a pioneer investor for pioneer activities pursuant to this resolution. A pioneer area shall not exceed 150,000 square kilometers. The pioneer investor shall relinquish portions of the pioneer area to revert to the international Area, in accordance with the following schedule:

(i) 20 percent of the area allocated by the end of the third year from the date of the allocation;

(ii) an additional 10 per cent of the area allocated by the end of the fifth year from the date of the allocation;

(iii) an additional 20 per cent of the area allocated or such larger amount as would exceed the exploitation area decided upon by the Authority in its rules, regulations and procedures, after eight years from the date of the allocation of the area or the date of the award of a production authorization, whichever is earlier.

(f) "area," "Authority," "activities in the Area" and "resources" shall have the meanings assigned to those terms under the Convention.

2. As soon as the Preparatory Commission begins to function, any State signatory of the Convention may apply to the Commission on its own behalf or on behalf of any State enterprise or entity or natural or juridical person specified in paragraph 1(a), for registration as a pioneer investor. The Commission shall register the applicant as a pioneer investor if the application:

(a) in the case of a State signatory, is accompanied by a statement certifying the level of expenditure made in accordance with paragraph 1(a), and, in all other cases, a certificate concerning such level of expenditure issued by a certifying State or States; and

(b) is in conformity with the other provisions of this resolution, including paragraph 5.

3. (a) Every application shall cover a total area, which need not be a single continuous area, sufficiently large and of sufficient estimated commercial value to allow two mining operations. The application shall indicate the co-ordinates of the area, defining the total area and dividing it into two parts of equal estimated commercial value and contain all the data available to the applicant with respect to both parts of the area. Such data shall include, inter alia,

information relating to mapping, sampling, the density of nodules and the composition of metals in them. In dealing with such data, the Commission and its staff shall act in accordance with the relevant provisions of the Convention and its Annexes concerning the confidentiality of data.

(b) Within 45 days of receiving the data required by subparagraph (a) above, the Commission shall designate the part of the area to be reserved in accordance with the Convention for the conduct of activities by the Authority through the Enterprise or in association with developing States. The other part of the area shall be allocated to the pioneer investor as a pioneer area.

4. No pioneer investor may be registered in respect of more than one pioneer area. In the case of a pioneer investor which is made up of two or more components, none of such components may apply to be registered as a pioneer investor in its own right or under paragraph 1(a)(iii).

5. (a) Any State signatory which is a prospective certifying State shall ensure, before making applications to the Preparatory Commission under paragraph 2, that areas in respect of which applications are made do not overlap with one another or with areas previously allocated as pioneer areas. The States concerned shall keep the Commission currently and fully informed of any efforts to resolve conflicts with respect to overlapping claims and the results thereof;

(b) Certifying States shall, prior to the entry into force of the Convention, ensure that pioneer activities are conducted in a manner compatible with it.

(c) In carrying out the conflict resolution procedure required under subparagraph (a) above, the prospective certifying States, including all potential claimants, shall resolve their conflicts by

negotiations within a reasonable period.
If such conflicts have not been resolved
by 1 March 1983, the prospective certifying States shall arrange for the submission of all such claims to binding
arbitration in accordance with UNCITRAL
Arbitration Rules to commence not later
than 1 May 1983 and to be completed by
1 December 1984. If one of the States
concerned does not wish to participate
in the arbitration, it shall arrange for
a juridical person of its nationality to
represent it in the arbitration. The
arbitration tribunal may, for good
cause, extend the deadline for the making of the award for one or more 30-day
periods.

(d) In determining the issue as to which applicant involved in a conflict shall be
awarded all or part of each area in conflict, the arbitral tribunal shall find
a solution which is fair and equitable,
having regard, with respect to each applicant involved in the conflict, to the
following factors:

(i) deposit of the relevant co-ordinates
with the prospective certifying
State or States not later than the
date of adoption of the Final Act or
1 January 1983, whichever is earlier;

(ii) the continuity and extent of past
activities relevant to each area in
conflict and the application area of
which it is a part;

(iii) the date on which each pioneer investor concerned or predecessor in
interest or component organization
thereof commenced activities at sea
in the application area;

(iv) the financial cost of activities measured in constant dollars relevant to
each area in conflict and to the application area of which it is a part;
and

(v) the time when activities were carried out and the quality of activities.

6. A pioneer investor registered pursuant to
this resolution shall, as from the date of such registration, have the exclusive right to carry out
pioneer activities in the pioneer area allocated to
him.

7. (a) Every applicant for registration as a
pioneer investor shall pay to the Commission a fee of $US 250,000. When the
pioneer investor applies to the Authority for a plan of work for exploration
and exploitation the fee referred to in
Annex III, article 13, paragraph 2 shall
be $US 250,000.

(b) Every registered pioneer investor shall
pay an annual fixed fee of $US 1 million
commencing from the date of the allocation of the pioneer area. The payments
shall be made by the pioneer investor
to the Authority upon the approval of
his plan of work for exploration and exploitation. The financial arrangements
undertaken pursuant to such plan of work
shall be adjusted to take account of the
payments made pursuant to this paragraph.

(c) Every registered pioneer investor shall
agree to incur periodic expenditures,
with respect to the pioneer area allocated to it, until approval of its plan
of work pursuant to paragraph 8, of an
amount to be determined by the Commission. The amount should be reasonably
related to the size of the pioneer area
and the expenditures which would be expected of a bona fide operator who intends to bring the area into commercial
production within a reasonable time.

8. (a) Within six months of the entry into
force of the Convention and certification by the Commission in accordance
with paragraph 11 hereof of compliance
with the provisions of this resolution,

575

the pioneer investor so registered shall apply to the Authority for a plan of work for exploration and exploitation, in accordance with the Convention. The plan of work in respect of such application shall comply with and be governed by the relevant provisions of the Convention and the rules, regulations and procedures of the Authority, including the operational requirements, the financial requirements and the undertakings concerning the transfer of technology. Accordingly, the Authority shall approve such application.

(b) When an application is made by an entity other than a State, pursuant to subparagraph (a), the certifying State or States shall be deemed to be the sponsoring State for the purposes of Annex III, article 4 of the Convention, and shall thereupon assume such obligations.

(c) No plan of work for exploration and exploitation shall be approved unless the certifying State is a party to the Convention. In the case of the entities referred to in paragraph 1(a)(ii), the plan of work for exploration and exploitation shall not be approved unless all the States whose natural or juridical persons comprise those entities are parties to the Convention. If any such State fails to ratify the Convention within six months after it has received a notification from the Authority that an application by it, or sponsored by it, is pending, its status as a pioneer investor or certifying State as the case may be, shall terminate, unless the Council, by a majority of three-fourths of its members present and voting decides to postpone the terminal date by a period not exceeding six months.

9. (a) In the allocation of production authorization, in accordance with article 151 of the Convention and Annex III, article 7, the pioneer investors who have obtained approval of plans of work for

exploration and exploitation, shall have priority over all applicants other than the Enterprise as contained in paragraph 2(c) of article 151. After each of the pioneer investors has obtained production authorization for its first mine site, the priority for the Enterprise contained in Annex III, article 7, paragraph 6 shall apply.

(b) Production authorizations shall be issued to each pioneer investor within 30 days of the date on which the pioneer investor notifies the Authority that it will commence commercial production within five years. If a pioneer investor is unable to begin production within the period of five years for reasons beyond its control, it shall apply to the Legal and Technical Commission for an extension of time. The said Commission shall grant such extension of time, for a period not exceeding five years and not subject to further extension, if it is satisfied that the pioneer investor cannot begin on an economically viable basis at the time originally planned. Nothing in this subparagraph shall prevent the Enterprise or any other pioneer applicant, who has notified the Authority that it will commence commercial production within five years, from being given a priority over any applicant who has obtained an extension of time under this subparagraph.

(c) If, upon being given notice, pursuant to subparagraph (b), that the Authority determines that the commencement of commercial production within five years would exceed the production ceiling in Article 151(2), the applicant shall hold a priority over any other applicant for the award of the next production authorization allowed by the production ceiling.

(d) In the event that two or more pioneer investors apply for production authorizations to begin commercial production

at the same time and article 151(a)
would not permit all such production to
commence simultaneously, the Authority
shall notify the pioneer investors concerned. Within three months of such
notification, they shall decide whether
and, if so, to what extent they wish to
apportion the allowable tonnage among
themselves.

(e) If, pursuant to subparagraph (d) above,
they decide not to apportion the available production among themselves, they
shall agree on an order of priority for
production authorizations, and all subsequent applications for production
authorizations will be granted after
those referred to in this subparagraph
have been approved.

(f) If, pursuant to subparagraph (d), they
decide to apportion the available production among themselves, the Authority
shall award each of them a production
authorization for such lesser quantity
as they have agreed. In each such case
the stated production requirements of
the applicant will be approved, and their
full production will be allowed as soon
as the production ceiling admits of additional capacity sufficient for the applicants involved in the competition. All
subsequent applications for production
authorizations will only be granted after
the requirements of this subparagraph
have been met and the applicant is no
longer subject to the reduction of production provided for in this subparagraph.

(g) If the parties fail to reach agreement
within the stated time period, the matter
shall be decided immediately by the .....
.................... in accordance with
the criteria set forth in article 7,
paragraphs 3 and 5 of Annex III.

10. (a) Any rights acquired by entities, natural
or juridical persons which possess the
nationality of or are effectively controlled by a State or States whose status

as certifying State has been terminated, shall lapse unless the pioneer investor alters its nationality and sponsorship within six months of the date of such termination, as provided for in subparagraph (c).

(b) A pioneer investor may alter its nationality and sponsorship from that prevailing at the time of its registration as a pioneer investor to that of any State party to the Convention which has effective control over the pioneer investor in terms of paragraph 1(a);

(c) Alterations of nationality and sponsorship pursuant to this paragraph shall not affect any right or priority conferred on a pioneer investor pursuant to paragraphs 6 and 8 of this resolution.

11. The Commission shall:

(a) provide pioneer investors with the certificates of compliance with the provisions of this resolution referred to in paragraph 8 hereof; and

(b) incorporate in its final report provided for in paragraph 10 of resolution No. I of the Conference, details of all registrations of pioneer investors and allocation of pioneer areas pursuant to this resolution.

12. In order to ensure that the Enterprise is able to carry out activities in the Area in such a manner as to remain in step with States and other entities:

(a) Every registered pioneer investor shall:

(i) carry out exploration at the request of the Commission in the area reserved pursuant to paragraph 3 of this resolution in connexion with its application for activities by the Authority through the Enterprise or in association with developing States, on the basis that the costs

so incurred plus interest thereon at the rate of 10 per cent per annum shall be reimbursed;

(ii) provide training at all levels for personnel designated by the Commission;

(iii) undertake prior to the entry into force of the Convention, to perform the obligations prescribed in the provisions of the Convention relating to transfer of technology;

(b) Every certifying State shall:

(i) ensure that the necessary funds are made available to the Enterprise in a timely manner in accordance with the provisions of the Convention, upon its entry into force; and

(ii) report periodically to the Commission on the activities carried out by it, by its entities or natural or juridical persons.

13. The Authority and its organs shall recognize and honour the rights and obligations arising from this resolution and the decisions of the Preparatory Commission taken pursuant to it.

14. Without prejudice to paragraph 13, this resolution shall have effect until the entry into force of the Convention.

15. Nothing in this resolution shall derogate from the provisions of Annex III, article 6, paragraph 3(c) of the Convention.

ANNEX V

Proposed modifications to document A/CONF/62/L.78

1. Article 150

(a) Delete the word "development" from subparagraph (a).

(b) Insert a new subparagraph (a) as follows:

(a) the development of the resources of the Area;

(c) Renumber the subparagraphs accordingly.

2. Article 155

Reformulate paragraph 3 as follows:

"the decision-making procedure applicable at the Conference shall be the same as that applicable at the Third United Nations Conference on the Law of the Sea. The Conference shall make every effort to reach agreement on any amendments by way of consensus, and there should be no voting on such matters until all efforts at consensus have been exhausted."

3. Article 161

Reverse the order of paragraph 1(a) and (b) and add the following to the end of new paragraph 1(a):

"as well as the largest consumer".

-----

A/CONF.62/L.132/
Add.1/Corr.1
23 April 1982

REPORT OF THE PRESIDENT TO THE CONFERENCE
IN ACCORDANCE WITH RULE 37 OF THE RULES OF PROCEDURE

Corrigendum

Annex IV, page 1, paragraph 1(a)(ii), line 1:

After juridical persons add 1/

---

1/    For their identity and composition see
"Sea-bed mineral resource development: recent
activities of the International Consortia" and
addendum, published by the Department of International Economic and Social Affairs of the
United Nations (ST/ESA/107).

-----

A/CONF.62/L.141
29 April 1982

REPORT OF THE PRESIDENT TO THE CONFERENCE

1. I hope this will be the last report which I shall make to the Conference. You will recall that on 23 April 1982, I submitted to you a report in accordance with rule 37 of the rules of procedure. That report is contained in document A/CONF.62/L.132 and Corr.1 and Add.1 and Corr.1. Yesterday and this morning, 53 delegations made statements on that report and on the proposals contained in the addendum to the report. This afternoon and this evening, I shall study carefully the records of that debate and, based upon my assessments of that record, I shall make an appropriate recommendation to the Plenary tomorrow morning.

2. After the exciting, momentous and, for me, exhausting events of last Monday, 26 April, I had wrongly assumed that my work was done. This was unfortunately not to be the case. The representatives of the Group of 77 and the representatives of the Eastern European (Socialist) Group approached me and Chairman Paul Bamela Engo to hold further informal consultations on the draft resolution governing preparatory investments in pioneer activities relating to polymetallic nodules, as contained in Annex IV of A/CONF.62/L.132/Addendum 1. In addition, the representatives of a number of industrialized countries requested Chairman Engo and me to hold further consultations on some remaining difficulties which they had on provisions of Part XI of the Draft Convention and its annexes. Following appropriate consultations Chairman Engo and I, with the able assistance of my good friend from Fiji, Ambassador Satya Nandan, held intensive informal consultations on 27 and 28 April. In this report, I shall attempt to give you an account of the results of those consultations.

The PIP Draft Resolution in Annex IV of A/CONF. 62/
L.132/Addendum 1

3. The representatives of the Group of 77 made three requests. First, they maintained that the size of the pioneer area contained in paragraph 1(e) is too large and should be reduced. This position was supported by Japan. The representatives of the Group

of 77 also requested that the relinquishment procedure in paragraph 1(e) should be accelerated and the
areas relinquished should not be in bits and pieces
but in contiguous areas.  Second, the Group of 77
requested that in paragraph 9(a), the Enterprise
should be guaranteed production authorization in respect of two mine sites instead of one, and that the
production authorization of the Enterprise should enjoy priority over the pioneer investors.  Third, the
Group of 77 requested the industrialized countries
that they should assist the Enterprise in financing
the exploration and exploitation of the second mine
site.

4.  The third demand of the Group of 77 was strongly
opposed by the Soviet Union and others, who argued
that this was an unacceptable attempt to reopen the
negotiations on financial matters which had been conducted in Negotiating Group 2 and which had been
settled.

5.  In respect of the first and second demands, a
deal was struck whereby in return for the Group of 77
not insisting on its position on paragraph 1(e), the
industrialized countries will agree that the Enterprise should have production authorization for two
mine sites, and such production authorization shall
enjoy priority over the pioneer investors.  This proposed reformulation of paragraph 9(a) is contained in
the addendum to this report.

Paragraph 1(a)(ii)

6.  In respect of paragraph 1(a)(ii), the Soviet
Union, supported by the other members of the Eastern
European (Socialist) Group made two complaints.
Their first complaint was that it was legally imper-
missible and inappropriate for an international diplo-
matic conference, such as this, to decide to grant the
status of a pioneer investor to private companies
which will be identified by means of a reference to a
United Nations document.  The legal opinion of the
Legal Counsel of the United Nations was sought.  Mr.
Suy's legal opinion and the reply of the Soviet Union
thereto are contained in document A/CONF.62/L.133.
The response of the Legal Counsel to the Soviet
Union's reply is contained in A/CONF.62/L.139.  The
United Nations Legal Counsel is of the opinion that
the approach adopted in paragraph 1(a)(ii) is legally

permissible and consistent with the practice of the United Nations. I concur with this opinion.

## The complaint that paragraph 1(a)(ii) is discriminatory

7. The second complaint of the Soviet Union and its colleagues from the Eastern European (Socialist) Group was that paragraph 1(a)(ii) discriminates against the States referred to in 1(a)(i) and 1(a)(iii). Their argument was that in the case of the States referred to in 1(a)(i) and 1(a)(iii), every State must sign the Convention before its State enterprise, its natural or juridical person could qualify as the pioneer investor. In the case of paragraph 1(a)(ii), if a consortium consists of four companies from four States, it is not required that all four States must sign the Convention before the consortia could be registered as a pioneer investor. On principle, there was merit in the Soviet complaint.

8. However, in return for this concession, the representatives of the Group of 77 were able to extract from the industrialized countries an even greater concession in paragraph 8(c). In paragraph 8(c), no plan of work for exploration and exploitation shall be approved for any of the consortia referred to in paragraph 1(a)(ii) unless all the States whose natural or juridical persons comprise those consortia are parties to the Convention. This requirement is even higher than that contained in the Draft Convention and in Annex III. For this reason, I believe that the concession by the Group of 77 in paragraph 1(a)(ii) is more than compensated by the concession by the industrialized countries in paragraph 8(c).

9. I should also like to point out that the principle of non-discrimination is a double-edged sword. The principle of non-discrimination means, in law, treating equals equally and giving differential treatment to those who are not equals. One could point out that the Soviet Union is a relative newcomer in the development of seabed mining technology, equipment, and expertise. One could almost point out that under paragraph 1(a)(i), the Soviet Union is guaranteed one mine site, whereas in Paragraph 1(a)(ii), the seven States, not counting Japan, have to share four mine sites.

## Proposed modifications to Part XI and Annex III

10. On the very first day of this session of the
Conference, I made a statement in which I reaffirmed,
on behalf of the Collegium, our commitment to work
for the adoption of the Convention, preferably by
consensus. With respect to the proposals of the
United States and the other co-sponsors of A/CONF.
62/L.121, I had informed the Conference of the parameters within which any productive negotiations
and consultations must be conducted. What are these
parameters? First, any proposed modification must
not call into question the fundamental framework and
elements of the existing text of Part XI and its
annexes. Second, any proposed modification must
take into account the interest of other countries
and must not be harmful to some or all of them.
Third, the proposed modification must be negotiated
within the framework and deadlines set out in document A/CONF.62/L.116. It is the desire of every
delegation in this Conference to have a Convention
which will be supported by all States, including the
United States. I believe I am right when I say that
the Conference is willing to pay a price in order to
obtain the support of the United States for the Convention. That price is not, however, an unlimited
one. It must be a reasonable price. It must be a
price which does not hurt the interest of other
countries, especially the developing countries.
Guided by these considerations, I have proposed in
the addendum to this report, a number of modifications to Part XI and to Annex III which, in my view,
do not hurt the interests of the developing countries
or the countries of the Eastern European (Socialist)
Group. The proposed modifications will enhance the
prospects that the United States and the other major
industrialized countries will join us in the adoption
of the Convention tomorrow and will subsequently sign
and ratify the Convention.

11. I will conclude my statement by making an appeal
to all the delegations in the Conference to support
the proposals contained in the addendum to this report. To the developing countries, I have this to
say. I know that what I am asking you to do is to
agree, essentially, to make a series of unilateral
concessions to the United States and other industrialized countries. But I ask you to bear in mind that
the concessions which I am asking you to make do not
hurt in any significant way, the interests of your

Group or of your countries. I believe it is a price
worth paying in order to enhance the prospects of
attracting universal support for our Convention. We
must also not forget that Part XI is not the only
part of our Convention. There are many other parts
of the Convention in which our countries have strong,
concrete, and vital interests. Because of the package-deal principle, we cannot adopt the one part
without the other. Let me give you an example to
illustrate my point. This Convention, if adopted,
is a landmark achievement for the landlocked States
in respect of their right of access to and from the
sea and freedom of transit.

12. To the United States and the other co-sponsors
of A/CONF.62/L.121, I address this appeal. I know
that the modifications which I have proposed to Part
XI and its annexes contained in the addendum to
A/CONF.62/L.132 and the addendum to this report look
meager compared to the demands in A/CONF.62/L.121. I
want to assure you that Chairman Engo and I have,
within the parameters which we set out for ourselves,
gone as far as we can to assist you. We believe that
these proposed modifications do address most of your
fundamental concerns, and we hope that it will be
possible for you to join the Conference tomorrow in
adopting the Convention.

13. To the members of the Eastern European (Socialist) Group, I address the following appeal. Nothing
that Chairman Engo and I have proposed, by way of
modifications to Part XI and its annexes, calls into
question the fundamental framework of the existing
text or is injurious to your interest. We appeal to
you to support our proposals.

14. Finally, I cannot conclude without paying a special tribute to the 11 good samaritans who co-sponsored document A/CONF.62/L.104. At a time when the Group
of 77 and the United States were locked in a confrontation, you came to our rescue. You built a bridge
between them. You opened up channels of communication
and dialogue. You have made it possible for Chairman
Engo and me to build upon your compromise proposals.

15. We have a rendezvous with history tomorrow.
With your help, your understanding, your cooperation,
and your good will, I am confident that we will succeed in keeping that rendezvous.

A/CONF.62/L.141/Add.1
28 April 1982

REPORT OF THE PRESIDENT TO THE CONFERENCE

Addendum

1. Proposed modification to document A/CONF.62/L.78

Unfair Economic Practices

Article 151 (2) bis

Rights and obligations relating to unfair economic practices under relevant multilateral trade agreements shall apply to the exploration and exploitation of minerals from the Area. In the settlement of disputes arising under this provision, States Parties which are Parties to such multilateral trade agreements shall have recourse to the dispute settlement procedures of such agreements.

Renumber the following articles accordingly.

2. Proposed modification to document A/CONF.62/L.78

Article 151

Reformulate paragraph 3 as follows:

The Authority shall have the power to limit the level of production of minerals from the Area, other than minerals from nodules, under such conditions and applying such methods as may be appropriate by adopting regulations in accordance with article 161, paragraph 7.

3. Proposed modification to document A/CONF.62/L.78

(a) In article 162(2)(n)(ii) insert the following sentences after the second sentence:

Priority shall be given to the adoption of rules, regulations and procedures for the exploration and exploitation of polymetallic nodules. Rules, regulations and procedures for the exploration and exploitation of any resource other than polymetallic nodules shall be adopted, within three years from the date of a request to the Authority by

any of its members to adopt such rules, regulations and procedures in respect of such
resource.

(b) In the last sentence, change the first word
"Such" to "All".

4. Proposed modification to document A/CONF.62/L.78,
article 155, paragraph 4

Alter the majority required from "two-thirds" to
"three-fourths".

5. Proposed modification to Annex III of document
A/CONF.62/L.78

(a) Add a new paragraph 3 (bis) to article 5
to read as follows:

3 (bis) If a sponsoring State is unable to ensure
the performance by the operator of the
undertakings referred to in paragraph 3,
the sponsoring State shall assume and
perform the operator's undertakings. If
the sponsoring State fails to carry out
its undertakings and a dispute arises in
relation thereto, the operator shall be
subject to the provisions of paragraph 4
of this Article.

(b) Renumber paragraphs 4 to 8 accordingly.

6. Proposed modification to Annex III in document
A/CONF.62/L.78

Reformulate the chapeau of paragraph 3 of article
6 as follows:

3. All proposed plans of work shall be dealt
with in the order in which they are received.
The proposed plans of work shall comply with
and be governed by the relevant provisions of
the Convention and the rules, regulations and
procedures of the Authority, including the
operational requirements, the financial contributions, and the undertakings concerning
the transfer of technology. If the proposed
plans of work conform to these requirements,
the Authority shall approve such plans of
work provided that they are in accordance

with the uniform and non-discriminatory requirements established by the rules, regulations and procedures of the Authority, unless:

7. Proposed modification to Annex IV of A/CONF.62/ L.132/Add.1

Reformulate paragraph 9(a) to read as follows:

9(a) In the allocation of production authorization, in accordance with article 151 of the Convention and Annex III, article 7, the pioneer investors who have obtained approval of plans of work for exploration and exploitation, shall have priority over all applicants other than the Enterprise which shall be entitled to production authorization for two mine sites including that referred to in article 151, paragraph 2(c). After each of the pioneer investors has obtained production authorization for its first mine site, the priority for the Enterprise contained in Annex III, article 7, paragraph 6 shall apply.

-----

A/CONF.62/L.141/
Add.1/Corr.1
30 April 1982

REPORT OF THE PRESIDENT TO THE CONFERENCE

Corrigendum

Page 2

Delete paragraph 5.

-----

APPENDIX H

VOTES CAST BY DELEGATIONS

ON THE ADOPTION OF THE TREATY TEXT

April 30, 1982

VOTES CAST BY DELEGATIONS ON THE ADOPTION OF THE TREATY TEXT, APRIL 30, 1982

| Country | Y | N | A |
|---|---|---|---|
| Afghanistan | Y | | |
| Albania | Y | | |
| Algeria | Y | | |
| Angola | Y | | |
| Antigua/Barbuda | Y | | |
| Argentina | Y | | |
| Australia | Y | | |
| Austria | Y | | |
| Bahamas | Y | | |
| Bahrain | Y | | |
| Bangladesh | Y | | |
| Barbados | Y | | |
| Belgium | | | A |
| Belize | Y | | |
| Benin | Y | | |
| Bhutan | Y | | |
| Bolivia | Y | | |
| Botswana | Y | | |
| Brazil | Y | | |
| Bulgaria | | | A |
| Burma | Y | | |
| Burundi | Y | | |
| Byelorussian SSR | | | A |
| Canada | Y | | |
| Cape Verde | Y | | |
| Centr.Afric.Rep. | Y | | |
| Chad | Y | | |
| DPR Korea | Y | | |
| Nauru | Y | | |

| Country | Y | N | A |
|---|---|---|---|
| Chile | Y | | |
| China | Y | | |
| Colombia | Y | | |
| Comoros | | | |
| Congo | Y | | |
| Costa Rica | Y | | |
| Cuba | Y | | |
| Cyprus | Y | | |
| Czechoslovakia | | | A |
| Dem.Kampuchea | Y | | |
| Dem. Yemen | Y | | |
| Denmark | Y | | |
| Djibouti | Y | | |
| Dominica | | | |
| Dominican Rep. | Y | | |
| Ecuador | Y | | |
| Egypt | Y | | |
| El Salvador | Y | | |
| Equat.Guinea | | | |
| Ethiopia | Y | | |
| Fiji | Y | | |
| Finland | Y | | |
| France | Y | | |
| Gabon | Y | | |
| Gambia | | | |
| German D.R. | | | A |
| Holy See | | | |
| Rep. of Korea | Y | | |

| Country | Y | N | A |
|---|---|---|---|
| Germany, F.R. | | | A |
| Ghana | Y | | |
| Greece | Y | | |
| Grenada | Y | | |
| Guatemala | Y | | |
| Guinea | Y | | |
| Guinea-Bissau | Y | | |
| Guyana | Y | | |
| Haiti | Y | | |
| Honduras | Y | | |
| Hungary | | | A |
| Iceland | Y | | |
| India | Y | | |
| Indonesia | Y | | |
| Iran | Y | | |
| Iraq | Y | | |
| Ireland | Y | | |
| Israel | | N | |
| Italy | | | A |
| Ivory Coast | Y | | |
| Jamaica | Y | | |
| Japan | Y | | |
| Jordan | Y | | |
| Kenya | Y | | |
| Kuwait | Y | | |
| Lao P.D.R. | Y | | |
| Kiribati | | | |
| San Marino | Y | | |

| Y | N | A | Country |
|---|---|---|---|
| Y | | | Lebanon |
| Y | | | Lesotho |
| | | | Liberia |
| Y | | | Libyan A.J. |
| | | A | Luxembourg |
| Y | | | Madagascar |
| Y | | | Malawi |
| Y | | | Malaysia |
| | | | Maldives |
| Y | | | Mali |
| Y | | | Malta |
| Y | | | Mauritania |
| Y | | | Mauritius |
| Y | | | Mexico |
| | | A | Mongolia |
| Y | | | Morocco |
| Y | | | Mozambique |
| Y | | | Nepal |
| | | A | Netherlands |
| Y | | | New Zealand |
| Y | | | Nicaragua |
| Y | | | Niger |
| Y | | | Nigeria |
| Y | | | Norway |
| Y | | | Oman |
| Y | | | Pakistan |
| Y | | | Liechtenstein |
| Y | | | Switzerland |
| Y | | | Panama |
| Y | | | Papua N Guinea |
| Y | | | Paraguay |
| Y | | | Peru |
| Y | | | Philippines |
| | | A | Poland |
| Y | | | Portugal |
| Y | | | Qatar |
| Y | | | Romania |
| Y | | | Rwanda |
| Y | | | Saint Lucia |
| Y | | | St. Vincent-Gren. |
| Y | | | Samoa |
| Y | | | Sao Tome/Principe |
| Y | | | Saudi Arabia |
| Y | | | Senegal |
| Y | | | Seychelles |
| Y | | | Sierra Leone |
| Y | | | Singapore |
| | | | Solomon Islands |
| Y | | | Somalia |
| | | | South Africa |
| | | A | Spain |
| Y | | | Sri Lanka |
| Y | | | Sudan |
| Y | | | Suriname |
| Y | | | Monaco |
| | | | Tonga |
| Y | | | Swaziland |
| Y | | | Sweden |
| Y | | | Syrian A.R. |
| | | A | Thailand |
| Y | | | Togo |
| Y | | | Trinidad-Tobago |
| Y | | | Tunisia |
| | N | | Turkey |
| Y | | | Uganda |
| | | A | Ukrainian SSR |
| | | A | U.S.S.R. |
| Y | | | U.A. Emirates |
| | | A | United Kingdom |
| Y | | | U.R. Cameroon |
| Y | | | U.R. Tanzania |
| | N | | United States |
| Y | | | Upper Volta |
| Y | | | Uruguay |
| | | | Vanuatu |
| | N | | Venezuela |
| Y | | | Viet Nam |
| Y | | | Yemen |
| Y | | | Yugoslavia |
| Y | | | Zaire |
| Y | | | Zambia |
| Y | | | Zimbabwe |
| Y | | | Namibia |
| | | | Tuvalu |

*130 YES*
*4 NO*
*17 ABSTAIN*

US STATEMENT MADE IN PLENARY:    April 30, 1982

by

Ambassador James L. Malone
Special Representative of the President
for the
Law of the Sea

Mr. President:

All of us here today recognize the critical importance of the world's oceans to mankind. We also recognize the importance of international agreements concerning the uses of the oceans. All countries represented here have worked long and hard, for over a decade, to come to such a comprehensive agreement. The United States helped initiate that process and has been a major participant in it.

Mr. President, I would like to expres the sincere appreciation of my delegation to the leadership of the Conference, the Collegium, and in particular, to you, Mr. President, for your untiring efforts in the search for a broadly acceptable package.

Just three months ago President Reagan reaffirmed the United States commitment to the multilateral treaty process for reaching agreement on the world's oceans. Within the context of an overall acceptable treaty, he also noted that those many provisions dealing with navigation, overflight, the continental shelf, marine research and environment, and other areas are basically constructive and in the interest of the international community. They are, of course, not perfect, but they do represent the product of hard negotiation and reasonable compromise.

At the same time, President Reagan announced that the United States had serious problems with elements of the deep seabed mining provisions and would seek changes to fulfill six broad objectives that would make the treaty acceptable to the United States. This conclusion was reached after a comprehensive, year-long review within the United States Government covering all aspects of the draft treaty.

My delegation came to this session willing to
work and negotiate with other countries to find
mutually acceptable solutions to the problems before
us. We proposed a set of amendments that would have
satisfied our objectives and, in our view, provided
a fair and balanced system to promote the development of deep seabed resources. In a spirit of compromise and conciliation, we made a further attempt
to find satisfactory solutions by revising our proposed amendments to take into account views expressed
by other delegations.

Three misconceptions have arisen about US motivations. I would like to address each of these
briefly.

The first misconception has been that the United
States was seeking essentially to nullify the basic
bargain in the draft treaty. This is not true.
Even if all of our proposed changes had been accepted,
there would still have been an international regulatory system for the deep seabeds and an international
mining entity. We have not tried to destroy the system at all, but rather to structure it in a way that
will best serve the interests of all nations by enhancing seabed resource development.

A second misconception has been that the primary
interest of the United States in the deep seabed regime related to protecting a few US business interests. That view has drastically misjudged the moti-
vation of the United States and its commitment to
certain principles.

Finally, many other countries, and even many
people in my own country, have believed that the
United States would, in the end, accept an unsatisfactory deep seabed regime because of the navigation
provisions that serve other national interests. That
view, as well, is false. We have consistently maintained that each part of the treaty must be satisfactory to us.

Mr. President, we came to this session determined
to work together to reach improvements that would accord with United States objectives and ensure a viable
seabed mining regime. I had hoped to be able to say
today that we had successfully concluded our task and
reached an acceptable outcome. Unfortunately, that is
not the case and I cannot make such a report.

Some modest improvements have been made in the draft treaty during this session. However, there has been an unyielding refusal on the part of some to engage in real negotiations on most of the major concerns reflected in the amendments proposed by the United States and co-sponsored by Belgium, the Federal Republic of Germany, France, Italy, Japan, and the United Kingdom. We appreciate that others put forward compromise proposals to try to bridge the gap, but these efforts did not succeed.

I do not wish to belabor the problems, but it is important that we understand clearly now far short of our objectives the conference has fallen.

First, we believe the seabed mining provisions would deter the development of deep seabed mineral resources. Economic development of these resources is in the interest of all countries. In a world in which rational economic development is so critical, particularly for developing countries, the treaty would create yet another barrier to such development. It would deny the play of basic economic forces in the market place.

Second, while there have been improvements to assure access to deep seabed minerals for existing miners, we do not believe that the seabed articles would provide the assured access for qualified future miners that is necessary to promote the economic development of these resources. The provisions would also create a system of privileges for the Enterprise that discriminate against private and national miners.

Third, the decision-making process in the deep seabed regime does not give a proportionate voice to those countries most affected by the decisions and, thus, would not fairly reflect and effectively protect their interests.

Fourth, the provisions allow for amendments to come into force for a State without its consent. While that may be possible for some political systems, it is clearly incompatible with United States processes for incurring treaty obligations. Moreover, after having made substantial investments in deep seabed mining, the choice of either accepting an amendment at some future time or being forced to withdraw from the treaty entirely is not acceptable.

596

Finally, the deep seabed regime continues to pose serious problems for the United States by creating precedents that are not appropriate. Provisions on mandatory transfer of technology and potential distribution of benefits to national liberation movements, in particular, raise these problems. These and other aspects, like production limitations, are also key problems for the US Congress.

In short, while the other provisions of the treaty are generally acceptable, I can come to no conclusion other than the fact that the treaty before us today does not satisfy any of the United States objectives in the deep seabed regime. This is why we were forced to vote against the treaty today, and why I will necessarily report to my Government that our efforts to achieve an acceptable deep seabed regime have not been successful. This is not a happy conclusion for the United States.

We recognize that many of us came to these negotiations with different perspectives and diverse interests. Indeed, there are even differences of opinion on the meaning of "the common heritage of mankind" and the consequences that flow from that concept.

Despite our differences, we have held to the conviction that negotiation and compromise could produce a convention serving the interests of all States. Unfortunately, in our view, the treaty before us does not meet those standards. The greatest tragedy of this treaty is that it will not bring more orderly and productive uses of the deep seabeds to reality. It also does not serve the broader goal of bringing the developed and developing countries closer together.

Thus, it is with particular regret that we have had to vote against the adoption of this treaty. We have not done so lightly, but for reasons of deep conviction and principle, which will continue to guide our actions in the future.

APPENDIX I

United Nations Department of Public Information
Press Section, United Nations, New York
Background Release SEA/498 3 December 1982

LAW OF SEA CONVENTION TO BE SIGNED IN JAMAICA
AT FINAL SESSION OF CONFERENCE, 6-10 DECEMBER

The new United Nations Convention on the Law of
the Sea will be opened for signature at meetings to
be held at Montego Bay, Jamaica, from 6 to 10 December 1982, by the Third United Nations Conference on
the Law of the Sea.

The Convention was adopted by the Conference on
30 April after nine years of negotiations in which
nearly 160 Governments took part. It defines a new
set of rules for virtually all uses of the oceans, including navigation, fisheries, mineral resource development, and scientific research. It seeks to protect
the world's seas from pollution and encourage rational management of their riches, so that their benefits
will be available on a just basis to all mankind.

The basic aim of the Convention is spelt out in
its preamble: the establishment of "a legal order for
the seas and oceans which would facilitate international communication and promote their peaceful uses,
the equitable and efficient utilization of their resources, the study, protection, and preservation of
the marine environment and the conservation of the
living resources thereof".

Two documents are to be signed at a formal ceremony at Montego Bay on 10 December which will mark the
conclusion of the Conference: the Convention with its
320 articles and nine annexes (document A/CONF.62/122)
and the Final Act of the Conference (document A/CONF.
62/121), a record of its proceedings and accomplishments since it opened at United Nations Headquarters,
New York, in 1973. The Final Act will include four
resolutions which the Conference adopted along with
the Convention in April, the first of which provides
for the establishment of a Preparatory Commission to
lay the groundwork for the main institutions to be
established when the Convention enters into force.

The Conference was convened in accordance with a
1970 resolution of the General Assembly (2750 C (XXV)).
It has been in session for 93 weeks from the time it
opened in December 1973 until it concluded its substantive work with the approval of final drafting
changes in September 1982.

(p. 2)

The forthcoming signing session was authorized
by the Assembly in a resolution adopted today.  It
will be held at Montego Bay at the invitation of the
Jamaican Government.  The meetings will be the final
part of the Conference's eleventh session.

The Convention and four related resolutions were
adopted as a package by a vote of 130 in favour to 4
against (Israel, Turkey, United States, Venezuela),
with 17 abstentions.

Until the final week of its decision-making session, the Conference avoided taking a vote on substantive issues.  This was in accordance with a rule
it had established in 1974, to seek consensus wherever
possible and to resort to voting only when it decided
that all efforts at consensus had been exhausted.
Adhering to this rule, the Conference negotiators
built a series of "mini-packages"--balanced compromises on contested issues ranging from seabed production policies to rules for marine scientific research
in offshore waters--which together made up the package
that became the Convention as a whole.  This "package-
deal" approach was in response to the General Assembly's 1973 decision that the Conference should adopt a
convention dealing with all matters relating to the
law of the sea, bearing in mind "that the problems of
ocean space are closely interrelated and need to be
considered as a whole".

Although it rejected three proposed amendments by
vote on 26 April, the Conference acted by consensus on
all of the elements that went into the Convention until the recorded vote requested by the United States
on 30 April, by which it adopted the text as a whole.

The Convention will be open for signature by all
States.  This includes the 157 Members of the United
Nations and the 11 other States which are now members
of one or more specialized agencies:  Democratic People's Republic of Korea, Holy See, Kiribati,

Liechtenstein, Monaco, Nauru, Republic of Korea, San Marino, Switzerland, Tonga and Tuvalu. These are the States which were entitled to full participation in the Conference. Actual attendance reached a total of 157 States at the session at which the Convention was adopted, held in New York from 8 March to 30 April (see round-up of session, Press Release SEA/494 of 30 April).

In addition to these 168 States, the Convention will be open to signature by Namibia, represented by the United Nations Council for Namibia, as well as by self-governing associated States and territories with legal competence over the matters governed by the Convention and by certain intergovernmental organizations. Included in the first category are the Cook Islands and Nieue, which have sent observers to a number of sessions of the Conference.

The international organizations entitled to sign and accede are those to which their member States have transferred legal competence over matters governed by the Convention, including competence to enter into treaties. The provision enabling such organizations to adhere was pressed by the members of the European Economic Community, which has power to regulate fisheries and certain other matters on behalf of its member States.

(p. 3)

The name of the new treaty, United Nations Convention on the Law of the Sea, was decided by the Conference at its most recent series of meetings, a resumed eleventh session held at United Nations Headquarters from 22 to 24 September. At those meetings, the Conference approved hundreds of textual changes recommended by its Drafting Committee to clarify and harmonize the text in its six official languages.

Jamaica was chosen by the Conference in September as host country for the signing session, after Venezuela withdrew an invitation it had submitted when the Conference held its first substantive session at Caracas in 1974. Venezuela, which withdrew its offer by letter dated 20 September, said it could not associate itself with the Convention for reasons of national interest.

Jamaica is also the host country designated in the Convention as the site for the International Seabed Authority, the main institution to be set up once the Convention enters into force. The precise location of the Authority's headquarters in Jamaica is to be considered by the Preparatory Commission.

The President of the Conference is Tommy T.B. Koh (Singapore). He was elected in March 1981 following the death in 1980 of H. Shirley Amerasinghe of Sri Lanka, who presided over the Conference during its first seven years.

The final meeting of the Conference will be addressed by Secretary-General Javier Pérez de Cuéllar, who is to fly from New York; by President Koh, and by the Prime Minister of Jamaica, Edward P.G. Seaga.

Final Act

The Montego Bay session will culminate on 10 December with a ceremony at which all representatives present will be called upon, in English alphabetical order, to sign on behalf of their Governments or organizations either or both of two documents: the Final Act of the Conference, and the Convention.

The Final Act of an international treaty-making conference contains the text of the instruments and resolutions adopted by the conference, and a formal account of the proceedings. The Final Act of the Law of the Sea Conference will follow this pattern. In signing it, Governments do not commit themselves to acceptance of the Convention. However, signature of the Final Act in this case will have a practical consequence: it will enable the signatory Government to send an observer to the Preparatory Commission, the body that is to prepare the ground for the Seabed Authority and the International Tribunal for the Law of the Sea, and draft regulations to govern preparatory seabed investments and future seabed exploitation.

Observers will be able to participate fully in the Commission's deliberations but not in its decisions. In order to become a full member of the Commission, with the right to vote, a State will have to sign or accede to
(p. 4)
the Convention. This

602

arrangement is set out in the resolution constituting
the Commission, adopted by the Conference in April and
included in the Final Act.

The Conference has adopted eight resolutions, all
of which will be in the Final Act. Four of these are
intended to complement the Convention: resolution I
establishes the Preparatory Commission and defines its
functions and powers; resolution II governs preparatory investment in seabed exploration and exploitation
by States and private consortia before the Convention
enters into force; resolution III deals with the
rights and interests of territories which have not
attained independence or self-government; and resolution IV gives recognized national liberation movements
the right to sign the Final Act.

One of the remaining four resolutions, also
adopted in April, contains recommendations for international assistance for the development of national
marine science, technology and ocean service infrastructures. The three other resolutions, adopted at
previous sessions, are a birthday tribute to the Latin
American Liberator Simón Bolívar, adopted at the Caracas session (1974); an expression of gratitude to
Venezuela as host for that session; and a tribute on
the 150th anniversary (1976) of the Amphictyonic Congress of Panama, convened to unify Latin America.

The Final Act will also contain a "Statement of
understanding concerning a specific method to be used
in establishing the outer edge of the continental margin". This was approved in April at the request of
Sri Lanka, which contended that the Convention's
rules for establishing the outer limits of the continental shelf would unfairly limit the breadth of its
shelf in the Bay of Bengal because of unusual geological features. The statement thus constitutes an exception to the rules set out in the Convention.

As specified in resolution IV, the national liberation movements which have been participating in the
Conference will be entitled to sign the Final Act as
observers. These are the movements recognized by the
League of Arab States and the Organization of African
Unity in their respective regions, and whose participation in the Conference as observers has been authorized by the General Assembly: the African National
Congress of South Africa, the Pan Africanist Congress
of Azania (South Africa), the South West Africa

People's Organization, and the Palestine Liberation
Organization. They will be entitled to participate
in the Preparatory Commission as observers.

## Signature and Ratification of Convention

Like any other treaty, the Law of the Sea Convention will have to be ratified or acceded to by a
specified number of States—60 in this case—before
it becomes law for the nations adhering to it. Signature is a step preliminary to ratification. It
does not legally bind Governments to adhere to the
Convention, but obliges signatories not to defeat its
objects and purposes. It normally indicates the signatory's intention to pursue the procedures dictated
by its national constitution or practice that will
lead to the deposit with the Secretary-General of an
instrument of ratification. The

(p. 5)

latter
process usually requires parliamentary approval and
may take years for some countries to complete. Instead of signing and later ratifying, Governments may
simply accede to the Convention without signing it;
the legal effect is the same.

The Convention will be open for signature for
two years at the Jamaican Ministry of Foreign Affairs
in Kingston. Governments will also be able to sign
it at United Nations Headquarters beginning 1 July
1983. It will be closed for signature at both places
on 9 December 1984 but will remain open indefinitely
for accession. Thus, there is no time limit within
which countries must adhere.

The Preparatory Commission is to be convened between 60 and 90 days after at least 50 States sign or
accede to the Convention. In the event that 50 signatures are recorded during the session at Montego
Bay, plans have been drawn up to hold the first session of the Commission at Kingston in March 1983 for
four weeks, with a possible extension by two weeks.

The Convention will enter into force one year
after it is signed or ratified by 60 States. At that
time the Seabed Authority and the Law of the Sea Tribunal will be formally established.

## Positions of Governments

The meeting at Montego Bay will provide an opportunity for Governments to state their position on the
Convention and especially their intentions with regard
to signing it.  Such statements will be made during
the first four days of next week, 6-9 December.  At
the time of signing or ratification, they may also
make declarations or statements with a view to harmonizing national laws and regulations with the provisions of the Convention.  However, article 310 expressly says that such declarations or statements must
"not purport to exclude or to modify the legal effect
of the provisions of this Convention in their application to that State party".

Another point on which States may make declarations at the time of signing or ratification concerns
their willingness to accept compulsory dispute settlement for certain types of disputes concerning the interpretation or application of the Convention.  Arti-
287 permits them to choose one or more of the following:  the International Tribunal for the Law of the
Sea, the International Court of Justice; and two types
of arbitral tribunals.  Article 298 permits States to
declare in writing that they do not accept any one or
more of such procedures in regard to disputes over
sea boundary delimitation, military and law enforcement activities, and disputes before the Security
Council.

In addition, an intergovernmental organization
authorized to sign the Convention may make a declaration specifying the matters governed by the Convention
in respect of which the organization's member States
have transferred legal competence to it.

(p. 6)

During the Conference's final year, delegations
had several opportunities to comment on aspects of the
Convention before it was adopted.  At nine meetings
between 30 March and 1 April, 112 speakers expressed
views on proposed changes in the draft.  At six meetings from 15 to 17 April, 87 speakers commented on
formal amendments submitted by delegations, most of
which were not pressed by their sponsors.  Forty-seven
States explained their positions on 30 April, immediately after the adoption of the Convention.

Many of the States supporting the Convention were of the view that, while the text was far from satisfying the interests of everyone, it represented the best that could be achieved after lengthy negotiations. A number of developing countries stressed that their group had made major concessions to the industrialized countries, particularly in regard to the seabed mining system.

The four States which voted against the Convention explained their stands immediately after the vote and in other oral and written statements to the Conference.

Israel said on 30 April that it could not accept any provision which granted any kind of standing to the Palestine Liberation Organization. In a written statement dated 15 September (document A/CONF.62/WS/ 33), it mentioned a number of other provisions that it could not support or that created difficulties, especially those bearing on maintenance of the freedom of the seas in respect of navigation and over-flight and as regard straits. Israel would make its final position known in due course, the statement added.

Turkey said it had voted against because the Conference had rejected its proposal to delete the article disallowing reservations to the Convention. That proposal, Turkey stated, would have accommodated countries which wanted to become parties to the Convention while safeguarding their vital interests. The amendment was rejected by 18 in favour to 100 against, with 26 abstentions. Voting in favour were Albania, Bolivia, China, Democratic Kampuchea, the Democratic People's Republic of Korea, Ecuador, Egypt, El Salvador, Guatemala, Oman, the Philippines, Romania, Saudi Arabia, Somalia, Turkey, the Upper Volta, Venezuela, and Yemen.

The United States, explaining its negative vote on 30 April, made five points: (1) the seabed mining provisions of the Convention would deter the development of deep seabed mineral resources; (2) access to those resources was not assured; (3) the countries most affected did not have a proportionate voice in decision making on seabed policies, with the result that their interests would not be fairly reflected and effectively protected; (4) the procedure whereby future amendments to seabed provisions could come into

force for a State without its consent was incompatible
with United States processes for incurring treaty obligations; and (5) the provisions on mandatory transfer of seabed technology, potential distribution of
benefits to national liberation movements, and production limitations posed key problems for the United
States Congress.

(p. 7)

Venezuela said on 30 April that it could not accept the articles on delimitation of maritime boundaries between States with opposite or adjacent coasts,
or the provision barring reservations. Alluding on
15 April to boundary delimitation issues with some of
its neighbours, Venezuela said that such issues should
be resolved by equitable agreement among the parties,
taking account of factors that varied from case to
case. Venezuela sponsored an amendment that would
have permitted reservations to the clauses in question, but did not press the amendment after the President indicated that there were no prospects for agreement on it.

On 24 September Argentina announced that it would
not sign either the Final Act or the Convention. It
cited objections to resolution III, on protection of
the rights of the people of a territory that had not
attained independence or self-government. On 30 April
after voting for the Convention, Argentina said it
would have voted against paragraph 2 of resolution
III, by which the Conference declared that, where
there was a dispute over sovereignty of a territory,
the parties should consult regarding the exercise of
those rights, with the interests of the territory's
people to be taken as a fundamental consideration.
Argentina favoured an earlier provision which, it
said, had been aimed at preventing the Powers controlling colonial or occupied territories from exercising
any rights that might consolidate such unlawful situations. The resolution, Argentina added, had no bearing on the Malvinas question, which was related to
decolonization.

Those abstaining in the vote on adoption of the
Convention were Belgium, Bulgaria, Byelorussia, Czech-
oslovakia, the German Democratic Republic, the Federal
Republic of Germany, Hungary, Italy, Luxembourg, Mon-
golia, the Netherlands, Poland, Spain, Thailand, the
Ukraine, the USSR, and the United Kingdom. Liberia

later announced that it wished to be recorded as abstaining. Albania, Ecuador, and the Holy See announced that they were not participating in the vote.

Belgium and the Federal Republic of Germany expressed disappointment with the seabed provisions, and Italy, the Netherlands, and the United Kingdom said the negotiations on this subject should have continued in view of the fact that consensus had not been achieved. However, the Federal Republic of Germany added that its position did not prejudge the question of future signature and ratification, and the Netherlands said it would carefully consider the question of signing. Spain expressed regret that the Conference had not accepted amendments it had submitted to the articles on transit passage through straits used for international navigation. It also objected to resolution III.

Bulgaria, the German Democratic Republic, Hungary, Mongolia, Poland, and the Soviet Union objected on 30 April that resolution II, on preparatory seabed investments, contained provisions which discriminated against the socialist countries. However, Poland and the Soviet Union announced, on 24 and 22 September, respectively, that they would sign the Convention.

(p. 8)

Thailand said the Convention would adversely affect its fishing industry in the exclusive economic zone; it also had difficulty with the maritime boundary delimitation provisions, but its abstention did not preclude the possibility that it might become a party later.

Of the countries which did not participate in the vote on the Convention, Albania said it was determined to defend its sovereignty over a 15-mile territorial sea, that the Convention violated the sovereign rights of coastal States by permitting passage of warships, that States were unjustly deprived of the right to enter reservations, and that the seabed provisions would allow the super-Powers, a small group of other industrialized countries, and a handful of transnational corporations to monopolize seabed resources.

Ecuador, which supported the concept of a 200-mile territorial sea throughout the Conference, said

the Convention's definitions of maritime spaces placed
archipelagos which formed part of a State's territory
--such as Ecuador's Galapagos Islands--in an unacceptable position.

Highlights of Convention

The Law of the Sea Convention consists of 17
parts and nine annexes. Their main features are summarized below.

I.    Use of terms:  The international seabed
area, activities in the area, pollution of the marine
environment and dumping are defined for the purposes
of the Convention.

II.    Territorial sea and contiguous zone:  Every
coastal State has sovereignty over its territorial sea,
up to 12 miles wide as from straight baselines running
along the coast.  Foreign vessels, including merchant
ships and warships, are permitted "innocent passage"
through these waters, defined as navigation that does
not prejudice the coastal State's peace, good order
or security.  In a further 12-mile area called the
contiguous zone, the coastal State can exercise the
control needed to prevent infringement of its customs,
fiscal, immigration or sanitary laws, and can punish
violators.

III.    Straits used for international navigation:
Vessels and aircraft of all nations may exercise
"transit passage" through straits.  This is defined
as freedom of navigation and overflight solely for
the purpose of continuous and expeditious transit,
without threat to the States on either side, which are
entitled to regulate navigation and other aspects of
passage.

IV.    Archipelagic States:  States made up of a
group or groups of closely related islands and inter-
connecting waters have sovereignty over a sea area
enclosed by straight lines drawn between the outermost
points of the islands, while the ships of all other
States enjoy the right of passage through sea lanes
designated by the archipelagic State.

V.    Exclusive economic zone:  Coastal States
have sovereign rights up to 200 miles from shore with
respect to resources and certain economic activities,
and also have specified types of jurisdiction over

scientific
                    (p. 9)
                            research and environmental
preservation, while all other States have freedom of
navigation and overflight, as well as freedom to lay
submarine cables and pipelines.  States are to cooperate for the conservation of highly migratory species including marine mammals (listed in annex I).
Landlocked States and "States with special geographical characteristics" have the right to participate in
exploiting part of the zone's fisheries when the
coastal State cannot harvest them all itself.  Delimitation of economic zones between States will be
"effected by agreement on the basis of international
law . . . in order to achieve an equitable solution".

          VI.  Continental shelf:  Coastal States have
sovereign rights over this national area of the seabed for the purpose of exploring and exploiting it,
without affecting the legal status of the water or
air space above.  The shelf extends at least to 200
miles from shore, and out to 350 miles or even beyond,
depending on the nature and configuration of the continental margin.  Coastal States will share with the
international community part of the revenue they de-
rive from exploiting oil and other resources from any
part of their shelf beyond 200 miles.  Delimitation
of overlapping shelves is to be on the same basis as
for the exclusive economic zone.  A Commission on the
Limits of the Continental Shelf will make recommendations to States on the shelf's outer boundaries
(annex II).

          VII.  High seas:  All States enjoy the tradition-
al freedoms of navigation, overflight, scientific research, and fishing in this area of the oceans beyond
national jurisdiction.  They will be obliged to adopt,
or cooperate with other States in adopting, measures
to manage and conserve living resouces.

          VIII. Regime of islands:  The territorial sea,
exclusive economic zone, and continental shelf of islands are to be determined in the same way as for
other land territory, but uninhabitable rocks will
have no economic zone or continental shelf.

          IX.  Enclosed or semi-enclosed seas:  States
bordering seas such as the Caribbean and the Mediterranean should cooperate on management of living

resources and on environmental and research policies and activities.

X.   Right of access of landlocked States to and from the sea and freedom of transit: The people and goods of States with no seacoast must be allowed to move through a neighbouring coastal State to reach and return from the sea, under mutually agreed terms.

XI.   International seabed area: All activities on the seabed area beyond national jurisdiction will be controlled by an International Seabed Authority, following the principle that the area and its re-sources are the common heritage of mankind. A paral-lel system will be established under which exploration and exploitation of deepsea minerals will be carried out by the Authority as well as by States and private and public corporations and consortia under contract with the Authority. The Authority will establish rules, regulations, and procedures for seabed mining, in accordance with basic conditions of prospecting, exploration and exploitation set out in the

(p. 10)

Convention (annex III). The Authority will have an Enterprise for mining (Statute in annex IV), as well as an Assembly, a Council, and a secretariat. A Sea-Bed Disputes Chamber of the International Tribunal will settle disputes and issue advisory opinions on request.

XII.   Protection and preservation of the marine environment: States are obligated to use "the best practical means at their disposal" to prevent and con-trol marine pollution from any source. They are to cooperate globally and regionally, notify one another of imminent or actual damage, and develop contingency plans against pollution. Technical assistance, moni-toring, and environmental assessment will be promoted. International rules and national legislation will be devised to prevent, reduce, and control pollution of the marine environment from land-based sources and activities on the oceans and seabed, including dumping. Enforcement will be the responsibility of coastal States, port States, and flag States, depending on the nature, source, and location of the offense. Safe-guards can be invoked against inappropriate enforce-ment actions. Ice-covered areas may be protected by special rules against pollution from vessels. States

will be liable for damage caused by violation of their
international obligations to combat marine pollution.
Warships will have sovereign immunity from environmental regulations imposed by other States, but the
States operating them must ensure that they act consistent with the Convention as far as practicable.
Obligations under other conventions on the protection
and preservation of the marine environment will not
be prejudiced by the new Convention.

XIII. Marine scientific research: All States
have the right to conduct ocean research for exclusively peaceful purposes. International cooperation
in this area is to be promoted through such means as
the publication and dissemination of information and
knowledge. All such research in the exclusive economic zone and on the continental shelf is subject to
the consent of the coastal State, but consent will
have to be given when the research is for peaceful
purposes and fulfills other criteria laid down in the
Convention. Scientific research installations or
equipment in the marine environment must not interfere with shipping routes and must bear identification markings and warning signals. States and international organizations are to be held responsible for
damage caused by their own research activities or for
action they take against the research conducted by
others when such action contravenes the Convention.
In the event of certain disputes, the researching
State may require the coastal State to submit to international conciliation on the ground that it was not
acting in a manner compatible with the Convention.

XIV. Development and transfer of marine technology: States are bound to promote marine technology
"on fair and reasonable terms and conditions", with
due regard for all legitimate interests, including the
rights and duties of holders, suppliers, and recipients of technology. International cooperation will be
promoted through the establishment of guidelines, criteria, and standards for technology transfer, coordination of international programmes, and cooperation
with international organizations. The establishment
and strengthening of national and regional marine
scientific and technological centres is to be promoted.

APPENDIX I

(p. 11)

XV. Settlement of disputes: States are obliged
to settle by peaceful means any disputes over the interpretation or application of the Convention. When
they cannot reach agreement on a bilateral basis, they
will have to submit most types of disputes to a compulsory procedure entailing a decision binding on all
sides. They will have four options: the International Tribunal for the Law of the Sea, to be established
under the Convention (statute in annex VI); the existing International Court of Justice; arbitration (annex
VII); and special arbitral procedures for particular
categories of disputes (annex VIII). Certain types of
disputes will have to be submitted to conciliation
(annex V), a procedure whose outcome is not binding on
the parties. States will have the option of declining
to accept compulsory settlement procedures for certain
types of disputes on especially sensitive matters such
as boundaries and military activities.

XVI. General provisions: States undertake to
discharge their obligations under the Convention in
good faith and without abusing their rights, and to
refrain from threatening or using force contrary to
international law. They are not bound to disclose
information contrary to their essential security interests. Coastal States have jurisdiction over
archaeological objects and objects of historical
origin found at sea up to the outer edge of their
contiguous zone (24 miles from shore).

XVII. Final provisions: The non-seabed provisions of the Convention can be amended by two-thirds
of the States parties, but the amendments will apply
only to those States which ratify or accede to them.
The seabed provisions can be amended with the approval
of the Assembly and the Council of the Authority, but
only if they do not prejudice the system of exploration and exploitation pending a review conference to
be held 15 years after commercial exploitation begins.
Sixty States must adhere before the Convention enters
into force. Intergovernmental organizations to which
States have transferred legal competence over matters
governed by the Convention can sign and accede to it
under specified conditions (annex IX).

APPENDIX II


Third United Nations Conference on the Law of the Sea
Document A/CONF.62/121 of 21 October 1982


FINAL ACT OF THE
THIRD UNITED NATIONS CONFERENCE ON THE LAW OF THE SEA


INTRODUCTION


1.  The General Assembly of the United Nations on 17
December 1970 adopted resolution 2749 (XXV) containing the Declaration of Principles Governing the Seabed and the Ocean Floor, and the Subsoil Thereof,
beyond the Limits of National Jurisdiction and resolution 2750 C (XXV) on the same date, wherein it decided to convene, in 1973, a Conference on the Law of
the Sea, which would deal with the establishment of
an equitable international regime--including an international machinery--for the area and the resources
of the seabed and ocean floor, and the subsoil thereof, beyond the limits of national jurisdiction, with
a precise definition of that area and with a broad
range of related issues including those concerning
the regimes of the high seas, the continental shelf,
the territorial sea (including the question of its
breadth and the question of international straits)
and contiguous zone, fishing and conservation of the
living resources of the high seas (including the
question of the preferential rights of coastal
States), the preservation of the marine environment
(including inter alia, the prevention of pollution),
and scientific research.

2.  Prior to the adoption of these resolutions, the
General Assembly had considered the item introduced
in 1967 on the initiative of the Government of Malta[1]
and had subsequently adopted the following resolutions on the question of the reservation exclusively
for peaceful purposes of the seabed and the ocean
floor, and the subsoil thereof, underlying the high
seas beyond the limits of present national jurisdiction, and the use of their resources in the interests
of mankind:

Resolution 2340 (XXII)  on 18 December 1967,
Resolution 2467 (XXIII) on 21 December 1968, and
Resolution 2574 (XXIV)  on 15 December 1969.

3. The General Assembly, by resolution 2340 (XXII),
established an Ad Hoc Committee to Study the Peaceful
Uses of the Seabed and the Ocean Floor beyond the
Limits of National Jurisdiction and, having considered its report,[2] established by resolution 2467 A
(XXIII) the Committee on the Peaceful Uses of the
Seabed and the Ocean Floor beyond the Limits of National Jurisdiction. The General Assembly, by resolution 2750 C (XXV), enlarged that Committee and requested it to prepare draft treaty articles and a
comprehensive list of items and matters for the Conference on the Law of the Sea. The Committee as thus
constituted held six session, and a number of additional meetings, between 1971 and 1973 at United Nations Headquarters in New York and at the Office of
the United Nations in Geneva. Having considered its
report[3] the General Assembly requested the Secretary-
General by resolution 2574 A (XXIV) to ascertain the
views of Member States on the desirability of convening, at an early date, a Conference on the Law of the
Sea.

4. Subsequent to the adoption of resolutions 2749
(XXV) and 2750 (XXV), the General Assembly, having
considered the relevant reports of the Committee[4]
adopted the following resolutions on the same
question:

Resolution 2881 (XXVI)    on 21 December 1971,
Resolution 3029 (XXVII)   on 18 December 1972, and
Resolution 3067 (XXVIII)  on 16 November 1973.

5. By resolution 3029 A (XXVII) the General Assembly
requested the Secretary-General to convene the first
and second sessions of the Third United Nations Conference on the Law of the Sea. The Secretary-General
was authorized, in consultation with the Chairman of
the Committee, to make such arrangements as might be
necessary for the efficient organization and administration of the Conference and the Committee, and to
provide the assistance that might be required in legal, economic, technical, and scientific matters.
The specialized agencies, the International Atomic
Energy Agency, and other inter-governmental organizations were invited to cooperate fully with the Secretary-General in the preparations for the Conference

and to send observers to the Conference.[5] The Secretary General was requested, subject to approval by the Conference, to invite interested non-governmental organizations having consultative status with the Economic and Social Council to send observers to the Conference.

6. By resolution 3067 (XXVIII) the General Assembly decided that the mandate of the Conference was the adoption of a Convention dealing with all matters relating to the Law of the Sea, taking into account the subject matter listed in paragraph 2 of General Assembly resolution 2750 C (XXV) and the list of subjects and issues relating to the Law of the Sea formally approved by the Committee, and bearing in mind that the problems of ocean space were closely interrelated and needed to be considered as a whole. By the same resolution, the General Assembly also decided to convene the first session of the Conference in New York from 3 to 14 December 1973 for the purpose of dealing with organizational matters, including the election of officers, the adoption of the agenda and rules of procedure of the Conference, the establishment of subsidiary organs and the allocation of work to these organs, and any other purpose within its mandate. The second session was to be held in Caracas, at the invitation of the Government of Venezuela, from 20 June to 29 August 1974 to deal with the substantive work of the Conference and, if necessary, any subsequent session, or sessions, were to be convened as might be decided upon by the Conference and approved by the Assembly.

## I. SESSIONS

7. In accordance with that decision and subsequently either on the recommendation of the Conference as approved by the General Assembly, or in accordance with decisions of the Conferences, the sessions of the Third United Nations Conference on the Law of the Sea were held as follows:

- First session held at United Nations Headquarters in New York, 3 to 15 December 1973;

- Second session held at Parque Central, Caracas, 20 June to 29 August 1974;

616

- Third session held at the Office of the United Nations in Geneva, 17 March to 9 May 1975;[6]

- Fourth session held at United Nations Headquarters in New York, 15 March to 7 May 1976;[7]

- Fifth session held at United Nations Headquarters in New York, 2 August to 17 September 1976;[8]

- Sixth session held at United Nations Headquarters in New York, 23 May to 15 July 1977;[9]

- Seventh session held at the Office of the United Nations in Geneva, 28 March to 19 May 1978;[10]

- Resumed seventh session held at United Nations Headquarters in New York, 21 August to 15 September 1978;[11]

- Eighth session held at the Office of the United Nations in Geneva, 19 March to 27 April 1979;[12]

- Resumed eighth session held at United Nations Headquarters in New York, 19 July to 24 August 1979;[13]

- Ninth session held at United Nations Headquarters in New York, 3 March to 4 April 1980;[14]

- Resumed ninth session held at the Office of the United Nations in Geneva, 28 July to 29 August 1980;[15]

- Tenth session, held at United Nations Headquarters in New York, 9 March to 24 April 1981;[16]

- Resumed tenth session held at the Office of the United Nations in Geneva, 3 to 28 August 1981;[17]

- Eleventh session held at United Nations Headquarters in New York, 8 March to 30 April 1982;[18]

- Resumed eleventh session held at United Nations Headquarters in New York, 22 to 24 September 1982.[19]

## II. PARTICIPATION IN THE CONFERENCE

8. Having regard to the desirability of achieving universality of participation in the Conference, the General Assembly decided by resolution 3067 (XXVIII) to request the Secretary-General to invite States Members of the United Nations or members of the specialized agencies or the International Atomic Energy Agency, and States parties to the Statute of the International Court of Justice, as well as the following States, to participate in the Conference: the Republic of Guinea-Bissau and the Democratic Republic of Viet Nam.

Participating at the sessions of the Conference were the delegations of: Afghanistan, Albania, Algeria, Angola, Antigua and Barbuda, Argentina, Australia, Austria, Bahamas, Bahrain, Bangladesh, Barbados, Belgium, Benin, Bhutan, Bolivia, Botwsana, Brazil, Bulgaria, Burma, Burundi, Byelorussian Soviet Socialist Republic, Canada, Cape Verde, Central African Republic, Chad, Chile, China, Colombia, Comoros, Congo, Costa Rica, Cuba, Cyprus, Czechoslovakia, Democratic Kampuchea, Democratic People's Republic of Korea, Democratic Yemen, Denmark, Djibouti, Dominica, Dominican Republic, Ecuador, Egypt, El Salvador, Equatorial Guinea, Ethiopia, Fiji, Finland, France, Gabon, Gambia, German Democratic Republic, Germany, Federal Republic of, Ghana, Greece, Grenada, Guatemala, Guinea, Guinea-Bissau, Guyana, Haiti, Holy See, Honduras, Hungary, Iceland, India, Indonesia, Iran, Iraq, Ireland, Israel, Italy, Ivory Coast, Jamaica, Japan, Jordan, Kenya, Kuwait, Lao People's Democratic Republic, Lebanon, Lesotho, Liberia, Libyan Arab Jamahiriya, Liechtenstein, Luxembourg, Madagascar, Malawi, Malaysia, Maldives, Mali, Malta, Mauritania, Mauritius, Mexico, Monaco, Mongolia, Morocco, Mozambique, Nauru, Nepal, Netherlands, New Zealand, Nicaragua, Niger, Nigeria, Norway, Oman, Pakistan, Panama, Papua New Guinea, Paraguay, Peru, Philippines, Poland, Portugal, Qatar, Republic of Korea, Romania, Rwanda, Saint Lucia, Saint Vincent and the Grenadines, Samoa, San Marino, Sao Tome and Principe, Saudi Arabia, Senegal, Seychelles, Sierra Leone, Singapore, Solomon Islands, Somalia, South Africa, Spain, Sri Lanka, Sudan, Suriname, Swaziland, Sweden, Switzerland, Syrian Arab Republic, Thailand, Togo, Tonga, Trinidad and Tobago, Tunisia, Turkey, Uganda, Ukrainian Soviet Socialist Republic, Union of Soviet Socialist Republics, United Arab Emirates, United Kingdom of Great Britain and Northern Ireland, United Republic of Cameroon, United Republic of Tanzania, United States of America, Upper

Volta, Uruguay, Venezuela, Viet Nam, Yemen, Yugoslavia, Zaire, Zambia, and Zimbabwe.[20]

9.  The Secretary-General was also requested by resolution 3067 (XXVIII) to invite interested intergovernmental and non-governmental organizations, as well as the United Nations Council for Namibia, to participate in the Conference as observers.

The specialized agencies and inter-governmental organizations participating as observers at the several sessions of the Conference are listed in the appendix hereto.

10.  On the recommendation of the Conference, by resolution 3334 (XXXIX), adopted on 17 December 1974, the General Assembly requested the Secretary-General to invite Papua New Guinea, the Cook Islands, the Netherlands Antilles, Niue, Suriname, the West Indies Associated States, and the Trust Territory of the Pacific Islands to attend future sessions of the Conference as observers or, if any of them became independent, to attend as a participating State.

The States and Territories participating as observers at the several sessions of the Conference are also listed in the appendix hereto.

11.  The Conference decided on 11 July 1974 to extend invitations to national liberation movements, recognized by the Organization of African Unity and the League of Arab States in their respective regions, to participate in its proceedings as observers.[21]

The national liberation movements participating as observers at the several sessions of the Conference are also listed in the appendix hereto.

12.  Consequent upon General Assembly resolution 34/92, the Conference decided on 6 March 1980[22] that Namibia, represented by the United Nations Council for Namibia, should participate in the Conference in accordance with the relevant decisions of the General Assembly.

## III.   OFFICERS AND COMMITTEES

13.  The Conference elected Hamilton Shirley Amerasinghe (Sri Lanka) as its President.  Subsequently,

at its seventh session, the Conference confirmed that
he was, and continued to be the President of the Conference although he was no longer a member of his
national delegation.[23] On the death of Hamilton
Shirley Amerasinghe on 4 December 1980, the Conference paid tribute to his memory at a special commem-
orative meeting on 17 March 1981 at its tenth session
(A/CONF.62/SR.144).[24]

14. The Secretary-General of the United Nations
opened the tenth session as temporary President.
The Conference elected Tommy T.B. Koh (Singapore) as
President on 13 March 1981.[25]

15. The Conference decided that the Chairmen and
Rapporteurs of the three Main Committees, the Chairman of the Drafting Committee, and the Rapporteur-
General of the Conference would be elected in a personal capacity and that the Vice-Presidents, the Vice-
Chairmen of the Main Committees, and the members of
the Drafting Committee should be elected by country.[26]

16. The Conference elected as Vice-Presidents, the
representatives of the following States: Algeria,
Belgium, replaced by Ireland during alternate ses-
sions (by agreement of the regional group concerned);
Bolivia; Chile; China; Dominican Republic; Egypt;
France; Iceland; Indonesia; Iran; Iraq; Kuwait;
Liberia; Madagascar; Nepal; Nigeria; Norway; Paki-
stan; Peru; Poland; Singapore, replaced by Sri Lanka
at the tenth session (by agreement of the regional
group concerned); Trinidad and Tobago; Tunisia;
Uganda; Union of Soviet Socialist Republics; United
Kingdom of Great Britain and Northern Ireland; United
States of America; Yugoslavia; Zaire; and Zambia.

17. The following Committees were set up by the Conference: the General Committee; the three Main Committees; the Drafting Committee, and the Credentials
Committee. The assignment of subjects to the plenary
and each of the Main Committees was set out in section III of document A/CONF.62/29.

The General Committee consisted of the President
of the Conference as its Chairman, the Vice-Presidents, the officers of the Main Committees, and the
Rapporteur-General. The Chairman of the Drafting
Committee had the right to participate in the meeting
of the General Committee without the right to vote.[27]

The Conference elected the following officers for the three Main Cojmittees which were constituted by all States represented at the Conference:

## First Committee

| | |
|---|---|
| Chairman | Paul Bamela Engo (United Repub. of Cameroon) |
| Vice-Chairmen | The representatives of Brazil, the German Democratic Republic, and Japan |
| Rapporteur | |

| | | |
|---|---|---|
| 1st & 2nd sessions | H.C. Mott | (Australia) |
| 3rd to 10th sessions | John Bailey | " |
| 11th session | Keith Brennan | " |

## Second Committee

| | |
|---|---|
| Chairman | |
| 1st & 2nd sessions | Andrés Aguilar (Venezuela) |
| 3rd session | Reynaldo Galindo Pohl (El Salvador) (by agreement of the regional group concerned) |
| 4th to 11th session | Andrés Aguilar (Venez.) |
| Vice-Chairmen | The representatives of Czechoslovakia, Kenya, and Turkey |
| Rapporteur | Satya Nandan (Fiji) |

## Third Committee

| | |
|---|---|
| Chairman | Alexander Yankov (Bulgaria) |
| Vice-Chairmen | The representatives of Colombia, Cyprus, and the Federal Republic of Germany |
| Rapporteur | |

| | |
|---|---|
| 1st & 2nd sessions | Abdel Magied A. Hassan |
| 3rd session | Manyang d'Awol |
| 4th & 5th sessions | Abdel Magied A. Hassan |
| 5th to 11th sessions | Manyang d'Awol (both from Sudan) |

The Conference elected the following officer and members of the Drafting Committee:

### Drafting Committee

| | |
|---|---|
| Chairman | J. Alan Beesley (Canada) |
| Members | The representatives of: Afghanistan; Argentina; Bangladesh (alternating with Thailand every year); Ecuador; El Salvador (replaced by Venezuela for the duration of the third session by agreement of the regional group concerned); Ghana; India; Italy; Lesotho; Malaysia; Mauritania; Mauritius; Mexico; Netherlands (alternating with Austria every session); Philippines; Romania; Sierra Leone; Spain; Syrian Arab Republic; Union of Soviet Socialist Republics; United Republic of Tanzania; and the United States of America. |

The Conference elected the following officers and members of the Credentials Committee:

### Credentials Committee

Chairman

| | |
|---|---|
| 1st session | Heinrich Gleissner (Austria) |
| 2nd & 3rd sessions | Franz Weidinger (Austria) |
| 4th to 11th session | Karl Wolf (Austria) |

| | |
|---|---|
| Members | The representatives of: Austria; Chad; China; Costa Rica; Hungary; Ireland; Ivory Coast; Japan; and Uruguay. |

Kenneth Rattray (Jamaica) was elected Rapporteur-General of the Conference.

18. The Secretary-General of the United Nations as Secretary-General of the Conference was represented by Constantin Stavropoulos, Under-Secretary-General, at the first and second sessions. Thereafter Bernardo Zuleta, Under-Secretary-General, represented the Secretary-General. David L.D. Hall was Executive Secretary of the Conference.

19. The General Assembly, by its resolution 3067 (XXVIII) convening the Conference, referred to it the reports and documents of the Committee on the Peaceful Uses of the Seabed and the Ocean Floor beyond the Limits of National Jurisdiction and the relevant documentation of the General Assembly. At the commencement of the Conference the following documentation was also before it:

(a) The provisional agenda of the first session of the Conference (A/CONF.62/1);

(b) The draft rules of procedure prepared by the Secretary-General (A.CONF.62/2 and Add.1-3), containing an appendix which embodied the "Gentleman's Agreement", approved by the General Assembly at its twenty-eighth session on 16 November 1973.

Subsequently, the Conference also had before it the following documentation:

(i) The proposals submitted by the delegations participating in the Conference, as shown in the Official Records of the Conference;

(ii) The reports and studies prepared by the Secretary-General;[28]

(iii) The informal negotiating texts and the draft Convention on the Law of the Sea and related draft resolutions and decisions drawn up by the Conference as hereafter set out.

## IV. DRAFTING COMMITTEE

20. The Drafting Committee commenced its work at the seventh session of the Conference with the informal examination of negotiating texts, for the purposes of refining drafts, harmonizing recurring words and expressions and achieving, through textual review, concordance of the text of the Convention in the six

languages.  The Committee was assisted in its informal work by six language groups comprising both members and non-members of the Drafting Committee, representing the six official languages of the Conference, each group being chaired by a coordinator [29] and
assisted by Secretariat linguistic experts.  The coordinators, under the direction of the Chairman of
the Drafting Committee, performed the major task of
harmonizing the views of the language groups and of
preparing proposals for the Drafting Committee,
through meetings open to both members and non-members
of the Drafting Committee.  In addition to the meetings held during the regular sessions of the Conference, the Committee held inter-sessional meetings as
follows:

- At United Nations Headquarters in New York,
  from 9 to 27 June 1980;

- At United Nations Headquarters in New York,
  from 12 January to 27 February 1981;

- At the Office of the United Nations in Geneva,
  from 29 June to 31 July 1981;

- At United Nations Headquarters in New York,
  from 18 January to 26 February 1982;

- At the Office of the United Nations in Geneva,
  from 12 July to 25 August 1982.

The Drafting Committee presented a first series of reports concerning the harmonization of recurring words
and expressions.[30]  The Committee presented a second
series of reports containing recommendations arising
out of the textual review of the Convention.[31]

V.  RULES OF PROCEDURE AND CONDUCT OF NEGOTIATIONS

21.  The Conference adopted its rules of procedure
(A/CONF.62/30) at its second session.[32]  The declaration incorporating the "Gentleman's Agreement" approved by the General Assembly,[33] made by the President
and endorsed by the Conference,[34] was appended to the
rules of procedure.  The declaration provided that:

"Bearing in mind that the problems of ocean
space are closely interrelated and need to be
considered as a whole and the desirability of

624

adopting a Convention on the Law of the Sea
which will secure the widest possible acceptance,

"The Conference should make every effort to
reach agreement on substantive matters by way of
consensus, and there should be no voting on such
matters until all efforts at consensus have been
exhausted."

22. The rules of procedure were subsequently amended
by the Conference on 12 July 1974,[35] on 17 March
1975[36] and on 6 March 1980.[37]

23. At its second session,[38] the Conference determined the competence of the three Main Committees by
allocating to the plenary or the Committees the subjects and issues on the list prepared in accordance
with General Assembly resolution 2750 C (XXV) A/CONF.
62/29). The Main Committees established informal
working groups or other subsidiary bodies which
assisted the Committees in their work.[39]

24. At the third session, at the request of the Conference, the Chairmen of the three Main Committees
each prepared a single negotiating text covering the
subjects entrusted to the respective Committee which
together constituted the Informal Single Negotiating
Text (A/CONF.62/WP.8, Parts I, II, and III), the
nature of which is described in the introductory note
by the President. Subsequently, the President of the
Conference, taking into consideration the allocation
of subjects and issues to the plenary and the Main
Committees submitted a single negotiating text on the
subject of settlement of disputes (A/CONF.62/WP.9).

25. At the fourth session of the Conference, following a general debate in the plenary on the subject,
as recorded in A/CONF.62/SR.58 to SR.65, at the request of the Conference [40] the President prepared a
revised text on the settlement of disputes (A/CONF.
62/WP.9/Rev.1) which constituted Part IV of the Informal Single Negotiating Text in document A/CONF.62.
WP.8. At the same session, the Chairmen of the Main
Committees each prepared a revised Single Negotiating
Text (A/CONF.62/WP.8/Rev.1, Parts I to III) and the
note by the President which is attached to the text
describes its nature.

26. During the fifth session, at the request of the Conference,[41] the President prepared a revised single negotiating text on the settlement of disputes (A/CONF.62/WP.9/Rev.2), which constituted the fourth part of the Revised Single Negotiating Text (A/CONF. 62/WP.8/Rev.1).

27. At its sixth session,[42] the Conference requested the President and the Chairmen of the Main Committees, working under the President's leadership as a team with which the Chairman of the Drafting Committee and the Rapporteur-General were associated,[43] which was subsequently referred to as "the Collegium",[44] to prepare an Informal Composite Negotiating Text (A/CONF.62/WP.10), covering the entire range of subjects and issues contained in Parts I to IV of the Revised Single Negotiating Text. The nature of the composite text so prepared was described in the President's memorandum (A/CONF.62/WP.10/Add.1).

28. At its seventh session, the Conference identified certain outstanding core issues and established seven negotiating groups (as recorded in (A/CONF.62/62) for the purpose of resolving these issues.[45] Each group comprised a nucleus of countries principally concerned with the outstanding core issue, but was open-ended.

The Chairmen of the Negotiating Groups were:

Negotiating Group on:

| | |
|---|---|
| Item 1 | Francis X. Njenga (Kenya) |
| Item 2 | Tommy T.B. Koh (Singapore |
| Item 3 | Paul Bamela Engo (United Republic of Cameroon), Chairman of the First Committee |
| Item 4 | Satya N. Nandan (Fiji) |
| Item 5 | Constantin A. Stavropoulos (Greece) |
| Item 6 | Andrés Aguilar (Venezuela), Chairman of the Second Committee |
| Item 7 | E.J. Manner (Finland) |

The Chairmen of the Negotiating Groups were to report on the results of their negotiations to the Committee or the plenary functioning as a Committee, as appropriate, before they were presented to the plenary.

29. The negotiations carried out at the seventh session and resumed seventh session of the Conference

were reported on by the President concerning the work
of the plenary functioning as a Main Committee, and
by the Chairmen of the Main Committees and the Negotiating Groups. These reports, together with the report of the Chairman of the Drafting Committee, were
incorporated in documents A/CONF.62/RCNG.1 and 2.[46]
The Conference also laid down criteria for any modifications or revisions of the Informal Composite Negotiating Text, which are set out in document (A/CONF.
62/62).

30.  At the eighth session a group of Legal Experts
was set up with Harry Wuensche (German Democratic
Republic) as its Chairman. [47]

31.  On the basis of the deliberations of the Conference (A/CONF.62/SR.111-SR.116) concerning the reports
of the President, the Chairmen of the Main Committees,
the Chairmen of the Negotiating Groups, and the Chairman of the Group of Legal Experts on consultations
conducted by them, a revision of the Informal Composite Negotiating Text (A/CONF.62/WP.10/Rev.1) was
prepared by the Collegium referred to in paragraph 27.
The nature of the text was described in the explanatory memorandum by the President attached to the text.

32.  At the resumed eighth session a further Group of
Legal Experts was set up with Jens Evensen (Norway)
as its Chairman.[48]

33.  The reports on the negotiations conducted at the
resumed eighth session by the President, the Chairmen
of the Main Committees, the Chairmen of the Negotiating Groups, and the Chairmen of the two Groups of
Legal Experts together with the report of the Chairman of the Drafting Committee were incorporated in a
memorandum by the President (A/CONF.62/91)

34.  At its ninth session, on the basis of the report
of the President concerning consultations conducted
in the plenary acting as a Main Committee (A/CONF.62/
L.49/Add.1 and 2), the Conference considered the
draft Preamble prepared by the President (A/CONF.62/
L.49) for incorporation in the next revision of the
Informal Composite Negotiating Text (A/CONF.62/WP.10/
Rev.1).  On the basis of the deliberations of the Conference (A/CONF.62/SR.125-SR.128) concerning the reports of the President, the Chairmen of the Main Committees, the Chairmen of the Negotiating Groups, and
the Chairmen of the Groups of Legal Experts on the

the consultations conducted by them, and the report of the Chairman of the Drafting Committee on its work, the Collegium[49] undertook a second revision of the Informal Composite Negotiating Text presented as the Informal Composite Negotiating Text/Rev.2 (in document A/CONF.62/WP.10/Rev.2), the nature of which was described in the President's explanatory memorandum attached to it.

35. At its resumed ninth session, on the basis of the deliberations of the Conference (A/CONF.62/SR. 134-SR.140) concerning the reports of the President and the Chairmen of the Main Committees on the consultations conducted by them, the Collegium prepared a further revision of the Informal Composite Negotiating Text. The revised text, titled "Draft Convention on the Law of the Sea (Informal Text)" (A/ CONF.62/WP.10/Rev.3), was issued together with the explanatory memorandum of the President (A/CONF.62/ WP.10/Rev.3/Add.1), which described the nature of the text.

36. The Conference also decided that the statement of understanding on an exceptional method of delimitation of the Continental Shelf applicable to certain specific geological and geomorphological conditions[50] would be incorporated in an annex to the Final Act.

37. The Conference decided that the tenth session was to determine the status to be given to the draft Convention (Informal Text).[51]

38. Following the deliberations of the Conference at its tenth and resumed tenth sessions (A/CONF.62/SR. 142-SR.155), the Collegium prepared a revision of the draft Convention on the Law of the Sea (Informal Text). The Conference decided that the text as revised (A/CONF.62/L.78) was the official draft Convention of the Conference, subject only to the specific conditions recorded in document A/CONF.62/114. At the resumed tenth session, the Conference decided that the decisions taken in the informal plenary concerning the seats of the International Seabed Authority (Jamaica) and the International Tribunal for the Law of the Sea (the Free and Hanseatic City of Hamburg in the Federal Republic of Germany) should be incorporated in the revision of the draft Convention); and that the introductory note to that resivion should record the requircments agreed upon when the decision concerning the two seats was taken (A/CONF.62/L.78)

39. Following consideration by the plenary[52]of the final clauses and in particular the question of entry into force of the Convention, the question of establishing a Preparatory Commission for the International Seabed Authority and the convening of the International Tribunal for the Law of the Sea was considered by the plenary at the ninth session. The President, on the basis of the deliberations of the informal plenary, prepared a draft resolution to be adopted by the Conference concerning interim arrangements, which was annexed to his report (A/CONF.62/L.55 and Corr.1). On the basis of the further consideration of the subject jointly by the plenary and the First Committee at the tenth, resumed tenth, and eleventh sessions of the Conference, the President and the Chairman of the First Committee presented a draft resolution (A/CONF. 62/C.1/L.30, annex I).

40. Following consideration at the eleventh session of the question of the treatment to be accorded to preparatory investments made before the Convention enters into force, provided that such investments are compatible with the Convention and would not defeat its object and purpose, the President and the Chairman of the First Committee presented a draft resolution contained in annex II to their report A/CONF.62/C.1/ L.30. The question of participation in the Convention was considered by the plenary of the Conference during the eighth to eleventh session, and the President presented a report on the consultations at the eleventh session in document A/CONF.62/L.86.

41. The eleventh session had been declared as the final decision-making session of the Conference.[53] During that session, on the basis of the deliberations of the Conference (A/CONF.62/SR.157-SR.166) concerning the report of the President (A/CONF.62/L.86) and the reports of the Chairmen of the Main Committees (A/CONF. 62/L.87, L.91 and L.92), on the negotiations conducted by them and the report of the Chairman of the Drafting Committee on its work (A/CONF.62/L.85 and L.89), the Collegium issued a memorandum (A/CONF.62/L.93 and Corr.1) containing changes to be incorporated in the Draft Convention on the Law of the Sea (A/CONF.62/ L.78), and document A/CONF.62/L.94 setting out three draft resolutions and a draft decision of the Conference which were to be adopted at the same time as the draft Convention.

The Conference determined that all efforts at
reaching general agreement had been exhausted.[54]
Throughout the preceding eight years of its work the
Conference had taken all decisions by consensus although it had exceptionally resorted to a vote only
on procedural questions, on questions concerning the
appointment of officials and on invitations to be
extended to participants in the Conference as
observers.

42.  On the basis of the deliberations recorded in
the records of the Conference (A/CONF.62/SR.167-
SR.182), the Conference drew up:

THE UNITED NATIONS CONVENTION ON THE LAW OF THE SEA

> RESOLUTION I on the establishment of the Prepara-
> tory Commission for the International Seabed
> Authority and for the International Tribunal
> for the Law of the Sea

> RESOLUTION II governing Preparatory Investment
> in Pioneer Activities relating to Polymetallic
> Nodules

> RESOLUTION III relating to territories whose
> people have not obtained either full indepen-
> dence or some other self-governing status rec-
> ognized by the United Nations or territories
> under colonial domination

> RESOLUTION IV relating to national liberation
> movements.

The foregoing Convention together with resolutions I to IV, forming an integral whole, was adopted
on 30 April 1982, by a recorded vote taken at the request of one delegation.[55] The Convention together
with resolutions I to IV was adopted subject to drafting changes thereafter approved by the Conference[56]
which were incorporated in the Convention and in resolutions I to IV, which are annexed to this Final Act
(annex I).  The Convention is subject to ratification
and is opened for signature from 10 December 1982
until 9 December 1984 at the Ministry of Foreign Affairs of Jamaica and also from 1 July 1983 until 9
December 1984 at United Nations Headquarters.  The
same instrument is opened for accession in accordance
with its provisions.

After 9 December 1984, the closing date for signature at United Nations Headquarters, the Convention
will be deposited with the Secretary-General of the
United Nations.

There are annexed to this Final Act:

The Statement of Understanding referred to in
paragraph 36 above (annex II); and the folowing resolutions adopted by the Conference:

Resolution paying tribute to Simón Bolívar the
Liberator (annex III);[57]

Resolution expressing gratitude to the President,
the Government, and officials of Venezuela (annex
IV)[58]

Tribute to the Amphictyonic Congress of Panama
(annex V);[59]

Resolution on Development of National Marine
Science, Technology, and Ocean Service Infrastructures (annex VI).[60]

## NOTES

1. United Nations General Assembly Official Records, 22nd
Session, Annexes, agenda item 92, document A/6695.

2. Ibid., 23rd Session, Annexes, agenda item 26,
document A/7230.

3. Ibid., 24th Session, Supplement Nos. 22 and 22A
(A/7622 and Corr.1 and A/7622/Add.1).

4. Ibid., 26th Session, Supplement No. 21 (A/8421; ibid.,
27th Session, Supplement No. 21 (A/8721 and Corr.1); and ibid.,
28th Session, Supplement No. 21 (A/9021 and Corr.1-3), vols. I–VI.

5. In addition it may be noted that the Conference was attended and assisted by observers from the United Nations Programmes and Conferences.

6. General Assembly resolution 3334 (XXIX) of 17 Dec. 1974.

7. General Assembly resolution 3482 (XXX) of 12 Dec. 1975.

8. Decision taken at the 69th meeting of the plenary Conference on 7 May 1976 (see Official Records of the Third United Nations Conference on the Law of the Sea, vol. V, A/CONF.62/SR.69).

9. General Assembly resolution 31/63 of 10 Dec. 1976.

10. General Assembly resolution 32/194 of 20 Dec. 1977.

11. Decision taken at the 106th meeting of the plenary on 19 May 1978 (see Official Records of the Third United Nations Conference on the Law of the Sea, vol. IX, A/CONF.62/SR.106).

12. General Assembly resolution 33/17 of 10 Nov. 1978.

13. Decision taken at the 115th meeting of the plenary on 27 April 1979 (see Official Records of the Third United Nations Conference on the Law of the Sea, vol. XI, A/CONF.62/SR.115).

14. General Assembly resolution 34/20 of 9 Nov. 1979.

15. Ibid.

16. General Assembly resolution 35/116 of 10 Dec. 1980, and decision taken at the 147th meeting of the plenary Conference on 20 April 1981 (A/CONF.62/SR.147).

17. General Assembly resolution 35/452 of 11 May 1981.

18. General Assembly resolution 36/79 of 9 Dec. 1981.

19. Decision taken at the 182nd meeting of the plenary Conference on 30 April 1982 (A.CONF.62/SR.182).

20. The list of States participating at each session is recorded in the appropriate report of the Credentials Committee.

21. Decision taken at the 38th meeting of the plenary Conference on 11 July 1974, Official Records of the Third United Nations Conference on the Law of the Sea, vol. 1, A/CONF.62/ SR.38.

22. <u>Ibid</u>., vol. XIII, A/CONF.62/SR.122/

23. 86th closed meeting of the plenary Conference held on 5 April 1978, in adopting resolution A/CONF.62/R.1 proposed by Nepal on behalf of the Asian Group; <u>ibid</u>., vol. IX, footnote on page 3.

24. The General Assembly of the United Nations paid tribute to the memory of Ambassador Hamilton Shirley Amerasinghe, President of the Conference since its inception, and prior to that, Chairman of the Committee on the Peaceful Uses of the Seabed and the Ocean Floor beyond the Limits of Nationsl Jurisdiction (A/35/PV.82). The General Assembly thereafter established a memorial fellowship in his name (resolution 35/116, paragraphs 1 and 2 of December 1980 and resolution 36/79, third preambular paragraph and paragraph 6, of 9 December 1981). See also A/36/697.

25. A/CONF.62/SR.142.

26. <u>Ibid</u>., vol. I, A/CONF.62/SR.2.

27. Decision taken at the 3rd meeting of the plenary Conference on 10 Dec. 1973 (see <u>Official Records of the Third United Nations Conference on the Law of the Sea</u>, vol. I, p. 9).

28. Economic implications of seabed mineral development in the international area: <u>ibid</u>., vol. III (A/CONF.62/25 dated 22 May 1974).

Economic implications of seabed mining in the international area: <u>ibid</u>., vol. IV (A/CONF.62/37 dated 18 Feb. 1975).

Description of some types of marine technology and possible methods for their transfer: <u>ibid</u>., vol. IV (A/CONF.62/C.3/L.22) dated 27 February 1975.

Draft alternative texts of the preamble and final clauses: <u>ibid</u>., vol. VI (A/CONF.62/L.13) dated 26 July 1976.

Annotated directory of inter-governmental organizations concerned with ocean affairs (A/CONF.62/L.14 dated 10 Aug. 1976.

Alternative means of financing the Enterprise: <u>ibid</u>., vol. VI (A/CONF.62/C.1/L.17) dated 3 Sep. 1976.

Costs of the Authority and contractual means of financing its activities, ibid., vol. VII (A/CONF.62/C.1/L.19) dated 18 May 1977.

Manpower requirements of the Authority and related training needs, ibid., vol. XII (A/CONF.62/82) dated 17 Aug. 1979.

Potential financial implications for States Parties to the future Convention on the Law of the Sea (A/CONF.62/L.65 dated 20 Feb. 1981.

Effects of the production limitation formula under certain specified assumptions (A/CONF.62/L.66) dated 24 Feb. 1981 and (A/CONF.62.L.66/Corr.1) dated 3 March 1981

Preliminary study illustrating various formulae for the definition of the continental shelf: ibid., vol. IX (A/CONF. 62/C.2/L.98) dated 18 April 1978; map illustrating various formulae for the definition of the continental shelf (A/CONF. 62/C.2/L.98/Add.1); calculation of areas illustrated beyond 200 miles in document A/CONF.62/C.2/L.98/Add.1, ibid., vol. IX, (A/CONF.62/C.2/L.98/Add.2) dated 3 May 1978; communication received from the Secretary of the Intergovernmental Oceanographic Commission: ibid., vol. IX (A/CONF.62/C.2/L.98/Add.3) dated 28 August 1978.

Study of the implications of preparing large-scale maps for the Third United Nations Conference on the Law of the Sea: ibid., vol. XI (A/CONF.62/C.2/L.99) dated 9 April 1979.

Study on the future functions of the Secretary-General under the Convention and on the needs of countries, especially developing countries, for information, advice, and assistance under the new legal regime (A/CONF.62/L.76) dated 18 Aug. 1981.

29. The coordinators of the language groups were as follows:

> Arabic language group: Mustafa Kamil Yasseen (United Arab Emirates), and Mohammad Al-Haj Hamoud (Iraq).
> Chinese language group: Wang Tieya (China), Ni Zhengyu (China), and Zhang Hongzeng (China).
> English language group: Bernard H. Oxman (United States) and Thomas A. Clingan (United States).
> Alternates: Steven Asher (United States) and Milton Drucker (United States).
> French language group: Tullio Treves (Italy).
> Alternate: Lucius Caflisch (Switzerland).
> Russian language group: F.N. Kovalev (USSR), P.N. Evseev (USSR), Yevteny N. Nasinovsky (USSR), and Georgy G. Ivanov (USSR).
> Spanish language group: José Antonio Yturriaga Barbarán (Spain), José Manual Lacleta Munoz (Spain), José Antonio

Pastor Ridruejo (Spain) and Luis Valencia Rodríguez (Ecuador).

30. A/CONF.62/L.56, A/CONF.62/L.57/Rev.1 and A/CONF.62/L.63/Rev.1. See Official Records of the Third United Nations Conference on the Law of the Sea, vols. XIII and XIV.

31. A/CONF.62/L.67/Add.1-16, A/CONF.62/L.75/Add.1-13, A/CONF.62/L.85/Add.109, A/CONF.62/L.142/Rev.1/Add.1 and A/CONF.62/L.152/Add.1-27.

32. Ibid., vol. 1, A/CONF.62/SR.24.

33. Official Records of the General Assembly Twenty-eighth Session, Plenary Meetings, 2169th meeting.

34. Official Records of the Third United Nations Conference on the Law of the Sea, vol. I, A/CONF.62/SR.19.

35. Ibid., vol. I A/CONF.62/SR.40.

36. Ibid., vol. IV, A/CONF.62/SR.52.

37. Ibid., vol. XIII, A/CONF.62/SR.122.

38. Ibid., vol. I, A/CONF.62/SR.15.

39. The First Committee appointed the following officers of the informal working groups set up by it between the second and eleventh sessions:

Christopher W. Pinto (Sri Lanka): Chairman of the informal body of the whole (decision of the first meeting of the First Committee) Official Records of the Third United Nations Conference on the Law of the Sea, vol. II; Chairman of the negotiating group on the system of operations, the regime and the conditions of exploration and exploitation of the Area, with a membership of 50 States, but open-ended (decision of the 14th to 16th meetings of the First Committee, ibid.).

S.P. Jagota (India) and H.H.M. Sondaal (Netherlands): Co-chairmen of the open-ended working group (decision of the 26th meeting of the First Committee, ibid., vol. VI).

Jens Evensen (Norway): Special Coordinator of the Chairman's informal working group of the whole on the system of exploitation (decision of the 38th meeting of the First Committee, ibid., vol. VII).

Satya N. Nandan (Fiji): Chairman of the informal
group on the question of production policies, established
under the auspices of Negotiating Group 1 referred to in
paragraph 28 hereunder (see 114th meeting of the General
Committee on 26 April 1979, ibid., vol. IX).

Paul Bamela Engo (United Republic of Cameroon):
Chairman of the First Committee, Francis X. Njenga (Kenya),
Tommy T.B. Koh (Singapore) and Harry Wuensche (German
Democratic Republic): Co-chairmen of the Working Group
of 21 on First Committee issues with the Chairman of the
First Committee as principal coordinator. The Working
Group consisted of 10 members nominated by the Group of
77, China, and 10 members nominated by the principal
industrialized countries with alternates for each group.
The Group was constituted with members and alternates as
necessary to represent the interests of the issue under
consideration (decision of the 45th meeting of the General Committee on 9 April 1979, ibid., vol. XI; see also
114th meeting of the plenary on 26 April 1979, ibid.,
vol. XI).

The Second Committee set up informal consultative
groups, at different stages, chaired by the three Vice-
Chairmen, the representatives of Czechoslovakia, Kenya,
and Turkey and by the Rapporteur of the Committee, Satya
N. Nandan (Fiji). (See statement by the Chairman of the
Second Committee, A/CONF.62/C.2/L.87 (ibid., vol. IV).
See also statement on the work of the Committee prepared
by the Rapporteur, A/CONF.62/C.2/L.89/Rev.1, ibid.).

The Third Committee appointed the following officers
of its informal meetings:

José Luis Vallarta (Mexico): Chairman of the informal
meetings on protection and preservation of the marine
environment (decision of the second meeting of the
Third Committee, ibid., vol. II).

Cornel A. Metternich (Federal Republic of Germany):
Chairman of the informal meetings on Scientific Re-
search and the Development and Transfer of Technol-
ogy (decision of the second meeting of the Third
Committee, ibid., vol. II; see also A/CONF.62/C.3/
L.16, ibid., vol. III).

40.  Decision taken at the 65th meeting of the plenary Conference on 12 April 1976, ibid., vol. V, A/CONF.62/SR.65.

41.  Ibid., vol. VI, A/CONF.62/SR.71.

42.  Ibid., vol. VII, A/CONF.62/SR.77-SR.79.

43.  Decision taken at the 79th meeting of the plenary Conference on 28 June 1977, ibid., vol. VII.

44.  President's explanatory memorandum attached to A/CONF. 62/WP.10/Rev.2, dated 11 April 1980.

45.  Official Records of the Third United Nations Conference on the Law of the Sea, vol. IX, A/CONF.62/SR.89 and 90. The descriptions of the items are recorded in A/CONF.62/62, ibid., vol. X.

46.  Ibid., vol. X.

47.  The Group of Legal Experts on the Settlement of Disputes relating to Part XI of the Informal Composite Negotiating Text was established by the Chairman of the First Committee in consultation with the President as reflected at the 114th meeting of the plenary and in A/CONF.62/C.1/L.25 and L.36, ibid., vol. XI.

48.  The Group of Legal Experts on the Final Clauses was established by the President to deal with the technical aspects of the Final Clauses after their preliminary consideration in the informal plenary as recorded at the 120th meeting of the plenary of 24 August 1979, ibid., vol. XII.

49.  As referred to in paragraph 27 above and in the President's explanatory memorandum attached to A/CONF.62/WP.10/Rev. 2.

50.  Decision taken at the 141st meeting of the plenary on 29 August 1980, ibid., vol. XIV, A/CONF.62/SR.141.

51.  Ibid., also referred to in A/CONF.62/BUR.13/Rev.1.

52.  At the resumed eighth session.

53.  In adopting the programme of work (A/CONF.62/116), ibid., A/CONF/62/SR.154.

54.  A/CONF/62/SR.174.

55.  Recorded vote taken at the request of the delegation of the United States of America, with two delegations not participating in the vote.  The result was 130 in favour, 4 against with 17 abstentions.

56. Decision taken by the Conference at the 182nd meeting of the plenary Conference on 30 April 1982 as well as its decision taken at the 184th meeting on 24 September 1982.

57. Draft resolution A/CONF.62/L.3 and Add.1-4 adopted by the Conference at the 43rd meeting of the plenary on 22 July 1974, *ibid.*, vol. I.

58. Draft resolution A/CONF/62/L.9, adopted by the Conference at the 51st meeting of the plenary on 28 August 1974, *ibid.*, vol. I.

59. Draft Tribute A/CONF.62/L.15 adopted by the Conference at the 76th meeting of the plenary on 17 September 1976, *ibid.*, vol. VI.

60. Draft resolution A/CONF/62/L.127 adopted by the Conference at the 182nd meeting of the plenary on 30 April 1982.


IN WITNESS WHEREOF the respresentatives have signed this Final Act.


DONE AT MONTEGO BAY this tenth day of December, one thousand nine hundred and eighty-two in a single copy in the Arabic, Chinese, English, French, Russian, and Spanish languages, each text being equally authentic. The original texts shall be deposited in the archives of the United Nations Secretariat.


The President of the Conference:


The Special Representatives of the
Secretary-General to the Conference:


The Executive Secretary of the Conference:

Annex I

RESOLUTION I

ESTABLISHMENT OF THE PREPARATORY COMMISSION FOR THE
INTERNATIONAL SEA-BED AUTHORITY AND FOR THE
INTERNATIONAL TRIBUNAL FOR THE LAW OF THE SEA

The Third United Nations Conference on the Law
of the Sea,

Having adopted the Convention on the Law of the
Sea which provides for the establishment of the International Seabed Authority and the International Tribunal for the Law of the Sea,

Having decided to take all possible measures to
ensure the entry into effective operation without undue delay of the Authority and the Tribunal and to
make the necessary arrangements for the commencement
of their functions,

Having decided that a Preparatory Commission
should be established for the fulfillment of these
purposes,

Decides as follows:

1. There is hereby established the Preparatory
Commission for the International Seabed Authority and
for the International Tribunal for the Law of the Sea.
Upon signature of or accession to the Convention by 50
States, the Secretary-General of the United Nations
shall convene the Commission, and it shall meet no
sooner than 60 days and no later than 90 days thereafter.

2. The Commission shall consist of the representatives of States and of Namibia, represented by
the United Nations Council for Namibia, which have
signed the Convention or acceded to it. The representatives or signatories of the Final Act may participate fully in the deliberations of the Commission as
observers but shall not be entitled to participate in
the taking of decisions.

3. The Commission shall elect its Chairman and
other officers.

4. The Rules of Procedure of the Third United Nations Conference on the Law of the Sea shall apply *mutatis mutandis* to the adoption of the rules of procedure of the Commission.

5. The Commission shall:

(a) prepare the provisional agenda for the first session of the Assembly and of the Council and, as appropriate, make recommendations relating to items thereon;

(b) prepare draft rules of procedure of the Assembly and of the Council;

(c) make recommendations concerning the budget for the first financial period of the Authority;

(d) make recommendations concerning the relationship between the Authority and the United Nations and other international organizations;

(e) make recommendations concerning the Secretariat of the Authority in accordance with the relevant provisions of the Convention;

(f) undertake studies, as necessary, concerning the establishment of the headquarters of the Authority, and make recommendations relating thereto;

(g) prepare draft rules, regulations and procedures, as necessary to enable the Authority to commence its functions, including draft regulations concerning the financial management and the internal administration of the Authority;

(h) exercise the powers and functions assigned to it by resolution II of the Third United Nations Conference on the Law of the Sea relating to preparatory investment;

(i) undertake studies on the problems which would be encountered by developing land-based producer States likely to be most seriously affected by the production of minerals derived from the Area with a view to minimizing their difficulties and helping them to make the

necessary economic adjustment, including studies on the establishment of a compensation fund, and submit recommendations to the Authority thereon.

6. The Commission shall have such legal capacity as may be necessary for the exercise of its functions and the fulfillment of its purposes as set forth in this resolution.

7. The Commission may establish such subsidiary bodies as are necessary for the exercise of its functions and shall determine their functions and rules of procedure. It may also make use, as appropriate, of outside sources of expertise in accordance with United Nations practice to facilitate the work of bodies so established.

8. The Commission shall establish a special commission for the Enterprise and entrust to it the functions referred to in paragraph 12 of resolution II of the Third United Nations Conference on the Law of the Sea relating to preparatory investment. The special commission shall take all measures necessary for the early entry into effective operation of the Enterprise.

9. The Commission shall establish a special commission on the problems which would be encountered by developing land-based producer States likely to be most seriously affected by the production of minerals derived from the Area and entrust to it the functions referred to in paragraph 5(i).

10. The Commission shall prepare a report containing recommendations for submission to the meeting of the States Parties to be convened in accordance with Annex VI, article 4, of the Convention regarding practical arrangements for the establishment of the International Tribunal for the Law of the Sea.

11. The Commission shall prepare a final report on all matters within its mandate, except as provided in paragraph 10, for the presentation to the Assembly at its first session. Any action which may be taken on the basis of the report must be in conformity with the provisions of the Convention concerning the powers and functions entrusted to the respective organs of the Authority.

12. The Commission shall meet at the seat of the Authority if facilities are available; it shall meet as often as necessary for the expeditious exercise of its functions.

13. The Commission shall remain in existence until the conclusion of the first session of the Assembly, at which time its property and records shall be transferred to the Authority.

14. The expenses of the Commission shall be met from the regular budget of the United Nations, subject to the approval of the General Assembly of the United Nations.

15. The Secretary-General of the United Nations shall make available to the Commission such secretariat services as may be required.

16. The Secretary-General of the United Nations shall bring this resolution, in particular paragraphs 14 and 15, to the attention of the General Assembly for necessary action.


RESOLUTION II


GOVERNING PREPARATORY INVESTMENT IN PIONEER ACTIVITIES RELATING TO POLYMETALLIC NODULES


The Third United Nations Conference on the Law of the Sea,

Having adopted the Convention on the Law of the Sea (the "Convention"),

Having established by resolution I the Preparatory Commission for the International Seabed Authority and for the International Tribunal for the Law of the Sea (the "Commission") and directed it to prepare draft rules, regulations and procedures, as necessary to enable the Authority to commence its functions, as well as to make recommendations for the early entry into effective operation of the Enterprise,

Desirous of making provision for investments by States and other entities made in a manner compatible with the international regime set forth in Part XI of

642

the Convention and the Annexes relating thereto, before the entry into force of the Convention,

Recognizing the need to ensure that the Enterprise will be provided with funds, technology, and
expertise necessary to enable it to keep pace with
the States and other entities referred to in the preceding paragraph with respect to activities in the
Area,

Decides as follows:

1. For the purposes of this resolution:

(a) "pioneer investor" refers to:

    (i) France, India, Japan, and the Union of
         Soviet Socialist Republics, or a state
         enterprise of each of those States or
         one natural or juridical person which
         possesses the nationality of or is ef-
         fectively controlled by each of those
         States, or their nationals, provided
         that the State concerned signs the Con-
         vention and the State or state enter-
         prise or natural or juridical person has
         expended, before 1 January 1983, an
         amount equivalent to at least \$US 30 mil-
         lion (United States dollars calculated in
         constant dollars relative to 1982) in
         pioneer activities and has expended no
         less than 10 percent of that amount in
         the location, survey, and evaluation of
         the area referred to in paragraph 3(a);

    (ii) four entities, whose components being
         natural or juridical persons[1] possess
         the nationality of one or more of the
         following States, or are effectively
         controlled by one or more of them or
         their nationals: Belgium, Canada, the

---

[1] For their identity and composition see "Seabed mineral resources development: recent activities of the
international Consortia" and addendum, published by
the Department of International Economic and Social
Affairs of the United Nations (ST/ESA/107 and Add.1).

Federal Republic of Germany, Italy, Japan, the Netherlands, the United Kingdom of Great Britain and Northern Ireland, and the United States of America, provided that the certifying State or States sign the Convention and the entity concerned has expended, before 1 January 1983, the levels of expenditure for the purposes stated in subparagraph (i);

(iii) any developing State which signs the Convention or any state enterprise or natural or juridical person which possesses the nationality of such State or is effectively controlled by it or its nationals, or any group of the foregoing, which, before 1 January 1985, has expended the levels of expenditure for the purpose stated in subparagraph (i);

The rights of the pioneer investor may devolve upon its successor in interest.

(b) "pioneer activities" means undertakings, commitments of financial and other assets, investigations, findings, research, engineering development and other activities relevant to the identification, discovery, and systematic analysis and evaluation of polymetallic nodules and to the determination of the technical and economic feasibility of exploitation. Pioneer activities include:

(i) any at-sea observation and evaluation which has as its objective the establishment and documentation of the nature, shape, concentration, location and grade of polymetallic nodules and of the environmental, technical, and other appropriate factors which must be taken into account before exploitation;

(ii) the recovery from the Area of polymetallic nodules with a view to the designing, fabricating, and testing of equipment which is intended to be used in the exploitation of polymetallic nodules;

(c) "certifying State" means a State which signs the Convention, standing in the same relation

to a pioneer investor as would a sponsoring
State pursuant to Annex III, article 4, of
the Convention and which certifies the levels of expenditure specified in subparagraph
(a);

(d) "polymetallic nodules" means one of the resources of the Area consisting of any deposit or accretion of nodules, on or just below
the surface of the deep seabed, which contain manganese, nickel, cobalt, and copper;

(e) "pioneer area" means an area allocated by
the Commission to a pioneer investor for
pioneer activities pursuant to this resolution. A pioneer area shall not exceed
150,000 square kilometres. The pioneer investor shall relinquish portions of the pioneer area to revert to the Area, in accordance with the following schedule:

(i) 20 percent of the area allocated by the
end of the third year from the date of
the allocation;

(ii) an additional 10 percent of the area allocated by the end of the fifth year
from the date of the allocation;

(iii) an additional 20 percent of the area allocated or such larger amount as would
exceed the exploitation area decided upon
by the Authority in its rules, regulations, and procedures, after eight years
from the date of the allocation of the
area or the date of the award of a production authorization, whichever is
earlier;

(f) "Area", "Authority", "activities in the Area"
and "resources" have meanings assigned to
those terms in the Convention.

2. As soon as the Commission begins to function,
any State which has signed the Convention may apply to
the Commission on its behalf or on behalf of any state
enterprise or entity or natural or juridical person
specified in paragraph 1(a) for registration as a pioneer investor. The Commission shall register the applicant as a pioneer investor if the application:

(a) is accompanied, in the case of a State which has signed the Convention, by a statement certifying the level of expenditure made in accordance with paragraph 1(a), and, in all other cases, a certificate concerning such level of expenditure issued by a certifying State or States; and

(b) is in conformity with the other provisions of this resolution, including paragraph 5.

3. (a) Every application shall cover a total area which need not be a single continuous area, sufficiently large and of sufficient estimated commercial value to allow two mining operations. The application shall indicate the coordinates of the area defining the total area and dividing it into two parts of equal estimated commercial value and shall contain all the data available to the applicant with respect to both parts of the area. Such data shall include, _inter alia_, information relating to mapping, testing, the density of polymetallic nodules, and their metal content. In dealing with such data, the Commission and its staff shall act in accordance with the relevant provisions of the Convention and its Annexes concerning the confidentiality of data.

(b) Within 45 days of receiving the data required by subparagraph (a), the Commission shall designate the part of the area which is to be reserved in accordance with the Convention for the conduct of activities in the Area by the Authority through the Enterprise or in association with developing States. The other part of the area shall be allocated to the pioneer investor as a pioneer area.

4. No pioneer investor may be registered in respect of more than one pioneer area. In the case of a pioneer investor which is made up of two or more components, none of such components may apply to be registered as a pioneer investor in its own right or under paragraph 1(a)(iii).

5. (a) Any State which has signed the Convention and which is a prospective certifying State

shall ensure, before making applications to
the Commission under paragraph 2, that areas
in respect of which applications are made do
not overlap one another or areas previously
allocated as pioneer areas. The States concerned shall keep the Commission currently
and fully informed of any efforts to resolve
conflicts with respect to overlapping claims
and of the results thereof.

(b) Certifying States shall ensure, before the
entry into force of the Convention, that
pioneer activities are conducted in a manner
compatible with it.

(c) The prospective certifying States, including
all potential claimants, shall resolve their
conflicts as required under subparagraph (a)
by negotiations within a reasonable period.
If such conflicts have not been resolved by
1 March 1983, the prospective certifying
States shall arrange for the submission of
all such claims to binding arbitration in
accordance with UNCITRAL Arbitration Rules
to commence not later than 1 May 1983 and to
be completed by 1 December 1984. If one of
the States concerned does not wish to participate in the arbitration, it shall arrange
for a juridical person of its nationality to
represent it in the arbitration. The arbitral tribunal may, for good cause, extend
the deadline for the making of the award for
one or more 30-day periods.

(d) In determining the issue as to which applicant involved in a conflict shall be awarded
all or part of each area in conflict, the
arbitral tribunal shall find a solution
which is fair and equitable, having regard,
with respect to each applicant involved in
the conflict, to the following factors:

(i) the deposit of the list of relevant co-
ordinates with the prospective certifying State or States not later than the
date of adoption of the Final Act or
1 January 1983, whichever is earlier.

(ii) the continuity and extent of past activities relevant to each area in conflict

and to the application area of which it
it a part;

(iii) the date on which each pioneer investor
concerned or predecessor in interest or
component organization thereof commenced
activities at sea in the application
area;

(iv) the financial cost of activities measured in constant United States dollars
relevant to each area in conflict and to
the application area of which it is a
part; and

(v) the time when those activities were
carried out and the quality of activities.

6. A pioneer investor registered pursuant to
this resolution shall, from the date of registration,
have the exclusive right to carry out pioneer activities in the pioneer area allocated to it.

7. (a) Every applicant for registration as a
pioneer investor shall pay to the Commission
a fee of $US 250,000. When the pioneer in-
vestor applies to the Authority for a plan
of work for exploration and exploitation the
fee referred to in Annex III, article 13,
paragraph 2, of the Convention shall be $US
250,000.

(b) Every registered pioneer investor shall pay
an annual fixed fee of $US 1 million commenc-
ing from the date of the allocation of the
pioneer area. The payments shall be made by
the pioneer investor to the Authority upon
the approval of its plan of work for exploration and exploitation. The financial arrangements undertaken pursuant to such plan
of work shall be adjusted to take account of
the payments made pursuant to this paragraph.

(c) Every registered pioneer investor shall agree
to incur periodic expenditures, with respect
to the pioneer area allocated to it, until
approval of its plan of work pursuant to paragraph 8, of an amount to be determined by

the Commission. The amount should be reasonably related to the size of the pioneer
area and the expenditures which would be expected of a bona fide operator who intends
to bring that area into commercial production within a reasonable time.

8. (a) Within six months of the entry into force
of the Convention and certification by the
Commission in accordance with paragraph 11,
of compliance with this resolution, the pioneer investor so registered shall apply to
the Authority for approval of a plan of work
for exploration and exploitation, in accordance with the Convention. The plan of work
in respect of such application shall comply
with and be governed by the relevant provisions of the Convention and the rules, regulations and procedures of the Authority, including those on the operational requirements, the financial requirements, and the
undertakings concerning the transfer of
technology. Accordingly, the Authority shall
approve such application.

(b) When an application for approval of a plan of
work is submitted by an entity other than a
State, pursuant to subparagraph (a), the
certifying State or States shall be deemed
to be the sponsoring State for the purposes
of Annex III, article 4, of the Convention,
and shall thereupon assume such obligations.

(c) No plan of work for exploration and exploitation shall be approved unless the certifying State is a Party to the Convention.
In the case of the entities referred to in
paragraph 1(a)(ii), the plan of work for exploration and exploitation shall not be approved unless all the States whose natural
or juridical persons comprise those entities
are Parties to the Convention. If any such
State fails to ratify the Convention within
six months after it has received a notification from the Authority that an application
by it, or sponsored by it, is pending, its
status as a pioneer investor or certifying
State, as the case may be, shall terminate,
unless the Council, by a majority of three
fourths of its members present and voting,

decides to postpone the terminal date for a
period not exceeding six months.

9.  (a) In the allocation of production authori-
    zations, in accordance with article 151 and
    Annex III, article 7, of the Convention, the
    pioneer investors who have obtained approval
    of plans of work for exploration and exploi-
    tation shall have priority over all appli-
    cants other than the Enterprise which shall
    be entitled to production authorizations for
    two mine sites including that referred to in
    article 151, paragraph 5, of the Convention.
    After each of the pioneer investors has ob-
    tained production authorization for its first
    mine site, the priority for the Enterprise
    contained in Annex III, article 7, paragraph
    6, of the Convention shall apply.

(b) Production authorizations shall be issued to
    each pioneer investor within 30 days of the
    date on which that pioneer investor notifies
    the Authority that it will commence commer-
    cial production within five years.  If a
    pioneer investor is unable to begin produc-
    tion within the period of five years for
    reasons beyond its control, it shall apply
    to the Legal and Technical Commission for an
    extension of time.  That Commission shall
    grant the extension of time, for a period
    not exceeding five years and not subject to
    further extension, if it is satisfied that
    the pioneer investor cannot begin on an eco-
    nomically viable basis at the time originally
    planned.  Nothing in this subparagraph shall
    prevent the Enterprise or any other pioneer
    applicant, who has notified the Authority
    what it will commence commercial production
    within five years, from being given a pri-
    ority over any applicant who has obtained an
    extension of time under this subparagraph.

(c) If the Authority, upon being given notice,
    pursuant to subparagraph (b), determines that
    the commencement of commercial production
    within five years would exceed the production
    ceiling in article 151, paragraphs 2 to 7, of
    the Convention, the applicant shall hold a
    priority over any other applicant for the

award of the next production authorization allowed by the production ceiling.

(d) If two or more pioneer investors apply for production authorizations to begin commercial production at the same time and article 151, paragraphs 2 to 7, of the Convention, would not permit all such production to commence simultaneously, the Authority shall notify the pioneer investors concerned. Within three months of such notification, they shall decide whether and, if so, to what extent they wish to apportion the allowable tonnage among themselves.

(e) If, pursuant to subparagraph (d), the pioneer investors concerned decide not to apportion the available production among themselves, they shall agree on an order of priority for production authorizations; and all subsequent applications for production authorizations will be granted after those referred to in this subparagraph have been approved.

(f) If, pursuant to subparagraph (d), the pioneer investors concerned decide to apportion the available production among themselves, the Authority shall award each of them a production authorization for such lesser quantity as they have agreed. In each case the stated production requirements of the applicant will be approved, and their full production will be allowed as soon as the production ceiling admits of additional capacity sufficient for the applicants involved in the competition. All subsequent applications for production authorizations will only be granted after the requirements of this subparagraph have been met and the applicant is no longer subject to the reduction of production provided for in this subparagraph.

(g) If the parties fail to reach agreement within the stated time period, the matter shall be decided immediately by the means provided for in paragraph 5(c) in accordance with the criteria set forth in Annex III, article 7, paragraphs 3 and 5, of the Convention.

10.   (a) Any rights acquired by entities or natural or juridical persons which possess the
nationality of or are effectively controlled
by a State or States whose status as certifying State has been terminated, shall lapse
unless the pioneer investor changes its nationality and sponsorship within six months
of the date of such termination, as provided
for in subparagraph (c).

(b) A pioneer investor may change its nationality and sponsorship from that existing at
the time of its registration as a pioneer
investor to that of any State Party to the
Convention which has effective control over
the pioneer investor in terms of paragraph
1(a).

(c) Changes of nationality and sponsorship pursuant to this paragraph shall not affect any
right or priority conferred on a pioneer investor pursuant to paragraphs 6 and 8.

11.   The Commission shall:

(a) provide each pioneer investor with the certificate of compliance with the provisions
of this resolution referred to in paragraph
8; and

(b) include in its final report required by paragraph 11 of resolution I of the Conference
details of all registrations of pioneer investors and allocations of pioneer areas
pursuant to this resolution.

12.   In order to ensure that the Enterprise is
able to carry out activities in the Area in such a
manner as to keep pace with States and other entities;

(a) every registered pioneer investor shall:

(i) carry out exploration, at the request of
the Commission, in the area reserved,
pursuant to paragraph 3 in connection
with its application, for activities in
the Area by the Authority through the
Enterprise or in association with developing States, on the basis that the

costs so incurred plus interest thereon at the rate of 10 percent per annum shall be reimbursed;

(ii) provide training at all levels for personnel designated by the Commission;

(iii) undertake before the entry into force of the Convention, to perform the obligations prescribed in the Convention relating to transfer of technology.

(b) every certifying State shall:

(i) ensure that the necessary funds are made available to the Enterprise in a timely manner in accordance with the Convention, upon its entry into force; and

(ii) report periodically to the Commission on the activities carried out by it, by its entities or natural or juridical persons.

13. The Authority and its organs shall recognize and honour the rights and obligations arising from this resolution and the decisions of the Commission taken pursuant to it.

14. Without prejudice to paragraph 13, this resolution shall have effect until the entry into force of the Convention.

15. Nothing in this resolution shall derogate from Annex III, article 6, paragraph 3(c), of the Convention.

RESOLUTION III

The Third United Nations Conference on the Law of the Sea,

Having regard to the Convention on the Law of the Sea,

Bearing in mind the Charter of the United Nations, in particular Article 73,

1. Declares that:

(a) In the case of a territory whose people have not attained full independence or other self-governing status recognized by the United Nations, or a territory under colonial domination, provisions concerning rights and interests under the Convention shall be implemented for the benefit of the people of the territory with a view to promoting their well-being and development.

(b) Where a dispute exists between States over the sovereignty of a territory to which this resolution applies, in respect of which the United Nations has recommended specific means of settlement, there shall be consultations between the parties to that dispute regarding the exercise of the rights referred to in subparagraph (a). In such consultations the interests of the people of the territory concerned shall be a fundamental consideration. Any exercise of those rights shall take into account the relevant resolutions of the United Nations and shall be without prejudice to the position of any party to the dispute. The States concerned shall make every effort to enter into provisional arrangements of a practical nature and shall not jeopardize or hamper the reaching of a final settlement of the dispute.

2. Requests the Secretary-General of the United Nations to bring this resolution to the attention of all Members of the United Nations and the other participants in the Conference, as well as the principal organs of the United Nations, and to request their compliance with it.

RESOLUTION IV

The Third United Nations Conference on the Law of the Sea,

Bearing in mind that national liberation movements have been invited to participate in the Conference as observers in accordance with rule 62 of its rules of procedure,

Decides that the national liberation movements, which have been participating in the Third United Nations

Conference on the Law of the Sea, shall be entitled
to sign the Final Act of the Conference, in their
capacity as observers.

Annex II

STATEMENT OF UNDERSTANDING CONCERNING A SPECIFIC METHOD
TO BE USED IN ESTABLISHING THE OUTER EDGE OF THE
CONTINENTAL MARGIN

The Third United Nations Conference on the Law
of the Sea,

Considering the special characteristics of a
State's continental margin where: (1) the average
distance at which the 200 metre isobath occurs is not
more than 20 nautical miles; (2) the greater proportion of the sedimentary rock of the continental margin lies beneath the rise; and

Taking into account the inequity that would result to that State from the application to its continental margin of article 76 of the Convention, in
that, the mathematical average of the thickness of
sedimentary rock along a line established at the maximum distance permissible in accordance with the provisions of paragraph 4(a)(i) and (ii) of that article
as representing the entire outer edge of the continental margin would not be less than 3.5 kilometres;
and that more than half of the margin would be excluded thereby;

Recognizes that such State may, notwithstanding
the provisions of article 76, establish the outer
edge of its continental margin by straight lines not
exceeding 60 nautical miles in length connecting fixed points, defined by latitude and longitude, at each
of which the thickness of sedimentary rock is not
less than 1 kilometre,

Where a State establishes the outer edge of its
continental margin by applying the method set forth
in the preceding paragraph of this statement, this
method may also be utilized by a neighbouring State
for delineating the outer edge of its continental
margin on a common geological feature, where its

outer edge would lie on such feature on a line established at the maximum distance permissible in accordance with article 76, paragraph 4(a)(i) and (ii),
along which the mathematical average of the thickness
of sedimentary rock is not less than 3.5 kilometres,

The Conference requests the Commission on the
Limits of the Continental Shelf set up pursuant to
Annex II of the Convention, to be governed by the
terms of this Statement when making its recommendations on matters related to the establishment of the
outer edge of the continental margins of these States
in the southern part of the Bay of Bengal.


Annex III


TRIBUTE TO SIMON BOLIVAR THE LIBERATOR

The Third United Nations Conference on the Law
of the Sea

Considering that 24 July 1974 marks a further
anniversary of the birth of Simón Bolívar, the Liberator, a man of vision and early champion of international organization, and a historic figure of universal dimensions,

Considering further that the work of Simón Bolívar the Liberator, based on the concepts of liberty
and justice as foundations for the peace and progress
of peoples, has left an indelible mark on history and
constitutes a source of constant inspiration,

Decides to pay a public tribute of admiration
and respect to Simón Bolívar the Liberator, in the
plenary meeting of the Third United Nations Conference on the Law of the Sea.

APPENDIX II

Annex IV

RESOLUTION EXPRESSING GRATITUDE TO THE PRESIDENT,
THE GOVERNMENT AND OFFICIALS OF VENEZUELA

The Third United Nations Conference on the Law
of the Sea,

Bearing in mind that its second session was held
in the city of Caracas, cradle of Simón Bolívar, Liberator of five nations, who devoted his life to
fighting for the self-determination of peoples, equality among States, and justice as the expression of
their common destiny,

Acknowledging with keen appreciation the extraordinary effort made by the Government and the people
of Venezuela, which enabled the Conference to meet in
the most favourable spirit of brotherhood and in unparalleled material conditions,

Decides

1. To express to His Excellency the President of
the Republic of Venezuela, the President and members
of the Organizing Committee of the Conference, and
the Government and people of Venezuela its deepest
gratitude for the unforgettable hospitality which they
have offered it;

2. To give voice to its hope that the ideals of
social justice, equality among nations and solidarity
among peoples advocated by the Liberator Simón Bolívar
will serve to guide the future work of the Conference.


Annex V

TRIBUTE TO THE AMPHICTYONIC CONGRESS OF PANAMA

The Third United Nations Conference on the Law
of the Sea, at its fifth session,

Considering that the current year 1976 marks the
one hundred and fiftieth anniversary of the Amphictyonic Congress of Panama, convoked by the Liberator

657

Simón Bolívar for the laudable and visionary purpose
of uniting the Latin American peoples,

Considering likewise that a spirit of universality prevailed at the Congress of Panama, which was
ahead of its time and which foresaw that only on the
basis of union and reciprocal cooperation is it possible to guarantee peace and promote the development of
nations.

Considering further that the Congress of Panama
evoked the prestigious and constructive Greek Amphic-
tyony and anticipated the ecumenical and creative
image of the United Nations,

Decides to render to the Amphictyonic Congress
of Panama, in a plenary meeting of the Third United
Nations Conference on the Law of the Sea, at its fifth
session, a public tribute acknowledging its expressive
historic significance.


Annex VI


RESOLUTION ON DEVELOPMENT OF NATIONAL MARINE SCIENCE,
TECHNOLOGY AND OCEAN SERVICE INFRASTRUCTURES

The Third United Nations Conference on the Law
of the Sea,

Recognizing that the Convention on the Law of
the Sea is intended to establish a new regime for the
seas and oceans which will contribute to the realization of a just and equitable international economic
order through making provision for the peaceful use
of ocean space, the equitable and efficient management and utilization of its resources, and the study,
protection, and preservation of the marine environment,

Bearing in mind that the new regime must take
into account, in particular, the special needs and
interests of the developing countries, whether coastal, landlocked, or geographically disadvantaged,

Aware of the rapid advances being made in the
field of marine science and technology, and the need

for the developing countries, whether coastal, landlocked, or geographically disadvantaged, to share in
these achievements if the aforementioned goals are to
be met,

Convinced that, unless urgent measures are taken,
the marine scientific and technological gap between
the developed and the developing countries will widen
further and thus endanger the very foundations of the
new regime,

Believing that optimum utilization of the new
opportunities for social and economic development offered by the new regime will be facilitated through
action at the national and international level aimed
at strengthening national capabilities in marine science, technology, and ocean services, particularly in
the developing countries, with a view to ensuring the
rapid absorption and efficient application of technology and scientific knowledge available to them,

Considering that national and regional marine
scientific and technological centres would be the
principal institutions through which States and, in
particular, the developing countries, foster and conduct marine scientific research, and receive and disseminate marine technology,

Recognizing the special role of the competent
international organizations envisaged by the Convention on the Law of the Sea, especially in relation to
the establishment and development of national and
regional marine scientific and technological centres,

Noting that present efforts undertaken within
the United Nations system in training, education and
assistance in the field of marine science and technology and ocean services are far below current requirements and would be particularly inadequate to
meet the demands generated through operation of the
Convention on the Law of the Sea,

Welcoming recent initiatives within international organizations to promote and coordinate their major international assistance programmes aimed at
strengthening marine science infrastructures in developing countries,

1. Calls upon all Member States to determine
appropriate priorities in their development plans

659

for the strengthening of their marine science, technology, and ocean services;

2. Calls upon the developing countries to establish programmes for the promotion of technical cooperation among themselves in the field of marine science, technology, and ocean service development;

3. Urges the industrialized countries to assist the developing countries in the preparation and implementation of their marine science, technology, and ocean service development programmes;

4. Recommends that the World Bank, the regional banks, the United Nations Development Programme, the United Nations Financing System for Science and Technology and other multilateral funding agencies augment and coordinate their operations for the provision of funds to developing countries for the preparation and implementation of major programmes of assistance in strengthening their marine science, technology, and ocean services;

5. Recommends that all competent international organizations within the United Nations system expand programmes within their respective fields of competence for assistance to developing countries in the field of marine science, technology, and ocean services and coordinate their efforts on a system-wide basis in the implementation of such programmes, paying particular attention to the special needs of the developing countries, whether coastal, landlocked, or geographically disadvantaged;

6. Requests the Secretary-General of the United Nations to transmit this resolution to the General Assembly at its thirty-seventh session.


The signature pages (not appended hereto) will be contained in the original of the Final Act in the form considered by the Conference in document FA/1/Add.1.

[Note: In accordance with the Secretary-General's practice, there will be only one signature block per page.]

Appendix

OBSERVERS PARTICIPATING AT THE CONFERENCE

States and territories

Cook Islands (3rd and 10th sessions)
Netherlands Antilles (3rd to resumed 7th ses-
sesions, resumed 8th session, 9th and 11th
sessions)
Papua New Guinea (3rd session)
Seychelles (5th session)
Suriname (3rd session)
Trust Territory of the Pacific Islands
(3rd to 11th sessions)

Liberation movements

African National Congress (South Africa)
African National Council (Zimbabwe)
African Party for the Independence of Guinea
and Cape Verde Islands (PAIGC)
Palestine Liberation Organization
Pan Africanist Congress of Azania (South Africa)
Patriotic Front (Zimbabwe)
Seychelles People's United Party (SPUP)
South West Africa People's Organization (SWAPO)

Specialized agencies and other organizations

International Labour Organization (ILO)
Food and Agricultural Organization of the
United Nations (FAO)
United Nations Educational, Scientific
and Cultural Organization (UNESCO)
Intergovernmental Oceanographic Commission (IOC)
International Civil Aviation Organization (ICAO)
World Health Organization (WHO)
World Bank
International Telecommunication Union (ITU)
World Meteorological Organization (WMO)
International Maritime Organization (IMO)
World Intellectual Property Organization (WIPO)

****

International Atomic Energy Agency (IAEA)

## Intergovernmental organizations

Andes Development Corporation
Asian-African Legal Consultative Committee
Commonwealth Secretariat
Council of Arab Economic Unity
Council of Europe
European Communities
Inter-American Development Bank
International Hydrographic Bureau
International Oil Pollution Compensation Fund
League of Arab States
Organization of African Unity
Organization of American States
Organization of Arab Petroleum Exporting
  Countries
Organization of the Islamic Conference
Organization for Economic Cooperation and
  Development
Organization of Petroleum Exporting Countries
Permanent Commission for the South Pacific
Saudi-Sudanese Red Sea Joint Commission
West African Economic Community

## Non-governmental organizations

### Category I

International Chamber of Commerce
International Confederation of Free Trade Unions
International Cooperative Alliance
International Council of Voluntary Agencies
International Council of Women
International Youth and Student Movement for the
  United Nations
United Towns Organization
World Confederation of Labour
World Federation of United Nations Associations
World Muslim Congress

### Category II

Arab Lawyers Union
Bahá'i International Community
Baptist World Alliance
Carnegie Endowment for International Peace
Commission of the Churches on International
  Affairs

Foundation for the Peoples of the South
  Pacific, Inc., The
Friends World Committee for Consultation
Inter-American Council of Commerce and Production
International Air Transport Association
International Association for Religious Freedom
International Bar Association
International Chamber of Shipping
International Commission of Jurists
International Cooperation for Socio-Economic
  Development
International Council of Environmental Law
International Council of Scientific Unions
International Federation for Human Rights
International Hotel Association
International Law Association
International Movement for Fraternal Union
  among Races and Peoples (UFER)
International Organization of Consumers' Unions
International Union for Conservation of Nature
  and Natural Resources
Latin American Association of Finance Development
  Institutions (ALIDE)
Mutual Assistance of the Latin American
  Government Oil Companies (ARPEL)
Pan American Federation of Engineering Societies
  (UPADI)
Pax Christi, International Catholic Peace
  Movement
Society for International Development (SID)
Women's International League for Peace and
  Freedom
World Alliance of Young Men's Christian
  Associations
World Association of World Federalists
World Conference on Religion and Peace
World Peace through Law Centre
World Young Women's Christian Association

### Roster

Asian Environmental Society
Center for Inter-American Relations
Commission to Study the Organization of Peace
Foresta Institute for Ocean and Mountain Studies
Friends of the Earth (F.O.E.)
International Institute for Environment and
  Development
International Ocean Institute
International Studies Association

National Audubon Society
Population Institute
Sierra Club
United Seamen's Service
World Federation of Scientific Workers
World Society of Ekistics

----

APPENDIX III


Statement by Ambassador Thomas Clingan
Head of the Delegation of the United States of America
at the Final Session of the
Third United Nations Law of the Sea Conference
Montego Bay, Jamaica on December 9, 1982


Mr. President, I wish first to express my delegation's gratitude for the generous hospitality of the Government of Jamaica, for its invitation to host these proceedings in this beautiful environment, and for the excellent arrangements it has provided. I would also like to express our appreciation to you, Mr. President, to the officers of the Conference, and to the members of the Secretariat, all of whom labored in these negotiations over many years.

Mr. President, I am here to sign, on behalf of the United States, the Final Act of the Convention. It had been our hope that we would be here for another purpose as well. The United States approached the work of the Conference early this year with renewed dedication and hope. As the President of the United States said on January 29, 1982, the United States remained committed to the multilateral process for seeking agreement on the law of the sea. With that in mind, the US delegation participated fully in the Eleventh Session, and sought a final result that would command global consensus. The Conference did not achieve that result.

The United States recognizes that certain aspects of the Convention represent positive accomplishments. Indeed, those parts of the Convention dealing with navigation and overflight and most other provisions of the Convention serve the interests of the international community. These texts reflect prevailing international practice. They also demonstrate that the Conference believed that it was articulating rules in most areas that reflect the existing state of affairs--a state we wished to preserve by enshrining these beneficial and desirable principles in treaty language.

Unfortunately, Mr. President, despite these accomplishments, the deep seabed mining regime that would be established by the Convention is unacceptable

and would not serve the interests of the international community.

The Conference undertook, for the first time in history, to create novel institutional arrangements for the regulation of seabed mining beyond the limits of national jurisdiction. It attempted to construct new and complex institutions to regulate the exploitation of these resources in a field requiring high technology that has not been fully developed and massive investments. We had all hoped that these institutions would encourage the development of seabed resources which, if left undeveloped, would benefit no one. A regime which would promote seabed mining to the advantage of all was the objective toward which we labored.

We regret that this objective was not achieved. Our major concerns with the seabed mining texts have been elaborated on in the records of this Conference and I will not use this occasion to repeat them. Suffice it to say, Mr. President, that along the road, some lost sight of what it was the world community had charged us to do. They forgot that, in the process of political interchange, the political and economic costs can become too high for some participants to bear. They forgot that, to achieve the global consensus we all sought, no nation should be asked to sacrifice fundamental national interests.

The result is that consensus eluded us on deep seabed mining. Each nation must now evaluate how it must act to protect its interests in the years to come.

We need not fear the future. In particular those elements which promote the general community interests with respect to navigation, and the conservation and utilization of resources within national jurisdiction, reflect long-standing practice. The expectations of the international community in these areas can and should be realized because we recognize that certain practices are beneficial to the community as a whole. For example, the Convention has recognized the sovereign rights of the coastal State over the resources of the Exclusive Economic Zone, jurisdiction over artificial islands, and jurisdiction over installations and structures used for economic purposes therein, while retaining the international status of the zone in which all States enjoy the

freedoms of navigation, overflight, the laying of submarine cables and pipelines, and other internationally
lawful uses of the sea, including military operations,
exercises, and activities. In addition, the Conference record supports the traditional US position concerning innocent passage in the territorial sea. The
rules that reflect the international community's expectations are sound and, therefore, they will endure.

Institutions, however, that do not command consensus and that are not beneficial to the community
as a whole raise serious problems. Under these circumstances, alternative ways of preserving national
access to deep seabed resources are necessary, just,
and permitted by international law.

As we begin the journey before us, we should face
the future devoid of rancor or recrimination, ready to
meet the challenges that lie ahead. Mr. President,
the United States faces the future in that spirit. In
the pursuit of its own legitimate and vital interests,
my country will act with responsibility and with
awareness of the interests of others. This very pursuit is necessary to the development of the resources
from which we can all benefit. Although States will
take different roads from here, I believe they share
a common goal--peace and the rule of law in the uses
of the world's oceans.

Mr. President, my delegation wishes to join the
many previous speakers in paying tribute to the memory
of the late Hamilton Shirley Amerasinghe of Sri Lanka,
who labored diligently as your predecessor in the
earlier stages of this Conference. None who knew him
will forget his warm and outgoing personality, his
wit, or his many significant contributions to the
work of the Conference.

In conclusion, on a personal note, let me express
my gratitude to you and, through you, to all concerned,
for the friendship and cooperation I have enjoyed
through the many years of this Conference. Thank you,
Mr. President.

APPENDIX IV


United Nation Department of Public Information
Law of the Sea Conference, Final Part of 11th Session
Montego Bay, Jamaica
Press Release SEA/MB/13 10 December 1982

ROUND-UP

NINE YEAR UNITED NATIONS CONFERENCE ON LAW OF THE SEA
      ENDS WITH SIGNING OF CONVENTION
      BY 119 DELEGATIONS AT MONTEGO BAY


First Session of Preparatory Commission To Begin
15 March in Kingston


        The Third United Nations Conference on the Law of
the Sea ended this afternoon following nine years of
work which culminated in the opening for signature today in Montego Bay, Jamaica, of the United Nations
Convention on the Law of the Sea.

        The new constitution for the world's oceans was
signed on the closing day by 118 countries and the
United Nations Council for Namibia.  No United Nations
convention has ever received such a large number of
signatures on the first day, and never before have a
majority of participants in a United Nations treaty-
making conference signed a convention as soon as it
was opened for signature.  Nearly 160 States have tak-
en part in the drafting of the Convention since the
Conference began in 1973.

        The Preparatory Commission for the main institu-
tions to be established under the Convention--the International Sea-Bed Authority and the International
Tribunal for the Law of the Sea--will hold its first
session at Kingston, Jamaica, beginning 15 March 1983.
The meeting was assured when the required 50 signatures to the Convention were affixed today.  All
States signing the Convention thereby become members
of the Commission.

        The announcement on the convening of the Prepara-
tory Commission was made by Secretary-General Javier
Pérez de Cuéllar, who flew to Montego Bay today to
make a closing statement at the Conference.  Mr. Pérez

de Cuéllar hailed the outcome of the Conference as a "a breath of fresh air at a time of serious crisis in international cooperation" and of decline in the use of international machinery for the solution of world problems.

The Prime Minister of Jamaica, welcoming the Conference to Jamaica at the start of its Montego Bay session on 6 December, described the Convention as "the only possible option". He said it provided "a solid basis for the political and economic development of the international community through collective right rather than individual might".

(p. A-2)

The President of the Conference, Tommy T.B. Koh, said on the closing day that States would be induced to support the Convention if the Preparatory Commission acted efficiently and objectively; but if it did not, the work of the Conference would have been in vain. Assessing the Conference's results, he stated: "We have strengthened the United Nations by proving that, with political will, nations can use the organization as a centre to harmonize their actions."

The meetings at Montego Bay were the final part of the Conference's eleventh session. They took place at the main hall of the Rose Hall Beach Hotel, on Jamaica's north coast facing the Caribbean Sea.

The Convention (document A/CONF.62/122 and corrigenda) was signed today by the following States: Algeria, Angola, Australia, Austria, Bahamas, Bahrain, Bangladesh, Barbados, Belize, Bhutan, Brazil, Bulgaria, Burma, Burundi, Byelorussia, Canada, Cape Verde, Chad, Chile, China, Colombia, Congo, Costa Rica, Cuba, Cyprus, Czechoslovakia, Democratic Republic of Korea, Democratic Yemen, Denmark, Djibouti, Dominican Republic, Egypt, Ethiopia, Fiji, Finland, France, Gabon, Gambia, German Democratic Republic, Ghana, Greece, Grenada, Guinea-Bissau, Guyana, Haiti, Honduras, Hungary, Iceland, India, Indonesia, Iran, Iraq, Ireland, Ivory Coast, Jamaica, Kenya, Kuwait, Lao People's Democratic Republic, Lesotho, Liberia, Malaysia, Maldives, Malta, Mauritania, Mauritius, Mexico, Monaco, Mongolia, Morocco, Mozambique, Nauru, Nepal, Netherlands, New Zealand, Niger, Nigeria, Norway, Pakistan, Panama, Papua New Guinea, Paraguay, Philippines, Poland, Portugal, Romania, Rwanda, Saint Lucia,

Saint Vincent and the Grenadines, Senegal, Seychelles, Sierra Leone, Singapore, Solomon Islands, Somalia, Sri Lanka, Sudan, Suriname, Sweden, Thailand, Togo, Trinidad and Tobago, Tunisia, Tuvalu, Uganda, Ukraine, USSR, United Arab Emirates, United Republic of Cameroon, United Republic of Tanzania, Upper Volta, Uruguay, Vanuatu, Viet Nam, Yemen, Yugoslavia, Zambia, and Zimbabwe.

In addition to these States, the Convention was also signed by the United Nations Council for Namibia and the Cook Islands.

The Convention will remain open for signature for two years, until 9 December 1984, at the Ministry of Foreign Affairs in Kingston, Jamaica, and from 1 July 1983 at United Nations Headquarters in New York. States may accede to the Convention at any time, with no time limit.

The signatures affixed today to the blue leather-bound volume contained in the text of the Convention's 320 artucles and nine annexes do not legally bind any Government. The Treaty will become binding on States which formally adhere to it through ratification or accession, as soon as it enters into force. This will happen one year after it is ratified or acceded to by 60 States.

(p. A-3)

Fiji has become the first State to ratify. Receipt of its instrument of ratification was announced today by President Koh.

In addition to the Convention (document A/CONF. 62/122 and corrigenda), delegations today signed the Conference's Final Act (document A/CONF.62/121)--the formal record of the Conference's work. This action does not imply any commitment by States in respect of the Conference's decisions, but it gives observer status in the Preparatory Commission to States which do not sign the Convention. Observers will be able to take part in the Commission's deliberations, but only States that sign the Convention can participate in its decision making.

The Final Act was signed by all States which signed the Convention, as well as by the following full participants in the Conference: Belgium, Benin,

Botswana, Ecuador, Equatorial Guinea, Federal Republic of Germany, Holy See, Israel, Italy, Japan, Jordan, Libya, Luxembourg, Oman, Peru, Republic of Korea,
Samoa, Spain, Switzerland, United Kingdom, United
States, Venezuela, and Zaire.

It was also signed by three Governments which had
observer status in the Conference: the Netherlands
Antilles, the Trust Territory of the Pacific Islands,
and the West Indies Associated States.

Also signing the Final Act were the European
Economic Community and the following national libera-
tion movements which participated in the Conference
as observers: the African National Congress of South
Africa, the Palestine Liberation Organization, the
Pan Africanist Congress of Azania, and the South West
Africa People's Organization.

The Law of the Sea Convention was adopted by the
Conference on 30 April by a vote of 130 in favour to
4 against, with 17 abstentions. The Conference held
the final part of its eleventh session at Montego Bay
from 6 to 10 December to hear statements of position
on the Convention and then open it for signature.

During four days devoted to hearing statements,
121 delegations presented their views on the Convention. Included among them were the President of Nauru,
the Prime Ministers of the Cook Islands and Netherlands
Antilles, two Deputy Prime Ministers, 11 Foreign Ministers, and 13 other Ministers.

Most of the speakers hailed the Convention as a
major achievement of international diplomacy, and a
number described it as the most significant multilateral treaty since the United Nations Charter,
signed at San Francisco in 1945.

(p. A-4)

Among the signatories were five of the 11 States
accorded a special status in the Conference-approved
scheme giving international sanction to "pioneer" seabed investors for exploration of the international
seabed area prior to the Convention's entry into force.
The five are Canada, France, India, the Netherlands,
and the Soviet Union. Of the six which did not sign,
the United States said the seabed mining provisions
were unacceptable; the United Kingdom said it would

seek improvements in these provisions; Italy thought the Preparatory Commission should help iron out difficulties in regard to seabed exploitation; Belgium and the Federal Republic of Germany said they were still studying the text; and Japan stated that the Convention "merits its support and signature" but was under review by its new Government.

Of the four countries other than the United States which voted against the Convention in April and did not sign today, Turkey and Venezuela cited objections to the provisions on maritime boundary delimitation, while Israel said it was still studying the text. Oman and Peru which voted in favour of the Convention in April, as well as Spain which abstained in the vote, said the text was still under study by their Governments. Switzerland, which also voted in favour, said its signature would depend on support for the Convention by other States. Ecuador, which did not sign and did not participate in the vote, re-iterated its position in support of a 200-mile territorial sea. The Holy See, another non-participant in the vote, reserved the right to sign and ratify. The Republic of Korea said it would sign as soon as domestic procedures were completed.

The Soviet Union and other socialist countries of Eastern Europe, which had abstained in the April vote on the ground that certain provisions of the pioneer investment scheme discriminated against them, were among the signatories of the Convention today, though they repeated their objections to the clauses in question.


(END OF PART A; PART B FOLLOWS)


(p. B-1)

Press Release SEA/MB/13 10 December 1982


Highlights of Convention

The main achievements of the Convention were outlined by President Koh in an address to the Conference on 6 December:


672

"First, the Convention will promote the maintenance of international peace and security, because it will replace a plethora of conflicting claims by coastal States with universally agreed limits on the territorial sea, on the contiguous zone, on the exclusive economic zone, and on the continental shelf.

"Second, the world community's interest in the freedom of navigation will be facilitated by the important compromises on the status of the exclusive economic zone, by the regime of innocent passage through the territorial sea, by the regime of transit passage through straits used for international navigation and by the regime of archipelagic sea-lanes passage.

"Third, the world community's interest in the conservation and optimum utilization of the living resources of the sea will be enhanced by the conscientious implementation of the provisions in the Convention relating to the exclusive economic zone.

"Fourth, the Convention contains important new rules for the protection and preservation of the marine environment from pollution.

"Fifth, the Convention contains new rules on marine scientific research which strike an equitable balance between the interests of the research States and the interests of the coastal States in whose economic zones or continental shelves the research is to be carried out.

"Sixth, the world community's interest in the peaceful settlement of disputes and the prevention of use of force in the settlement of disputes between States has been advanced by the mandatory system of dispute settlement in the Convention.

"Seventh. the Convention has succeeded in translating the principle that the resources of the deep seabed constitute the common heritage of mankind into fair and workable institutions and arrangements.

(p. B-2)

"Eighth, though far from ideal, we can nevertheless find elements of international equity in the Convention, such as revenue-sharing on the continental shelf beyond 200 miles, giving landlocked and

673

geographically disadvantaged States access to the
living resources of the exclusive economic zones of
their neighbouring States, the relationship between
coastal fishermen and distant-water fishermen, and
the sharing of the benefits derived from the exploitation of the resources of the deep seabed."

(A fuller description of the Convention's provisions is contained in the background press release
on the Montego Bay session, SEA/498 of 3 December.)

Adopted along with the Convention, and contained
in the Final Act, are four resolutions. The first
establishes the Preparatory Commission for the Seabed
Authority and the Law of the Sea Tribunal. The second
governs preparatory investments in pioneer activities
by States and private consortia relating to polymetallic nodules on the deep seabed. The third resolution
deals with the rights and interests of territories
which have not attained independence or self-government. The fourth accords to recognized national liberation movements the right to sign the Final Act.

The Conference adopted by acclamation one further
resolution at Montego Bay, expressing "profound gratitude for the exceptional hospitality" extended to it
by the Government and people of Jamaica.

### Views of Delegations

The 121 statements by delegations which preceded
the signing included both ceremonial and substantive
declarations. Tributes were paid to key figures in
the history of the Convention, notably Arvid Pardo of
Malta, who in 1967 first pressed for United Nations
action to have deep seabed resources recognized as a
common heritage of mankind; Hamilton Shirley Amerasinghe of Sri Lanka, President of the Conference for
its first six years, until his death in 1979; and his
successor in the presidency, Mr. Koh of Singapore.
Mr. Pardo received a standing ovation when he appeared
at the podium of the Conference on its next-to-last
day.

(p. B-3)

Many of the representatives who have attended the
Conference since its beginning spoke of its nine years
of difficult labours over a path which began at Caracas, Venezuela, with the first substantive session in

1974, continued in New York and Geneva, and returned to the Caribbean for the conclusion of its work. Recalling this journey in his opening statement on 6 December, President Koh remarked that when the Conference began, "there were many who told us that our goal was too ambitious and not attainable. We have proven the skeptics wrong, and we have succeeded in adopting a Convention covering every aspect of the uses and resources of the seas".

The Convention was described by speakers from all regional and interest groups as a monumental achievement in international law, codifying existing rules and devising new ones to meet modern circumstances. Burundi saw it as substituting harmony and the rule of law for the chaos that had prevailed with respect to the uses of the oceans. In Denmark's view, the Convention was a major step in the development of North-South relations and an essential contribution to international stability and world order. Egypt believed it would assist in developing international cooperation and help minimize unjust competition in the exploitation of the sea's resources.

For the Gambia, the Convention was "the best codification, modification, simplification, modernization, reform and systematic development of the international law of the sea". Japan described the text as the best possible compromise which the Conference could have achieved. Poland thought it would remove the causes of many international disputes and fill many legal loopholes. For Saint Vincent and the Grenadines, the Convention, by clearly spelling out rights, provided the basis for reducing conflict and ensuring greater peace and security. Senegal also thought it would make a major contribution to peace. The Solomon Islands said the display of international unity represented by the Convention was encouraging to small island nations. Sri Lanka saw it as having the highest potential of any instrument in history to serve as the foundation for peace, social justice, and good order. To Switzerland, the many mutual concessions in the Convention reflected the concern of the vast majority of States to see order rather than anarchy reign in the sea.

Several countries contrasted the old law of the sea with the new. Thus, the Ivory Coast regarded the earlier "freedom of the seas" doctrine as an instrument for maintaining the predominance of the most

powerful maritime Powers and said it must be replaced
by the notion of the "fraternal sea". Morocco remarked that the previous law of the sea conventions,
signed at Geneva in 1958, had not taken account of
realities. Whereas rules of international law were
dictated in the past by the big Powers, said the
Philippines, the new Convention set out rules formulated by the combined will of the great majority of
States. Uganda saw it as the most important symbol
to date of a new democratic era in the development of
international law--a change from the time when a few
States imposed their own order on the world.

(p. B-4)

A number of speakers, including Democratic
Yemen, Grenada, and the Niger, saw the Convention,
and particularly the Seabed Authority, as an important step toward the establishment of the new international economic order that developing countries
have been seeking. But some developing countries believed, in the words of Mauritius, that they obtained
"a raw deal", because the benefits to developed countries from exploitation of the exclusive economic
zone and the continental shelf would far exceed those
of the developing countries. In the same vein,
Sierra Leone thought African countries had little to
benefit from the Convention because it sacrificed the
principle that ocean resources were the common heritage of mankind and showed no preference for the
equitable distribution of resources. On the other
hand, Togo observed that, for the first time, a large
number of developing countries, particularly in
Africa, had decided on rules to govern their mutual
relations in matters of maritime transport and the
exploitation of seabed and ocean resources. Liberia
called on the international community to help the
developing countries, particularly in Africa, to exploit their seabed resources through training, manpower, joint ventures, and technology transfer.

A number of countries which signed the Convention urged that States which had not yet done so,
should take no unilateral actions contrary to the new
treaty. In particular, they objected to the plan for
a so-called "mini-treaty" among potential seabed mining countries in the West, aimed at mutual recognition of mining claims put forward under national
legislation.

Peru, speaking on this aspect for the "Group of 77" developing countries, said that any measure in regard to the international seabed area taken through national legislation or multilateral agreement incompatible with the Convention "would be without international validity and would lead the rest of the States to adopt, for their part, the measures necessary to protect their interests". In the view of Bangladesh, no State, no matter how powerful or technically advanced, should be permitted unilaterally to exploit the area which the Convention defined as the common heritage of mankind. Lesotho stated that the international area was free from State sovereignty and could not be appropriated by any State or person. Countries must prevent the exploitation of the ocean's riches by a handful of States, said Libya. Zambia regarded such action as "using the might of technology in taking advantage of the weak".

This point was also made by speakers from other groups. Thus, Australia said, "Mining the seabed outside the Convention would be highly divisive, and the country concerned would incur the hostility of the bulk of the world." Byelorussia condemned what it called the United States' agreement with three other Western States to seize the most promising seabed sectors.

The United States, however, said that, under the circumstances, "alternative ways of preserving national access to deep seabed resources are necessary, just, and permitted by international law".

(p. B-5)

A number of countries urged the United States and other industrialized countries to reconsider their decision not to sign the Convention. The United States was committing a grave error in isolating itself from the rest of the world by refusing to sign, said Cuba, citing an article in Foreign Affairs by Leigh S. Ratiner, former member of the United States delegation to the Conference. Fiji hoped that the United States position was a "temporary aberration" from its traditional support for international law. The United States had much more to gain from the Convention and should not pursue other arrangements with like-minded States, Malaysia argued. Singapore felt that the countries which had declared their intention not to sign, including those which

were strong advocates of international law, should reconsider.  In the words of Suriname, "The major industrialized States cannot just pick up their marbles and walk away, just because they did not get everything they might have wanted."  The United Republic of Cameroon remarked that the United States could not afford the discomforts of isolation, especially over a treaty in which the negotiations accorded priority to its declared vital interests.

Nigeria addressed a similar appeal to the United Kingdom, expressing the hope that its position constituted only a temporary separation, not a divorce, from the rest of the Commonwealth.

The United States told the Conference that, while it could not accept the seabed provisions of the Convention, most other parts reflected prevailing international practice and would endure.  However, other participants endorsed the view of President Koh that States could not "pick what they like and disregard what they do not like" in the Convention, or "claim rights under the Convention without being willing to assume the correlative duties".  Canada feared that if States could arbitrarily select the rights and responsibilities under the Convention which they would recognize or deny, any prospect for global cooperation on vital issues might be ended.  The Ukraine regretted what it described as the United States' refusal to uphold agreements reached about the seabed.  The Soviet Union remarked that "the Convention is not a basket of fruit from which one can pick only those which one fancies."

A related aspect addressed by several speakers was the effects of the Convention on countries which did not adhere to it.  In the view of the Federal Republic of Germany, States could not be subject to obligations under the Convention until they had ratified it; until then, they could rely on and be bound by the generally recognized practice of States as contained in conventions already in force.  In a similar vein, the United Kingdom held that existing rights, such as those that derived from freedom of the high seas, as well as existing conventional law, would remain.

The Dominican Republic, on the other hand, held that while the Convention could have legal effects

only for its parties, its norms and principles would
serve as guidelines for non-parties, as well. Finland considered that the benefits of the Convention
could be enjoyed only by States that adhered to it.
Making the point in more specific terms, Iran said
that only States parties would be entitled to benefit
from contractual rights with respect to transit passage through straits used for international navigation, the concept of the exclusive economic zone, and
the international seabed area.

(p. B-6)

Sweden, which cited a number of features in the
Convention that were not to its benefit, observed
nonetheless that to accept certain rules which might
not appear fully consistent with the short-run national interest might prove wise in the long fun.

Several countries pointed to the possibility of
future revision of parts of the Convention. The Holy
See believed that "through some modicum of complex
international negotiating processes, an essential
consensus may still subsequently be arrived at."
Calling on States to put aside misgivings, Ireland
considered that any shortcomings in the Convention
could be met by adaptation and ultimately remedied
by review. The Netherlands said it would seek adjustments during the preparatory stage in the provisions for the mandatory transfer of seabed technology
from private and State mining entities to the Seabed
Authority and developing countries. The United Kingdom said it wanted to explore with others the prospects for improvements in the seabed provisions, including technology transfer. Looking further into
the future, Kenya welcomed provisions permitting an
orderly review of the Convention to ascertain if it
had worked satisfactorily in the matter of seabed exploration and exploitation.

However, Indonesia regretted that certain industrialized countries were still demanding concessions
which went beyond the limits of possible accommodation. Yugoslavia thought the developing countries
had already reached the upper limit of concessions
in regard to the common heritage principle.

Several countries looked to the Preparatory Commission as a vehicle for achieving an accommodation
that would enable additional States to adhere to the

Convention. Austria felt that much would depend on
the Commission's faithfulness to the principles of
consensus and comprehensiveness of approach. "If the
Preparatory Commission adopts a realistic and pragmatic attitude," said Canada, "the future is assured."
Chile also thought that the future of the Convention
would greatly depend on how the Commission proceeded.
Colombia urged that the Commission work to facilitate
universality rather than make it more difficult. In
France's view, imperfections with regard to technology transfer and the financing of the Authority should
be corrected by the Commission when it drafted the
rules, regulations, and procedures for the future mining system. Italy thought the Commission should take
a pragmatic approach in ironing out difficulties with
regard to seabed mining. Norway believed that the
Commission's work might be crucial in making the Convention universal. Uruguay also thought the Commission could play a role in that regard by the wise use
of its powers.

Many States presented their interpretations and
comments on various substantive provisions of the Convention. Under article 310, such statements must
"not purport to exclude or to modify the legal effect
of the provisions of this Convention in their application to that State party". In this connection,
Chad warned that States must not make restrictive interpretations that would deprive the Convention of
substance, since the text was an indivisible whole.

(p. B-7)

Many of the comments related to the future system for exploiting the seabed area beyond national
jurisdiction. While some developing countries welcomed this part of the Convention as offering them
access to resources that might otherwise be taken exclusively by technologically advanced nations, others
expressed misgivings. Algeria, for example, thought
the provisions for protecting preparatory seabed investments and on the composition and functioning of
the Authority gave advantages to developed countries
sometimes far removed from the objectives of the new
international economic order. In China's view, the
resolution on pioneer investors went too far to meet
demands of a few industrialized nations and their
companies. Iraq would have preferred to see a seabed
regime that was immune from monopolies by a handful
of States. Pakistan considered that the major

beneficiaries would be a few industrialized countries.
In the view of the United Republic of Tanzania, private companies would have almost automatic access to
seabed resources, while loopholes would impede the
availability of capital and technology to the Authority's Enterprise.

Several industrialized countries expressed different misgivings about the seabed regime. Belgium
said the spirit of compromise had not been respected
to the same extent for the seabed provisions as for
other aspects of the Convention. The Federal Republic of Germany mentioned its previous criticism of
provisions on technology transfer, production limitation, financial burdens deriving from the operation
of the system, and the procedure for future review of
this part of the Convention. Italy feared that the
institutions projected for the seabed, by their number and complexity, would have difficulty in ensuring
a viable system of exploitation. The United States
said the system was "unacceptable and would not serve
the interests of the international community".

Czechoslovakia said that if the present legal
regime had been accepted, the oceans' wealth would
have been monopolized by some of the most industrialized States, and the differences between the poorest
and richest countries would have grown. Viet Nam believed that the Conference had given the United States
"exorbitant privileges" in regard to pioneer investors.

In other comments on the seabed, India announced
that it had already spent the amount ($30 million)
required for designation as a pioneer investor and
would submit to the Preparatory Commission the results
of its surveys in the Central Indian Basin of the
Indian Ocean. The Republic of Korea said it looked
forward to organizing joint ventures with other newly
industrializing and developing countries to exploit
the seabed. Tunisia thought the Authority should
play a role      (p. B-8)   in preventing over-exploitation of the common heritage and unilateral exploitation by certain States which might be tempted to place
self-interest above the interests of humanity.

Gabon and Zaire, land-based producers of minerals of the type found on the seabed, reiterated their
concern at the production limitation formula in the
Convention and the provision for a compensation

681

scheme to protect such countries from economic harm
resulting from seabed exploitation.

A number of States which had unsuccessfully
sought to amend the draft Convention in order to require prior notification or authorization for the innocent passage of foreign warships through the territorial sea, repeated their support for that position
in the interest of coastal State security. Benin regretted that coastal States had had to accept omission of such a clause, at the price of their security.
The Democratic People's Republic of Korea, Romania,
and the Sudan contended that coastal States had the
right to safeguard their security interests in regard
to the passage of warships through their territorial
waters. Malta said it went along with the compromise
on this point and reserved the right to submit a declaration. Saint Lucia regretted what it described as
the vagueness of the text on this point. The United
Arab Emirates disagreed with the article as it stood.
Vanuatu regretted that the text permitted vessels
carrying nuclear weapons and materials to pass through
the territorial sea. In Yemen's view, the passage of
warships through the territorial waters of a small developing country was a violation of its sovereignty.

Brazil said that while the economic interests of
coastal States were well protected in the Convention,
the text was much less explicit concerning their security interests in the area between 12 and 200 miles
because it had been impossible to overcome the intransigence of the great naval Powers.

Spain referred to objections it had raised at
the Conference in April to articles on transit passage
of straits used for international navigation.

A number of island countries and others welcomed
the Convention's provisions on the 200-mile exclusive
economic zone. The Cook Islands noted that its zone
of 1,360,000 square kilometres surrounded a land mass
of 94 square miles. Costa Rica said it was already
applying its law requiring license fees for vessels
fishing for highly migratory species such as tuna.
Ecuador stated that recognition of coastal State sovereignty over the resources of the zone and continental shelf had been an important conquest by those
States. Iceland said the provisions on the zone represented "formidable results" for a country so dependent on the sea. Mexico saw the rights of coastal

States over the resources as part of the permanent effort to secure full exercise of sovereignty over their natural resources.

(p. B-9)

Nauru was grateful to the United Nations "for making it possible for us to legislate for a tract of sea around our island to a definite extent internationally recognizable, to claim as our own to exploit and fish for the economic well-being of our people". New Zealand cautioned that small Pacific island States would obtain full benefit from their zones only if more powerful States were prepared to respect their international obligations. Somalia opposed what it described as efforts by certain States to internationalize the zone by distorting certain provisions of the Convention.

Cape Verde was of the view that the exclusive economic zone concept prejudiced the national interest of countries such as itself which had advocated or established a larger territorial sea.

Bulgaria said it accepted the establishment of the economic zone as an essential concession to coastal States, which for their part should avoid damaging the interests of other States.

Some States commented on the provisions in the Convention which call for delimitation of overlapping economic zones and continental shelves "on the basis of international law . . . in order to achieve an equitable solution". The Bahamas said it would have preferred a clear statement that the median line between two countries' coasts should be the mandatory factor in determining where maritime boundaries should lie. Guyana said countries must be on guard against "attempts to insinuate into bilateral relations, under the guise of maritime delimitation, disputes and controversies which owe their inspiration to ambitions rooted in territorial aggrandizement". Venezuela reaffirmed its objection to the delimitation provisions.

Four Mediterranean States voiced differing views on the application of the Convention's rules to enclosed and semi-enclosed seas. Israel said it was not satisfied that some of the Convention's major concepts were fully applicable in such seas. Turkey took the position that maritime boundary delimitation in

such seas could be settled only through agreement of the parties, on the basis of equity. On the other hand, Cyprus opposed attempts to create particular rules for such seas in derogation from the rules of the Convention; and Greece said any attempt to apply certain provisions to the exclusion of others, or to prevent application in certain regions, must be excluded as contrary to the Convention.

A number of archipelagic States welcomed the Convention's provisions giving them extended jurisdiction over the waters around their islands. Papua New Guinea observed that the Convention did not take account of the concerns of such States that freedom of navigation through specified parts of archipelagic waters must be consistent with considerations of security, national unity, and resource jurisdiction of the archipelagic State.

(p. B-10)

A number of landlocked and geographically disadvantaged States, as well as some of the neighboring coastal States, commented on the provisions regarding access by the geographically disadvantaged to the sea and to the exclusive economic zones of other States.

Among the landlocked and geographically disadvantaged States, Bahrain said it would have preferred the provisions to be more effective, and Bhutan said those States had had to be satisfied with very little. The German Democratic Republic remarked that the effective exercise of its rights as a geographically disadvantaged State was a matter of immediate economic importance, in view of the burdens its deepsea fishing industry had had to shoulder as a result of the introduction of exclusive economic zones. Hungary also saw the landlocked States as losers on such issues as the economic zone and the outer limits of the continental shelf, which reduced the area of the common heritage. Mongolia regarded the fisheries access rights of landlocked States as very limited. Nepal was not wholly satisfied with the provisions on transit rights of landlocked countries and on their access to fisheries in the economic zones of neighbouring countries. For Paraguay, the Convention ensured the right of landlocked countries to exploitation of neighbouring countries' economic zones. Trinidad and Tobago considered that accommodation should have been made for States which had

traditionally and habitually fished in certain areas. The Upper Volta felt that the Convention's concern for the interests of such States was not everywhere evident.

Among coastal States with landlocked neighbours, Angola stressed that transit rights and access to the sea and its resources were matters to be negotiated rather than questions of inherent right. Similarly, Mauritania and Pakistan stated that such access could take place only on the basis of bilateral or regional agreements.

Finally, a number of countries praised the dispute settlement provisions of the Convention, and some announced their selection of preferred mechanisms--a choice given them under articles 287 and 298. Barbados, however, voiced support for compulsory and binding procedures and said it was not pleased with the less-binding procedures contained in the Convention.

In a written statement submitted to the Conference (document A/CONF.62/WS/35), Argentina said it would be unable to sign the Convention or the Final Act because of objections to the Conference's resolution III, adopted in April, on the rights and interests of territories which have not attained independence or self-government. Argentina stated that, as the Malvinas and South Sandwich and South Georgia Islands formed an integral part of Argentine territory, it did not recognize the right or title of any other State relating to resources alleged to be protected by that resolution.

APPENDIX V

United Nations Department of Public Information
Law of the Sea Conference, Final Part of 11th Session
Montego Bay, Jamaica
Press Release SEA/MB/14 10 December 1982

CLOSING STATEMENT BY THE PRESIDENT
OF CONFERENCE ON THE LAW OF THE SEA

Following is the text of the statement today by
the President of the Third United Nations Conference
on the Law of the Sea, Tommy T.B. Koh, at the closing
meeting of the Conference at Montego Bay, Jamaica:

Dear colleagues, we have created a new record in
legal history. Never in the annals of international
law has a Convention been signed by 119 countries on
the very first day on which it is opened for signature. Not only is the number of signatories a remarkable fact, but just as important is the fact that the
Convention has been signed by States from every region
of the world: from the North and from the South, from
the East and from the West, by coastal States as well
as landlocked and geographically disadvantaged States.
I believe that the overwhelming support for this Convention is a vindication of the consensus procedure
by which we have worked. I am happy to inform the
Conference that Fiji is the first State to have ratified the Convention. I urge all the other signatories
to ratify the Convention as soon as possible so that
we will have the required 60 ratifications within the
next two years. I must also urge the States which
shall become parties to this Convention to ensure that
their domestic laws are brought into compliance with
it.

Dear colleagues, during the last four days I have
listened attentively to the statements made by the 120
delegations.

I would like to highlight the major themes which
I have found in those statements.

(p. 2)

First, delegations have said that the Convention
does not fully satisfy the interests and objectives
of any State. Nevertheless, they were of the view
that it represents a monumental achievement of the
international community, second only to the United
Nations Charter. The Convention is the first comprehensive treaty dealing with practically every
aspect of the uses and resources of the seas and the
oceans. It has successfully accommodated the competing interests of all nations.

The second theme which has emerged from the
statements is that the provisions of the Convention
are closely inter-related and form an integral package. Thus it is not possible for a State to pick
what it likes and to disregard what it does not like.
It was also said that rights and obligations go hand
in hand, and it is not permissible to claim rights
under the Convention without being willing to shoulder
the corresponding obligations.

The third theme I have heard is that this Convention is not a codification Convention. The argument that, except for Part XI, the Convention codi-
fies customary law or reflects existing international
practice is factually incorrect and legally insup-
portable. The regime of transit passage through
straits used for international navigation and the
regime of archipelagic sea lanes passage are two examples of the many new concepts in the Convention.
Even in the case of article 76 on the continental
shelf, the article contains new law in that it has
expanded the concept of the continental shelf to include the continental slope and the continental rise.
This concession to the broad-margin States was in return for their agreement for revenue-sharing on the
continental shelf beyond 200 miles. It is therefore
my view that a State which is not a party to this
Convention cannot invoke the benefits of article 76.

(p. 3)

The fourth theme relates to the lawfulness of any
attempt to mine the resources of the international
Area of the seabed and ocean floor. Speakers from
every regional and interest group expressed the view
that the doctrine of the freedom of the high seas can

provide no legal basis for the grant by any State of
exclusive title to a specific mine site in the international Area.  Many are of the view that article 137
of the Convention has become as much a part of customary international law as the freedom of navigation.
Any attempt by any State to mine the resources of the
deep seabed outside the Convention will earn the universal condemnation of the international community
and will incur grave political and legal consequences.
All speakers have addressed an earnest appeal to the
United States to reconsider its position.  The United
States is a country which has, throughout its history,
supported the progressive development of international
law and has fought for the Rule of Law in the relations between States.  The present position of the
United States Government toward this Convention is,
therefore, inexplicable in the light of its history,
in the light of its specific law of the sea interests,
and in the light of the leading role which it has
played in negotiating the many compromises which have
made this treaty possible.

A final theme which has emerged from the statements concerns the Preparatory Commission.  Now that
the required number of States have signed the Convention, the Preparatory Commission for the establishment of the International Seabed Authority and the
International Tribunal for the Law of the Sea will begin its work in March next year.  Many speakers have
attached great importance to its work.  The Commission
will have to adopt the rules and procedures for the
implementation of resolution II relating to pioneer
investors.  It will, inter alia, draft the detailed
rules, regulations and procedures for the mining of
the seabed.  If it carries out its work in an efficient, objective, and businesslike manner, we will
have
(p. 4)
a viable system for the mining of the
deep seabed.  This will induce those who are standing
on the sidelines to come in and support the Convention.  If, on the other hand, the Preparatory Commission does not carry out its tasks in an efficient,
objective, and practical manner, then all our efforts
in the last 14 years will have been in vain.  In carrying out its work, the Commission should also pay
strict regard to economy, to the avoidance of waste,
and to efficiency.  In order to enable it to get off
to an early start, I will request the Secretary-

General and his staff to assist the Commission by undertaking the necessary preparatory work.

Dear colleagues, today is a day for celebration. We celebrate the successful conclusion of our collective endeavour. We have strengthened the United Nations by proving that with political will, nations can use the organization as a center to harmonize their actions. We have shown that with good leadership and management the United Nations can be an efficient forum for the negotiation of complex issues. We celebrate the victory of the Rule of Law and of the principle of the peaceful settlement of disputes. Finally, we celebrate human solidarity and the reality of interdependence which is symbolized by the United Nations Convention on the Law of the Sea.

I declare the Third United Nations Conference on the Law of the Sea closed.